21st International Conference on Cognition and Exploratory Learning in Digital Age (CELDA 2024)

Zagreb, Croatia
26-28 October 2024

Editors:

Demetrios G. Sampson
Dirk Ifenthaler
Pedro Isaias
Luis Rodrigues

ISBN: 979-8-3313-0936-7

Printed from e-media with permission by:

Curran Associates, Inc.
57 Morehouse Lane
Red Hook, NY 12571

Some format issues inherent in the e-media version may also appear in this print version.

Printed with permission by Curran Associates, Inc. (2025)

For permission requests, please contact International Association for Development of the Information Society (IADIS) at the address below.

International Association for Development of the Information Society (IADIS)
Rua Sao Sebastiao Da Pedreira
No. 100, 30, 1050-209
Lisbon, Portugal

Phone: 351 21 3151373
Fax: 351 21 3151244

secretariat@iadis.org

Additional copies of this publication are available from:

Curran Associates, Inc.
57 Morehouse Lane
Red Hook, NY 12571 USA
Phone: 845-758-0400
Fax: 845-758-2633
Email: curran@proceedings.com
Web: www.proceedings.com

21st International Conference on Cognition and Exploratory Learning in Digital Age

CELDA 2024

Zagreb, Croatia ■ 26-28 October

PROCEEDINGS

EDITED BY:

Demetrios G. Sampson

Dirk Ifenthaler

Pedro Isaías

iadis

international association for development of the information society

21st INTERNATIONAL CONFERENCE
on

COGNITION AND EXPLORATORY LEARNING IN THE DIGITAL AGE (CELDA 2024)

PROCEEDINGS OF THE 21st INTERNATIONAL CONFERENCE on

COGNITION AND EXPLORATORY LEARNING IN THE DIGITAL AGE (CELDA 2024)

ZAGREB, CROATIA

OCTOBER 26 - 28, 2024

Organised by

iadis

international association for development of the information society

As a member of Crossref (a non-profit membership organization for scholarly publishing working with the purpose to make content easy to find, link, cite and assess) each published paper in this book of proceedings will be allocated a DOI (Digital Object Identifier) number for its fast and easy citation and indexation.

Edited by Demetrios G. Sampson, Dirk Ifenthaler and Pedro Isaías

Associate Editor: Luís Rodrigues

TABLE OF CONTENTS

FULL PAPERS

SHORT PAPERS

REFLECTION PAPER

FOREWORD

These proceedings contain the papers of the 21st International Conference on Cognition and Exploratory Learning in the Digital Age (CELDA 2024), held in Zagreb, Croatia, from 26 to 28 October 2024 and organized by the International Association for Development of the Information Society (IADIS).

The CELDA conference aims to address the main issues concerned with evolving learning processes and supporting pedagogies and applications in the digital age. There have been advances in both cognitive psychology and computing that have affected the educational arena. The convergence of these two disciplines is increasing at a fast pace and affecting academia and professional practice in many ways.

Paradigms such as just-in-time learning, constructivism, student-centered learning and collaborative approaches have emerged and are being supported by technological advancements such as simulations, virtual reality and multi-agent systems. These developments have created both opportunities and areas of serious concerns. This conference aims to cover both technological as well as pedagogical issues related to these developments. Main tracks have been identified. However innovative contributions that do not easily fit into these areas will also be considered as long as they are directly related to the overall theme of the conference – cognition and exploratory learning in the digital age.

The following areas are represented in the submissions for CELDA 2024:

- Acquisition of Expertise
- Assessing Progress of Learning in Complex Domains
- Assessment of Exploratory Learning Approaches
- Assessment of Exploratory Technologies
- Cognition in Education
- Collaborative Learning
- Educational Psychology
- Exploratory Technologies (Simulations, VR, i-TV, etc.)
- Just-in-Time and Learning-on-Demand
- Learner Communities and Peer-Support
- Learning Communities & Web Service Technologies Pedagogical issues related with Learning Objects
- Learning Paradigms in Academia
- Learning Paradigms in the Corporate Sector
- Life-long Learning
- Student-centered Learning
- Technology and Mental Models
- Technology
- Learning and Expertise
- Virtual University

The CELDA 2024 Conference received 66 submissions from more than 25 countries. Each submission was reviewed in a double-blind review process by at least two independent reviewers to ensure quality and maintain high standards. Out of the papers submitted, 40 were accepted as full papers for an acceptance rate of 61%; 14 were accepted as short papers and 1 was accepted as a reflection paper. Authors of the best published papers in the CELDA 2024 proceedings will be invited to publish extended versions of their papers in a book from Springer.

In addition to the presentation of full, short and reflection papers, the conference also includes one keynote presentation from an internationally distinguished researcher. We would therefore like to express our gratitude to this year keynote speaker: Dr. Panagiotis Kampylis, Greek National Documentation Centre, Greece.

A successful conference requires the effort of many individuals. We would like to thank the members of the Program Committee for their hard work in reviewing and selecting the papers that appear in this book. We are especially grateful to the authors who submitted their papers to this conference and to the presenters who provided the substance of this meeting. We wish to thank all members of our organizing committee.

Last but not least, we hope that everybody enjoyed the presentations and we invite all participants for next year's edition of the International Conference on Cognition and Exploratory Learning in the Digital Age.

Pedro Isaías, Universidade Aberta (Portuguese Open University), Portugal and
The University of New South Wales (UNSW – Sydney), Australia
Conference Chair

Demetrios G. Sampson, University of Piraeus, Greece
Dirk Ifenthaler, University of Mannheim, Germany & Curtin University, Australia
Program Co-Chairs

October 2024

PROGRAM COMMITTEE

CONFERENCE CHAIR

Pedro Isaías, Universidade Aberta (Portuguese Open University), Portugal
and The University of New South Wales (UNSW – Sydney), Australia

PROGRAM CO-CHAIRS

Demetrios G Sampson, University of Piraeus, Greece
Dirk Ifenthaler, University of Mannheim, Germany & Curtin University, Australia

COMMITTEE MEMBERS

Ah-Choo Koo, Multimedia Univerisity, Malaysia
Alke Martens, University of Rostock, Germany
Allan Jeong, Florida State University, USA
Anthony Y. H. Liao, Asia University, Taiwan
Barbara Lockee, Virginia Tech, USA
ChanMin Kim, Penn State University, USA
Charalampos Karagiannidis, University of Thessaly, Greece
Charlotte Baez, St. Gallen University of Teacher Education, Switzerland
Charoula Angeli-Valanides, University of Cyprus, Cyprus
Chien Sing Lee, Sunway University, Malaysia
Chun-Wang Wei, Kaohsiung Medical University, Taiwan
Dirk Tempelaar, Maastricht University, Netherlands
Farshad Badie, Berlin School of Business & Innovation (BSBI), Germany
Giuliana Guazzaroni, MI, Italy
Jay Loftus, Michigan State University, USA
Josef Buchner, St. Gallen University of Teacher Education, Switzerland
Juan Felipe Calderon, Universidad Andres Bello, Chile
Julie-Ann Sime, Lancaster University, United Kingdom
Katherine Sinitsa, Int. Res. Training Center for Info. Technologies and Systems, Ukraine
Kuo-Liang Ou, National Tsing Hua University, Taiwan
Kyparissia Papanikolaou, School of Pedagogical and Technological Education, Greece
Lence Miloseva, Goce Delcev University, Macedonia
Luis Anido, University of Vigo, Spain
Maiga Chang, Athabasca University, Canada
Mike Joy, University of Warwick, United Kingdom
Min Kyu Kim, Georgia State University, United States
Ming-Chi Liu, Feng Chia University, Taiwan
Miriam Mulders, University of Duisburg-Essen, Germany
Mohammad Khalil, University of Bergen, Norway
Monica Divitini, Norwegian University of Science and Technology, Norway
Muhittin Sahin, University of Mannheim, Germany
Patrick Blumschein, University of Education Freiburg, Germany
Patrick Jost, Vorarlberg University of Applied Sciences, Austria
Radu Vasiu, Politehnica University of Timisoara, Romania

Sanghoon Park, University of South Florida, USA
Stamatios Papadakis, University of Crete, Greece
Stefanie Schallert-vallaster, St. Gallen University of Teacher Education, Switzerland
Tobias Hoelterhof, Catholic University of Applied Sciences, Germany
Vincent Barre, Le Mans University, France
Yen-Ting Lin, National Pingtung University, Taiwan

KEYNOTE LECTURE

TEACHING LIKE SOCRATES: THE TIMELESS ART OF QUESTIONING FOR FOSTERING CREATIVE THINKING IN THE AI ERA

Dr. Panagiotis Kampylis,
Greek National Documentation Centre, Greece

Abstract

This keynote delves into how the Socratic method -a teaching approach that revolves around asking deep, thought-provoking questions- could be a cornerstone of effective teaching and learning in the AI era. We will examine how this timeless method, when combined with generative AI, can offer personalised and adaptive learning experiences and foster creative and critical thinking. The keynote aims to provide insights into how the blending of ancient wisdom with modern technology could transform teaching, creating an engaging and intellectually stimulating environment for students in the AI era.

Full Papers

USING LARGE LANGUAGE MODELS FOR ACADEMIC WRITING INSTRUCTION: CONCEPTUAL DESIGN AND EVALUATION OF THE SOCRAT PROJECT

Lukas Spirgi and Sabine Seufert
University of St. Gallen
St.Jakob-Strasse 21, CH-9000 St.Gallen, Switzerland

ABSTRACT

Academic writing has undergone significant evolution due to advancements in AI. Students are leveraging AI in diverse ways for their studies. This study introduces a course design (SOCRAT) to teach students genre-based academic writing through AI. Genre-based academic writing is an educational strategy instructing students in the writing techniques and norms pertinent to their specific academic disciplines. AI is utilised as a personal training system and research assistant in this proposed course design. Students require cognitive and metacognitive knowledge to effectively work with AI tools. The SOCRAT design is based on the concept of mastery learning to ensure that students build their competencies. An initial evaluation of the prompts developed for this design indicates that LLM can particularly assist students in analysing their written text and providing suggestions for enhancement. This can help students develop their genre-based writing skills. The models are not yet convincing for other types of tasks where the LLMs are required to give exact answers.

KEYWORDS

Academic Writing, Artificial Intelligence (AI), Text Genres, Large Language Model (LLM), Co-Creation

1. INTRODUCTION

Since November 2022, the swift proliferation of the robust chatbot ChatGPT has sparked widespread concerns, especially within academic institutions, regarding the potential misuse by students to produce texts without substantial effort. Potential drawbacks include the rise in plagiarism, surface-level learning, and reliance on such tools (Seufert et al., 2024). Several studies have examined how students benefit from ChatGPT and its impact on universities (Spirgi et al., 2024; von Garrel et al., 2023).

There are often calls for more oral examinations in the current discussion about using generative AI models such as ChatGPT in education. These are intended to ensure learners have analysed the topic in depth. Some universities even abolish qualification theses such as bachelor theses altogether (Zenthöfer, 2023).

Nevertheless, teaching academic writing remains essential in higher education, as it provides students with essential critical thinking and practical communication skills applicable across different fields. Incorporating large language models (LLMs) into academic writing pedagogy can enhance this pedagogical endeavour by providing tailored feedback and illustrative examples, thereby accelerating skill acquisition and proficiency (Seufert et al., 2024).

2. PROBLEM DEFINITION AND RESEARCH METHODOLOGY

As the introduction to the article shows, the advent of generative AI is massively transforming academic writing. Despite the support provided by AI tools, students must still be able to write academic texts. The article pursues the following goals based on the genre-based academic writing theory (Thoreau, 2006).

1. Developing a design for teaching students genre-based academic writing with the support of AI tools.

2. To assess how well current LLMs cope with the prompts developed for the design.

The research methodology utilised in this study is design-based research, known for its effectiveness in generating sustainable innovations in education and teaching (McKenney & Reeves, 2018). A design (SOCRAT) is being developed to show how academic writing skills can be taught in the first semester using AI in higher education. The design is based on the theory of genre-based writing and the skills students need to learn to work effectively with AI tools (Seufert et al., 2024; Thoreau, 2006). In order to identify the types of tasks that today's LLMs are good at, several prompts have been tested that can be used in the SOCRAT design. Criteria for evaluating the performance of each task were defined in advance. For the evaluation, 12 LLMs were selected. These models were selected based on performance, parameter size, and licence. The Hugging Face leaderboard was employed to evaluate the collective performance of the LLMs (Hugging Face, 2024). The interaction with the LLMs uses the zero-shot method, meaning the models must answer the question without context or examples. Table 1 lists the models tested. Each model is given a number. These numbers are used in the following.

Table 1. Selected LLMs

Nr.	LLM	Nr	LLM	Nr.	LLM
1	Yi-34B-Chat	5	Claude 2.1	9	OpenHermes-2.5-Mistral-7B
2	Mixtral-8x-7B-v0.1	6	Openchat-3.5	10	Nous-Hermes-13b
3	Mistral-Medium	7	Lama-2-70b-chat-hf	11	Gpt-4-1106-turbo-preview
4	Bard-jan-24-gemini-pro	8	Zephyr	12	Gpt-3.5-turbo-0125

Chapter 3 presents the theoretical foundations on which the SOCRAT design was developed. Chapter 4 presents the design developed and the results of the language models tested. A discussion of the implications follows this.

3. THEORETICAL BACKGROUND

3.1 Genre-Based Instruction to Develop Academic Writing Skills

Genre-based academic writing is a methodology in educational practice that focuses on teaching students the writing skills and conventions specific to their academic disciplines. This approach is precious in higher education, where developing research competence is crucial. The genre-based framework is grounded in the understanding that different academic fields have distinct forms of communication, and mastering these is key to academic and professional success (Seufert et al., 2024).

In higher education, students must learn various text genres to use correctly and complete their studies successfully. The term "genre" was coined by Thoreau (2006). He defines a genre as writing with a specific style, a specific target group of readers and a clear purpose. A genre, therefore, encompasses a functional perspective whereby specific social conventions, linguistic features and rhetorical structures of the text must be considered (Hyland, 2003). Each genre has its schematic structure. Genre approaches have been seen in recent decades as new ways of teaching and learning writing (Badger & White, 2000). They combine features and perspectives of more traditional approaches, such as the product-oriented (focus on linguistic knowledge, with particular attention to the appropriate use of vocabulary, syntax and cohesive devices) and the process-oriented approaches (focus on linguistic skills, e.g. drafting, planning, revising and editing text, rather than on linguistic knowledge). The genre approach has also become more prevalent in higher education in recent years to promote writing skills specifically (Kruse, 2016). Depending on the type of writing, students face varying expectations. However, students may struggle to fulfil these expectations due to the lack of standardised terminology for describing academic genres (Kruse et al., 2015).

A distinction can also be made between academic text genres with specific social functions, each of which entails different types of tasks in teaching (Seufert et al., 2024). Nesi and Gardner (2012) analyse various English universities' substantial assortment of student texts. They categorised these texts into 90 distinct genres, subsequently organised into 13 genre families. These genre families are based on five different social functions (Kruse, 2016):

- demonstration of knowledge and understanding (genres example: explanation)
- ability to make informed and independent arguments (genres example: essays)
- development of research skills (genres example: literature reviews)
- preparation for professional action (genres example: case reports)
- writing for oneself and others (genres example: narrative accounts)

An example of genre knowledge for writing an academic paper is the CARS model, which defines how a good introduction is written. John Swales formulated the CARS model after a comprehensive analysis of journal articles spanning diverse academic disciplines, aiming to enhance the quality of research introductions (J. M. Swales, 1990). The model outlines the typical structure used in crafting the introductory sections of scholarly research studies. According to the model, three rhetorical moves are employed to ascertain the research's background, motivation, and focal point: 1) Establishing a Territory, 2) Establishing a Niche, and 3) Occupying a Niche. For each of the three defined moves, the model shows how it can be implemented when writing an abstract (J. Swales, 2014)

The notion of text genres outlined here could serve as a foundational framework for elucidating and methodically fostering collaboration with AI-driven systems for research and writing within higher education (Seufert et al., 2024).

3.2 Knowledge Base for AI-based Academic Writing

To work effectively with AI writing tools, a variety of knowledge are required, as shown in Figure 1. (Seufert et al., 2024). The cognitive knowledge required consists of the following aspects (Seufert, 2024). Rhetorical knowledge pertains to the style's intent, the author's stance, and their understanding of the intended audience. Formal knowledge encompasses the culturally endorsed frameworks, etiquette, and norms regarding language selection within a given context. Subject-specific knowledge pertains to the information acquired within particular academic disciplines or areas of study. Procedural knowledge refers to how certain things are done, e.g. the steps involved in writing a text, such as researching and writing (Tardy et al., 2020). Interdisciplinary knowledge involves integrating concepts and content from various disciplines or subjects. Epistemic knowledge entails comprehending how seasoned professionals think and operate within their domains. This comprehension empowers learners to perceive the purpose and practicality of their acquired knowledge (OECD, 2020).

In addition to cognitive knowledge, metacognition is becoming increasingly crucial through collaboration with AI tools. Metacognition consists of two aspects: understanding one's thought processes and learning (metacognitive knowledge) and the skill to employ this understanding to manage and oversee one's learning journey (metacognitive regulation) (Seufert, 2024). Specifically, metacognitive knowledge is vital in assessing the outcomes produced by generative AI tools. Users must pose a series of inquiries to assess the output. The initial question concerns whether the output must adhere to truth (conditional knowledge). Subsequently, users must evaluate whether they possess the expertise required to determine the accuracy of the output (declarative knowledge) (Sabzalieva & Valentini, 2023).

Both students' cognitive knowledge and metacognition can be trained with AI tools. For example, an AI tutor can be used to train students' genre knowledge. At the same time, new technologies, incredibly generative AI with natural language dialogues, make it possible to promote better metacognitive knowledge, which was previously difficult to train. For example, learners can use generative AI as training systems, e.g. for a Socratic dialogue or as a dynamic evaluator to map thought processes and open up new ways of learning (Seufert, 2024).

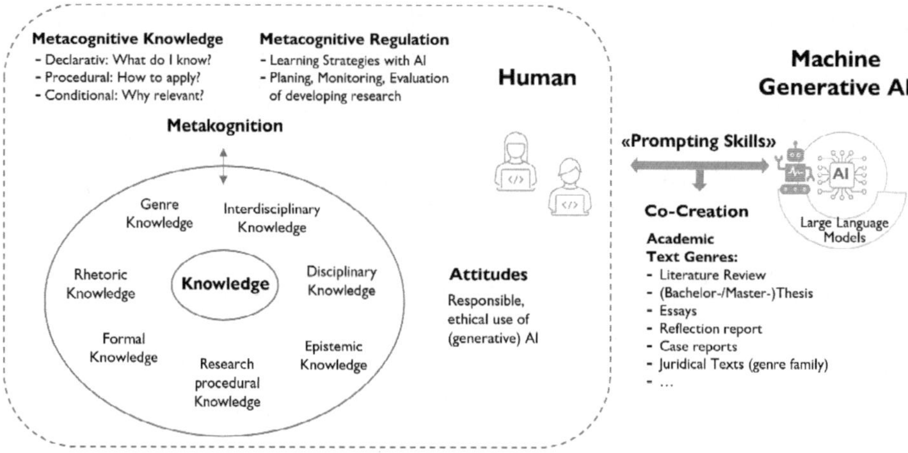

Figure 1. Type of knowledge for AI co-creation (Seufert, 2024)

4. RESULTS

4.1 Project SOCRAT (System of Critical Reasoning and Thesis)

4.1.1 Objectives of the SOCRAT Design

The SOCRAT (System of Critical Reasoning and Thesis) project aims to enhance students' research abilities during their initial semester at university. These essential skills are introduced through a compulsory introductory course attended by all students. In particular, the skills developed should make it easier for first-year students to start their studies. Additionally, the design empowers students to work with the AI tool.

4.1.2 SOCRAT as Training and Research Assistant

The course curriculum encompasses fundamental knowledge (as shown in Figure 2), such as various text genres and overarching research paradigms, as well as practical skills for designing, executing, and disseminating research projects. In the course's first part (Orientation Phase), students must build up the necessary specialist knowledge. This includes, above all, the cognitive knowledge presented in Chapter 3.1. In the second part of the course, students must apply what they have learnt by writing a systematic literature review. In this part of the course, students will go through the stages of planning their research, creating their insides and publishing their work.

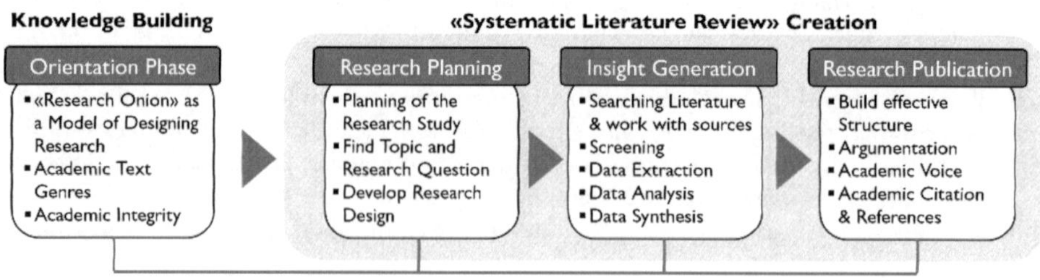

Figure 2. Stages and content of the SOCRAT design

The course consists of two parts and is structured according to Bloom's Mastery Learning (MT) concept. Mastery learning states that students should achieve a level of mastery in basic knowledge before moving on to new topics. If mastery is not achieved, students are given extra help to learn and revise, then retested (Bloom, 1968).

The use of AI in the two phases of the course is illustrated in Figure 3. First, the focus is on building research skills. In particular, the AI can provide personalised feedback, meaning each student is supported individually. The AI becomes a personalised training system. In addition to the necessary genre knowledge, students learn to use AI tools in academic writing. In particular, learning prompting skills is fundamental. At the end of the first phase, students sit a closed-book examination to test their acquired skills. Students who pass the exam enter the second phase of the course. The second part of the course requires students to apply and demonstrate these skills by working with AI to write their systematic literature review. The students write a scientific article in collaboration with the AI. This corresponds to the concept of "augmentation" (Jarrahi, 2018). This concept aims to create a working partnership between man and machine, where both can contribute their respective strengths. (Jarrahi, 2018; Seufert et al., 2019).

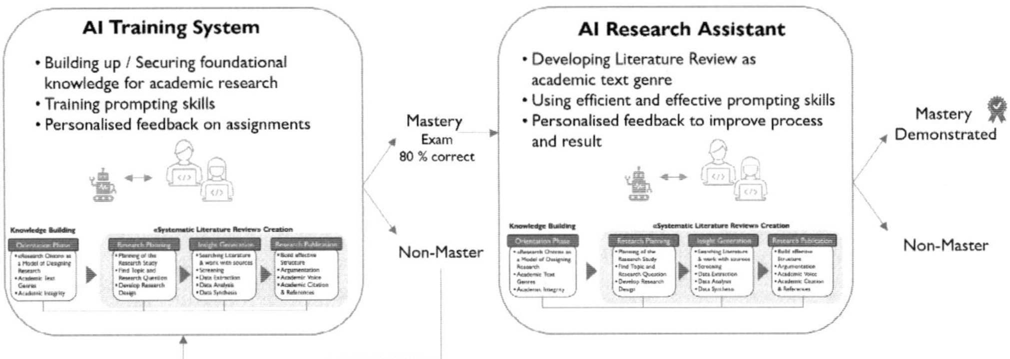

Figure 3. SOCRAT Design

The CARS model exemplifies the genre knowledge taught in SOCRAT Design. This model can illustrate an AI's role as a training system or a research assistant. Crafting an introduction for an academic article is a pivotal step in producing scholarly work. Structuring an introduction within a systematic literature review is an aspect of genre knowledge. When AI is utilised as a personal training system, it elucidates the principles of the CARS model and its potential applications within a systematic literature review framework. As a personal research assistant, AI answers students' queries about their texts and provides suggestions for more effective implementation of the CARS model in their systematic literature review introduction.

4.2 Evaluation of the Prompts Design Created for the SOCRAT Design

In the course design (SOCRAT) presented, AI plays an important role: in the first part as a personalised training system and in the second part as a personalised research assistant. The students use different prompts in the two roles of the AI. The next step is to test which types of prompts work well with the current state of the technology. The CARS model (see Chapter 3.1) is used as an example of genre knowledge to assess how well current LLMs cope with the prompts developed for the design. The performance of LLMs will be evaluated through two test series. The first trial contains tasks from lower taxonomy levels and is used to sort out unusable LLMs. The LLMs had to evaluate already written introductions in the second test series. The second test is exclusively assigned to language models who have completed the first task.

Table 2. Test procedure overview

Test series		Sample task for the LLMs
1	(9 tasks each in German and English)	• Name the 3 main moves in the CARS (Creating a Research Space) model by Swales. • What does the acronym CARS stand for in Swales's CARS model?
2	(6 tasks each in German and English)	• The following text is an introduction to a research paper. Analyse this introduction according to the CARS model developed by Swales. For the three moves, "establish a territory", "establish a niche", and "occupying the niche", state exactly where they begin and where they end. For each move, name every single phrase that is typical for this move.

4.2.1 Evaluation of LLMs in Test Series 1

As shown in previous chapters, this test requires LLMs to answer questions about the CARS model. The tasks with a low taxonomy level were sometimes solved very inaccurately. The LLMs are rated as adequate and inadequate based on their performance. A total of five models were rated unsatisfactory, and seven models were rated sufficient. Models 1, 6, 7, 8, 9, and 10 are unsuitable for the SOCRAT design due to poor performance in the first task. Specifically, Model 1 is imprecise, Model 6 has a high error rate, Model 7 struggles with German, and Models 8 and 9 answer too few questions correctly. Models 2, 3, 4, 5, 11, and 12 suit the SOCRAT design. Model 11 answered all questions correctly, while Model 12 also performed very well.

4.2.2 Evaluation of LLMs in Test Series 2

The LLMs were given a pre-written introduction, based on which the LLM had to solve the tasks described in Table 3. These are all tasks of higher taxonomy levels ('analysis' or 'evaluation'). In this section, the prompts used for the test are shown in italics.

Table 3. Tasks of the second test series

Task set	
1	Identify and label the three CARS moves in a given instruction.
2	Identify which of the three moves is missing in the given instruction.
3	Complete the introduction based on input from the student.
4	Support in improving the introduction by giving Feedback
5	Compare introductions and improve one of them.
6	Find weak points in the introduction and improve them.

The first task, in which the LLMs had to mark a CARS move's exact start and end points, was poorly solved. The LLMs could not achieve the accuracy promoted in the prompt: *"...For the 3 moves "establish a territory", "establish a niche", "occupying the niche", state exactly where they begin and where they end..."*. Task 2 was particularly badly solved when the prompts were written in English. All models have not understood the task. All LLMs solved task 3 very well. The prompt for task 3 described the task as follows: *"You are a tutor in a university course on academic writing. The students have learnt to write introductions according to the CARS model by Swales, but they need some help from time to time. The following is an incomplete introduction..."*. The assistance provided by the LLMs was very valuable. The support of the LLMs was precious to the students. The LLMs wrote excellent supplements to the given introduction. The prompt for task 4 was built similarly to the prompts for task 3. Task 4 was also solved well by all LLMs. The prompt explicitly stated that no complete solution should be proposed. *"... Provide the student with suggestions about how she can edit the text. Only write a few sentences on your own. For the major part of the sentences, you only provide support for the editing, but no complete solution..."*. The feedback provided is considered to be very helpful for the students. Tasks 5 and 6 were moderately well-solved. Many weaknesses were inherent in the instructions given to the LLM for completing tasks 5 and 6. All models offered valuable improvement suggestions. However, not all weaknesses were identified. It could be presumed that the LLMs would have discovered even more weaknesses if they had been queried again. Nevertheless, this was not pursued due to the zero-shot approach.

The following observations can be made on the individual models: Model 2 distinguished itself with coherent and concise answers in this evaluation, while Model 3 offered clear and actionable feedback. The lengthy responses of Model 4 were less disruptive, and Model 5 provided the most valuable feedback with its concise answers. Model 11 continued to be the top performer, whereas the feedback from Model 12 was perceived as less valuable.

5. DISCUSSION AND OUTLOOK

The SOCRAT design was developed based on the theory of genre-based writing. Care has been taken to foster the necessary skills for students to work with AI tools. Design not only promotes cognitive knowledge but also metacognitive knowledge. Structuring the courses according to Bloom's mastery learning concept ensures all students achieve the required competencies.

The two test series demonstrate the technical capabilities of the LLMs in performing the tasks of a personal training system and a personal research assistant. The objective was to ascertain whether the SOCRAT design could be implemented. The findings indicate that, in principle, six different LLMs can execute the tasks. Interestingly, it appears that even free language models can accomplish the assigned tasks, which could be particularly beneficial for educational institutions given the often limited public budgets.

The language models had to solve tasks at different levels of Bloom's taxonomy (Bloom, 1976). LLMs better solve certain types of tasks than others. In particular, tasks 3 and 4 of the second test series were solved very well by the LLMs. The LLMs must provide feedback or write texts based on student input in these two tasks. In this type of task, the focus is less on the precision of the answers and more on whether the LLMs relate well to the given introduction. In these types of tasks, the output of the language models can vigorously promote the development of students' competencies by conveying cognitive knowledge and stimulating metacognition. The LLMs provide food for thought and encourage students to scrutinise their work.

The LLMs still have difficulties solving task types, such as task 1 of the current test series. The LLMs cannot mark the exact start and end of a move of the CARS model. Precision is difficult for the LLM to realise. This problem can also be seen in the first test series in which certain LLMs have already been sorted out. A high level of response accuracy is essential, especially for tasks with a low taxonomy level.

Our experiments with the LLMs also show that the design of the prompt is particularly critical to the quality of the output. The language in which the prompt is written also significantly influences the quality of the output. Most LLMs were trained with more English than German data. It is necessary to empower students to formulate precise and accurate prompts. These skills should be taught alongside the technical knowledge in the initial part of the course. For students to formulate precise prompts, they must correctly understand the basics from the first part of the course, such as genre knowledge.

The zero-shot approach was used to test the LLMs, meaning no follow-up questions were asked. However, the authors assume that follow-up questions could improve the performance of the LLMs in text analysis.

6. CONCLUSION

Numerous studies suggest that the advent of AI fundamentally transforms academic writing (Boyd-Graber et al., 2023; Seufert et al., 2024; Spirgi et al., 2024). Students already use AI tools in their studies (von Garrel et al., 2023). Despite this, it remains crucial for students to master the art of scientific research. The rapid advancements in AI necessitate adaptations in university teaching programs. This article presents the theoretical foundations of genre-based writing, defines the competencies required to work with AI tools, and introduces the SOCRAT design. The two test series demonstrated that several LLMs can already perform the tasks of a personal training system or serve as personal research assistants. However, the performance of the LLMs varies for different types of tasks. The LLMs excel when tasked with making suggestions for improvement. It turns out that LLMs can be effectively used as tutors to promote the development of students' competencies. In other areas, the performance of LLMs is subpar.

Recognising that students can only effectively use AI tools if they possess the necessary knowledge to formulate precise prompts and evaluate the results is crucial. The design of the course and the tasks play a pivotal role in developing the student's skills. The next step involves testing the SOCRAT design with a select group of students.

REFERENCES

Badger, R., & White, G. (2000). A process genre approach to teaching writing. *ELT Journal, 54*(2), 153–160. https://doi.org/10.1093/elt/54.2.153

Bloom, B. S. (1968). *Learning for Mastery: Instruction and Curriculum* (BR-6-2556). https://files.eric.ed.gov/fulltext/ED053419.pdf

Bloom, B. S. (Ed.). (1976). *Beltz-Studienbuch: Vol. 35. Taxonomie von Lernzielen im kognitiven Bereich* (5. Aufl., 17. - 21. Tsd). Beltz.

Boyd-Graber, J., Okazaki, N., & Rogers, A. (2023). *ACL 2023 policy on AI writing assistance.* https://2023.aclweb.org/blog/ACL-2023-policy/

Hugging Face. (2024). *Open LLM Leaderboard.* https://huggingface.co/spaces/HuggingFaceH4/open_llm_leaderboard

Hyland, K. (2003). *Second language writing. ACLS Humanities E-Book.* Cambridge University Press. https://doi.org/10.1017/CBO9780511667251

Jarrahi, M. H. (2018). Artificial intelligence and the future of work: Human-AI symbiosis in organisational decision making. *Business Horizons*, *61*(4), 577–586. https://doi.org/10.1016/j.bushor.2018.03.007

Kruse, O. (2016). Wissenschaftliches Schreiben forschungsorientiert unterrichten. In A. Hirsch-Weber & S. Scherer (Eds.), *Wissenschaftliches Schreiben in Natur- und Technikwissenschaften* (pp. 29–53). Springer Fachmedien Wiesbaden. https://doi.org/10.1007/978-3-658-12211-9_3

Kruse, O., Meyer, H., & Everke Buchanan, S. (2015). *Schreiben an der Universität Konstanz : Eine Befragung von Studierenden und Lehrenden.* https://doi.org/10.21256/zhaw-55

McKenney, S., & Reeves, T. C. (2018). *Conducting Educational Design Research.* Routledge. https://doi.org/10.4324/9781315105642

Nesi, H., & Gardner, S. (2012). *Genres across the disciplines: Student writing in higher education. The Cambridge applied linguistics series.* Cambridge University Press.

OECD. (2020). *Lernkompass 2030: OECD-Projekt Future of Education and Skills 2030 Rahmenkonzept des Lernens.* https://www.oecd.org/education/2030-project/contact/OECD_Lernkompass_2030.pdf

Sabzalieva, E., & Valentini, A. (2023). *Chatgpt and artificial intelligence in higher education: Quick start guide.* Organisation des Nations unies pour l'éducation, la science et la culture (UNESCO); Institut international de l'UNESCO pour l'enseignement supérieur en Amérique latine et dans les Caraïbes / International Institute for Higher Education in Latin America and the Caribbean (IESALC). https://eduq.info/xmlui/handle/11515/38828

Seufert, S. (2024). Zukunft Bildung: Auswirkungen generativer KI auf Bildungssysteme. In S. Seufert & S. Handschuh (Eds.), *Generative Künstliche Intelligenz: ChatGPT und Co für Bildung, Wirtschaft und Gesellschaft* (1. Auflage, pp. 139–164). Schäffer-Poeschel Verlag.

Seufert, S., Burkhard, M., Gubelmann, R., Niklaus, C., & Handschuh, S. (2024). Hochschulbildung: KI-basiertes Forschen und Schreiben. In S. Seufert & S. Handschuh (Eds.), *Generative Künstliche Intelligenz: ChatGPT und Co für Bildung, Wirtschaft und Gesellschaft* (1. Auflage, pp. 197–214). Schäffer-Poeschel Verlag.

Seufert, S., Guggemos, J., Meier, C., & Helfritz, K. (2019). *Augmentation. Personalentwicklung in der digitalen Transformation - Ergebnisse einer empirischen Studie.* Deutsche Gesellschaft für Personalführung. https://www.alexandria.unisg.ch/handle/20.500.14171/98945

Spirgi, L., Seufert, S., Delcker, J., & Heil, J. (2024). Student Perspectives on Ethical Academic Writing with ChatGPT: An Empirical Study in Higher Education. *Proceedings of the 16th International Conference on Computer Supported Education*(Volume 2), 179–186.

Swales, J. (2014). Create a research space (CARS) model of research introductions. *Writing About Writing: A College Reader*, 12–15.

Swales, J. M. (1990). *Genre analysis: English in academic and research settings*. Cambridge University Press.

Tardy, C. M., Sommer-Farias, B., & Gevers, J. (2020). Teaching and Researching Genre Knowledge: Toward an Enhanced Theoretical Framework. *Written Communication*, *37*(3), 287–321. https://doi.org/10.1177/0741088320916554

Thoreau, M. (2006). *Write on track: A guide to academic writing*. Pearson Education New Zealand.

von Garrel, J. von, Mayer, J., & Mühlfeld, M. (2023). *Künstliche Intelligenz im Studium Eine quantitative Befragung von Studierenden zur Nutzung von ChatGPT & Co.* https://opus4.kobv.de/opus4-h-da/frontdoor/deliver/index/docId/395/file/befragung_ki-im-studium.pdf

Zenthöfer, J. (2023, December 1). Erste Uni schafft Bachelorarbeiten ab. *Frankfurter Allgemeine Zeitung,* 2023. https://www.faz.net/aktuell/karriere-hochschule/hoersaal/ki-und-plagiate-erste-uni-schafft-bachelorarbeiten-ab-19353621.html

LARGE LANGUAGE MODEL DETUNING IN LEARNING CONTENT UNDERSTANDING

Tsubasa Minematsu and Atsushi Shimada
Kyushu University, Japan

ABSTRACT

In using large language models (LLMs) for education, such as distractors in multiple-choice questions and learning by teaching, error-containing content is used. Prompt tuning and retraining LLMs are possible ways of having LLMs generate error-containing sentences in the learning content. However, there needs to be more discussion on how to tune LLMs for specific lecture content. Such discussions help control LLMs and for developing educational applications. In this study, we aim to train a detuned LLM that only states incorrect things, considering the limitations of prompt-based approaches such as prompt injection. Our method detunes LLMs by generating datasets that confuse LLMs. To evaluate our method, we asked the detuned LLM to solve multiple-choice questions to evaluate whether it answered the questions incorrectly or not. We also evaluate how many errors are contained in the sentences generated by the LLM to investigate how their knowledge of lecture content is degraded regarding factuality.

KEYWORDS

Large Language Model, Data Poisoning, Data Augmentation

1. INTRODUCTION

LLMs are not just theoretical concepts, but practical tools that can be applied to learning support and teacher support (Kasneci et al., 2023). Their high performance in text generation is shown in their practicality. In addition, their applicability to various natural language processing applications is remarkable, thanks to leveraging recent techniques such as prompt engineering and in-context learning. With LLM applications such as OpenAI's ChatGPT, we can quickly develop various practical applications such as question generation (Raina & Gales, 2022) and tutoring systems by LLMs (Mollick & Mollick, 2023). Mollick & Mollick (2023) provide seven examples of practical applications of LLMs as tutors and students and their relationship to educational theory.

The required abilities of such LLMs are different depending on their role. To support learners as a teacher, the LLM understand the learning content more correctly than the learners. Like learning-by-teaching (Kirschner & Hendrick, 2020; Matsuda et al., 2010), when a learner evaluates the texts generated by a LLM, it is acceptable for the LLM to produce sentences that contain mistakes. Such LLMs can provide a learning environment in which students interact with each other in a person-to-person-like dialogue, asking additional questions and pointing out mistakes.

The reasonable way for generating sentences containing errors is to constrain the LLM with prompts such as "Answer the question incorrectly" and "Explain the topic incorrectly". However, in our preliminary investigation, it was easy to get the constrained LLMs with the above prompt to explain correctly. After the LLM gave an incorrect explanation using the above prompt, this finding was produced by asking the LLM for the correct explanation again, like "Explain correctly". This second input for getting correct information can be regarded as a type of prompt injection such as "*ignore the above...*" (Crothers et al., 2023). In other words, even though a system administrator adds such constraints, learners can easily pull out the correct content when interacting with the LLM in a student role. Such attack methods have been studied to degrade the model performance (Crothers, Japkowicz, & Viktor, 2023; Shu et al., 2023). The task is to adjust the LLM to produce incorrect sentences. However, few discussions and developments exist on LLM performance degradation in educational applications. It is necessary to discuss how LLMs' abilities are limited for controlling LLMs.

As our research question, this study investigates whether LLMs can disrupt knowledge of previously acquired learning content. For the investigation, we propose a detuning method that directly disrupts an LLM's knowledge to degrade performance by a fine-tuning approach regarding the factuality and correctness of generated sentences. In this study, we detuned the knowledge of terms explained in lecture materials for a lecture on data science. Since there is no training dataset of incorrect sentences for the specific lecture, we develop automatic wrong sentence generation methods for the detuning dataset. For the RQ, we set the following RQs. (RQ1) Does the proposed method allow the LLM to generate incorrect content? (RQ2) What methods effectively degrade the LLM? As the evaluation criteria of our method, we used the number of wrong answers in multiple-choice questions because large-scale datasets of multiple-choice questions are used for LLM performance assessment (Yue et al., 2023). In addition, we manually evaluated the errors in the sentences generated by the LLMs. Furthermore, we discuss the results of the detuning process and the issues related to improving the efficiency of detuning.

2. RELATED WORK

Large language model for education. In recent years, the development of large-scale language models has progressed rapidly, and researchers from both companies and research institutions have proposed various large language models (Zhao et al., 2023). Their ability to generate sentences outperforms that of conventional language models, and the development of applications that take advantage of language models, such as ChatGPT, is accelerating. The field of education is no exception (Kasneci et al., 2023), and many educational applications of LLM are being proposed, such as question generation (Raina & Gales, 2022), foreign language learning (Young & Shishido, 2023) and tutoring (Mollick & Mollick, 2023). Different applications can be developed by inputting instructions to the LLM as prompts. This simplicity is different from the development of ITS and other systems. However, LLM's sentence generation is dependent on the training data. When domain knowledge not included in the training data is needed for adapting to lectures, the lack of knowledge can be added to LLMs by retrieval augmented generation (RAG) (Lewis et al., 2020) or finetuning. In this study, we aim to decrease LLM's performances, which cannot be achieved by augmenting knowledge with existing public data. Therefore, we generate poison data for detuning.

Adversarial attack for natural language processing. There are attack methods to cause LLM malfunctions and degrade LLM's performance. Identifying these vulnerabilities helps in enhancing the security and reliability of LLMs. The attack methods include prompt injection (Crothers et al., 2023). LLMs trained by third parties, especially companies, are tuned not to generate objectionable content. However, Zou et al. propose automatically generating adversarial prompts that allow objectionable content to be generated (Zou, Wang, Kolter, & Fredrikson, 2023). On the other hand, including harmful data (poison data) in the training of LLMs can cause inappropriate behavior in the trained LLMs (Wan, Wallace, Shen, & Klein, 2023; Shu et al., 2023). Wan et al. propose replacing the correct output label with the wrong poison label for input texts containing specific phrases. (Wan et al., 2023). In this attack method, only the inclusion of the specific phrases in the input text affects the prediction accuracy of the LLM. Shu et al. also propose generating adversarial responses by conveying the adversary's instructions to the LLM and the regular user's instructions (Shu et al., 2023). The LLM automatically uses pairs of user instructions and adversary responses as poison data for training. In this study, like Shu et al.'s method, we generate adversarial responses as poison data. The responses are related to incorrect understanding generated automatically from lecture materials.

3. DATA GENERATION FOR DETUNING LLM

This study aims to reduce the ability of pre-trained LLMs to generate sentences regarding factuality and correctness. Figure 1 shows our approach overview. A well-trained LLM learns word generation probabilities based on training data. As shown in Figure 1(a), to generate incorrect content such as "LLM is developed for image processing", we apply a fine-tuning approach using a small dataset with incorrect sentences. This fine-tuning process degrades the LLM performance regarding the factuality and correctness of generated sentences. Therefore, we call this process detuning (degradation by fine-tuning).

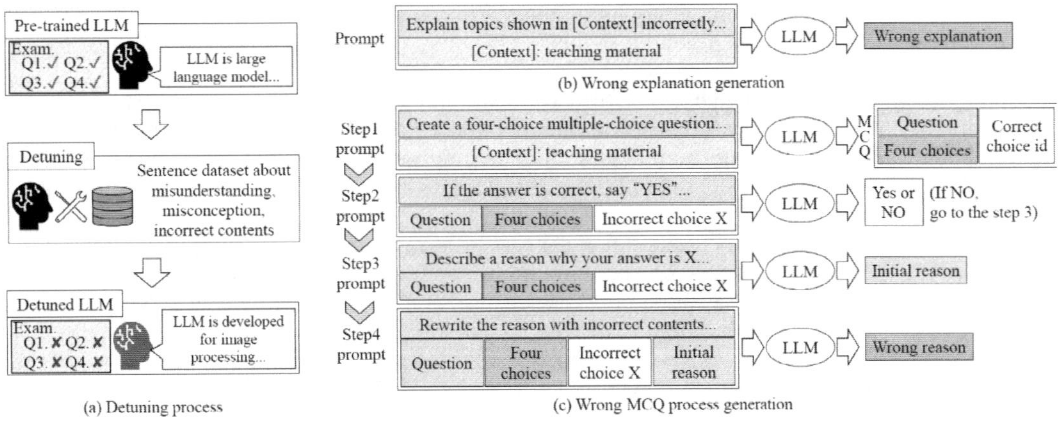

Figure. 1. Overview of detuning LLM and detuning data generation

We automatically construct a dataset with incorrect sentences about the learning content for detuning the LLM. Using the detuning dataset, the LLM's weight parameters change in the detuning process to increase the probability of generating incorrect sentences. When generating the detuning dataset, grammatical errors are unacceptable in this study because they are not directly related to disrupting LLM's knowledge of specific lecture content. It is also unacceptable to ignore learning context. For example, when asking the LLM to solve a problem, it is meaningless if the response from the LLM is always "Hello" ignoring the context. We use the lecture material as a context for data generation by pre-trained LLMs to generate sentences that are grammatically correct and consistent with the lecture content.

We propose two data generation methods for generating erroneous knowledge. First, from the viewpoint of wrong sentence generation for lecture materials, we propose wrong explanation generation (WEG), which incorrectly explains the topic shown in the lecture materials. Second, from the viewpoint of generating wrong answers to multiple-choice questions, we propose wrong MCQ process generation (WPG), which generates a wrong answering process based on wrong reasons.

3.1 Wrong Explanation Generation

As shown in Figure 1(b), in WEG, the well-trained LLM takes sentences from lecture materials as context and generates the wrong explanations. Any lecture material written in natural language can be used. However, lecture materials can be separated due to the limited number of input tokens in the LLM. WEG was executed for each slide page since slide-based learning materials were used in this study.

The prompts include an instruction part about the WEG and the context of the lecture material. The instruction part includes instruction sentences to give output format information and an incorrect explanation according to the context. An initial part of the instruction [1] is "Explain topics shown in [Context] with deliberately incorrect content.". The context part of the instruction contains the sentences extracted from one page of slide-based learning material. The generated sentences are used for the detuning process without post-processing.

3.2 Wrong MCQ Process Generation

In WPG, the wrong MCQ process corresponds to reasons why a choice was selected to answer a multiple-choice question. Such reasoning is used to enhance the performance of LLM, as in CoT (Wei et al., 2022). However, WPG tries to generate wrong reasons, and we expect that wrong reasoning leads to performance degradation. WPG is a complex task compared to WEG. Referring to the prompt design policy 3 (Sondos Mahmoud Bsharat, 2023), we divide this generation process into four steps. As shown in

[1] The full prompts in our method are shown in https://bit.ly/celda24PTM.

Figure 1(c), step 1 involves the generation of MCQs, step 2 entails the verification of MCQ answers, step 3 is dedicated to the initial generation of reasons, and step 4 focuses on the rewriting of reasons. WPG provides a pair of one MCQ, reasons when selecting an incorrect choice, and the incorrect choice number based on one page of slide-based material.

In step 1, MCQs are generated based on the lecture material. Like WEG, the well-trained LLM takes a page of slide-based material as context. It generates a question related to the content, four choices, and one correct answer choice number. The instruction begins: "Create a four-choice multiple-choice question based on the provided [Context]." Note that a one-shot MCQ example is included in the prompt for formatting purposes.

In step 2, the LLM receives the generated question, the four choices, and the answer number. It verifies whether its choice is correct or incorrect. An initial part of the instruction is "If the answer is correct, say YES, otherwise NO." The answer choices marked as wrong in step 2 are used in step 3.

In step 3, the LLM generates a reason for its choice in answering the question. The LLM takes the question, the four choices, and the number marked as wrong in step 2. It generates the reason for choosing that choice number. An initial part of the instruction is "Describe a reason why your answer is choice {#choice}", where {#choice} is the choice number. However, since there is no explicit instruction here to include incorrect sentences, the LLM might not generate incorrect sentences efficiently.

In step 4, erroneous sentences are generated by instructing LLM directly, like WEG. The LLM accepts the reason generated in step 3 and the context in step 3. The LLM rewrites one sentence at a time to increase the chance of including the incorrect reason. An initial part of the instruction is "Rewrite [Target] with a deliberately incorrect content.".

After step 4, we can obtain MCQs, reasons when selecting an incorrect choice, and the incorrect choice number. By combining those generated sentences, detuned datasets can be constructed. Details are described in Section 4.1. However, in our preliminary evaluation, we identified a bias in the distribution of incorrect choice numbers. Therefore, we rearranged the order of the four choices to equalize the frequency of incorrect choice numbers in the dataset as post-processing. In addition, we replace "choice X" with "this choice" when the reasons contain "choice X", where X is a number because the order of the choice is changed.

4. EXPERIMENTAL SETTINGS

We evaluated the effectiveness of the detuning process and the detuning data generation methods regarding the degradation of LLMs' factuality and correctness. First, we generated the detuning datasets using WEG and WPG, and then a well-trained LLM was detuned by using the detuning datasets. The details of the detuning settings are described in Section 4.1. The LLMs detuned by the different datasets conducted two tasks: answering for MCQ and explaining lecture content to evaluate the effectiveness of our dataset generation methods. The evaluation aimed to investigate whether our detuning process degraded LLMs. In addition, we analyzed what component of our method was effective for the detuning. The details of the evaluation settings are described in Section 4.2 and 4.3.

4.1 Detuning Setting

In this experiment, we used the slide-based lecture material in lectures at our institution to generate detuning datasets. The lectures were on data science introduction and included content for beginners, from data analysis basics to machine learning outlines. The number of lecture materials was seven, and the total number of pages was 410.

In WEG and WPG, we used GPT-4 (gpt-4-preview-1104) in OpenAI. The temperature, top p, and other parameters were set to 1.0, 0.0, and default values. Note that the temperature was 0.0 in WPG's step 2 because the expected outputs were YES or NO. When executing WEG and WPG, the average number of characters generated is 542.05 and 452.98, respectively. After WEG and WPG, we constructed three datasets: the WEG, WPG, and WPG(init) datasets. The WPG(init) dataset consists of initial reason statements generated in step 3 of WPG. We investigated how LLM was degraded and the effectiveness of the degradation by comparing WEG and WPG datasets. In addition, we focused on the effectiveness of step 4 of WPG by comparing WPG and WPG(init) datasets.

The data format for the detuning followed OpenAI's API. In WEG, the first ten characters of the generated sentence were formatted as input tokens and the remaining as output tokens. Three types of detuning samples were formatted in WPG. The first sample focused on generating reasons. The input contained the generated MCQ and the instructions for reasoning it. The output contained the corresponding generated reason. The second sample focused on answering MCQs. The input contained the generated MCQ, reasons, and instructions for answering it. The output was the answer choice number. Like WEG, the third sample focused on generating incorrect sentences directly. The input contained the first ten characters of the reason sentence. The output contained the remaining. Note that the last part of the reason tends to contain a statement about the choice, such as "therefore, this choice is correct". It is unnecessary in tasks such as "Please explain X". Therefore, we used 75% of the sentences from the beginning of the reason in the third sample.

We used GPT-3.5 (gpt-3.5-turbo) as a detuned target model. The GPT-3.5 was detuned by the WEG, WPG, and WPG(init) datasets. As the training hyperparameters, we set the epoch to 8, the learning rate multiplier in OpenAI's API to 2.0, the batch size of WEG to 1, and the batch size of WPG/WPG(init) to 8. Since the size of the detuning dataset was different for each dataset, the number of epochs and batch size were configured to achieve roughly equal numbers of training steps across datasets. The size of the WEG dataset was 410, and WPG/WPG(init) were 3168. Therefore, the number of iterations was approximately 3200.

4.2 MCQ Evaluation Setting

The detuned LLMs were evaluated based on their ability to answer MCQs. One of the authors, a data science lecturer, developed the MCQs for this evaluation. Each MCQ featured four choices and was structured around the question, such as, "Which is the correct explanation for X?" We used 106 MCQs related to lecture material topics in data science.

We compared the correct answer rates of four different LLMs: GPT-3.5, and the three detuned LLMs. GPT-3.5 was used as the baseline model. In this evaluation, we aimed that the detuned LLMs had lower rates than GPT-3.5. All the LLMs used the same prompt to answer MCQs. The instruction is "Please respond to the following question. You should display your answer number only."

4.3 Explanation Evaluation Setting

We evaluated the explanation ability of the detuned LLMs to investigate whether they learned incorrect content and explained lecture topics incorrectly. Compared to the MCQ evaluation, this evaluation focused on what knowledge LLM learned. In this evaluation, we asked the three detuned LLMs to explain keywords of data sciences. The 11 selected keywords were the main topics in each lecture material such as "Quantitative and Qualitative Data," and "Artificial Intelligence".

The explanations by the detuned LLMs were evaluated on a sentence-by-sentence basis manually. We referred to the evaluation criteria by Liu et al. (2022).

- *Grammaticality*: Wherever the generated sentences are grammatical or not.
- *Relevance*: Whether the generated sentences are relevant to the explanation of the given keyword.
- *Factuality*: Whether the generated sentences are factually correct or not. The explanations should be generally adequate, even if there are exceptions, such as unusual cases.

These criteria were binary labels "Agree" = 1 and "Disagree" = 0. Factuality is the most important criterion in this evaluation. The criterion directly shows whether the knowledge of the detuned LLM is disrupted. Grammaticality and relevance are also assessed, as demonstrating the absence of grammatical errors and irrelevant explanations are required for assessing factuality. Note that we expected that the detuned LLMs would be sufficient in grammaticality because our detuning datasets were generated from GPT-4.

The two evaluators evaluated the generated explanations based on the three criteria. We recruited a lecturer of data science and an information science research student in our institution as evaluators. There is no reward. The lecturer was the same as the MCQ developer. The research student belonged to our Graduate School of Information Science, was familiar with pattern recognition, and had enough knowledge of the lecture material in this study. We did not tell the research student that the LLMs were detuned. As training for the evaluation, they practiced the evaluation using some examples prepared for this training and agreed on the results of each evaluation.

Table 1. Correct answer rate (CAR) in MCQ evaluation. WEG, WPG, and WPG(init) mean the detuned LLM by each dataset

LLM	GPT-3.5	WEG	WPG	WPG(init)
CAR (%)	76.42	49.52	11.32	11.32

Table 2. The agreement of the two evaluators and the mean score in grammaticality, relevance, and factuality in the explanation evaluation

Metric	Grammaticality	Relevance	Factuality
Agreement (%)	97.7	100	83.0
Mean score	0.989	1.00	0.580

Detuned LLM	WEG	WPG	WPG(init)
Agree (%)	56.9	0.0	83.3
Either one agree (%)	29.2	3.9	15.0
Disagree (%)	13.8	96.1	1.7

We instructed the detuned LLMs to "Explain keyword in data science in about five sentences in Japanese." Note that we added an instruction to the prompt to control the number of sentences to balance the number of assessments. The three detuned LLM by the WEG, WPG, and WPG(init) datasets generated 65, 51, and 60 sentences (3475, 3316, and 3280 characters), respectively. Therefore, the evaluators assessed 176 sentences.

5. EXPERIMENTAL RESULTS

5.1 Evaluation Results

MCQ evaluation. Table 1 shows the correct answer rate for the MCQs comparing the four LLMs. The correct answer rate was calculated by dividing the correct responses by the total number of questions (106 questions). Note that, once, the detuned LLM by WEG could not be answered due to formatting errors. We instructed that the output format was only number using the prompt. The response was removed.

We confirmed that our detuning process could reduce the performance of the MCQ answering task. All the detuned LLMs demonstrated lower correct answer rates than GPT-3.5. GPT-3.5, as the baseline, demonstrated a 76.42% correct answer rate. In WEG, the correct answer rate decreased by about 17%. In WPG and WPG(init), the correct answer rate decreased by about 65%. Therefore, the WPG and WPG(init)-LLMs demonstrated lower correct answer rates than the WEG-LLM. The result indicates the effectiveness of task-specific detuning. The WPG dataset did not contain incorrect contents for the MCQ answering process.

Explanation evaluation. To assess the evaluators' agreement on the explanation evaluation, we calculated the agreement on grammaticality, relevance, and factuality by dividing the number of their same decisions by the total number of evaluated sentences. In addition, the scores by the evaluators were calculated to investigate the quality of the generated sentences. The results are shown in Table 2. These agreements were shown between 80% and 100%. Factuality's agreement was lower than one of grammaticality and relevance. The Cohen's kappa was $\kappa = 0.65$ in factuality. Based on the above consideration, we conclude that the agreement is acceptable in the explanation evaluation.

Regarding grammaticality and relevance in Table 2, the mean scores were nearly 1.0. For almost all explanations of grammar and relevance, both evaluators decided that the quality was sufficient. This result means that the detuning dataset contained grammatically sufficient sentences, and the detuning process did not lose the ability to understand the natural language enough to communicate with us as expected. We concluded that the generated explanations were quality enough to analyze factuality, our main criterion.

According to Table 3, we observed differences in the number of incorrect explanations generated by the detuned LLMs, comparing the three datasets. The WPG(init)-LLM generated a few explanations containing incorrect contents, and 83.3% of the explanations satisfy factuality. On the other hand, most of the explanations generated by the WPG-LLMs did not satisfy facticity. The results of the detuned LLM by WEG were also intermediate between the results of the WPG and WPG(init). Therefore, the WPG process was the most effective in degrading LLM for factuality.

These results imply that this may reflect the number of incorrect sentences in each dataset. WPG(init) was a dataset built from sentences of initial reasons before explicit instructions to include incorrect reasons in the WPG process. Therefore, this means it is consistent with containing few incorrect explanations in this evaluation's results. In the WEG process, the well-trained LLM (GPT-4) directly generated incorrect explanations from learning material in a single instruction. On the other hand, the WPG process was multi-stage. In step 4, a corresponding incorrect reason sentence was generated for each initial reason sentence, which made it more likely to contain incorrect sentences.

5.2 Discussion and Limitation

According to Table 1 and Table 3, the detuned LLM by the WPG dataset achieved the degradation of LLMs in terms of answering MCQs incorrectly and giving incorrect explanations, which is the answer of RQ1. In addition, the detuned LLMs by the WPG(init) and WEG were partially degraded. Depending on the data generation method, the effectiveness of the detuning was different, which is the answer of RQ2. In Table 1, the WPG(init)-LLM showed the lowest correct answer rate, while it could explain the keywords in data science lectures correctly in Table 3. The WPG(init) results imply that the task type of the dataset can effectively control the abilities of LLMs. In other words, it is essential to design the assessment items to restrict these abilities and consider whether data generation or dataset construction for the restriction is possible. The WEG results demonstrated less degradations than WPG results in both MCQ and explanation evaluation. We consider that the number of incorrect sentences in detuning datasets is crucial in controlling LLM degradation. This insight is instrumental in controlling LLMs' abilities (e.g., a medium level of understanding). However, our method did not specifically focus on degrading specific knowledge and the level of competency in this study. Such flexible degradation methods are a future challenge.

Our technical limitation is the guarantee of the accuracy of the generation of MCQs in step 1 of the WPG. Hallucination is generally a challenge for LLMs. In our study, the choices generated by the LLM as incorrect choices can be correct. In order to alleviate this problem, the WPG process reconfirms the choices in step 2 with more simple task prompts than in step 1. According to Table 1, we believe that the effect of the hallucination on choice is minor; however, when we asked GPT-4 to answer the MCQs in the same experimental setting as in Section 4.2, the correct answer rate was 89.6%. Therefore, improving the accuracy of MCQ generation is essential to guarantee the stability of WPG. In addition, our evaluation has the other limitations. We made the MCQs to evaluate the four LLMs. However, our MCQs only evaluate the lower levels, such as remembering and understanding, in Bloom's taxonomy (LW et al., 2001). In order to control LLM flexibly, it is necessary to incorporate tasks related to higher-order cognitive levels into the data generation. Alternatively, we can use the MCQs for assessing high-order thinking (Jovanovska, 2018).

We expect learning-by-teaching environments with the detuned LLM to be helpful, such as correcting incorrect explanations generated by the detuned LLM. To improve the contents provided by the detuned LLM, we need to evaluate whether the generated sentences contain beneficial incorrect content for learners, such as mistakes that learners are likely to make. The following two sentences used in the explanation evaluation were generated by the WPG-LLMs: (1) "Unstructured data refers to data organized strictly according to a regular format within a specific data model or relational database." and (2) "Data visualization is a culinary doctrine that uses different spices' colors and aromas to represent information to make particularly complex recipes and cooking procedures easier to understand." The explanation in the learning material uses an analogy between data analysis and cooking. The detuned dataset can contain such words related to cooking. Sentence (1) is a mistake about structured data. While it can help confirm concepts, Sentence (2) contains incorrect information that data science course learners would not make. Assessing such biases is important in controlling detuned LLMs as student models.

6. CONCLUSION

We proposed a detuning method that disrupts LLM knowledge according to learning content, such as lecture material. In the data poison-based attack method, we have developed a wrong explanation generation that incorrectly explains the contents of lecture materials and a wrong MCQ process generation that generates incorrect answer processes for multiple-choice questions. In the experiments, MCQ evaluation and explanation evaluation were conducted. The results showed that WPG had the lowest MCQ correct answer rate and could generate incorrect explanations. In the future, we investigate data generation methods that connect cognitive models to data generation tasks, such as Bloom's taxonomy, to flexibly limit LLMs' abilities.

ACKNOWLEDGEMENT

This work was supported by JST, PRESTO Grant Number JPMJPR236A, Japan.

REFERENCES

Crothers, E. N., Japkowicz, N., & Viktor, H. L. (2023). Machine generated text: A comprehensive survey of threat models and detection methods. *IEEE Access, 11*, 70977-71002.

Jovanovska, J. (2018). Designing effective multiple-choice questions for assessing learning outcomes. *Infotheca - Journal for Digital Humanities, 18* (1), 25–42.

Kasneci, E., Sessler, K., Küchemann, S., Bannert, M., Dementieva, D., Fischer, F., . . . Kasneci, G. (2023). Chatgpt for good? on opportunities and challenges of large language models for education. *Learning and Individual Differences, 103*, 102274.

Kirschner, P., & Hendrick, C. (2020). *How learning happens: Seminal works in educational psychology and what they mean in practice.* Routledge.

Lewis, P., Perez, E., Piktus, A., Petroni, F., Karpukhin, V., Goyal, N., . . . others (2020). Retrieval-augmented generation for knowledge-intensive nlp tasks. *Advances in Neural Information Processing Systems, 33*, 9459–9474.

Liu, J., Liu, A., Lu, X., Welleck, S., West, P., Le Bras, R., . . . Hajishirzi, H. (2022). Generated knowledge prompting for commonsense reasoning., *Proceedings of the 60th annual meeting of the association for computational linguistics (volume1: Long papers)* (pp. 3154–3169).

LW, A., DR, K., PW, A., KA, C., Mayer, R., PR, P., . . . MC, W. (2001). *A taxonomy for learning, teaching, and assessing: A revision of bloom's taxonomy of educational objectives.*

Matsuda, N., Keiser, V., Raizada, R., Tu, A., Stylianides, G., Cohen, W. W., & Koedinger, K. R. (2010). Learning by teaching simstudent: Technical accomplishments and an initial use with students. In *Intelligent tutoring systems: 10th international conference, part i 10* (pp. 317–326).

Mollick, E., & Mollick, L. (2023). Assigning ai: Seven approaches for students, with prompts. *ArXiv, abs/2306.10052.*

Raina, V., & Gales, M. (2022). Multiple-choice question generation: Towards an automated assessment framework. *arXiv preprint arXiv:2209.11830.*

Shu, M., Wang, J., Zhu, C., Geiping, J., Xiao, C., & Goldstein, T. (2023). On the exploitability of instruction tuning. In *Thirty-seventh conference on neural information processing systems.*

Sondos Mahmoud Bsharat, Z. S., Aidar Myrzakhan. (2023). Principled instructions are all you need for questioning llama-1/2, gpt-3.5/4. *arXiv preprint arXiv:2312.16171.*

Wan, A., Wallace, E., Shen, S., & Klein, D. (2023). Poisoning language models during instruction tuning. In *Proceedings of the 40th international conference on machine learning.*

Wei, J., Wang, X., Schuurmans, D., Bosma, M., Xia, F., Chi, E., . . . others (2022). Chain-of-thought prompting elicits reasoning in large language models. *Advances in Neural Information Processing Systems, 35,* 24824– 24837.

Young, J. C., & Shishido, M. (2023). Investigating openai's chatgpt potentials in generating chatbot's dialogue for english as a foreign language learning. *International Journal of Advanced Computer Science and Applications, 14* (6).

Yue, X., Ni, Y., Zhang, K., Zheng, T., Liu, R., Zhang, G., . . . Chen, W. (2023). *Mmmu: A massive multi-discipline multimodal understanding and reasoning benchmark for expert agi.*

Zhao, W. X., Zhou, K., Li, J., Tang, T., Wang, X., Hou, Y., . . . Ji-Rong Wen, J. (2023). A survey of large language models. *ArXiv, abs/2303.18223.*

Zou, A., Wang, Z., Kolter, J. Z., & Fredrikson, M. (2023). *Universal and transferable adversarial attacks on aligned language models.*

EVIDENCE-BASED CONTENT DESIGN AND VALIDATION FOR CYBERSECURITY GAMES

Nicolai Plintz[1] and Dirk Ifenthaler[1, 2]
[1]*University of Mannheim, Germany*
[2]*Curtin University, Australia*

ABSTRACT

This study aims to develop a preliminary model for the content validation of serious games, specifically to assess two cybersecurity games designed for children aged 8-13 years as part of the Erasmus+ project "SuperCyberKids". Using a scoping review of databases from pedagogy, psychology, and computer science, we identified current trends in creating and validating content for serious games. The study proposes a three-phase model for content validation: initialization, theoretical content validation, and practical content validation. This model is intended to ensure that serious games meet the defined learning objectives and provide effective learning experiences. Subsequently, we conducted a survey with N=20 experts based on the scoping review, who were asked to evaluate the content of two cybersecurity games, Spoofy and Nabbovaldo. The results showed that both games generally provided good protection across the content topics.

KEYWORDS

Game-Based Learning, Serious Games, Cybersecurity

1. INTRODUCTION

Serious games are becoming increasingly popular and are being used in a wide variety of educational contexts. There is a wide range for the use of serious games, for instance, financial education (Hoseiny & Niknafs, 2020), the medical field (Roman et al., 2020), cultural safety training (Pimentel et al., 2022), and cybersecurity (Manganello et al., 2023). However, serious games and game-based learning are not new phenomena and have a long tradition (Eseryel et al., 2011; Plass et al., 2016). Serious games appeared over fifty years ago and can be described as games whose main purpose is not purely entertainment (Loh et al., 2015; Abt, 1987). In general, serious games as an intervention appear to be well-researched in terms of cognitive, metacognitive, and affective-motivational learning outcomes (Eseryel et al., 2014; Barz et al., 2024), as well as their influence on motivation (Zou et al., 2021), engagement, emotions (Lei et al., 2022), and potential in assessment (Eseryel et al., 2014). But there are still some challenges left, on the one hand, that the competencies to be taught are not always clear and, on the other hand, how to integrate existing games into a curriculum (Wastiau et al., 2009). While other reviews focus more on measuring learning outcomes (Acquah & Katz, 2020) or the impact of a specific domain (Noroozi et al., 2020; Gao & Sun, 2020), there seems to be a gap in the validation of the content of serious games, for instance in terms of embedding them in existing learning scenarios. What emerges, however, is that the origin of the content and the conception of such games are not always transparent (e.g., Duffull & Peterson, 2020; Sousa & Rocha, 2019). As part of the [anonymized project name], teachers and school heads are provided with two games to be examined for holistic coverage. The evaluation aims to determine which competencies cannot be taught through the games to create further materials and content. A scoping review was conducted to address this gap, followed by the proposed strategy for validating the two cybersecurity games. To focus on content validation to create an appropriate strategy for our game evaluation, we used the following research questions:

RQ1: Are there standard processes for creating the content for serious games?

RQ2: What content validation strategies are used in connection with serious games?

RQ3: Which components and processes are necessary to develop and implement a holistic model for the content validation of serious games?

RQ4: How can the developed holistic model effectively validate the content of two specific serious games?

2. METHODOLOGY

2.1 Scoping Review

We used leading educational, psychology, and informatics databases for the scoping literature review: Science Direct, ERIC, Web of Science, and IEEE Xplore. A dualistic search string was applied. To reflect the different facets of "Serious Games," the search string included different synonyms and components. The outcome search string included different modules for analyzing the content. For instance, competency or content analytics. Search String focused on GBL: ("Serious Game*" OR "Educational Game*" OR "Learning Game* OR "Digital Game*" OR "Game-Based Learning") Search String focused on Content evaluation ("Competency Evaluation" OR "Content Analys*" OR "Qualitative Analys*" OR "Thematic Analy*"). Our search included scientific literature published by June 2024 and was confined to articles that were published within the last five years. The inclusion criteria were to involve a game or a framework for evaluating the content of games. In addition, we included studies relating to an iterative design process were also included. In other words, studies in which a game was conceptualized or developed and the content was iteratively adapted. Books, theses, and studies that were not in English have been excluded. In sum, $N = 181$ studies were identified. After removing the duplicate, $N = 148$ were left. After carrying out the title and abstract search, $N = 50$ remained. After screening the full-text papers, $N = 18$ articles were finally included. From the included studies, we extracted the type of games, content analysis strategies that were carried out, and the criteria to develop the content of the games.

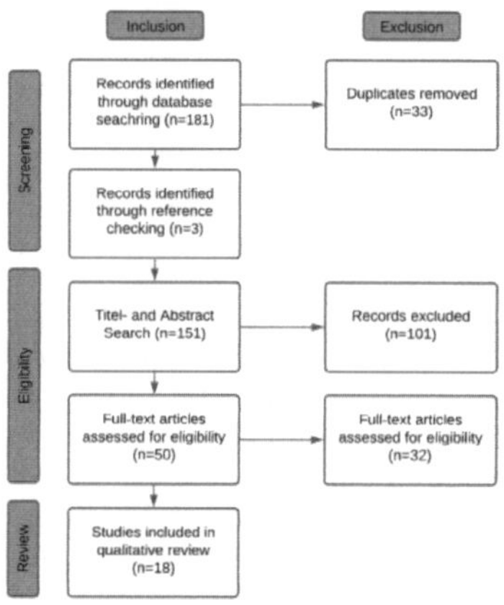

Figure 1. Flow-Chart Scoping Review

2.2 Content Evaluation

After we had created the content evaluation strategy, we conducted a survey with professionals (N=20) to test and evaluate the content of the two cybersecurity games, Spoofy and Nabbovaldo. N=10 professionals for Nabbovaldo and N=10 for Spoofy for each game. We recruited professionals from the areas of education (N=13), cybersecurity (N=1), and cybersecurity education (N=6) to validate the content. The participants in the Spoofy group were mainly aged between 18 and 29 (n=5) and 30 and 39 (n=2), followed by 40 and 49 (n=2) and 50 and 59 (n=1). In the Nabbovaldo group, the age distribution was as follows: 18-29 years (n=3), 30-39 years (n=6), 40-49 years (n=1). In terms of professional expertise, almost half had more than seven years of professional experience. This longevity of experience suggests that participants could provide informed and thoughtful assessments. Geographically, the participants gained their experience in different countries: ten in Germany, three in Italy, two in Estonia, two in Bulgaria, and one person each in Russia, the USA, Estonia, and Türkiye. This geographical diversity brought a variety of perspectives to the evaluation and allowed for a comprehensive analysis of the game Spoofy and Nabbovaldo.

3. RESULTS

3.1 Are there Standard Processes for Creating the Content for Serious Games?

The content creation methodologies can be narrowed down to three main areas. These range from the use of experiential knowledge from experts (Arboleya-Garcia & Miralles, 2022; Andreoli et al., 2017) to the use of scientific literature (Tinôco et al., 2022; Roman et al., 2020; Hodges et al., 2021; Neuwelt & Kearns, 2021) and the use of multilevel methods (Ingadottir et al., 2022; Leong et al., 2021; Pimentel et al., 2022). Multi-level methods usually combine empirical knowledge and domain-specific knowledge from professionals using literature. It is striking that these methods also involve the end-users (Leong et al., 2021; Pimentel et al., 2022). Holistic approaches to content creation also emphasize the involvement of domain and content experts (Andreoli et al., 2017). Occasionally, the approach is reversed in that developing serious games itself should contribute to learning success (Ke, 2014). The development of learning objectives by SME for development also appears to be an approach for developing content for serious games (Arboleya-Garcia & Miralles, 2022). An extension of this approach could be the integration of serious games into the curriculum and the use of existing learning objectives (Duffull & Peterson, 2020; Hodges et al., 2021).

3.2 What Content Validation Strategies are used in Connection With serious games?

Content validation strategies are essentially linked to the creation of serious games and should involve different stakeholders, such as content experts, pedagogical experts, game designers, and developers (Andreoli et al., 2017). Questionnaires are one of the main methods for evaluating content (Calderón & Ruiz, 2015; Sousa & Rocha, 2019; Mhadhbi et al., 2024), but interviews and participant reflections are also frequently used (Pimentel et al., 2022). Dedicated questionnaires on content topics are rare, and content validation questions often appear only sporadically (e.g., Mhadhbi et al., 2024). These questionnaires tend to focus on a holistic evaluation of the games, frequently neglecting content validation. These findings are consistent with the results of the scoping review by Pistono and colleagues (2022), who identified eleven frameworks for creating and validating serious games. The evaluation tends to focus more on design. These findings are consistent with this scoping review. Some authors tend to conduct usability tests, for example, for age appropriateness (Ingadottir et al., 2022) or in terms of design and gameplay (Leong et al., 2021), and consider elements of content evaluation (Daoudi, 2022). Andreoli and colleagues (2017) propose a more content-based evaluation through pre- and post-tests to measure learning gains (Calderón & Ruiz, 2015). Several options have emerged: one option is to compare with the learning objectives as part of a pilot study (Arboleya-Garcia & Miralles, 2022), and another is a validation carried out in advance by experts. For example, Neuwelt and Kearns (2021) had a validation carried out by experts before the introduction of their escape room. Another method is to have certain materials, such as practice-oriented use cases, evaluated by experts. In the study by Tinôco and colleagues (2022), experts validated the clinical cases, with a minimum agreement of 80% required. If this was not achieved, the use cases were adjusted.

In summary, a dual approach to content validation is promising. Based on the findings of this scoping review, we developed the following content evaluation strategy: First, we used a systematic review to extract all cybersecurity skills necessary for the age group (Plintz & Ifenthaler, 2023) and converted them into competencies. In the next step, we checked whether a basic offer for teaching the topics was available by converting the relevant cybersecurity competencies into "The game introduces to...". As a final step, we plan to conduct pre- and post-tests as part of a pilot study.

3.3 Which Components and Processes are Necessary to Develop and Implement a Holistic Model for the Content Validation of Serious Games?

No holistic model for the content validation of serious games stands out from the scoping review. However, if the content elements of the individual studies are summarized, an initial framework can be created. Thus, content validation can comprise three phases: initialization phase, theoretical content validation, and practical content validation. In the initialization phase for the validation of the content of the games, learning objectives for comparison should first be defined or extracted. These objectives can be created by SMEs (e.g., Arboleya-Garcia & Miralles, 2022; Andreoli et al., 2017), from scientific literature (e.g., Tinôco et al., 2022; Roman et al., 2020; Hodges et al., 2021; Neuwelt & Kearns, 2021) and/or from curricular learning objectives (Andreoli et al., 2017). In the second phase, a first content validation could be carried out. This first validation should check whether a serious game is theoretically available to achieve the learning objectives. This could be done by professionals in different ways, for instance piloting with professionals (Neuwelt and Kearns, 2021), interviews or reflection from professionals (Pimentel et al., 2022), or surveying professionals (e.g., Calderón & Ruiz, 2015; Sousa & Rocha, 2019; Mhadhbi et al., 2024; Duffull & Peterson, 2020). In the third phase, the practical content validation, the end users should also be involved (e.g., Leong et al., 2021; Pimentel et al., 2022). Here, a pre-and post-test could be used to evaluate whether the content can be taught (Calderón & Ruiz, 2015). Figure 2 provides an overview of a potential initial model.

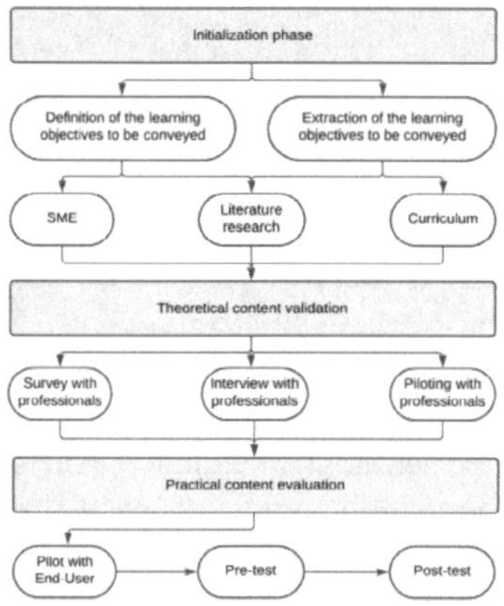

Figure 2. Initial Content Evaluation Framework for Serious Games

3.4 How can the Developed Holistic Model Effectively Validate the Content of Two Specific Serious Games?

As an initialization phase, we extracted the skills that 8–13-year-olds should have in the field of cybersecurity from the literature, using a study that had already been carried out. This included a skill extraction from the scientific literature as part of a systematic review and a subsequent validation by a Delphi study (Plintz & Ifenthaler, 2023). This was then translated into learning objectives or, rather, competence statements. These serve as a basis and function as learning objectives. In the next step, an expert survey was conducted as part of the theoretical content validation. The survey study with professionals evaluates the content coverage conveyed by the serious games Nabbovaldo and Spoofy. We have carried out an analysis of the mean value, the percentage of agreement (PA), and the ratio of agreement to disagreement (PAD). We categorized the data based on these three indicators to create a mapping. Table 1 provides an overview of the categorization logic.

Table 1. Coverage Criterion

Coverage Criterion	**Good Coverage Criterion**	**Moderate Coverage Criterion**	**Poor Coverage Criterion**
Percentage of Agreement (PA)	PA > 75%	75% ≥ PA < 50%	PA ≤ 50%
Ratio Agree disagree (PAD)	PAD > 80% Ratio: 5:1 and higher	80% ≥ PAD < 75% Ratio: 4:1	PAD ≤ 75% Ratio: 3:1 and lower
Mean value (MV)	MV > 2,6	2,6 ≥ MV < 2,3	MV ≤ 2,3

A mean value (MV) above 2.6 is required for good coverage, indicating high overall agreement. The percentage of agreement (PA) must be above 75%, placing it in the top quartile. Moderate coverage requires a positive value, meaning total agreement is at least half of all responses. Values below this threshold indicate poor coverage. The agreement to disagreement (PAD) ratio should exceed 80%, ensuring a higher than 4:1 ratio and minimizing ambiguity. If the ratio is 3:1 or lower (≤ 75%), it indicates poor coverage, as the results show ambiguity among professionals. Therefore, there are three assessment criteria for each competency item. These criteria are then divided into sections to carry out the assessment, which categorizes coverage into different levels: good, moderate-good, moderate, moderate-poor, and poor coverage. The coverage level for each item is detailed in Table 2.

Table 2. Base of the Coverage Level

Coverage Level	Criteria
Good Coverage	3 criteria good coverage, or 2 criteria good coverage + 1 criteria moderate coverage
Moderate-Good Coverage	2 criteria moderate coverage + 1 criteria good coverage
Moderate Coverage	3 criteria moderate coverage, or 1 criterion good coverage + 1 criterion moderate coverage + 1 criterion poor coverage
Moderate-Poor Coverage	2 criteria moderate coverage + 1 criteria poor coverage
Poor Coverage	3 criteria poor coverage, or 2 criteria poor coverage + 1 criterion good coverage, or 2 criteria poor coverage + 1 criterion moderate coverage

Concerning the games, different approaches are recommended depending on the coverage. In the area of good coverage and moderate-good coverage, the games can be used to teach the content. In the area of moderate coverage, it is recommended to use additional materials or not to use them alone to teach the competencies addressed. In the area of moderate-poor or poor coverage, it is recommended to use additional or alternative materials.

The average score across all categories and items for Spoofy was 2.72 combined with a PAD of 93.51% and a PA of 77.84%, this indicates generally good coverage. Table 3 provides a detailed overview of the participants' responses and illustrates the distribution of scores in the different categories.

Table 3. Evaluation of the cybersecurity game Spoofy

Spoofy											
	Abusive Content										
	I1	I2	I3	I4	I5	I6	I7	I8	I9	I10	
Total "Agree"	7	3	9	9	9	7	7	9	8	4	
Total "Disagree"	1	2	0	0	1	1	0	0	0	1	
Total "Neutral"	2	5	1	1	0	2	3	1	2	5	
Percentage agreement	70%	30%	90%	90%	90%	70%	70%	90%	80%	40%	
Ratio of Agree and Disagree	88%	60%	100%	100%	90%	88%	100%	100%	100%	80%	
Mean value in points	2,6	2,1	2,9	2,9	2,8	2,6	2,7	2,9	2,8	2,3	
Mean value per categorie	2,66										
	Data Privacy and Data Awareness							Frauds			
	I11	I12	I13	I14	I15	I16	I17	I18	I19	I20	I21
Total "Agree"	8	9	8	9	10	7	9	5	10	10	7
Total "Disagree"	0	0	0	0	0	1	0	2	0	0	1
Total "Neutral"	2	1	2	1	0	2	1	3	0	0	2
Percentage agreement	80%	90%	80%	90%	100%	70%	90%	50%	100%	100%	70%
Ratio of Agree and Disagree	100%	100%	100%	100%	100%	88%	100%	71%	100%	100%	88%
Mean value in points	2,8	2,9	2,8	2,9	3	2,6	2,9	2,3	3	3	2,6
Mean value per categorie	2,84							2,73			
	Malicious Code						Preventing Technologies				
	I22	I23	I24	I25	I26	I27	I28	I29	I30		
Total "Agree"	10	10	8	9	8	8	8	8	4		
Total "Disagree"	0	0	0	0	1	1	0	0	1		
Total "Neutral"	0	0	2	1	1	1	2	2	5		
Percentage agreement	100%	100%	80%	90%	80%	80%	80%	80%	40%		
Ratio of Agree and Disagree	100%	100%	100%	100%	89%	89%	100%	100%	80%		
Mean value in points	3	3	2,8	2,9	2,7	2,7	2,8	2,8	2,3		
Mean value per categorie	2,85						2,63				
	Safety										
	I31	I32	I33	I34	I35	I36	I37				
Total "Agree"	4	10	7	8	8	7	7				
Total "Disagree"	3	0	2	0	0	2	0				
Total "Neutral"	3	0	1	2	2	1	3				
Percentage agreement	40%	100%	70%	80%	80%	70%	70%				
Ratio of Agree and Disagree	57%	100%	78%	100%	100%	78%	100%				
Mean value in points	2,1	3	2.5	2.8	2.8	2.5	2.7				
Mean value per categorie	2,63										

The analysis of the survey with professionals showed that the game Spoofy has a solid overall coverage of the content taught. Nevertheless, there are areas in some specific items that should be highlighted. Poor coverage was found for the following items: I2: The game introduces children to classifying online content according to age appropriateness, I10: The game introduces children to developing and implementing strategies for coping with negative experiences, I30: The game introduces children to using software tools to protect digital devices. At the same time, there is a general inconsistency in the following items, which indicates that this content may not be sufficiently conveyed: I18: The game introduces children to the topic of intellectual property, I31: The game introduces children to sex-related cyber threats. Due to these inconsistencies, the content on intellectual property and sex-related cyber threats should be provided separately and in detail to ensure that these important topics are also adequately communicated. In summary, the expert survey shows that the game Spoofy performs well in most areas. Still, specific content in the items mentioned should be improved and addressed separately to ensure comprehensive and effective teaching.

Table 4. Evaluation of the cybersecurity game Nabbovaldo

Nabbovaldo										
	Abusive Content									
	I1	I2	I3	I4	I5	I6	I7	I8	I9	I10
Total "Agree"	8	5	7	7	5	4	8	9	10	5
Total "Disagree"	1	3	0	0	0	2	2	0	0	1
Total "Neutral"	1	2	3	3	5	4	0	1	0	4
Percentage agreement	80%	50%	70%	70%	50%	40%	80%	90%	100%	50%
Ratio of Agree and Disagree	89%	63%	100%	100%	100%	67%	80%	100%	100%	83%
Mean value in points	2,7	2,2	2,7	2,7	2,5	2,2	2,6	2,9	3	2,4
Mean value per categorie	2,59									

	Data Privacy and Data Awareness							Frauds			
	I11	I12	I13	I14	I15	I16	I17	I18	I19	I20	I21
Total "Agree"	10	10	5	7	7	3	8	7	7	6	8
Total "Disagree"	0	0	0	1	0	0	0	1	0	0	0
Total "Neutral"	0	0	5	2	3	7	2	2	3	4	2
Percentage agreement	100%	100%	50%	70%	70%	30%	80%	70%	70%	60%	80%
Ratio of Agree and Disagree	100%	100%	100%	88%	100%	100%	100%	88%	100%	100%	100%
Mean value in points	3	3	2,5	2,6	2,7	2,3	2,8	2,6	2,7	2,6	2,8
Mean value per categorie	2,70							2,68			

	Malicious Code						Preventing Technologies		
	I22	I23	I24	I25	I26	I27	I28	I29	I30
Total "Agree"	10	10	10	9	9	5	5	8	6
Total "Disagree"	0	0	0	1	0	1	0	0	0
Total "Neutral"	0	0	0	0	1	4	5	2	4
Percentage agreement	100%	100%	100%	90%	90%	50%	50%	80%	60%
Ratio of Agree and Disagree	100%	100%	100%	90%	100%	83%	100%	100%	100%
Mean value in points	3	3	3	2,8	2,9	2,4	2,5	2,8	2,6
Mean value per categorie	2,85						2,63		

	Safety						
	I31	I32	I33	I34	I35	I36	I37
Total "Agree"	7	10	7	8	6	9	6
Total "Disagree"	0	0	1	1	2	0	2
Total "Neutral"	3	0	2	1	2	1	2
Percentage agreement	70%	100%	70%	80%	60%	90%	60%
Ratio of Agree and Disagree	100%	100%	88%	89%	75%	100%	75%
Mean value in points	2,7	3	2,6	2,7	2,4	2,9	2,4
Mean value per categorie	2,67						

A similar picture emerges for the game Nabbovaldo, with an overall score of 2.68 across all categories and items combined with a PAD of 93.45% and a PA of 73.24%, this indicates also a generally good coverage. Malicious code seems to be best covered. Nabbovaldo also seems to provide good coverage in Safety, for instance, there is an entire agreement for I32: The game introduces children to online etiquette and behavior, and all participants agree. The following items showed poor coverage: I2: The game introduces children to classifying online content based on age appropriateness. The game introduces children to detecting online risks and threats that require the assistance of an adult (I6). The game introduces children to use strategies to protect persistent data (I16). All in all, there seems to be at least a slightly positive coverage for the categories. Good and comprehensive coverage appears to be provided for the area of malicious code. However, there still seems to be potential for improving protection against these threats through the category of preventing technologies.

4. DISCUSSION AND CONCLUSION

The development and validation of serious games, especially in content evaluation, is a complex process closely linked to various methods and approaches. The results of our scoping review show that three options are being used more and more for developing content for games as well as for their evaluation of the content: the application of expert knowledge (e.g. Arboleya-Garcia & Miralles, 2022; Andreoli et al., 2017), the inclusion of scientific literature as a basis (e.g. Tinôco et al., 2022; Roman et al., 2020; Hodges et al., 2021; Neuwelt & Kearns, 2021) and multilevel approaches (e.g. Ingadottir et al., 2022; Leong et al., 2021; Pimentel et al., 2022). A similar picture emerges in the area of evaluating the content of the games (Calderón & Ruiz, 2015; Sousa & Rocha, 2019; Mhadhbi et al., 2024). Implicit content is often conveyed, and it is difficult to classify it precisely (Rowe et al., 2015), as there is an interconnectivity between the areas (Papanastasiou et al., 2017). Our scoping review also supports the results of Andrew and colleagues (2023), who state that the study design and evaluation methods often make it difficult to generalize the results. In addition, content experts and educators, such as teachers or curriculum designers, should be involved in the content design and evaluation of serious games (Andreoli et al., 2017). This is why we propose an initial three-phase model for the content evaluation of serious games. These consist of an initialization phase (definition of knowledge to be conveyed), a theoretical content validation (can the defined learning objectives be theoretically achieved through the learning offer), and a subsequent practical evaluation (does an actual knowledge transfer take place). However, there are a bunch of limitations. First of all, the initial model is only based on a theoretical foundation and needs empirical validation. In addition, the scoping review may not include all relevant studies due to the chosen databases and the date limitation. Also, the initialization phase must be more strictly defined to avoid ambiguity in the evaluation of the questions. Furthermore, the pilot study raised some possible challenges, such as recruiting potential participants and using scales. In order to make the results more selective and definable, a 3-point Likert scale should not be used, and the participants should be given a list of term definitions in advance. In summary, future research should focus more on comparing the skills of existing games and curricula in order to close the existing gap in the validation of the content of serious games. With regard to the two cybersecurity games and the evaluation procedure, there are indications that ambiguity should be minimized by defining the competencies more precisely. To avoid this, a free text field for feedback should be provided in addition to the questionnaire. At the same time, the next step in the model must be to evaluate whether the learning offer is actually provided by the games. To this end, we will also be conducting a pilot study for both games in the future, which will include a pre- and post-test.

ACKNOWLEDGEMENT

This work was co-funded by the Erasmus+ Programme of the European Union under Project No. 101087250 - ERASMUS-EDU-2022-PI-FORWARD.

REFERENCES

Abt, C. C. (1987). Serious games. University Press of America.

Acquah, E. O., & Katz, H. T. (2020). Digital game-based L2 learning outcomes for primary through high-school students: A systematic literature review. *Computers & Education, 143*, 103667. https://doi.org/10.1016/j.compedu.2019.103667

Andreoli, R., Corolla, A., Faggiano, A., Malandrino, D., Pirozzi, D., Ranaldi, M., ... & Scarano, V. (2017). A framework to design, develop, and evaluate immersive and collaborative serious games in cultural heritage. *Journal on Computing and Cultural Heritage (JOCCH), 11*(1), 1-22. https://doi.org/10.1145/3064644

Arboleya-García, E., & Miralles, L. (2022). 'The game of the sea': An interdisciplinary educational board game on the marine environment and ocean awareness for primary and secondary students. *Education Sciences, 12*(1), 57. https://doi.org/10.3390/educsci12010057

Barz, N., Benick, M., Dörrenbächer-Ulrich, L., & Perels, F. (2024). The effect of digital game-based learning interventions on cognitive, metacognitive, and affective-motivational learning outcomes in school: A meta-analysis. *Review of Educational Research, 94*(2), 193-227.

Calderón, A., & Ruiz, M. (2015). A systematic literature review on serious games evaluation: An application to software project management. *Computers & Education, 87*, 396-422. https://doi.org/10.1016/j.compedu.2015.07.011

Daoudi, I. (2022). Learning analytics for enhancing the usability of serious games in formal education: A systematic literature review and research agenda. *Education and Information Technologies, 27*(8), 11237-11266. https://doi.org/10.1109/ISECON.2018.8340460

Duffull, S. B., & Peterson, A. K. (2020). Students' perceptions of playing a serious game intended to enhance therapeutic decision-making in a pharmacy curriculum. *Currents in Pharmacy Teaching and Learning, 12*(11), 1348-1353.

Eseryel, D., Ge, X., Ifenthaler, D., & Law, V. (2011). Dynamic modeling as cognitive regulation scaffold for complex problem solving skill acquisition in an educational massively multiplayer online game environment. *Journal of Educational Computing Research, 45*(3), 265-287. https://doi.org/10.2190/ec.45.3.a

Eseryel, D., Law, V., Ifenthaler, D., Ge, X., & Miller, R. B. (2014). An investigation of the interrelationships between motivation, engagement, and complex problem solving in game-based learning. *Journal of Educational Technology & Society, 17*(1), 42–53. https://www.j-ets.net/collection/published-issues/17_1

Gao, F., Li, L., & Sun, Y. (2020). A systematic review of mobile game-based learning in STEM education. *Educational Technology Research and Development, 68*, 1791-1827. https://doi.org/10.1007/s11423-020-09787-0

Hodges, G. W., Oliver, J. S., Jang, Y., Cohen, A., Ducrest, D., & Robertson, T. (2021). Pedagogy, partnership, and collaboration: A longitudinal, empirical study of serious educational gameplay in secondary biology classrooms. *Journal of Science Education and Technology, 30*, 331-346. https://doi.org/10.1007/s10956-020-09868-y

Hoseiny, S., & Niknafs, A. (2020, December). Study of the Serious Games Capacity in Promoting Financial Literacy. In *2020 International Serious Games Symposium (ISGS)* (pp. 81-87). IEEE. https://doi.org/10.1109/ISGS51981.2020.9375426

Ingadottir, B., Blondal, K., Thue, D., Zoega, S., Thylen, I., & Jaarsma, T. (2017). Development, usability, and efficacy of a serious game to help patients learn about pain management after surgery: An evaluation study. *JMIR Serious Games, 5*(2), e6894. https://doi.org/10.2196/31471

Ke, F. (2016). Designing and integrating purposeful learning in game play: A systematic review. *Educational Technology Research and Development, 64*, 219-244. https://doi.org/10.1007/s11423-015-9418-1

Lei, H., Wang, C., Chiu, M. M., & Chen, S. (2022). Do educational games affect students' achievement emotions? Evidence from a meta-analysis. *Journal of Computer Assisted Learning, 38*(4), 946-959. https://doi.org/10.1111/jcal.12664

Leong, C., Liesaputra, V., Morrison, C., Parameswaran, P., Grace, D., Healey, D., ... & Houghton, L. A. (2021). Designing video games for nutrition education: A participatory approach. *Journal of Nutrition Education and Behavior, 53*(10), 832-842. https://doi.org/10.1016/j.jneb.2021.07.001

Manganello, F., Città, G., Denaro, P., Earp, J., Fante, C., Ifenthaler, D., & Janka, L. (2023). Toward a game-based cybersecurity training for young students: the SuperCyberKids project. *BOOKOF*, 103.

Mhadhbi, H., Horta, L. M., Ims, J., Draper-Rodi, J., Mansfield, H., Shaw, R., Rinne, S., Cleland Silva, T., Metsälä, E., & Ménard, M. (2024). Perceived benefits and limitations of game-based simulation education by osteopathy students in early clinical training: A preliminary mixed methods study. *International Journal of Osteopathic Medicine, 53*, 100726. https://doi.org/10.1016/j.ijosm.2024.100726

Neuwelt, P. M., & Kearns, R. A. (2021). Playing the game: Interactively exploring journeys into primary care. *Wellbeing, Space and Society, 2*, 100045. https://doi.org/10.1016/j.wss.2021.100045

Noroozi, O., Dehghanzadeh, H., & Talaee, E. (2020). A systematic review on the impacts of game-based learning on argumentation skills. *Entertainment Computing, 35*, 100369. https://doi.org/10.1016/j.entcom.2020.100369

Papanastasiou, G. P., Drigas, A. S., & Skianis, C. (2017). Serious games in preschool and primary education: Benefits and impacts on curriculum course syllabus. *International Journal of Emerging Technologies in Learning*, 12(1). https://doi.org/10.3991/ijet.v12i01.6065

Pimentel, J., López, P., Correal, C., Cockcroft, A., & Andersson, N. (2022). Educational games created by medical students in a cultural safety training game jam: a qualitative descriptive study. *BMC Medical Education, 22*(1), 805. https://doi.org/10.1186/s12909-022-03875-w

Pistono, A., Santos, A., & Baptista, R. (2022). A qualitative analysis of frameworks for training through Serious Games. *Procedia Computer Science, 204*, 753-759. https://doi.org/10.1016/j.procs.2022.08.091

Plass, J. L., Homer, B. D., & Kinzer, C. K. (2015). Foundations of game-based learning. *Educational psychologist, 50*(4), 258-283. https://doi.org/10.1080/00461520.2015.1122533

Plintz, N. B., & Ifenthaler, D. (2023). *SuperCyberKids Learning Framework* (Deliverable No. D2.1). European Commission, Erasmus+ Programme. Project No. 101087250 - ERASMUS-EDU-2022-PI-FORWARD. Retrieved from https://www.supercyberkids.eu/deliverables/

Roman, P., Rodriguez-Arrastia, M., Molina-Torres, G., Márquez-Hernández, V. V., Gutiérrez-Puertas, L., & Ropero-Padilla, C. (2020). The escape room as evaluation method: A qualitative study of nursing students' experiences. *Medical Teacher, 42*(4), 403-410. https://doi.org/10.1080/0142159X.2019.1687865

Rowe, E., Asbell-Clarke, J., Baker, R.S. (2015). Serious Games Analytics to Measure Implicit Science Learning. In: Loh, C., Sheng, Y., Ifenthaler, D. (eds) Serious Games Analytics. Advances in Game-Based Learning. Springer, Cham. https://doi.org/10.1007/978-3-319-05834-4_15

Sousa, M. J., & Rocha, Á. (2019). Digital learning: Developing skills for digital transformation of organizations. *Future Generation Computer Systems, 91*, 327-334. https://doi.org/10.1016/j.future.2018.08.048

Tinôco, J. D. D. S., Silva, L. S. D., Medeiros, T. M. D., Grande, M. E. G., Guedes, M. L. D. A., Fernandes, M. I. D. C. D., & Lira, A. L. B. D. C. (2023). "Enfermeiro Diagnosticador" board game for teaching diagnostic reasoning in nursing: A quasi-experimental study. *Acta Paulista de Enfermagem, 36*, eAPE00001. https://doi.org/10.37689/acta-ape/2023AO000111

Wastiau, P., Kearney, C., & Van den Berghe, W. (2009). How are digital games used in schools. *European Schoolnet*, 1-174.

Zou, D., Zhang, R., Xie, H., & Wang, F. L. (2021). Digital game-based learning of information literacy: Effects of gameplay modes on university students' learning performance, motivation, self-efficacy and flow experiences. *Australasian Journal of Educational Technology, 37*(2), 152-170. https://doi.org/10.14742/ajet.6682

INTEGRATING GAZE DATA AND DIGITAL TEXTBOOK READING LOGS FOR ENHANCED ANALYSIS OF LEARNING ACTIVITIES

Ken Goto[1], Li Chen[2], Tsubasa Minematsu[3] and Atsushi Shimada[2]
[1]Graduate School of Information Science and Electrical Engineering, Kyushu University,
[2]Faculty of Information Science and Electrical Engineering, Kyushu University,
[3]Promotion Office for Data-Driven Innovation, Kyushu University,
744 Motooka, Nishi-ku, Fukuoka 819-0395, Japan

ABSTRACT

Learning logs collected by digital educational systems, increasingly deployed in educational settings, include clickstream logs recorded through page transitions in teaching materials and digital marker logs recorded by drawing a marker. A challenge with these learning logs is their low temporal and spatial resolutions. This paper proposes a system that generates a high-resolution learning log (HLL) by utilizing learners' gaze information obtained through webcam-based eye tracking. We also propose methods for analyzing learners' learning-theme browsing patterns using HLL. The HLL retains the attention time of the learning-themes on the learning material and viewing time in and out of the screen. Utilizing the HLL allows learners' attention transitions to be captured over time. Compared with traditional topic-based learning log analysis methods, HLL offers a more granular analysis of detailed learning theme browsing patterns.

KEYWORDS

Learning Log, Eye Tracking, Non-negative Matrix Factorization

1. INTRODUCTION

In the field of education, various e-learning systems, including digital textbooks, have been introduced and utilized as alternatives to traditional paper-based textbooks. This change made it possible to record and analyze data reflecting how learners engage in learning in the form of learning logs stored in a database. In recent years, digital learning materials have become widespread, and learning logs that record the access to and operation of these materials have become the subject of analysis. In courses utilizing digital learning materials, learning logs are automatically collected to represent learners' reading behaviors, including critical reading strategies (Majumdar et al., 2021). The learning logs collected included clickstream logs, recorded at each page transition, and digital marker logs.

Clickstream logs are easily collected through page transitions. However, because log collection depends on learner interactions, the temporal resolution is not necessarily high. The spatial resolution was at the page level, and a more detailed resolution was not available. This makes it difficult to analyze learning behaviors at the level of areas of interest or specific learning themes on each page. Digital marker logs have higher spatial resolution than clickstream logs because they are recorded at the text level within the page. However, they only focused on specific keywords within a page. In addition, because digital marker logs are recorded based on the learners' active actions, the number of recorded logs is limited. Therefore, the temporal resolution is low.

To address these issues, this study proposes the development of a system that generates a high-resolution learning log (HLL) by utilizing learners' gaze data obtained through webcam-based eye tracking. By combining gaze data with reading logs of digital textbook and content information within pages, the system aims to create HLLs with superior temporal and spatial resolutions. Learners' gaze data can be related to their visual and cognitive focus, providing additional insights into the understanding and interpretation of reading strategies and processes. Compared to traditional hardware-based eye tracking, web camera-based eye tracking is low-cost and easily applicable to large audiences, such as in lectures.

2. RELATED WORK

2.1 Eye-Tracking in Education

Eye-tracking is widely used to study learners' visual attention and its impact on learning. For example, the eye-mind hypothesis assumes a direct link between visual and cognitive focus; thus, eye-tracking can be used to infer cognitive load, information processing patterns, and cognitive effort (Just & Carpenter., 1980). In Just and Carpenter's theoretical model, reading comprehension consists of multiple processes, including word encoding, lexical access, semantic role assignment, and the integration of information. Eye movement data traced using eye-tracking technology can be converted into eye-fixation time. Based on a theoretical model, eye movement data effectively explain reading strategies and processes.

Recently, more studies have emphasized applying eye-tracking in education and developing eye-tracking technology. Emerging patterns have been highlighted in the use of eye-tracking for educational research, such as applying cognitive and attention theories, measuring visual attention and cognitive load, and using advanced data analysis technology (Ke et al., 2024). In addition, a multimodal model that predicted student collaboration satisfaction was evaluated using Facial Action Units (AU), Head Pose (Pose), and Eye Gaze (Gaze) while interacting with a game-based learning environment (Acosta et al., 2024). While eye-tracking offers detailed insights into learners' behavior and cognitive processes, challenges remain regarding equipment costs, complexity, and accurate data interpretation.

In this study, we combined learner's gaze data with reading logs to enhance temporal and spatial resolution and provide insights into understanding their reading patterns and processes.

2.2 Learning Behavior Analysis by Learning Theme

Various learning logs have been recorded in e-learning systems used in the field of education. These learning logs are stored in association with the learners to indicate their learning activities. As a result, most existing learning analyses utilizing learning logs are "learner-based," which focuses on each learner's overall learning activities and makes it difficult to identify the well-learned and not well-learned topics. Therefore, "learner-based" learning log analysis is ineffective for educational support when teachers need to understand the learning status of lesson content or review lesson plans.

To address this issue, research on expressing and analyzing learning behavior patterns from a topic-based perspective proposes a "learning-topic-based" analysis method (Wang et al., 2022). This method represents learning activities by learning topics in a matrix of learning-topics × learning activities and applies Non-negative Matrix Factorization (NMF) to the matrix to analyze learning behavior patterns by topic. However, there are challenges to the aggregation of learning behaviors based on learning topics. In this study, the time spent viewing a learning topic was aggregated as the total viewing time of the pages containing that topic. For example, if the learning topic "Fourier Transform" is included on page 1 and page 5, with viewing times of 100 seconds and 800 seconds, respectively, the viewing time for "Fourier Transform" would be aggregated as 900 seconds. This can result in overestimation if the learner was not focused on "Fourier Transform" within the material. By applying the proposed method, NMF can be applied to a matrix of learners × learning-topics, with viewing time as an element, allowing the analysis of learners' viewing patterns by learning topic. However, due to the above-mentioned, it is considered difficult to analyze detailed viewing patterns of learners beyond the page level. In addition, it is difficult to grasp the transition of the learning themes of interest over time in the NMF-based analysis of browsing patterns of learning themes because it analyses browsing patterns within a certain period (e.g., the entire lecture). In this paper, we propose an analysis of the browsing patterns of learning themes using HLL, which enables a detailed analysis of browsing patterns and visualization of the transitions of attention to learning themes based on eye movements.

3. METHOD

The system proposed in this paper uses WebGazer (Papoutsaki et al., 2016), a webcam-based eye-tracking tool, and BookRoll (Ogata et al., 2015) as digital textbooks. Figure 1 shows the overall system structure. First, the learner accesses BookRoll educational material and then calibrates WebGazer. The system uses WebGazer to estimate the gaze points. The system then records the viewpoint and BookRoll reading logs and combines them with BookRoll text to generate the HLL. By leveraging HLL, we conducted learning analyses, such as visualizing time-series data of targeted learning themes and analyzing browsing patterns using NMF.

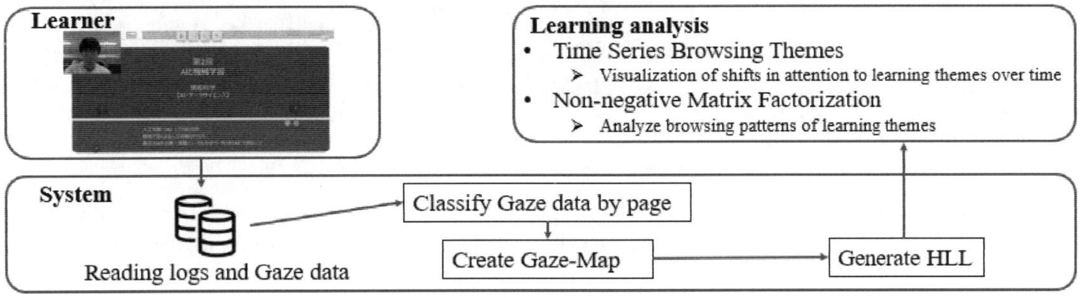

Figure 1. System overview

3.1 Recording of Gaze Points

First, the learner begins browsing BookRoll, and the system simultaneously records the estimated x and y gaze coordinates, username displayed on BookRoll, and timestamp. This resulted in recording four pieces of data (name, x, y, and time). BookRoll records a clickstream log as the learners' reading logs. From the clickstream logs, the start and end times of viewing each page for each learner and the viewing time can be calculated. For this process, we used OpenLA (Murata et al., 2020), a library used to form the learning data. By comparing the start and end viewing times of each page with the recorded time of each gaze point, it was possible to determine which gaze points viewed which pages. This allowed us to assign a page number to each learners' gaze point, as shown in Table 1.

Table 1. Learners gaze points

id	name	x	y	Time	Page
1	S_1	500.000	250.000	2024-01-01 10:30:00	1
2	S_1	200.000	300.000	2024-01-01 10:30:00	1

3.2 Creation of Gaze-Map

This section describes the creation of a Gaze-Map in the format shown in Table 2. First, the gaze points classified by page were divided into gaze point groups at specified times. Then, by using Kernel Density Estimation (Terrel et al., 1992), we calculated Attention, the learner's attention in each of the nine 3 × 3 regions, from the divided gaze point groups. WebGazer uses a webcam to estimate the gaze points, which is less accurate than dedicated eye-tracking hardware. Dividing the screen into 3 × 3 areas in this study allowed for the generation of HLL with reasonable accuracy and spatial resolution despite the trade-off with lower spatial resolution. We then describe a method for creating a Gaze-Map that retains the calculated Attention, the number of all gaze points, the number of off-screen gaze points among the segmented gaze points, and the number of seconds of gaze points used.

Kernel Density Estimation (KDE) is a nonparametric method for estimating data distribution. Figure 2 shows the flow for estimating the distribution of gaze points. First, for the gaze points classified by page in Section 2.1, the gaze points were divided into gaze point groups at the specified times. In this system, gaze points are divided by the number of gaze points every 30 seconds or when a page switch occurs. Subsequently, a matrix with zero text length was created, and a 2D Gaussian kernel was added to the matrix corresponding to the gazing point coordinates and divided by the number of viewpoints. This yielded a matrix that represented the probability density of the gaze point. The resulting matrix of the probability densities was divided into 3 × 3 areas. For each of the divided areas, all values in the area were added to obtain a 3 × 3 matrix. This was recorded in the Attention column of the Gaze-Map. Attention is a 3 × 3 matrix representing the probability density of each of the nine areas of interest.

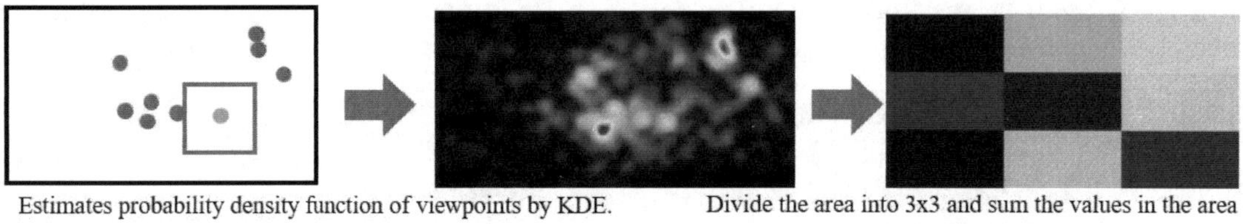

Figure 2. Flow of calculating Attention

The number of all divided gaze points is denoted as points, the number of gaze points outside the matrix as off-points, and the duration of gaze points as GazeTime. These data were referred to as Gaze-Maps.

Table 2. Gaze-Map format

Userid	Page	Time	Attention	points	off-points	GazeTime
A_U1	1	2024-01-01 10:30	[[0.005, 0.15, 0.20], …]	900	15	30
A_U1	1	2024-01-01 10:31	[[0.10, 0.30, 0.00], …]	150	10	5

3.3 HLL Generation with Gaze-Map and BookRoll

By mapping Gaze-Map to BookRoll text, we can log the learning themes that learners are focusing on. This section details the creation of the HLL, which includes learners' areas of interest, specific learning themes, viewing times for these themes, in-screen viewing times, and off-screen viewing times. Table 3 presents the HLL format. This was achieved by categorizing learning themes in BookRoll text by area and aligning them with the Gaze-Map data.

Figure 3 shows the flow of identifying the learning theme of interest by matching Gaze-Maps and text information from BookRoll. First, learning themes were identified, and a list of learning themes by area was created. Next, the learning theme corresponding to the area with the highest Attention in the Gaze-Map was recorded in the word column of the HLL as the theme that received the most attention. If there are multiple learning themes corresponding to the highest-valued area in the Gaze-Map, one HLL is generated for each keyword; and thus, multiple HLLs are generated.

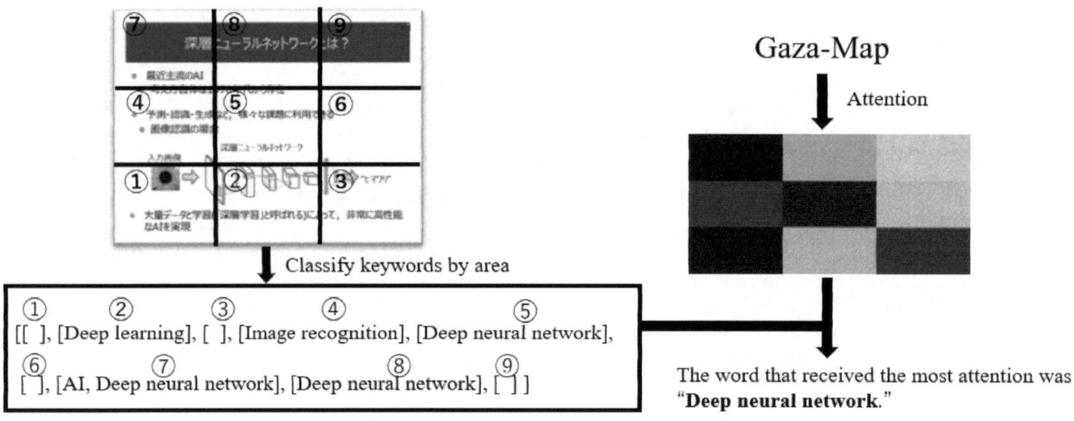

Figure 3. Flow of mapping Gaze-Map to BookRoll

Gaze-Map records the number of all gaze points (points), number of off-view-points (off-points), and number of seconds used for each gaze point (GazeTime). From this, view time (the time spent gazing at the learning theme of interest in the HLL), onview (in-screen attention time), and offview (off-screen attention time) were calculated. These values are calculated using the following equations:

$$onview = GazeTime \times (points - offpoints)/points$$

$$offview = GazeTime \times offpoints/points$$

$$viewtime = onview \times \max(Attention)/sum(Attention)$$

Table 3. HLL format

Userid	Page	Time	Attention	Word	view-time	offview	onview
A_U1	1	2024-01-01 10:30	[[0.005, ...], ...]	Recognition	11.1	0.5	29.5
A_U1	1	2024-01-01 10:30	[[0.005, ...], ...]	Specific AI	11.1	0.5	29.5

4. LEARNING ANALYSIS UTILIZING HLL

4.1 Visualization of Viewed Learning Themes

By visualizing the learning theme on the vertical axis and time on the horizontal axis on a heat map, it was possible to understand the shift in attention to the learning theme over time. The HLL records the learner, time, learning theme, and viewing time. Therefore, it was possible to calculate the time spent viewing a learning theme at a specific time. A time-series heat map can be created by calculating the browsing time of the learning themes at each time of day from the HLL and arranging them in a time series. By utilizing the HLL of all learners, it is possible to observe the transition in the attention of all learners, and by utilizing the HLL of individual learners, it is possible to observe the transition in the attention of each individual learner. This enables us to visually understand the themes that interest students as well as those that do not.

4.2 Factor Analysis by Non-Negative Matrix Factorization

The learner × learning-theme matrix shown in Table 4 was created using HLL. Each element represents the browsing time during which the learners focus on a learning theme. In the learner × learning-theme matrix based on previous study, the element of the matrix is page-based browsing time. By utilizing the HLL, it is possible to create a learner × learning-theme matrix whose elements are gaze-based learning theme browsing times.

Table 4. Learner × Learning-theme matrix

Learner	Theme1	Theme2	Theme3	Theme4	• •
Learner A	10	40	100	80	• •
Learner B	20	5	150	70	• •
• •	• •	• •	• •	• •	• •

For the two-dimensional matrix created above, matrix decomposition was performed by applying NMF with the scale of each column set to [0-1] by min-max normalization.

5. EXPERIMENT RESULT

A viewing experiment was conducted with 45 learners utilizing the "Information Science" course material offered at the authors' university. After WebGazer calibration, participants viewed the 45-page material for 30 minutes. While reading, the participants were asked to keep Bookmark, Memo, Marker, Getit, and NotGetit. Table 5 shows the mean and standard deviation of the learning logs and HLL per participant.

Table 5. Average and standard deviation of the number of learning logs recorded in the experiment

	BookMark	Memo	Marker	Getit	NotGetit	Next+Prev	HLL
Avg	4.29	0.98	29.49	48.18	1.51	170.87	**327.86**
Std	4.93	2.37	20.45	16.62	2.12	53.52	**85.45**

As described in Section 4.1, the HLL can visualize transitions in the learning themes viewed by learners. Figure 4 shows the transitions of attention themes for all learners during the 30-minute experiment.

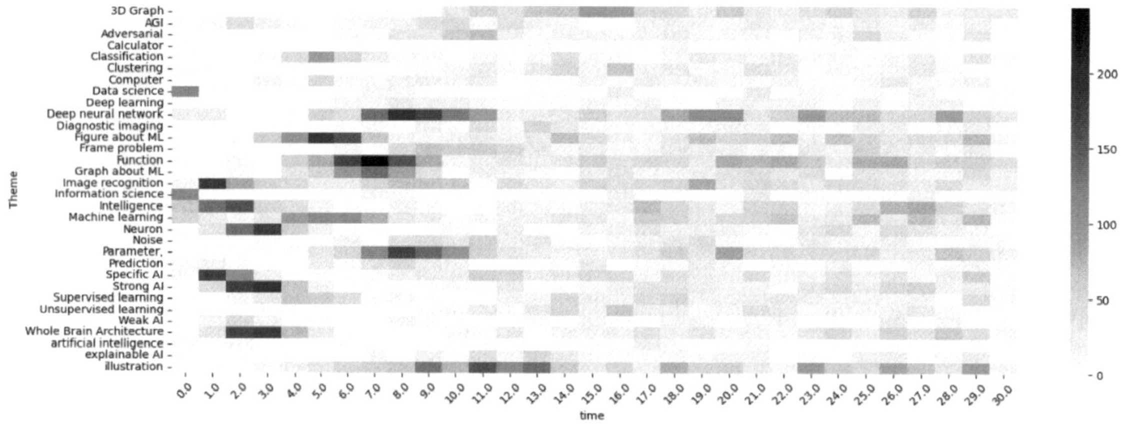

Figure 4. The transitions of all learners' themes of interest

Figure 5 shows the learning-theme × factor matrix obtained by applying NMF to the learner × learning-theme matrix (45 × 35). The number of factors was set to five. The left matrix in Figure 5 is a decomposition of the learner × learning-theme matrix with the HLL view-time as an element. The right matrix in Figure 5 is a decomposition of the learner × learning-theme matrix with browsing time as an element, calculated based on previous study.

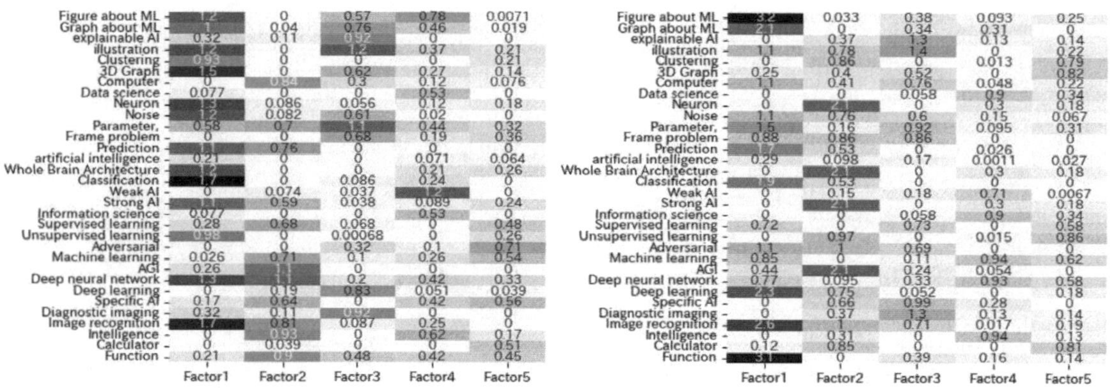

Figure 5. Decomposition of the learner × theme matrix created using HLL view-time (left) and the page view-time (right)

6. DISCUSSION

6.1 Evaluation of Temporal and Spatial Resolution of HLL

Table 6 shows the percentage improvement in the number of learning logs recorded by the HLL compared with conventional learning logs based on the results in Table 5. BookMark is the log of a page to be reviewed, and the spatial resolution is at the page level. HLL improved the number of records by 7542.42% compared with BookMark. Memo is the log of key points and questions, and its spatial resolution is at the textual level. The number of HLL records increased by 33355.10% compared with Memo. Marker is the log of the text on the page, and its spatial resolution is at the textual level. The number of HLL records increased by 1011.77% compared with Marker. Getit and NotGetit are logs that indicate whether each page was "understood" or "not understood," and their spatial resolution is at the page level. The number of HLL records increased by 580.49% and 21612.58% compared with Getit and NotGetit, respectively. Next+Prev are clickstream logs. Next is recorded when the next page is opened, and Prev is recorded when returning to the previous page. The spatial resolution of these logs is at the page level. The number of HLL records increased by 91.88% compared with Next+Prev. The HLL has a higher spatial resolution than other learning logs because it retains information on areas of interest and learning themes. The HLL has an increased number of records compared with conventional learning logs, indicating a superior temporal resolution.

Table 6. Percentage improvement in HLL records compared with conventional logs

	BookMark	**Memo**	**Marker**	**Getit**	**NotGetit**	**Next+Prev**
Improvement (%)	7542.42	33355.10	1011.77	580.49	21612.58	91.88

6.2 The Utility of Browsing Pattern Analysis

From Figure 4, it is possible to identify a shift in the attention of learner to learning themes over time. We can see that the specific learning theme was the continuous focus of attention until 14 minutes after the start of the experiment. This indicates that in the first half of the experiment, all the learners' attention shifted to the same learning theme. However, from 15 minutes until the end of the experiment, attention was distributed to many learning themes. This suggests that the learners may finish reading the experimental material in approximately 14 minutes, and then brow the pages they were interested in. By utilizing HLL, the transition in learners' attention can be visualized in a time-series heat map to confirm learners' learning-theme browsing patterns for teaching materials. It is possible to analyze whether the learning themes that teachers consider important are viewed by learners. Learners' reading time and attention are affected by the complexity of the text content. Generally, more difficult content increases the cognitive load, requiring more time to process and comprehend information (Just & Carpenter. 1980). Therefore, learning themes on which learners spend more time indicate that they pay more attention to information processing. In future instructional designs, other data (such as pre-tests or regular reflections) should be combined to determine learners' understanding and provide support.

From Figure 5, it is possible to understand the learners' learning theme browsing patterns. Learners with strong values for each factor had a pattern of viewing the learning themes that co-occurred with each factor. In the previous study, the factors had strong values for learning themes contained within the same page. This is because the elements of the learner × learning-theme matrix were calculated from page viewing time. From the learning-theme × factor matrix on the right of Figure 5, we can confirm that Factor 2 shows browsing patterns of "neurons," "strong AI," "whole brain architecture," and "AGI." However, these learning themes are on the same page, and it is not possible to obtain the browsing patterns of the learning themes across pages. When we look at the learning theme × factor matrix obtained by decomposing the learner × theme matrix created using HLL, we can confirm Factor 1 has a co-occurrence relationship with "Classification," "Image recognition," etc. Factor 2 has a co-occurrence relationship with "AGI," "Deep neural network," and "Intelligence." Factor 3 has a co-occurrence relationship with "Illustration," "Parameters," and so on. Factor 4 has a co-occurrence relationship with "Weak AI," "Figure about ML," "Data science," etc. Factor 5 has a co-occurrence relationship with "Adversarial," "Machine learning," "Specific AI," and so on. The matrices created utilizing HLL are calculated based on eye-gazing time, which allows us to analyze the viewing patterns of learning themes across pages compared with previous studies. Identifying connections between learning themes can deepen the understanding of the interactions and differences between different concepts.

7. CONCLUSION

In this study, we propose the HLL, a learning log with excellent temporal and spatial resolution, and learning behavior analysis utilizing the HLL. The experimental results showed that HLL had better temporal and spatial resolution than other learning logs. In addition, the HLL made it possible to visualize the transition of the viewed learning themes in the time series. This enables instructors to improve lecture materials and lectures by understanding contents to which learners do not pay attention. In addition, the results of the pattern analysis of learning-theme browsing using NMF showed the possibility to analyze browsing patterns among pages better than in previous studies. However, the accuracy of HLL is dependent on the web camera-based eye-tracking system and the calibration performed by the learners. Therefore, it is necessary to discuss the selection of the eye-tracking tools used and the implementation of appropriate calibration methods.

As for the future work, first, it is necessary to analyze the relationship between learner gaze and learning behavior. HLL retains both on-screen and off-screen viewing time. We will analyze the relationship between these learners' gaze behaviors and learning behaviors. Second, HLL has great potential in offering new insights such as better understanding learners' difficulties, understanding, or misconceptions, as well as providing some emotional cues. However, the HLL is used mainly as a research tool. In our future work, it is expected to integrate this method into authentic learning environments, to assess learners' cognitive and emotional skills or learning strategies through multimodal data and provide some intervention based on the evidence.

ACKNOWLEDGEMENT

This work was supported by JST CREST Grant Number JPMJCR22D1 and JSPS KAKENHI Grant Number JP22H00551, Japan.

REFERENCES

Acosta, H., Lee, S., Mott, B., Bae, H., Glazewski, K., Hmelo-Silver, C. and Lester, J. (2024). Multimodal learning analytics for predicting student collaboration satisfaction in collaborative game-based learning. In: B. Paaßen and C. Demmans Epp, eds. Proceedings of the 17th International Conference on Educational Data Mining. Atlanta, Georgia, USA, July 2024. International Educational Data Mining Society, pp. 224-235.

Just, M.A. and Carpenter, P.A. (1980). A theory of reading: from eye fixations to comprehension. Psychological Review, 87(4), pp. 329.

Ke, F., Liu, R., Sokolikj, Z., Dahlstrom-Hakki, I. and Israel, M. (2024). Using eye-tracking in education: review of empirical research and technology. Educational Technology Research and Development, pp. 1-36.

Majumdar, R., Bakilapadavu, G., Majumder, R., Chen, M.A., Flanagan, B. and Ogata, H. (2021). Learning analytics of humanities courses: Reader profiles in critical reading activities. Research and Practice in Technology Enhanced Learning, 16(1), pp. 25.

Murata, R., Minematsu, T. and Shimada, A. (2020). OpenLA: Library for Efficient E-book Log Analysis and Accelerating Learning Analytics. International Conference on Computer in Education (ICCE 2020), pp. 301-306.

Ogata, H., Yin, C., Oi, M., Okubo, F., Shimada, A., Kojima, K. and Yamada, M. (2015). E-Book-based learning analytics in university education. International Conference on Computer in Education (ICCE 2015), pp. 401-406.

Papoutsaki, A., Sangkloy, P., Laskey, J., Daskalova, N., Huang, J. and Hays, J. (2016). WebGazer: Scalable Webcam Eye Tracking Using User Interactions. Proceedings of the 25th International Joint Conference on Artificial Intelligence (IJCAI). AAAI, pp. 3839-3845.

Terrell, G.R. and Scott, D.W. (1992). Variable kernel density estimation. The Annals of Statistics, pp. 1236-1265.

Wang, J., Minematsu, T., Taniguchi, Y., Okubo, F. and Shimada, A. (2022). Topic-Based Representation of Learning Activities for New Learning Pattern Analytics. International Conference on Computers in Education 2022 (ICCE2022), Vol. 1, pp. 268-278.

EXPLORING STUDENT PERCEPTION AND INTERACTION USING CHATGPT IN PROGRAMMING EDUCATION

Boxuan Ma, Li Chen and Shin'ichi Konomi
Kyushu University, Japan

ABSTRACT

Generative artificial intelligence (AI) tools like ChatGPT are becoming increasingly common in educational settings, especially in programming education. However, the impact of these tools on the learning process, student performance, and best practices for their integration remains underexplored. This study examines student experiences and interactions using ChatGPT in a beginner-level Python programming course through a combination of questionnaire responses and student-ChatGPT dialogue data analysis. The findings reveal a generally positive student reception toward ChatGPT, emphasizing its role in enhancing the programming education experience. Additionally, by clustering and analyzing the types of prompts students use, we identify four distinct patterns of ChatGPT usage and compare the performance outcomes associated with each pattern. This empirical research provides a deeper understanding of AI-enhanced programming education, offering valuable insights and suggesting pathways for future research and practical applications.

KEYWORDS

Generative AI, ChatGPT, Python, Programming Education

1. INTRODUCTION

The advent of generative artificial intelligence (AI) tools, such as ChatGPT, has introduced transformative changes across various sectors, including education (Chen et al., 2024). These tools have the potential to reshape the way educators approach teaching and how students engage with learning materials. In the context of programming education, the integration of AI tools marks a significant shift in how teaching and learning are conceptualized and implemented (Rahman and Watanobe, 2023; Malinka et al., 2023). Traditionally, programming courses have emphasized hands-on practice and the development of problem-solving skills through iterative learning. However, with AI tools now capable of generating code, providing instant feedback, and even debugging, the role of the instructor and the learning process itself is evolving. While these advancements offer new opportunities for personalized learning and efficient problem-solving, they also raise critical questions about the role and effectiveness of AI in enhancing student learning outcomes.

One primary concern voiced by educators and students alike is the potential for over-reliance on AI tools, which could impede the development of critical thinking and problem-solving skills (Tlili et al., 2023). The ease with which AI can generate solutions may discourage students from engaging fully with the problem-solving process, leading to a surface-level understanding rather than a deep mastery of programming concepts (Skjuve et al., 2023). This concern is not unfounded, as the crux of programming education lies in nurturing a mindset capable of breaking down complex problems and devising innovative solutions—skills that might atrophy if students become overly dependent on AI-generated answers. Furthermore, the influence of AI on student behavior and learning processes is still not fully understood, making it essential to investigate these dynamics more thoroughly. This concern underscores the need for a deeper understanding of how AI influences student performance and their overall approach to learning in programming courses. Understanding these questions is crucial for educators to develop strategies that integrate AI tools to support, rather than undermine, the educational objectives of programming courses (Kasneci et al., 2023).

This research investigates the impact of ChatGPT on student experiences and learning outcomes in an introductory Python programming course to address these concerns, it mainly focuses on two research questions:

RQ1: How do students perceive the use of ChatGPT in programming learning, and how does it impact their learning experiences?

RQ2: How do students use ChatGPT, and how do different types of ChatGPT usage influence their performance?

To answer these questions, we first analyze student perceptions and experiences with ChatGPT through questionaries (RQ1). Then, using the student-GPT interaction data, we further analyzed the types of prompts students used to explore how students give prompts to use ChatGPT in class. Through cluster analysis, we identified four different patterns of ChatGPT usage and compared different types of ChatGPT usage's impacts on student performance (RQ2). This study contributes to the growing body of research on AI-enhanced education by offering insights into how ChatGPT affects student learning in programming. Our findings deepen our understanding of AI's role in education and suggest practices for integrating these tools into programming curricula.

2. RELATED WORK

2.1 ChatGPT's Ability to Enhance Programming Education

Recent studies have highlighted ChatGPT's ability to handle common programming challenges with impressive results, such as code generation, program repair, and code summarization (Rajala et al. 2023). Additionally, a recent work (Phung et al. 2023) systematically compared GPT models with human tutors and found that they approach human-level performance in Python programming tasks and real-world buggy programs. In addition, ChatGPT has proven valuable in providing feedback on programming assignments and helping students apply theoretical knowledge in practice. Previous works demonstrated the model's effectiveness in generating personalized feedback, which students rated positively (Pankiewicz and Baker, 2023). Overall, ChatGPT's capabilities as a programming assistant extend beyond automation, showing significant promise in educational applications as well.

2.2 Students' Perception of Using ChatGPT for Programming

Numerous studies have explored students' perspectives on using ChatGPT in programming education (Biswas, 2023; Humble et al., 2023; Yilmaz et al., 2023; Shoufan, 2023; Ma et al., 2024). These studies have recognized both the advantages and drawbacks of employing ChatGPT for programming learning. Their findings indicate that students view ChatGPT as a useful tool, noting its ability to respond quickly and effectively to questions, thereby reducing time spent on researching solutions. Students also appreciate its clear explanations and well-organized responses (Ma et al., 2024), whether they are trying to grasp concepts or solve programming problems, such as identifying errors and guiding corrections (Ghimire and Edwards, 2024). However, the studies also highlight some disadvantages mentioned by students. Many are aware of the occasional incorrectness in ChatGPT's responses or that it may not always provide the answers students need, particularly in programming contexts where multiple solutions exist (Shoufan, 2023; Ma et al., 2024). Additionally, many students are concerned that relying on ChatGPT might make them overly dependent on it, thereby reducing their ability to think critically and learn independently (Yilmaz et al., 2023; Ma et al., 2024).

2.3 Impact of Students Using ChatGPT for Programming

Researchers have also examined whether using ChatGPT influences student performance. Recent studies (Brender et al. 2024) revealed that students who used ChatGPT performed similarly to those who did not have access to the tool. Other research has evaluated the quality of AI-assisted student solutions to programming tasks (Qureshi, 2023). However, the research consistently indicates that while ChatGPT may enhance task performance and completion rates, it does not significantly deepen understanding (Kazemitabaar et al., 2023). Further investigation is needed to better understand how students interact with ChatGPT and its impact on both learning outcomes and task performance.

3. METHOD

Table 1. Pre-questionnaire and post-questionnaire items

Pre-questionnaire items
Q1 How familiar are you with ChatGPT?
• I can explain everything about it • I can explain it to some extent • I somewhat understand it
• I don't understand it well • I don't know it at all
Q2 Do you use ChatGPT?
• I am using it • I used to use it but not anymore • I haven't used it but plan to use it in the future
• I don't use it and have no plans to use it in the future
Q3 What is your level in Python programming?
• Beginner • Intermediate • Advanced
Q4 Do you think using ChatGPT to learn Python programming is beneficial or detrimental?
• I think it is positive • I rather think it is positive • I am neutral • I rather think it is negative • I think it is negative
Post-questionnaire items
Q1 Is ChatGPT helpful for learning programming? (5-point likert scale)
Q2 Will you keep using ChatGPT for learning programming? (5-point likert scale)
Q3 Will you use ChatGPT often? (5-point likert scale)
Q4 Will you recommend ChatGPT to friends? (5-point likert scale)
Q5 How do you think ChatGPT can help with programming learning? (Multiple answers allowed)
• Correct programming code • Answer programming questions • Provide examples of programming code
• Offer learning advice and resources • Explain programming concepts
Q7 What are the advantages of using ChatGPT for programming learning? (Open-ended Question)
Q8 What are the limitations or disadvantages of using ChatGPT for programming learning? (Open-ended Question)
Q9 How could ChatGPT be improved to better assist with programming learning? (Open-ended Question)

This study aims to investigate students' experiences with ChatGPT within a university Python programming exercise course and employs a mixed-methods approach with both quantitative and qualitative data to answer our research questions. Students are allowed to use ChatGPT freely throughout the class. They can log into a web-based interface that leverages the GPT-4 API, allowing them to engage in conversations directly through this platform. All the conversations between students and ChatGPT were collected for analysis.

3.1 Participants and Context

A total of 36 undergraduate students enrolled in a Python programming course at our university participated in this study. The participants included 34 freshmen, 1 sophomore, and 1 junior, with 19 identifying as male and 17 as female. IRB approval in our university was obtained for the study. The course, spanning fourteen weeks, covers the fundamentals of the Python programming language. Each week, students attend a 90-minute lesson. The first 45 minutes of each session are dedicated to instruction, utilizing presentations and e-books, followed by 45 minutes of hands-on programming assignments related to that week's topic. Students need to complete programming assignments (e.g., write a specific function based on the requirements) and submit their solutions through the Learning Management System (LMS), which automatically checks and records all interactions and code submissions.

3.2 Data Collection and Analysis

At the beginning of the course, we asked all participants to fill out a pre-questionnaire to collect demographics such as major and gender. We also asked about their programming experiences and their familiarity with ChatGPT. After the class, we conducted a post-questionnaire, which gathered students' opinions about their experience of using ChatGPT for programming learning. A 5-point Likert scale (1-completely disagree, 5-completely agree) is used to measure different aspects of the students' opinions toward using ChatGPT for learning programming. Also, open questions were developed to determine students' viewpoints on the use of ChatGPT for programming learning purposes. All question items are shown in Table 1. Students were instructed to use ChatGPT freely throughout the class, after each class, they were asked to record their dialogue data with GPT and submit them to LMS. Note that not all participants contributed equally to the dataset, some students did not engage sufficiently with the LMS, resulting in incomplete data for certain weeks. We attempt to answer our research questions by analyzing the data collected from student prompts, ChatGPT responses, and surveys. Through questionnaires, we first explored students' perspectives on the role ChatGPT played. Next, we analyzed ChatGPT prompts obtained from the students and conducted a cluster analysis to find the students' common usage patterns. Finally, we compared the performance of the students in different clusters. The details and results will be described in the next section.

4. RESULTS

4.1 Analysis of Questionnaires

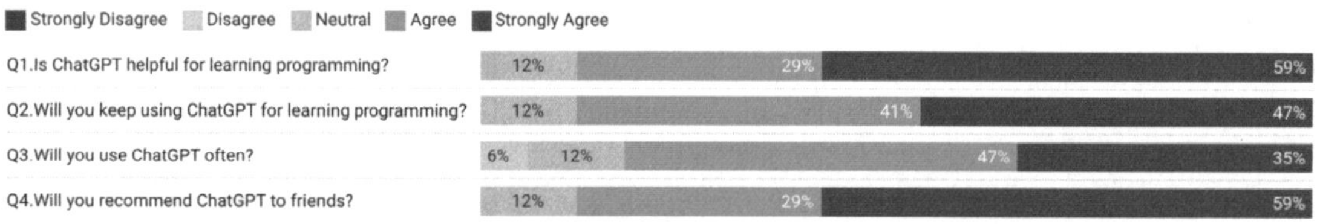

Figure 1. Students' responses to post-questionnaire

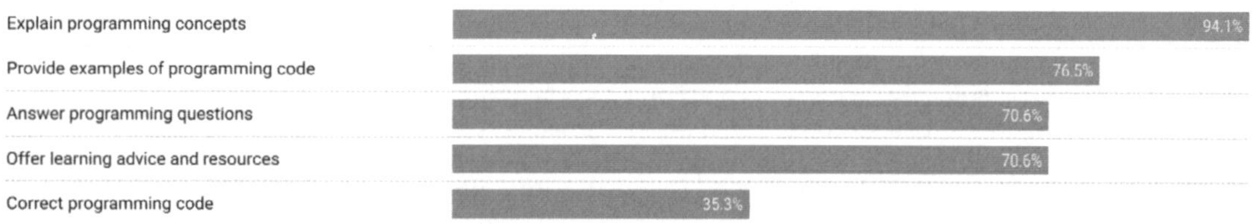

Figure 2. Students' responses on how ChatGPT can help with programming learning

The pre-questionnaire reveals that most respondents are familiar with ChatGPT, a significant portion (86.1%) reported having some knowledge, while 13.9% reported low or no understanding (Q1). This is not surprising as 88.9% of respondents are using ChatGPT or have used it before, and only 11.1% of respondents have not used it yet (Q2). Also, a majority of respondents are beginners in Python programming (75%), and 25% are reported as intermediate or advanced. Overall, the perceived impact of ChatGPT on learning (Q4) was generally positive, with 80.5% viewing it as beneficial to some extent.

Figure 1 shows the post-questionnaire results. There is overwhelming support for ChatGPT as a beneficial tool in learning programming, with most respondents in agreement (Q1, 58.8% strongly agree, 29.4% agree, 11.8% neutral and no respondent disagreed). Similarly, there is a high intention to continue using ChatGPT for learning programming (Q2), with 47.1% strongly agree and 41.2% agree to continue its use. Furthermore, most respondents plan to use ChatGPT frequently in the future for programming learning (Q3, 47.1% strongly agree, and 35.2% agree), and the majority of respondents agree to recommend ChatGPT to their friends (Q4, 58.8% strongly agree and 29.4% agree). This suggests that users find value in ChatGPT's capabilities for their learning needs. Overall, the data reflects a highly positive reception of ChatGPT among learners in programming courses. Additionally, Figure 2 illustrates the perceived usage of

ChatGPT in programming learning. The highest percentage, 94.1%, indicates that ChatGPT helps provide code examples. 76.5% believe that ChatGPT aids in explaining programming concepts. Equal portions of respondents, at 70.6% each, believe that ChatGPT aids in answering programming questions and correcting programming code. This highlights its role in offering practical coding assistance and clarification on tasks. Analysis of the dialogue data shows that students frequently use ChatGPT as a debugging tool, especially when they are working on programming exercise activities. Lastly, 35.3% of respondents value ChatGPT for offering learning advice and resources.

Our open-ended questions revealed that students find ChatGPT useful due to its ability to quickly identify and correct coding errors, provide clear explanations, and offer helpful suggestions. However, they also noted limitations, such as incorrectness in its responses, which is confusing, particularly when its answers differ from those given by teachers. Additionally, students mentioned that ChatGPT sometimes provides overly advanced information, making it difficult to follow. There is also a concern that over-reliance on ChatGPT might hinder the development of fundamental programming skills by encouraging shortcuts. To enhance its effectiveness, students suggested improving the correctness and relevance of ChatGPT's responses, incorporating step-by-step explanations, and aligning its guidance more closely with classroom content.

4.2 Analysis of Interactions

4.2.1 Prompt types

Table 2. Categorized prompt types and descriptions

Prompt Types	Description
Code Verification	Ask for verification the correctness of code.
Conceptual Question	Ask questions about programming-related conceptual knowledge.
Asking for Advice/Learning Resources	Request advice or resources for learning.
Code Correction	Ask for debugging and correction of errors in the code.
Error Message Interpretation	Request interpretation of the meaning and causes of error messages.
Code Implementation Questions	Ask specific questions related to code implementation.
Code Generation	Request the generation of code snippets for specific requirements.
Asking for example	Request example code for specific concepts or functionalities.
Code Optimization	Request the improvement of existing code based on specific needs.
Code Explanation	Ask for explanation of the functionality and purpose of the code.

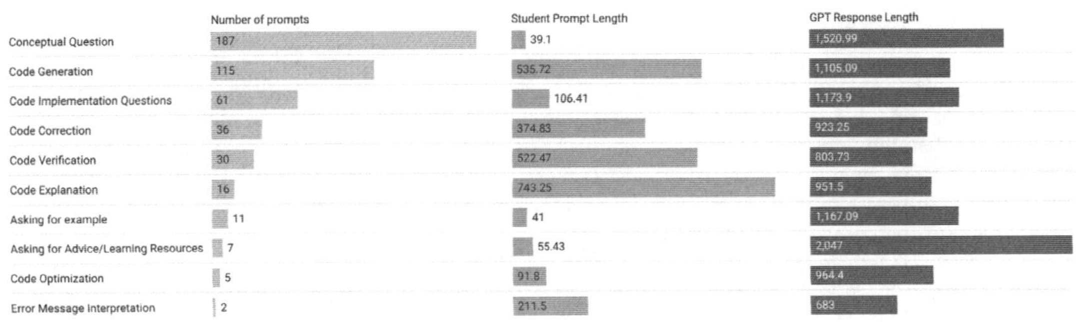

Figure 3. Count of various types and length of prompts and responses

To better understand the utilization of ChatGPT in the class, we analyzed 470 ChatGPT prompts obtained from the students. Although some previous work has categorized student prompts, their classifications were generally broader, often dividing prompts into just three or four categories (Ghimire and Edwards, 2024;

Brender et al. 2024). To gain a more nuanced understanding of student behavior, we conducted a detailed review of the interactions between students and ChatGPT, leading to a more granular classification of student prompts. This resulted in ten distinct categories of prompts, which are summarized in Table 2.

Figure 3 illustrates the distribution of various types of prompts submitted by students. Conceptual questions, requests for code generation, and code implementation questions were the most common types of prompts. The figure also shows the average length of prompts sent by students. We found that the average prompt lengths for code explanation, code generation, code verification, and code correction are significantly higher than those for other prompt types. This is expected, as students typically include the code itself in these prompts. In contrast, other types of prompts tend to have an average length of fewer than 200 characters. In contrast to the diversity in the average length of prompts, we found that all prompts received fairly long responses (more than 600 characters). A careful examination reveals that GPT provides detailed answers across different prompt types, often including examples and explanations, underscoring its role as a comprehensive and supportive tool in the learning process. Among these, prompts asking for advice or resources elicited the longest GPT responses (2,047 characters), while conceptual questions received the second longest responses, averaging 1,520.99 characters.

4.2.2 Cluster Analysis

Table 3. Clustering results of students' prompts

Prompt Types	**Conceptual Learners (C1)**	**Code Verifiers (C2)**	**Practical Coders (C3)**	**AI-Reliant Coders (C4)**
	Mean (SD)	**Mean (SD)**	**Mean (SD)**	**Mean (SD)**
Code Verification	2.02% (0.21)	**80.00% (1.41)**	4.33% (0.35)	6.48% (0.54)
Conceptual Question	**75.60% (1.44)**	0.00% (0.00)	7.39% (0.39)	1.03% (0.14)
Asking for Advice/Learning Resources	1.88% (0.14)	0.00% (0.00)	**8.75% (0.36)**	2.05% (0.29)
Code Correction	3.70% (0.20)	10.00% (0.71)	**21.03% (0.41)**	10.19% (0.69)
Error Message Interpretation	0.31% (0.04)	0.00% (0.00)	**3.17% (0.34)**	0.00% (0.00)
Code Implementation Questions	7.64% (1.21)	0.00% (0.00)	**33.86% (0.98)**	14.71% (0.31)
Code Generation	2.18% (0.15)	10.00% (0.71)	11.63% (0.18)	**62.24% (1.67)**
Asking for example	**5.01% (0.19)**	0.00% (0.00)	0.00% (0.00)	0.00% (0.00)
Code Optimization	0.33% (0.03)	0.00% (0.00)	**1.43% (0.12)**	0.00% (0.00)
Code Explanation	1.33% (0.09)	0.00% (0.00)	**8.41% (0.20)**	3.30% (0.17)

Table 4. The percentage of students in each cluster

Category	**C1**	**C2**	**C3**	**C4**
Percentage of students	46.2%	11.5%	23.1%	19.2%

Following previous work (Brender et al. 2024), we calculated for each student the percentage of prompts in each category and then used k-means clustering. In order to identify the optimal number of clusters, we have performed the elbow method, and the number of clusters is set to 4 based on the results. Table 3 shows the results including four clusters: Conceptual Learners (C1), Code Verifiers (C2), Practical Coders (C3), and AI-Reliant Coders (C4), and the percentage of students in each cluster are shown in Table 4. We give each cluster a name based on the results.

Conceptual Learners: Cluster 1 is dominated by students who primarily focus on understanding programming concepts. These students are less concerned with debugging or validating their code, likely preferring to focus on the broader conceptual frameworks of programming. With 75.60% of their prompts categorized under Conceptual Questions, they are heavily invested in deepening theoretical understanding.

Code Verifiers: Cluster 2 is characterized by a strong emphasis on ensuring code correctness, with a striking 80.00% of prompts focused on Code Verification. These students are highly detail-oriented, often seeking to validate their code and ensure it functions as intended. This cluster also shows a moderate engagement with Code Correction (10.00%) and Code Generation (10.00%), while the complete lack of engagement in Conceptual Questions and other categories suggests that these students prioritize practical coding tasks over theoretical learning.

Practical Coders: Cluster 3 includes students who exhibit a balanced approach, with significant engagement across several categories, particularly Code Implementation Questions (33.86%) and Code Correction (21.03%). These students are highly practical, focusing on the application of their coding knowledge and the refinement of their code. They also show notable involvement in Code Explanation (8.41%), indicating that they often seek to understand the purpose and functionality of their existing code.

AI-Reliant Coders: Cluster 4 is named AI-Reliant Coders, with 62.24% of their prompts centered on code generation. After examining their dialogue details, we found that these students frequently copy and paste their coding problems directly into ChatGPT, depending on the AI to generate entire solutions with minimal manual input. When issues arise, they often rely on GPT to correct errors and validate the code, until their code successfully passes, this finding is aligned with previous work (Qureshi, 2023). This is also evident in their moderate engagement with Code Implementation Questions (14.71%) and Code Correction (10.19%), showcasing their preference for using GPT for generating code and also using GPT for refining and debugging it.

4.2.3 Student Academic Performance

Table 5. Students' performance of different clusters

	Category	C1	C2	C3	C4
Assignments (Full marks=150)	Mean (SD)	144.85 (7.94)	147.48 (3.01)	144.80 (5.66)	148.27 (0.97)
Final Grade (Full marks=5)	Mean (SD)	4.42 (0.51)	4.00 (0.00)	4.50 (0.55)	4.00 (0.00)

Table 5 shows students' performance across different clusters. It includes data on the total assignment scores (out of 150) accumulated over 12 weeks and final grades (with letter grades S, A, B, C, F converted to numerical values 5, 4, 3, 2, 1), with both mean and standard deviation provided for each cluster. Given the non-normal distribution of the data, we used the Mann-Whitney U test to compare the performance between every two groups. For assignments, AI-Reliant Coders (C4) and Code Verifiers (C2) outperformed those in the other clusters, achieving higher mean scores. For AI-Reliant Coders, who likely relied heavily on ChatGPT for generating solutions directly translates to high performance in assignments, as the AI's output is often correct. Code Verifiers appear to have written their code and then used ChatGPT for verification and debugging. This allows them to correct errors before submission, which significantly increases the accuracy of their code. However, the final course grades, which provide a more holistic evaluation of student performance, revealed that Practical Coders (C3) and Conceptual Learners (C1) earned higher grades compared to C2 and C4. They achieved higher final grades likely due to their comprehensive understanding of concepts and balanced engagement in both theoretical and practical aspects of the course, which are key components of a holistic evaluation beyond just assignment scores. While the Mann-Whitney U test indicated no statistically significant differences in performance across the clusters, these findings offer valuable insights into integrating AI tools in programming courses.

5. CONCLUSION

This study delves into ChatGPT's role in Python programming learning, focusing on student perceptions and interactions. Through questionnaires, we first explored students' perspectives on the role ChatGPT played. Next, we analyzed ChatGPT prompts obtained from the students and conducted a cluster analysis to find the students' common usage patterns. Finally, we compared the performance of the students in different clusters. By analyzing the questionnaire data, our research provides insights into effectively integrating LLMs into programming education. The results suggest that students value ChatGPT as a beneficial tool that assists them and enhances their learning experiences in program learning. Interaction data analysis indicated detailed interaction between students and ChatGPT.

There are some limitations to this study. First, the sample size is relatively small, which limits the generalizability of the results. Second, while our analysis methods identified different patterns, these clusters may not accurately represent students' true intent, as they might be influenced by factors such as the ability to provide high-quality prompts, the context in which the prompts were used, and student ' s prior knowledge and experience. Further validation with additional data is required to confirm these findings. In addition, although we compared the performance of different students, the absence of a closed-format test limits the results. For future work, we plan to collect and analyze more data to further explore the effects on student behavior and learning outcomes. We will also focus on a detailed examination of students' code quality after using ChatGPT, as well as an in-depth analysis of ChatGPT's responses.

ACKNOWLEDGEMENT

This work was supported by JSPS KAKENHI Grant Numbers JP20H00622 and JP24K20903.

REFERENCES

Biswas, S. (2023). *Role of ChatGPT in computer programming.: ChatGPT in computer programming.* Mesopotamian J. Comput. Sci. 2023, 8–16.

Brender, J., El-Hamamsy, L., Mondada, F., & Bumbacher, E. (2024). *Who's Helping Who? When Students Use ChatGPT to Engage in Practice Lab Sessions.* In *International Conference on Artificial Intelligence in Education* (pp. 235-249). Cham: Springer Nature Switzerland.

Chen, L., Li, G., Ma, B., Tang, C., Okubo, F., Shimada, A. (2024). *How do strategies for using ChatGPT affect knowledge comprehension?.* Springer, Cham. In *International Conference on Artificial Intelligence in Education* (pp. 151-162). Cham: Springer Nature Switzerland.

Ghimire, A., & Edwards, J. (2024). *Coding with AI: How are tools like chatgpt being used by students in foundational programming courses.* In *International Conference on Artificial Intelligence in Education* (pp. 259-267). Cham: Springer Nature Switzerland.

Humble, N., et al. (2023). *Cheaters or AI-enhanced learners: Consequences of ChatGPT for programming education.* Electron. J. e-Learn.

Kasneci, E., et al. (2023). *ChatGPT for good? on opportunities and challenges of large language models for education.* Learn. Individ. Differ. 103, 102274.

Kazemitabaar, M., Chow, J., Ma, C.K.T., Ericson, B.J., Weintrop, D., Grossman, T. (2023). *Studying the effect of AI code generators on supporting novice learners in introductory programming*. In: CHI'2023, pp. 1–23. ACM.

Ma, B., Chen, L., Konomi, S. (2024). *Enhancing programming education with ChatGPT: a case study on student perceptions and interactions in a Python course.* In *International Conference on Artificial Intelligence in Education* (pp. 113-126). Cham: Springer Nature Switzerland.

Malinka, K., Peres´ıni, M., Firc, A., Hujn´ak, O., Janus, F. (2023). *On the educational impact of ChatGPT: is artificial intelligence ready to obtain a university degree?* In: Proceedings of the 2023 Conference on Innovation and Technology in Computer Science Education, vol. 1. pp. 47–53.

Pankiewicz, M., Baker, R.S. (2023). *Large language models (GPT) for automating feedback on programming assignments.* arXiv preprint arXiv:2307.00150.

Phung, T., et al. (2023). *Generative AI for programming education: benchmarking ChatGPT, GPT-4, and human tutors.* Int. J. Manag. 21(2), 100790.

Qureshi, B. (2023). *Exploring the use of ChatGPT as a tool for learning and assessment in undergraduate computer science curriculum: opportunities and challenges.* In: 9th International Conference on e-Society, e-Learning and e-Technologies, pp. 7–13. https://doi.org/10.1145/3613944.3613946

Rahman, M.M., Watanobe, Y. (2023). *Chatgpt for education and research: opportunities, threats, and strategies.* Appl. Sci. 13(9), 5783.

Rajala, J., Hukkanen, J., Hartikainen, M., Niemel¨a, P. (2023). *"Call me Kiran"-ChatGPT as a tutoring chatbot in a computer science course.* In: Proceedings of the 26th International Academic Mindtrek Conference, pp. 83–94.

Shoufan, A. (2023). *Exploring students' perceptions of ChatGPT: thematic analysis and follow-up survey.* IEEE Access.

Skjuve, M., Følstad, A., Brandtzaeg, P.B. (2023). *The user experience of ChatGPT: findings from a questionnaire study of early users.* In: Proceedings of the 5th International Conference on Conversational User Interfaces, pp. 1–10.

Tlili, A., et al. (2023). *What if the devil is my guardian angel: Chatgpt as a case study of using chatbots in education.* Smart Learn. Environ. 10(1), 15.

Yilmaz, R., Yilmaz, F.G.K. (2023). *Augmented intelligence in programming learning: examining student views on the use of ChatGPT for programming learning.* Comput.Hum. Behav. Artif. Hum. 1(2), 100005.

UNPACKING THE THREE SPHERES OF INTEREST IN A BLENDED INTENSIVE PROGRAMME: COLLABORATIVE LEARNING, BLENDED LEARNING AND INTERNATIONALISATION

Alice Barana[1], Antonino Cambria[1,2], Marina Marchisio Conte[1] and Enrico Spinello[3]
[1]*Department of Molecular Biotechnology and Health Sciences, University of Turin, Piazza Nizza 44, 10153 Torino, Italy*
[2]*High Defence Study Centre, Piazza della Rovere, 83, 00165 Roma, Italy*
[3]*Education and Training Command and School of Applied Military Studies, Via Arsenale 22, 10121 Torino, Italy*

ABSTRACT

As innovative activities and methodologies bloom in the panorama of education, three areas of particular interest in the security and defence education field are collaborative learning, blended learning, and internationalisation. These elements are the pillars of Blended Intensive Programmes (BIPs), short mobility activities that combine residential and online phases in a collaborative environment. This study aims to understand the effects of collaborative learning, blended learning, and internationalisation on security and defence education. The context of the research is a set of BIPs designed and implemented by the Interdepartmental University School of Strategic Sciences of the University of Turin in the 2022/2023 and 2023/2024 academic years. The sample is composed of 209 students who filled out a questionnaire about the effectiveness of the learning modalities and the outcomes achieved after attending one of the seven BIPs. The methodology adopted is the thematic analysis of the students' open answers, chosen to highlight the impact of collaborative learning, blended learning, and internationalisation on their academic path. The results show the effects of elements combination, such as the development of critical thinking and transversal skills, which are fundamental in the officers' training.

KEYWORDS

Blended Intensive Programmes, Blended Learning, Collaborative Learning, Internationalisation, Military Education

1. INTRODUCTION

The military education landscape is not just a field, but an ever-expanding galaxy, dotted with many new stars that promise a flourishing future. It serves as a guiding star for many actors in the field of education, including students, teachers, and staff. These stakeholders need to continually broaden their horizons and scrutinise new educational elements, methodologies, instrumentations, and activities that can add value to the educational sphere. This sphere, which plays an extremely important role in the military over the long term, is the first step that every military officer, as well as civilians, go through before putting boots on the ground of operation. Its role is vital to be efficient and must be maintained over time since it must lead to benefits in terms of saving time and costs, employment of personnel, and maintaining high professional standards (Gell 2017; Paile-Calvo 2016; Marchisio and Spinello 2021; Barana et al. 2024). A new educational format which blends new methodologies, new tools and new approaches in the field of military education is the Blended Intensive Programme, BIP. The design of BIPs includes several elements considered innovative and efficient to meet the needs of the armed forces through the blended learning, collaborative learning and internationalisation (Barana et al. 2024; Cambria et al. 2023a). The three elements' international blueprint can spread the defence and security culture in the military environment and in the civilian and European spheres of education. Therefore, it is necessary to understand how these new methodologies evolve and analyse the early results to see how they can be improved and how it is suitable to adapt them to be as efficient as possible. In this way, a management and quality check process can control where programmes are going and also understand the modalities of evolution and which quality effects would be produced. Once these effects are identified and compared with the practical needs of the armed forces, they can be improved, tailored and adapted. For this reason, the paper attempts to analyse the results collected from the responses given by the students' final feedback during 7 BIPs conducted at the Interdepartmental University School of Strategic Sciences (SUISS) of the University of Turin in cooperation with the IT-Army Education and Training Command and School of Applied Military Studies (ETC&SAMS) concerning their experience and contact with courses that implemented blended learning, internationalisation, and collaborative learning. These elements merged are important because they can produce new efficient and effective methodologies in learning and teaching, especially in military education. (Laal and Laal 2012; Wilson and Wilson 2019; Namyssova 2019; Barana et al. 2024).

This paper aims to understand the effects of innovative approaches based on blended learning, collaborative learning, and internationalisation in defence and security education. The methodology is based on a thematic analysis. The research group wants to track other studies or experiences dealing with these elements, with the aim of introducing the seeds of investigative purpose in the academic research landscape and the outcomes of innovative research results in the field of military education. The following section reports the theoretical framework on the topics, consolidating the most important terms of the research and defining and describing them for subsequent use in the practical research process. The methodology section highlights the research question and explains the coding and merge process step by step, trying not to overlook possible methodological gaps and explicitly setting out the research question. In the fourth part, the results section, a representation of the results of the thematic analysis is shown, and quantitative results are structured in a matrix to analyse data and create graphs, later discussed in the fifth part. Lastly, conclusions are drawn, answering the research question and highlighting possible future research programmes using this paper as a stepping stone for further research and contribution to other papers.

2. THEORETICAL FRAMEWORK

It is important to involve military students in blended learning, collaborative learning, and internationalisation activities to develop highly professional personnel ready to operate, able to interact, and comfortable with national and international colleagues. Similar methodologies can affect the young officers' aptitude when managing their operational career by training in any place and at any time. Still, above all, they can satisfy the needs of the armed forces with cost reduction and specialised training personnel (Barana et al. 2024). The European frameworks (EU 2016; Gell 2017) state that it is important to include blended, collaborative, and internationalisation experiences, but there are not many examples. It is still a fertile ground that this work could contribute to nurture.

2.1 Blended Intensive Programmes

Blended Intensive Programmes are a new Erasmus+ 2021-2027 Programme funding scheme. They consist of international educational activities that combine virtual collaboration and short physical mobility, proposing "challenge-based" activities. Intensive mixed programs must assign at least 3 ECTS credits to students and involve the participation of at least three universities from three European Union Member States.

2.2 Collaborative Learning

Collaborative learning (CL) is a powerful classroom approach used in different contexts, from classroom games and project work to team-building activities. Working collaboratively helps students gain knowledge from the interaction. When the interaction is on a higher level, the CL helps students build knowledge through discussion, peer collaboration, interaction and evaluation (Kimmerle et al. 2021; Onrubia and Engel 2009). A comprehensive definition was provided by Laal and Laal (2012), who defined Collaborative Learning as follows: "CL is an educational approach to teaching and learning that involves groups of learners working together to solve a problem, complete a task, or create a product. In the CL environment, the learners are challenged both socially and emotionally." Collaborative knowledge construction is a multi-level approach that requires individual students to take on cognitive responsibilities. During this process, students become aware of their shared knowledge and develop collective knowledge (Barana et al., 2023; Lund, 2019). Wilson and Wilson (2019), after Johnson et al. (2007), advocated a theory of social interdependence, where three ways in which students can learn in a context of reciprocal relationships were proposed: they can work together cooperatively to achieve their learning goals; they may compete against each other; or they may work individually. In military education, collaboration is an important indicator in developing officer and civilian actors' professional paths. Their roles will be complementary and useful for both parties one day. Let officers and civilians collaborate since they are in the educational and vocational training path is strategic. Education cooperation and knowledge exchange foster a wide range of aspects in the learning process to increase global competitiveness, help tackle global challenges, transform higher education through capabilities and capacity building, and nurture equality (Cambria et. al, 2023b).

2.3 Blended Learning

The handbook (EU 2021) explains that blended learning (BL) in formal education happens when a school, educator, or learner takes more than one approach to the learning process: blending school sites and distance learning environments. The most important element is when the institution blends different learning tools, including digital (e.g., online platforms, instruments such as artificial intelligence, digital environments, and the delivery of lessons) and non-digital tools. Through BL in multiple contexts, students experience the possibility to be independent and autonomous in their learning and study at their own pace. They can be the owners of their personal laboratory where it is possible to experiment with new forms of learning. BL classes include integrating the face-to-face session and the online learning phase, which is assumed to involve students in active learning through diverse learning approaches (Cambria et al. 2023c; Namyssova et al. 2019). In the context of military environment and education, young officers and new leaders must be able to perform their duties in mixed environments and manage digital tools on a master level. These activities allow students to get used to digital learning environments and exploit their massive potential. In line with this description and definition, BL is a flexible approach that helps improve the inclusiveness of education (EU 2021).

2.4 Internationalisation

One of the first aspects that highlight the importance of this third ingredient is stated in the definition as follows: "The intentional process of integrating an international, intercultural or global dimension into the purpose, functions and delivery of post-secondary education, to enhance the quality of education and research for all students and staff and to make a meaningful contribution to society" (De Wit et al. 2015). The quality that people want to seek is measured in terms of increasing the number of exchanges, the mutual recognition, the use of Erasmus mobility, the opening of national educational opportunities to young European officers, and the learning and teaching about Europe and its defence, such as the creation of common modules as well as the promotion of learning foreign languages (Paile-Calvo 2016; Gell 2015). It also allows them to practice oral communication and leadership skills and develop critical thinking, problem-solving, and creativity. All these features and elements in the career of personnel in the field of security and defence pave the way for greater integration and coherence of our future actions in favour of peace and security (Gell 2017). Internationalisation (I) answers the needs expressed by the current scenarios depicted by EU, NATO and UN. The aim is to develop officers' ability to work in any international operating theatre with colleagues worldwide, to fit into different cultural contexts, and to create collaborative networks (Marchisio and Spinello 2021; Cambria et al. 2023b).

3. METHODOLOGY

The research question we want to answer with this paper is the following: what effects do blended learning, collaborative learning, and internationalisation have in the context of BIPs applied in military education?

In 2012, the IT-Army Staff invited the ETC&SAMS to join the "European Initiative for the exchange of young officers, inspired by ERASMUS" programme, also known as Military ERASMUS or EMILYO, in line with the rules established by the Implementation Group. The first Erasmus exchange program was launched (2013-2014) (Marchisio and Spinello 2021). The first Common Module on Common Security and Defence Policy (CSDP) was organised in December 2013. Based on this experience, the first BIPs were launched in 2023 (Cambria et al. 2023b). In 2024, BIPs were developed and improved per the ERASMUS+ 2021-2027 criteria. These programmes were designed and implemented to merge the paramount elements of BL, CL, and I within the condensed environment of Military Education. For this study, we considered the 7 BIPs held at the

SUISS during the 2022/2023 and 2023/2024 academic years: 2 editions of "Biosafety and Bioterrorism" (Bio&Bio); 2 editions of "Problem Solving and Critical Thinking" (PSCT), 2 editions of "Law of Armed Conflict" (LOAC) and one edition of "Common Security and Defence Policy" (CSDP). During the creation, management, and development of the BIPs at the SUISS, a digital learning environment was used to deliver theoretical lessons and create a digital environment where participants could meet and put the knowledge gained into practice. The digital tools were also used during the residential and practical phases. The BIPs were attended by 290 students, of which 40% were international, and 60% were local students; 35% were civilian, and 65% were military personnel; 41% were female, and 59% were male students. The data were collected through a final questionnaire that students were asked to fill out at the end of each BIP after the exam. In particular, the study focuses on questions Q5, Q6, Q7, Q10, and Q11, which were included in the questionnaires of all the 7 BIPs. The items were formulated to collect the motivation and engagement of the students immersed in the activity. The items related to CL were designed to understand how students interacted among themselves. The question related to I aims to investigate the opportunities and the critical moments the students faced during the activities in international environments, especially considering the hyperconnected world we live in. The items related to BL investigate how students used digital tools to solve problems in a blended environment. They are listed in Table 1 and organised according to the area of interest.

Table 1. Questions selected for the analysis

N°	Text	Area
Q5	What activities did you carry out? Indicate shortly the goal, the role and the main contribution.	CL
Q6	What was accomplished by your team?	CL
Q7	How did you take advantage of the international interaction and collaboration with peer students from different countries?	I
Q10	What technology and virtual tools did you use?	BL
Q11	Did you use Artificial Intelligence tools during the BIP? If so, briefly explain how it helped you.	BL

The research approach of this study is based on the thematic analysis applied to the set of student responses. Thematic analysis is a method for identifying, analysing and reporting patterns within data. It minimally organises and describes the data set in rich detail (Braun and Clarke 2006). Thematic analysis can be an essentialist or realist method, which reports experiences, meanings and the reality of participants, or it can be a constructionist method, which examines how events, realities, meanings, experiences and so on are the effects of a range of discourses operating within society. It can also be a 'contextualist' method, sitting between the two poles of essentialism and constructionism, in which case it is characterised by theories such as critical realism (Braun and Clarke, 2006). We have decided to apply the middle way, i.e., contextualism, and the various steps taken will be explained in the following paragraphs.

The first step was to collect and organise all the answers to the selected items of the final questionnaire of the seven BIPs mentioned earlier. This phase consists of familiarising ourselves with data: transcribing data in an Excel file, reading them, and noting initial ideas. All the answers were analysed, trying to summarise the effects of CL, BL, and I on security and defence education through annotations. Once all the answers were analysed, we moved on to the thematic analysis's second step: generating initial codes, which consists of coding interesting features of the data systematically across the entire data set and collating data relevant to each code. To do this, brief sentences were formulated for each area of analysis (CL, BL, and I) that reflected the main elements included in the students' responses. Lastly, descriptive statistics were run to highlight the occurrence of the various codes.

4. RESULTS

Through the thematic analysis process, we obtained nine codes organised by category. Three belong to the area of CL, two to the area of BL, and four to the area of I. They were created in such a way as to describe concisely the effects of BL, CL, and I on learning.

The three codes related to Collaborative Learning were the following:

- **CL1: Work closely together to solve the problem.** It contains/includes all the answers that refer to the students' joint effort in achieving the set objective and solving the task, which could be solving a problem or creating a presentation. The answers also address the proper student role and one's contribution to achieving the goal.

- **CL2: Build knowledge process through discussion, interaction and peer collaboration.** It concerns a more advanced state of response, which implies higher phases of collaborative knowledge construction through discussions, debates, and presentations. Therefore, all answers that reported training or improvement due to an exchange of discussions were included in this group. For a practical example, those who gave answers such as "*stimulating the working process and giving the right direction to the team*" or "*we were discussing and creating a final product in the group with the exchange of ideas*" were coded with CL2.
- **CL3: Gain theoretical and practical knowledge.** It concerns a more general aspect, where knowledge is acquired in a theoretical and practical manner but without specifying the method. This code indicates that, by working in a group and collaborating, it was possible to acquire both practical and theoretical training.

The two codes related to Blended Learning are the following:

- **BL1: Use of a Virtual Learning Environment**. It identifies all those response areas that involve using any learning management system or virtual environment during the various courses. Moodle, SELENE, and the SUISS learning platform are examples of virtual environments. All answers addressing such elements were coded with this sentence.
- **BL2: Use digital tools for enhancing interaction**. It aims to codify all those answers that refer to the use of digital tools, such as ChatGPT, PowerPoints, Canvas and other digital tools that increase interaction and achieve a result in solving the assigned tasks of solving the problems or delivering public presentations. These were tools that they needed to use collaboratively to provide a common solution to tasks assigned to the group altogether.

The four codes related to Internationalisation are the following:

- **I1: Foster and practice a foreign language**. It concerns one of the most critical consequences of international activities: practising, improving, and using a foreign language, which also breaks down linguistic barriers. Linguistic barriers are also a significant obstacle to work mobility. Students appreciated the opportunity to practice and use English during WGs, lessons and public presentations.
- **I2: Interact with foreign cultures and develop transversal skills and competencies**. It categorises a wider selection of answers. It includes all those that mention the interaction between cultures for the development of transversal skills. Moreover, task sharing based on the specialities of foreign personnel is an element of selection in this area.
- **I3: Develop critical thinking.** It collects the most student responses. It includes answers that involve an exchange of opinions, ideas, experiences, and points of view, which are fundamental elements of the critical thinking process. For this reason, answers such as "*an exchange of ideas*", "*share points of view*", or "*exchange opinions*" were assigned this code.
- **I4: Expand one's knowledge internationally**. It refers to something general about an international overview. It aims to collect and codify all answers that include a cognitive aspect of other nations' cultures, situations, and historical events, expanding participants' knowledge internationally.

Once this phase was completed, we moved on to the following steps, thus creating a thematic map to delineate an analysis that culminated into the drafting of the conclusions. After collecting the 290 responses, a quantitative analysis was conducted to compute the frequencies and percentages of the codes. Results are shown in Table 2. The answers that could not be coded with the identified codes were labelled "Empty answers." No reference to the effects of CL, BL, or I could be detected in these answers.

Table 2. Frequency and Percentage of the codes in line with the answers provided by the students

Codes	Frequency	Percentage
Collaborative Learning		
CL1: Work closely together to solve the problem	148	51%
CL2: Build knowledge process through discussion, interaction and peer collaboration	79	27,2%
CL3: Gain theoretical and practical knowledge	59	20,3%
Empty answer	4	1,4%
Total	290	100%
Blended Learning		
BL1: Use of a Virtual Learning Environment	57	19,7%

BL2: Use digital tools for enhancing interaction	81	27,9%
Empty answer	152	52,4%
Total	290	100%
Internationalisation		
I1: Foster and practice a foreign language	88	30,3%
I2: Interact with foreign cultures and develop transversal skills and competencies	73	25,2%
I3: Develop critical thinking	90	31%
I4: Expand one's knowledge internationally	35	12,1%
Empty answer	4	1,4%
Total	290	100%

The responses show the students' engagement with the activities, although the sample comprises students who participated in different BIPs about different topics and with different teachers and teaching modalities. In Table 3, we report some significant examples of students' answers coded, organised by thematic area.

Table 3. Examples of students' answers per code

Code	Examples	BIP
CL1	"We worked in group to achieve a common goal; my role was the spokesperson so I would curate the final aspects of the press release and the presentation."	Bio&Bio 2024
CL2	"I was Echo's Head of the Industrial Development Organisation, but also, I did a lot of the speaking in the presentation. I came with the proposals of what actions the organisation should take. I, but also one of my colleagues, helped with the math problems and explained to the others the mathematical process"	PSCT 2024
CL2	"I attended all the lectures and I did not hesitate to ask questions whenever I needed. I kept my personal notes. In the workshop I participated actively in the structure of argument and the presentation."	LOAC 2023
CL2	"We had to discuss issues regarding security and to find a solution or express our opinion. We had to research, form our own opinion, discuss, and present the final result"	CSDP 2024
CL3	"I was the biological analyst in our group. I had to study the scenario carefully and try to find out what was the kind of the contagion that has spread through the nation. I also did an experiment with a fluorescent agent and samples taken from the river in our scenario."	Bio&Bio 2024
BL1	"E-learning and Moodle. I also used powerpoint to make a presentation"	LOAC 2024
BL2	"Especially Chat GPT. But not in the sense that is the instrument that has to work for us, but for support and to have a faster response"	PSCT 2023
BL2	"Only on the biology lessons, because they were more specific than my skills"	Bio&Bio 2023
I1	"It was an opportunity to enhance my English-speaking skills and discuss the aspects of LOAC"	LOAC 2024
I2	"Improve language skills. See how people from other countries respond to the same problem"	LOAC 2024
I3	"I had the chance to speak English and ameliorate the fluency, and also to exchange experiences and personal knowledge. It was unique to investigate the cultural differences and approaches to problem solving and communication"	PSCT 2024
I3	"We exchanged different points of view on this delicate subject as protection of cultural property or civilians."	LOAC 2024
I3	"I had the opportunity to share different opinions (somewhat culturally based) and to find common ground."	LOAC 2023
I4	"I talked with professors and students from other countries inside and outside the school. It was interesting to learn new things from them."	CSDP 2024

5. DISCUSSION AND CONCLUSIONS

A common element observed from the students' responses is that the combination of CL, BL, and I creates high student engagement and satisfaction. It can be seen from the contents and the type of responses given. Considering the examples of students' answers presented in the previous paragraph, one can perceive the feeling of belonging to the group and the immersion in the task assigned to solve altogether (PSCT 2023, PSCT 2024, Bio&Bio 2024). Immersion in working groups in contact with foreign officers, military personnel, and students with other backgrounds allowed the participants to be motivated. From the results, a good percentage of students (51%) highlighted in their responses the necessity to work in groups and solve the tasks assigned.

The use of digital tools is both an aid in facilitating problem solving, but also an excellent, always accessible source from which to draw information that can then be useful for student growth and learning. Almost 50% of students reported using digital environments and tools efficiently. The other half of the students did not mention the use of the tools, probably because one in the group was elected to use that tool. This shows a good division of tasks among the members of the groups to minimise the efforts and maximise the results.

To top it off, the phenomenon of internationalisation and contact with other cultures and foreign personnel provides an excellent opportunity to improve one's language skills quickly and focus on a specific topic. This allows students to not only break down language barriers but also develop critical thinking skills as a result of exchanging experiences, viewpoints, and opinions. Indeed, 61% of students' responses reported the usefulness of international learning in improving language skills and exchanging opinions, thus consequentially developing critical thinking. The peculiar example reported for code I4 shows that there was also the possibility of increasing knowledge with international inputs. Even if this percentage was around 12%, it is possible to say that the predisposition for in-depth analysis with teachers and peers who gained a different background is present among the students. In the internationalisation area, another important element is that 25% of students were trying to achieve and improve those transversal skills that someone can learn with experience (e.g., the capacity to talk about different cultures in international environments, or the capacity to recognise the values of personnel from another country and try to make them feel better, the capacity to understand some way of thinking and anticipate some outcomes, the capacity to mediate conflicts that can rise in a discussion). This experience did not only draw from the face-to-face lessons but, as written in some responses, also from the time spent visiting together, during the time for homework at home or during the time spent out the lessons.

The feature that makes the BIPs unique and innovative is the union and fusion of CL, BL, and I. This creates a student-centred learning environment focused on the students' learning journey. Motivation, engagement, simulation, and teamwork are facilitators that allow students to integrate their cultural and academic background with a significant experience for their future. Almost 98% of students' answers show they benefited from the courses with different highlighted aspects. Indeed, only 1,4% left empty answers or wrote something that could not be coded. The reason may be a lack of interest in the activity or in completing the questionnaire.

In military education, the characteristics of BIPs make them optimal mobility experiences that do not affect operational activities with excessive costs. Moreover, civilian-military collaboration in an international perspective and sharing a European security and defence culture are precious learning occasions in officers' training. It is crucial to evaluate how these innovative training modalities can help develop officers' mindsets, availability, and adaptability for the missions they will have to undertake. The BIPs can be fertile ground for expressing how the complex environment of theoretical knowledge is translated into the concrete form of experience and practice in the real world. Students must build their knowledge in a social and collaborative environment, thus becoming useful for their entire community (Cambria et al. 2023b). The results allow us to affirm that CL promoted the development of skills such as teamwork, communication and problem solving in a real and practical context. Indeed, almost 71% of students collaborated and participated actively in the knowledge-building process. I exposed officers to different cultures and perspectives, preparing them to operate in a global environment, and almost the entire sample (98%) of students was aware that the BIPs are great opportunities for making experience. The BL combined traditional teaching methods with digital technologies, offering a more flexible and personalised approach to learning, and half (50%) of the students affirmed it in their answers. These approaches can help create well-rounded officers and civilians ready to face the complex challenges of the modern world. From the analysis of the answers, 98% of the sample found some opportunities to exploit in the BIPs. Therefore, the BIPs can be considered valuable for the student's career path; they are an opportunity to be introduced to a new and innovative learning approach. This air of innovation answers the current context and scenarios that EU Member States and other institutions face.

To sum up, the answers of the students who participated in these seven BIPs have shown that CL, BL, and I can bring significant innovations to the field of Military Education. We are on the brink of a new beginning of exploratory learning and innovative didactic methodologies. The advantages are very clear in terms of efficiency and effectiveness. BIPs are safe laboratories where it is possible to gain a wide range of experiences, skills and knowledge specific to the military environment without suffering from the critical consequences of mistakes made in the real world. The acquisition of transversal skills and soft skills adds value to the initiative, allowing the students to gain theoretical knowledge and put that knowledge into practice. Thus, they acquire awareness and capabilities to interact in a complex, volatile, and uncertain environment. To develop this study further, we will organise interviews with participants in future BIPs to gain an in-depth understanding of the effects of CL, BL, and I on their career paths and to map specific teaching modalities to the various effects.

This work, in a long-term view, stresses the importance of developing the three components to become pillars in the world of military education. The research is a stepping stone for further analyses and comparison with the experience evolution over the years. The paper shows a picture of an evolving analysis process that absorbs various elements of education and tries to make them unique through combination and design related to Military Education.

REFERENCES

Barana, A., et al. (2023). Investigating the Knowledge Co-Construction Process in Homogeneous Ability Groups during Computational Lab Activities in Financial Mathematics, *Sustainability*, Vol. 15, No. 18, p. 13466. https://doi.org/10.3390/su151813466

Barana, A., et al. (2024). Detecting blended learning, collaborative learning and internationalisation in military education: a systematic literature review, *Proceedings of 18th International Conference on e-Learning and Digital Learning 2024 and Sustainability, Technology and Education 2024*. Budapest, Hungary, pp. 137-144.

Braun, V. and Clarke, V. (2006). Using thematic analysis in psychology, *Qualitative Research in Psychology*, Vol. 3, No. 2, pp. 77-101, https://doi.org/10.1191/1478088706qp063oa

Cambria, A., et al. (2023a). Educational Innovation in Hybrid Warfare, *Proceedings of 16th International Conference Of Education, Research And Innovation*. Seville, Spain, pp. 9433-9440. https://dx.doi.org/10.21125/iceri.2023.2432

Cambria, A., et al. (2023b). Blended Intensive Programs for Fostering Collaboration and Knowledge Exchange In Security And Defence Education. *Proceedings of 16th International Conference of Education, Research and Innovation*. Seville, Spain, pp. 9441-9448. https://dx.doi.org/10.21125/iceri.2023.2433

Cambria, A., et al. (2023c). Higher Education training activities in international environments for developing skills of civil-military cooperation. *Proceedings of the 20th International Conference on Cognition And Exploratory Learning In The Digital Age.* Madeira Island, Portugal, pp. 402-406

De Wit, H., et al. (2015). Internationalisation of higher education: A study for the European parliament. Brussels: *European Parliament Policy Department B: Structural and Cohesion Policies*

EU European Commission. (2016). Learning Opportunities and Qualifications in Europe – Information about courses, work-based learning and qualifications. Brussels. Available from: https://ec.europa.eu/ploteus/content/descriptors-page.

EU European Commission, Directorate-General for Education, Youth, Sport and Culture. (2021). Blended learning for high quality and inclusive primary and secondary education. *Publications Office of the European Union*. https://data.europa.eu/doi/10.2766/237842.

Johnson, D. W., et al. (2007). The state of cooperative learning in postsecondary and professional settings. *Educational Psychology Review*, Vol. 19, No. 1, pp. 15–29.

Gell, H. (2015). Increase of Students' personal Development by Internationalisation. *Habilitation Process at the University of Defence Brno*, Faculty of Military Leadership Czech Republic, Brno.

Gell, H. (2017). Increase of Military Leadership Skills and Competences of future Leaders by Internationalisation, *Scientific Journal "Economics & Management"*, Brno, February

Kimmerle, J., Fischer, F., & Cress, U. (2021). Argumentation and knowledge construction. In U. Cress, C. Rosnoja, & H. (Eds.), *International handbook of computer-supported collaborative learning* (pp. 183–198). Springer International Publishing. https://doi.org/10.1007/978-3-030-65291-3_10.

Laal, M. and Laal, M. (2012). Collaborative Learning: What is it? *SciVerse ScienceDirect Procedia, Social and Behavioral Sciences*, Vol. 31, pp. 491-495. https://doi.org/10.1016/j.sbspro.2011.12.092.

Lund, K. (2019). Building and regulating cognitive, linguistic, and interactional aspects of knowledge between the individual and the group. *Computers in Human Behavior*, Vol. 100, No. 1, pp. 370–383. https://doi.org/10.1016/j.chb.2019.04.013

Marchisio, M. and Spinello, E. (2021). Internationalisation for Enhancing The European Security And Defence Higher Education. *Proceedings of International Conference e-Learning 2021*, Virtual, pp. 99-106.

Namyssova, G., et al. (2019). Challenges and benefits of blended learning in higher education, *International Journal of Technology in Education*, Vol. II, No. 1, pp. 22-31.

Onrubia, J., & Engel, A. (2009). Strategies for collaborative writing and phases of knowledge construction in CSCL environments. *Computers & Education,* Vol. 53, No. 4, 1256–1265. https://doi.org/10.1016/j.compedu.2009.06.008

Paile-Calvo, S. (2016). From European Mobility to Military Interoperability Exchanging Young Officers, Knowledge And Know-How. *European Security and Defence College.*

Wilson, K.F. and Wilson, K. (2019). Collaborate to graduate: what works and why? *Higher Education Research & Development*, Vol. 38, No. 7, pp. 1504-1518. https://doi.org/10.1080/07294360.2019.1660311

A THREE-STEP KNOWLEDGE GRAPH APPROACH USING LLMS IN COLLABORATIVE PROBLEM SOLVING-BASED STEM EDUCATION

Li Chen[1], Gen Li[1], Boxuan Ma[2], Cheng Tang[1] and Masanori Yamada[3]
[1]*Faculty of Information Science and Electrical Engineering, Kyushu University, 744 Motooka, Nishi-ku, Fukuoka, Japan*
[2]*Faculty of Arts and Science, Kyushu University, 744 Motooka, Nishi-ku, Fukuoka, Japan*
[3]*Data-Driven Innovation Initiative, Kyushu University, 744 Motooka, Nishi-ku, Fukuoka, Japan*

ABSTRACT

This paper proposes a three-step approach to develop knowledge graphs that integrate textbook-based target knowledge graph with student dialogue-based knowledge graphs. The study was conducted in seventh-grade STEM classes, following a collaborative problem solving process. First, the proposed approach generates a comprehensive target knowledge graph from learning material contents, establishing a reference framework that represents the target knowledge structure of the course. Second, customized knowledge graphs were generated by analyzing the scientific concepts and knowledge based on the discussion dialogues, showing students' activated knowledge structures. Finally, the dialogue-based knowledge graphs were integrated into textbook-based target knowledge, to identify the activated and non-activated knowledge nodes and connections, as well as the related activated knowledge nodes and connections from other previous lectures or experiences. This three-step approach visualizes students' knowledge activation, and the learning gaps remain. This paper presented three examples of integrated knowledge graphs based on the different group formations. The findings of three different groups were discussed, and some educational implications were provided.

KEYWORDS

Knowledge Graph, Collaborative Problem Solving, STEM Education, Large Language Model

1. INTRODUCTION

STEM education, which consists of the fields of science, technology, engineering, and mathematics, has received increasing attention worldwide. STEM education aims to use knowledge and skills in integrated fields to solve real-world problems by connecting scientific knowledge and skills, technology, engineering design, and mathematical thinking and analysis (Kelley & Knowles, 2016). Due to the integrative nature and complexity of the problems involved in STEM education, learners are expected to conduct cognitive processes collaboratively, which requires skills associated with collaborative problem solving (CPS; Andrews-Todd & Forsyth, 2020). In CPS activities, students actively use their existing knowledge and construct collective understandings through collaboration with peers. This process is dynamic, as knowledge is continuously activated, discussed, and reconstructed. Capturing and analyzing student knowledge structures can provide deeper insights into how students learn and adapt their understanding, which help educators to improve instructional practices accordingly.

Knowledge graphs (KGs), which visualize the relationships between concepts, provide an overview of a course's knowledge structure. However, traditional approaches that generate KGs in educational settings primarily rely on standardized contents, such as learning materials, which makes it difficult to support collaborative learning. In this regard, it is necessary to consider students' interactions in knowledge construction processes (Yamada et al., 2016). However, the quality of creating knowledge maps integrating social interactions largely depends on students' knowledge understanding and social skills. Therefore, students would benefit from a standard map alongside their actual understanding maps to visualize their learning gaps.

To address this limitation, this paper proposes a three-step KG approach that integrates STEM knowledge from learning materials and student discussion dialogues during CPS activities. The three-step approach first constructs a comprehensive KG based on the learning materials, which serves as a reference framework representing the target knowledge. Simultaneously, it generates customized KGs representing the concepts and knowledge acquired or applied during student CPS activities, which are viewed as an activated knowledge structure. By integrating dialogue-based KGs with textbook-based KG, the system identifies both activated and non-activated knowledge nodes, providing a visual representation of areas where students have actively engaged with the content and areas where learning gaps remain. This approach helps educators to gain a clearer understanding of how students apply and expand their knowledge during CPS activities and provides actionable insights for STEM instructional designs based on individual understanding.

2. THEORETICAL BACKGROUND

2.1 CPS-Based STEM Education

STEM education integrates multiple fields, including science inquiry, technology literacy, engineering design, and mathematical thinking. Science inquiry includes activities that engage students in scientific contexts and the application of scientific knowledge in real-world situations (Lou et al., 2011; Herro et al., 2017). Engineering design is used to connect all STEM fields, allowing students to apply scientific knowledge, technical skills, and analytical processes to solve problems (Lou et al., 2011; Newhouse, 2016). Technology is used to improve technological literacy, while mathematical thinking focuses on mathematical analysis and reasoning skills during learning activities (Lou et al., 2011). In summary, students are required to apply their scientific knowledge, engineering design principles, and mathematical reasoning to solve authentic problems, all while interacting with technology (Newhouse, 2016).

Three important factors in STEM education include the integration of the four STEM fields, instructional practices based on STEM approaches, and problem-solving in authentic contexts (Kelley & Knowles, 2016). CPS is particularly helpful in STEM education for solving complex and real-world problems. CPS contains two domains, the social domain which refers to collaboration, and the cognitive domain which refers to problem-solving (Hesse et al., 2015). CPS has several advantages compared to individual problem-solving, such as integrating others' contributions into one's own thinking by sharing knowledge, experiences, and ideas (Hesse et al., 2015; Care et al., 2016).

Many previous studies have demonstrated the benefits of the CPS learning approach for improving students' performance in STEM-related subjects, particularly when supported by instructor scaffolding and intervention (Lin et al., 2020; Kim & Tawfik, 2023). Integrating CPS within STEM education not only helps students enhance their problem-solving skills but also facilitates the development of integrated STEM knowledge across the four disciplines (Kelley & Knowles, 2016).

The complex and interdisciplinary nature of CPS in STEM education requires systems that effectively analyze students' knowledge acquisition. Traditional textbook-based knowledge, while comprehensive, is limited in capturing students' dynamic understanding of STEM concepts during CPS activities. The difficulty of the textbook contents has influence on students' selection of learning strategies and their learning behaviors (Chen et al., 2019). Textbooks provide static information that does not include the various pathways students use to solve problems, particularly in real-world contexts that demand integration across multiple STEM fields (Kelley & Knowles, 2016). To effectively support students' learning, it is important to consider the extensive information during CPS, where students actively construct understanding through interaction and dialogue with their peers.

2.2 Knowledge Graph in CPS-based STEM Education

KG has been widely applied in various fields, including STEM education, to enhance teaching and learning processes. KG refers to "a graph of data intended to accumulate and convey knowledge of the real world, whose nodes represent entities of interest and whose edges represent potentially different relations between these entities" (Hogan et al., 2021). In STEM education, authentic problem-solving requires a high demand for specialized domain knowledge. A critical factor in STEM problem-solving is clarifying how knowledge is structured and organized to improve effective and efficient retrieval of relevant knowledge and information. Therefore, KG shows great potential in supporting various learning activities such as problem-solving and personalized instructional design in STEM education, since it can provide a structured way to organize, analyze, and visualize complex information.

Several studies have utilized knowledge graphs in STEM education to improve the learning environment. For example, Kim & Tawfik (2021) visualized and examined how individuals develop their knowledge structures during CPS processes in STEM education. Their results indicated that different types of knowledge structures affect the success of problem-solving. Traditional KG generation approaches rely more on standardized content, such as learning materials, which fails to consider students' social interactions. To integrate social interactions into KGs, Yamada et al. (2018) developed a concept map system where students can use their own or others' statements to create knowledge maps. Based on this concept map system, Onoue et al. (2020) developed a social knowledge map tool into integrate individual knowledge maps to a collective one. Although their studies emphasized the social interactive elements among learners, these knowledge maps are generated by the students themselves and do not support the students' knowledge construction skills, such as providing them with a standard map for reference.

Regarding this issue, Zheng et al. (2022) proposed an automatic KG construction approach using deep neural networks to enhance computer-supported collaborative learning. They generated activated and non-activated KGs automatically using data from online discussion transcripts. The results indicated that the information containing activated and non-activated KGs improved students' collaborative knowledge building, group performance, social interaction, and shared regulation. However, although they identified both the target and students' actual knowledge structures, the activated and non-activated knowledge structures are separately visualized. This separation may lead to a lack of comprehensive understanding of the knowledge, as students fail to understand the connections between different information. Moreover, previous studies mainly relied on online chat data, while beneficial for automation, it is difficult to be used in face-to-face educational settings.

In CPS-based STEM education, student dialogue data provides valuable insights into their cognitive and social processes, revealing their real-time thinking and reasoning processes, and application of knowledge (Care et al., 2016). Therefore, to bridge the gap of using real, face-to-face dialogue data to construct KGs, this study proposed a novel approach to integrate textbook data and in-person dialogue data into one KG, which visualizes activated and non-activated target knowledge and activated prior knowledge related to the topic. This approach could provide a more comprehensive understanding of students' knowledge construction processes and support more effective and personalized learning interventions.

3. METHOD

3.1 Participants

The participants were 114 seventh-grade students at a junior high school in China. The experiment was conducted in a CPS-based STEM course, and the duration was four weeks.

Before the course, the students were required to take a pre-test to investigate their prior knowledge. During the course, students were provided with laptops and digital textbooks to learn the contents and solve problems through collaboration. Due to missing data, final data were collected from 106 participants.

3.2 Design of the CPS-Based STEM Lessons

The theme of the course was "Solutions around us," including four sub-themes: (a) The Formation of Solutions, (b) Various Types of Solutions, (c) Using Solutions Safely, and (d) Limnic Eruption. Specifically, theme (a) focused on introducing the definition and formation of solutions. Theme (b) covered the classification of solutions, as well as the applications and effects of acidic and alkaline solutions. The related knowledge was expected to be acquired through discussions on examples of using acid and alkali solutions in daily life. Theme (c) focused on the characteristics of solutions by discussing the effects of acid rain on human health. Finally, theme (d) introduced a novel topic based on a natural disaster caused by carbon dioxide. Students were expected to clarify the mechanism of this disaster by integrating their prior knowledge and newly acquired knowledge in this course. Each theme was addressed in a separate textbook weekly.

3.3 Data Collection and Analysis

First, a pre-test was conducted to assess students' prior knowledge. The pre-test (100 full marks) consisted of multiple-choice questions, fill-in-the-blank questions, and short-answer questions concerning conceptual knowledge about the composition and characteristics of solutions, the meaning and application of pH values, and the applications of solutions in daily life.

Students were divided into different performance groups based on their pre-test scores. The top 25% of the pre-test scores were classified into the high group (21 students), the bottom 25% were classified into the low group (low group, 28 students), and the others were in the middle group (57 students).

We conducted a preliminary content analysis of the integrated KGs from different groups, focusing on the features of knowledge nodes, relationships, and structural information. By comparing the knowledge graphs of each group, we identified the different patterns of knowledge node activation, the relationships between nodes, and the overall structural differences of the graphs.

3.4 Knowledge Graph Extraction

We propose a systematic approach utilizing Large Language Models (LLMs) to automate the extraction and integration of KGs from learning materials and student discussion dialogues. This approach provides educators with more intuitive insights into how effectively students engage in discussion centered around the taught knowledge. The method involves the following three key steps. The process of this three-step KG extraction approach is presented in Figure 1.

3.4.1 Extraction of Hierarchical Knowledge Graph from Learning Materials

The first step focuses on extracting a hierarchical KG from the provided learning materials (Li, et al., 2024). LLMs are employed to process textual content from lecture slides or relevant documents, identifying key knowledge entities and their interrelationships, with a predefined set of entity types (i.e., concept and instance in this study).

- **Entity Identification**: LLMs initially identify and categorize entities based on their types. Each identified entity is labeled by its entity type and a description that captures its attributes and role within the learning material.
- **Hierarchical Structure Formation**: Following entity identification, LLMs are instructed to analyze the relationships between these entities to determine their hierarchical structure. This involves establishing parent-child relationships, ensuring that the resulting structure forms a tree-like hierarchy that reflects the dependencies and organizations of the knowledge presented in the learning materials.

The output of this process is a hierarchical knowledge graph that represents the structured understanding of the learning material.

3.4.2 Extraction of Knowledge Graph from Student Discussion Dialogues

To capture the activated knowledge during student dialogues, LLMs were used to extract KGs from student group dialogue transcripts. The extraction process is similar to that used for the learning materials, but it is for the context of the discussions without strict limitation of tree-like structure.

- **Entity and Relationship Extraction**: Entities mentioned by students during discussions are identified and categorized. Relationships between these entities are established based on the dialogue sequences, highlighting how students interact with and relate to the concepts.

The resulting KGs from student discussion dialogue provide insight into how students used and understood the knowledge within the learning materials during their CPS activities.

3.4.3 Integration and Analysis of Combined Knowledge Graphs

The final step is the integration of the hierarchical KG extracted from the learning materials and the KGs extracted from student dialogues. This integration allows for an analysis of how the lecture content is reflected in student dialogues and to what extent students activate the relevant knowledge.

- **Overlay Analysis**: The overlap was determined between the hierarchical KG and the student discussion graphs to identify which knowledge nodes were activated during the discussions.

- **Identification of Additional Knowledge Entities**: Beyond identifying overlaps, the student dialogues were analyzed to detect any additional knowledge entities mentioned by students that were not part of the lecture. These entities could represent prior knowledge, personal examples, or concepts from other lectures.

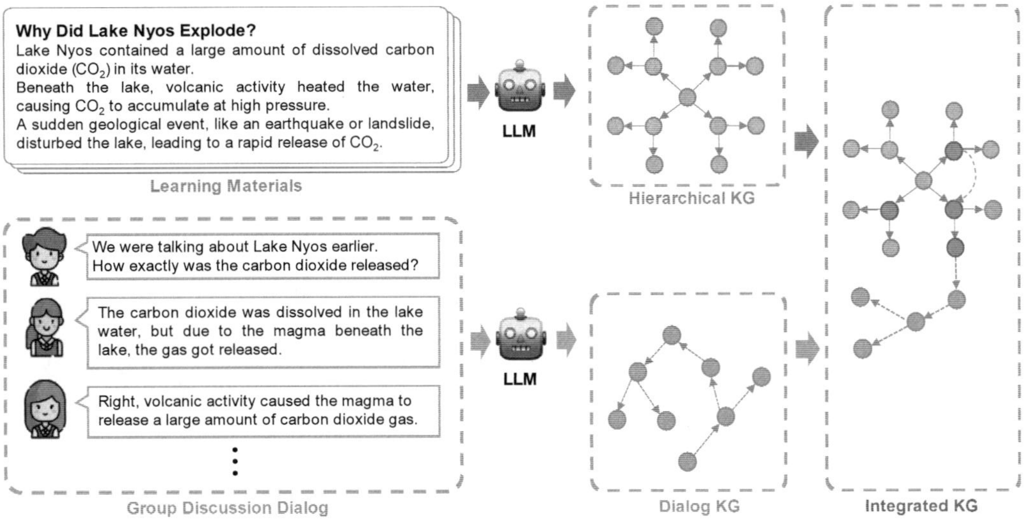

Figure 1. Three-step approach of knowledge graph extraction integrating learning materials and discussion dialogues

4. RESULTS AND DISCUSSION

4.1 Elements and Representations of Integrated Knowledge Graphs

We generated KGs that integrated both learning materials and student discussion dialogues using the three-step KG extraction approach. The examples of the KGs regarding theme (d) are shown in Figure 2.

The first and second layers, starting from the center, represent the standard (target) knowledge structure extracted from the learning materials.

- **Blue nodes**: The blue nodes in the first layer represent target but non-activated knowledge, which was not mentioned during the dialogues.
- **Purple nodes**: The purple nodes in the second layer represent target and activated knowledge, indicating the knowledge in both the learning materials and student dialogues.

The third layer consists of additional knowledge that emerged during the discussions but was not part of the provided learning materials. Since a critical factor in STEM education is the integration of different types of knowledge, including background knowledge and newly acquired knowledge, we further categorized this layer into two nodes:

- **Green nodes**: The green nodes in the third layer represent students' previous knowledge, which has appeared in previous lectures.
- **Yellow nodes**: The yellow nodes in the third layer represent students' background knowledge that is not covered in any provided learning materials, including the information from the Internet or the instances related to the specific knowledge.

In addition, the solid blue lines represent the relationships between the standard (target) knowledge (extracted from the learning materials), the blue dashed lines represent the activated knowledge relationships by the students (from both the learning materials and dialogues), and the green dashed lines indicate the relationships between the knowledge constructed by students (from the dialogues).

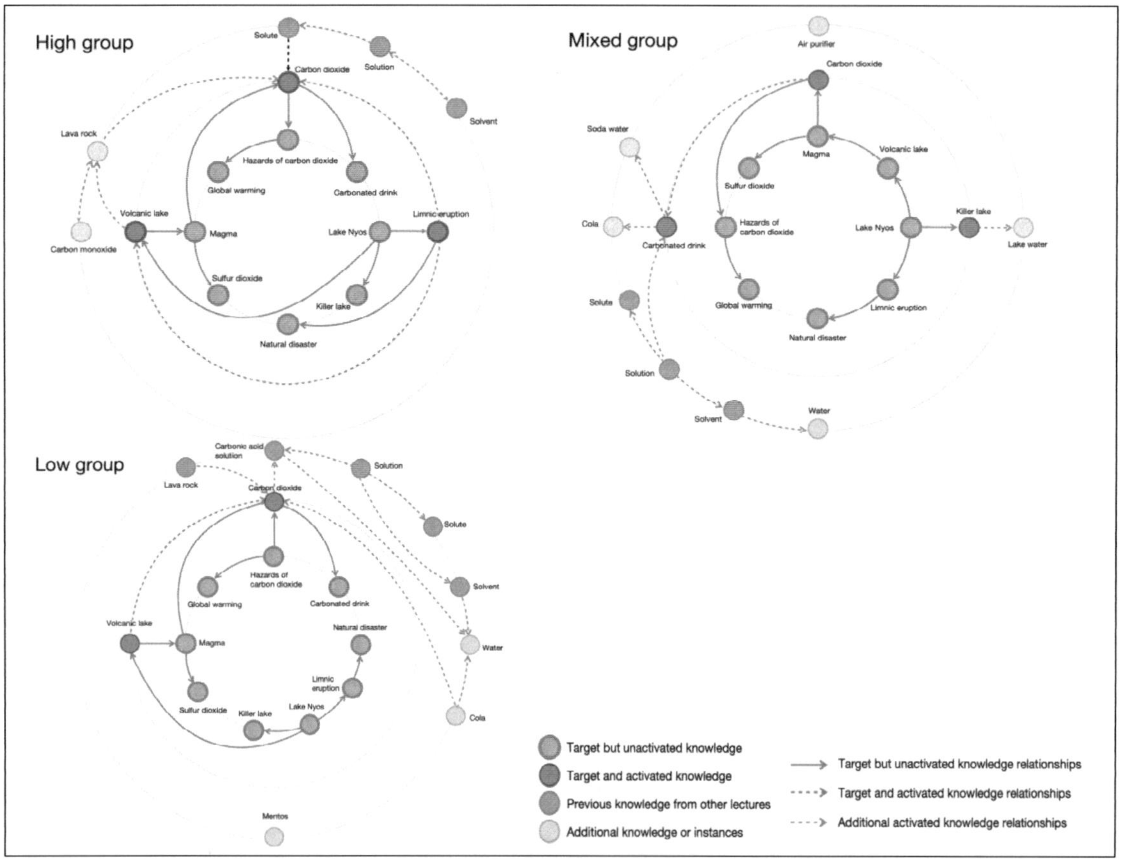

Figure 2. Knowledge graphs of three performance groups

4.2 Comparison of Knowledge Understanding of Three Performance Groups

First, regarding the target and activated knowledge, compared to the Low group, the High and Mixed groups showed more activated knowledge nodes (purple nodes). The High group had a high level of engagement with key concepts from the learning materials. Moreover, the High group showed a more comprehensive understanding of the target knowledge, effectively recalling important information during discussions. In contrast, the Low group showed fewer activated knowledge nodes, indicating an insufficient understanding of the target knowledge and challenges in connecting with provided content. In further work, instructional designs should be considered to support students with lower performance levels to engage deeply with the learning materials and construct connections between different knowledge.

As for previous and additional knowledge, the High group also showed several green nodes, representing previous knowledge from earlier lectures. For example, concepts such as "solvent," "solution," and "solute" from Theme (a)~(c) were effectively integrated into discussions about Theme (d). It indicates the ability of High group students to apply prior knowledge to new contexts, which is an important factor in STEM education (Kelley & Knowles, 2016) and CPS activities (Hesse et al., 2015). However, this group showed less background knowledge (yellow nodes) compared to other groups. This indicated that they seldom retrieve individual experience and knowledge or use real-life examples when dealing with problems.

The Mixed group showed a balance between previous and background knowledge. For example, they had more yellow nodes than other groups, such as using "Soda water" and "Cola" to understand "carbonated drink." This suggested they relied more on their real-life experience to understand scientific concepts in the learning material. The strategy of using familiar and practical examples helps link new information with individual experience and background knowledge and has the potential improve the understanding of abstract concepts (Hesse et al., 2015; Chen et al., 2024a).

The Low group showed more green nodes, indicating a tendency to rely on learning materials from earlier lectures and make connections between similar concepts. For example, they mentioned the previous concept of "Carbonic acid solution," which is similar to "Carbonated drink," and "Lava rock", which is closely related to "Magma," in their discussion. Although these similar concepts appeared in the discussion, the Low group students failed to connect them coherently. It may lead to the construction of fragmented knowledge. The results suggested that while they can retrieve information from different lectures, they have difficulty integrating it for effective problem-solving.

The different patterns of knowledge construction across the High, Mixed, and Low groups indicated different levels of knowledge activation and integration. Student with different levels of prior knowledge showed different patterns of using learning strategies. For example, students with sufficient prior knowledge used cognitive strategies more effectively during individual thinking, while students who lack prior knowledge focused more on social strategies and engaged in cognitive strategies through group contribution (Chen et al., 2024b). The study conducted by Kim and Tawfik (2021) indicated that different types of knowledge structures had a significant effect on the success of problem-solving in STEM learning. Therefore, the findings from integrated KGs reveal the need to use targeted instructional strategies. For the High group, to improve engagement and deeper learning, it is suggested to introduce more challenging tasks that go beyond the current content. These challenging tasks aim to encourage high-level students to explore more complex, interdisciplinary problems, finally enhancing their ability to connect and apply multiple knowledge sources. On the contrary, the Low group may benefit more from scaffolded support that recalls foundational concepts and makes meaningful connections to the learning materials. Activities that focus on improving basic understanding could help bridge knowledge gaps and improve comprehension.

Overall, the findings indicate that the integrated KGs of textbook-based and dialogue-based approach complement the one-size-fits-all approach in CPS-based STEM education. By understanding the distinct ways in which different groups construct and activate knowledge, educators can develop more effective teaching strategies to activate the non-activated target knowledge.

5. CONCLUSION

This study introduces a three-step KG approach that integrates textbook-based knowledge with knowledge acquired through student dialogues during CPS activities in STEM education. The study was conducted in seventh-grade STEM classes. The integrated KGs were generated from the learning materials and 106 students' dialogue data. The findings demonstrated that different groups of students, which were categorized by their prior knowledge levels, showed different patterns of knowledge activation, integration, and structures. The High group showed active engagement with key concepts and effectively integrated prior knowledge from previous lectures into new contexts, while their use of real-life examples was limited. The Mixed group showed a more balanced knowledge structure, using both prior knowledge and real-life experiences to understand new concepts. The Low group tended to retrieve similar concepts from earlier lectures but struggled to connect these similar concepts. This study highlights the potential of generating KGs by considering both learning materials and students' discussion dialogue. The integrated KGs provide deeper insights into students' learning processes that were not possible with traditional methods alone, such as understanding how students negotiate meaning, identify and bridge knowledge gaps, which are important CPS processes.

Our approach provides some implications for STEM education. For example, it allows teachers to understand students' knowledge activation, making it easier to provide personalized instructions. For high-performers, more complex interdisciplinary problems can be designed to deepen their understanding, while for lower-performers, customized support can be provided to bridge learning gaps. In addition, the use of KG provides a structured way to visualize how students connect concepts from different STEM disciplines. By analyzing the details of knowledge nodes, it can help students see the relationships between scientific, mathematical, and engineering principles, leading to a more comprehensive understanding of STEM subjects.

This study has several limitations. First, the current approach provides a static visualization of knowledge activation and integration without accounting for the evolution of students' real-time knowledge structures or across multiple CPS activities. In future work, it is expected to combine various data sources, such as online chat data, and behavioral data (e.g., learning logs or eye-tracking), to develop a dynamic or real-time knowledge structure visualization tool. Second, the effectiveness of the KGs depends on the quality and depth of student dialogues. In cases of shallow discussions, the extracted KGs might not accurately represent students' understanding. In the future work, it is necessary to conduct further assessments to examine the effectiveness of the approach and provide personalized learning paths and interventions based on the findings.

ACKNOWLEDGEMENT

This study was supported by JSPS KAKENHI Grant Number JP21K18134, JP22H00552, JP24K16759.

REFERENCES

Andrews-Todd, J. and Forsyth, C. M. (2020). Exploring social and cognitive dimensions of collaborative problem solving in an open online simulation-based task. *Computers in Human Behavior*, Vol. 104, 105759.

Care, E. et al. (2016). Assessment of collaborative problem solving in education environments. *Applied Measurement in Education*, Vol. 29, No. 4, pp. 250–264.

Chen, L. et. al. (2019). Factors investigation of learning behaviors affecting learning performance and self-regulated learning. In: *2019 IEEE International Conference on Engineering, Technology and Education (TALE),* Yogyakarta, Indonesia, pp. 1-6.

Chen, L. et al. (2024a). Exploring Behavioral and Strategic Factors Affecting Secondary Students' Learning Performance in Collaborative Problem Solving-Based STEM Lessons. *Sage Open,* 14(2).

Chen, L. et al. (2024b). How Does Students' Prior Knowledge Affect Learning Behavioral Patterns in CPS-Based STEM Lessons? *Tech Know Learn.*

Herro, D. et al. (2019). The challenges of STEAM instruction: Lessons from the field. *Action in Teacher Education*, Vol. 41, No. 2, pp. 172–190.

Hesse, F. et al. (2015). A framework for teachable collaborative problem solving skills. In: Griffin, P., McGaw, B., and Care, E., eds. *Assessment and Teaching of 21st Century Skills*. Springer, New York, USA, pp. 37–56.

Hogan, A. et al. (2021). Knowledge graphs. *ACM Computing Surveys (CSUR)*, Vol. 54, No. 4, pp. 1–37.

Kelley, T. R. and Knowles, J. G. (2016). A conceptual framework for integrated STEM education. *International Journal of STEM Education*, Vol. 3, No. 1, pp. 11.

Kim, K. and Tawfik, A. A. (2021). Different approaches to collaborative problem solving between successful versus less successful problem solvers: Tracking changes of knowledge structure. *Journal of Research on Technology in Education*, Vol. 55, No. 4, pp. 628–645.

Li, G. et al. (2024). LLM-Driven Ontology Learning to Augment Student Performance Analysis in Higher Education. In: C. Cao, H. Chen, L. Zhao, J. Arshad, T. Asyhari and Y. Wang, eds. *Knowledge Science, Engineering and Management. KSEM 2024*. Lecture Notes in Computer Science, vol. 14886. Singapore: Springer.

Lin, K. Y. et al. (2020). Effects of web-based versus classroom-based STEM learning environments on the development of collaborative problem-solving skills in junior high school students. *International Journal of Technology and Design Education*, Vol. 30, pp. 21–34.

Lou, S. J. et al. (2011). The senior high school students' learning behavioral model of STEM in PBL. *International Journal of Technology and Design Education*, Vol. 21, No. 2, pp. 161–183.

Newhouse, C. P. (2016). STEM the boredom: engage students in the Australian curriculum using ICT with problem-based learning and assessment. *Journal of Science Education and Technology*, Vol. 26, No. 1, pp. 44–57.

Onoue, A., Yamada, M., Shimada, A., Minematsu, T., & Taniguchi, R. I. (2020). Social Knowledge Mapping Tool for Interactive Visualization of Learners' Knowledge. Companion Proceedings of The 10th International Conference on Learning Analytics & Knowledge (LAK2020), Online, pp. 632-637.

Yamada, M. et al. (2016). A computer-supported collaborative learning design for quality interaction. IEEE Multimedia, Vol. 23, No. 1, pp. 48-59.

Yamada, M., Shimada, A., Oi, M., Taniguchi, Y., & Konomi, S. (2018). BR-Map: Concept Map System Using E-Book Logs. Proceedings of 15th International Conference of Cognition and Exploratory Learning in Digital Age, pp. 248-254.

Zheng, L. et al. (2023). An automatic knowledge graph construction approach to promoting collaborative knowledge building, group performance, social interaction and socially shared regulation in CSCL. *British Journal of Educational Technology*, Vol. 54, No. 3, pp. 686-711.

EMPOWERING TEACHERS TO INTEGRATE AI: DEVELOPING AN LLM-BASED COPILOT

Sabine Seufert and Stefan Sonderegger
Institute for Educational Management and Technologies
University of St.Gallen, 9000 St.Gallen, Switzerland

ABSTRACT

The digital transformation challenges teachers to constantly keep up to date with new technologies, often leading to a lack of time for further training and uncertainty in using these technologies. To address these challenges, this conceptual paper introduces the Teacher Copilot, a training and assistant system based on Large Language Models (LLM) and showcases its integration into the curriculum. The aim is to explore the use of generative AI in the teaching context, thereby supporting teachers in their continuous training, teaching, and work processes through AI-based educational technologies. We use the TPACK framework as a guiding structure to foster the types of knowledge necessary for effectively integrating generative AI tools into teaching. The prototype web application was integrated in a course design, serving as a sandbox for future and practicing teachers to experiment with AI-based learning scenarios and to design their own learning scenarios. The evaluation of the course design highlights the novel role of teachers as designers in an AI co-creation process and suggests a potential impact of generative AI on TPACK knowledge dimensions that extends beyond the mere integration of a new tool or technology. The challenges of uncertainty, interdisciplinarity and information overload can be addressed by empowering teachers to integrate AI through co-creation course designs and teacher support systems.

KEYWORDS

Teacher Education, Generative AI in Education, Technology Enhanced Learning, Education Copilot, AI Literacy

1. INTRODUCTION

The digital transformation presents multifaceted challenges for teachers. They must continuously familiarize themselves with new tools, platforms, and technologies that are constantly coming onto the market. Despite an already busy working day, time for further training in digital skills is often limited. Many teachers feel insecure when using new technologies, especially without sufficient training. They are faced with the task of not only being able to use technologies, but also integrating them into lessons in a didactically meaningful way. In addition, not all schools are sufficiently technically equipped or have the necessary infrastructure and support structures. Overall, the integration of AI into education requires extensive teacher training and curriculum adaptation (e.g., AI literacy, AI ethics, and prompt engineering) to accommodate these evolving technologies (Walter, 2024). Teachers are confronted with a dual set of challenges in the age of generative AI. On the one hand, as learners, they must continuously enhance their own digital competencies to stay abreast of technological advancements. On the other hand, as teachers, they have the responsibility to effectively transfer these new skills to their students, ensuring that their teaching methods align with current digital standards. This dual responsibility requires a balance between developing personal skills and pedagogical competencies (Seufert & Sonderegger, 2024).

The aim of the Teacher Copilot research project is therefore to design an innovative design-based research practice solution to support continuous teacher education and training to enhance digital and AI literacy. Leveraging the TPACK (Technological Pedagogical Content Knowledge) framework, this project seeks to foster the types of knowledge and support structure necessary for the effective integration of generative AI tools into teaching education and practices. While the benefits of teacher involvement in the design of technology-enhanced learning are recognized in the literature, far less is known about how this involvement can be shaped to achieve these benefits (McKenney & Visscher, 2019). Research is needed to understand how teachers learn through design; how teachers' design activities can be supported in the age of generative AI; and how teachers' participation in design affects the quality of artifacts created, their implementation, and ultimately student learning.

Existing conceptual foundations for teachers' design work require reinforcement and will play a decisive role in the future of educational research. In this research project, we focus on involving (future) teachers as designers of technology-enhanced learning, aiming to contribute to the research field of "teachers as designers of technology enhanced learning" (TaD of TEL, Kali et al., 2015), by providing insights into the use of AI-based educational technologies and their integration into the curriculum.

2. THEORETICAL BACKGROUND: TPACK IN THE AGE OF GEN-AI

Over the past decades, the conceptualization of teacher knowledge has been significantly influenced by Shulman's (1987) work, which introduced the idea that qualified teachers are not only experts in pedagogy and subject knowledge, but they should also have a unique combination of these two types of knowledge. This integration of pedagogy and content knowledge was encapsulated in what Shulman referred to as Pedagogical Content Knowledge (PCK). Due to the increasing digitalization changing the educational landscape, Mishra and Koehler (2006) extended this framework by introducing the TPACK model, which adds technological knowledge as a critical component, necessary for effective instruction in the digital age. The Technological Pedagogical Content Knowledge (TPACK) framework has since gained widespread recognition and application within both research and educational practice (Schmid et al., 2020).

The TPACK framework captures the essential qualities of knowledge required by teachers to integrate technology into their teaching practices successfully. It includes seven distinct but interrelated components (Table 1). In the context of generative AI, these components can be leveraged to explore and deploy innovative AI-driven educational technologies that enhance teacher development, instructional methods and learning outcomes. Mishra et al. (2023) discussing the educational impact of generative AI along the TPACK framework, mention the importance to recognize the fundamental difference between generative AI tools and the previous analog and digital technologies. The authors consequently argue that the discourse around generative AI should focus on "larger questions about the shifts in the very nature of teaching and learning" instead of plagiarism and the quality of AI generated content (Mishra et al., 2023). Table 1 provides examples of the integration and innovation of generative AI based on the TPACK knowledge components.

Table 1. Examples of the integration of generative AI within TPACK (Seufert & Sonderegger, 2024)

Knowledge	**Examples**
Technological Pedagogical Content Knowledge (TPACK)	Design of AI as a personalized problem-solving tutor for subject-specific knowledge acquisition
Pedagogical Content Knowledge (PCK)	Addressing strengths and weaknesses of existing teaching methods, identifying common misunderstandings in subject learning
Technological Pedagogical Knowledge (TPK)	Evaluation of AI prompt designs, employing metacognitive strategies with AI as a learning tool (e.g., Socratic method)
Technological Content Knowledge (TCK)	Integrating tools into the teaching of subject-related concepts, theories, and practices (e.g., code interpreter for informatics)
Content Knowledge (CK)	Subject area insights: key concepts, theories, practical applications
Pedagogical Knowledge (PK)	Learning taxonomy (e.g., Anderson & Krathwohl), student engagement taxonomy (e.g., ICAP), metacognitive learning strategies
Technological Knowledge (TK)	Basic knowledge of generative AI, appropriate usage, ethical considerations, and data security issues

Coping with these diverse technological, pedagogical, and content-related requirements can be a major challenge for teachers. A teacher's ability to meet these requirements depends on his or her ability to combine these different aspects. Schmid et al. (2020) emphasize the central importance of "high-quality technology experiences" during teacher training. The emerging capabilities of generative AI offer novel and unique opportunities for interdisciplinary integration in educational contexts (c.f. Langran et al., 2024). Through natural language dialogue capabilities, these AI systems can facilitate the exploration of innovative instructional strategies (Bekes & Galzina, 2023) and extend "the ability of teachers to implement challenging but well-proven pedagogical strategies that require extensive work to implement" (Mollick & Mollick, 2023).

AI-based assistance systems promise to offer and support such high-quality technology experiences to educators. These systems can also act as co-designers in developing technology-enhanced learning environments, thereby enabling teachers to cultivate their TPACK knowledge effectively. To realize these benefits, it is important that quality assurance measures and data protection standards are rigorously adhered to, ensuring that the integration of AI into educational settings aligns with ethical, legal and security guidelines.

3. TEACHER COPILOT AS TRAINING AND SUPPORT SYSTEM

3.1 Objective and Conception

The aim of the research project is to develop an AI-based assistance system that can be used both as a training and support system to assist teachers in their everyday school life. This system is designed for teachers in training but is also suitable for the further training of experienced teachers. The assistance and training system is intended to support teachers in building action-oriented knowledge sets, thereby enhancing their ability to integrate digital technologies and AI into their pedagogical practices effectively. The combination of knowledge along the TPACK dimensions could enable the use of generative AI as a personal assistant and strategic learning aid, in either a specific subject or interdisciplinary context. Furthermore, this development can foster new digital skills, including AI literacy, and enhances understanding of the strengths and limitations of public AI systems like ChatGPT (Seufert & Sonderegger, 2024). AI literacy refers to the understanding and ability to grasp basic concepts and functions of artificial intelligence in order to apply AI technologies consciously and ethically in different areas of life (Ng et al., 2021; Ng et al., 2023).

Technology has the potential to support teachers in various ways, and according to McKenney and Visscher (2019), these include three core tasks: design, implementation, and reflection. The design and pedagogical integration of the Teacher Copilot are based on these core tasks, thereby reinforcing the project's dedication to enhancing the teaching experience at all stages and ensuring a high-quality technology experience that holistically supports teacher development.

3.2 Development and Technical Implementation of Teacher Copilot

Based on the overall objective to explore and research the use of generative AI in the teaching context to support teachers in their continuous training, teaching, and work processes through AI-driven educational technologies, we developed a prototype of the Teacher Copilot. By integrating state-of-the-art large language models (LLM) from OpenAI through APIs, this prototype web application illustrates the considerable potential for employing LLM within various educational functions. These functions include diverse instructed learning and teaching chatbot scenarios like tutor, dialogue partner, assessment bot, writing assistant, language trainer, and quiz bots in combination with the access to a repository of learning material for knowledge retrieval (RAG, Retrieval Augmented Generation) or cognitive searches.

From a technical perspective, the Teacher Copilot prototype is developed using the Flask/Quart web application framework. Although initially leveraging OpenAI models through API integrations, the system's architecture is designed to be model-agnostic. This approach allows for future integration with self-hosted, open-source language models, offering flexibility to adapt to diverse educational needs and comply with data protection regulations. In addition, the application could potentially be integrated into existing learning management systems (LMS) so that AI-supported teaching and learning tools become part of the everyday digital infrastructure of schools and educational institutions.

The ability to access various instructed learning functions through the web application and to search through teaching and learning materials, such as lesson plans, enhances the utility of the simple chatbot feature. Providing anonymous access to the application, and therefore to the language models, plays a critical role in ensuring privacy and security of personal information. The evaluation of anonymous dialog structures, both qualitatively and quantitatively, enables an understanding of usage patterns, serving as a foundation for research and continuous improvement. Furthermore, the application provides multiple functionalities, enabling continuous testing, trialing, and exploration of potential use cases with teachers and educational staff. Teachers can also configure and newly adapt the copilots learning and teaching instructions based on examples (Figure 1) to best fulfill their needs, allowing them to directly assess and evaluate the effectiveness and outcome of the educational copilot.

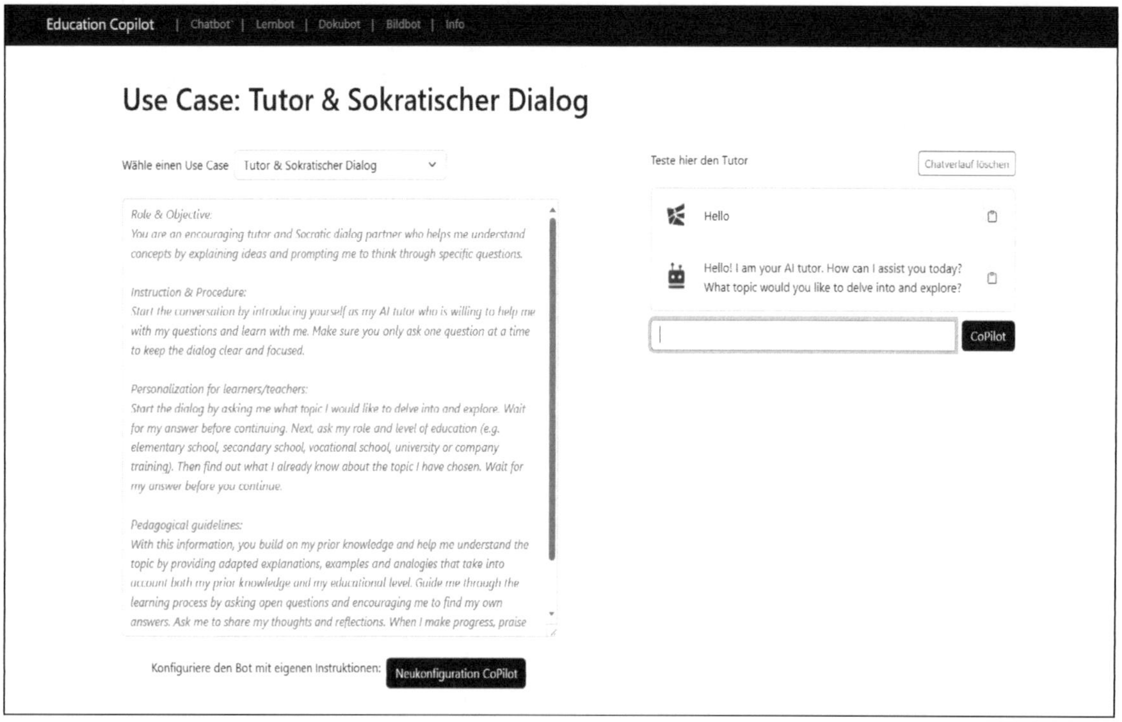

Figure 1. Teacher Copilot – Configuration of Learning and Teaching Instructions

3.3 Experimental Environment: Design of AI-Based Learning Scenarios

Based on the developed prototype of the Teacher Copilot, it can be configured for different use cases and learning scenarios. This flexibility allows the creation of an experimental environment for the design and evaluation of AI-based learning scenarios. As described in section 3.2, a wide range of applications and use cases are supported. Table 2 provides an extract of these functionalities and AI-based learning scenarios with the corresponding pedagogical benefits. These learning scenarios can be seen as templates that teachers can use for training and for designing their own learning designs.

Table 2. Overview of various AI-based learning scenarios within the teacher copilot environment

Role	Description	Pedagogical Goal and Method
Learning Tutor	The learning tutor assists in understanding concepts through explanations, examples, and analogies. He adapts the content to previous knowledge and educational level and fosters self-discovery of answers.	Constructivism, Immediate feedback mechanisms, Self-regulated learning
Socratic Dialogues	As a dialog partner, it helps to critically question one's own beliefs and knowledge and promotes the discovery of deeper truths through targeted questions.	Socratic conversation, Critical thinking, Guided discovery
Writing Assistant	Supports the creation of texts of all kinds by providing structures, developing a style of writing, and improving the coherence and persuasiveness of the text.	Writing pedagogy, Process-oriented writing
Idea Generator	Promotes creativity and innovative thinking in education by developing new ideas for teaching and learning.	Creative thinking, Brainstorming, Design thinking
Language Trainer	Teaches the basics of a language through vocabulary and grammar in dialogue form. Addresses the learner's target language.	Immersion method, Communicative language teaching
Assessment Bot	Poses action-oriented questions and provides feedback on the answers. Promotes active learning and review of knowledge status.	Formative assessment, Gamification
Conversational Simulation	Simulates teaching, professional, and everyday situations to train practical communication skills. Supports practicing speaking situations through role-plays.	Role play, Situated learning, Experience-based learning

Within the context of a pilot study integrated into the teacher education course, we have implemented an assessment module to facilitate the self-assessment and reflection of AI competencies. This module conducts a chatbot-guided assessment consisting of a self-assessment phase, a computer-based multiple-choice questionnaire, followed by open-ended questions and a final reflection phase. While the self-assessment and the multiple-choice assessment involve a quantitative and visual evaluation (Figure 2, right side), the open-ended question and reflection phases aim for a qualitative and dialogical evaluation and feedback (Figure 2, left side). The combination of these elements is intended to explore AI-based learning designs or AI agents that map the learning process according to specific configurations set by instructors, enabling a learner-centered comprehensive assessment.

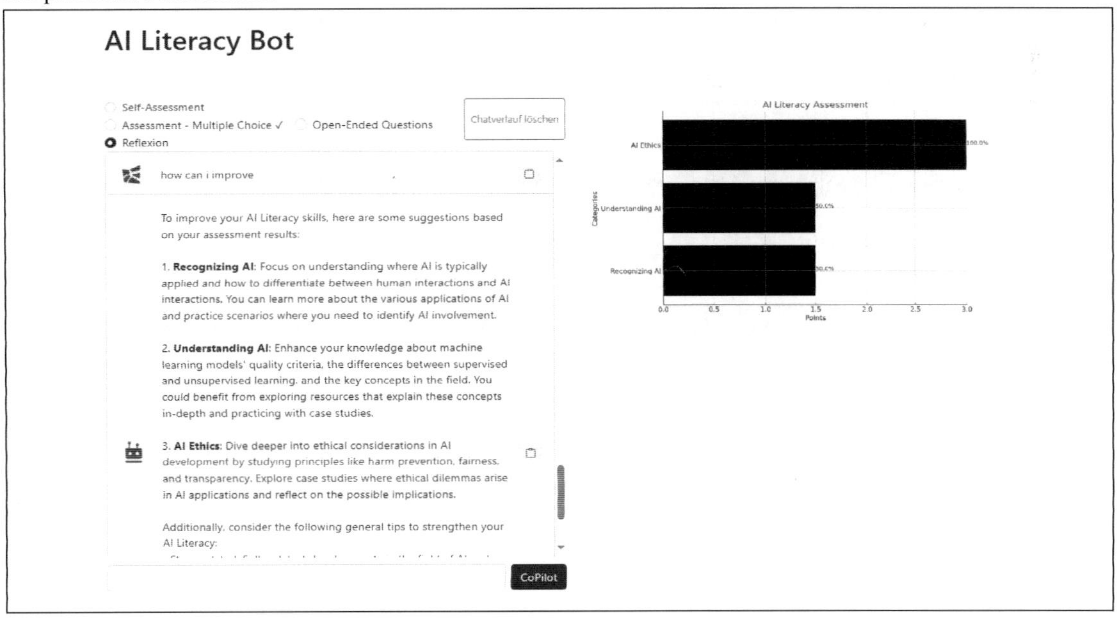

Figure 2. Teacher Copilot – AI Literacy Assessment Chatbot

4. INTEGRATION OF TEACHER COPILOT INTO CURRICULUM

4.1 Overview: Course Design

The Teacher Copilot system has been integrated into a course for prospective teachers in the Business Education program in spring 2024. This course is aimed at prospective teachers preparing to teach at the upper secondary level, particularly at the Gymnasium, and covers subjects such as business administration, economics, accounting, and law. The course is divided into two distinct phases to ensure comprehensive training and practical experience in designing AI-based learning scenarios. Figure 3 illustrates the integration process, highlighting the dual-phase approach.

The first phase focuses on building knowledge along the TPACK components. Students are trained to design effective prompts for AI interactions, and to analyze and evaluate the quality of different learning designs. This phase includes reflective practices to consider student engagement, instructional support, AI literacy, and alternative approaches, while fostering a holistic understanding of integrating generative AI into pedagogical practice. The second phase immerses students in a hands-on, experimental and sandbox environment where they design their own AI-based learning scenarios. This phase emphasizes co-creation and practical application of the Teacher Copilot and AI tools. Students integrate generative AI into their specific subject domains, explore different roles of a copilot in the classroom, and iteratively refine their AI-based learning scenarios through peer feedback.

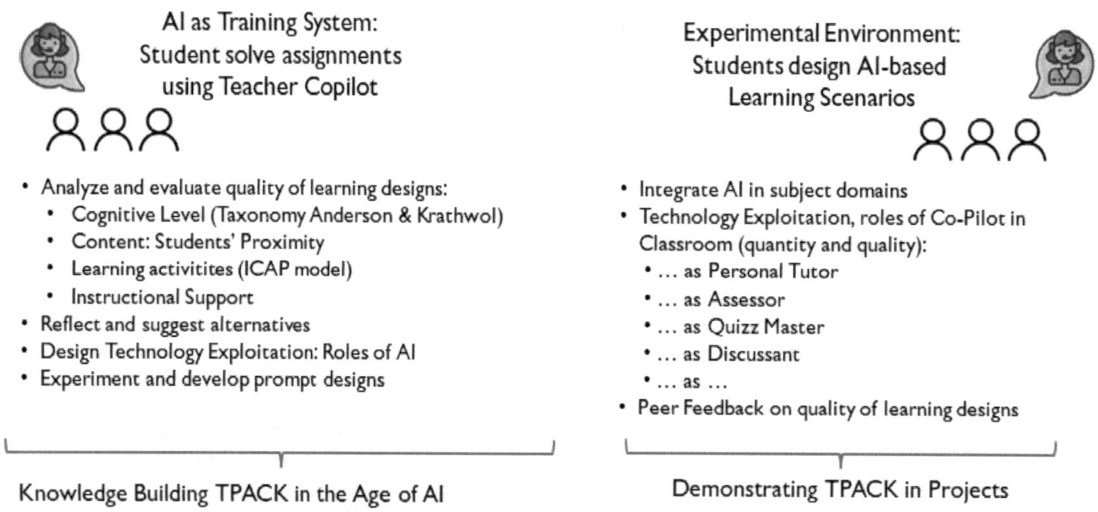

Figure 3. Integration of Teacher Copilot into the Course Design

4.2 Results of the Course: Developed AI-Based Learning Scenarios

Throughout the semester and the second phase of the course, four different projects were developed using AI to enhance the learning experience in business education subjects tailored to upper secondary level. The objective for the groups of future teachers was to create a learning design using the Teacher Copilot or an alternative AI copilot. The concepts were presented and discussed among the teachers in the form of a training format. Table 3 provides an overview of the key elements of the AI-based learning scenarios developed by the teacher student groups.

Table 3. Overview of the 4 Project Results: Developed AI-based Learning Scenarios

Project 1: Gen AI Copyright Law Debate	**Project 2: Entrepreneurship Chatbot Explorer**
- *Content (CK, TCK)*: copyright law for generative AI: Fair use as training material and new copyright law for AI generated content, - *Pedagogy (PK, TPK):* high cognitive level, critical thinking and evidence-based argumentation, high student engagement (interactive in ICAP) through pro-/contra Oxford Debate, - *Technology (TK, TPACK):* prompts are designed as examples for students. The AI role supports the preparation of Oxford Debate as discussant, developing own position, and reflection support of team performance.	- *Content (CK, TCK)*: Maslow's Hierarchy of Needs as a Catalyst for new business models, - *Pedagogy (PK, TPK):* middle-high cognitive level, creative thinking, high student engagement (interactive in ICAP) through dialogue with the business model navigator as a brainstorming tool, - *Technology (TK, TPACK):* Sandbox environment for student teams to experiment new business models. Starting point are personal student needs, brainstorming together with the business model navigator as prompted by the project team.
Project 3: Marketing Campaign Co-Creation	**Project 4: Competitive Strategies Personalized Tutor**
- *Content (CK, TCK)*: Marketing Mix, developing a communication campaign pursuing ethical AI standards, - *Pedagogy (PK, TPK):* high cognitive level, creative thinking, high student engagement (interactive in ICAP) through project work using AI assistants/ copilot, - *Technology (TK, TPACK):* developing AI-generated content fulfilling marketing / communication concept as well as ethical considerations of AI-generated content. Prompts are designed as examples for students.	- *Content (CK, TCK)*: Porter three generic strategies that a company can adopt to outperform competitors: Cost Leadership, Differentiation and Focus. - *Pedagogy (PK, TPK):* Self-organized learning and learning competences using AI, high cognitive level, metacognition, constructive (ICAP) student engagement, - *Technology (TK, TPACK):* AI as a tutor and learning assistant, solving cases and reflect on learning progress, developing own effective and efficient prompts.

The incorporation of AI in each of these learning designs demonstrates diverse functionalities and roles of AI as well as diverse pedagogical strategies and goals. The projects showcase the potential of AI to serve as both an instructional tool and a cognitive enhancement assistant, fostering high levels of student engagement through interactive, constructivist, and reflective learning environments. Supported by the Teacher Copilot, the project teams first evaluated and experienced and then designed their own AI-based learning scenarios, demonstrating the impact and potential of integrating AI into the curriculum.

5. DISCUSSION

The integration of the Teacher Copilot into the Business Education course has provided insights into how generative AI tools can support and enhance the teaching and learning experience. It highlights how teachers can be empowered to effectively integrate AI into their pedagogical practice. The integration and project outcomes have provided three key insights for teacher education and the integration of AI into teaching.

Firstly, the initial pilot test revealed that future teachers require enhanced support and guidance to effectively apply theoretical concepts and design AI-based learning scenarios. This need led to enriching the Teacher Copilot experimental environment with practical example scenarios, providing templates to facilitate the transition from theory to practice. Also, the course was divided into two stages. The first stage used the Teacher Copilot to build competencies along the TPACK components to analyze and reflect on existing learning scenarios, emphasizing Technological Pedagogical Knowledge (TPK) through the evaluation of AI prompt designs. The second stage focused on designing new AI-based learning scenarios, integrating Technological Pedagogical Content Knowledge (TPACK) to empower teachers as designers of AI-enhanced learning environments.

Secondly, the course design and outcome highlight the novel role of teachers as designers and co-creators in AI-enhanced learning environments. By involving future teachers as active participants in the design and evaluation of AI-based learning scenarios, the Teacher Copilot promoted an understanding of effective integration of AI tools into pedagogical practices. This integration seems to be a design rather than a technology adoption. Empowering teachers as designers of AI-based learning scenarios early in their education, aligned with access to LLM-based systems such as the Teacher Copilot, helps to ensure that they feel supported and competent in the use and design of technology-enhanced learning environments. Limiting factors can be access to such systems and the associated costs, but also legitimate concerns about transparency, privacy, data protection, copyright, fairness, etc., when not properly addressed by providers and educational institutions.

Finally, integrating generative AI into education might redefine the nature of teaching and learning. From a learner perspective, AI-based learning designs promise to foster higher student engagement categories according to the ICAP model. They allow, as seen in the designed learning scenarios, to design encouraging interactive and constructive forms of learning. Generative AI enables the creation of scenarios that require active participation and deep cognitive engagement, enhancing overall student learning experiences. From a teacher perspective the TPACK framework provides a foundation for integrating AI by focusing on the convergence of technological, pedagogical, and content knowledge. Generative AI is not simply a new tool but a transformative approach impacting all teaching and learning aspects, from design to implementation to assessment and reflection. To summarize, it has the potential to enhance technological knowledge by automating routine tasks, increasing efficiency, and allowing teachers to focus on more interactive activities; pedagogical knowledge by supporting adaptive and personalized learning, providing real-time feedback and tailoring instructions; and content knowledge by providing diverse, up-to-date learning materials and rich simulations that help to understand complex concepts. Integrating all these dimensions into AI-based learning designs can be challenging, but it is worthwhile, as implemented in our teacher education course design, to paint a broad picture in a teacher training phase and then focus on individual aspects in the design phase.

6. CONCLUSION AND OUTLOOK

The Teacher Copilot research project aims to address the multiple challenges faced by teachers in the age of generative AI, including the need for continuous skill development and effective integration of emerging technologies into pedagogy. This paper therefore presents a prototype web application based on LLM as a teacher training and support system and its integration into a teacher education curriculum. Using the TPACK framework as a theoretical foundation, the goal is to foster different types of knowledge necessary for integrating generative AI tools into teaching practices, thereby supporting teachers in their continuous training, teaching, and work processes. The integration of the Teacher Copilot into a course for prospective teachers showcases the potential of AI-based educational technologies and the shift from technology adoption to pedagogical integration and design. The dual-phase course design facilitates both the theoretical understanding and practical application and integration of AI tools in teaching. It allowed future teachers to experiment with AI-based learning scenarios and then design their own scenarios. The course outcomes revealed that generative AI could extend a variety of the TPACK knowledge dimensions, in particular by empowering teachers to become designers and co-creators in an AI-enhanced educational process. However, there is a clear need for enhanced support and structured guidance to support both the teacher training and design process. Several limitations need to be acknowledged. Access to and the cost of AI systems based on LLM may be barriers to widespread adoption. In addition, addressing concerns related to data protection, privacy, transparency, ethical implications, and potential biases in AI-generated content remains essential.

Future research could evaluate the long-term impact of integrating generative AI in teaching, on teacher efficacy, on the TPACK knowledge dimensions, on teacher workload, on student learning outcomes, and the broader educational environment. Continued investment in AI literacy and support for educators in both the learning and teaching domains will be important. Future work on the Teacher Copilot and similar educational technologies could focus on broader functionality, scalability, and contextual adaptability. Further developments should also include training and support for curriculum integration including ethical, legal, organizational, and technical information. Through continuous iteration and feedback, the Teacher Copilot aims to empower teachers in their dual roles as learners and educators, ensuring the meaningful integration of generative AI into educational practice. By carefully addressing these challenges and exploring the potential of generative AI, education systems can work towards a more adaptive and technologically integrated learning environment, enhancing both teacher and student experiences.

REFERENCES

Anderson, L. W., & Krathwohl, D. R. (Eds.). (2001). *A Taxonomy for Learning, Teaching, and Assessing: A Revision of Bloom's Taxonomy of Educational Objectives*. Longman.

Bekes, E. R., & Galzina, V. (2023). Exploring the Pedagogical Use of AI-Powered Chatbots Educational Perceptions and Practices. *2023 46th MIPRO ICT and Electronics Convention (MIPRO)*, 636–641. https://doi.org/10.23919/MIPRO57284.2023.10159734

Kali, Y., McKenney, S. & Sagy, O. (2015). Teachers as designers of technology enhanced learning. *Instr Sci 43*, 173–179. https://doi.org/10.1007/s11251-014-9343-4

Langran, E., Searson, M., & Trumble, J. (2024). Transforming Teacher Education in the Age of Generative AI. *Exploring New Horizons: Generative Artificial Intelligence and Teacher Education, 2.* https://www.learntechlib.org/primary/p/223928/

McKenney, S., & Visscher, A. J. (2019). Technology for teacher learning and performance. Technology, *Pedagogy and Education, 28*(2), 129–132. https://doi.org/10.1080/1475939X.2019.1600859

Mishra, P., & Koehler, M. J. (2006). Technological pedagogical content knowledge: A framework for teacher knowledge. *Teachers' college record, 108*(6), 1017–1054.

Mishra, P., Warr, M., & Islam, R. (2023). TPACK in the age of ChatGPT and Generative AI. *Journal of Digital Learning in Teacher Education, 39*(4), 235-251. https://doi.org/10.1080/21532974.2023.2247480

Mollick, E. R., & Mollick, L. (2023). Using AI to Implement Effective Teaching Strategies in Classrooms: Five Strategies, Including Prompts. *The Wharton School Research Paper.* http://dx.doi.org/10.2139/ssrn.4391243

Ng, D. T. K., Leung, J. K. L., Chu, S. K. W., & Qiao M. S. (2021). Conceptualizing AI Literacy: an exploratory review. *Computers and Education: Artificial Intelligence, 2.* 100041. https://doi.org/10.1016/j.caeai.2021.100041

Ng, D. T. K., Wu, W., Leung, J. K. L., Chiu, T. K. F. & Chu, S. K. W. (2023). Design and validation of the AI literacy questionnaire: The affecitve, behavioural, cognitive and ethical approach. *British Journal of Educational Technology.* https://doi.org/10.1111/ bj et .13 411

Schmid, M., Brianza, E., & Petko, D. (2020). Developing a short assessment instrument for Technological Pedagogical Content Knowledge (TPACK.xs) and comparing the factor structure of an integrative and a transformative model. *Computers & Education, 157*, 103967. https://doi.org/10.1016/j.compedu.2020.103967.

Seufert, S., & Sonderegger, S. (2024). Generative KI in der Lehrerbildung: "Teacher Copilot" als Assistenz- und Trainingssystem für Lehrkräfte. In S. Seufert & S. Handschuh (Hrsg.), *Generative künstliche Intelligenz : ChatGPT und Co für Bildung, Wirtschaft und Gesellschaft* (S. 215–228). Schäffer-Poeschel Verlag.

Shulman, L. (1987). Knowledge and teaching: Foundations of the new reform. *Harvard educational review, 57*(1), 1-23.

Walter, Y. (2024). Embracing the future of Artificial Intelligence in the classroom: the relevance of AI literacy, prompt engineering, and critical thinking in modern education. *International Journal of Educational Technology in Higher Education*, 21(1), 1–29. https://doi.org/10.1186/s41239-024-00448-3

ENHANCING LEARNING AND SKILLS IN THE DIGITAL AGE: DIGITAL BLOOM AND PLATFORMS IN MUSIC EDUCATION

Sri Hermawati Dwi Arini[1*] and Tuti Tarwiyah Adi[2]

Music Education Department, Universitas Negeri Jakarta

[1]Jl. Pendidikan Raya, Komp. IKIP Duren Sawit, Blok BZ No.1, Jakarta Timur 13440, Indonesia

[2]Jl. Carita I/ 252 Blok VII, Bumi Bekasi Baru Utara, Bekasi Utara 17114, Indonesia

ABSTRACT

In the current era of Society 5.0, technology is being used to enhance the quality of human life. This concept is in line with the ideas presented by Churches in 2009 when revising Bloom's Taxonomy, which evolved into Digital Bloom. In addition, the changing era also underscored the competencies that students need to acquire as stated by Trilling and Fadel in 2008. They categorized learning skills into two main domains, namely life and career, and learning and innovation. The arts education paradigm in Indonesia has long emphasized expressive competence, aesthetic experience, and the analysis of meaning. However, specific problems in music education arise from an overemphasis on psychomotor aspects while ignoring the cognitive domain of learning and assessment. Art education material in Indonesia is divided among music theory, expression, appreciation, and creativity. Following this, integrating technology into learning has several benefits such as sustainability, publication, as well as interaction among students, universities, and countries, which can be achieved through collaboration for mutual progress. By engaging in digital learning activities following Bloom's principles, students not only acquire knowledge but also important social values and enhance their digital literacy. Therefore, the purpose of this article is to provide valuable knowledge about digital literacy through the application of digital Bloom. The scope of the discussion includes digital Bloom concept and development through activities using platforms. In conclusion, the implementation of Digital Bloom has been found to enhance students' argumentation and collaboration skills, leading to the development of social values. Additionally, documentation, publication, and interactive activities are facilitated through digitalization.

KEYWORDS

Bloom Digital, Platforms, Learning, Innovation Skills, Digital Literacy

1. INTRODUCTION

In Society 5.0 era, the education plays a crucial role in enhancing the quality of human resources, and digitization influences rapid technological advancements. Digitization is a process that describes increasing social implications with the assistance of computers, media, and new communication platforms for education, economic, societal, and cultural activities (Schumacher & Erol, 2016). One of the skills developed by the government is digital literacy, which is required for living, learning, and working in a society where communication and access to information are increasingly facilitated through technology.

1.1 The Critical Thinking and Metacognitive Concept

Why is critical thinking essential in teaching arts education?

Critical thinking is the ability to analyze ways of thinking that include reasoning, analysis, evaluation, decision-making, and problem-solving.

---

*shermawati@unj.ac.id

Bloom's taxonomy (1956) has undergone revision and development, notably revised by Anderson and Krathwohl for levels C4-C6. This taxonomy was later expanded by Sousa, who added discussions on complexity and difficulty. Ausubel further contributed by classifying low and high-level thinking skills, leading to the final digital spectrum of Bloom's taxonomy in 2008 described by Churches.

Bloom is related to assessment as well as the teaching and learning process. In Bloom taxonomy, the cognitive domain is reported as only one, but in the revision, Anderson & Krathwohl showed two dimensions, namely knowledge and cognitive process. Knowledge dimension is categorized into factual, conceptual, procedural, and metacognition.

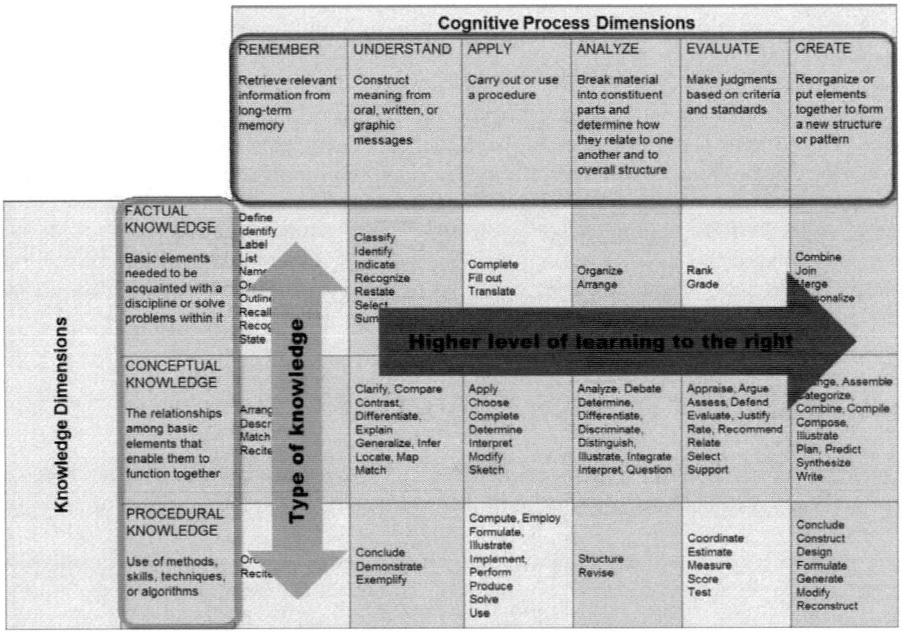

Figure 1. Knowledge Dimension and cognitive Process Dimension
Resources : Benton, 2014

The verbs in the teaching and learning process are analyzed through the application of Bloom Digital. Tarricone (2011) stated that metacognition is a critical thinking center, and according to Benton (2014), it involves self-assessment of understanding, knowledge acquisition, and thought processes. Based on the explanation of knowledge and cognitive process dimension, higher order thinking skill is not only at C4-C6, but also at C1.

According to (Trilling & Fadel, 2009), the 21st-century skills are grouped into three categories, namely life and career, learning and innovation, as well as information media and technology skills. In addition, mastery of IT (Information Technology) in the 21st century has become essential for all students, and the most recent advancement in this area is Digital Bloom Taxonomy.

The paradigm of art education in Indonesia has long emphasized expressive competence, aesthetic experience, and meaning analysis. A specific issue in music education is that it focuses only on psychomotor aspects and neglects the cognitive domain in learning and assessment.

The integration of technology in learning includes documentation, particularly in Art and Culture Education where text preservation is achieved through digitization. This ensures that texts spanning centuries are well-preserved and accessible, serving as invaluable cultural heritage for future generations. Traditional works of art that were previously in the form of tapes, CDs, and files can now be safely preserved through digitization. In addition to documentation, another positive aspect that can be obtained is publication. Digitization facilitates the publication of thoughts, study results, and traditional works of art. This includes students' written work through blogging, websites, and Instagram which are enhanced by interactive methods. Students learn to argue (comment), collaborate, and review through interactive methods, as well as exchange content between schools, universities, and countries.

2. WRITING PURPOSE

This writing aimed to provide an explanation and knowledge about digital literacy through the application of digital Bloom.

3. TECHNOLOGY INTEGRATION

In current era, digital media has revolutionized learning, including the development of art and exhibitions. Previously, every activity was limited by space and time, but currently, the restriction has been removed. Digital technology serves as a classroom, as well as a source and medium of learning. Following this, learning activities with Bloom are not only to achieve higher-order thinking skills but also to create a classroom with various suitable platforms, and social media applications can be used to showcase learning outcomes. The changes focus on expressing art to develop and promote new ways of artistic expression in the virtual world, which tend to foster creativity. The integration of art and digital technology in education, as well as the application of digital Bloom and platforms are forms of adaptation that need to be carried out because all aspects of life are related to digital realm. Furthermore, Art education needs to integrate digital technology as a medium, source of learning, and means of publication. With the application of digital Bloom, learning processes can be tailored to the expected competency achievements, hence, art educators need to master digital literacy.

4. THE CONCEPT OF BLOOM DIGITAL

Bloom's cognitive framework was pioneered by Bloom, suggesting that as science advances, higher and more important dimensions, such as creating, will be discovered. Therefore, Anderson and Krathwohl revised Bloom's levels.

According to (Churches, 2008), generations change continuously, and times change with technology. Consequently, Bloom's theory has been adapted to current conditions and demands. Additionally, Bloom's Digital Taxonomy is a development of the original Bloom's Taxonomy and involves creating learning activities in a digital environment. This framework focuses on utilizing digital tools within a learning environment to facilitate various cognitive processes, including achieving, recalling, understanding, applying, analyzing, evaluating, and fostering creativity. Following this, it also emphasizes the use of these tools as mediums rather than the central focus of the taxonomy.

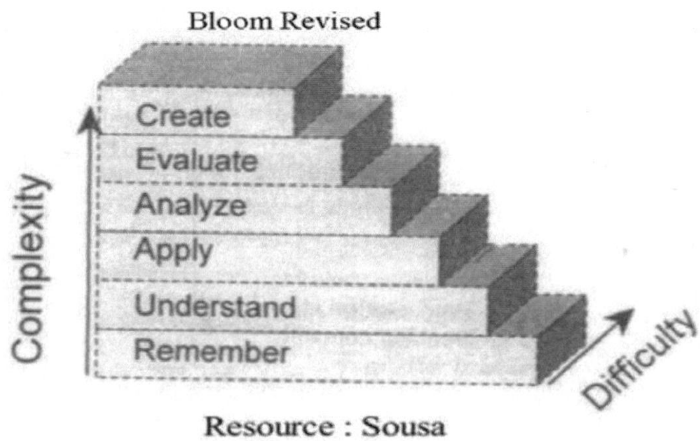

Figure 2. Bloom's revised digital taxonomy map

The higher the competency to be achieved, the more multi-tasking, complex, and difficult the learning and thinking activities will become when applying Bloom's digital taxonomy.

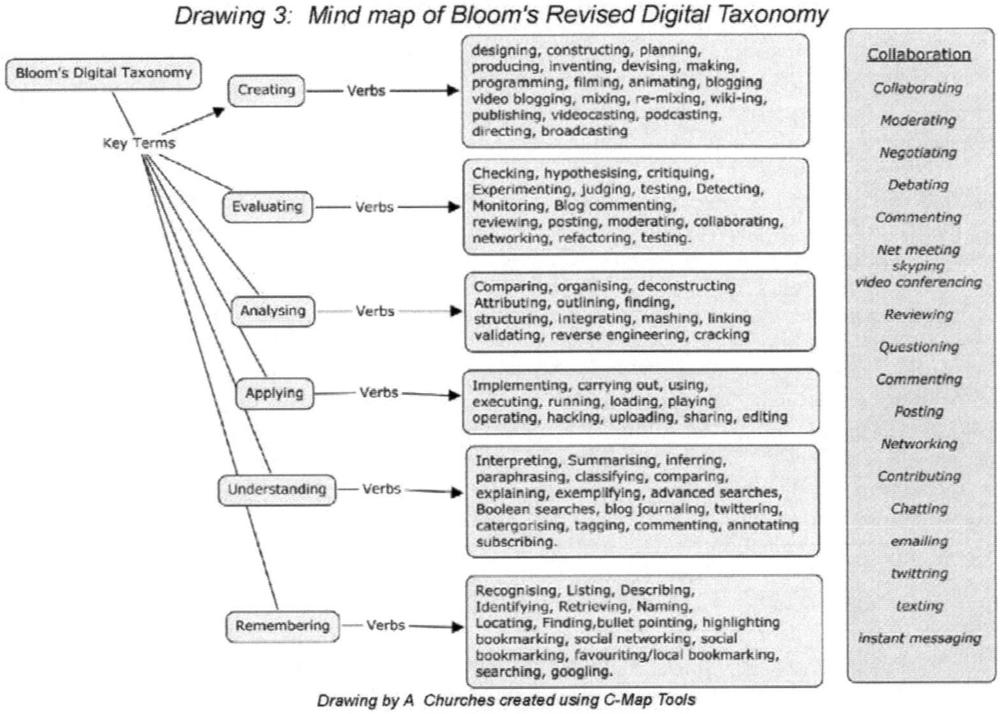

Figure 3. Mind map of Bloom's Revised Digital Taxonomy map.

By using Bloom Digital, it is necessary to encourage student success in higher education.

5. IMPLEMENTATION OF BLOOM DIGITAL VIA PLATFORMS

Chong (2011) showed the impact of integrating blogs in music learning using Bloom's Digital Taxonomy, as shown below:

1. Students can actively engage by providing responses in the comment section.
2. Students can analyze the differences between non-Western and Western classical modes by observing musical traditions from specific time periods through video content shared via blogging tasks.

In their study, (Chong, 2011) stated that teachers need to create instructional strategies to facilitate learning using blogs. In the application of Bloom Digital, students submitted assignments on the blog according to the "assignment room" given (using and organizing).

Furthermore, (Chong, 2011) showed music learning with blogging activities via Web 2.0. Each student uploaded the assigned task to the blog and then analyzed it through checking and assessing by providing comments. All blogs were configured with others, hence they received feedback from other blogs.

Barrio et al. (2016) showed the application of digital Bloom and collaborative work through the Moodle platforms. Students joined forums and exchanged ideas by sending comments, images, and/or audio media (posting and organizing).

Sastre et al. (2013) showed learning art of music through collaboration with Web 2.0, as shown below:

- Students were introduced to platforms 2.0 which was used for collaborative learning (googling).
- Student identified the most suitable platforms for collaboration, such as Wikis and WordPress, through analysis and evaluation)
- Student discussed the selection of suitable musical instruments for performances via blog comments in the WordPress comments section.

Salavuo (2008) concluded that learning music through social networks with the application of Bloom Digital allowed students to send their work to online platforms (uploading), get feedback (in the form of comments), discuss, ask questions, provide answers, as well as engage in music-related arguments (collaborating, criticizing and judging).

Fung & Cheung (2008) claimed that the incorporation of group work in teaching and intervention can effectively foster students' critical thinking skills. Wang & Cheng (2013) stated that critical thinking is an essential skill for students, emphasizing that preservice teachers must understand the concept of critical teaching and how to develop critical thinking, especially in investigating data and discussions.

According to Stupple et al. (2017), critical thinking is important in higher education because developing this skill can predict academic achievement. Lou, Shi Jer, Guo, Recognizing Chinese musical instruments and their classification patterns, including wind, stringed, psaltery, and percussion instruments, as well as their structures, through the "Panorama of Chinese Musical Instruments" feature (classifying and using).

- Being able to click on one of the desired musical instruments to see a picture of that instrument and click on the link at the bottom of the page to view the entire musical performance.

There is an evaluation feature where students are asked to classify Chinese musical instruments based on type, method of playing, or by matching instruments with their names (problem solving and testing).

In the blackboard, students were divided into several groups and the task was to analyze the uniqueness of composers in music periods, namely Pre-Classical, Classical, and Early Romantic. Students can discuss using the online face-to-face features provided (operating, result, and comparing).

There was an evaluation feature, where students were asked to classify musical instruments based on type or how to play, or by matching Chinese musical instruments and their names (resolving problems and testing).

Moccozet et al. (2013) showed the use of the Musimage platforms in learning classical music appreciation for students:

- Observe explanations about the use of classical music in soundtracks (exploring images, music, and short film clips) and compare with other students (comparing and reviewing).

Coutinho & Lindeman (2013) demonstrated music learning with Web 2.0 and Podcasts in the application of Bloom's Digital Taxonomy, as shown below:

- Students were introduced to an informative audio podcast called 'A Little Diversion' that served as an introduction to Audacity, a Web 2.0 software enabling the creation of audio podcasts (recognition and results).

Lou et al. (2011)showed the features that students use on CAMI in implementing Bloom Digital:

- This included recognizing Chinese musical instruments, and understanding the classification patterns, including wind, stringed, psaltery, and percussion instruments along with their structures through the "Panorama of Chinese Musical Instruments" (classifying and using) feature.
- Students can click on one of the desired instruments and see a picture or click on the link at the bottom of the page to see the entire musical performance.

Fillimon et al. (2019) showed students can search for music history with the help of Alexa and use games in learning and assessment process.

Cho et al. (2019) showed the process that students go through in implementing Bloom Digital included:

- Listening to songs uploaded to the application, and there were 13 music titles embedded (using the app).
- Writing notes about music, including analytical (analyzing rhythm, melody, harmony, form, tempo, dynamics, and timbre of music), aesthetic (writing down special parts, characteristics, and musical instruments that might be used, writing down why), and sensory (explain any images or direct objects while listening to music), write short essays and create a picture of music heard (analyzing, result, and reviewing).

6. SOCIAL VALUE

Socially, through argumentation activities, the critical processes of collaborating individuals were influenced by social and environmental factors. Davis et al. (2016) suggested using classroom debates to promote critical thinking, communication, and collaboration (Lampert, 2006).

Regarding digital literacy and its diverse skills set, it is important to recognize the heterogeneity inherent in these abilities. The classroom environment can be designed to improve students' achievement, specifically in cultural contexts (Giroux & Simon, 1988). This included deliberate efforts to shape the generation of knowledge and identities within specific social dynamics. This was similar to Roth (2005) who stated that students have the opportunity to participate actively in improving their learning through dialogue. The educational value of collaboration (teamwork) is also an impact of the application of digital Bloom's taxonomy.

Culturally, the documentation of heritage cultural artifacts, such as traditional works of art through digitalization can serve as learning resource, like websites and digital gamelans. Furthermore, the cultural values do not change, only the changes broaden the scope previously limited by time and location. This cultural shift gives rise to two positive outcomes, namely (1) the wealth of cultural heritage can now be preserved and shared globally through digitalization, and (2) digitalization facilitates the creation of interactive content, such as resources for appreciating cultural festivals and tourism strategies. Schools lacking traditional musical instruments can learn digital traditional music, which becomes meaningful within Bloom framework.

7. CONCLUSION

Bloom's digital taxonomy enriches critical thinking because it applies higher-order thinking skills.

- Students can explore their skills.
- Students are ready to face changing times and technological advances.
- Higher-order and critical thinking skills can be realized with Bloom Digital.
- With Bloom Digital, teachers are ready to teach higher-order thinking skills.

The application of Bloom Digital in learning empowers students to actively engage in inquiry-based activities. This included tasks like making comparisons, argumentation, and collaboration, which are higher-order thinking skills competency. Furthermore, students benefited from social, cultural, and collaborative learning experiences facilitated by digitalization through networks. Learning activities that use Bloom Digital in higher-order thinking skills included comparing, result, structuring, integrating, experimenting, judging, blog commenting, reviewing, posting, collaborating, networking, producing, publishing, podcasting, directing, and broadcasting. These activities were facilitated through platforms like Bloom Digital Blog Web 2.0, Instagram, Blakeboard, moodle, CMI, Musimage, apexa, ARMG, hence, the application of Bloom Digital increased digital literacy, learning, and skills.

REFERENCES

Barrio, F. G., Rivas Rebaque, B., & Gértrudix Barrio, M. (2016). Analysis of Musical Learning Experiences Through The Use of Digital Applications of Students in The Degree in Early Childhood Education. *INTED2016 Proceedings, 1*(March), 3255–3262. https://doi.org/10.21125/inted.2016.1759

Benton Carol W. (2014). Thinking about Thinking ANSI/NISO Z 39-48, 1992, United Stated Of America.

Cho, S., Baek, Y., & Choe, E. J. A strategic approach to music listening with a mobile app for high school students. *International Journal of Music Education, 37*(1), 132–141, (2019). DOI: https://doi.org/10.1177/0255761418819016

Chong, E. K. M. (2011). Blogging Transforming music learning and teaching Reflection of a teacher – researcher. *Journal of Music, Technology and Education, 3*(2), 167-181. https//doi.org/10.1386/jmte.3.2-3.167_1

Churches, A. (2008). Bloom's Digital Taxonomy. https://www.pdst.ie/sites/default/files/BloomDigitalTaxonomy-AndrewChurches.pdf

Coutinho, C., & A. Lindeman, C. (2013). Web. 2.0 Technologies in music education in Portugal : Using podcast for learning. *Computers in the Schools, 28*(1), 56-74, DOI : https//doi.org/10.1080/07380569.2011.552043

Davis, K., Zornick, M. L. W., Roland, J., & Wade, M. M. (2016). *Using debate in the classroom encouraging critical thinking, communication and collaboration.* Routledge, New York.

Filimon, M., Iftene, A., & Trandabăț, D. Using games and smart devices to enhance learning geography and music history. *Proceedings of the 28th International Conference on Information Systems Development*, (2019): Information Systems Beyond 2020, ISD 2019

Fung, D. C. L., To, H., & Leung, K. (2016). The influence of collaborative group work on students development of critical thinking: the teacher in facilitating group discussions. *Pedagogies: An International Journal. 11*(2), 146-166.

Giroux, H.A., & Simon, R. (1988). Schooling, Popular culture and a Padagogy of Possibility. *Journal of Education, 170*(1). https://www.jstor.org/stable/42741800

Lampert, N. (2006). Critical thinking dispositions as an outcome of art education. *Studies in Art Education, 47*(3), 215-228, (2006).

Lou, S. J., Guo, Y. C., Zhu, Y. Z., Shih, R. C., & Dzan, W. Y. (2011). Applying computer-assissted musical instruction to music appreciation course: An example with chinese musical instruments. *Turkish Online Journal of Educational Technology, 10*(1), 45–57, (2011).

Moccozet, L., Tardy, C., Lakhdar, A., Rentsch, R., & Wirth, M. (2013). Musimage: Using social multimedia to engage pupils in classical music appreciation. *2013 International on Interactive Collaborative Learning (ICL), September*, 164-170, https//doi.org/10.1109/ICL2013.6644564

Roth, W. M. (2005). *Being and becoming in the classroom.* Ablex Publishing, Wesport, Connecticut.

Salavuo, M. (2008). Social media as an opportunity for pedagogical change in music education. *Journal of Music, Technology and Education, 1*(2), 121–136. https://doi.org/10.1386/jmte.1.2and3.121_1

Sastre, J., Cerda, J., Garcia, W., Hernandez, C. A., Lloret, N., Murillo, A., Pico, D., Serrano, J. E., Scarani, S., & Dannenberg, R. B. (2013). New Technologies for Music Education. *2013 Second International Conference on E-Learning and E- Technologies in Education (ICEEE),* September, 149–154. https://doi.org/10.1109/ICeLeTE.2013.6644364

Schumacher, A., Sihn, W., & Erol, S. (2016). Automation, digitization and digitalization and their implications for manufacturing processes. *The International Scientific Conference on Innovation and Sustainability, 28/29 October, 6, (2016)*. https://www.researchgate.net/publication/ 318877006.

Stupple, E. J. N., Maratos, F. A., Elander, J., Hunt, T. E., Cheung, K. Y. F., & Aubeeluck A. V. (2017). Development of the critical thinking toolkit (critt): A measure of student attitudes and beliefs about critical thinking. *Thinking Skills and Creativity Journal 23*, 91-100.

Tarricone, P. (2011). *The Taxonomy of Metacognition*. Psychology Press. https://psycnet.apa.org/record/2011-16104-000

Trilling, B., & Fadel, C. (2009). *21st Century Skills: Learning for Life in Our Times.* John Wiley & Sons, San Francisco, CA.

Wang, Y. L., & Cheng, Y. (2013). Construction of online informal learning environment based on digital bloom. *Applied Mechanics and Materials,* 241-244, 2996-2999, https//doi.org/10.4028/www.scientific.net/AMM.241

LEVERAGING CHATGPT FOR AUTOMATED KNOWLEDGE CONCEPT GENERATION

Tianyuan Yang, Baofeng Ren, Chenghao Gu, Boxuan Ma and Shin'ichi Konomi
Kyushu University, Japan

ABSTRACT

As education increasingly shifts towards a technology-driven model, artificial intelligence systems like ChatGPT are gaining recognition for their potential to enhance educational support. In university education and MOOC environments, students often select courses that align with their specific needs. During this process, access to information about the knowledge concepts covered in a course can help students make more informed decisions. However, manually constructing this knowledge concept information is a labor-intensive and time-consuming task. In this paper, we explore the capability of ChatGPT in generating relevant knowledge concepts from course syllabi and evaluate the accuracy and consistency of these AI-generated concepts against course content using four assessment techniques at both the concept level and course level. We investigate the feasibility of using ChatGPT-generated concepts as a direct educational resource, as well as their potential integration into broader educational technologies, such as interpretable course recommendation systems.

KEYWORDS

Educational Data Mining, Large Language Models, Knowledge Concepts

1. INTRODUCTION

In university and MOOC environments, learners typically have the autonomy to select courses based on their interests and educational goals. The concepts covered within a course play a pivotal role in informing these decisions, as they provide learners with insights into the course content and any prerequisites required (Ma et al., 2024). Institutions often provide students with detailed information to facilitate informed decision-making to help learners, including course syllabi and the key concepts associated with each course. However, course syllabi are usually prepared by instructors or academic departments, which is time-consuming and labor-intensive (Pan et al., 2017).

As educational paradigms continue to advance and increasingly integrate technology-driven methodologies, the role of AI systems such as ChatGPT in augmenting educational practices has garnered significant attention. Within the educational sphere, ChatGPT has been employed for generating simple code snippets and brief texts (Ehara, 2023), with studies suggesting that it delivers surprisingly high-quality outputs across a variety of tasks. Recently, there have been attempts to generate course-related information using AI models like ChatGPT in research (Gupta et al., 2023). However, despite its promising capabilities, ChatGPT's responses may still harbor factual inaccuracies or logical inconsistencies. For tasks such as code generation, essay composition, and other extensive text-based projects, educators or subject matter experts can typically review and rectify these errors. Nevertheless, when it comes to more straightforward outputs, such as course syllabi or lists of related knowledge concepts, even experienced educators may find it challenging to identify subtle inaccuracies (Alexander et al., 2023; Perkins et al., 2024).

In response to these challenges, our research aims to explore the feasibility of using ChatGPT to automatically generate high-quality knowledge concepts. In this paper, we explore the feasibility of applying ChatGPT within the educational domain, with a particular focus on its ability to generate relevant concepts from course syllabi. Our objective is to automatically extract key concepts that a course is designed to cover by inputting the course syllabus into ChatGPT, employing carefully designed prompt. This approach not only saves time but also reduces the need for extensive data collection, providing students with a more efficient way to understand and choose courses. The concepts generated by ChatGPT are subsequently compared to manually extracted knowledge concepts in a multi-dimensional analysis of their relevance. This comparison aims to evaluate the potential of ChatGPT in autonomously generating course-specific knowledge concepts. To determine the feasibility of utilizing ChatGPT-generated concepts as a direct educational resource for students and as a foundation for further technology-driven educational strategies, we employed two distinct levels of assessment. Our study addresses several critical questions:

- RQ1: How closely do the ChatGPT-generated knowledge concepts from course syllabi align with those manually generated by academic departments?
- RQ2: Are the ChatGPT-generated concepts comprehensible from a human perspective?
- RQ3: Can the ChatGPT-generated concepts accurately represent the core content of the course?

By investigating these questions, we aim to contribute to the growing body of knowledge regarding the application of AI technologies in education. Our findings indicate that ChatGPT is capable of generating high-quality knowledge concepts that not only assist students in understanding course content but also provide valuable insights for the development of more effective AI-driven educational tools, such as course recommender systems. This approach offers significant time savings and reduces the effort required for the manual generation of knowledge concepts.

2. RELATED WORK

The emergence of large language models (LLMs) like ChatGPT has opened new possibilities in education, including generating educational content, providing personalized learning experiences, and enhancing educational tools. Research has increasingly explored LLMs in various educational applications, such as course recommendation, content generation, and addressing data sparsity (Wu et al., 2024). For example, Yang et al. (2024) used ChatGPT to expand course concepts, enhancing the transparency and explainability of course recommendations. Ehara (2023) investigated the effectiveness of GPT-generated concepts in enhancing the explainability of course recommendations. The study found that while these concepts generally align with recognized curricular content, further refinement is required due to inconsistencies in accuracy. Barany et al. (2024) examined ChatGPT's potential in qualitative codebook development, comparing manual, automated, and hybrid approaches to assess their impact on code quality, reliability, and coding efficiency in educational research. Castleman et al. (2023) explored how integrating domain knowledge bases into GPT-based intelligent tutoring systems affects their accuracy and pedagogical abilities, finding that enhanced knowledge base access improves these systems' comprehension and communication, though they still fall short of human experts. Lin et al. (2024) focused on using GPT models, specifically through prompting and fine-tuning, to automatically generate explanatory feedback in tutor responses, aiming to improve tutor training programs' quality and effectiveness. Beyond its direct application in educational scenarios, ChatGPT can also be integrated into a range of educational tools.

The use of ChatGPT in course recommendation systems has become increasingly popular. Course recommendation in educational environments poses a multifaceted challenge, influenced by diverse factors such as career aspirations, skill enhancement goals, and credit requirements (Ma et al., 2021). Previous research (Wagner et al., 2023; Jiang et al., 2023; Yang et al., 2023) has leveraged various types of information to improve recommendation accuracy, but these efforts often encounter the challenge of data sparsity in educational datasets. Our research addresses this issue by automatically generating supplementary information through ChatGPT.

Despite these advancements, challenges persist in the application of LLMs in education. As highlighted by our study and others, the uncertainty surrounding the accuracy and relevance of AI-generated content underscores the necessity for ongoing improvement. Ensuring that LLM-generated concepts accurately reflect course content and effectively meet students' learning needs remains a crucial focus for future research. Our work explores the usability of ChatGPT for generating course knowledge concepts, which could potentially address the issue of data sparsity in educational datasets and, accordingly, enhance the performance of course recommendation systems.

3. METHOD

3.1 Dataset

In this paper, we utilized a dataset collected from the XuetangX MOOC platform Yu et al. (2020). After preprocessing the dataset, it included 683 courses and 25,161 distinct knowledge concept entities. Each course in the dataset is associated with a course description and several related knowledge concepts. An illustrative example of course information in the dataset is shown in Table 1. Based on the course information provided, we prompted GPT to generate the corresponding knowledge concepts for each course.

Table 1. An example of course information in XuetangX dataset

Course Name	Manual Knowledge Concept	Course Description
Principles and Development of Database Systems	Minimum Spanning Tree; Database Technology; Shortest Path	Database technology is a core component of various information systems such as business processing systems, e-commerce systems, management information systems, office automation systems, and big data application systems. It is also a crucial technical means for efficiently managing and utilizing data resources in an information society, supporting business processing, data analysis, information services, scientific research, and decision-making management. The educational objectives of this course are to help learners grasp the principles and development techniques of database systems, and cultivate students' engineering abilities in database design, programming, and innovative applications, thereby establishing their competencies in database application system development.

3.2 Prompting Structure

We utilized ChatGPT-3.5 to generate relevant knowledge concept entities for each course. To ensure that the responses were both accurate and engaging, we prompted ChatGPT to "respond as a teacher." When generating the knowledge concepts, we provided ChatGPT with the course name, course description, and existing knowledge concepts. The prompt used in our experiments is presented in Table 2.

Table 2. Prompt for generating knowledge concepts for each course

Role	Content
System	You are responded as a teacher to output relevant knowledge concepts of each course. Your task is to analyze course information to generate appropriate knowledge concepts to help students understand course content based on the course name, course description, and the relevant concepts. Extract and generate keywords that summarize the knowledge concepts related to the course content. Respond with the keywords in Chinese, separated by spaces.
User	Continue extracting the relevant concepts for the following course by considering the course description, cour name, and existing concepts from a similar perspective. Course Name: {course name} Existing Concepts: {existing concepts} Course Description: {desc}
Assistant	**Response of ChatGPT-generated course knowledge concepts**

After designing prompts to generate course knowledge concepts using ChatGPT, we successfully generated a total of 27,120 distinct knowledge concepts, a figure comparable to the number of manually generated concepts. This equivalence in quantity enables us to conduct a follow-up assessment without introducing bias related to discrepancies in the number of concepts, thereby ensuring a more accurate and fair evaluation. Since the dataset was entirely in Chinese, the knowledge concepts generated were also in Chinese. For readability in this paper, we have translated these concepts into English. We select some representative manual concepts and ChatGPT-generated concepts as shown in Table 3.

Table 3. The examples of manual concepts and ChatGPT-generated concepts

Course Name	Manual Concepts	ChatGPT-generated Concepts
Calculus	Exponential; Median Theorem; Polynomials; Fourier Series	Functions; Closed Interval; Definite Integral; Limit; Calculus
Pathophysiology	Infectious Disease; Bronchial Asthma; Myocardial Infarction	Disease Process; Metabolism; Systemic Pathophysiology
Introduction to Logic	Formal System; Dialectics of Nature; Axiomatization; Classification	Formal System; Dialectics of Nature; Objective Law; Ambiguity
Big Data Machine Learning	Optimization; Decision Problem; Random Variable; Convolution	Statistical Learning; Image Segmentation; Decision Theory
Principles of Economics	Cash; Policy; Consumer; Entrepreneur; Inflation; Redistribution Policy	Cash; Psychology; Market; Resource Allocation; Government Intervention
Principles and Development of Database Systems	Minimum Spanning Tree; Database Technology; Shortest Path	Database Technology; Big data application system; Database design

3.3 Evaluation

After generating the knowledge concepts for each course using ChatGPT, we evaluated the quality of the concepts generated by ChatGPT both at the conceptual level and the course level to determine their usability. While previous research (Ehara, 2024) has predominantly focused on concept-level assessment, and overlooking course-level evaluation, we contend that course-level assessment is equally critical. When selecting courses, students typically consider the overall knowledge offered by the course rather than focusing on individual concepts in isolation. Our concept-level assessments concentrated on the semantic similarities between individual concepts, whereas our course-level assessments examined the coherence and relevance of the concepts generated for the course as a whole. Specifically, we utilized a pre-trained term embedding corpus provided by Song et al. (2018). This corpus enabled us to obtain embeddings for each concept. By calculating the spatial distance between the embeddings of different concepts, specifically using cosine similarity, we were able to identify similar concepts.

4. RESULT

4.1 Concept-Level Similarity (RQ1 & RQ2)

In the first evaluation, we assessed the quality of the concepts generated by GPT at the concept level. We calculated each ChatGPT-generated concept's similarity to all other concepts in the dataset and identified the Top-K most similar concepts. We then determined how many of these similar concepts belonged to the same course as the GPT-generated concept. The underlying assumption is that concepts belonging to the same course are inherently more similar. This evaluation provided insight into the semantic coherence of the GPT-generated concepts within the context of each course.

The result of concept-level similarity is shown in Figure 1, which presents four histograms showing the distribution of match ratios for the Top-K similar concepts generated by GPT, where K is set to 10, 20, 50, and 100. The match ratio represents the proportion of similar concepts generated by GPT that also belong to the same course as the manual course concept. We can observe that (1) Across all four histograms, the majority of concepts have a low match ratio, concentrated between 0.1 and 0.3. This suggests that most of the top K similar concepts generated by GPT are only moderately aligned with the manual course concepts in the same course. (2) The concept-level evaluation shows that while GPT can generate related concepts, the relevance to the original course decreases as more similar concepts are considered. This could reflect the challenge GPT faces in accurately capturing the specific context or nuances of the course content.

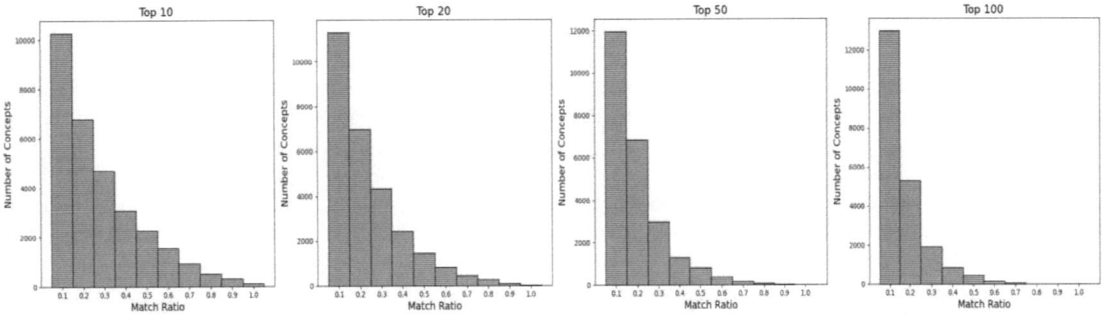

Figure 1. The distribution between match ratio and the number of concepts under different Top-K similar concepts

Given the challenges associated with accurately assessing the quality of concepts using only existing NLP techniques, we employed expert scoring to evaluate the knowledge concepts generated by GPT, thereby enhancing the credibility of our assessment. The evaluation process involved two experts independently scoring each automatically generated knowledge concept based on their expertise. To ensure the fairness of the assessment, we randomly selected 10,000 concepts across various domains due to the large volume of generated concepts. A 5-point scale was utilized, where higher scores indicated greater alignment of the generated concepts with the curriculum content. Given the diverse range of concepts sampled, the expert evaluation was informed by a combination of course descriptions, manually generated concepts, and ChatGPT-generated advice.

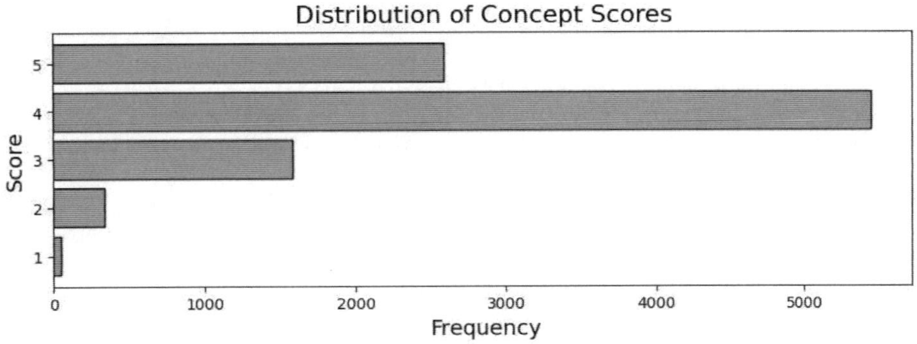

Figure 2. The distribution between expert scoring evaluation

The result of expert scoring is shown in Figure 2, which illustrates the distribution of expert scoring evaluation for 10,000 GPT-generated concepts, evaluated on a 5-point scale based on their relevance to the corresponding course. We can observe that (1) Only a small number of concepts received a score of 1 or 2, indicating minimal or no relevance to the course. Conversely, the majority of concepts were scored as 4, reflecting significant relevance and alignment within the same domain as the course. (2) The results from this expert evaluation indicate that GPT is largely capable of generating course knowledge concepts with high relevance, as evidenced by the concentration of scores at 4 and 5. However, the presence of a notable portion of mid-range scores indicates that there are still inconsistencies in concept relevance. These findings support the feasibility of using GPT-generated concepts in educational contexts, but they also highlight the need for further refinement to consistently achieve the highest levels of relevance and alignment.

Notably, the expert scoring evaluation experiment demonstrates that the GPT-generated concepts are indeed usable at the concept level, as evidenced by the high relevance scores assigned by experts. However, these findings present a contrast to the results from the earlier similarity-based evaluation. The discrepancy between the two outcomes suggests that the similarity experiment might be constrained by the limitations of similarity calculations, which rely heavily on embedding-based methods. These methods may not fully capture the nuanced and context-specific relationships between concepts, leading to lower similarity scores despite the expert evaluations indicating strong relevance. This highlights the importance of incorporating multiple evaluation approaches to fully understand the utility of AI-generated content in educational applications.

4.2 Course-Level Consistency Evaluation (RQ3)

Next, we evaluated the generated concepts at the course level. Using pre-trained word embeddings, we computed the embeddings for both the manual course concepts and the GPT-generated concepts. For each course, we aggregated the embeddings of the manual concepts and the GPT-generated concepts separately. We then calculated the Top-K most similar courses for each course, based on both the manually generated and GPT-generated concept embeddings. By comparing the overlap between the two Top-K lists, we assessed the consistency of similar courses identified by the manually generated and ChatGPT-generated concepts. The manual course concept-based similarity was treated as the ground truth, providing a benchmark to evaluate the utility of the GPT-generated concepts.

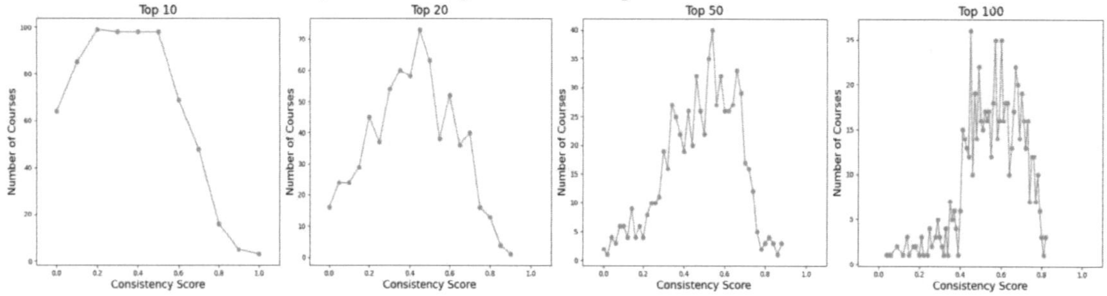

Figure 3. The distribution of consistency scores across different Top-K values (10, 20, 50, 100)

Figure 3 presents the distribution of consistency scores across different Top-K values (10, 20, 50, 100). The consistency score reflects the overlap between the lists of similar courses generated based on the manual course concepts and those generated using GPT-generated concepts. We can observe that the course-level evaluation results suggest that GPT-generated concepts are generally consistent with the manual course concepts when identifying similar courses. The high consistency scores across various K values indicate that the GPT-generated concepts can reliably represent the course content, making them useful for educational purposes.

We conducted a further course-level evaluation to determine whether the Top-K similar courses identified by GPT-generated concept embeddings corresponded with those identified by embeddings derived from manually created course concepts. Specifically, we calculated the cosine similarity between the embeddings derived from the GPT-generated concepts and those from the manually generated concepts, recording whether the original course was among the Top-K similar courses. A hit was recorded as 1, and a miss as 0. Hit Ratio (HR) analysis to further assess the effectiveness of GPT-generated concepts at the course level. The hit ratio measures the proportion of cases where the Top-K similar courses identified using GPT-generated concepts include the course identified using the manual concepts as a ground truth. This provides a direct measure of the alignment between the two sets of similar courses.

Table 4. The result of hit ratio (HR@K) analysis in different K values

Top-K	10	20	50	100
HR (%)	42.6061	48.6091	56.9546	63.9824

The result is shown in Table 4, we observe that (1) The hit ratio analysis supports the findings from the consistency score evaluation, demonstrating that GPT-generated concepts exhibit a high degree of alignment with manually generated course concepts. Therefore, GPT-generated concepts hold significant potential for enhancing course recommendation systems, especially when used in conjunction with a broader analysis that includes more similar courses. (2) As the value of K increases from 10 to 100, there is a steady improvement in the Hit Ratio, rising from approximately 42.6% at K=10 to 63.9% at K=100. This trend indicates that the GPT-generated concepts increasingly align with the original course content as a larger set of similar courses is considered. The growing Hit Ratio suggests that GPT-generated concepts become more reliable and consistent when the comparison includes more courses, demonstrating their potential to effectively capture the essential features of course content.

4.3 Discussion

The comprehensive evaluation of GPT-generated concepts involved four distinct yet complementary analyses: the concept-level similarity, expert scoring evaluation, the consistency score and the hit ratio. These analyses collectively provide a comprehensive understanding of the alignment and reliability of GPT-generated concepts concerning the manually generated course concepts.

The results from these four analyses suggest that GPT-generated concepts are generally effective in representing the content and context of courses, particularly at a broader, thematic level. While there may be some limitations in capturing finer details or specific nuances, the overall alignment with manual concepts reflected in both the consistency scores and hit ratios supports the use of GPT-generated concepts in educational applications. This result aligns with the previous research (Ehara, 2023). These concepts can reliably identify courses with similar content, making them a valuable tool for tasks such as course recommendation, curriculum development, and personalized learning pathways.

The evaluations indicate that GPT-generated concepts can serve as a useful complement to traditional concept-generation methods, particularly in large-scale educational environments where the need for automated, scalable solutions is paramount. However, for applications requiring high precision and specificity, further refinement of the GPT model's output may be necessary to ensure closer alignment with course-specific details.

We note that several researchers have attempted to leverage ChatGPT to address issues related to data sparsity in education, particularly in the context of interpretable course recommendation systems. Yang et al. (2024) have utilized ChatGPT to expand course concepts, aiming to enhance the transparency and interpretability of these systems. We argue that by providing well-defined and contextually relevant concepts to describe course content, AI-generated concepts can significantly aid students in understanding why certain courses are recommended to them. However, as observed in our evaluation, variations in the accuracy and relevance of these concepts indicate that further refinement is necessary to ensure that these systems can reliably recommend courses that genuinely meet students' learning needs and goals.

5. CONCLUSION

This study investigated the potential of GPT to generate knowledge concepts for educational purposes, evaluating the generated concepts through both concept-level and course-level analyses. The results indicate that GPT-generated concepts are generally of high quality, with expert evaluations confirming their relevance and utility at the concept level. However, the similarity-based evaluation revealed some discrepancies, likely due to the limitations of embedding-based similarity calculations, which may not fully capture the nuanced relationships between concepts. Despite these challenges, our findings suggest that GPT-generated concepts offer a promising solution for automating the time-consuming task of manual concept generation, holding significant potential for enhancing educational practices. As educational paradigms increasingly embrace personalized and technology-driven approaches, GPT-generated concepts could play a vital role in supporting direct teaching applications, potentially streamlining content creation and improving learning outcomes.

While our results are encouraging, it is important to note that GPT-generated concepts are not yet ready for direct implementation without further refinement. The variability in accuracy and relevance observed in our evaluations indicates that additional optimization is needed to ensure these concepts consistently meet the high standards required for educational use.

This study acknowledges some limitations, notably the lack of an efficient solution to the variability in the quality of ChatGPT-generated concepts. Although the generated concepts were validated through four assessment strategies, we did not conduct sufficient user studies to determine if students find these concepts reasonable. Future work will involve user evaluations to assess the applicability of these concepts in educational settings. Additionally, we aim to leverage this information to enhance digital education, such as by constructing a more informative knowledge graph for improving course recommendation systems to better guide student course selection.

ACKNOWLEDGEMENT

This work was supported by JST SPRING, Grant Number JPMJSP2136, JSPS KAKENHI Grant Numbers JP20H00622 and JP24K20903.

REFERENCES

Alexander, K., Savvidou, C., & Alexander, C. (2023). Who wrote this essay? Detecting AI-generated writing in second language education in higher education. *Teaching English with Technology*, Vol. 23, No. 2, pp. 25-43.

Barany, A., Nasiar, N., Porter, C., Zambrano, A. F., Andres, A. L., Bright, D., ... & Baker, R. S. (2024). ChatGPT for Education Research: Exploring the Potential of Large Language Models for Qualitative Codebook Development. In *International Conference on Artificial Intelligence in Education*. pp. 134-149.

Castleman, B. and Turkcan, M. K. (2024). Examining the Influence of Varied Levels of Domain Knowledge Base Inclusion in GPT-based Intelligent Tutors. In *Proceedings of the 17th International Conference on Educational Data Mining*. Atlanta, Georgia, USA, pp. 649-657.

Ehara, Y. (2023). Measuring Similarity between Manual Course Concepts and ChatGPT-generated Course Concepts. *Proceedings of the 16th International Conference on Educational Data Mining*. Bengaluru, India, pp. 474-476.

Gupta, P., Raturi, S., & Venkateswarlu, P. (2023). Chatgpt for designing course outlines: A boon or bane to modern technology. *Available at SSRN 4386113*.

Jiang, L., Liu, K., Wang, Y., Wang, D., Wang, P., Fu, Y., & Yin, M. (2023). Reinforced explainable knowledge concept recommendation in MOOCs. *ACM Transactions on Intelligent Systems and Technology*, Vol. 14, No. 3, pp. 1-20.

Lin, J., Chen, E., Han, Z., Gurung, A., Thomas, D. R., Tan, W., ... & Koedinger, K. R. (2024). How Can I Improve? Using GPT to Highlight the Desired and Undesired Parts of Open-ended Responses. *arXiv preprint arXiv:2405.00291*.

Ma, B., Lu, M., Taniguchi, Y., & Konomi, S. I. (2021). CourseQ: the impact of visual and interactive course recommendation in university environments. *Research and practice in technology enhanced learning*, Vol. 16, No.18, pp. 1-24.

Ma, B., Lu, M., Taniguchi, Y., & Konomi, S. I. (2021). Investigating course choice motivations in university environments. *Smart Learning Environments*, Vol. 8, pp. 1-18.

Ma, B., Yang, T., & Ren, B. (2024). A Survey on Explainable Course Recommendation Systems. In *12th International Conference, DAPI 2024, Held as Part of the 26th HCI International Conference, HCII 2024*. Washington, DC, USA, pp. 273-287.

Pan, L., Wang, X., Li, C., Li, J., & Tang, J. (2017). Course concept extraction in moocs via embedding-based graph propagation. In *Proceedings of the Eighth International Joint Conference on Natural Language Processing*. Vol 1, pp. 875-884.

Perkins, M., Roe, J., Postma, D., McGaughran, J., & Hickerson, D. (2024). Detection of GPT-4 generated text in higher education: Combining academic judgement and software to identify generative AI tool misuse. *Journal of Academic Ethics*, Vol. 22, No. 1, pp. 89-113.

Song, Y., Shi, S., Li, J., & Zhang, H. (2018). Directional skip-gram: Explicitly distinguishing left and right context for word embeddings. In *Proceedings of the 2018 Conference of the North American Chapter of the Association for Computational Linguistics: Human Language Technologies*. Vol 2, pp. 175-180.

Wagner, K., Merceron, A., Sauer, P., & Pinkwart, N. (2023). Can the Paths of Successful Students Help Other Students with Their Course Enrollments?. In *Proceedings of the 16th International Conference on Educational Data Mining*. Bengaluru, India, pp. 171-182.

Wu, L., Zheng, Z., Qiu, Z., Wang, H., Gu, H., Shen, T., ... & Chen, E. (2024). A survey on large language models for recommendation. *World Wide Web*, Vol. 27, No. 5, pp. 60.

Yang, T., Ren, B., Ma, B., Khan, M. A. Z., He, T., & Konomi, S. I. (2024). Making Course Recommendation Explainable: A Knowledge Entity-Aware Model using Deep Learning. In *Proceedings of the 17th International Conference on Educational Data Mining*. Atlanta, Georgia, USA, pp. 658-663.

Yang, Y., Zhang, C., Song, X., Dong, Z., Zhu, H., & Li, W. (2023). Contextualized knowledge graph embedding for explainable talent training course recommendation. *ACM Transactions on Information Systems*, Vol. 42, No. 2, pp. 1-27.

Yu, J., Luo, G., Xiao, T., Zhong, Q., Wang, Y., Feng, W., ... & Tang, J. (2020). MOOCCube: A large-scale data repository for NLP applications in MOOCs. In *Proceedings of the 58th Annual Meeting of the Association for Computational Linguistics*. pp. 3135-3142.

DEVELOPMENT OF TWO APPLICATIONS FOR ACOUSTIC EDUCATION FOR ARCHITECTURAL DESIGNERS

Mari Ueda[1], Yuichi Tsumoto[2] and Tetsuo Tanaka[1]
[1]*Dept. of Information Media, Faculty of Information Technology, Kanagawa Institute of Technology*
1030 Shimo-ogino, Atsugi, Kanagawa, 243-0292, Japan
[2]*Account Department 1 ,Kansai Office, NOMURA Co., Ltd.*
Parks Tower 19th floor, 2-10-70 Nambanaka, Naniwa-ku, Osaka 556-0011, Japan

ABSTRACT

According to architectural designers, although they are aware of the sound environment when designing spaces, in many cases visual (design) and cost (cost-effectiveness, etc.) were the predominant factors.
In many cases, the visual (design) and cost aspects (cost-effectiveness, etc.) were dominant. The tacit rule for evaluating the sound environment was that a quiet space with no noise was somehow better. Futhermore, when space designers have meetings with clients, they are consulted that although they can present photographs, it is difficult to explain comfort other than visual elements. Even if they have attended classes on sound environment at university, it seems to be difficult for architectural designers who are not specialised in sound to concretely verbalise and articulate the image of the sound environment in their own consciousness. Therefore, the authors considered that, in order for architectural designers to design spaces with consideration for sound, it is important for them to make it their own thing, such as their own senses, to absorb knowledge before learning the knowledge of acoustics, and to show it objectively and clearly. Therefore in this study, two applications were developed: an application to raise architectural designers' awareness of the sound environment and a reverberation sensation training application.

KEYWORDS

Architectural Designers, Acoustic Education, Acoustic Environment, Reverberation Time

1. INTRODUCTION

According to architectural designers, although they are aware of the sound environment when designing spaces, in many cases visual (design) and cost (cost-effectiveness, etc.) were the predominant factors.

In many cases, the visual (design) and cost aspects (cost-effectiveness, etc.) were dominant. The tacit rule for evaluating the sound environment was that a quiet space with no noise was somehow better. However, recently, sound environment design focusing on indicators other than quietness, such as speech privacy-conscious sound environment design in hospitals and pharmacies, and sound environment design of commercial spaces to ensure liveliness, has also been conducted (Astolfi, 2004), (Joerg, 2016), (Kang, 2002). We have also conducted studies on sound environment design guidelines that take into account the anonymity of the sound environment (Maruyama, 2020). As described above, there is a need not only for quietness, but also for appropriate sound environment design for specific applications. Especially in multi-group conversation spaces such as restaurants, it is also important that the space is 'comfortable for conversation' in addition to visual elements.

On the other hand, when architectural designers have meetings with clients, they are consulted that although they can present photographs, it is difficult to explain comfort other than visual elements. Even if they have attended classes on sound environment at university, it seems to be difficult for architectural designers who are not specialised in sound to concretely verbalise and articulate the image of the sound environment in their own consciousness. Therefore, the authors considered that, in order for architectural designers to design spaces with consideration for sound, it is important for them to make it their own thing, such as their own senses, to absorb knowledge before learning the knowledge of acoustics, and to show it objectively and clearly. Therefore in this study, two applications were developed: an application to raise architectural designers' awareness of the sound environment and a reverberation sensation training application.

2. APPLICATION FOR EVALUATING THE SOUND ENVIRONMENT IN RESTAURANTS

2.1 Application Overview

In order to help architectural designers to optimise their design in consideration of sound, a sound environment assessment application for restaurants was developed to firstly trigger awareness of the sound environment. We developed a restaurant sound environment application for members of the design team of NOMURA Corporation, one of the leading architectural design firms in Japan. They are a design team that has designed spaces for many national and international restaurants (Ueda, 2024).

Figure 1 shows the screen where the user registers information on the sound environment.

The information to be registered is the situation at the time of the sound environment evaluation, the shop, the seating area and the user's (evaluator's) subjective opinion. Table 1 shows the details of each item.

Figure 1. Example of the sound environment assessment sheet input screen

Table 1. Evaluation items to be assessed in the application

Circumstances	Date, Noise level, Number of visitors
Shop	Shop name, Address, Business type, BGM, BGM genre
Seats	Capacity, Seat type, Seat distance, Seating area, Ceiling height, Open terrace availability, Open kitchen, Floor, wall, and ceiling materials, Table top and chair seat materials
Photo	Photos of the inside of the shop
Subjective evaluation	Ease of speaking, Liveliness, Difficulty in hearing, Reverberation

NOMURA Design Team architectural designers can reaffirm how they feel in any space by simultaneously evaluating physical data such as noise level, presence or absence of background music, seating size and distance between seats, as well as their own subjectivity. By collecting and sharing a large number of these evaluations, we believe that it is possible to clarify the relationship between physical characteristics and subjectivity.

The noise level is measured by other applications (for iPhone: Sound Level Analyzer Lite Decibel Meter, TOON, LLC/Android: SPL Meter, keuwlsoft) and is input by the user. We will also consider adding a measurement function to this application.

2.2 Brief Summary of the User Evaluation and Results

On subjective awareness: architectural designers' assessment of the sound environment of the restaurants and bars they visit on a daily basis led to the following statements. 'I used to focus on visuals such as wall materials and lighting, but the task of evaluating the sound environment using the app has made me more aware of the sound environment'. 'I had never been aware of noisy restaurants before, but using the app, I now realise that there are noisy environments and environments where it is difficult to have a conversation, and sound environments where it is easy to have a conversation.'

At the moment, the evaluation has only been carried out by about 30 architectural designers from NOMURA Corporation but it appears that awareness of the sound environment has been raised.

On evaluation tools: original applications seem to be more motivating for evaluation than evaluations using Google Forms or Excel. In Japan, there are several web applications for sharing restaurant evaluations.

Issues related to evaluation: Regarding the evaluation item 'reverberation', feedback such as 'I cannot get a sense of reverberation (echo)' and 'There are individual differences in the sense of reverberation' were reported.

2.3 Application Configuration

This application is implemented as a web application as shown in Figure 2. Firebas is a mobile and web application back-end service (BaaS: Backend as a Service) provided by Google, consisting of several product groups (Firebase). Firebase Authentication is used to implement authentication functions, Cloud Firestore is a document-oriented database for data storage and management, Firebase Hosting is used for web hosting, and Cloud Storage is used for image storage. The Google Maps Platform is also used for the implementation of the Google Maps Platform geo-targeting system. The geocoding service of the Google Maps Platform is used to convert latitude and longitude into addresses.

The implementation on the client side uses HTML, JavaScript and CSS, as in general web applications. In addition, the Firebase SDK for accessing Firebase services and UIKit, a front-end framework (CSS and JavaScript library) widely used in web production, are used. The Maps JavaScript API is used to access geocoding services.

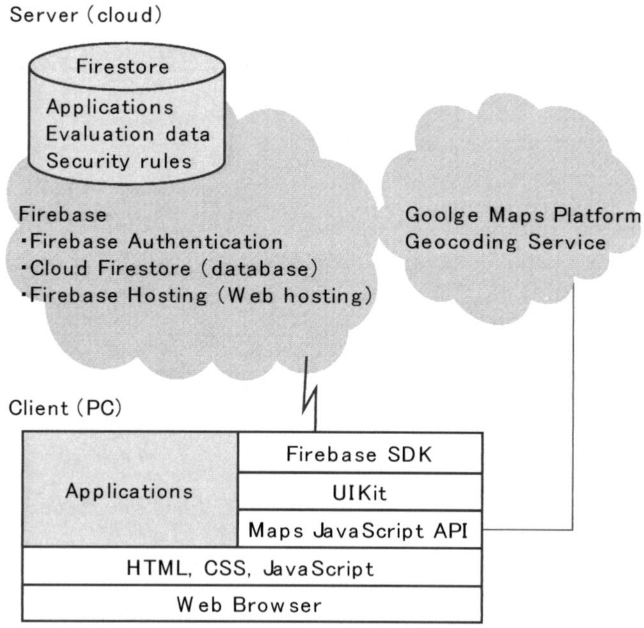

Figure 2. System configuration

3. DEVELOPMENT OF A REVERBERATION TIME TRAINING APPLICATION

In the previous chapter, we developed an application for evaluating the sound environment of restaurants and cafés so that architectural designers, who have given priority to visual design, can become aware of the sound environment when designing their spaces. As a result, opinions were heard that it was difficult to get a sense of 'reverberation (echo)' at the same time as the awareness-raising application, and that there were individual differences in the sense of reverberation. This led to the discussion that it is necessary to grasp the reverberation sensation sensitively at the same time as raising awareness of the sound environment. In this chapter, a reverberation training application for spatial designers was developed and tested on architectural designers, referring to the training for grasping the volume and frequency of ear training to foster sound perfection.

3.1 Application Overview

The application consists of a function for registering user profiles, a training function for listening to sounds and answering their reverberation time (1), a training function for listening to two sounds and answering the one with the longer reverberation time (2), and a history display function for these two types of training (Iwamiya, 2003), (Kawahara, 2016).

Figure 3 shows the screen of the training function (1), and Figure 4 shows its history screen. When the user clicks the start button on the training screen, a sound is played. The user selects the reverberation time with a button. This is repeated ten times, and the answer is registered by clicking the Register button. The history screen shows the training date and time, the correct answer, the answer, the correct answer and the difference between the correct answer and the answer for each session.

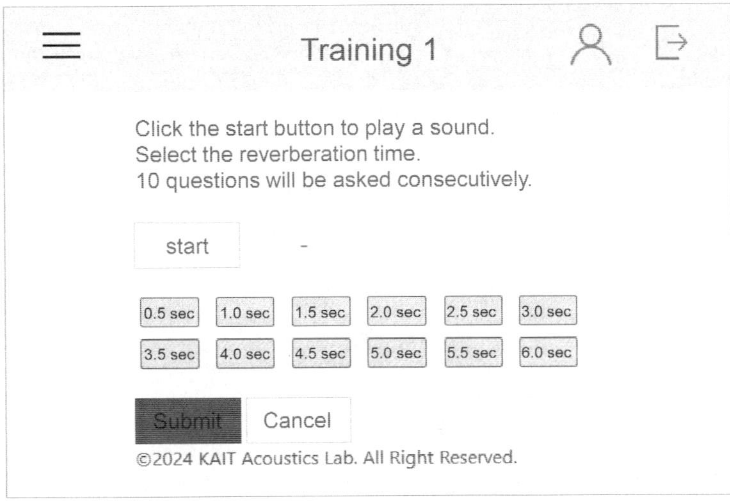

Figure 3. Example of training 1 screen

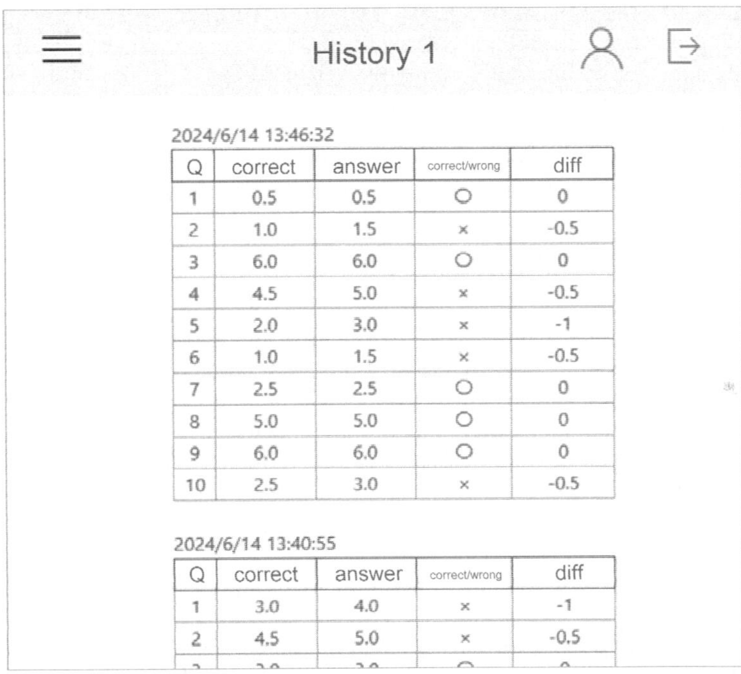

Q	correct	answer	correct/wrong	diff
1	0.5	0.5	○	0
2	1.0	1.5	×	-0.5
3	6.0	6.0	○	0
4	4.5	5.0	×	-0.5
5	2.0	3.0	×	-1
6	1.0	1.5	×	-0.5
7	2.5	2.5	○	0
8	5.0	5.0	○	0
9	6.0	6.0	○	0
10	2.5	3.0	×	-0.5

Q	correct	answer	correct/wrong	diff
1	3.0	4.0	×	-1
2	4.5	5.0	×	-0.5

Figure 4. Example of training 1 history screen

Figure 5 shows an example of the screen of the training function (2). When the start button is clicked, the sound is played twice. The user clicks on the button with the longer reverberation. This is repeated ten times, and the answer is registered by clicking the Register button. The history screen shows the training date and time, the 10 correct answers, the answer, and the correct or incorrect answer.

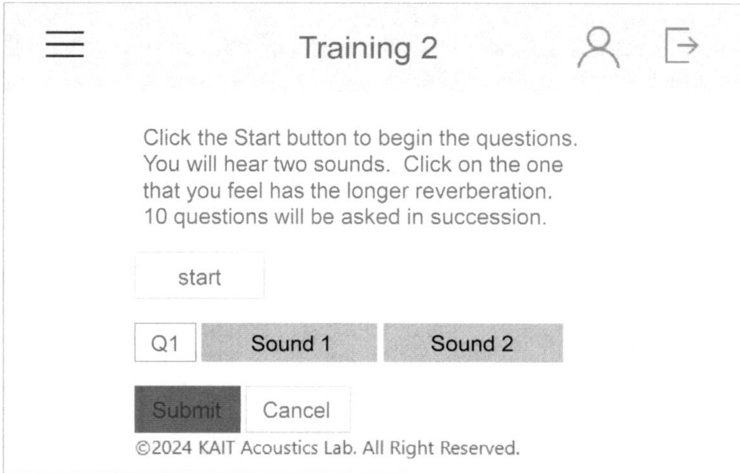

Figure 5. Example of training 2 screen

3.2 Feedback at the Moment from Architectural Designers

The reverberation training application is currently being used by spatial designers, who have given feedback such as 'the actual reverberation time is far different from what I had imagined in my head' and 'the sense of long reverberation was different for each person, but through training I expect that the team's sense of reverberation will be consistent to some extent'. The training is expected to make the team's sense of resonance more consistent to a certain extent.

3.3 Application Configuration

This application is implemented as a web application in the same way as Figure 2. Firebase is a mobile and web application back-end service (BaaS: Backend as a Service) provided by Google, consisting of several product groups. Firebase Authentication is used to implement authentication functions, Cloud Firestore is used for data storage and management, and Firebase Hosting is used for web hosting.

The client-side implementation uses HTML, JavaScript and CSS, as in general web applications. In addition, the Firebase SDK for accessing Firebase services and UIKit, a front-end framework (CSS and JavaScript library) widely used for web production, are used.

4. CONCLUSION

In this study, as a first step to enable spatial designers to concretely verbalise and clarify the image of the sound environment in their consciousness, we developed a sound environment evaluation application for restaurants to trigger their awareness of the sound environment. During the evaluation, many of the space designers stated that it was difficult to evaluate reverberation and resonance, and that the feeling seemed to differ from person to person even when talking (among designers). The reverberation training application is currently being used by spatial designers, and their impressions include: 'The actual reverberation time is far different from what I thought in my head' and 'The sense of long reverberation was different for each person, but I expect that the team's sense of reverberation will be consistent to some extent through training. The training is expected to make the team's sense of resonance more consistent to a certain extent.

Currently, the designers are actually using the application to evaluate the sound environment of various restaurants. In the future, it is planned to investigate whether there are any changes in awareness before and after the use of the application and how it is actually utilised. In addition, by combining this reverberation training with the sound environment evaluation application described in the previous report, the awareness of space designers towards the sound environment will be broadly promoted.

REFERENCES

Astolfi. A., et al. (2004). "Good Acoustical Quality in Restaurants: A Compromise between Speech Intelligibility and Privacy." Proceedings of International Conference on Acoustics, ICA 2004, 1201-1204.

https://firebase.google.com/

Iwamiya, S., et al. (2003). "Technical Listening Training: Improvement of sound sensitivity for acoustic engineers and sound designers". Acoustical Science and Technology. 24. 27-31.

Joerg, B., et al. (2016). "Privacy-Aware Acoustic Assessments of Everyday Life," JAES Volume 64 Issue 6, pp. 395-404; June.

Kang, J. (2002). "Numerical modelling of speech intelligibility in dining spaces." Applied Acoustics 2002, 63, 1135-1333.

Kawahara, K., et al. (2016). "Training course for instructors of technical listening training," Acoust. Sci. & Tech., 37, 185–186.

Maruyama, N., et al. (2020). "Assessing the ease of conversation in multi-group conversation spaces: Effect of background music volume on acoustic comfort in a café," Building Acoustics 27(2), 137–153.

Rindel, J. H., et al. (2012). "Acoustical capacity as a means of noise control in eating establishments." Proceedings of BNAM 2012, Odense, Denmark.

Rindel, J. H., et al. (2010). "Verbal communication and noise in eating establishments, Applied Acoustics 71, 1156-1161.

Ueda, M. et al. (2024). "Development of a restaurant sound environment assessment application to provide acoustic education for space designers." Proceedings of The Acoustical Society of Japan Spring Meetings 2024(in Japanese).

ASSESSMENT OF BARRIERS TO EDUCATIONAL TECHNOLOGY ACCEPTANCE

Stephen Downes
National Research Council Canada
Ottawa, Canada

ABSTRACT

This paper reports on literature related to the assessment of barriers to educational technology assessment. It surveys the development of technology acceptance models from social cognitive theory and innovation diffusion theory through to a unified theory that considers performance expectancy, effort expectancy, and social influence. Because risk is a significant factor in technology assessment, this paper outlines risk assessment processes, beginning with the Fine-Kinney method through to derivation of a risk matrix. Finally, it considers factors related to the validation of technology acceptance survey assessments.

KEYWORDS

Technology, Assessment, Risk, Validity, Model, Education

1. INTRODUCTION

Institutions introducing educational technology to staff and students frequently encounter resistance and negative responses. From learning management systems to automated assessment to large language models, new innovations are often met with a less than enthusiastic response. Often, studies and surveys are undertaken to understand the reasons for these concerns. But there isn't a single set of metrics available to assist in this task.

This paper reports on a study undertaken to study the barriers to technology acceptance in an institutional training environment. The purpose of this assessment is to review criteria for an evaluation of a survey assessing reasons for teacher hesitance to use new learning technologies. It does not report on the study itself, but on the considerations applied as part of the process of validation of the survey instrument. The results of this investigation offer useful advice to others considering similar assessments in the future.

To that end, three major sets of criteria were considered: first, technology assessment models, in order to identify the scope of considerations; second, risk assessment models, to understand how potential harms from new technology may be understood, and third, methods and approaches for the assessment of the reliability and validity of the survey instrument.

2. ACCEPTANCE MODELS

Technology acceptance and diffusion models describe and explain the adoption and deployment of new tools and applications. Adoption theory describes the choices individuals make and is understood in terms of behaviour change. Diffusion theory considers the spread of a technology over time across an organization (Straub, 2009, 627).

These models are largely based in social cognitive theory and describe two major roles for social learning: vicarious experience through modelling (Bandura, 1963, 607), and vicarious experience mediated through the use of a technology (Bandura, 2001, 17). Major factors influencing acceptance decisions include: attention to the behaviour, whether it is retained or recollected, whether it can be reproduced successfully, and whether the agent is motivated to do it again (Straub, 2009, 629).

2.1 Innovation Diffusion Theory

Rogers' Innovation Diffusion Theory (1962) describes five stages of evaluation of an innovation: awareness of the innovation, persuasion of its benefits, decision to adopt the innovation, implementation of the decision, and confirmation of the innovation process. These happen in individuals at different times, resulting in Rogers' 'innovation diffusion curve', which describes the progress of an innovation through early adopters, mainstream and late adopters or laggards.

Adoption is "a decision to make full use of technology innovation as the best course of action available" where innovation is "anything that is perceived as new from the perspective of the adopters and is described by Rogers by five characteristics: relative advantage, compatibility, complexity, traceability, and observability" (Rogers, 1995, 5; Granić, 2023, 184-5). Following Bandura, Rogers also describes the channels of communication through which an innovation is modelled, and the social system, that is, the "a set of interrelated units that are engaged in joint problem-solving to accomplish a common goal" (Rogers, 1995, 23) in which the adoption decision takes place.

2.2 Theory of Planned Behavior

"A person's intention to perform (or not to perform) a behaviour is the immediate determinant of that action" (Azjen, 1985, 12). Changes in intention can be caused by changes in the salience of belief, new information, changes in confidence or commitment, individual differences such as skills, willpower, emotions and compulsions, or external factors such as time, opportunity, and dependence on others.

2.3 Technology Acceptance Model

"A person's intention to perform (or not to perform) a behaviour is the immediate determinant of that action" (Azjen, 1985, 12). Changes in intention can be caused by changes in the salience of belief, new information, changes in confidence or commitment, individual differences such as skills, willpower, emotions and compulsions, or external factors such as time, opportunity, and dependence on others.

Table 1. Factor Analysis of Perceived Usefulness and Ease of Use. By the author; adapted from Davis, 1989, p. 331 (Table 7, Study 2)

Scale Items		Factor 1 (Usefulness)	Factor 2 (Ease of Use)
Usefulness			
1	Work More Quickly	.91	.01
2	Job Performance	.98	−.03
3	Increase Productivity	.98	−.03
4	Effectiveness	.94	.04
5	Makes Job Easier	.95	−.01
6	Useful	.88	.11
Ease of Use			
1	Easy to Learn	−.20	.97
2	Controllable	.19	.83
3	Clear & Understandable	−.04	.89
4	Flexible	.13	.63
5	Easy to Become Skillful	.07	.91
6	Easy to Use	.09	.91

Over time, the original model by was extended through the addition of other constructs (Granić, 2023, 186ff): perceived enjoyment, conformity behaviour, and self-esteem (Yu, 2020); perceived playfulness (Lin and Yeh, 2019); and privacy, infrastructure, institutional support, and access devices (Aburagaga, Agoyi, and Elgedawy (2020)

The Decomposed Theory of Planned Behavior (DTPB) combines TPB and TAM to depict specific beliefs as decomposed into belief constructs (Taylor & Todd, 1995, 147). Factors that impact the acceptance and usage of a technology include: attitude (perceived ease to use, perceived usefulness, and compatibility), subjective norm (peer influence and superior influence), and perceived behavioural control factors (self-efficacy, resource-facilitating conditions, and information technology support).

2.4 Concerns-Based Adoption Model

According to Straub (2009) "technology adoption is a complex, inherently social, developmental process; individuals construct unique yet malleable perceptions of technology that influence their adoption decisions. Thus, successfully facilitating technology adoption must address cognitive, emotional, and contextual concerns." Accordingly, the Concerns-Based Adoption Model (CBAN) "includes three diagnostic, judgement-free components, the Stages of Concern (SoC) survey; Levels of Use (LoU) interviews; and Innovation Configuration Maps (ICM). Through 35 survey items, the SoC survey identifies individual attitudes and beliefs of change agents and how they align with the innovation" (Olson, et al., 2020, 50) while the LoU identifies stages of use of the innovation, ranging from 'novice' to 'advanced user'.

2.5 Unified Theory of Acceptance and Use of Technology

Following a review of technology acceptance models (including those listed above), Venkatesh, et al. (2003) extracted common factors tested a model called the Unified Theory of Acceptance and Use of Technology (UTAUT), "which posits three direct determinants of intention to use (performance expectancy, effort expectancy, and social influence) and two direct determinants of usage behavior (intention and facilitating conditions). Significant moderating influences of experience, voluntariness, gender, and age were confirmed as integral features of UTAUT" (Ibid., 467).

2.6 Barriers to Technology Adoption

While the acceptance models discussed above focus on factors influencing technology adoption, it is often useful to focus on the barriers specifically, as for example by Reid (2014). "Unavailable technology is an obvious barrier. Less obvious are the reliability and complexity of available instructional technologies. Because these can be complex, faculty with poor self-efficacy may be reluctant to try them. If a technology is unreliable, faculty turning away from it will influence others to do the same" (386-7).

A comparison of the specific categories identified by Reid and the factors discussed in the acceptance models will reveal a significant degree of overlap. In Reid, however, the point of view or perspective of the person adopting technology assumes greater importance. For example, "Leadership may not understand the complexities of the technologies, or the time needed to master them" (394). This creates a need to study technology adoption from the perspective of different and specific roles within the organization.

3. RISK MANAGEMENT

3.1 Risk Assessment Models

In many cases, teachers are hesitant to adopt new tools because of perceived risks. Assessments of this hesitation need to be informed by the teachers' understanding of risks. A risk assessment profile should be employed to provide a complete description.

These models are largely based in social cognitive theory and describe two major roles for social learning: vicarious experience through modelling (Bandura, 1963, 607), and vicarious experience mediated through the use of a technology (Bandura, 2001, 17). Major factors influencing acceptance decisions include attention to the behaviour, whether it is retained or recollected, whether it can be reproduced successfully, and whether the agent is motivated to do it again (Straub, 2009, 629).

3.2 Fine-Kinney method

The Fine-Kinney method of risk assessment (Fine, 1971; Kinney, 1976) calculates a risk score based on the product of scores for probability, exposure, and consequences. Each is weighted equally; later modifications vary the weighting.

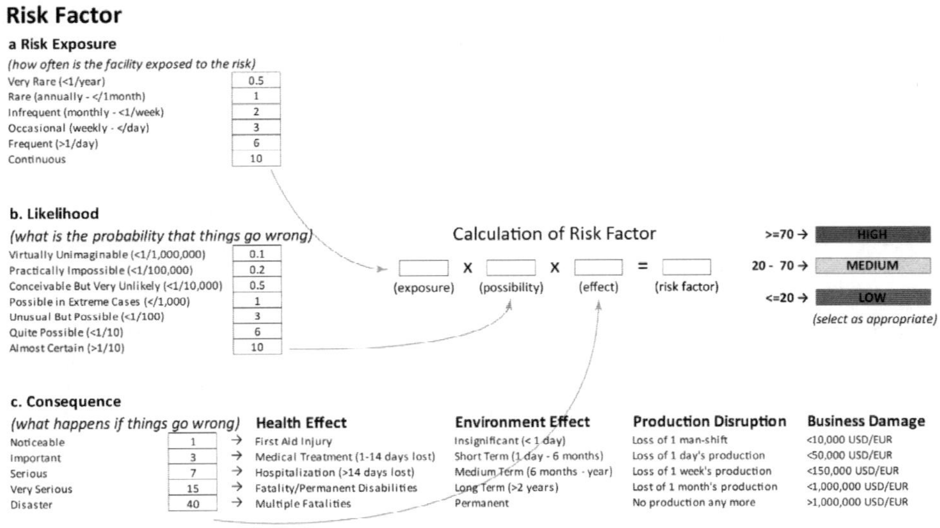

Figure 1. Risk Factors. By the Authors. Adapted from Enhesa. https://support.enhesa.com/hc/en-us/articles/360043232272-Fine-Kinney-Risk-Ranking-Methodology

3.3 Analytical Hierarchy Process Model

The Analytical Hierarchy Process model is a method for weighting and combining multiple goals or outcomes and multiple criteria in order to obtain weighted outcomes (Harker, 1989, 8). Risks are assessed using a risk classification scheme organizing risk factors according to categories, for example, 'acts of god', 'financial', 'design', etc., with subfactors being identified under each, forming a hierarchy (Mustafa and Al-Bahar, 1991, 48).

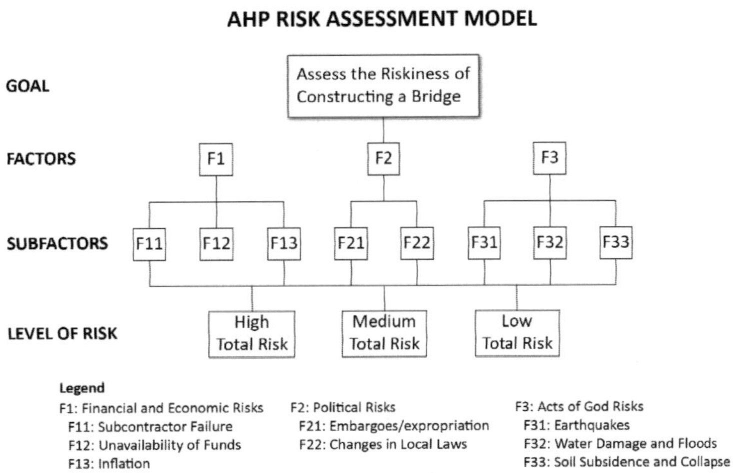

Figure 2. AHP Risk Assessment Model. By the authors. Adapted from Mustafa and Al-Bahar, 1991, 48

3.4 Risk Matrix

A risk matrix combines the first two elements of the Fine-Kinney model. For example, the U.S. Department of Defense describes it as follows: "Consistent predefined likelihood and consequence criteria provide a structured means for evaluating risks so decision makers and program office staff can make objective comparisons" (DOD, 2017, 23). Risks may be further weighted by other factors, for example, cost to mitigate (Ibid. 29). A red-yellow-green colour scheme is characteristically employed to illustrate the final risk score. A risk assessment may be combined with an 'opportunity management' calculation in order to weight benefits in addition (Ibid. 43).

Having the teacher perform the risk assessment as described by one of these three models will focus an understanding of their concerns and the basis for their objection.

4. VALIDATION

Studies such as the one described in this report are subject to the reliability and validity assessment to determine how well they measure the phenomena they are investigating; as commonly understood, reliability refers to the consistency of a measure, while validity refers to the accuracy of a measure. The measures surveyed here consider both aspects, and the list is drawn both from formal studies of research assessment (AERA, 2014) as well as literature related to more specific forms of assessment.

4.1 Content Validity

An assessment of content validity concerns the degree of correlation of test scores with external criteria (Cureton (1951) in Sireci, 1998, 88) and includes elements of content representativeness and content relevance (Messick, 1975) or process (Tenopyr, 1977).

Content validity involves assessing whether the questions in the survey cover the entire range of issues or concepts being studied. This is done by having subject matter experts review the survey questions to ensure that they are relevant, appropriate, and comprehensive (Olsen, 2010, 136).

4.2 Construct Validity

Construct validity is similar to content validity, though it refers specifically to the structure or construction of the concept intended to be measured. This construct may be depicted using a Rasch model, which defines how data should be structured in order to obtain measurements from it. In a Likert survey, where respondents the option that best describes their attitudes, beliefs, and experiences, the Rasch model measures such factors as the unidimensionality and local independence of those options (Yamashita, 2022, 4).

Construct validity may be assessed by testing the survey and comparing the results with established measures of the same concept. This may be represented as a mapping of the questions in the survey or questionnaire to the structure of the concept being measured, and determination that response options do not overlap or extend beyond the construct being measured.

4.3 Criterion Validity

Wikipedia defines criterion validity, or criterion-related validity, as "the extent to which an operationalization of a construct, such as a test, relates to, or predicts, a theoretical representation of the construct - the criterion". For example, if the test measures X as a barrier to Y, then in a model of the concept, the unmitigated presence of X would predict an absence of Y.

The American Educational Research Association (AERA, 2014, 29) recommends that "the description of each criterion variable should include evidence concerning its reliability, the extent to which it represents the intended construct (e.g., task performance on the job), and the extent to which it is likely to be influenced by extraneous sources of variance." In any systems model, this extent may be high. That is, to continue the example, the description considers additional or alternative explanations for the absence of Y.

Criterion validity involves comparing the survey results with another established measure of the same construct to ensure that they are consistent (Fink, 2010). For example, if a survey is measuring job satisfaction, the results could be compared with another established job satisfaction scale.

4.4 Test-Retest Reliability

Typically, test-retest reliability involves administering the survey twice to the same group of people and comparing the results to ensure that they are consistent. This is done to assess the stability of the survey over time. As AERSA (2014, 39) states, "The overall reliability/precision, given error variance due to the sampling of forms, occasions, and raters, can be estimated through a test-retest study involving different forms administered on different occasions and scored by different raters."

In some cases, it may be impractical to administer the same survey to the same people, as the application of the survey the first time may influence responses the second time, particularly when the survey is administered in the context of a focus group. In such a case, it may be sufficient to administer the same survey twice to the same type of people. The focus of test-retest is to assess the questions, not the specific individuals; "Information about random fluctuations in scores is essential for understanding the reliability of change scores—that is, for distinguishing random short-term score differences from true improvements or deteriorations over time" (Polit, 2014, 1714).

4.5 Internal Consistency

Internal consistency involves assessing the extent to which the questions in the survey are measuring the same construct. For example, if some questions are asking about the objective existence of an entity, and other questions are asking about a respondent's perceptions of an entity, the questions are not measuring the same construct. Assessment of internal consistency may be considered conceptually, as in the example just given, or by using statistical techniques such as coefficient alpha to assess the inter-correlation between the survey items (Cronbach, 1951).

The coefficient alpha is "an internal-consistency reliability coefficient based on the number of parts into which a test is partitioned (e.g., items, subtests, or raters), the interrelationships of the parts, and the total test score variance." It is also called Cronbach's alpha and, for dichotomous items, KR-20 (AERA 2014 217). The internal-consistency coefficient is "an index of the reliability of test scores derived from the statistical interrelationships among item responses or scores on separate parts of a test" (AERA 2014 220).

To assess the internal-consistency coefficient a method such as the split-halves method may be employed, where "scores on two more-or-less parallel halves of the test (e.g., odd-numbered items and even-numbered items) are correlated, and the resulting half-test reliability coefficient is statistically adjusted to estimate reliability for the full-length test" (AERA 2014 35-36).

5. DISCUSSION

This paper survey three major sets of factors related to the assessment of barriers to technology acceptance. While it does not set out to prescribe any particular approach or set of survey questions, it identifies major parameters such studies should encompass. The first section reviewed the progress of technology acceptance models, cumulating with UTAUT, and the need to consider performance expectancy, effort expectancy, and social influence along with two direct determinants of usage behavior: intention and facilitating conditions. It also detailed the construction of a risk matrix and a method for weighting and combining multiple goals or outcomes and multiple criteria. Finally, it considered several methods for survey instrument validation to ensure all and only factors related to technology acceptance are measured.

Though these sets of considerations are well-known by those with experience in the field, it is unusual to see all these sets of factors considered in published studies of teacher and student attitudes with respect to the adoption of new technology. Hence, they are collected here and offered as a model for the assessment of surveys and studies of technology adoption.

REFERENCES

American Educational Research Association (AERA). (2014). Standards for Educational and Psychological Testing. https://www.testingstandards.net/uploads/7/6/6/4/76643089/9780935302356.pdf

Bandura, A., Ross, D., & Ross, S. A. (1963). Vicarious reinforcement and imitative learning. The Journal of Abnormal and Social Psychology, 67(6), 601–607. doi:10.1037/h0045550

Bandura A. (2001). Social cognitive theory: an agentic perspective. Annual Review of Psychology. 2001;52:1-26. doi: 10.1146/annurev.psych.52.1.1. PMID: 11148297.

Cronbach, Lee J. (1951). "Coefficient alpha and the internal structure of tests". Psychometrika. Springer Science and Business Media LLC. 16., 3): 297–334. https://link.springer.com/article/10.1007/BF02310555

Davis, F. D. (1989), "Perceived usefulness, perceived ease of use, and user acceptance of information technology", MIS Quarterly, 13, 3): 319–340. https://www.jstor.org/stable/249008

Department of Defense (DED), U.S. (2017). Department of Defense Risk, Issue, and Opportunity Management Guide for Defense Acquisition Program. https://web.archive.org/web/20170704192215/https://www.acq.osd.mil/se/docs/2017-RIO.pdf#page=36

Fine, W. T. (1971). Mathematical evaluations for controlling hazards. Journal of Safety Research, 3(4), 157–166. https://apps.dtic.mil/sti/citations/AD0722011

Fink, A. (2010). Survey Research Methods. In International Encyclopedia of Education, Third Edition, Penelope Peterson, Eva Baker, Barry McGaw, eds., pp. 152-160. Elsevier. https://doi.org/10.1016/B978-0-08-044894-7.00296-7

Granić, A. (2023). Technology Acceptance and Adoption in Education. In: Zawacki-Richter, O., Jung, I., eds) Handbook of Open, Distance and Digital Education. Springer, Singapore. https://doi.org/10.1007/978-981-19-2080-6_11

Harker, P. (1989). The Art and Science of Decision Making: The Analytic Hierarchy Process. In The Analytic Hierarchy Process, pp.3-36. Springer-Verlag, Editors: Bruce L. Golden, Edward A. Wasil, Patrick T. Harker. https://www.researchgate.net/publication/263735008_The_Art_and_Science_of_Decision_Making_The_Analytic_Hierarchy_Process

Kinney, G. F., & Wiruth, A. D. (1976). Practical risk analysis for safety management, pp. 1–20. Naval Weapons Center. https://apps.dtic.mil/sti/citations/ADA027189

Kokangül, A., Polat, U., and Dağsuyu, C. (2017). A new approximation for risk assessment using the AHP and Fine Kinney methodologies. Safety Science, Volume 91, 2017, 24-32. https://doi.org/10.1016/j.ssci.2016.07.015

Messick, S. (1975). The standard problem: Meaning and values in measurement and evaluation. American Psychologist, 30(10), 955–966. https://doi.org/10.1037/0003-066X.30.10.955

Mustafa, M. A. and Al-Bahar, J. F. (1991). Project risk assessment using the analytic hierarchy process. IEEE Transactions on Engineering Management, vol. 38, no. 1, 46-52, Feb. 1991, doi: 10.1109/17.65759. https://ieeexplore.ieee.org/document/65759

Olson, K., Lannan, K., Cumming, J., MacGillivary, H. & Richards, K. (2020). The Concerns-Based Adoption Model and Strategic Plan Evaluation: Multiple Methodologies to Understand Complex Change. Educational Research: Theory and Practice, 31(3), 49-58. https://files.eric.ed.gov/fulltext/EJ1274351.pdf

Polit, D.F. (2014). Getting serious about test–retest reliability: a critique of retest research and some recommendations. Quality of Life Research 23, 1713–1720. https://doi.org/10.1007/s11136-014-0632-9

Reid, P. (2014). Categories for barriers to adoption of instructional technologies. Education and Information Technologies 19:383–407. DOI 10.1007/s10639-012-9222-z. Published online: 11 November 2012. Springer Science+Business Media New York 2012.

Sireci, S.G. (1998) The Construct of Content Validity. Social Indicators Research, Vol. 45, No. 1/3, Validity Theory and the Methods Used in Validation: Perspectives from Social and Behavioral Sciences, Nov., 1998), pp. 83-117. https://www.jstor.org/stable/27522338

Sträub, E.T. (2009). Understanding Technology Adoption: Theory and Future Directions for Informal Learning. Review of Educational Research, June 2009, Vol. 79, No. 2, pp. 625-649. D01: 10.3102/0034654308325896

Taylor, S. and Todd, P.A. (1995). Understanding Information Technology Usage: A Test of Competing Models. Information Systems Research, Vol. 6, No. 2, JUNE 1995), pp. 144-176.

Tenopyr, M. L. (1977). Content-construct confusion. Personnel Psychology, 30(1), 47–54. https://doi.org/10.1111/j.1744-6570.1977.tb02320.x

Venkatesh, V., Morris, M., Davis, G., and Davis, F. (2003). User Acceptance of Information Technology: Toward a Unified View. MIS Quarterly Vol. 27 No. 3, pp. 425-478. https://www.academia.edu/72868491/User_Acceptance_of_Information_Technology_Toward_a_Unified_View

Yamashita, T. (2022). Analyzing Likert scale surveys with Rasch models. Research Methods in Applied Linguistics, Volume 1, Issue 3, 2022, 100022, ISSN 2772-7661. https://doi.org/10.1016/j.rmal.2022.100022

MEASURING COMPUTATIONAL THINKING – DEVELOPING A SHORT PERFORMANCE TEST FOR HIGHER EDUCATION

Josef Guggemos[1*], Roman Rietsche[2*], Stephan Aier[3], Jannis Strecker[3] and Simon Mayer[3]
[1]*Department of Vocational Education and Training, University of Education Schwäbisch Gmünd, Germany*
[2]*Institute for Digital Technology Management, Bern University of Applied Sciences, Switzerland*
[3]*School of Computer Science, University of St.Gallen, Switzerland*
**Josef Guggemos and Roman Rietsche contributed equally*

ABSTRACT

Technological advancements, particularly in artificial intelligence, significantly transform our society and work practices. Computational thinking (CT) has emerged as a crucial 21st-century skill, enabling individuals to solve problems more effectively through an automation-oriented perspective and fundamental concepts of computer science. To ensure the effective integration of CT into educational curricula, it is crucial to develop efficient assessment frameworks that allow teachers to measure and promote student CT proficiency. Therefore, our aim is to develop a short test to measure CT among undergraduate students. To this end, we consider two performance tests: the Computational Thinking test (CTt) and the Algorithmic Thinking Test for Adults (ATTA). We use items from both instruments to compile a short test. Based on a sample of 290 second-year non-computer science undergraduate students, we provide evidence on the quality of our test. Besides classical test theory, we apply item response theory, namely Rasch modeling, and confirmatory factor analysis. Our test shows favorable properties, e.g., Cronbach's alpha > .75, and may be suitable for the efficient assessment of CT across higher education programs.

KEYWORDS

Computational Thinking, Assessment, Rasch-scaling, Performance Test, Higher Education

1. INTRODUCTION

Far-reaching technological changes are shaping our society and ways of working (Zhang et al., 2024). Key drivers for these changes are advances in the field of computing (Wing, 2008). From an educational point of view, it is vital to determine and develop the skills necessary for success in such an environment. Among others, computational thinking (CT) is regarded as a key 21st-century skill (Voogt et al., 2015; Wing, 2006). Wing conceptualized CT as "solving problems, designing systems, and understanding human behavior, by drawing on the concepts fundamental to computer science" (2006, p. 33).

Much research has been carried out on CT in K–12 settings (Lu et al., 2022). This includes conceptualizations and delineations of CT (Shute et al., 2017), CT instruction (Hsu et al., 2018), and CT assessment (Tang et al., 2020). Although there is substantial evidence regarding CT in K–12 settings, research on CT in higher education is only gradually evolving (Zhang et al., 2024). Higher education should contribute to student employability (Cheng et al., 2022; Lu et al., 2022). Hence, in an increasingly digital environment, CT may be important to achieve this goal (ISTE, 2015).

A prerequisite for quantitative CT research (in higher education) are assessment instruments that can capture a student's level of CT and track its development (Lye & Koh, 2014). In comparison to self-assessments, that are subjective by nature, test instruments (tests) have the advantage that they objectively measure performance instead of self-efficacy (Lafuente Martínez et al., 2022). They offer an upper bound for students' actual proficiency (Bühner, 2011). CT tests are available for K–12 and adults (Lafuente Martínez et al., 2022; Román-González et al., 2017; Zhang et al., 2024); however, studies on the assessment of CT in higher education primarily address computer science students (Lu et al., 2022). Hence, these tests may not be well-suited for students in other domains because they may be too difficult for such students.

Beyond its research applications, assessing student CT proficiency at the start of a course offers substantial benefits. It enables instruction tailored to individual learning needs, allowing lecturers to allocate their limited time more efficiently to students who require additional support. Moreover, tutors could focus on those students with lower test scores. Such measures can support study success (Ifenthaler & Yau, 2020). However, test time is often an issue in higher education (Schlax et al., 2020). Current CT tests typically require a minimum of 45 minutes to complete. Administering both a pre-test and a post-test would necessitate dedicating time equivalent to an entire lecture. This may be impractical within the constraints of a standard course schedule. Overall, there is a need for a short test to assess the CT proficiency of students in higher education outside the disciplines of STEM. Against this background, we raise the following research question:

RQ: How can the computational thinking proficiency of undergraduate students be tested efficiently?

To answer this question, section two reviews the conceptual basis of CT, the state of CT research in higher education, and suitable CT tests. We do not consider instruments for large-scale assessment, like the International Computer and Information Literacy Study (ICILS) (Fraillon et al., 2019). Instead, we focus on freely available tests that researchers and educators may use to measure CT in higher education. Due to the importance of CT interventional studies in higher education (Jong & Jeuring, 2020), instruments should be suitable for pre-post, or longitudinal designs. Section three presents our method and sample. Section four discusses the results.

Our research makes three substantial contributions. First, we offer a validated short test that efficiently assesses CT. This means it achieves an internal consistency reliability greater than .75 with only 11 dichotomous items. Second, we provide empirical evidence that our test items are suitable for undergraduate students in the social sciences, i.e., non-STEM. Third, our test ensures fairness and non-discrimination in CT assessment in terms of gender, which is essential for equitable education and research.

2. STATE OF THE ART

2.1 Computational Thinking

A core set of CT facets can be identified that specifies this concept (Lyon & Magana, 2020; Shute et al., 2017). Table 1 summarizes this core set.

Table 1. Core facets of CT

Abstraction	"simplifying from the concrete to the general as solutions are developed" (Barr & Stephenson, 2011, p. 52)
Algorithmic thinking	using "a step-by-step procedure for taking input and producing some desired output" (Wing, 2008, p. 3718)
Automation	"process in which a computer is instructed to execute a set of repetitive tasks quickly and efficiently compared to the processing power of a human" (Lee et al., 2011, p. 33)
Decomposition	"breaking problems down into smaller parts that may be more easily solved" (Barr & Stephenson, 2011, p. 52)
Debugging	"find your own mistakes and fix them" (Hsu et al., 2018, p. 299)
Generalization	"move from specific to broader applicability" (Selby & Woollard, 2013, p. 4)

2.2 Computational Thinking in Higher Education

Literature reviews are available about CT in higher education, in general, and about CT assessment, in particular.

Jong and Jeuring (2020) reviewed 49 articles that examine various interventions aimed at developing CT skills in students. The authors identified the types of interventions, their effectiveness, and how they are evaluated. They found that CT is often taught through programming assignments and that the interventions are evaluated in diverse ways, making comparisons of the findings challenging. Additionally, they noted that interventions are rarely adapted to students' actual proficiency levels. The authors suggest using standardized instruments for evaluating effectiveness and better aligning interventions with students' proficiency levels.

Lyon and Magana (2020) reviewed 13 studies. They analyzed the pedagogical designs and research methods used. The review highlights the need for more research on how students get involved in CT processes or how teaching can improve CT in undergraduate students. Many of the reviewed studies report the positive effects of interventions used to foster CT. However, these studies regularly rely on self-reported metrics. The authors stress the importance of robust definitions and sound measurement instruments to evaluate CT interventions in higher education. Their work emphasizes the growing interest in CT research in higher education.

Lu et al. (2022) reviewed 33 studies about CT assessment in higher education. Most studies targeted undergraduate students, particularly those majoring in computer science. Other groups include in-service teachers and students from various STEM fields, indicating a strong emphasis on technical disciplines. They categorized CT assessment types, including block-based assessments, knowledge/skill tests, self-assessments, text-based programming projects, and academic achievements in computer science courses. Interviews and observations were also utilized to assess CT. The review highlighted challenges in distinguishing between computational thinking skills and computer science skills, with some studies confounding the two. The review identified a need for CT assessments in higher education with an emphasis on research that develops validated assessment instruments.

Zhang et al. (2024) performed a meta-review comprising 11 literature reviews about CT assessment. The major finding of this study is that there is an increase in the number of studies about CT assessment in higher education. A plethora of constructs is available to be included in CT assessments. However, no systematic investigation of the tools or instruments exists regarding the nature of the constructs being assessed. Although there is an (increasing) interest in CT assessment in higher education, issues remain about the methodological rigor and systematic evaluation of interventions.

2.3 Computational Thinking Tests

Shute et al. (2017) point to the Computational Thinking test (CTt) as an internationally established standardized CT assessment instrument. Román-González et al. (2017, 2018) have developed and validated a CTt for secondary students. The authors rely on the CT framework of Brennan and Resnick (2012). It is consistent with the core CT facets (see Table 1). *Abstraction* is covered as visual code blocks representing the problems, including conditionals and variables. *Algorithmic thinking* is necessary because all tasks require sequencing steps to come to a solution. *Automation* is captured by means of loops. *Decomposition* manifests itself in the use of functions to split up the problems into more manageable elements. *Debugging* is necessary because students are required to identify mistakes in provided sequences of code blocks. *Generalization*, however, is not directly addressed by the CTt. For assembling visual code blocks, the authors utilize the *code.org* platform (https://code.org/), which is similar to Scratch (Hsu et al., 2018, p. 302). The test comprises 28 selected response items, can be taken online, and takes about 45 minutes. No programming experience is necessary, which makes this CTt a very flexible instrument. The authors validated their CTt using a sample of 1,251 Spanish 5th to 10th grade students and classical test theory. The reliability of the test is sufficiently high (Cronbach's alpha = .79). Evidence for the suitability of pre-post designs is available (Zhao & Shute, 2019).

In addition to the large amount of time required for the CTt, its main drawback may be that the items are too easy for higher education students. Guggemos et al. (2019) developed a version of the CTt, comprising 26 items, geared towards upper-secondary level students. Five easy items of the initial CTt version were replaced by five more difficult ones. The authors validated the test using 202 students from upper secondary education. They demonstrated Rasch scalability of their CTt version (including unidimensionality) and reported a WLE-reliability of 0.81. Moreover, a proficiency level model was presented, with which the difficulty of items can be predicted. This facilitates the development of new items with a desired difficulty based on validated difficulty drivers (e.g., conditionals and functions). Evidence for the suitability of the test for longitudinal studies is available (Guggemos, 2021). Although this test yields compelling psychometric characteristics, several items may be too easy for higher education students. This is problematic because for a short CT test, a good fit between proficiency and item difficulty is important (Bühner, 2011).

Lafuente Martínez et al. (2022) developed and validated an Algorithmic Thinking Test for Adults (ATTA) following internationally accepted standards (AERA et al., 2014). The ATTA covers core CT facets (see Table 1): Algorithmic thinking, decomposition, abstraction, pattern recognition, and debugging. It is suitable for assessing people with or without content knowledge about computer science and coding skills in post-secondary education settings. The required test time is about 70 minutes. Cronbach's alpha equals .84. The authors also performed confirmatory factor analyses and concluded the unidimensionality of the ATTA. A drawback of the ATTA may be that it is overall too difficult for undergraduate students in fields outside of STEM. Moreover, the required test time of about 70 minutes for the full version may be a drawback in tertiary education settings.

In summary, combining items from the CTt version for upper-secondary level students (Guggemos et al., 2023) with items from the ATTA may be a good approach for compiling a short test for undergraduate students. The combination may be possible because both tests cover implicitly (CTt) and explicitly (ATTA) the core CT facets (see Table 1). Selecting items from both tests might yield a set of items with a good fit between item difficulty and student proficiency.

3. METHOD

3.1 Compiling the Test

Both the CTt and ATTA have been shown to be unidimensional. Hence, on the content level, all items from either the CTt or ATTA would be suitable for a short CT test. However, the item that elicits the most information about a student's proficiency has an expected probability of a correct answer of 50% (Bühner, 2011). In the Wright map, this is represented by the same Logit value for a person as well as an item. The authors screened the CTt and ATTA items and their reported difficulty (Guggemos et al., 2023; Lafuente Martínez et al., 2022). In combination with data on drivers for item difficulty in CT (Guggemos et al., 2023), a good ex-ante approximation of item difficulty may be possible. Since student CT proficiency substantially varies, a sufficiently broad spectrum of items is necessary. In Rasch modeling, Logit values usually range between ± 2 Logit (Boone, 2016). Using a step of 0.25 Logit, in an optimal case, 17 items would cover the entire proficiency spectrum (± 2 Logit). Overall, we selected 18 items based on predicted item difficulty and predicted student CT proficiency.

3.2 Sample and Data Collection

Overall, 290 second-year students from the course "Fundamentals and Methods of Computer Science for Business Studies" at the University of St.Gallen act as a sample. The sample size is sufficient for Rasch modeling (Şahin & Anıl, 2017). The course aims to provide students with foundational knowledge and practical skills in computer science, covering programming, databases, web applications, networking, data science, and machine learning. It follows a structured setup that includes graded weekly quizzes, assignments, project work, and close tutorial support.

Data collection was performed at the beginning of the semester. Prior to performing the test, we collected data on the characteristics of the students. On average, the students were 23.34 years old (SD = 2.22, min = 20, max = 32), and 40% identified themselves as female. We also asked the participants to self-assess their skills in various areas on a ten-point scale: computer skills (M = 4.76, SD = 2.10), programming skills (M = 2.36, 1.86), mathematical skills (6.00, SD = 1.84), English skills (7.65, SD = 1.51), and native language skills (M = 9.11, SD 1.10). During the course's first lecture, the students were asked to perform the test. The lecturer supervised the students and ensured an adequate test environment. The test time was 20 minutes.

To collect the data, we used our own developed multiple-choice assessment and feedback application (LOOM), which over 2000 students have used over the past five years (Rietsche et al., 2018; Ritz et al., 2023). We selected this app because it provides an integrated end-to-end process with a high-quality user experience for various test items.

We used two testlets. Students were randomly assigned to the testlets ($n_1 = 149$, $n_2 = 141$). Each group performed seven unique items, and four anchor items that were identical in both groups, resulting in 11 items per student and, overall, 18 items for both groups (7 + 7 + 4). The items were presented to the students in random order. The anchor items permit locating all the students and items on one logit scale (Boone, 2016). All items are in English and are available here: https://tinyurl.com/yhf6jca8. Figure 1 shows the easiest item (item 14) and Figure 2, the most difficult one (item 18).

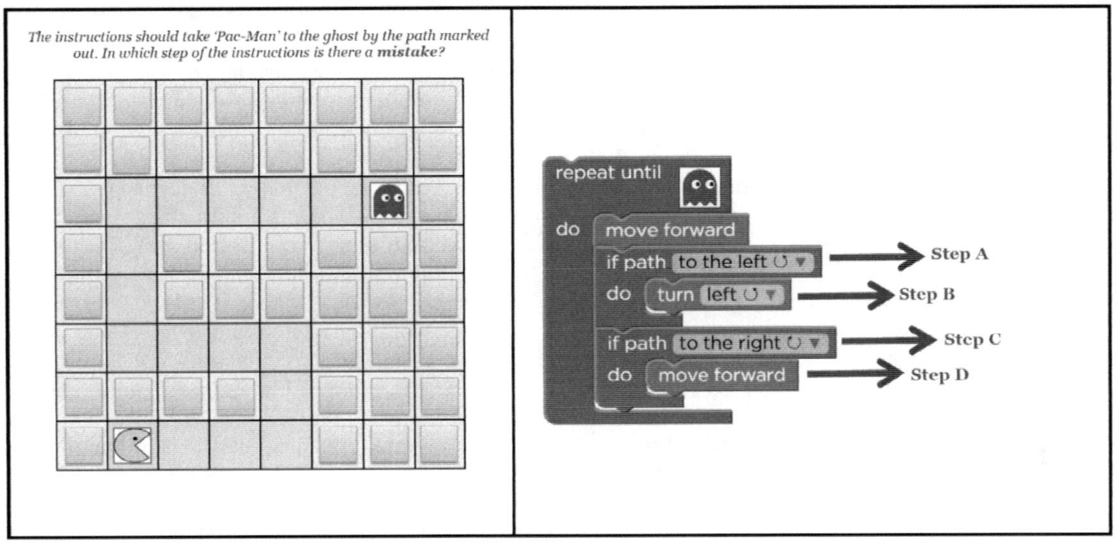

Correct answer: Step D.

Figure 1. Item 14 from the test (taken from the CTt)

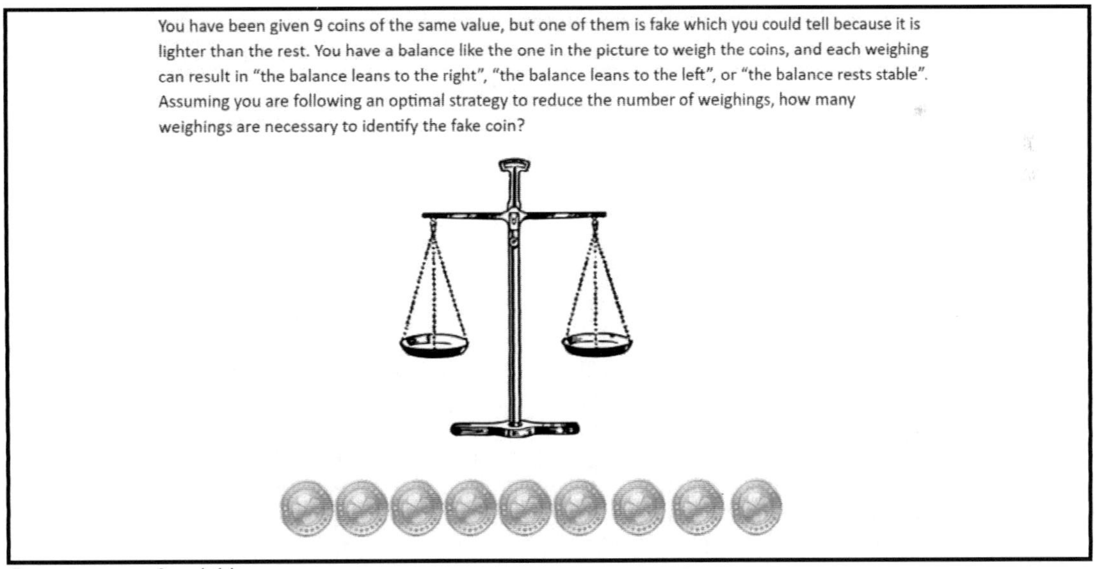

Correct answer: 2 weighings.

Figure 2. Item 18 from the test (taken from the ATTA)

3.3 Psychometric Test Validation

Due to the favorable characteristic of specific objectivity, we aim at Rasch modeling. This aligns with Zhang et al. (2024), who call for more rigor in research about CT assessment. The main advantage of Rasch modeling is that students (proficiency) and items (difficulty) can be located on a common (Logit) scale that allows for a criterion-referenced test interpretation (Hartig & Frey, 2013). For assessing Rasch scalability and the quality of our test, we rely on the recommendations of Boone (2006). We use a Wright map to evaluate the fit between item difficulty and student CT proficiency. Based on differential item functioning (DIF) analyses, we identify items that may discriminate specific sub-groups (AERA et al., 2014). We use gender (male/female) and the median of students' self-reported skills, e.g., mathematical and programming skills, as split criteria. Based on the median of each self-assessed skill, we form two groups: above-median students and the remainder. We regard DIF less than .43 Logit as negligible, between .44 and .64 as moderate, and greater than .65 as large (Penfield & Algina, 2006).

To check for item homogeneity (unidimensionality), we conduct confirmatory factor analysis ('lavaan' 0.6-18 package in R, Rosseel, 2012) with CT as a single factor. We use a robust maximum likelihood estimator. This, compared to a weighted least squares estimator, allows us to consider missing data by design. The following values serve as cut-off values (van de Schoot et al., 2012): acceptable fit: CFI and TLI >0.90, RMSEA <0.08, SRMR <0.10; good fit: CFI and TLI >0.95, RMSEA <0.05, SRMR <0.06. Since we combined two instruments, we specifically check if a two-dimensional model with the CTt and ATTA as factors fits the data better than a unidimensional model. To compare the competing models, we use the Haughton Bayesian information criterion (HBIC) and the SPBIC variant that is based on a scaled unit information prior and hence more general than the BIC (Lin et al., 2017).

After having checked Rasch scalability, we examine if the items meet the cut-off values applied in the PISA studies (OECD, 2017, pp. 131–134) using the R package 'TAM 4.2-21' (Robitzsch et al., 2024): The deviance from the item discrimination implied by the Rasch model is evaluated utilizing weighted mean square error (wMNSQ = Infit). It should lie between 0.8 and 1.2. The point-biserial correlation should be above 0.30. The percentage of correct answers should fall between 20% and 90%. Not more than 10% of missing data should be present.

Finally, we provide EAP/PV- and WLE-reliability as a measure for overall test reliability from the item response theory context. To ensure comparability with available test instruments, we also report Cronbach's alpha and McDonald omega total from classical test theory; these values should be greater than .70 (Sarstedt et al., 2023).

4. RESULTS

4.1 Psychometric Validity

Table 2 summarizes the characteristics of the test items. The standard deviation of the students' CT proficiency equals 1.60 Logit (mean standardized to zero), with a minimum of -3.61 and a maximum of 3.97 Logit. The mean item difficulty is 0.32 Logit (SD = 1.09). This, and the Wright map (see Figure 3), point to a good fit of item difficulty and CT proficiency. Concerning DIF effects, only negligible DIF appears for gender. However, there are, in parts, large DIF effects in terms of students' self-assessed skills.

The assumption of item homogeneity (unidimensionality) of the test is justified: SB–$\chi^2(144) = 48.67$ ($p = .291$), CFI = 0.984, TLI = 0.980, RMSEA = 0.026, SRMR = 0.049. The non-significant χ^2-test and the fit values point to a good fit. This might also indicate local stochastic independence of the items. A two-dimensional model with the CTt and ATTA as factors fits worse than the one-dimensional model (when considering model complexity): SPBIC = 2,487 and HBIC = 2,417 vs. SPBIC = 3,693 and HBIC = 3,579. Moreover, the latent correlation between the ATTA and CTt equals .941, i.e., these factors can hardly be empirically separated.

Concerning the cut-off values from the PISA studies, in general, all items show good values (see Table 2). The wMNSQ lies between 0.85 and 1.20. The point-biseral correlations are higher than 0.30, except for item 18 (see Figure 2), which is by far the most difficult item. The percentage of correct answers for the items lies between 0.759 and 0.215, again except for item 18 (0.121). Moreover, item 7 is also slightly too difficult (0.195). Every student fully processed the items, i.e., the proportion of missing values is smaller than 10%. EAP/PV-reliability equals 0.77, and WLE-reliability 0.69. For the first testlet, Cronbach's alpha equals .77 and McDonald's omega total .80. For the second testlet, the values are .75 and .78, respectively. Hence, a short test with 11 items may yield a sufficient reliability for research purposes (>.70).

Table 2. Item difficulty, fit, and DIF-effects of the test (testlet design with two testlets with $n_1 = 141$ and $n_2 = 149$)

						DIF effect					
Item	θ	s.e. θ	wMNSQ	Pt.bis.	P+	Female	Comp.	Prog.	Native	English	Math
1	1.105	0.200	1.002	0.485	0.309	-0.304	0.045	**-1.042**	0.162	-0.275	0.019
2	0.064	0.190	0.916	0.616	0.497	-0.035	-0.028	0.300	-0.355	-0.094	0.093
3	-0.412	0.194	1.016	0.574	0.584	-0.110	-0.376	-0.206	0.247	*-0.596*	**0.919**
4	0.607	0.192	1.116	0.449	0.396	0.366	0.298	-0.421	-0.273	-0.172	-0.058
5*	-0.866	0.145	0.946	0.616	0.662	-0.251	0.128	**0.697**	-0.098	0.010	0.225
6*	0.273	0.136	0.978	0.560	0.459	0.264	0.431	0.300	-0.217	*-0.584*	-0.316
7	1.871	0.228	1.201	0.273	0.195	0.197	0.383	-0.306	-0.343	-0.107	-0.252
8	1.720	0.221	1.016	0.437	0.215	-0.047	0.038	**-0.629**	0.348	*-0.689*	*-0.457*
9	0.461	0.191	1.093	0.484	0.423	-0.432	-1.517	*-0.485*	-0.196	-0.268	**0.677**
10*	-1.290	0.154	0.845	0.684	0.728	0.084	-0.340	0.117	0.160	0.160	-0.341
11*	-0.231	0.138	1.006	0.565	0.552	-0.089	**0.850**	0.234	0.318	-0.316	0.211
12	-0.275	0.198	1.049	0.553	0.560	0.205	-0.385	0.174	*0.521*	**-0.715**	0.275
13	-0.555	0.202	0.862	0.662	0.610	0.224	*0.529*	0.428	*-0.557*	**-0.889**	-0.408
14	-1.516	0.230	0.845	0.666	0.759	-0.020	-0.141	**-0.896**	-0.216	**0.668**	*-0.490*
15	0.733	0.200	1.053	0.504	0.376	0.308	0.427	*0.518*	**0.986**	0.119	0.168
16	0.498	0.197	1.099	0.482	0.418	0.300	-0.166	-0.147	*0.480*	0.005	**-1.020**
17	0.895	0.202	1.052	0.474	0.348	-0.266	-0.250	0.165	**-1.364**	**-0.857**	*-0.530*
18	2.583	0.281	1.157	0.253	0.121	-0.395	0.075	**1.199**	0.395	**4.599**	**1.287**
Min	-1.516	0.136	0.845	0.253	0.121	-0.432	-1.517	-1.042	-1.364	-0.889	-1.020
Max	2.583	0.281	1.201	0.684	0.759	0.366	0.850	1.199	0.986	4.599	1.287

Note. Items in bold are from the ATTA (7-11, 16-18) and all other items are from the CTt. Items marked with an asterisk are anchoring items. DIF effects in italic are moderate, DIF effects in bold are large.
θ = difficulty, s.e. = standard error, wMNSQ = weighted mean square error, Pt.bis. = point biserial correlation, P+ = correct responses.

5. DISCUSSION

This research addresses a critical gap in CT research within higher education, particularly for non-STEM students, by developing an efficient assessment environment. By doing so, this study contributes to the better assessment and tracking of factors that are relevant in enhancing student employability and participation in an increasingly digital society. To this end, we used items from the CTt that is aimed at (upper) secondary level students, as well as the ATTA that addresses adults.

The students in the sample show a very broad proficiency spectrum ranging from -3.61 to 3.97 Logit. Usually, Logit values range between ± 2 Logit (Boone, 2016). This shows the challenge to develop a test with items of suitable difficulty for all students. To illustrate the range: An item that students with medium proficiency (Logit = 0) solve with an expected probability of 50% is solved by the top performers with an expected probability of 98%. The worst-performing students solve this item with an expected probability of 3%. As performance cannot be manipulated by the test takers towards a higher test score (providing a valid test procedure), the top-performing students may be indeed highly proficient in CT. The finding of a small proportion of students highly proficient in CT is consistent with the ICILS among secondary level students (Fraillon et al., 2019). The low-performing students may not necessarily be poor in CT. Since we tested the students in a low-stakes environment, a lack of test motivation may also explain their poor results (Simzar et al., 2015).

As the Wright map indicates, our set of 18 items meets the students' proficiency spectrum reasonably well. Except for the very high and very low performing students (>|2.0| Logit) there is, in general, an item included that could be solved with an expected probability of 50%. Hence, we were successful in developing an efficient test. Further items could be developed with an expected difficulty greater than 3.5 Logit to precisely measure CT among students with very high CT proficiency. To this end, further items from the ATTA could be used. More importantly, items may be necessary to precisely measure the CT of students with low CT proficiency (<-2.0 Logit). To this end, further items from the CTt can be used. The Wright map can also be utilized to set proficiency standards (Guggemos et al., 2023). If the standard, for instance, is 2.0 Logit, it may not be necessary to measure CT above this level with high precision; rather, in this case, it may be sufficient to ascertain that students are above this level.

Since there is not much room for improvement in terms of person-item fit, adaptive testing may be a viable option to achieve a desired precision with less test time (Chang, 2015). In this case, the item set is not tailored to a specific group but to the individual student. Our research may be a first step towards adaptive testing of CT as the test is, in general, Rasch scalable, which implies specific objectivity. However, considerably more items would be required for adaptive tests than is currently the case.

Logit	Student	Items
4.0		
	XXX	
3.5		
3.0		
2.5	XXXXXXXXX	**18**
2.0		
	XXXXXXXX	**7**
1.5	XXXXXXXXXXX	**8**
	XXXXXXXXXXXXXXXXXXXX	
1.0	XXXXXXXXXXXXXXXXXXXXXX	1
	XXXXXXXXXXXXXXXXXXXXXX	17
0.5	XXXXXXXXXXXXXXXXXXXXX	4 15
	XXXXXXXXXX	6 **9** **16**
0.0	XXXXXXXXXXXXXXXXXXXXXXXXXXXXXXXXXXXXXXXXXXXXXXXX	2
	XXXXXXXXXXXXXXXX	**11**
-0.5	XXXXXXXXXXXXXXXX	3 12
	XXXXXXXXXXXX	13
-1.0	XXXXXXXXXX	5
	XXXXXXXXXX	
-1.5	XXXXXXXX	**10**
	XXXX	14
-2.0		
	XXXXX	
-2.5	XXXXX	
-3.0		
-3.5	XXXXXXXXXXXXXXXXX	
	XXXXXXXXXXXXX	
-4.0		

Figure 3. Wright map. Items in bold are from the ATTA; all other items are from the CTt

Concerning the test evaluation, the remarkable DIF effects have to be mentioned. In particular, the DIF effect of item 18 for students with above-median self-reported English skills is noteworthy (DIF = 4.6 Logit). Item 18 is the most difficult one (2.6 Logit). No student with above-median self-reported English skills solved this item correctly, which explains the high DIF effect. The high difficulty of item 18 can also explain the DIF effects regarding self-reported programming and mathematical skills. Further, there is only negligible DIF in terms of gender. This is important because gender differences play an essential role in CT research (Torres-Torres et al., 2024).

Concerning the cut-off values applied in the PISA studies, the items are (almost) within range, except for item 18. The reason for this may be the high item difficulty in combination with the low item discrimination. High item difficulty is, in general, negatively associated with item discrimination (Bühner, 2011). Item 18 could have been removed. However, against the backdrop of the broad proficiency spectrum in our sample, we opted against removing this item.

As demonstrated, the CTt and ATTA are compatible. A unidimensional model yielded the best fit. Both tests are freely available (for research purposes), which allows researchers to cover a very broad CT proficiency spectrum by combining these two tests. This may be important for studies of CT development across the lifespan. Our research therefore opens up avenues for investigating the long-term impact of CT interventions and educational strategies, contributing to evidence-based practices in education. Our test may be particularly suitable for this endeavor as it does not require specific prior knowledge, such as a programming language.

Having demonstrated Rasch-scalability of the combined CTt and ATTA test, the proficiency level model of Guggemos et al. (2023) could be extended to higher education. Such a proficiency level model could help curriculum development and to communicate test results in higher education. Concerning curriculum development, it could be specified what kind of tasks with what cognitive operations students should be systematically able to master after an intervention. When communicating the test results, it could be stated the kind of cognitive operations the student is not able to master but which are required by the curriculum.

Regarding the CTt, Román-González et al. (2018) demonstrated the predictive validity for academic performance and instructional sensitivity. For the ATTA, such evidence is not available. Future research should investigate the predictive validity and instructional sensitivity of the ATTA or those of our test.

Although our test may be suitable for many purposes, we agree with Román-González et al. (2019) that only a combination of instruments may yield a comprehensive picture of CT. Our test may be complemented with self-assessment instruments that capture self-efficacy and can capture CT on a broader scale. Such an instrument may be the Computational Thinking Scales (see Guggemos et al., 2023).

6. CONCLUSION

Valid and economic test instruments are important for formative and summative assessment. We developed a short test for undergraduate students' computational thinking (CT). To this end, we combined the Computational Thinking test and the Algorithmic Thinking Test for Adults. Both performance tests cover generally accepted core facets of CT. Our test shows, in general, good psychometric properties, both in terms of classical test theory and item response theory. The fit between item difficulty and students' CT proficiency is good. The only weakness is some differential item functioning (DIF) effects concerning students' self-assessed skills, e.g., in mathematics. However, there is no substantial DIF concerning gender. All items are selected response and can, therefore, be coded in an economic and objective way. Overall, it may be a suitable instrument to test undergraduate students' CT skills with a reasonable amount of test time (about 20 minutes). Internal consistency reliability (Cronbach's alpha and McDonald's omega total) is greater than .75. In sum, our test may be valuable for research purposes as CT is an important 21st-century skill and may be considered in a variety of research designs. Moreover, our test can be used to ascertain the level of students' CT at the beginning of a course. The obtained information can help lecturers to tailor the course content and offer support to specific students.

REFERENCES

AERA, APA, & NCME. (2014). *Standards for educational and psychological testing*. American Educational Research Association. https://eric.ed.gov/?id=ED565876

Barr, V., & Stephenson, C. (2011). Bringing computational thinking to K-12. *ACM Inroads*, *2*(1), 48–54.

Boone, W. J. (2016). Rasch Analysis for Instrument Development: Why, When, and How? *CBE Life Sciences Education*, *15*(4). https://doi.org/10.1187/cbe.16-04-0148

Brennan, K., & Resnick, M. (2012). New frameworks for studying and assessing the development of computational thinking. *American Educational Research Association Meeting, Vancouver, BC, Canada*, 1–25.

Bühner, M. (2011). *Einführung in die Test- und Fragebogenkonstruktion [Introduction to test and questionnaire construction]* (3rd ed.). Pearson Studium.

Chang, H.-H. (2015). Psychometrics behind Computerized Adaptive Testing. *Psychometrika*, *80*(1), 1–20. https://doi.org/10.1007/s11336-014-9401-5

Cheng, M., Adekola, O., Albia, J., & Cai, S. (2022). Employability in higher education: a review of key stakeholders' perspectives. *Higher Education Evaluation and Development*, *16*(1), 16–31. https://doi.org/10.1108/HEED-03-2021-0025

Fraillon, J., Ainley, J., Schulz, W., Friedman, T., & Duckworth, D. (2019). *Preparing for life in a digital world: IEA International Computer and Information Literacy Study 2018 international report*. International Association for the Evaluation of Educational Achievement (IEA). https://www.iea.nl/publications/study-reports/preparing-life-digital-world

Guggemos, J. (2021). On the predictors of computational thinking and its growth at the high-school level. *Computers & Education*, *161*, 104060. https://doi.org/10.1016/j.compedu.2020.104060

Guggemos, J., Seufert, S., & Román-González, M. (2019). Measuring computational thinking - adapting a performance test and a self-assessment instrument for German-speaking countries. *Proceedings of the 16th International Conference Cognition and Exploratory Learning in the Digital Age (CELDA)*, 183–191. https://doi.org/10.33965/celda2019_201911L023

Guggemos, J., Seufert, S., & Román-González, M. (2023). Computational Thinking Assessment – Towards More Vivid Interpretations. *Technology, Knowledge and Learning*, *28*, 539–568. https://doi.org/10.1007/s10758-021-09587-2

Hartig, J., & Frey, A. (2013). Benefits and limitations of modeling competencies by means of Item Response Theory (IRT). *Zeitschrift Für Erziehungswissenschaft*, *16*(S1), 47–51. https://doi.org/10.1007/s11618-013-0386-0

Hsu, T.-C., Chang, S.-C., & Hung, Y.-T. (2018). How to learn and how to teach computational thinking: Suggestions based on a review of the literature. *Computers & Education*, *126*, 296–310. https://doi.org/10.1016/j.compedu.2018.07.004

Ifenthaler, D., & Yau, J. Y.-K. (2020). Utilising learning analytics to support study success in higher education: a systematic review. *Educational Technology Research and Development*, *68*(4), 1961–1990. https://doi.org/10.1007/s11423-020-09788-z

ISTE. (2015). *Computational thinking: leadership toolkit*. https://www.iste.org/computational-thinking

Jong, I. de, & Jeuring, J. (2020). Computational Thinking Interventions in Higher Education. In N. Falkner & O. Seppala (Eds.), *Koli Calling '20: Proceedings of the 20th Koli Calling International Conference on Computing Education Research* (pp. 1–10). ACM. https://doi.org/10.1145/3428029.3428055

Lafuente Martínez, M., Lévêque, O., Benítez, I., Hardebolle, C., & Zufferey, J. D. (2022). Assessing Computational Thinking: Development and Validation of the Algorithmic Thinking Test for Adults. *Journal of Educational Computing Research*, *60*(6), 1436–1463. https://doi.org/10.1177/07356331211057819

Lee, I., Martin, F., Denner, J., Coulter, B., Allan, W., Erickson, J., Malyn-Smith, J., & Werner, L. (2011). Computational thinking for youth in practice. *ACM Inroads*, *2*(1), 32. https://doi.org/10.1145/1929887.1929902

Lin, L.-C., Huang, P.-H., & Weng, L.-J. (2017). Selecting Path Models in SEM: A Comparison of Model Selection Criteria. *Structural Equation Modeling: A Multidisciplinary Journal*, *24*(6), 855–869. https://doi.org/10.1080/10705511.2017.1363652

Lu, C., Macdonald, R., Odell, B., Kokhan, V., Demmans Epp, C., & Cutumisu, M. (2022). A scoping review of computational thinking assessments in higher education. *Journal of Computing in Higher Education*, *34*(2), 416–461. https://doi.org/10.1007/s12528-021-09305-y

Lye, S. Y., & Koh, J. H. L. (2014). Review on teaching and learning of computational thinking through programming: What is next for K-12? *Computers in Human Behavior*, *41*, 51–61. https://doi.org/10.1016/j.chb.2014.09.012

Lyon, J. A., & Magana, J. A. (2020). Computational thinking in higher education: A review of the literature. *Computer Applications in Engineering Education*, *28*(5), 1174–1189. https://doi.org/10.1002/cae.22295

OECD. (2017). *PISA 2015 Technical Report*. OECD Publishing.

Penfield, R. D., & Algina, J. (2006). A generalized DIF effect variance estimator for measuring unsigned differential test functioning in mixed format tests. *Journal of Educational Measurement*, *43*(4), 295–312. https://doi.org/10.1111/j.1745-3984.2006.00018.x

Rietsche, R., Duss, K., Persch, J. M., & Söllner, M. (2018). Design and Evaluation of an IT-Based Formative Feedback Tool to Foster Student Performance. In *Thirty Ninth International Conference on Information Systems (ICIS),* San Francisco, CA, USA.

Ritz, E., Rietsche, R., & Leimeister, J. M. (2023). How to Support Students' Self-Regulated Learning in Times of Crisis: An Embedded Technology-Based Intervention in Blended Learning Pedagogies. *Academy of Management Learning & Education*, *22*(3), 357–382. https://doi.org/10.5465/amle.2022.0188

Robitzsch, A., Kiefer, T., & Wu, M. (2024). *Package 'TAM'.* https://cran.r-project.org/web/packages/TAM/TAM.pdf

Román-González, M., Moreno-León, J., & Robles, G. (2019). Combining assessment tools for a comprehensive evaluation of computational thinking interventions. In S. C. Kong & H. Abelson (Eds.), *Computational thinking education* (pp. 79–98). Springer. https://doi.org/10.1007/978-981-13-6528-7_6

Román-González, M., Pérez-González, J.-C., & Jiménez-Fernández, C. (2017). Which cognitive abilities underlie computational thinking? Criterion validity of the Computational Thinking Test. *Computers in Human Behavior*, *72*, 678–691. https://doi.org/10.1016/j.chb.2016.08.047

Román-González, M., Pérez-González, J.-C., Moreno-León, J., & Robles, G. (2018). Can computational talent be detected? Predictive validity of the Computational Thinking Test. *International Journal of Child-Computer Interaction*, *18*, 47–58. https://doi.org/10.1016/j.ijcci.2018.06.004

Rosseel, Y. (2012). lavaan: An R package for structural equation modeling. *Journal of Statistical Software*, *48*(2), 1–36. https://doi.org/10.18637/jss.v048.i02

Şahin, A., & Anıl, D. (2017). The Effects of Test Length and Sample Size on Item Parameters in Item Response Theory. *Educational Sciences: Theory & Practice*, *17*, 321–335. https://doi.org/10.12738/estp.2017.1.0270

Sarstedt, M., Hair, J. F., & Ringle, C. M. (2023). "PLS-SEM: indeed a silver bullet" – retrospective observations and recent advances. *Journal of Marketing Theory and Practice*, *31*(3), 261–275. https://doi.org/10.1080/10696679.2022.2056488

Schlax, J., Zlatkin-Troitschanskaia, O., Happ, R., Pant, H. A., Jitomirski, J., Kühling-Thees, C., Förster, M., & Brückner, S. (2020). Validity and fairness of a new entry diagnostics test in higher education economics. *Studies in Educational Evaluation*, *66*, 100900. https://doi.org/10.1016/j.stueduc.2020.100900

Selby, C. C., & Woollard, J. (2013). *Computational thinking: The developing definition.*

Shute, V. J., Sun, C., & Asbell-Clarke, J. (2017). Demystifying computational thinking. *Educational Research Review*, *22*, 142–158. https://doi.org/10.1016/j.edurev.2017.09.003

Simzar, R. M., Martinez, M., Rutherford, T., Domina, T., & Conley, A. M. (2015). Raising the stakes: How students' motivation for mathematics associates with high- and low-stakes test achievement. *Learning and Individual Differences*, *39*, 49–63. https://doi.org/10.1016/j.lindif.2015.03.002

Tang, X., Yin, Y., Lin, Q., Hadad, R., & Zhai, X. (2020). Assessing computational thinking: A systematic review of empirical studies. *Computers & Education*, *148*, 103798. https://doi.org/10.1016/j.compedu.2019.103798

Torres-Torres, Y.-D., Román-González, M., & Perez-Gonzalez, J.-C. (2024). Didactic strategies for the education of computational thinking from a gender perspective: A systematic review. *European Journal of Education*, *59*(2), Article e12640. https://doi.org/10.1111/ejed.12640

van de Schoot, R., Lugtig, P., & Hox, J. (2012). A checklist for testing measurement invariance. *European Journal of Developmental Psychology*, *9*(4), 486–492. https://doi.org/10.1080/17405629.2012.686740

Voogt, J., Fisser, P., Good, J., Mishra, P., & Yadav, A. (2015). Computational thinking in compulsory education: Towards an agenda for research and practice. *Education and Information Technologies*, *20*(4), 715–728. https://doi.org/10.1007/s10639-015-9412-6

Wing, J. M. (2006). Computational thinking. *Communications of the ACM*, *49*(3), 33–35. https://doi.org/10.1145/1118178.1118215

Wing, J. M. (2008). Computational thinking and thinking about computing. *Philosophical Transactions. Series A, Mathematical, Physical, and Engineering Sciences*, *366*(1881), 3717–3725. https://doi.org/10.1098/rsta.2008.0118

Zhang, X., Aivaloglou, F., & Specht, M. (2024). A Systematic Umbrella Review on Computational Thinking Assessment in Higher Education. *European Journal of STEM Education*, *9*(1), 1–13. https://doi.org/10.20897/ejsteme/14175

Zhao, W., & Shute, V. J. (2019). Can playing a video game foster computational thinking skills? *Computers & Education*, *141*, 103633. https://doi.org/10.1016/j.compedu.2019.103633

ADVANCING COLOUR PERCEPTION: EXPLORING YOUNG CHILDREN'S COLOUR DISCRIMINATION IN MIXED REALITY

Patrick Jost, Elias Berchtold and Sebastian Rangger

Human-Centred-Technologies Research Centre, FHV University of Applied Sciences, Dornbirn, Austria

ABSTRACT

One of the world's most famous pyramids is not located in Egypt but is on a music album cover by the band Pink Floyd. However, not a pyramid but a prism, the iconic image of a beam of light turning into a rainbow is a powerful symbol that captures the complexities of colour perception across cultures and individuals. This study examines how children can discern colour gradations in mixed reality (MR) environments, utilising the widely employed Farnsworth-Munsell 100 Hue Test. The MR version of the test, adapted for use with the Meta Quest 3, was evaluated with 52 children aged between 5 and 17 years. The results revealed significant differences in colour discrimination among age groups. Younger children had more difficulty distinguishing hues, particularly in the green-blue spectrum. The findings also demonstrate the applicability of MR-based colour assessments for younger children, providing a fast-screening alternative to traditional physical colour vision testing. The study's outcomes are conclusively synthesised, highlighting their implications for colour discrimination in educational settings.

KEYWORDS

Virtual Reality Color Vision Test, Mixed Reality, Children's Color Discrimination, Educational Technology, Farnsworth-Munsell Hue Test, Color Vision Screening

1. BACKGROUND AND RESEARCH AIMS

With the growing prevalence of mobile devices, screens, and VR/MR environments in daily life, many activities depend on digital representations. Musicians compose on tablets, children engage with digital textbooks, and meetings occur in virtual spaces. Studies show that head-mounted displays (HMDs) offer different colour rendering than traditional computer monitors or touchscreens. This is due to the proximity of the display to the user's eyes and the immersive nature of the experience (Toscani et al., 2019). For example, due to different viewing distances, a 24-inch Full HD monitor approximately corresponds to 63, a 4K monitor to 126, and the HMD Meta Quest 3, used in this study, to 20 pixels per degree. HMDs can also allow for specific control of external light with the video passthrough function, or even block environmental light entirely, which can influence colour perception differently from touchscreens and monitors (Siess et al., 2018).

Consequently, studying colour vision must extend to head-mounted displays (HMDs). Many jobs now require acute digital colour discrimination. In healthcare, accurate colour perception is crucial for diagnosis and interpreting colour-enhanced images (Ashton & Leppard, 2021; Brant & Helms, 2012). In transportation, it ensures safety by correctly interpreting digital signals (Blundell et al., 2020; Friedrich & Vollrath, 2022; Gibb et al., 2016; Mollon, 1982). The fashion industry relies on precise colour vision for quality control (Sekhri, 2022), and education benefits from understanding colour's impact on cognition and learning (Brooker & Franklin, 2016). Colour vision deficiency (CVD) affects about 1 in 12 boys and 1 in 200 girls worldwide (Birch, 2012; Gordon, 1998). Red-green colour blindness, the most common type, includes protanopia (lack of red photoreceptors) and deuteranopia (lack of green photoreceptors). Blue-yellow colour blindness (tritanopia) and complete colour blindness (achromatopsia) are rarer (Birch, 2012; Mollon, 1982; Paramei, 2012; Richardson et al., 2008). Given the impact of colour on learning (Brooker & Franklin, 2016; Duyan & Unver, 2016; Otto & Askov, 1968), this research focuses on colour discrimination skills in schoolchildren using mixed reality environments. The Farnsworth Munsell 100 Hue Test (FM100) is a key tool for assessing colour discrimination.

Used for over 70 years, it involves arranging 85 movable caps into a gradient to evaluate the ability to distinguish and arrange different shades of colour (Farnsworth, 1943) (Figure 1).

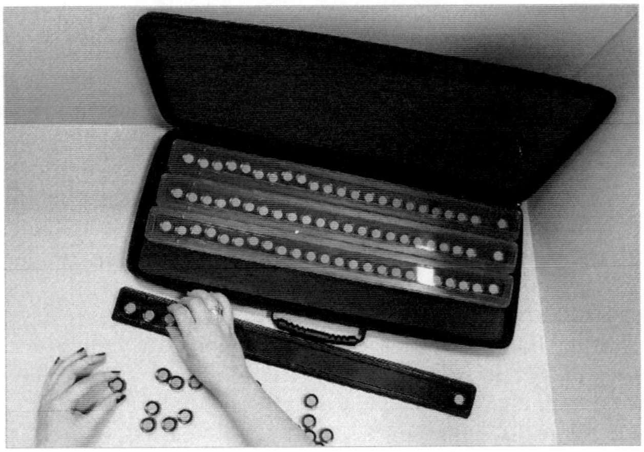

Figure 1. Physical Farnsworth–Munsell Hue Colour Vision Test. Courtesy of Gabriela P. (2019), Wikimedia Commons (CC BY 4.0)

The four colour gradient trays are (1) red-yellow, (2) yellow-green, (3) green-blue, and (4) blue-red. Many online versions of this test are simplified, using fewer than 20 hues per row. Widely used in industries to evaluate colour discrimination skills, the physical test serves as the basis for exploring mixed reality colour discrimination in schoolchildren.

1.1 Colour Discrimination in Children: Reality and Mixed Reality Environments

Understanding colour discrimination in children is critical, especially within educational settings where early cognitive and sensory development is paramount. Distinguishing between highly similar colours is necessary in various instructional contexts, such as fashion design education, where learners are required to recognise fine chromatic differences to develop harmonious palettes and achieve the desired visual effects (Quattrer et al., 2020), and in vision research utilising virtual reality environments, where colour accuracy and subtle variations in visual stimuli are essential for realistic perception and effective training (Ong et al., 2020; Toscani et al., 2019).

In this context, the physical FM100 test has been applied and studied across different age groups. Verriest et al. (1982) and Mäntyjärvi (2001) provided normative data indicating a developmental trajectory where colour discrimination abilities improve with age, peaking at around 19 years (Kinnear & Sahraie, 2002; Ling & Dain, 2018). The U-shaped performance curve identified by Kinnear and Sahraie (2002) reveals that colour discrimination improves from childhood, peaks in late adolescence, and declines in older age. This pattern underscores the need for age-specific colour discrimination assessment and intervention strategies. Additionally, the yellow-green and green-blue axes/trays have been found particularly challenging for children and adults, likely due to the physiological and perceptual properties of the human eye (Cranwell et al., 2015; Moreland, 1989). In educational contexts, colour is leveraged to enhance learning outcomes.

Cranwell et al. (2015) demonstrated that performance on the FM100 test is significantly related to nonverbal IQ, underscoring its cognitive demands. Research further indicates that strategically using colour in educational materials can improve memory retention and learning efficiency (Elliot & Maier, 2014; Witzel & Gegenfurtner, 2018). For example, Elliot (2015) and Kaya & Epps (2004) found that specific colours can influence cognitive performance and emotional states, impacting learning efficiency. Inclusivity in educational material design is crucial, incorporating high contrast, patterns, and other visual cues to accommodate variations in colour perception (Ali et al., 2021; Sushil et al., 2017). CVD studies highlight the importance of early screening to ensure that children are not disadvantaged in tasks requiring accurate colour perception (Chandak et al., 2017; Karunanayake et al., 2021). Adaptive learning strategies that recognise these variations allow educators to tailor instruction methods, employing assistive technologies or providing additional support for students who struggle with colour discrimination (Birch, 2012; Diachenko et al., 2022). Combining visual and textual information has been shown to enhance comprehension and retention (Mayer, 2020; Sweller, 2010).

In real-world settings, aside from educational material, the use of colour in classroom design has also shown a significant impact on children's attention and engagement (Duyan & Unver, 2016; Gaines & Curry, 2023). In digital learning environments, the quality and type of display can affect colour perception as well, making it crucial to design digital content that is accessible and effective for children with and without CVD. Research in colour discrimination testing on computer screens confirmed the age-related performance curve found in the physical tests (Kinnear & Sahraie, 2002), with colour discrimination skills peaking in late adolescence while declining in older adults again (Ling & Dain, 2018; Paramei, 2012). Emerging technologies offer adaptable colour control, such as entirely simulated learning environments in virtual and mixed reality scenarios, allowing the real world to pass through the HMD. However, studies show that colour attributes in immersive VR environments can impact cognitive performance, as do different interaction variants (Jost et al., 2019; Xia et al., 2023).

Regarding colour perception and discrimination skills in 3D immersive environments, Cwierz et al. (2021) conducted an FM100 colour test in fully calibrated VR for adults. They found that both the physical and VR tests are similarly functional, though the VR test was somewhat more difficult, likely due to the challenges of using HMDs. In alignment with the higher cognitive demands found for VR learning tasks, their results also highlight the potential for viable colour discrimination assessments in immersive 3D scenarios.

Understanding colour discrimination in children across various real-world, screen and mixed reality settings is essential for developing effective educational strategies and materials. The FM100 test presents as a critical tool for this purpose. With adaptations for quicker assessments oriented on the digital variants offered online, it could provide an accessible rapid-screening approach. In an applicable form, it could help identify exceptional colour vision skills early in school or during engaging MR experiences tailored to each age group and provide for more controllable assessment settings via HMDs.

1.2 Research Objectives

To explore colour discrimination skills of school children and learn more about the applicability of colour vision assessment in immersive digital environments. This study extends traditional colour vision research by examining how colour discrimination skills vary between younger and older school-age children in a mixed reality environment experienced through an HMD and its relation to physical colour vision testing. The FM 100 Hue Test serves as the foundation for the study that explores two research objectives:

1. Explore colour discrimination skill differences between younger children (ages 5-9) and older children (ages 10-17) when engaging in a mixed reality colour sorting task based on the FM100 test. Specifically, the study will examine colour differentiation ability in the four colour gradient trays (Red-Yellow, Yellow-Green, Green-Blue, Blue-Red) and evaluate total error rates.
2. Investigate the overall tendency in age-group colour discrimination change between the mixed reality variant and the conventional FM100 test. Therefore, assessing the relation of physical and mixed reality colour discrimination performance, as experienced through HMD, and its applicability as a fast-screening tool for colour vision at schools and extracurricular events.

2. EMPIRICAL RESEARCH METHODOLOGY

2.1 HMD Specifications and Fast-Screening Considerations

Computer screens employ colour management and colour spaces to display colours accurately. Without proper colour management, colours like "Maximum (255,0,0) red" can vary significantly between screens due to differences in subpixels and pixel density[1]. In HMDs, pixel density further affects colour accuracy, impacting how closely pixels are placed. Colour spaces, such as sRGB and Adobe RGB, define the range of displayable

[1] https://developer.oculus.com/resources/colour-management-guide

colours and white points. The white point is the reference white used in the colour space, indicating the colour temperature of white. For example, sRGB uses a D65 white point, corresponding to a colour temperature of approximately 6500 Kelvin, resembling average daylight.

Notably, Oculus and Meta Quest HMDs use a D75 white point, corresponding to a colour temperature of approximately 7500 Kelvin. This higher colour temperature results in slightly bluer tones than the standard D65 white point used in sRGB displays. Despite consumer displays, including HMDs, not being ideal for absolute colour accuracy, they are suitable for relative colour difference assessments due to their close adherence to the sRGB Rec.709 standard. The Meta Quest 3 HMD was selected for its accessibility, advanced hardware, and affordability, making it suitable for large-scale colour vision tests and fast-screening at schools and events. Other HMDs, like the Apple Vision Pro, offer more advanced technology but are less accessible and significantly more expensive. Features of the Meta Quest 3, such as hand-tracking, offer intuitive interaction with virtual objects important for an MR FM100 test, such as picking and placing colour caps for sorting and higher quality video passthrough of the surroundings for spatial orientation reducing risks when many children group or queue to take part in the colour vision assessment event. The Meta Quest 3 weighs 515g, has 2064 x 2208 pixels per eye, a 120Hz refresh rate, and a 110° x 96° field of view with an RGB stripe subpixel layout that contributes to a consistent arrangement of red, green, and blue subpixels[2].

2.2 Creating and Configuring the Mixed Reality Colour Discrimination Task

The colour test application was developed using the Unity game engine and deployed as an Android APK for the Meta Quest 3. Various plugins were utilised to implement robust hand tracking and enable passthrough functionality, including the XR Interaction Toolkit, Open XR, and AR Foundation. The application aimed to be as physically accurate as possible by using the default Linear colour space. Light settings were calibrated to be close to the D65 standard, providing a neutral white light without an intense colour temperature that could introduce an unwanted tint to the scene. The test setup was minimalistic to avoid distractions. It consisted of a grey table, a wooden board on top, and 10 cap slots per colour gradient tray. Each of the four colour gradient trays, aligned with the physical FM100 test, was presented separately to the participant for sorting (Figure 2).

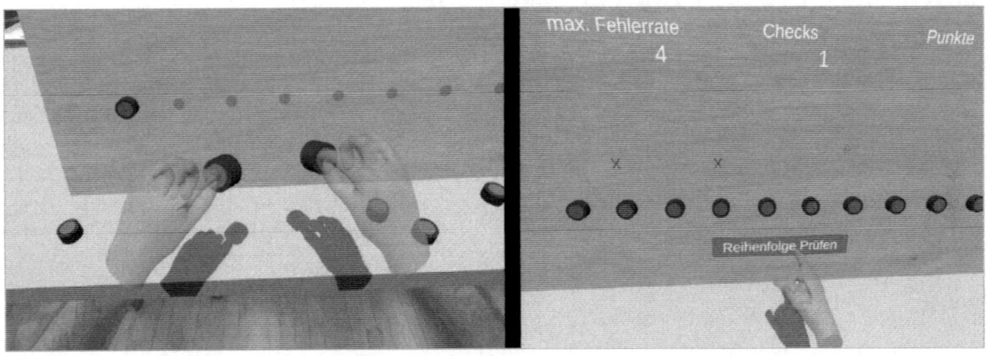

Figure 2. Mixed reality colour vision task based on the FM100 hue test with reduced colour caps (40 from 85) for quick screening with school children. Image captured from the HMD by the authors

At the start of each session, the first and last caps were pre-placed on the board. Participants then picked up one of the remaining eight caps on the table and placed them to create a seamless colour gradient per tray by judging the colour. Thanks to the activated passthrough feature, the real-world surroundings were visible during the MR setup. Interaction with the scene was intuitive, as hand tracking was used for picking and placing the caps, eliminating the need for additional controllers. Participants could grab and place the caps using their hands, similar to the physical FM100 test (Figure 2, left). A sound effect played when a cap was correctly placed in a corresponding slot on the board, with different tunes indicating correct or incorrect final solutions.

Caps could be re-arranged if necessary. Once all caps were placed, the tray could be checked, indicating which pins were correctly placed. Participants could then adjust the placement of the caps and perform another check. After sorting all four trays correctly, a final high score was calculated and displayed to the participants.

[2] https://developer.oculus.com/quest

Each time the app started, the first and last caps were placed on the board. All that was left to do for the participant was to pick up one of the remaining 8 caps on top of the table and place them accordingly to create a seamless colour gradient per tray by judging the colour. While doing this task, the real-world surroundings can be seen in this MR setup thanks to the activated passthrough. Interacting with the scene was intuitive, with hand tracking allowing the pick and placement of the caps, and no additional controllers were required.

As with the physical FM100, participants could grab and place the caps using their hands (Figure 2). A sound effect would play when a cap was placed in a corresponding slot on the board. A different tune would play, depending on whether the final solution was correct or wrong.

If necessary, caps already placed could still be removed and placed again at a new location. If all caps were placed, this tray could be checked to indicate which pins were placed correctly. The user could then take action to adjust the placement of the pins again and perform another check. When all 4 trays were sorted correctly, a final high score was calculated and shown to the participants. The MR app was based on a smaller variant of the FM100 hue test, commonly used for online colour tests, and is also available on the official physical test publisher's website[3]. In this variant, there are 10 colours with a fixed start & end point and 4 different colour trays:

Table 1. Mixed reality FM100 colour gradients and cap colour values by tray (hexadecimal code)

red-yellow	b2766f	b17466	ae725f	a8745a	a87452	a8794e	a97e4c	a78244	a28946	9d8e48
yellow-green	97914b	8d9352	86955c	7e9760	7c9567	699a71	649a76	5b947a	589480	529687
green-blue	4e9689	4c9691	4a9696	4a9698	52949f	6090a5	688fa7	6c8aa6	7489a7	7b84a3
blue-red	8484a3	8d85a3	9483a0	99819d	9f7f98	a9798b	ae7787	b1757f	b3757a	b37673

We chose this setup because the completion time is quicker and more fitting to fast-screen queues of school children waiting to participate, compared to a full FM100 colour set with more than twice the number of caps to place.

2.3 Research Design and Data Collection

The field test was planned to be conducted during a big event at our university, showcasing research practices and projects to young children. The colour test setup was situated in one of the many rooms featuring various projects. Over six hours, visitors continuously participated in the colour test, often forming a line to wait for their turn. Initially, three stations with HMDs and instructors were available, but due to higher-than-expected demand, we later switched to two stations to allow one HMD to recharge.

The setup included three Meta Quest 3 HMDs, with tablets mirroring the participants' views. The three instructors assisted the children with putting on and adjusting the HMDs for comfort. A computer screen displayed a leaderboard with the top 10 best scores, and another showed a loop of a typical playthrough of the colour test app. The high score calculation considered error rate, error distance, time, and submission count. While not subjected to scientific evaluation, the high score was included to engage young participants and encourage participation.

When first starting the app, a disclaimer and opt-in screen were displayed on the HMD and the mirrored tablet screen, explaining what data we collect and how we use it. For children below 14, the parents also had to agree to participate. Furthermore, the participant could input a nickname and choose an age group range. We offered 8 age groups from 5 to 64 years in case some parents and grandparents also want to participate. The order in which the four gradient trays were presented to each participant was calculated randomly. The first and last caps of the presented gradient were already fixed in place, and the other eight colour caps were randomly spawned in the front area of the table (Figure 2, left). The participant could pick up each of them, judge their colour shaded, and place it in a socket at the decided place in the gradient. After completing all 4 colour trays of the FM100, the headset sent its data to our server secured by https protocol. It would then be visible on the computer screen, and the young participants could see their rank. The HMD was ready for other visitors to participate. In accordance with the *first* research objective, it was hypothesised that there would be a difference between the age groups

[3] https://www.colorlitelens.com/images/huetest/Farnsworth100.html

regarding MR colour discrimination performance across the colour trays. Respectively, the null hypothesis for the field study was established as:

H_0: 'There is no significant difference in colour discrimination error rates between younger children (ages 5-9) and older children (ages 10-17) for each colour tray (RedYellow, YellowGreen, GreenBlue, BlueRed) and in total error rates.'

Moreover, concerning the *second* research aim, the colour discrimination between the younger and older children was expected to show similar improvement (mean error percentage improvement) in the MR colour test compared to the findings of the traditional physical FM100 with a full colour cap set. For this, the comprehensive existing results from literature were screened (Kinnear, 1970; Kinnear & Sahraie, 2002; Mäntyjärvi, 2001; Verriest et al., 1982) with finding the results of Kinnear and Sahraie (2002) providing data for the respective age-groups for comparative descriptive analysis.

3. RESULTS

3.1 Participation

Many of the participants were very young (age-group 5 to 9) and used an HMD for the first time. After a short introduction, the participants found it easy to use and understand, thanks to the intuitive hand tracking and MR passthrough (Figure 3).

Figure 3. Mixed reality colour vision task based on the FM100 hue test with reduced colour caps (40 from 85) for quick screening with school children. Image captured from the HMD by the authors

We removed participants who did not finish all rounds or had already done the test before. This is an important step because, in contrast to the traditional test where there is only one final check, in our MR variant, each tray could be readjusted until all colours are at their correct location on the board before progressing to the next gradient. After cleaning, 52 valid data sets were put forward for analysis (Table 2).

Table 2. Participation in the FM100 MR fast-screening colour vision app for school children

Age group	*participants (n)*	*red-yellow*	*yellow-green*	*green-blue*	*blue red*	*total*
5-9	19	55.47	56.11	50.79	56.68	219.05
10-17	33	48.82	53.27	57.48	56.42	216.00

Note. The table shows the number of participants per age group and their mean completion time (seconds) for each colour tray and the total

3.2 Mixed Reality Colour Discrimination Performance

For analysis regarding the first research aim, statistical analysis ($\alpha = 0.05$) involved independent samples t-tests of the mean error rates per cap using IBM SPSS Statistics version 29. Stratified bootstrapping (10,000 samples, bias-corrected and accelerated) was applied to account for non-normality in the data distribution (Field, 2018), as indicated by the Shapiro-Wilk test ($p < 0.05$) with equality of variances assumable for all measures (Levene's test $p > 0.05$). The descriptive statistics and results, including bootstrapped standard errors, t-statistics, p-values, and 95% confidence intervals (*CIs*), are summarised in Table 3.

Table 3. Mean error rates and statistical results of MR colour discrimination performance between age groups

Colour tray	*M* per cap and (total) [5-9]	*M* per cap and (total) [10-17]	*M diff.* per cap	*95% CI lower*	*95% CI upper*	*M total* change in %	*t*	*p*	*Cohen's d*
total	0.39 (12.6)	0.30 (9.64)	-0.09	-0.20	0.02	-23.7	-1.72	0.10	-0.48
red-yellow	0.24 (1.95)	0.25 (2.00)	0.01	-0.13	0.14	2.56	0.10	0.92	0.03
yellow-green	0.34 (2.74)	0.26 (2.09)	-0.08	-0.24	0.07	-23.7	-1.05	0.30	-0.31
green-blue	0.57 (4.53)	0.36 (2.88)	-0.21	-0.35	-0.05	-36.4	-2.70	0.01	-0.79
blue-red	0.43 (3.42)	0.33 (2.67)	-0.09	-0.26	0.07	-21.9	-1.12	0.26	-0.31

Note. Mean error rates per cap are calculated per movable colour cap: 8 per tray, 32 in the total MR FM100

The results revealed significant differences between the two age groups for the green-blue (tray 3) error rate per cap. The younger children show a significantly higher mean error rate per cap ($M = 0.57$) compared to the older children ($M = 0.36$), $t = -2.7$, $p = 0.01$, with a moderate to large effect size of Cohen's $d = -0.8$. In the other colour gradient trays and the overall mean error rate, the colour discrimination capability was not statistically different between the two age groups (Figure 4).

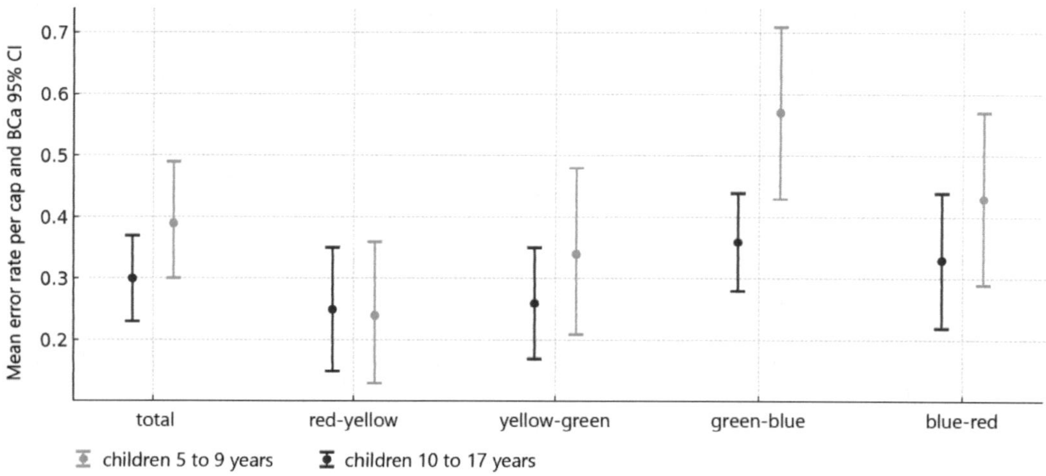

Figure 4. Mixed reality colour discrimination performance between children aged 5-9 and 10-17 years

As the MR colour differentiation of the younger children (5 to 9) differs significantly in the gradient from blue to green, the results suggest rejecting H_0 and indicate an age-related improvement, particularly in discriminating these colour shadings towards an older age between 10 and 17. Notably, a tendential improvement of colour discrimination skill was reflected in the results for all colour gradients of the FM100 test, except the red-yellow gradient (Figure 5).

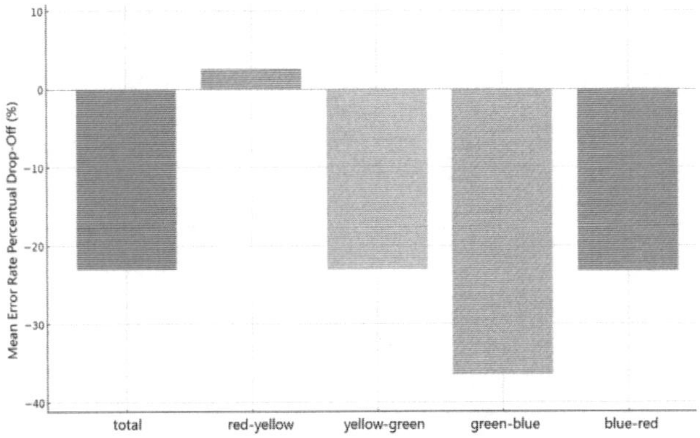

Figure 5. Percentual drop-off in the mean error rate between children aged 5-9 and 10-17 in total and within the colour trays of the MR test

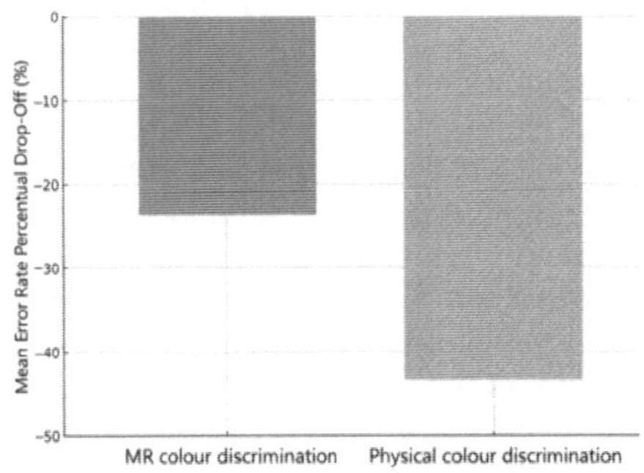

Figure 6. Percentual drop-off (total mean error rate) from ages 5-9 to 10-17; MR test compared to Physical FM100 by Kinnear and Sahraie (2002)

Regarding the second research objective, the descriptive analysis (Figure 6) reveals a pronounced drop-off in mean errors for both the MR colour discrimination test (M_{change} = -23.7) and the physical FM100 test across all 85 colour caps (M_{change} = -43.4), highlighting age-group improvement. The improvement is more prominent with the physical FM100.

4. DISCUSSION

4.1 Implications Regarding Children's Colour Discrimination Skills in Education

The findings on the research objectives of this study both provide implications for educational practices, particularly in how colour discrimination skills are assessed and understood in school-age children within mixed reality environments. As established in previous literature, colour plays a crucial role in educational settings by enhancing learning outcomes and cognitive processes (Brooker & Franklin, 2016; Elliot & Maier, 2014).

Regarding the *first research objective*, the current study extends this understanding by demonstrating that children's ability to discriminate colours, especially in challenging gradients like green-blue, improves with children's age in MR environments in line with the findings of both physical (Kinnear & Sahraie, 2002; Verriest et al., 1982) and digital screen-based (Ling & Dain, 2018) colour discrimination tests. Educational implications arise from the observed differences in colour discrimination skills between younger (5-9 years) and older (10-17 years) children. Specifically, the significant differences in the green-blue gradient suggest that educational interventions should consider age-specific strategies for teaching and assessing colour perception abilities (Cranwell et al., 2015). For instance, early screening of colour discrimination skills in MR environments can identify children who may benefit from targeted educational support or interventions tailored to their developmental stage. The results underline previous findings that green-blue colour hues pose a challenge for colour discrimination (Moreland, 1989). This study particularly highlights these difficulties for younger children between the ages of 5 and 9, with significant improvements observed in children aged 10 to 17, consistent with results from screen-based colour discrimination studies (Ling & Dain, 2018). In addition, the results demonstrate that this holds true also for mixed reality scenarios that blend digital colour renderings with real-world passthrough visuals.

With the *second research objective*, the study further explored this comparability of MR-based colour discrimination assessments with the traditional physical FM100 test. While the error rates were generally higher in the MR environment compared to the physical test, the drop-off in error rates between age groups was less pronounced in MR than in the physical FM100. This finding aligns with previous research in virtual environments, which also reported higher error rates than physical testing methods (Cwierz et al., 2021). The lower drop-off in error rates between age groups in MR can be attributed to the challenges posed by MR environments, such as interacting with virtual objects. However, unlike fully synthetic VR, MR allows for more natural interaction using hand-tracking technology together with the visual perception of real-world elements, which may facilitate better performance in colour discrimination tasks compared to fully rendered VR settings and using controllers. Future research can explore insightful comparative studies between VR and MR FM100 assessments, building on the contributions of this study. Furthermore, this study's findings demonstrate the potential of an accessible MR-based test based on the simplified FM100 as a fast-screening tool for colour discrimination in school settings and extracurricular events. Despite higher error rates compared to physical tests, the expected drop-off in error rate between age-groups and the corresponding profile within the four colour trays support the suitability of the MR test for screening of exceptional colour discrimination skills and CVD in scenarios showcased in this study.

MR colour vision screening using a commercial HMD, therefore, offers a practical alternative for quick assessments, aligning with the needs of educational environments where efficiency and accessibility are crucial (Chandak et al., 2017). The comparable drop-off in error rates and expected results across age groups and colour gradients shows that using an MR test with a commercial HMD can effectively screen children's colour discrimination challenges. This highlights the applicability of MR-based testing in educational screening protocols using the demonstrated configuration, especially since the average completion time for the MR FM100 test is less than four minutes per child (Table 2).

4.2 Limitations

While this study provides valuable insights, it also has some limitations. Our MR setup differed from the traditional FM100 test by including a timer, high score display, and larger cap distances for hand tracking. We used fewer colours for an accessible, child-friendly variation, which might affect sensitivity. Each of the four colour trays was presented individually and could be repeated with feedback until correctly sorted, potentially impacting results. We did not pre-screen for CVD in the children, while the physical FM100 study held for comparison excluded these individuals. This may contribute to the lower error drop-off rate in our MR test. While the MR CVD test, as demonstrated in this study, can provide for rapid pre-screening of colour discrimination skill peculiarities, it is not a medical application. Thus, detected anomalies require follow-up and further thorough investigation using the physical FM100 test or other standard diagnostic procedures. Despite these limitations, the study suggests promising potential for MR-based colour discrimination testing, highlighting the need for further research with larger, diverse samples and controlled environments.

5. CONCLUSION

This study explored colour discrimination skills in schoolchildren using mixed reality (MR) environments compared to traditional FM100 tests. Significant age-related differences were found, especially in the green-blue colour gradient, with younger children showing higher error rates. These findings underscore the need for age-specific educational strategies. Despite the expected higher overall error rates in MR tests, the consistent patterns of age-related improvement indicate MR's potential as a fast-screening tool for colour vision in educational contexts. The MR test's accessibility and engaging format, associated with the fast completion time of under four minutes, make it a practical alternative to traditional methods. The study advances our understanding of colour discrimination in children within MR environments, offering valuable insights for educational practices. Integrating MR technology enables educators to identify and support diverse colour perception abilities, enhancing learning outcomes and cognitive development. Future research should further explore and refine its applicability across different age groups and settings.

ACKNOWLEDGEMENT

This research has been partially funded by the Austrian Research Promotion Agency FFG through the COIN Project SimLern, #898080.

REFERENCES

Ali, Q., Heldal, I., Helgesen, C. G., Krumina, G., Costescu, C., Kovari, A., Katona, J., & Thill, S. (2021). Current challenges supporting school-aged children with vision problems: A rapid review. *Applied Sciences*, *11*(20), 9673.

Ashton, R., & Leppard, B. (2021). *Differential Diagnosis in Dermatology* (5th ed.). CRC Press. https://doi.org/10.1201/9780429023248

Birch, J. (2012). Worldwide prevalence of red-green color deficiency. *Journal of the Optical Society of America. A, Optics, Image Science, and Vision*, *29*(3), 313–320. https://doi.org/10.1364/JOSAA.29.000313

Blundell, J., Scott, S., Harris, D., Huddlestone, J., & Richards, D. (2020). With flying colours: Pilot performance with colour-coded head-up flight symbology. *Displays*, *61*, 101932.

Brant, W. E., & Helms, C. A. (2012). *Fundamentals of Diagnostic Radiology*. Lippincott Williams & Wilkins.

Brooker, A., & Franklin, A. (2016). The effect of colour on children's cognitive performance. *British Journal of Educational Psychology*, *86*(2), 241–255. https://doi.org/10.1111/bjep.12101

Chandak, N. R., Daigavane, S. V., & Sharma, S. R. (2017). Screening of colour vision deficiency in school children of Wardha District. *Indian Journal of Clinical and Experimental Ophthalmology*, *3*(1), 80–84.

Cranwell, M. B., Pearce, B., Loveridge, C., & Hurlbert, A. C. (2015). Performance on the Farnsworth-Munsell 100-Hue Test Is Significantly Related to Nonverbal IQ. *Investigative Ophthalmology & Visual Science*, *56*(5), 3171–3178. https://doi.org/10.1167/iovs.14-16094

Cwierz, H., Díaz-Barrancas, F., Llinás, J. G., & Pardo, P. J. (2021). On the Validity of Virtual Reality Applications for Professional Use: A Case Study on Color Vision Research and Diagnosis. *IEEE Access*, *9*, 138215–138224. IEEE Access. https://doi.org/10.1109/ACCESS.2021.3118438

Diachenko, I., Kalishchuk, S., Zhylin, M., Kyyko, A., & Volkova, Y. (2022). Color education: A study on methods of influence on memory. *Heliyon*, *8*(11), e11607. https://doi.org/10.1016/j.heliyon.2022.e11607

Duyan, F., & Unver, R. (2016). A research on the effect of classroom wall colours on student's attention. *A/Z : ITU Journal of Faculty of Architecture*, *13*, 73–78. https://doi.org/10.5505/itujfa.2016.57441

Elliot, A. J. (2015). Color and psychological functioning: A review of theoretical and empirical work. *Frontiers in Psychology*, *6*. https://doi.org/10.3389/fpsyg.2015.00368

Elliot, A. J., & Maier, M. A. (2014). Color psychology: Effects of perceiving color on psychological functioning in humans. *Annual Review of Psychology*, *65*, 95–120. https://doi.org/10.1146/annurev-psych-010213-115035

Farnsworth, D. (1943). The Farnsworth-Munsell 100-hue and dichotomous tests for color vision. *Journal of the Optical Society of America*, *33*, 568–578.

Field, A. (2018). *Discovering Statistics Using IBM SPSS Statistics* (5th Edition). Sage Publications.

Friedrich, M., & Vollrath, M. (2022). Urgency-Based color coding to support visual search in displays for supervisory control of multiple unmanned aircraft systems. *Displays*, *74*, 102185.

Gabriela P. (2019). *Farnsworth–Munsell Hue Color Vision Test, Material and Finishing Laboratory* [Graphic]. Wikimedia Commons. https://commons.wikimedia.org/wiki/File:Farnsworth%E2%80%93Munsell_Hue_Color_Vision_Test,_Material_and_Finishing_Laboratory.jpg

Gaines, K., & Curry, Z. (2023). The Inclusive Classroom: The Effects of Color on Learning and Behavior. *Journal of Family and Consumer Sciences Education*, *29*(1), Article 1. https://natefacs-ojs-ttu.tdl.org/natefacs/article/view/72

Gibb, R., Gray, R., & Scharff, L. (2016). *Aviation Visual Perception: Research, Misperception and Mishaps*. Routledge. https://doi.org/10.4324/9781315568584

Gordon, N. (1998). Colour blindness. *Public Health*, *112*(2), 81–84. https://doi.org/10.1038/sj.ph.1900446

Jost, P., Cobb, S., & Hämmerle, I. (2019). Reality-based interaction affecting mental workload in virtual reality mental arithmetic training. *Behaviour & Information Technology*, 1–17. https://doi.org/10.1080/0144929X.2019.1641228

Karunanayake, A., Weerasuriya, M. A., & Wijekoon, W. M. C. D. (2021). The prevalence of colour vision deficiency, parent-reported, and child reported difficulties among 10- to 16-year-old school children in the Galle education zone, Sri Lanka. *Galle Medical Journal*, *26*(4). https://doi.org/10.4038/gmj.v26i4.8067

Kaya, N., & Epps, H. H. (2004). Relationship between color and emotion: A study of college students. *College Student Journal*, *38*(3), 396–405.

Kinnear, P. R. (1970). Proposals for scoring and assessing the 100-HUE test. *Vision Research*, *10*(5), 423–433. https://doi.org/10.1016/0042-6989(70)90123-9

Kinnear, P. R., & Sahraie, A. (2002). New Farnsworth-Munsell 100 hue test norms of normal observers for each year of age 5–22 and for age decades 30–70. *British Journal of Ophthalmology*, *86*(12), 1408–1411.

Ling, B. Y., & Dain, S. J. (2018). Development of color vision discrimination during childhood: Differences between Blue–Yellow, Red–Green, and achromatic thresholds. *JOSA A*, *35*(4), B35–B42.

Mäntyjärvi, M. (2001). Normal test scores in the Farnsworth–Munsell 100 hue test. *Documenta Ophthalmologica*, *102*, 73–80.

Mayer, R. (2020). *Multimedia Learning*. Cambridge University Press.

Mollon, J. D. (1982). Color vision. *Annual Review of Psychology*, *33*, 41–85. https://doi.org/10.1146/annurev.ps.33.020182.000353

Moreland, J. D. (1989). Unipolar, Bipolar and Other Errors in the Farnsworth-Munsell 100-Hue Test. In B. Drum & G. Verriest (Eds.), *Colour Vision Deficiencies IX: Proceedings of the ninth symposium of the International Research Group on Colour Vision Deficiencies, held at St. John's College, Annapolis, Maryland, U.S.A., 1–3 July 1987* (pp. 397–405). Springer Netherlands. https://doi.org/10.1007/978-94-009-2695-0_44

Ong, S. C., Pek, L. C. (Ivy), Chiang, T. L. (Carol), Soon, H. W., Chua, K. C., Sassmann, C., Razali, M. A. B., & Koh, T. C. (Victor). (2020). A Novel Automated Visual Acuity Test Using a Portable Head-mounted Display. *Optometry and Vision Science*, *97*(8), 591–597. https://doi.org/10.1097/OPX.0000000000001551

Otto, W., & Askov, E. (1968). The Role of Color in Learning and Instruction. *The Journal of Special Education*. https://doi.org/10.1177/002246696800200204

Paramei, G. V. (2012). Color discrimination across four life decades assessed by the Cambridge Colour Test. *Journal of the Optical Society of America. A, Optics, Image Science, and Vision*, *29*(2), A290-297. https://doi.org/10.1364/JOSAA.29.00A290

Quattrer, M., Zonatti, W. F., & Gouveia, A. P. S. (2020, March). Color Lab IFRJ: Practical color exercises for fashion courses. *Color Culture and Science Journal*. https://doi.org/10.23738/CCSJ.120107

Richardson, P., Saunders, K., & McClelland, J. (2008). Colour Vision Testing Made Easy: How Low Can You Go? *Optometry in Practice*, *9*(1), 17.

Sekhri, S. (2022). *Textbook of fabric science: Fundamentals to finishing*. PHI Learning Pvt. Ltd.

Siess, A., Wolfel, M., & Haffner, N. (2018). Color Preference Differences between Head Mounted Displays and PC Screens. *2018 International Conference on Cyberworlds (CW)*, 25–32. 2018 International Conference on Cyberworlds (CW). https://doi.org/10.1109/CW.2018.00018

Sushil, K., Mandira, M., Binod, R., Arun, D., & Rani, G. (2017). Prevalence of Congenital Colour Vision Deficiency (CVD) in School Children of Bhaktapur, Nepal. *Int J Med Sci Clin Invent*, 8–11.

Sweller, J. (2010). Element Interactivity and Intrinsic, Extraneous, and Germane Cognitive Load. *Educational Psychology Review*, *2*(22), 123–138.

Toscani, M., Gil, R., Guarnera, D., Guarnera, G., Kalouaz, A., & Gegenfurtner, K. R. (2019). Assessment of OLED Head Mounted Display for Vision Research with Virtual Reality. *2019 15th International Conference on Signal-Image Technology & Internet-Based Systems (SITIS)*, 738–745. 2019 15th International Conference on Signal-Image Technology & Internet-Based Systems (SITIS). https://doi.org/10.1109/SITIS.2019.00120

Verriest, G., Van Laethem, J., & Uvijls, A. (1982). A new assessment of the normal ranges of the Farnsworth-Munsell 100-hue test scores. *American Journal of Ophthalmology*, *93*(5), 635–642. https://doi.org/10.1016/0002-9394(82)90432-8

Witzel, C., & Gegenfurtner, K. R. (2018). Color Perception: Objects, Constancy, and Categories. *Annual Review of Vision Science*, *4*(1), 475–499. https://doi.org/10.1146/annurev-vision-091517-034231

Xia, G., Henry, P., Chen, Y., Queiroz, F., Westland, S., & Cheng, Q. (2023). The effects of colour attributes on cognitive performance and intellectual abilities in immersive virtual environments. *Computers in Human Behavior*, *148*, 107853. https://doi.org/10.1016/j.chb.2023.107853

IMPLEMENTATION AND EVALUATION OF A CHATBOT IN A BUSINESS COURSE IN HIGHER EDUCATION

Pedro Isaias[1], Tania Hoque[1] and Paula Miranda[2]
[1]*Universidade Aberta – Portuguese Open University*
Lisbon, Portugal
[2]*Instituto Politécnico de Setúbal, ESTSetúbal*
Setúbal, Portugal

ABSTRACT

While the higher education sector is continuously searching for innovative technologies, the use of chatbots requires extensive research and careful consideration of their pedagogical value. The lessons learned from lecturers who experiment with chatbots can constitute important evidence to support their use. This paper presents a chatbot specifically designed for a Higher Education course, named RESOURCEbot, its mechanics and workflows. This chatbot was used in a university course to assist the students with recommendations of relevant research papers. It is also presented the chatbot´s evaluation. The evaluation of the RESOURCEbot derived from a questionnaire that was distributed among the students to assess their opinions about the experience of using a chatbot, its performance and their intention to use chatbots in educational settings. The results highlighted some of RESOURCEbot's limitations, such as some difficulty in understanding the students' prompts, but overall they reflected the students' positive opinions concerning its ease of use, and the value and pertinence of its recommendations.

KEYWORDS

Chatbots, Artificial Intelligence, Higher Education, Technology Evaluation

1. INTRODUCTION

Chatbots present unprecedented opportunities for education in terms of communication and information. They're accessible and offer scalability, while providing important possibilities for personalised learning (Wollny et al., 2021). Chatbots can be defined as "intelligent computer systems designed to mimic human conversation to enable automated guidance and support [using] natural language processing and machine learning" (Caldarini et al., 2022, p. 1), with applicability to various areas (Smutny & Schreiberova, 2020). Chatbots, can improve the engagement of students, assist the personalisation of the learning process, support lecturers and provide valuable information about students' behaviour (Kuhail et al., 2023). They have the potential to offer a more equative and interactive learning experience (Koyuturk et al., 2023) as well as to provide valuable feedback to the learners (Sáiz-Manzanares et al., 2023). At the same time, more studies are highlighting the need to examine the ethical and security implications of their use (Fulgencio, 2024).

A fundamental aspect of using technology for educational purposes is to assess if its impact was, in fact, pedagogically beneficial. This paper presents the evaluation results of RESOUCEbot, a chatbot, implemented, in a curricular unit, within an undergraduate course, to provide recommendations on which research papers, the students should use. It intends to examine the students' perception about its use in a twofold research question: what were the strengths and limitations of RESOURCEbot and what improvement can be introduced in the future to enhance its educational value? The paper begins by examining the use of chatbots in higher education and exploring students' perceptions of their use. It then describes the implementation of RESOURCEbot and outlines the research methods. The ensuing section presents the results and precedes the discussion and conclusion.

2. CHATBOTS FOR EDUCATIONAL PURPOSES

Since chatbots can provide support to multiple users at the same time, they are a more productive and more affordable alternative to human operators. The evolution of technology has facilitated their implementation improving their flexibility and simplifying their maintenance. In addition, these advancements in artificial intelligence have enhanced their capacity to emulate human dialogue (Caldarini et al., 2022).Chatbots can be categorised into informative, chat-based or conversational, and task-based (Adamopoulou & Moussiades, 2020). Chatbots are being used in education to improve student services, to improve engagement, and to reduce the financial cost of administrative tasks (Abbas et al., 2022). Wollny et al. (2021) study concluded that chatbots are being used in education mainly for the improvement of skills, to enhance the efficiency of education and to increase learners' motivation, and they have three pedagogical roles: learning, assistance and mentoring. Some examples include Coding Tutor, which assists students with writing software code (Hobert, 2019); Mondly, Andy, John Bot, and Buddy.ai, designed for language teaching (Belda-Medina & Kokošková, 2023); and Jill Watson, a chatbot that acts like a teaching assistant to address students questions regarding the course content (Kakar et al., 2024). In learning settings, chatbots can be teacher-oriented or service-oriented (Abbas et al., 2022).

There are several aspects at the origin of some scepticism concerning chatbots, including mistrusting its capacities, and insufficient socio-emotional intelligence (Bilquise et al., 2024). The challenge of the deployment of chatbots, in educational environments, relates to those associated with the use of AI in general, and that is to achieve a balance between harnessing its potential and fostering an implementation that is both responsible and ethical (Adıgüzel et al., 2023). When implemented in practice, for educational purposes, chatbots present some challenges, they lack sufficient resources to answer appropriately to the students' questions, there can be a mismatch between the type of chatbot and the task requirements, poor conversational design, low-quality content (Tlili et al., 2023).

Several studies propose methods for the evaluation of chatbots (Belda-Medina & Kokošková, 2023)(Koyuturk et al., 2023)(Abbas et al., 2022). There is a panoply of methodologies that can be used for evaluating the implementation of the chatbots, some studies portray an evaluation that is more focused on the students, while others concentrate on the actual performance of the chatbot, using a variety of strategies. Radziwill and Benton (2017) study presented a summary of previous research on chatbot evaluation, listing the quality attributes, which can be classified into efficiency (performance), effectiveness (functionality and humanity) and satisfaction (affect, ethics and behaviour, and accessibility). The evaluation criteria can also be mainly focused on the efficiency of the chatbots outputs and assess the completeness and accuracy of its responses (Govender, 2024). The assessment of the interactions of the students with the chatbot can use posts from discussion boards, students' grades, course access and conversation logs (Song et al., 2019).

Students encouraging perceptions and their willingness to use chatbots will have a positive impact in its deployment (Bilquise et al., 2024). The research on this subject has voiced different perspectives, taken from several studies that describe implementation experiments. Some studies have also appraised students views and concluded that their satisfaction levels were only moderate with students highlighting the need for improvement in areas such as adjusting to users' needs, including interactive multimedia, and enhancing speech functionalities (Belda-Medina & Kokošková, 2023). Some students remain reticent regarding the use of chatbots and find it difficult to trust them for essential support, to obtain information and for guidance (Bilquise et al., 2024).

In contrast, there is previous research that portrays mainly positive views. Sáiz-Manzanares et al. (2023) examined students' satisfaction with the use of chatbots for self-regulated learning and concluded that the students considered the chatbot to be a valuable tool for concentrating their questions on the specific concepts of the subject and for reflecting on their own learning process. In Hobert (2019) paper the students rated a chatbot that assist them with computer coding, as being a valuable addition to the course. The chatbot was characterised as being helpful and a useful support in understanding the content. On the other hand, they highlighted some limitations at the level of the excessive guidance, the capacity to understand their questions and the type of feedback that was offered. Similarly, Huang et al. (2019) conclusion of the evaluation of students perception demonstrates that they were satisfied with the chatbot in terms of minimising their feelings of isolation, increasing collaborative learning and improving conceptual learning. At the same time, some design limitations became evident, such as insufficient support when the students answered incorrectly and the quality of the content of the chatlogs.

3. RESOURCEBOT

RESOURCEbot (Resource Optimization and Selection for Education bot) is a pedagogical innovation that has been developed under the project HYBOT - Enhancing hybrid teaching in higher education through chatbots, a EU funded project of which Universidade Aberta (Portuguese Open University) is a consortium member, having also the following partners: Fachhochschule des Mittelstands (FHM) - University of applied Sciences, Germany; Université Côte d'Azur (UCA), France; Tallinn University, Estonia; Kaunas University of Technology (KTU), Lithuania; Trainings-Online Gesellschaft für E-Portale mbH, Germany (associated partner). RESOURCEbot has been specifically developed for the course Innovation and Knowledge Management, a semester course of the Master's Degree in Management offered by Universidade Aberta. RESOURCEbot´s goals are to act as a recommendation system to help students to select resources for their assignment under a specific course activity. Students interacted with the bot in English in order to enquire it regarding the available selected resources for that activity. Both natural language as well as choice menus (prompts) were available for students to interact with the system.

3.1 RESOURCEbot Mechanics

An immediate and accurate response can be generated including offering suggestions of resources. This virtual assistant can support lecturers and learners in numerous ways. Many researchers identified the tremendous benefits of integrating AI chatbots in educational settings (Labadze et al., 2023). The RESOURCEbot was developed to assist students in finding relevant resources, as is described in the system flow chart in figure 1.

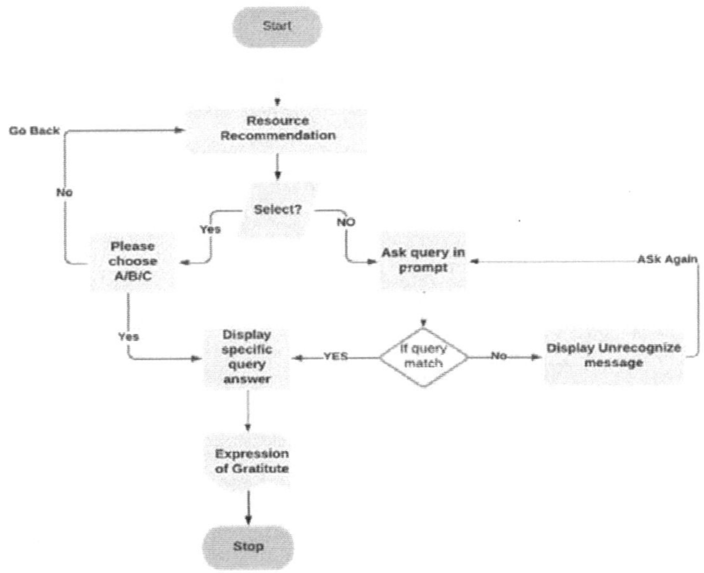

Figure 1. Flow chart of RESOURCEbot

The chatbot window was available on the Moodle webpage. The welcome message and recommendations for resources appeared on the display and then the recommendation feature interpreted the menus to inspire and guide students to interact with the chatbot. The menus can boost engagement for learners as they can minimise the potential confusion (Hew et al., 2023). The menus have several selection criteria, filters, and results. At this point, it is not necessary to ask questions in a prompt. However, if the users want to return to the start menu, they can use the back option. The user can ignore the offered menus and ask queries in the prompt directly. If the input query matches the intent, then the result will given to the user. Otherwise, the system will display an "unrecognised message" text, asking the user to try again. Once the desired result is obtained the chatbot displays a message of gratitude.

3.2 Chatbot Internal System Workflow

The RESOURCEbot´s internal system workflow had six phases (figure 2).

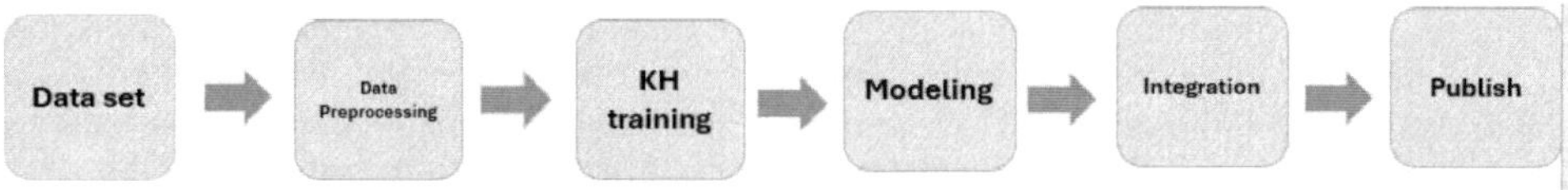

Figure 2. Chatbot´s internal system workflow diagram

Firstly, a data set was prepared to implement this chatbot. Dataset preparation is one of the crucial stages of building any system (Abdelmoiz et al., 2024). The resources were to be recommended according to the search query, therefore an Excel sheet was prepared with the dataset: 13 resources were analysed and categorised according to their abstract, keywords, title, publication date, resource type, author name, etc. The second step, data preprocessing, in this case, entailed the normalization of a dataset. Cleaning and removing corrupt or inaccurate records from the dataset is necessary to improve a system's quality and performance. Modifying and replacing any irrelevant information is part of data preprocessing. Finally, the data in the Excel sheet was converted to text data. With concern to Knowledge Hub (KH) training, the Melibo framework developed an AI-driven tool named Knowledge Hub to facilitate a wide range of information. The user interface of this platform is easy to use which can be beneficial in increasing engagement for non-technical people. It doesn't require high knowledge of technology. Three options are available to train this hub: text, web and file analyser. In the training phase, text analyser was used to increase knowledge and the preprocessed text data in the text analyser section was inputted.

The modelling step involved designing a chat flow using the Melibo framework and involved several phases. Firstly, a chat flow was selected in the create chat option, to design the model. Figure 3 describes the connecting nodes with the knowledge hub. Node one contains the possible questions asked by students. In this step, a large number of potential questions should be input to enrich the chatbot knowledge (Hew et al., 2023).

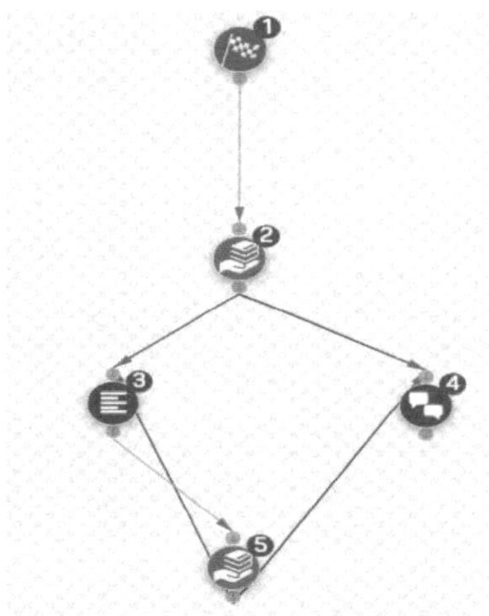

Figure 3. Chat flow Model

The training phase should continue until it gives the green signal. The red signal means the training is poor, orange indicates not sufficient. Node number two contains the knowledge hub symbol. In node number two the knowledge pieces and variables are selected. The configuration of this node is the search setting and general setting. The search settings function provides the custom search results of the input query. General settings have the function of GPT version selection, in this case the GPT-4 version was used.

The fifth phase, integration, entails merging with the Moodle webpage once the modelling is completed. It is possible to customise the chatbot according to the desired design, by choosing the name, colour, language, and other options. In the HTML tag, the API was merged in Moodle webpage. Finally, the last phase is where the users can see the chatbot logo on the webpage. After clicking the logo the chat window will open and users can see the console window. Initially, potential menus were given to the students to inspire them to conduct the chatbot (figure 4).

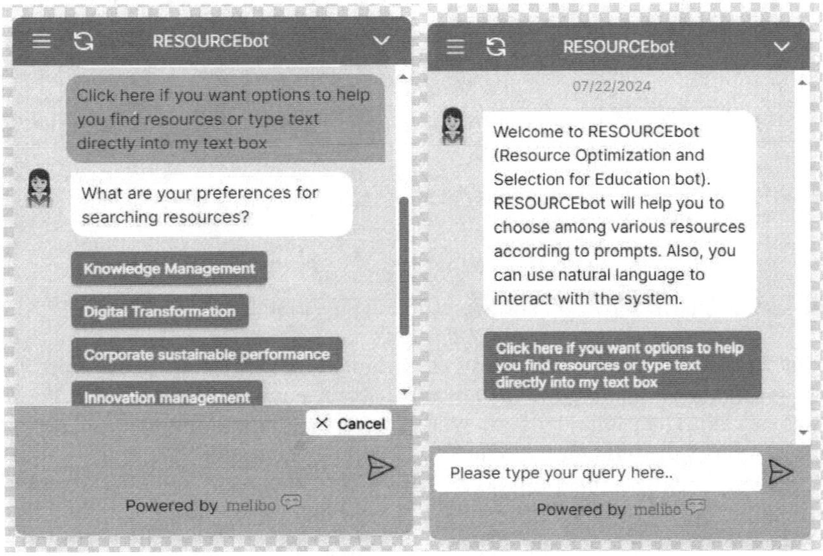

Figure 4. Outlook of RESOURCEbot

After publishing, every chat was monitored by using a Melibo tool named Bot Gym. It is possible to teach the bot if the output result gives wrong information (Hew et al., 2023). The improvement continued after the publication of the chatbot. It was important to understand how students were interacting with the system, and what kind of keywords they were using. The chatbot was trained in possible keywords, such as ID, resource number, document number, but not all keywords could be anticipated. Many students were searching using the word "article", for example, "find me the article number 3 details". In this case, since the bot was unfamiliar with the word, it displayed an "unrecognised message" in return. The RESOURCEbot was then trained with the word "article". This process was continuous during the test case of the chatbot.

4. RESOURCEBOT EVALUATION: STUDENTS' PERSPECTIVE

Following the application of the RESOURCEbot, a questionnaire was distributed among the students to assess their experience with the chatbot, and its performance. A total of 16 students completed the questionnaire. Most students (12) had already used chatbots, 6 of them only rarely and the other 6 on a regular basis. Only 2 students had no knowledge of what chatbots were, and 2 students knew what they were, but had never used them before. Hence, most were familiar with chatbots, prior to RESOURCEbot's implementation. In addition, most students (10) used them in the personal arena, 6 for educational purposes, 4 students used them professionally and 1 student stated that he/she used them on e-commerce websites.

The remaining questions were focused on the experience with the RESOURCEbot specifically. Firstly, the students responded to a Likert scale question, which assessed several dimensions of the RESOURCEbot performance (figure 5).

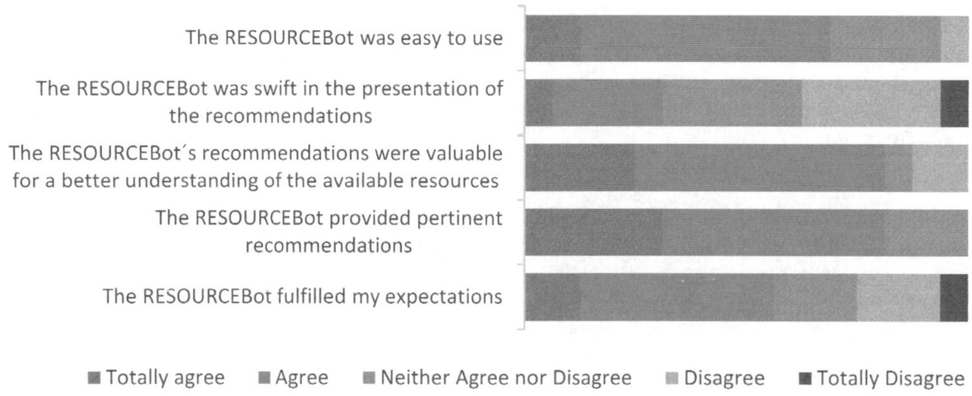

Figure 5. Students´ views about the RESOURCEbot performance

As can be seen in the chart above, most students found the RESOURCEbot easy to use (11), though 4 were neutral about its ease of use and 1 disagreed. With regard to swiftness, only 5 students considered the chatbot to be fast, while 5 were neutral in this question, 5 disagreed and 1 totally disagreed. The value of the recommendations for a better understanding of the available resources, on the other hand, were a subject that the majority agreed (13). The neutral position was selected by 1 respondent and 2 disagreed. Most students also found the recommendations to be pertinent (13) and only 3 students were neutral. Furthermore, 9 respondents stated that the RESOURCEbot fulfilled their expectations, but 3 students were neutral, 3 disagreed and 1 totally disagreed. The performance of RESOURCEbot was equally assessed with 2 open-ended questions regarding its strengths and limitations.

In the open-ended question about its positive aspects, the students reinforced its ease of use and the fact that it provided access to valuable information. They also mentioned its role in saving time, since it presented a swifter strategy to access the relevant papers, and its efficiency in providing pertinent recommendations: "direct recommendation of the most adequate papers" (student 9). In addition, some students highlighted its innovative nature, its flexibility and its role in supporting the task "innovation and a supporting tool" (student 12). The main trends in these open-ended responses were coherent with the opinions voiced in the Likert scale items. When asked about the limitations, the students focused on the difficulties that the chatbot had with understanding the requests, due to language restrictions. Some of the terms that were used by the students weren't understood by the chatbot, as described by some students: "Sometimes it doesn't understand what we write" (student 11); " I had some language problems with the chatbot. For example, I asked "Do you have any resource on the topic X?" and the chatbot was not able to process the request…and I found out that it was enough to change the term "resource" (…) I had this problem three times, where I've used basic terms and the chatbot did not understand, I had to guess the term the chatbot knew, through synonyms" (student 4). Furthermore, some respondents highlighted the incompleteness of the responses: "it should give 8 resources for the determined criteria and it only gives 6 or 7" (student 10). Others cited its technological immaturity and mentioned that there was not enough time to explore the chatbot, due to the deadline of the activity.

After appraising the strengths and limitations of the RESOURCEbot, the students were asked to suggest additional resources. Some responded by numerating general improvements based on limitations, such as better interface or more accurate responses. Nonetheless, the majority of the students did suggest specific resources: communication in natural language, higher number of papers, available in other languages, such as Portuguese, access to previous questions, and proactive recommendations. As student 15 stated "the capacity to interact with quality in natural language" and student 13 added "I would like that it had more papers. It only has 13". A few students also suggested the addition of other functionalities related to the papers it recommends, more specifically, a summary of the papers, analysis of tables and figures, ability to take notes and the possibility of translation.

The Likert scale question also included two items to assess the students future intention to use chatbots in the curricular unit where the RESOURCEbot was deployed and in the course in general (figure 6).

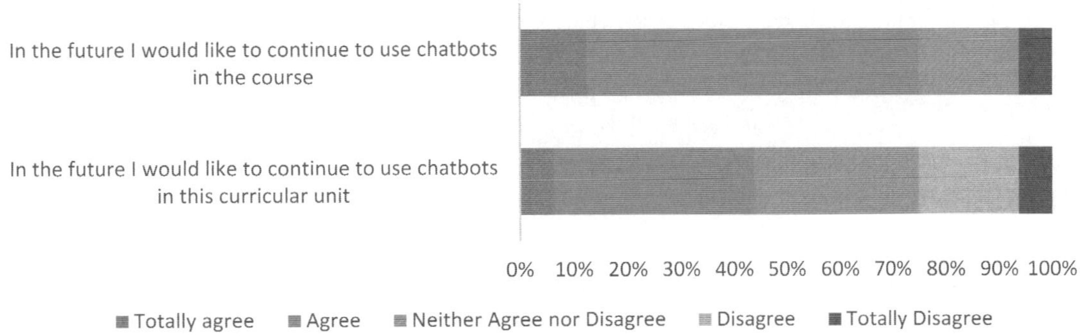

Figure 6. Students' intention to continue to use chatbots

The students showed a stronger intention to use chatbots in the course rather than in the curricular unit. The prospective use of chatbots in the course was supported by 12 of the students, 3 respondents were neutral and 1 totally disagreed. On the other hand, only 7 students showed their intention to continue to use chatbots in the curricular unit, while 5 were neutral, 3 disagreed and 1 totally disagreed. The students were asked if they were likely to recommend the RESOURCEbot to a peer. Only 3 students stated that they were extremely likely to recommend and 4 stated that they were very likely to recommend. Three students selected a more moderate position, stating that they were somewhat likely to recommend. On the opposite side of the spectrum, 5 students said that they were not very likely and 1 not likely at all.

The final question of the survey asked the students to leave any additional comments to the use of RESOURCEbot. Six students did not provide comments. The remaining students said that they liked the experience, that it was a new for them and that it was a good initiative. They thanked the lecturer and stated that it has room for improvement, but that in the future it can be a valuable tool for the students. As student 16 stated: "I understand RESOURCEbot in this context is still growing and being changed, but I strongly believe it can truly be a force for objectivity and assistance to students (…) I have explored, and I believe, I have taken from this bot a lot of information that was very helpful and insightful".

5. DISCUSSION AND CONCLUSION

Chatbots can be used in higher education for numerous purposes, such as to enhance communication and to access more relevant information. This paper focused on the use of RESOURCEbot, a chatbot that was developed to act as a recommendation system.

The analysis of the questionnaire shows that the use of RESOURCEbot was perceived by most students as being mainly positive. The students highlighted its ease of use, the value and relevance of its recommendations and they felt that their expectations were met. On the other hand, they identified some limitations, as in previous studies (Tlili et al., 2023), such as its difficulty in understanding some of the prompts. Overall, the majority of the students stated that they would like to continue to use chatbots in the course.

Despite this study's limitations, more specifically, its limited scope and small sample size, it constitutes an example of AI use in higher education and it can contribute to assist the design of an educational chatbot. The results revealed student's openness to the use of AI in educational settings and they illustrated the potential of this technology. This study can be used as a stepping stone for prospective research on learning and teaching with AI and it can encourage other lecturers to venture into the deployment of this technology in their courses. On the other hand, the difficulties reported by the students seem to support the scepticism that exists around chatbots' actual capacities, as argued in the literature (Bilquise et al., 2024). These difficulties can equally be examined as valuable insight that can pave the way for future improvements in chatbots development and implementation.

Given that the outcomes of the RESOURCEbot's deployment were mainly positive, future research can focus on improving the characteristics of the chatbot, to enhance its performance and improve its interaction with the students. Moreover, future studies can examine the use of chatbots for other purposes in higher education, with more in-depth research methods, and with other stakeholders, such as lecturers, developers and higher education institutions.

REFERENCES

Abbas, N., Whitfield, J., Atwell, E., Bowman, H., Pickard, T., & Walker, A. (2022). Online chat and chatbots to enhance mature student engagement in higher education. *International Journal of Lifelong Education*, *41*(3), 308-326.

Abdelmoiz, M. M., Mostafa, M. M., & Soliman, T. H. (2024). Developing an Educational Chatbot for Scientific Data Management Course Using DialogFlow. *Appl. Math*, *18*(3), 629-640.

Adamopoulou, E., & Moussiades, L. (2020). Chatbots: History, technology, and applications. *Machine Learning with applications*, *2*, 100006.

Adıgüzel, T., Kaya, M. H., & Cansu, F. K. (2023). Revolutionizing education with AI: Exploring the transformative potential of ChatGPT. *Contemporary Educational Technology.*

Belda-Medina, J., & Kokošková, V. (2023). Integrating chatbots in education: insights from the Chatbot-Human Interaction Satisfaction Model (CHISM). *International Journal of Educational Technology in Higher Education*, *20*(1), 62.

Bilquise, G., Ibrahim, S., & Salhieh, S. E. M. (2024). Investigating student acceptance of an academic advising chatbot in higher education institutions. *Education and Information Technologies*, *29*(5), 6357-6382.

Caldarini, G., Jaf, S., & McGarry, K. (2022). A literature survey of recent advances in chatbots. *Information*, *13*(1), 41.

Fulgencio, S.-V. (2024). Developing Effective Educational Chatbots with GPT: Insights from a Pilot Study in a University Subject. *Trends in Higher Education*, *3*(1), 155-168.

Govender, R. G. (2024). My AI students: Evaluating the proficiency of three AI chatbots in completeness and accuracy. *Contemporary Educational Technology*, *16*(2), ep509.

Hew, K. F., Huang, W., Du, J., & Jia, C. (2023). Using chatbots to support student goal setting and social presence in fully online activities: learner engagement and perceptions. *Journal of Computing in Higher Education*, *35*(1), 40-68.

Hobert, S. (2019). Say hello to 'coding tutor'! design and evaluation of a chatbot-based learning system supporting students to learn to program. In *Fortieth International Conference on Information Systems, Munich.*

Huang, W., Hew, K. F., & Gonda, D. E. (2019). Designing and evaluating three chatbot-enhanced activities for a flipped graduate course. *International Journal of Mechanical Engineering and Robotics Research.*

Kakar, S., Maiti, P., Taneja, K., Nandula, A., Nguyen, G., Zhao, A., Nandan, V., & Goel, A. (2024). Jill Watson: Scaling and Deploying an AI Conversational Agent in Online Classrooms. International Conference on Intelligent Tutoring Systems,

Koyuturk, C., Yavari, M., Theophilou, E., Bursic, S., Donabauer, G., Telari, A., Testa, A., Boiano, R., Gabbiadini, A., & Hernandez-Leo, D. (2023). Developing effective educational chatbots with chatgpt prompts: Insights from preliminary tests in a case study on social media literacy. *arXiv preprint arXiv:2306.10645.*

Kuhail, M. A., Alturki, N., Alramlawi, S., & Alhejori, K. (2023). Interacting with educational chatbots: A systematic review. *Education and Information Technologies*, *28*(1), 973-1018.

Labadze, L., Grigolia, M., & Machaidze, L. (2023). Role of AI chatbots in education: systematic literature review. *International Journal of Educational Technology in Higher Education*, *20*(1), 56.

Radziwill, N. M., & Benton, M. C. (2017). Evaluating quality of chatbots and intelligent conversational agents. *arXiv preprint arXiv:1704.04579.*

Sáiz-Manzanares, M. C., Marticorena-Sánchez, R., Martín-Antón, L. J., Díez, I. G., & Almeida, L. (2023). Perceived satisfaction of university students with the use of chatbots as a tool for self-regulated learning. *Heliyon*, *9*(1).

Smutny, P., & Schreiberova, P. (2020). Chatbots for learning: A review of educational chatbots for the Facebook Messenger. *Computers & Education*, *151*, 103862.

Song, D., Rice, M., & Oh, E. Y. (2019). Participation in online courses and interaction with a virtual agent. *International Review of Research in Open and Distributed Learning*, *20*(1).

Tlili, A., Shehata, B., Adarkwah, M. A., Bozkurt, A., Hickey, D. T., Huang, R., & Agyemang, B. (2023). What if the devil is my guardian angel: ChatGPT as a case study of using chatbots in education. *Smart learning environments*, *10*(1), 15.

Wollny, S., Schneider, J., Di Mitri, D., Weidlich, J., Rittberger, M., & Drachsler, H. (2021). Are we there yet?-a systematic literature review on chatbots in education. *Frontiers in artificial intelligence*, *4*, 654924.

ENHANCING ARTISTIC EDUCATION WITH AI: THE HAMLET WORKSHOP

Franco Ripa di Meana[1], Andrea Guidi[1], Alberto Giretti[2], Massimo Vaccarini[2], Matteo Zambelli[3] and Dilan Durmus[2]
[1]*Rome Fine Arts Academy, Via di Ripetta, 222 – 00186 Rome, Italy*
[2]*Marche Polytechnic University, Via Brecce Bianche, 60131 Ancona, Italy*
[3]*Florence University, Department of Architecture, DiDA, Via della Mattonaia, 8, 50121 Florence, Italy*

ABSTRACT

This paper presents a methodology for exploring the potential of artificial intelligence in supporting divergent thinking within academic arts education. Thirteen students from Rome Fine Arts Academy engaged with excerpts from Shakespeare's "Hamlet," using artificial intelligence (AI) tools such as °'°Kobi, Chat GPT, and Midjourney to develop interpretations and derivative artworks through a structured yet flexible exploration process. Preliminary findings highlight positive participant engagement, with evidence pointing to the emergence of divergent thinking. Participants' feedback revealed a significant distinction between their experiences with AI tools like Chat GPT and the features of °'°Kobi, suggesting that interactions with °'°Kobi facilitate easier creative exploration and engagement. The workshop's methodology provides a comprehensive framework for integrating AI-assisted tools with focus groups and collaborative educational work through artistic expression.

KEYWORDS

AI, Art Education, Workshop, Creativity, Divergent Thinking

1. INTRODUCTION

The workshop was designed as an activity with research and educational objectives within a structured academic framework. Thirteen students from diverse artistic backgrounds—including Multimedia Arts, Set Design, and Painting—engaged in the analytical and creative interpretation of selected scenes from Shakespeare's "Hamlet."

The process was enhanced by the AI tool °'°Kobi (°'°Kobi, 2024), a web-based AI tool designed to facilitate creative thinking catalysing the emergence of collective intelligence in communities of practice. Participants could also use other AI tools such as Chat GPT. Creative outputs, including artworks and individual documentation of the related artistic process were published on the Research Catalogue, an online repository for artistic research (Research Catalogue, 2024)

From a research perspective, the workshop served as a live study to identify and observe divergent thinking in artistic processes. We particularly focused on gathering data to understand how participants analysed, drew inspiration, and developed thematic elements of literary texts into novel creative outputs while being supported by AI tools. By examining the interactions between students and the AI, we aim to study divergent thinking, as inferred from their chat interactions with the AI.

The educational component of the workshop was designed to provide students with experience in artistic creation and interpretation. Students engaged with excerpts from "Hamlet" through a structured yet open-ended task that encouraged them to develop personal artistic responses to the text. This approach aimed to challenge individual creativity while stimulating students' collaborative skills, as participants shared and developed their analysis of the proposed text and their creative outputs collectively.

2. ENHANCING LEARNING IN ARTISTIC EDUCATION

The integration of Artificial Intelligence (AI) into educational paradigms has increasingly gained interest over recent years, providing innovative pathways for enhancing learning experiences across various disciplines. This literature review examines the current role of AI in education, particularly in creative and artistic fields, exploring the opportunities, challenges, and implications of such integration. The review also delves into further foundational aspects of the workshop such as collaborative and experiential learning.

2.1 Opportunities and Challenges for AI in Artistic Education

AI serves as a foundational aspect of the workshop proposed in this research, assisting participants in the ideation phase and creating the conditions to observe divergent thinking in their creative activities.

Ouyang and Jiao (2021) proposed three paradigms of AI in education: AI-directed, AI-supported, and AI-empowered learning. Their research emphasises how AI can shift educational practices from traditional teacher-centred models to more experiential and student-centred approaches, thereby fostering greater student agency and creativity. Similarly, Liang et al. (2020) highlighted various applications of AI in educational settings, such as intelligent tutoring systems, adaptive learning environments, and collaborative creative writing platforms. These AI applications have been shown to enhance student engagement, provide personalised learning experiences, and support the development of critical thinking.

AI tools can act as co-creators, generating ideas and suggestions that students can refine, thereby supporting creativity and expanding imaginative capacities (Berns & Colton, 2020). Chen (2020) explores how AI tools can support art education by providing methods for artistic exploration and creation. They highlight the potential of AI to act as a co-creator, offering suggestions and generating ideas that students can refine and build upon. This perspective aligns with findings from other scholars, such as Berns and Colton (2020), who discuss the bridging of generative deep learning and computational creativity, emphasising AI's capability to generate novel ideas and facilitate creative processes. Moreover, studies by Giretti et al. (2023) have discussed the incorporation of large language models (LLMs) like CHAT GPT into the educational methodologies used in art and design education to support creative thinking. AI tools can act as co-creators, generating ideas and suggestions that students can refine, thereby supporting creativity and expanding imaginative capacities (Berns & Colton, 2020). Furthermore, Habib et al. (2017) examined the role of AI in supporting various teaching and learning. They found that AI tools could provide substantial support for creative tasks, facilitating a deeper understanding of artistic concepts and creating a more interactive learning environment. Goksel and Bozkurt (2019) provide a comprehensive overview of AI applications in education, focusing on art education. They discuss how AI can support personalised learning and creative exploration, but also highlight significant barriers, including the complexity of developing AI tools that effectively replicate human artistic processes, and the ethical concerns related to AI's role in creative fields.

Significant challenges arise, including the ethical implications of AI-generated art and the necessity for teachers to adapt to new technologies while maintaining artistic integrity and originality in students' work. Rudolph et al. (2023) examines the disruptive impact of AI assistants like ChatGPT in higher education, including art education. They note improvements in AI-generated content quality and its potential to change teaching methodologies, while also addressing challenges such as the need for a robust conceptual structure to guide AI integration and the regulatory implications for educational institutions. Greenhalgh (2023) explores the practical applications of generative AI tools in higher education classrooms, providing insights into how these tools can assist in the ideation and brainstorming phases of creative projects. He also discusses the challenges of integrating these technologies effectively into curricula, ensuring they enhance rather than detract from the educational experience. Cetnic and She (2021) discuss the technical and creative challenges of using AI in visual arts. They highlight the limitations of current AI systems in fully understanding the nuanced aspects of art, such as style and context, and call for more sophisticated models to better mimic human creativity and interpretation.

2.2 Experiential Learning and Divergent Thinking

The practical nature of the workshop as well as the interaction with the AI were designed to facilitate experiential learning. Connecting Experiential Learning and Project-Based Learning, as discussed by Eisner

(2002), encourages students to engage deeply with their work through practical, real-world projects, emphasising active learning and collaboration, making it effective in art and design education. Kolb's Experiential Learning Theory proposes that learning is a cyclical process involving concrete experience, reflective observation, abstract conceptualization, and active experimentation (Kolb, 1984). Greene (1995) emphasises how hands-on experiences and reflective practice drive meaningful engagement through art-based inquiry promoting creativity, critical thinking, and cultural appreciation.

Focus groups occurring in the workshop were conceived to facilitate collaborative learning. Collaborative learning in art education involves students working together, sharing their creative processes, and critiquing each other's work. This approach is meant to facilitate a deeper understanding of artistic concepts and broader cultural and social contexts. Scager et al. (2016) highlight the benefits of collaborative learning, noting that it promotes higher engagement, motivation, and the development of interpersonal and cognitive skills. Experiential learning can effectively occur through collaborative activities, as they allow learners to engage in meaningful dialogue, share diverse perspectives, and collaboratively solve problems, thereby enhancing their learning experience (Smith & MacGregor, 1992).

By engaging students in creative tasks, we aimed to stimulate their creativity and create the conditions to observe the dynamics of divergent thinking. Divergent thinking, a component of creativity (Runco, 2014; Torrance, 1966), involves generating multiple, unique solutions to open-ended problems. According to Runco (2012), divergent thinking is an indicator of creative potential and encompasses key dimensions such as fluency, flexibility, originality, and elaboration. In the context of art and design education, experiential learning models play a significant role in supporting creativity. The integration of AI, particularly Large Language Models (LLMs), in education holds potential for enhancing divergent thinking. Berns and Colton (2020) suggest that AI can act as a catalyst for expanding imaginative capacities and creative practice by providing diverse perspectives.

3. °'°KOBI

The Hamlet Workshop incorporated a variety of tools designed to enhance participants' engagement and individual and collaborative activities. Among the AI tools available to participants was the °'°Kobi system. The °'°Kobi system is a knowledge system (Giretti et al. 2022) designed to facilitate creative exploration and deep engagement with artistic content by leveraging AI to interpret queries and recontextualize results. Results are based on a database of qualified artistic research publications from Research Catalogue constituting its system knowledge base. °'°Kobi uses large language models to organise such knowledge into relational structures that encompass multiple semantic contexts (Giretti et al. 2023).

From the user's point of view, the AI's responses are displayed through a graphic user interface, which includes a text and a vocal interface built upon the browser's speech API. This dual-mode interface allows users to engage in accessible terminological searches, expanding the modes of interactions with the system and enriching the user interactive experience.

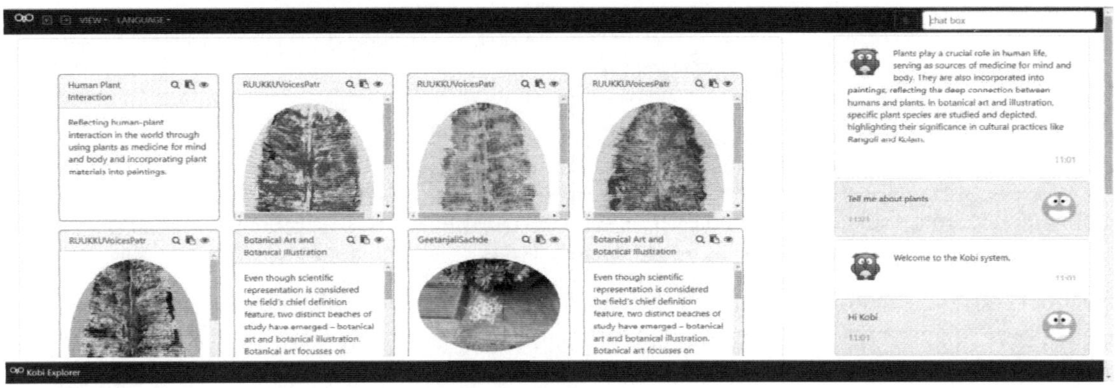

Figure 1. The °'°Kobi chat interface. Users can type their queries in the top-left chat box. Responses are displayed below the chat box and pronounced by a synthetic voice through text-to-speech. They can include related media such as images

Users initiate dialogue by proposing topics of discussion, such as 'search for ...' or 'tell me about ...'. The system then searches the semantic latent space of the knowledge base to receive information semantically close to the search topic. Such contents form the basis for generating the context of the discussion with the AI. By crafting narratives and providing explanations based on the user's semantic position, this approach ensures that the AI provides relevant and contextually enriched information grounded on qualified artistic references. As shown in Fig.1, the system provides text responses to user queries (a text-to-speech functionality is also available). Additionally, it retrieves and displays relevant media from the knowledge base. This media includes text and images related to the user's query. The system is designed to open new interpretative horizons to the topics proposed by the user to the AI. This, of course, is not guaranteed, and depends to a great degree on the kind of knowledge that builds °'°Kobi's knowledge base. Its current knowledge is based on artistic publications, enabling it to generate contexts that offer critical interpretations and novel content. Artistic research publications have proven to likely trigger divergent conversations, as the system tends to interpret the subject's query with greater flexibility. For example, research on the topic of ghosts and music may return a reply contextualised on spectralism, a late 20th-century approach to musical composition that focuses on the analysis of sound spectra.

4. PARTICIPANTS & DATA COLLECTION

The study involved thirteen participants, mostly from Italy (eleven individuals), with one participant each from China and Persia. The average age among the participants was 25 years old, with an even gender distribution of approximately half female and half male. Students participating in the workshop earned educational credits akin to those of a standard academic course.

Detailed chat logs between participants and the Kobi AI conversational agent captured interactions that provided insights into how the AI facilitated creative thinking and guided participants toward new ideas. This data is the subject of quantitative analysis evaluating the divergence of themes and topics in the participants' interactions with the AI. This involved observing the shifts in dialogue trajectories as participants explored various themes in "Hamlet" or related these themes to other texts and ideas through AI prompts. A forthcoming analysis will measure how each interaction with the AI led to potentially new lines of inquiry.

Data collected for qualitative analysis includes recordings of all focus group sessions, which provided a source of data on how participants' thoughts evolved through interaction and collaboration. In addition to the discussions, the study monitored the number and types of artistic outputs, including photographs, drawings, and digital art. These outputs served as a visual representation of how the themes of "Hamlet" were interpreted and expressed artistically by each participant. Collectively, this qualitative data aims to offer a detailed view of the creative dynamics within the workshop, revealing both the individual and collective learning outcomes facilitated by the structured activities and interactions.

At the conclusion of the activities, participants filled out anonymous structured questionnaires evaluating the workshop.

5. THE AMLETH WORKSHOP

The workshop began on March 8th. Participants were introduced to the goals, tasks, and assessed their familiarity with "Hamlet." They identified and discussed features of the text and were assigned to represent their interpretations through various forms, including written pieces, multimedia elements, or visual arts. All creations had to maintain a clear connection to the original text's themes. By the second session on March 15th, they refined their projects with feedback and discussed the role of AI tools they used in sparking ideas. By March 22nd, they prepared for final presentations of their work.

5.1 First Session

The initial meeting was set in a classroom setting where participants were oriented about the workshop goals, confirmed their understanding via consent forms, and assessed their familiarity with "Hamlet" through a baseline questionnaire. This questionnaire explored their exposure to the play, live performances, and related artistic works.

Researchers clarified the nature of the workshop's tasks. It was emphasised that the first session was meant to focus on extracting and discussing themes within the text. Researchers leading the activity highlighted several examples of such themes, including the dynamics of the father/son relationship, the existential contrast between ghosts and humans, and the complex layers of communication evident within the play. These examples helped to illustrate the depth and variety of elements that participants could consider.

The workshop activities started with a curated exploration of Shakespeare's "Hamlet," focusing on Act One, scenes 4 and 5—the central dialogue between Hamlet and the Ghost. These scenes were selected to emphasise the fundamental relationships and scenarios of the literature work, rather than the intricate details of the plot, facilitating a focused analysis by the participants. Participants were expected to connect intuitively with the mythical aspects of the characters, particularly Hamlet, regardless of their familiarity with the overall play. This approach aimed to provoke deeper thought about character motivation and thematic significance rather than plot mechanics.

For the reading session, each participant received the text printed in both English and a highly regarded Italian translation by Cesare Garboli, ensuring accessibility and comprehension. To enhance the classroom setting for discussions and group activities, tables were reorganised from the traditional row distribution into a more collaborative configuration. Instead of rows, researchers arranged the tables in a circle shape layout. This setup enhanced visibility and interaction, supporting group dynamics and fostering an inclusive environment for discussion and idea sharing.

The reading session was designed to establish a common baseline of concepts, observations, and details drawn from the text of "Hamlet." Initially, participants were invited to identify and share a particular theme from the text that resonated with them. They had complete autonomy in their choices, which could range from a specific word or phrase, a character relationship, or a broader thematic concept. This exercise encouraged participants to engage with the material on a personal level, sparking a diverse range of perspectives right from the beginning. In a subsequent round of discussion, participants contributed their own insights, building on the initial features identified by the researchers. This iterative dialogue allowed the group to integrate their interpretations. The session continued with a concise tutorial on the °'°Kobi chat interface and Research Catalogue editor interface.

5.2 Second and Third Sessions

Subsequent sessions on March 15th and 22nd revolved around the development and presentation of artistic projects.

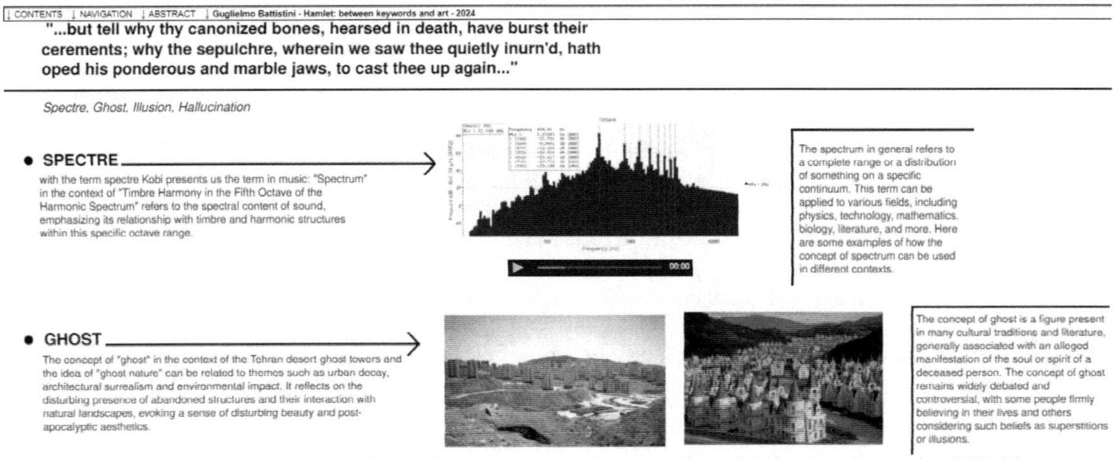

Figure 2. Screenshot of a participant's brainstorming document from the ideation phase using °'°Kobi

During the second session, participants were asked to report on their ideation and craft activities over the past week and discuss the progress of their tasks. The feedback shared was particularly insightful, highlighting the value of °'°Kobi in facilitating participant interactions and enhancing their creative processes (see Figure 2 for a screenshot of a participant's brainstorming document from the ideation phase using °'°Kobi). Participants discussed °'°Kobi's agency in sparking new ideas, connections and unexpected insights, thereby enriching their initial creative concepts.

It was also agreed that the Research Catalogue publications should not only showcase original artistic material but also document the creative process participants underwent, using various tools, including but not limited to °'°Kobi. This approach aimed to provide a comprehensive view of both the final outputs and the developmental journey of each participant, capturing the evolution of their ideas and the influences of their interactions with the AI.

During the third session, participants presented their final creative work. Some examples of these creative outputs are shown in Figure 3. Several examples were shared during the session, as well as material documenting the ways in which participants engaged with the text excerpts from Amleth and AI tools. The session closed with an informal review of °'°Kobi's system usability, where participants provided feedback on their experiences using °'°Kobi. This feedback highlighted various user requests and insights.

Figure 3. Examples of creative outputs from the workshop. © Anonymous. Used with permission under CC BY-NC-ND.

6. INITIAL INSIGHTS AND LIMITATIONS

Feedback from participants indicated a high level of satisfaction with the structure of the workshops and technology's role in enhancing their creative explorations. The ability of AI tools such as °'°Kobi to suggest novel associations and ideas was particularly valued.

Participants declared in the anonymous questionnaire that their engagement with the workshop topics was notably high, with 50% expressing the highest interest and 40% a high level of interest; only 10% reported no interest. Similarly, 60% felt highly engaged by the workshop, 30% moderately so, and only 10% found it not engaging. The workshop was considered significantly enriching to their educational journey by most participants, with 70% affirming it absolutely provided useful tools, information, and stimuli, and 30% agreeing generally. Overall, the workshop was evaluated as very stimulating and engaging by 80% of the participants, 10% found it stimulating, and 10% considered it boring and unappealing.

During focus groups, when asked to describe their experience in the AI-assisted sessions, students highlighted the supportive role of AI, particularly °'°Kobi, in their creative processes. Such feedback has significant implications for the context of this paper. Firstly, it supports the premise that AI could be integrated into educational settings to enhance learning experiences in an art educational context. Students' positive perceptions indicate that AI is seen as a beneficial tool in their creative processes. The feedback provides evidence that aligns with theoretical concepts discussed in the paper, such as the benefits of experiential learning and the role of AI in supporting artistic education. Their experience suggests that °'°Kobi supported creativity, offering perspectives and insights during students' creative work.

Participants' feedback highlights a clear distinction between their experiences with AI tools, such as Chat GPT, and °'°Kobi, framing a comparative discussion that underscores the advantages of °'°Kobi approach to AI in supporting creativity in art education. Participants noted that while Chat GPT provided precise responses, it lacked the flexibility and creativity needed for artistic exploration. °'°Kobi was appreciated for its ability to support creative processes by offering the re-contextualisation of concepts. Participant 7 provided a specific example to illustrate their point. They mentioned that when using the word 'hallucination', "°'°Kobi gave a philosophical context, whereas Chat GPT provided a more psychological interpretation". Participant 1 stated that many of the results from Chat GPT were not of interest as the responses were "much more scientific and targeted to the exact query". Furthermore, Participant 1 mentioned that the precision of Chat GPT felt "anti-creative," a sentiment echoed by Participant 7, who found Chat GPT more suitable for "strictly academic use." Participant 2 found °'°Kobi extremely functional as "it responded to the need for using artificial intelligence in an artistic way".

Participant 10 compared their experiences with °'°Kobi and Midjourney. They found Midjourney more disappointing and less immediate compared to °'°Kobi, which had "its own style" and "offered more variation due to the different contents from various artists". The textual parts in °'°Kobi were found to be much more stimulating. They elaborated on their workflow, noting that in both Midjourney and °'°Kobi, they worked in cycles where the output informed the next input. It was more common for °'°Kobi to inspire a prompt for Midjourney rather than the other way around.

This distinction is important in the context of the paper because it validates the hypothesis that °'°Kobi's design and functionality are suited for supporting creativity in art education. The feedback from participants aligns with the theoretical framework presented in the paper, which emphasises a possible role for AI tools in supporting divergent thinking and creativity in art education.

Despite the positive outcomes, there are limitations that must be critically reflected upon. One significant limitation is the relatively small sample size of the workshop, which consisted of only thirteen participants. While the feedback is insightful, it may not be fully representative of the broader population of art students. This limitation calls for caution in generalizing the findings to larger educational contexts or different cultural backgrounds. To address this point, current research efforts are actively engaged in conducting similar workshops with a more diverse and larger group of participants to validate and extend the findings.

A further limitation relates to the nature of the data presented. Much of the current data is based on self-assessments provided by participants through structured questionnaires and focus group discussions. While these self-assessments offer valuable insights into participants' experiences and perceptions, they are inherently subjective and may not fully capture the nuances of how AI tools like °'°Kobi influence the creative process. We are currently conducting both quantitative and qualitative analyses to further validate and deepen the understanding of the data. Detailed chat logs between participants and the °'°Kobi AI, recordings of focus group sessions, and analyses of artistic outputs are being reviewed to evaluate the semantic divergence of themes, the evolution of ideas, and the overall impact of AI on the participants' creative processes. This ongoing analysis is expected to support the objective understanding of the workshop's outcomes.

7. CONCLUSIONS

In this paper we presented a workshop-based approach that integrates AI tools in enhancing artistic education at Rome Fine Arts Academy. By combining individual AI-assisted activities with collaborative discussions, participants engaged with Shakespeare's "Hamlet" and produced creative outputs published in the Research Catalogue. Participants benefited from a structured yet flexible framework that encouraged personal artistic responses to the text while facilitating collaborative exploration. The °'°Kobi system played a crucial role in this process, providing a platform for semantic exploration and creative idea generation to stimulate students' divergent thinking. The Research Catalogue served as an essential tool for documenting and publishing the creative outputs, ensuring that the developmental journey was comprehensively recorded and accessible for further academic inquiry.

Data from participants' feedback reinforces the argument for innovative methodologies in art education. It suggests that incorporating AI tools like °'°Kobi can lead to more engaging and stimulating educational experiences, potentially setting a precedent for future use of the tool in pedagogical approaches. The positive students feedback highlights the possibility of developing AI tools that are user-friendly and tailored to the needs of learners, underscoring the potential for AI assistants to be learning partners in art settings.

Future research will focus on a detailed quantitative and qualitative analysis of the data collected to evaluate the full impact of AI during students' activities in the workshop. This includes examining the role of AI in facilitating and observing divergent thinking and understanding how AI tools like °'°Kobi can be optimised to support artistic processes in academic settings. The insights gained from this study will contribute to the ongoing development of AI-assisted educational frameworks, aiming to enrich the learning experiences of students in the arts. Subsequent research may involve rigorous, controlled experiments across a broader range of educational environments including art, design and architecture. These studies may incorporate structured questionnaires aligned with cognitive theories to gain a deeper understanding of how generative AI impacts artistic learning outcomes. These experiments will aim to refine the application of AI in education, ensuring that the tools enhance creativity and learning outcomes and are adaptable to different educational contexts and student demographics.

REFERENCES

Bern, S., & Colton, S. (2020). Bridging Generative Deep Learning and Computational Creativity. *In proceedings of the International Conference on Computational Creativity (ICCC).*

Cetinic, E., & She, J. (2021). Understanding and creating art with AI: Review and outlook. arXiv. Cornell University, Ithaca, NY. https://arxiv.org/abs/2102.09109

Chen, W., Shidujaman, M., Jin, J., & Ahmed, S. U. (2020). A methodological approach to create interactive art in artificial intelligence. *In HCI International 2020 -- Late Breaking Papers: Cognition, Learning and Games* (pp. 13-31). Springer International Publishing.

Eisner, E. W. (2002). *The Arts and the Creation of Mind.* Yale University Press, New Haven, CT.

Giretti, A., Lemma, M., Zambelli, M., & Ripa di Meana, F. (2022). Knowledge Mapping for Creative Thinking. *In Proceedings of the International Conference on Cognition and Exploratory Learning in the Digital Age (CELDA).*

Giretti, A., Durmus, D., Vaccarini, M., Zambelli, M., Guidi, A., & Ripa di Meana, F. (2023). Integrating Large Language Models in Art and Design Education. *In Proceedings of the International Conference on Cognition and Exploratory Learning in the Digital Age (CELDA).*

Goksel, N., & Bozkurt, A. (2019). Artificial intelligence in education. *In Handbook of Research on Learning in the Age of Transhumanism* (pp. 224-236). IGI Global, Hershey, PA, USA.

Greene, M. (1995). Releasing the imagination: *Essays on education, the arts, and social change*. Jossey-Bass, San Francisco, CA, USA.

Greenhalgh, N. (2023). How Can AI Tools Like ChatGPT Be Used in Higher Education? Daniels College of Business, University of Denver, Denver, CO, USA.

Habib, S., Vogel, T., Anli, X., & Thorne, E. (2024). How does generative artificial intelligence impact student creativity? *Journal of Creativity, 34*(1), 100072.

Kobi (2024). https://www.kobidev.it

Kolb, D. A. (1984). *Experiential Learning: Experience as the Source of Learning and Development*. Prentice Hall, Englewood Cliffs, NJ, USA.

Liang, J. C., Hwang, G. J., Chen, M. R. A., & Darmawansah, D. (2023). Roles and research foci of artificial intelligence in language education: an integrated bibliographic analysis and systematic review approach. *Interactive Learning Environments, 31*(7), 4270-4296.

Ouyang, F., & Jiao, P. (2021). Artificial intelligence in education: The three paradigms. *Computers and Education: Artificial Intelligence, 2*, 100020. Elsevier, San Diego, CA, USA.

Phillips, K. W., Northcraft, G. B., & Neale, M. A. (2006). Surface-level diversity and decision-making in groups: When does deep-level similarity help? *Group processes & intergroup relations*, 9(4), 467-482.

Research Catalogue (2024). https://www.researchcatalogue.net/.

Rudolph, J., Tan, S., & Aspland, T. (2023). Editorial 6 (2): Personal digital assistant or job killer? Generative AI and the teaching profession in higher education. *Journal of Applied Learning and Teaching*, 6(2), 07-16.

Runco, M. A., & Acar, S. (2012). Divergent thinking as an indicator of creative potential. *Creativity research journal*, 24(1), 66-75.

Runco, M. A. (2014). Creativity: *Theories and themes: Research, development, and practice* (2nd ed.). Elsevier Academic Press, San Diego, CA, USA.

Scager, K., Boonstra, J., Peeters, T., Vulperhorst, J., & Wiegant, F. (2016). Collaborative learning in higher education: Evoking positive interdependence. *CBE—Life Sciences Education*, Vol. 15, No. 4, article 69.

Smith, B. L., & MacGregor, J. T. (1992). What is collaborative learning. *In Collaborative Learning: A Sourcebook for Higher Education*. National Center on Postsecondary Teaching, Learning, and Assessment. University Park, PA, USA.

Torrance, E. P. (1966). *The Torrance Tests of Creative Thinking – Norms-Technical Manual Research Edition – Verbal Tests, Forms A and B – Figural Tests, Forms A and B*. Personnel Press, Princeton, NJ, USA.

EXPLORING COMPUTING PARADIGMS AND THEORETICAL PERSPECTIVES ON PROGRAMMING AND COMPUTATIONAL THINKING IN MATHEMATICS EDUCATION

Said Hadjerrouit
University of Agder
Faculty of Technology and Sciences, Department of Mathematical Sciences
4604 Kristiansand, Norway

ABSTRACT

This article aims to problematize the role of programming in mathematics education. Problematizing involves acknowledging a deeper complexity in the understanding of programming than originally perceived and questioning its assumed value in mathematics education. This approach entails identifying its underlying paradigmatic assumptions in relation to computational and mathematical thinking, as well as theoretical perspectives that offer different angles on issues inherent to programming. In essence, problematizing programming does not simply endorse its assumed utility as a powerful tool. Instead, it involves questioning programming in the context of mathematical and computational thinking, computer programs, and their meaningful integration into the teaching and learning of mathematics. Problematization challenges the notion of programming solely as a 'powerful digital resource' urging a critical evaluation of its role and potential impacts in mathematics education.

KEYWORDS

Computational Thinking, Computer Programs, Mathematical Thinking, Paradigm, Programming

1. INTRODUCTION

Programming has recently become a mandatory subject in Norwegian schools as the country seeks to prepare teachers with the skills to teach programming and computational thinking. The increased integration of programming into school mathematics has led to its expanded implementation in universities, prompting a need to explore its contribution both to secondary school and undergraduate mathematics education (Gueudet et al., 2023; Gueudet, 2022; Gueudet et al., 2020; Hadjerrouit & Hansen, 2022; Hansen & Hadjerrouit, 2023). Stakeholders and decision-makers assume that the use of programming as a digital resource in mathematics education will positively enhance mathematical learning and teaching.

To critically examine this assumption, it is essential to consider the 'problematic' aspects inherent in programming. This entails not simply accepting programming as an obvious solution to mathematical teaching and learning. Rather, it involves questioning the paradigmatic assumptions of programming in relation to computational and mathematical thinking. It also entails exploring diverse theoretical perspectives that provide alternative approaches to addressing the inherent issues in programming. This problematization of programming leads to three interrelated research questions:

a) *What paradigmatic assumptions shape the understanding of computer programs (CPs) and computational thinking (CT)?*
b) *What distinct attributes define computational thinking (CT), mathematical thinking (MT), and programming, and how are they interrelated?*
c) *Which theoretical perspectives provide meaningful constructs for integrating mathematical thinking (MT), computational thinking (CT), and programming into mathematics education?*

This article is structured as follows. Firstly, the concept of "problematic," which serves as a roadmap for problematizing programming, is defined. Secondly, the paradigms of computer programs (CPs) are outlined.

Thirdly, the relationships between mathematical thinking (MT), computational thinking (CT), and programming are described. Next, theoretical perspectives for integrating MT, CT, and programming into mathematics education are presented. Lastly, the article concludes with a discussion on a potential paradigmatic shift or computational turn resulting from increased use of programming in mathematics education.

2. THE PROBLEMATIC OF PROGRAMMING

The concept of "problematic" ("problématique" in French) was invented in 1949 by the philosopher G. Bachelard in his book "*Le rationalisme appliqué*" and has inspired prominent philosophers and their ideas, such as M. Foucault's concept of episteme, G. Deleuze's reflections on the "Problem-Idea" in his main doctoral thesis "Difference and Repetition" (1968).

A 'problematic' (as a noun) "is not simply a set of questions. It is rather the matrix or the angle from which it will become possible and even necessary to formulate a certain number of precise problems" (Maniglier, 2012, p. 21). To problematize is not to try to tell the "truth" about programming, as if there were properties of programming out there waiting for educators and researchers to discover them; to problematize is to try to solve specific, singular problems related to programming in correlation to mathematics education. With other words, a 'problematic' is rather the perspective from which it becomes possible and necessary to formulate a certain number of precise problems (Maniglier, 2012).

Moreover, the concept of problematic initiates a critique of the subject–object relation in the explanation of thought in general and of science in particular. According to Maniglier (2012) referring to Bachelard, to think is not to tell and describe the truth about any particular given objects (be these living beings or material things, e.g., programming in this case), as if there is correspondence of thought to a mind-independent world out there waiting for researchers and educators to lay their attention on it; to think is to try to solve specific, singular problems.

Accordingly, there are only singular problems, which simultaneously determine the subject to think and the object to be thought. Bachelard (1949, p. 56) pointed out that 'we must first posit the object as a subject of the problem, and the subject of the cogito as a consciousness of the problem'. In other words, neither objects nor subjects, neither things nor minds, exist primarily. There are only problems, which constitute the very possibility of the correlation between subjects and objects (Maniglier, 2012).

Applied to programming, problematizing involves not simply accepting programming as a given solution that inherently benefits the learning and teaching of mathematics. Problematizing requires initiating critical reflection on computer programs (CPs) in correlation to computational thinking (CT). By reversing this correlation and applying it to mathematics education, we can think about what we want to achieve in terms of learning and teaching and consider critically how programming and computational thinking (CT) might support mathematical thinking (MT).

In summary, by beginning with computer programs (CPs) and exploring the correlations between mathematical thinking (MT), computational thinking (CT), and programming, we can better identify the paradigmatic assumptions underlying programming in relation to mathematics teaching and learning. This approach allows us to offer appropriate theoretical perspectives that may challenge the current status of programming in mathematics education.

3. COMPUTING PARADIGMS

This section of the paper addresses the first research question: *What paradigmatic assumptions shape the understanding of computer programs (CPs) and computational thinking (CT)?*

To address this question, it is important to note that mathematics education is still not well informed by paradigms of programming and computer programs (CPs) from computer science education. Upon closer examination of the research literature, it becomes evident that there exists a deficiency in interdisciplinary perspectives and linkages between the disciplines of computer science and mathematics education concerning paradigmatic foundations of computer programs (CPs), computational thinking (CT), and programming in general. This deficiency leads to a restricted understanding of the affordances and constraints of CPs, as diverse paradigms and theories offer varied insights and perspectives on programming. Clearly, neglecting to critically examine these matters can hinder the progression of knowledge and restrict the comprehension of the potential benefits of programming within mathematics education.

Given this background, it appears that many novice teacher and student programmers have no appropriate paradigm of CPs, and, as a result, they are faced with immediate and challenging (sometimes "brutal") feedback while programming on conclusions drawn from their erroneous paradigm, especially when using an advanced programming language like Python.

Clearly, teaching and learning programming supposes an effective paradigm and the reading and appropriation of experienced people's CPs. Reading well-designed CPs improves vocabulary, understanding, and communication skills. Moreover, making mistakes when developing CPs increases syntactical and semantical awareness, and computational thinking (CT) as the very basis of CPs.

There are several paradigms of CPs that connect ontology with epistemological and methodological issues (Eden, 2007; Rapaport, 2020; Turner, 2014). Firstly, the rationalistic paradigm, which considers CPs as abstract mathematical entities, and writing CPs is a mathematical activity. From an epistemological point of view, deductive reasoning is the only accepted method for investigating CPs.

Secondly, the technocratic paradigm argues that CPs are ontologically concrete entities. From an epistemological point of view, knowledge about CPs emanates only from experience and posteriori procedures.

Thirdly, from the perspective or the scientific paradigm, CPs cannot ontologically be reduced neither to concrete nor to abstract entities, and writing CPs combines priori and posteriori procedures, that is deductive and inductive reasoning.

Finally, the linguistic paradigm considers CPs ontologically as linguistic objects fixed by the grammar of their language with a technological manifestation. Epistemologically, knowledge about CPs is determined by the syntactic and semantic definitions and their technological constructions.

Some specific questions arise from considering these paradigms: What is the nature of CPs that are mathematical? technocratic? scientific? linguistic? or a combination of these? Do CPs imply a new philosophy of objects (or artefacts) that are purely computational? Is there a computational ontology, epistemology, and methodology? To what extent are these relevant for studying CPs in relation to learning and teaching mathematics? What theoretical perspectives are most appropriate to address these issues? And finally, what is the link that connects the paradigms?

Based on these considerations, it is argued that CT is the link that connects CPs with the paradigms. CT is not a discipline, per se, but "it must be understood in its proper context, which is that of CS" (Computer Science) (Lodi & Martini, 2021, p. 884-885). In this regard, CT is transversal to the paradigms, but cannot be reduced to this role (Ibid). There is CT for and inside the rationalistic paradigm, but also within the other paradigms.-But this does not mean that CT is only instrumental to these paradigms. CT is rather transversal because it has a proper epistemological identity. Hence, it can be considered as an epistemological lens and a set of attributes for understanding computational objects (Figure 1).

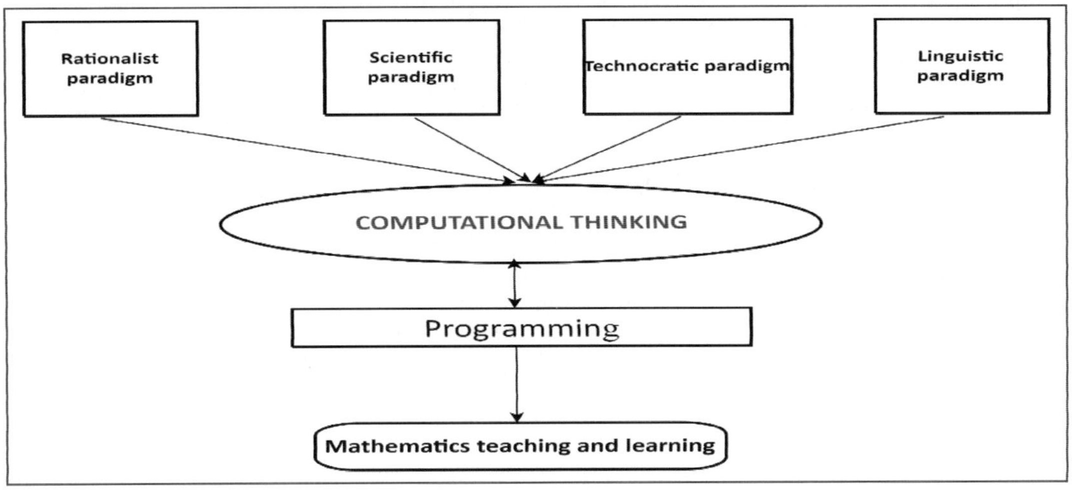

Figure 1. CT as epistemological lens and transversal to computing paradigms

4. COMPUTATIONAL THINKING (CT), MATHEMATICAL THINKING (MT), PROGRAMMING AND THEIR RELATIONSHIPS

This section addresses the second research question: *What distinct attributes define computational thinking (CT), mathematical thinking (MT), and programming, and how are they interrelated*? The question aims to explore the relationships between MT, CT, and programming in the context of mathematical problem-solving.

4.1 Computational Thinking (CT)

CT was originally defined by Papert (1980) on how to utilize programming as a tool for children to think and learn with. With the emergence of a new wave of CT, Wing (2006, p. 33) argues that CT represents a "universally applicable attitude and skill set everyone, not just computer scientists". CT is the thought process involved in "formulating a problem and expressing its solution(s) in such a way that a computer – human or machine – can effectively carry out" (ibid). But still, no established definition of CT exists yet, even though several descriptions share central attributes (Denning & Tedre, 2021; Elicer & Tamborg, 2023; Hadjerrouit & Hansen, 2022; Shute et al., 2017; Weintrop et al., 2016). These attributes are the capacity to *think algorithmically* as a means of problem-solving; the *breaking down of problems* into their constituent parts; *generalization* by identifying similarities; abstraction to simplify problems by removing extraneous details, and *evaluation* to ensure the suitability of the problem-solving approach (Csizmadia et al., 2015).

4.2 Mathematical Thinking (MT)

Likewise, there is no consensus on an exact definition of MT. Similar terms are "mathematical reasoning" and "mathematical abilities". MT consists of "beliefs about math, problem solving processes, and justification for solutions". MT involves the "application of math skills to solve math problems, such as equations and functions" (Shute et al. 2017, p. 145). More generally, MT includes algebraic, geometric, numerical, and modelling reasoning. However, despite the lack of established definitions, MT and CT share several commonalities: Mathematical modelling, problem-solving, data analysis, statistics, and probability (Shute et al., 2017; Weintrop, 2016). Mathematical modelling provides a foundation for the use and development of CT. Problem-solving is common both to MT and CT, and data analysis requires numerical thinking.

4.3 Programming and Coding

Programming as a multi-step iterative process that spans over problem analysis, designing a solution, evaluating its effectiveness, and implementing the solution through coding. As such, programming is part of the broader concept of CT (Saqr et al., 2021). Coding itself is part of the broader concept of programming and represents the step in the programming process where instructions are coded in a programming language. Coding is often used by organizations looking to deliver 'coding knowledge' to teachers (e.g., code.org).

4.4 Programming and Natural Languages

Programming languages use artificial languages with a strict grammar, logical, precise syntax and semantics, and no tolerance for errors. In contrast, natural languages have a loose and flexible syntax and semantics that allow for creativity and variation. Additionally, a natural language is neither informational nor communicational. It is something quite different, it is the transmission of "order-words" (Deleuze & Guattari, 1987). With other words, it "(…) tells us what we 'must' think, retain, expect, (…)" (Ibid). Although there are substantial differences between programming and natural languages, some critical questions emerge from these considerations: Do programming languages influence our thought processes? Is programming a tool that shapes the practices of teaching and learning mathematics? A point is common to both languages, namely: Like reading literature of high-quality in English or French, learning programming entails engaging with well-designed CPs and adopting the expertise of good programmers. This process not only enhances vocabulary, syntactical and semantical awareness, but also fosters better understanding and communication skills.

4.5 Programming and Algebra: Commonalities and Differences

An illustration of both commonality and difference between MT and programming can be seen in the assignment sign '=' in programming and the equal sign '=' in algebra (Figure 2).

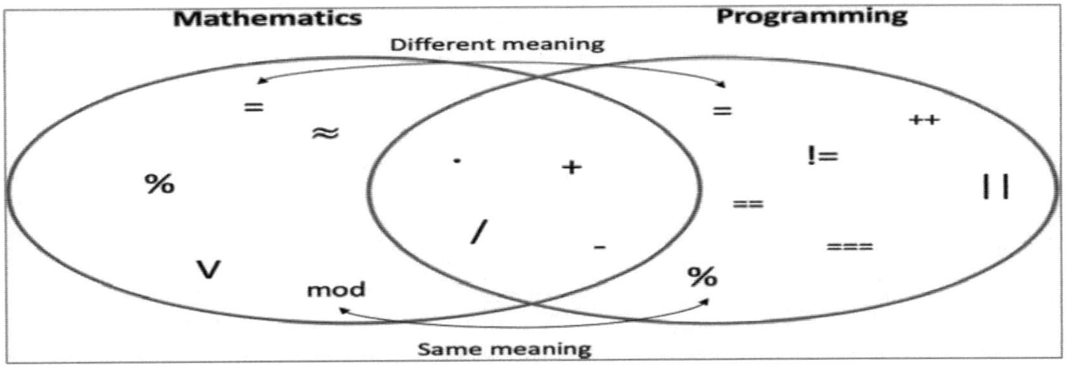

Figure 2. The sign '=' and '%' in programming vs. the sign '=' and 'mod' in algebra (Bråting et al., 2022, p. 301)

The symbol '=' is interpreted as a command to compute a new value (e.g., in Python) and as an equivalence relation in algebra (mathematics). The key difference is that an assignment is temporal, while an equivalence relation is timeless and holds universally. Consequently, '=' in algebra may require didactic effort from students to transition from an operational to a relational understanding. Clearly delineating the differences in the meaning of '=' could facilitate the development of algebraic thinking through contrasting examples and promoting accuracy awareness. In contrast, 'mod' and '%' have the same meaning in both mathematics and programming.

4.6 A Reciprocal Approach for Connecting MT, CT and Programming

Connecting MT, CT, and programming (P) in a reciprocal way is at the heart of tackling mathematical problem solving. However, according to the literature, the reciprocal way of connecting CT, MT, and programming makes up only 10.7% of all relations (Wu & Yang, 2022). One-way connections (from CT/P to MT, and from MT to CT/P) constitute the overwhelming majority (about 90%). A model of connecting MT, CT, and programming in a reciprocal way is elaborated by Hansen and Hadjerrouit (2023). The following figure (Figure 3) illustrates the model used in university undergraduate mathematics education.

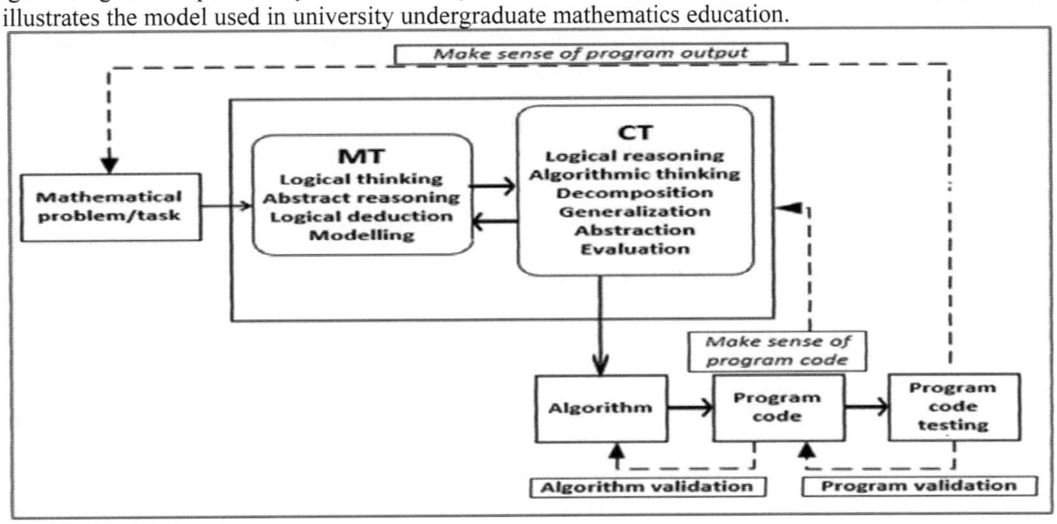

Figure 3. Reciprocal connections between MT, CT and programming

The model highlights four points. Firstly, it is a pre-requisite that students have a good understanding of mathematical concepts and a capability for abstract reasoning and logical deduction to benefit from CT. Secondly, CT should enable students to logically analyze, abstract, and decompose a mathematical problem and design an algorithm before programming it. Thirdly, students should be able to translate the mathematical solution and associated algorithm into programming code that can be tested and evaluated. Finally, the solution process should be generalized to a variety of similar problems. This is not a linear model starting from a mathematical problem and ending up with program code testing. It is rather an iterative and reciprocal model with feedback to previous steps to make sense of the program output and validating the algorithm.

5. THEORETICAL PERSPECTIVES ON INTEGRATING PROGRAMMING INTO MATHEMATICS EDUCATION

This section addresses the third research question: "*Which theoretical perspectives provide meaningful constructs for integrating MT, CT, and programming into mathematics education?*" For a comprehensive exploration of this question, it is essential to show how theoretical perspectives provide different angles to operationalizing programming and CPs, in relation to MT and CT, as discussed in research question 2.

CPs can be operationalized as digital resources, tools for thinking and exploration, artifacts (such as Geogebra, Numbas, or Excel) to be transformed into instruments, or a collection of various artifacts comprising programming constructs (such as if-then-else, repeat, while/do, for-loops, variables, arrays, etc.). If so, how do CPs mediate between subjects (teachers, students) and objects (mathematical teaching and learning)? We might also inquire whether there is a distinction between digital tools like GeoGebra and CPs. Lastly, we might consider whether CPs could be regarded as computational objects with a distinct ontology, or even as actants with agency in accordance with Actor-Network Theory.

There exist numerous theoretical perspectives with meaningful constructs that are particularly pertinent for exploring the integration of CT and programming into the teaching and learning of mathematics. More specifically, several theories provide suitable constructs for integrating CT and programming, each offering insights into different research directions. Furthermore, these theories can be combined and aligned to comprehensively analyze the role of CT and programming in mathematics education.

A first category of theories includes constructionism (Papert & Harel, 1991), socio-cultural theories such as Activity Theory (AT) relying on the concept of mediation (Vygotsky, Leont'ev, Engeström), situated learning theories such as Wenger's Communities of Practice (CoP), and other related theories outside mathematics education.

A second category of theories are those that are technology-focused (Sinclair et al., 2022), such as Anthropological Theory of Didactics (Chevallard's ATD), Theory of Didactical Situations (Brousseau's TDS), Instrumental Approach (Trouche's IA), and Documentational Approach to Didactics (Trouche's & Gueudet's DaD), and similar theories such as Instrumental Orchestration. In addition, general technology-based frameworks can be considered, such as TPACK, MDTK or PTK.

More specifically, we need to understand how programming is integrated into the subject-object relation. In constructivist theories, this relation is non-dialectical, and CPs are essentially passive. In contrast, the relation is dialectical in theories such as IA, DaD, TMS, and AT. In terms of AT, the subject-tool dialectic is crucial because the act of programming cannot be reduced solely to what the subject (teacher, student) can do or to what the CPs do. Programming is done by a subject interacting with the CP. Wertsch (1998) uses the term 'Subject-acting-with-mediational-means' to characterize this relation, the mediational means being the CPs.

Other theories may address programming from a slightly different angle, such as Radford's Theory of Objectification, Theory of Semiotic Mediation (Bartoloni-Bussi & Mariotti), or Gibson's Affordance Theory to address affordances and constraints of CPs in a mathematical education setting.

Is there another option beyond non-dialectical and dialectical relations? This is where the third category of theoretical perspectives comes into play, such as Latour's Actor-Network-Theory (ANT) and Distributed Cognition. These provide a third type of relation between subjects and objects, one that acknowledges distributed agency across both humans and non-humans. A CP is not merely a passive tool or artifact but an active participant in the creation of mathematical knowledge. Viewed through this perspective, CPs can be seen as non-human agents, sharing agency alongside human actors, thereby distributing agency across both.

Lastly, a fourth category of theories explores programming-related issues encompassing ethics, gender, social justice, and climate change. Postmodern theories like Critical Discourse Theory, Michel Foucault's concept of power dynamics ("knowledge is power"), and Jacques Derrida's deconstruction theory can offer insights into the political and ethical dimensions of programming.

Figure 4 illustrates the various theoretical perspectives in mathematics education that integrate MT in relation to CT, programming, and coding.

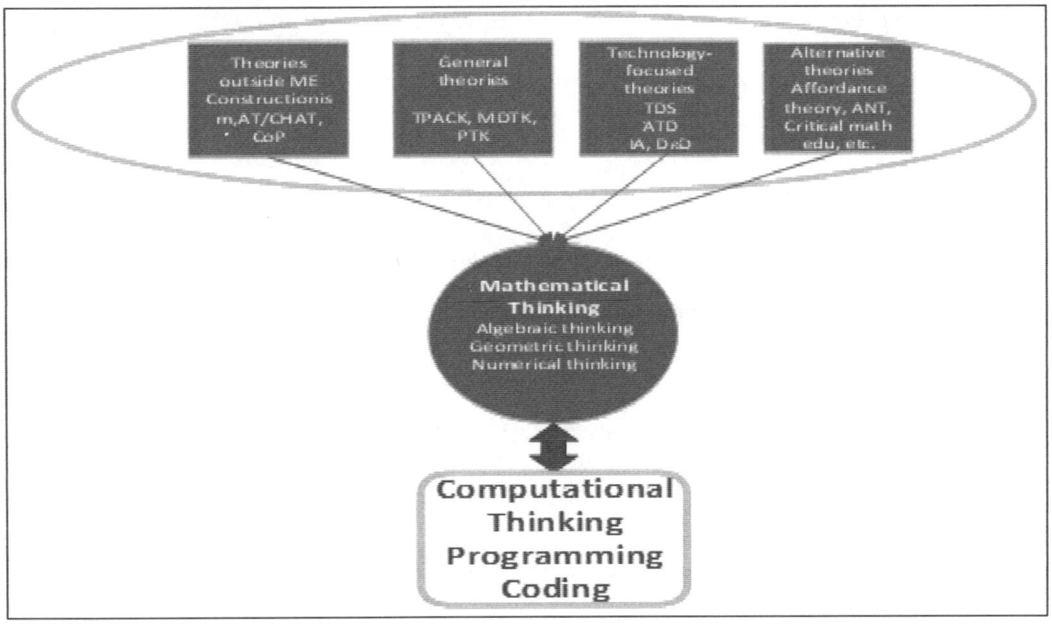

Figure 4. Theoretical perspectives for integrating MT, CT and programming into in mathematics education

6. CONCLUSIONS AND FUTURE WORK

This paper outlines a pathway for integrating programming into mathematics education using theoretical frameworks and computer paradigms in relation to CT and MT. The key constructs of the theories can be applied to operationalize CPs in diverse ways, such as using them as tools for thinking and exploration, artifacts, mediational means, or non-human agents. Consequently, it is crucial for researchers to comprehend the affordances and constraints of each theory to identify the perspectives that enable the formulation of specific problems and research questions that address the various angles from which programming and CPs are viewed.

However, existing theories may not adequately capture all the distinctive aspects of programming. Therefore, a critical question emerges for future investigation: "*Are we experiencing a paradigm shift as outlined by Kuhn (1962), or a computational turn similar to Lerman's sociocultural turn (Lerman, 2000)*?" A paradigm shift occurs when researchers adopt a new paradigm, leading to shifts in the meanings of key concepts like agency, which evolves from a solely human domain to one shared between humans and non-humans, as exemplified by Actor-Network-Theory. This shift may reframe CPs as non-human agents and could diminish student and instructor agency in educational contexts.

A computational turn involves a renewed focus or reorientation of research toward computational objects, prompting a reconsideration of key concepts like artifact, mediation, and subject-object dialectic. This opens new research directions in mathematics education by linking the turn to computational ontology, epistemology, and methodology. Consequently, researchers need to realign their work by concentrating on renewing constructs such as artifact and mediation and connecting them to computational objects.

Another future research direction for exploring programming involves using generative AI tools, like ChatGPT, as virtual instructors. These AI tools could undergo tailored training to align with specific learning objectives and determine how to effectively engage them for assistance. In mathematics education, students might find value in utilizing AI during the coding process. Much like human educators in some cases, AI tools can offer immediate feedback and assistance in syntax error detection, thereby enhancing the coding experience. Incorporating AI tools for code evaluation could potentially shift the focus towards developing students' higher-order cognitive skills, including MT, CT, and advanced problem-solving strategies.

REFERENCES

Bachelard, G. (1949). *Le rationalisme appliqué* (translated as *Reason Applied*). Presses Universitaires de France (PUF).

Bråting, K., et al. (2022). Mathematical competencies and programming: The Swedish case. In U.T. Jankvist & E. Geraniou (Eds). *Mathematical Competencies in the Digital Era*, vol. 20 (pp. 293-310). Springer.

Csizmadia, A., et al. (2015). Computational thinking: A guide for teachers. Retrieved from https:// eprints.soton.ac.uk/424545/1/150818_Computational_Thinking_1_.pdf

Deleuze, G., & Guattari, F. (1987). *A thousand plateau*. Minneapolis. University of Minnesota Press, 1987.

Deleuze, G. (1968). *Différence et répétition* (translated as *Difference and Repetition*). Presses Universitaires de France (PUF).

Denning, P.J., & Tedre, M. (2021). Computational thinking: A disciplinary perspective. *Informatics in Education 20*(1), pp. 361–390.

Eden, A. (2007). Three paradigms in computer science. *Minds and Machines 17*(2), pp.135–167.

Elicer, R., & Tamborg, A. (2023). A critical case study on the implementation of computational thinking in mathematics education. *Implementation and Replication Studies in Mathematics Education 3*, pp. 44–74.

Gueudet, G., et al. (2023). Learning programming for mathematical investigations: an instrumental and community of practice approach. *Research in Mathematics Education*, pp. 1-26.

Gueudet, G., et al. (2022). Understanding how students learn programming for mathematical inquiry at university: Schemes and social-individual dialectics. In J. Hodgen, et al. (Eds.). *Proceedings of CERME12*, (pp.2411-2418).

Gueudet, G., et al. (2020). Programming as an artefact: What do we learn about university students' activity? In T. Hausberger, et. al. (Eds.). *Proceedings of INDRUM 2020* (pp. 443–452).

Hadjerrouit, S., & Hansen, N.K. (2022). Undergraduate mathematics students engaging in problem-solving through computational thinking and programming: A case study. In D. Ifenthaler; P. Isaías, & D. G. Sampson (2022). *Orchestration of Learning Environments in the Digital World* (pp. 197-214). Springer.

Hansen, N.K, & Hadjerrouit, S. (2023). Analyzing students' computational thinking and programming skills for mathematical problem solving. In D. Ifenthaler; P. Isaías, & D. G. Sampson (2023). *Open and Inclusive Educational Practice in the Digital World, Cognition and Exploratory Learning in the Digital Age* (pp. 155-173). Springer.

Kuhn, T. (1962). *The structure of scientific revolutions*. University of Chicago Press.

Latour, B. (2005). *Reassembling the social: An introduction to Actor-Network-Theory*. Oxford University Press.

Lerman, S. (2000). The social turn in mathematics education. In J. Boaler (Ed.). *Multiple Perspectives on Mathematics Teaching and Learning* (pp.19-44). Ablex Editors.

Lodi, M., & Martini, S. (2021). Computational thinking, between Papert and Wing. *Science & Education 30*, pp. 883–908.

Maniglier, P. (2021). What is a problematic? Dossier: Bachelard and the concept of problematic. *Radical Philosophy 173*, pp. 21–23.

Rapaport, W.J. (2020). Syntax, semantics, and computer programs. *Philosophy & Technology 33*, pp. 309–321.

Papert, S., & Harel, I. (1991). *Constructionism*. Norwood, NJ: Ablex Publishing.

Papert, S. (1980). *Mindstorms - Children, computers, and powerful ideas*. New York: Basic Books, Inc.

Sinclair, N., et al. (2022). Revisiting theories that frame research on teaching mathematics with digital technology. In: A. Clark-Wilson et al. (2022). *The Mathematics Teacher in the Digital Era* (pp. 391–418). Springer.

(da) Rosa, S., et al. (2016). Philosophy of computer science and its effect on education towards the construction of an interdisciplinary group. *Clei Electronic Journal 19*(1), pp. 1-19.

Shute, V.J., et al. (2017). Demystifying computational thinking. *Educational Research Review*, pp. 1-10.

Turner, R. (2014). Programming languages as technical artifacts. *Philos. Technol. 27*, pp. 377–397.

Weintrop, D. (2016). Defining computational thinking for mathematics and science classrooms. *Journal of Science Education and Technology 25*, pp. 127–147.

Wing, J. M. (2006). Computational thinking. *Communication of the ACM, 49*(3), pp. 33–35.

Wu, W.-R., & Yang, K.-L. (2022). The relationships between computational and mathematical thinking: A review study on tasks. *Cogent Education 9*(1), pp. 1-19.

A FIGHT AGAINST THE FORGETTING CURVE

Müslüm Atas, Helmut Lindner, Thomas Strametz, Fatima Jammoul, Johannes Feiner
and Antonius Metry Saad
Institute of Software Design and Security, FH JOANNEUM, Austria

ABSTRACT

With the rapid growth of digital education, e-learning has become essential for offering accessible and flexible learning opportunities. This paper investigates strategies to achieve long-term learning outcomes and reduce study time in e-learning. It explores various techniques, including self-testing, spaced repetition, and the serial position effect, tailored to both visual and auditory learners. The study compared the effectiveness of these strategies, revealing that self-testing and spaced repetition improve learning and combat forgetting. However, in this context, the serial position effect did not show a noticeable impact on learning outcomes.

KEYWORDS

Didactics, e-Learning, Forgetting Curve, Serial-Position-Effect

1. INTRODUCTION

The COVID-19 pandemic posed numerous challenges across various domains, necessitating innovative solutions to overcome them (Pratama et al., 2020). Particularly, the education and industry sectors experienced major changes as they shifted towards remote learning and telecommuting to keep their activities going. For instance, a research (Agency, 2021) conducted in Austria highlights that, during the pandemic, approximately 45% of primary and secondary schools and 60% of high schools transitioned to distance learning. One of the main difficulties students faced during this shift was organizing their courses, effectively managing their time, and understanding the course material.

In response to these challenges and to uphold educational quality, institutions increasingly relied on video conferencing tools and e-learning applications. The application of e-learning tools in particular became increasingly popular during the pandemic (Lynch, 2020), as they enable students to interact with course materials according to their individual schedules. Moreover, e-learning applications offer distinct advantages beyond traditional learning methods, such as facilitating self-assessment and identifying areas of weakness. Another limitation of traditional learning is the issue of forgetting. Ebbinghaus (Ebbinghaus, 1913) addressed this issue by conducting multiple case studies to illustrate the forgetting curve, which shows that a significant portion of acquired knowledge is lost within 24 hours.

Taking advantage of the widespread use of smartphones, which provide flexibility regarding location and time, enhances the effectiveness of e-learning applications even more. Motivated by these advantages, we have developed a mobile e-learning application that supports students at an Austrian university during their course. Due to the fact that the pilot study of the application takes place in Austria, an Android application was developed, as this is the most frequently used mobile operating system (Statista, 2024).

The goal of our E-Learning application is to help students prepare for exams and remember course material in the long term. But developing such applications presents significant challenges, as they must adapt to various contexts such as the type of learning material, learning types (visual or auditory), question formats (single or multiple choice), and numerous other factors. To address these challenges and meet learner requirements, multiple versions of the application were developed and tested.

Initially, the application was tailored to different learning types. According to Vester (Vester, 1992), there are four main learning types: auditory, visual, haptic, and intellectual, whereby auditory and visual being the most common (Özbaş, 2013), (Bradford, 201AD). Consequently, two distinct applications were designed for these predominant learning types, each differing in their approach. For visual learners, correct answers were visually highlighted, while for auditory learners, correct answers were acoustically repeated multiple times.

Furthermore, an effective learning strategy was developed to counter the forgetting. For example, systematically repeating incorrectly answered questions has proven highly effective (Ebbinghaus, 1913), (Hartwig and Dunlosky, 2012). Moreover, the way in which this repetition is done, significantly impacts its effectiveness. For example, the order of the individual questions or answers can influence forgetting. The psychological phenomenon "serial-position effect" (Murdock Jr, 1962) states that the first and last items in a long list are generally memorised more effectively than those in the middle. This phenomenon was also used in our app to counteract the forgetting curve. The incorrectly answered questions were placed at the beginning and end of the question list to make it easier to remember the correct answers.

This paper is organized as follows: In Section 2 we review related work and give insights on the background for the ideas used in the e-learning application. Section 3 describes the setup for the pilot study and how different strategies were employed to fight the forgetting curve. In Section 4 the data obtained from the pilot study is analyzed and gives insight into potential future improvements on the application. We conclude in Section 5.

2. BACKGROUND / RELATED WORK

Despite controversy about the importance of learning types (Looß, 2001), (De Bruyckere, Kirschner and Hulshof, 2015), (Kirschner, 2017) we focus on two of the four suggested learning types (German term: *Lerntypen*) by Frederic Vester. Learners which are said to be of visual learning type constitute 65% of the population followed by auditory learning types. The influence of visual versus auditory learning on recall, analysed using a memory test, is discussed in Lindner, Blosser and Cunigan (2009). Ebbinghaus investigated the human process of forgetting information (Murre and Dros, 2015, p.4-11). Items shown first or last within a series of items can be remembered best. Concerning forgetting, the term *Ebbinghaus Speed* was coined by Subirana, Bagiati and Sarma (2017).

To confirm success of learning, assessments are used. Self assessment, as discussed in Hartwig and Dunlosky (2012), is an important way for feedback and reflection. This can be supported by mobile apps. Hence, we try the same approach as discussed in Schimanke, Mertens and Vornberger (2014): maximise learning outcomes with a mobile game or an e-learning app in our case. The positioning of questions influences the process of remembering. This phenomena is called *serial positioning effect* (Murdock Jr, 1962) and can be a means to mitigate Ebbinghaus' forgetting curve. Even before Covid the life long learning (LLL) was found to be necessary in modern society (Schäfer, 2017, p. 4-5). Since then, the way of learning has shifted into an foremost remote and an even more selfdirected process.

For e-learning applications, the use of gamification elements enhance the motivation of learners (Zecri, Ouzzif and El El Haddioui, 2021). One important approach is to provide mobile personalised learning environments (mPLEs) on smartphones (Humanante-Ramos, García-Peñalvo and Conde-González, 2016). The implementation of an Android mobile app, as discussed in the upcoming Sections, was designed according to core features needed to ask questions according to the relevant algorithms, but also to motivate usage by providing push-notification. For improved usability and user experience (UX) the interfaces have to be designed in a human suitable way. To create accessible and usable GUIs see the ten heuristics by Nielsen (1995).

3. METHOD

The concept and implementation of the mobile app seeks to answer the two following research questions:

1. Has the use of the e-learning application improved the understanding of students?
2. Has the serial positioning effect aided the understanding?

In order to evaluate these questions, we conducted a pilot study. To quantify the effectiveness of the app, participants of the study should diligently make use of the app on a daily basis and subsequently participate in an independent examination of the learned material to assess how much information was retained. Thus, a group of students should be selected, who have to take an exam independent of the app. The provided learning application then supports students during the two week studying phase prior to the exam. The learning app itself supports both auditory and visual learning types by switching to either an auditory (spoken answers) or a visual (questions and answers as text) mode for the quiz, depending on the learning type of the participant.

3.1 Target Group & Preparation

For this pilot a cohort of 37 students from the part-time degree program "Software Design and Cloud Computing" at the University of Applied Science "FH JOANNEUM" was selected. Together they participated in the course "Webtechnologies", where the mobile app was designed to help them prepare for the final exam. Prior to the learning phase, the students had to take a test (Philognosie, 2023) to identify which type of learner they are. As a result of the test, every student got a percentage showing their affiliation to each of the learning types. They were subsequently classified as either an auditory or a visual learner according to the results of this test, which then influenced the setup for the learning app.

3.2 The Pilot Study

The pilot study started on 14th of January 2023 and lasted until 27th of January 2023. The final exam for the course was held on 28th of January 2023. The students were exhorted to use the mobile app every day during this timeframe to help prepare for the exam as a form of a distributed practice learning strategy (Ebbinghaus, 1913). Questions were organized in "Learning Units" or "Quizzes", each of them consisting of ten questions. To avoid cheating, each question had to be answered within thirty seconds. To discourage students from studying only during the last few days prior to the exam, one could only complete a singular learning unit per day. This also homogenizes the dataset and allows for more comparability between each students improvements over time. Thirty-two persons took part in the study by using the application at least once. These participants were separated into four groups in order to differentiate the results according to their learning type and the impact of the serial positioning effect. First, the participants were split into two groups according to their learning type. To isolate any impact of the serial positioning effect, these two groups were both further split into two groups, where one group had their questions arranged to use the serial positioning effect and the other's questions were arranged randomly. In order to fight the forgetting curve, questions may be repeated in subsequent quizzes, which is known as spaced repetition (Schimanke, Mertens and Vornberger, 2014). Thus, the same question is typically reviewed more than once, though not necessarily in consecutive learning units.

Table 1. Classification of participants for the pilot study

Group	Learning Type	Learning Strategy
AS	auditory	serial positioning
AR	auditory	random positioning
VS	visual	serial positioning
VR	visual	random positioning

3.3 Creating a Learning Unit

A learning unit or quiz is comprised of ten unique questions, which are chosen from a predefined questionnaire. For a learning unit questions are selected by an algorithm, which assures that each question is used conforming to a uniform distribution. In order to implement the depicted learning strategies as in Table 1, questions are organized for each user into queues by their status. The status is either "new" which means this question has not been used in a prior learning unit, "correct" which means the question was answered correctly before or "false", which means the answer was last answered incorrectly. Initially all questions (a subset of the questionnaire) will be put into Queue1 ("new" questions). Figure 1 shows the queue structure used to organize questions for a specific user.

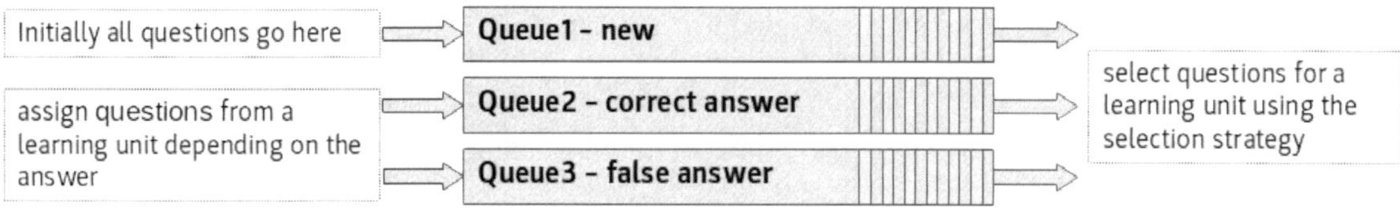

Figure 1. Queues used to manage questions

Building a learning unit consists of these steps:

1. Select questions using a selection strategy.
2. Position questions within a learning unit using serial positioning or random positioning.
3. Execute learning unit.
4. Send answered questions to queues dependent on the respective answer (correct/incorrect).

Question Selection Strategy

Questions for a new learning unit are selected using FIFO (First-in First-out) queues. The selection of questions from these queues is controlled by the following algorithm:

```
//Find 10 Questions for a learning unit
1. take (a) questions from Queue3 (0 <= a <= 2)
2. take (b) questions from Queue1  (0 <= b <= 10-a)
if (b < 10-a)
  take (c) questions from Queue2 (0 <= c <= 10-a-b)
  if (c < 10-a-b)
    take (d) questions from Queue3 (3 <= d <= 10)
```

The operation `take (n)` removes `n` questions from a queue and appends them to the quiz. After the questions for a quiz have been selected, their order in the learning unit is determined. Questions from Queue3 (wrong answer in previous quizzes) will be positioned within the learning unit using either serial or random positioning. The learning unit is ready for use when selection and positioning of the questions have been completed. The user runs the quiz and has to answer the questions, depending on the answer the questions will be reassigned to Queue2 (correct answer) or Queue3 (wrong answer) for further usage in later learning units.

4. RESULTS

The application was tested on a group of students enrolled in a class on Webtechnologies, with the goal to support them in the two weeks prior to their final exam. Predictably, out of the 37 enrolled students, eight motivated students used the app more than six times, 15 less than six times and 14 students refused to use the app at all. Only the set of eight students which used the app frequently and the 15 students which used the app infrequently are considered in our results. Motivating students to participate in the quizzes was done using push-notifications, which proved to be effective on some students. It is important to recall, that the application was not the same for all students. Participants were separated into groups according to their learning type affinity (visual or auditory), in line with the results of a prior taken affinity test for their learning type, i.e., each student was assigned the learning type that scored higher in this affinity test. Furthermore, in order to assess the effectiveness of making use of the serial positioning effect, the participants were again split into two groups. Groups AS and VS utilized the serial position effect by placing incorrectly answered questions at the beginning (primacy effect) or at the end (recall effect). Incorrectly answered questions from members of Groups AR and VR appeared without a concrete placement strategy in subsequent tries. This leads to a dataset with four distinct groups, which we will be analyzing in this chapter.

In total, 116 test attempts are recorded and available for analysis. Each test attempt contains ten questions and a score between 0 and 100 which reflects number of correctly answered questions.

4.1 Data Analysis

In this subsection, we aim to investigate two major questions:

1. Has the use of the e-learning application improved the understanding of students?
2. Has the serial positioning effect aided the understanding?

To answer the first question, we consider two ways to evaluate a student's understanding: on the one hand, we may consider the overall score achieved in each attempt at the quiz and on the other hand, we consider the overall grade. The latter is determined by each student's performance in a final exam, whose questions may coincide with the questions of the learning units. However, the final exam also includes open ended questions, where the understanding of the subject is tested in more detail. As seen on the left of Figure 2, the mean of the exam score increases significantly with each attempt, showing a clear learning trend with the sharpest upwards slope after 3 attempts. Due to the diverse group of participating students, this curve may be biased by previous experience. As seen on the right of Figure 2, students who reported to "know a bit" prior to the class, started out with higher scores than their counterparts. One can however see that after the 4th attempt, the gap between students with and without previous experience has diminished clearly, indicating a success of the app to homogenize the knowledge level within the class. It must be emphasized again, that the app was only introduced towards the end of the class, two weeks prior to the final exam, and only two lectures followed after its introduction. Thus, the reduction of the gap between the score curves is not biased by lectures in between.

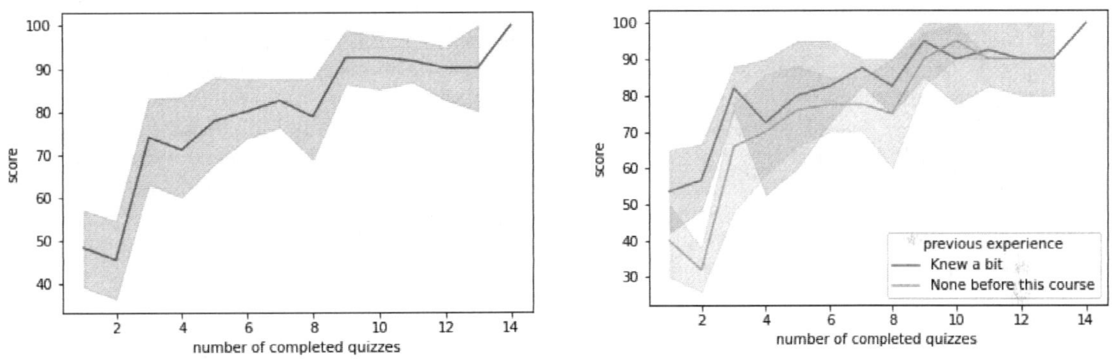

Figure 2. Mean improvement of quiz scores over attempts (left) and stratified by previous experience (right)

On the other hand, the influence on the final grade can be seen in Figure 3. As is clear on the left of the figure, the participants can be roughly separated in two groups. If a participant has taken the test more than 6 times, they are flagged as a *frequent_user*. The distribution of the grades between these two groups, as seen on the right of Figure 3, shows some differences. Indeed, infrequent users show a wider variance in their grades, while frequent users tend to mostly get the best grade (1), with one user each obtaining a different grade (2) and (4), respectively. Thus, while students who didn't frequently use the app didn't necessarily fail, they tended to show more variance in their final grades.

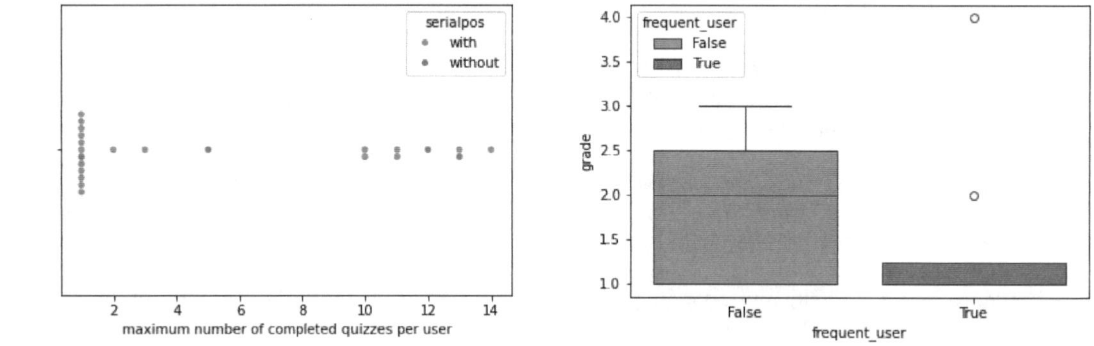

Figure 3. Number of quizzes per user (left) and resulting grades for frequent and infrequent users (right)

With respect to the serial positioning effect, the data cleaning unfortunately yielded a very imbalanced dataset. Out of the 23 remaining participants, only 4 had the chance to test the application without the serial positioning effect. Thus, it is not possible to give a funded statistical reasoning on whether the serial positioning effect has yielded a different distribution in grades than its counterpart. This was tested using a one-sided Mann-Whitney Test to test for equal distributions ($p = 0.33$). This test was chosen to accommodate the lack of a normal distribution in the data as well as the very small sample size.

Nevertheless, it is possible to compare the answering accuracy of questions asked multiple times in order to gain insights related to the serial position effect. Figure 4 compares the serial positioning groups (AS + VS) and the random positioning groups (AR + VR) in terms of accuracy (y-axis) over the number of question attempts (x-axis). The blue line denotes the accuracy of questions placed at the beginning (primacy) or the end (recall) while the red line represents the accuracy of the remaining questions. The serial positioning groups show a steady increase of accuracy for primacy and recall questions which indicates a learning effect for wrongly answered questions in previous tries. The random positioning group does not reveal a noticeable difference between the primacy/recall and the remaining questions which should not be the case anyway as all questions are placed randomly in this group.

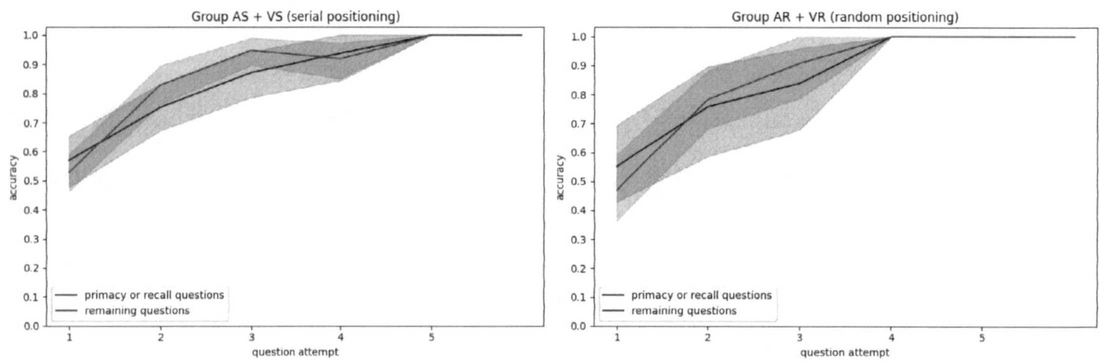

Figure 4. Comparison of the primacy/recall effect of questions answered multiple times in serial and random positioning groups

The Mann-Whitney Test was also used to investigate whether there was a difference in the distributions of the grades between frequent and infrequent users. This test also showed no strong significance ($p = 0.13$). This may be due to the fact that a bias in expertise lifted the average of the infrequent users. Only 4 out of 14 users, who indicated having some prior experience with the material, used the app frequently.

Among students who reported having no prior experience, 5 out of 9 were infrequent users, which is a much more even split.

All in all, while there appears to be very little statistical significance in these small groups, infrequent users showed larger variance in their final grades in comparison to frequent users as seen in Figure 3. Additionally, the use of the app helped bridge the gap between students who had prior experience and students who had none.

5. CONCLUSION AND OUTLOOK

In modern learning environments, using e-learning tools can provide great benefits to learners. The authors discuss an e-learning quiz app, that aims to counteract the forgetting curve by making use of the serial positioning effect. The app was tested on students preparing for an exam and results show clearly that students who used the app regularly had on average very good grades and students with little to no prior knowledge very quickly bridged the gap to more experienced students. Unfortunately, no clear statistical significant difference between including or excluding a strategy to use the serial positioning effect has been achieved. The authors believe that this is due to the very small sample size and lack of clear commitment of the participants. In order to improve participation and diligence by students, a more extended study could be performed in the coming year. The use of the application could be encouraged by allocating a small amount of bonus points that count towards the course. A larger dataset with more consistent participants could help get a clearer picture on potential serial positioning effects. Additionally, one could collect data regarding the students reception of the e-learning tool in an extensive study to investigate the differences in experiences within the groups. Besides, some researchers (De Bruyckere, Kirschner and Hulshof, 2015), (Kirschner, 2017) have criticized the validity of learning types as a learner characteristic, arguing that the emphasis should instead be placed on universally effective learning strategies. Future research should therefore focus on learning strategies that are effective regardless of individual learning styles.

In order to improve understanding, the handling of mistakes is crucial. This prototype does not expand upon falsely answered questions. An improved prototype could also include explanations as to why the given answer was wrong. This extention could result in faster improvements of the quiz scores and, subsequently, better scores on the final exam.

REFERENCES

Agency, A. P. (2021) *Corona — School During Distance Learning and Shift Work*. Available at: https://science.apa.at/power-search/2754993624251251132 (Accessed: January 5, 2024)

Bradford, W. C. (201AD) "Reaching the Visual Learner: Teaching Property Through Art," *The Law Teacher*, 11

De Bruyckere, P., Kirschner, P. A. and Hulshof, C. (2015) *Urban Myths about Learning and Education*. 1st ed. ELSEVIER ACADEMIC PRESS INC

Ebbinghaus, H. (1913) *Memory: A Contribution to Experimental Psychology*. Teachers College, Columbia University. Available at: https://openlibrary.org/books/OL14022573M/Memory

Hartwig, M. K. and Dunlosky, J. (2012) "Study Strategies of College Students: Are Self-testing and Scheduling Related to Achievement?," *Psychonomic Bulletin & Review*, 19(1), pp. 126–134. Available at: DOI: 10.3758/s13423-01-0181-y

Humanante-Ramos, P. R., García-Peñalvo, F. J. and Conde-González, M. Á. (2016) "PLEs in Mobile Contexts: New Ways to Personalize Learning," *IEEE Revista Iberoamericana de Tecnologias del Aprendizaje*, 11(4), pp. 220–226. Available at: DOI: 10.1109/RITA.2016.2619121

Kirschner, P. A. (2017) "Stop Propagating the Learning Styles Myth," *Computers & Education*, 106, pp. 166–171. Available at: DOI: 10.1016/j.compedu.2016.12.006

Lindner, K., Blosser, G. and Cunigan, K. (2009) "Visual Versus Auditory Learning and Memory Recall Performance on Short-term Versus Long-term Tests," *Modern Psychological Studies*, 15(1), pp. 39–46. Available at: https://scholar.utc.edu/mps/vol15/iss1/6/

Looß, M. (2001) "Lerntypen? Ein pädagogisches Konstrukt auf dem Prüfstand," *Die Deutsche Schule*, 93(2), pp. 186–198. Available at: DOI: 10.25656/01:27550

Lynch, M. (2020) "E-Learning During A Global Pandemic," *Asian Journal of Distance Education*, 15, pp. 189–195

Murdock Jr, B. B. (1962) "The Serial Position Effect of Free Recall," *Journal of experimental psychology*, 64(5), p. 482-483. Available at: DOI: 10.1037/h0045106

Murre, J. M. J. and Dros, J. (2015) "Replication and Analysis of Ebbinghaus' Forgetting Curve," *PLOS ONE*, 10(7), pp. 1– 23. Available at: DOI: 10.1371/journal.pone.0120644

Nielsen, J. (1995) *10 Usability Heuristics for User Interface Design*. Available at: https://www.nngroup.com/articles/ten-usability-heuristics/ (Accessed: April 29, 2024)

Özbaş, S. (2013) "The Investigation of the Learning Styles of University Students," *The Online Journal of New Horizons in Education*, 3(1), pp. 53–58

Philognosie, G. (2023) *Lerntypentest: Welcher Lerntyp bin ich?*. Available at: https://www.philognosie.net/lerntypen/lerntypen-test-welcher-lerntyp-bin-ich (Accessed: May 6, 2024)

Pratama, H. *et al.* (2020) "The Trend in Using Online Meeting Applications for Learning During the Period of Pandemic COVID-19: A Literature Review," *Journal of Innovation in Educational and Cultural Research*, 1(2), pp. 58–68. Available at: DOI: 10.46843/jiecr.v1i2.15

Schäfer, E. (2017) "Lebenslanges Lernen. Erkenntnisse und Mythen über das Lernen im Erwachsenenalter," *Zeitschrift Hochschule und Weiterbildung (ZHWB)*, pp. 68–69. Available at: DOI: 10.1007/978-3-662-50422-2

Schimanke, F., Mertens, R. and Vornberger, O. (2014) "Spaced Repetition Learning Games on Mobile Devices: Foundations and Perspectives," *Interactive Technology and Smart Education*, 11, p. 201–202. Available at: DOI: 10.1108/ ITSE-07-2014-0017

Statista (2024) *Most Common Smartphone Operating Systems in Austria as of March 2024*. Available at: https://www.statista.com/forecasts/1001220/most-common-smartphone-operating-systems-in-austria (Accessed: January 5, 2024)

Subirana, B., Bagiati, A. and Sarma, S. (2017) "On the Forgetting of College Academics: at Ebbinghaus Speed?," in *Proc. 9th International Conference on Education and New Learning Technologies (Edulearn 2017)*, pp. 8908–8918

Vester, F. (1992) *Denken, Lernen, Vergessen: was geht in unserem Kopf vor, wie lernt das Gehirn, und wann lässt es uns im Stich?*. Deutscher Taschenbuch Verlag

Zecri, E., Ouzzif, M. and El El Haddioui, I. (2021) "Study of the Use of Gamification Elements in e-Learning Applications," in *Proc. 4th International Conference on Networking, Information Systems & Security (NISS 2021)*. Association for Computing Machinery, pp. 1–5. Available at: DOI: 10.1145/3454127.3456591

AN EMPIRICAL STUDY ON THE IMPACT OF IMMERSIVE VIRTUAL REALITY ON ENHANCING INTERCULTURAL SENSITIVITY

Mahnaz Moallem and Folashade Agbolade
Towson University
8000 York Rd. Towson, MD 21252-0001, United States

ABSTRACT

Virtual reality (VR) is a computer-generated three-dimensional environment representing the real or imaginary world with the virtual world through various sensory channels. The multisensory immersion feature of VR (Immersive VR-I-VR) reduces the user's awareness of what is happening in the surroundings. The use of immersive virtual reality interventions to enhance cognitive, social, and emotional knowledge and skills has increased. Nevertheless, while VR is used for professional training in various fields, its application in higher education and teacher education has only evolved recently. This study aimed to develop and test the implementation of an I-VR intervention to enhance teacher education students' cultural sensitivity. It used a systematic empirical approach, collecting quantitative and qualitative evidence. The findings indicated that immersive virtual reality (VR) intervention improves intercultural sensitivity or intercultural competence, significantly contributing to educational practices and technological applications in cultural learning.

KEYWORDS

Immersive Virtual Reality, Cultural Competence in Teacher Education, Cultural Sensitivity in Digital Age, As, Effectiveness of Immersive Virtual Reality

1. INTRODUCTION

Virtual reality (VR) is a computer-generated three-dimensional (3-D) environment representing the real or imaginary world with the virtual world through various sensory channels (e.g., visual, auditory, and kinesthetic) to achieve a sense of immersion. The multisensory immersion feature of VR (Immersive VR) via the latest head-mounted displays (i.e., HTC Vive or Oculus Rift) reduces the user's awareness of what is happening in the surroundings (Huang et al., 2021). Immersive VR (I-VR) provides the perception of being present in a non-physical world, allowing the human brain to believe it is somewhere it is not (Freina & Ott, 2015). Thus, total learner immersion happens when, due to a deep mental and/or physical state of engagement, senses suspend the belief that the person is in the non-physical world. The use of immersive virtual reality interventions to enhance cognitive, social, and emotional knowledge and skills has increased due to the release of more advanced and affordable VR technologies. As an immersive yet safe learning environment, immersive VR offers enormous potential for growth in learning and holds considerable promise for enhancing youth and adult education. However, while VR has been used extensively for professional training in various fields (e.g., industry, health, military, neuroscience, psychology, biology, etc.), its application in higher education and teacher education has only evolved recently (McGarr, 2020). Thus, limited studies have explored the use of immersive VR for learning and teaching.

Intercultural competence (IC) has been defined in various ways but generally refers to the ability to interact effectively and appropriately in an intercultural context (Deardorff, 2006). Developing IC improves teachers' understanding of students with different world views (cognitive), enables them to regulate thoughts, emotions, and reactions (affective), and enhances tolerance for ambiguity to effectively build bridges across cultural diversity (Akdere et al., 2021). Intercultural sensitivity is the foundation of IC (Hammer, 2011), which refers to understanding cultural differences and similarities that strongly affect values, learning, and behavior (Stafford et al., 1997) and appreciating and embracing increasing diversity. Cultural sensitivity starts with recognizing differences between cultures and acknowledging that these variations are demonstrated in how individuals communicate and relate to one another. It also refers to the subjective experience of cultural difference, which is the foundation of the developmental model of intercultural sensitivity developed by Bennett (1993). The developmental model suggests stages, and with each stage, the person moves to a deeper level of cultural sensitivity. Hence, cultural sensitivity is more than awareness and requires viewing all human beings as unique humans and realizing that their experiences, beliefs, values, and language affect their perceptions. In other words, while intercultural knowledge and awareness represent the cognitive component of the learning process, intercultural sensitivity deals with the social and emotional empathy or affective dimensions of IC (Chen & Starosta, 2000; Li et al., 2022).

Increasingly, researchers have begun to explore the benefits and applications of immersive VR, particularly on the affective dimensions of learning in higher education learning and training environments. However, although a growing body of literature shows that immersive VR technology is effective for learning technical and scientific subjects—cognitive components (Daniela & Lytras, 2019), empirical studies on VR technology for social, emotional, and attitudinal learning are rare. The literature is unclear on whether, how, and to what extent I-VR develops intercultural proficiency. In light of this gap, this study projected that I-VR would offer authentic and situated learning experiences by enabling immersions in authentic and previously inaccessible multicultural learning spaces, placing students in unfamiliar cultural contexts, and creating a sense of being physically present in a non-physical setting (Blyth, 2018).

2. REVIEW OF THE LITERATURE

The literature review points to a few studies that examined the effectiveness of I-VR in enhancing intercultural sensitivity and emotional empathy. Li, Shing IP, Wong, and Lam (2020) investigated if immersive virtual reality (VR) content could enhance intercultural sensitivity in Hong Kong youth (15-20 years). Using the Oculus Go headset, 67 students participated in VR scenarios on ethnic identity. Pre-post tests showed improved intercultural sensitivity, particularly in engagement, confidence, and attentiveness. Similarly, Li, Lo Kon, and Shing Ip (2022) conducted a randomized study with 80 participants assigned to VR, video, and control groups. The VR group retained intercultural sensitivity improvements better than the video group. Sense of presence and emotional empathy predicted these changes. Akdere, Achenson, and Jiang (2021) examined VR as a learning tool for IC in 46 first-year STEM students using Oculus Rift. The VR simulation improved cultural knowledge and self-assessment of IC. Shadiev, Wang, and Huang (2023) explored the perceptions of 21 university students from China and Uzbekistan on VR intercultural learning activities. The study significantly improved knowledge, attitude, skills, and awareness. Gao and colleagues (Gao et al., 2021) investigated the impact of I-VR on learning different cultures among 50 English-language Chinese students. Although no significant impact on knowledge retention or cultural sensitivity was found, participants preferred VR for learning about festival culture. Overall, these studies indicate that I-VR's sense of presence and emotional engagement results in the enhancement of intercultural sensitivity in participants (e.g., Akdere et al., 2021; Gao et al., 2021; Li et al., 2020; Li et al., 2022; Shadiev et al., 2020). However, even though short exposure to the I-VR environment (compared to long-term exposure to different cultural settings in interventions such as study abroad) and highlighting intercultural awareness in recent studies has shown to improve cultural sensitivity in youth and adults, it is imperative to explore the impact of exposing students to longer and a sequence of I-VR learning activities with an emphasis on both cognitive and emotional empathy with the inclusion of deliberate mental engagement through pre-post reflection opportunities.

This study aimed to develop and test implementing an immersive VR intervention to enhance teacher education students' cultural sensitivity. It further assessed the efficacy of I-VR as a medium to develop empathy, emotion, motivation, and desire to understand, appreciate, and accept differences among cultures. It specifically answered the following questions:

- How does I-VR affect the development of teacher education students' intercultural sensitivity through immersive experience and self-reflection, and does the experience change students' understanding, perspectives, attitudes, and values?
- What is the efficacy of I-VR as a medium to enhance cultural awareness (knowledge and sensitivity (empathy))? How is the immersive experience perceived?
- Does being present and immersed in the virtual cultural space improve motivation and interest in learning more about culture?

- What is the impact of the I-VR intervention on intercultural sensitivity with a specific focus on the sense of presence and emotional experience?

3. METHODOLOGY

The study used a systematic empirical approach to answer its questions. It collected quantitative and qualitative evidence using calibrated instruments under defined and replicable conditions.

3.1 Participants of the Study

The study involved 20 volunteer preservice teachers, 17 females and three males, aged between 18 and 42. Ethnically, the group included 5 African Americans, 3 Asians, 11 Whites, and 1 participant from another background. The participants' majors were predominantly in elementary education (12), with others in pre-elementary (1), special education (1), and secondary education (6). Regarding technology proficiency, 50% of participants rated it adequate, 45% high, and 5% very high. The use of technology tools was varied: 40% had experience with VR headsets, 5% with VR applications, 5% with AR headsets, and 30% had no experience with these tools. Experience levels with VR technology were mostly at the beginner level (60%), followed by novice (30%), intermediate (5%), and advanced (5%). Participants' assessments of VR's effectiveness highlighted its potential for enhancing teaching and learning, creating hands-on environments, and simulating real-world situations for teacher preparation.

3.2 Immersive VR Intervention

The design of the I-VR intervention focused on creating a four-session I-VR learning process that progressively immersed students in the lives of those who may not share the same cultural and social norms. A Blackboard course shell was created for the intervention. To create the four-session consecutive learning environment, researchers reviewed the existing 360 video content and evaluated them for relevancy and quality using the following criteria: 1) cultural authenticity--accurately represent the cultures and avoid stereotyping 2) diverse perspectives--offer various cultural experiences, 3) cultural respect--promote respect for different cultures, 4) production quality-- video resolution, audio clarity, and overall VR experience, and 5) cultural awareness and empathy--foster empathy and an appreciation of cultural differences. The learning environment was to use problem orientation to prepare the students to focus on both cognitive and emotional cultural competence, encouraging reflective thoughts.

The *first session* offered a 45-minute I-VR learning experience. The first 30 minutes focused on utilizing the VR equipment and becoming comfortable with the *Engage VR*. The second 15 minutes offered five high-quality 360 virtual reality video tours (10 minutes each) from www.airpano.com for participants to choose one to view. *Session two* consisted of a 45-minute lesson and a 12-minute video entitled "*The Cultural Iceberg*." The video was played after starting the participants with a problem statement that made them think about their future classroom with its diverse student population. Five open-ended post-video reflective questions were developed to be completed after viewing the "The Cultural Iceberg" video. The *third* 45-60-minute *session* focused on immigration as a complex and multi-faceted phenomenon. The following four emotionally engaging videos on why people immigrate were selected: "*Displaced (10 minutes-360),*" "*My Home, Shatila (4 minutes-360),*" "*I am a Refugee (6 minutes),*" and "*Students' Immigrant Stories (6 minutes)*"). Two pre-post-video reflective questions were developed to guide participants in their exploration. *Session four* focused on the topic of immigrants' experiences and perspectives. A 12-minute NPR video entitled "*An Immigrant Family Moves through Generation Trauma*" and a recorded series of 360 video interviews of the first- and second-generation student immigrants currently enrolled in various programs at the university to speak about their experiences as a learner were selected for this session. One of the researchers, a first-generation immigrant, conducted 360 video interviews, which were recorded. While a protocol with a few open-ended questions was used, the interview used a conversational and sharing format to make interviewees comfortable.

3.3 Data Collection Instruments

Data was collected using numerous validated and reliable equipment.
The *Cultural Competence Scale*: A 14-item Likert scale created by AAC&U for US universities. The instrument is easy to use and assesses student intercultural learning after intercultural learning activities, which this study examined. The 6-point scale measures "openness (2 items)," "curiosity (2 items)," "communication (2 items)," "empathy (2 items)," "worldview (2 items)," and "self-awareness (4 items)."

Presence Questionnaire (PQ) version 3 was created by Witmer, Jerome, and Singer (2005) to quantify virtual presence. Presence is psychological awareness in the virtual world. Version 3 of the PQ employs a seven-point Likert scale. The 29 elements are grouped into four categories: interaction, sensory fidelity, adaptation/immersion, and interface quality. According to Witmer, Jerome, & Singer (2005), the PQ has a Cronbach's alpha of.84 for all item combinations. Multiple subscale concept items showed internal consistency (Witmer et al., 2005). Given the VR setting, 21 of 29 3-point scale items were selected for the research (9 for subscale "involvement," 4 for "sensory fidelity," 6 for "adaptation/immersion," and two for "interface quality."

Visual Realism, Motivation, and Usability: The researchers used ten questions from Lipp et al. (2021) 14-item VR Realism instrument and removed four Audience Appearances subscale items to create the 5-point scale. It assesses VR's visual realism. Ten items measuring scene realism (5 items), audience behavior (4 items), and sound realism (1 item) were combined with ten items measuring user interface usability and ten items measuring motivation and interest (adopted from VR usability testing surveys developed by other researchers).

We also collected self-reflection questions to test intercultural sensitivity. Self-report data was supplemented by open-ended interviews and observations. After the intervention, students shared their ideas, personal stories, and cultural sensitivity experiences in a brief Engage VR interview room conversation. Researchers might record sessions for analysis using Engage VR.

3.4 Procedure

The first session offered a 45-minute I-VR learning experience. The lab facilitator helped students log in to the LMS course, complete the consent form, put on the headset, practice operating VR headsets and hand controllers, and log into the *Engage-VR* application (for which they used instructions to create an account before the session), create a personalized avatar, interact with various objects in the *Engage VR* hub room, and become comfortable in the environment using the VR equipment. For the second 15 minutes, after taking a few minutes break, the participants viewed their selected 360 VR virtual tours by putting on the Meta Quest Pro or Meta Quest 2 headset again and logging into the *Engage VR* blank room. After viewing the 360 VR video tour, the participants were instructed to take off the headset and return to the LMS course to complete the *Realism, Motivation, and Usability* questionnaire and informally share their experiences regarding ease of use and confidence after practicing VR technology. For the second 45-minute session, the participants logged into the LMS course, completed the *Intercultural Competence Scale*, and reviewed the lesson's problem statement. They were then assisted in putting on the headset, logging into *Engage VR*, and going to the interview room to view "*The Cultural Iceberg*" video, which took about 12 minutes. Once finished, they were instructed to take off the headset and return to the LMS course to respond to the post-video reflective questions. For the third 45-60-minute session, the participants were asked to log into the LMS course first to complete a series of open-ended reflective questions asking them to think about the concept of immigration. The participants then used their headsets to log into the *Engage VR* blank room to watch four short videos. The participants were advised to take breaks between each video if needed. After viewing the videos, participants returned to the LMS course and completed post-video reflective questions. Like the previous sessions, for lesson four, participants logged into the LMS course, read the orientation description for the lesson, put on the headset, logged into the *Engage VR* blank room, and viewed the 12-minute NPR video followed by a short break. They then viewed the recorded 360 video interviews of the first- and second-generation student immigrants. After viewing the videos and taking another short break, participants were assisted in moving to *Engage VR*, the interview room. The facilitator asked them to share their thoughts, personal stories, and experiences with cultural sensitivity. They were informed that their conversation was recorded. After session four, the participants returned to the LMS course and completed the post-IC and VR Presence surveys.

3.5 Data Analyses

IBM SPSS Statistics was used to analyze the quantitative data. Descriptive statistics were administered for the 20 participants' *Presence and Visual Realism Motivation and Usability Questionnaire*s. Paired sample t-tests were used to compare the participants' IC before and after the intervention. A significance level of 0.05 (i.e., 95% confidence level) was used across all sample t-test analyses. Discourse analysis was used to understand how participants discussed and framed their VR experiences in their responses to the reflective questions. Participants' choice of words and descriptions of their perspectives, views, and feelings were further examined for the nuances of language and context and how they perceived and constructed ideas about different cultures. The participants' narrative responses were triangulated with quantitative results.

4. RESULTS

A paired-sample t-test was used to compare the means between the pre-intervention and the post-intervention IC scale (see Table 1).

Table 1. The pre-and post-survey statistics on the Intercultural Competence (IC) Scale

N= 20	Pre-Intervention		Post-Intervention	
	Mean	SD	Mean	SD
Openness	8.75	2.75	9.85	2.25
Curiosity	8.50	2.52	9.70	2.23
Communication	7.90	2.38	9.55	2.13
Empathy	8.55	2.76	10.05	2.48
Worldview	8.45	2.31	9.55	2.06
Self-Awareness	17.95	5.03	21.05	4.32

The paired-sample t-test shows that mean differences were significantly different in the categories of "openness," "communication," "worldwide," and "self-awareness" (see Table 2). Although the mean differences in the categories of "curiosity" and "empathy" were insignificant, the mean scores showed a noticeable increase. Furthermore, the voluntary participation in the intervention suggests the presence of some pre-intervention empathy and curiosity.

Table 2. Results of paired-sample t-test for intercultural competence scale

	Mean Diff	SD	SEM	t	df	p
Openness	1.10	2.27	0.15	2.17	19	0.043*
Curiosity	1.20	2.98	0..67	1.80	19	0.088
Communication	1.65	2.64	0.59	2.79	19	0.012*
Empathy	1.50	3.52	0.79	1.91	19	0.072
Worldwide	1.10	2.25	0.50	2.19	19	0.041*
Self-Awareness	3.10	4.76	1.07	2.91	19	0.009*

*p < 0.05; **p < 0.01; ***p < 0.001.

The content analysis of responses to the post-reflection questions confirmed changes in participants' openness, communication, worldviews, and self-awareness. After viewing "The Cultural Iceberg" video, responses to the question "What are some visible aspects of the culture, and how do they differ from underlying, less visible aspects?" showed that 75% of participants recognized the underlying or invisible aspects of cultures and used languages such as beliefs, values, feelings, and norms to explain them. In response to the reflective question of how their own beliefs and assumptions impacted their perceptions and interactions with people from different cultural backgrounds, 90% of participants directly or indirectly acknowledged misunderstanding or misinterpreting the behaviors of individuals from different cultures.

The quantitative analysis of the 3-point scale *Presence Questionnaire* (PQ) shows the participants' view of the VR environment. The combined items for each subscale show that participants find the I-VR environment natural, highly responsive, and consistent with real-world experience. They also thought the sound and auditory aspects of the environment and adaptations, or immersion, were acceptable, did not think there were delays in their actions, all their senses were engaged in the experience, and thought they could control devices during the tasks (see Table 3).

Table 3. Descriptive statistics for the sense of presence in the VR environment

Subscale (# items)	N	Minimum	Maximum	Mean (SD)
Involvement (9)	17	16.00	27.00	22.9 (3.3)
Sensory (4)	18	9.00	12.00	11.28 (.90)
Adaptability (6)	18	13.00	18.00	16.67 (1.6)
Interface (2)	18	2.00	6.00	2.89 (1.13)
Valid N (Listwise)	17			

The 5-point *Realism, Motivation, and Usability* questionnaire also measured various aspects of the I-VR environment, including participants' positive emotions (motivation and interest) (see Table 4). Overall, participants rated the various aspects of the environment highly and were emotionally positive about the I-VR environment, finding it natural, realistic, fun, engaging, and motivating.

Table 4. Descriptive statistics assessing realism, motivation, and usability of I-VR

Subscale (# items)	N	Minimum	Maximum	Mean (SD)
Scene Realism (5)	20	19.00	25.00	22.0 (1.92)
Audience Behavior (4)	20	11.00	20.00	16.3 (2.81)
Sounds Realism (1)	20	3.00	5.00	4.4 (.60)
Usability (10)	20	22.00	37.00	27.6 (3.83)
Positive Emotion (10)	20	32.00	48.00	41.3 (5.04)
Valid N (Listwise)	20			

The further exploration of the item-by-item descriptive statistics for the five items in the "Audience Behavior" showed that the mean score for the item asked, "behavior of virtual humans in virtual reality space was authentic," was lower (Mean = 3.70; SD = 1.08) compared with other items that mean scores were between 4.40 to 4.10). Also, not all usability items were scored highly (see Table 5), and while the participants felt comfortable and confident operating the equipment, VR technology was challenging to learn, and technical support was needed to use it.

Table 5. Descriptive statistics assessing the usability of I-VR

Usability Items (N = 20) 5-point scale	M	SD
I thought the VR technology was easy to use.	1.75	.716
I found the VR technology unnecessarily complex.	2.55	1.39
I think I would need support of a technical person to be able to use the VR technology.	2.05	1.14
I felt very uncomfortable/unconfident when operating the equipment.	4.05	.825
I would think most people would learn to use this system very quickly.	2.20	1.00
I thought the user interface placed too close was uncomfortable to use.	2.15	.875
I thought the user interface placed too far was difficult to use.	2.10	.936
I found the system very awkward to use.	3.85	1.03
I felt very confident using the VR technology.	2.70	1.21
I needed to learn a lot of things before I could get going with the equipment.	4.65	.489

Linear regression was also calculated for the IC scores as a dependent variable, and a 10-item survey measured interest and motivation as an independent variable. The linear regression analysis showed that interest and motivation in I-VR did not significantly predict cultural competence, measured by 14 items in four categories ($F(1, 18) = 0.246$, $p = 0.626$).

The analysis of observation notes and informal conversation after each session suggested that participants enjoyed learning via the I-VR environment, as demonstrated by returning voluntarily for the second, third, and fourth sessions with no attrition. Nevertheless, while participants may have been highly interested and motivated to learn via immersive virtual reality, this linear regression showed that motivation did not significantly predict participants' cultural competence or the learning outcomes from the training. Nevertheless, the qualitative data confirmed that the lab facilitator's assistance played a significant role in participants' utilizing the equipment comfortably and confidently.

4.1 Qualitative Results

Analysis of the responses to lesson three pre- and post-reflective questions revealed more information about the qualitative changes in participants' intercultural understanding. For example, the participants' language, perception, and assumptions about student immigrants show some development. In the pre-session, one of the reflective questions was, "Why do you think individuals and families immigrate from their home countries to come to the United States?" A common response thread was to "have a better life, "more opportunities," or a "more stable economy." However, in post-reflective responses, the common thread expanded to include "search for safety," "security for their families," "access to food and water," and "avoid war and political conflicts." Expansion of their understanding was also notable in their responses to post-reflective questions in lesson four, where they pointed to the importance of immigrants' identity, respect for their cultures, understanding of the sacrifice they make to immigrate, and how they could relate to their experiences. Another post-session reflection question asked participants, "How can the process of immigration impact family dynamics and relationships, positively or negatively? How does the process of immigration impact children, their experiences, and their relationships with others in schools? The participants' responses acknowledged the need to understand different cultures and respect their values and experiences. However, they seemed to struggle to provide concrete examples of how immigration impacts children and their family dynamics. Lesson four's post-reflection asked participants questions about their feelings and reactions to the recorded interviews of the first- and second-generation student immigrants at the university. The responses were personal and emotional and demonstrated empathy, connection, surprise, respect, and worldview about people from different cultures. The range of emotions and reactions showed the development of cultural sensitivity, which was also observed in mean differences in the IC scale. Furthermore, the last two sessions and the immigrant students' experiences resonated with the participants more. The stories participants shared in the final VR interview demonstrated a deeper understanding of how their actions as future teachers could impact their students' lives. ***(Due to page limitation, tables of excerpts were eliminated)***

5. DISCUSSION & CONCLUSION

The study developed and pilot tested an immersive VR intervention to enhance teacher education students' intercultural sensitivity. It investigated the efficacy of I-VR as a medium to develop empathy, emotion, motivation, and desire to understand, appreciate, and accept differences among cultures. The results showed that participants' IC and sensitivity enhanced after participating in four progressively immersive VR sessions. This result is consistent with the findings of the previous studies (Akdere et al., 2021; Li et al., 2020; Li et al., 2022). Specifically, as reflected on the IC subscales of openness, communication, worldview, and self-awareness, the differences were statistically significant, demonstrating the intervention's effectiveness in increasing participants' preparedness to be open-minded and recognize their own presumptions about intercultural differences and similarities. The significant change in the "self-awareness" items of IC ("I am aware of my own cultural rules and biases," "I can describe my personal cultural rules and biases," and "I actively seek to improve my understanding of complicated differences between cultures") points to efficacy and affordability of I-VR learning environments and offering an alternative approach compared with less accessible, costly study abroad programs that have shown effectiveness in improving IC. Nonetheless, a repeated delayed measure should also be administered to ensure the longer retention of cultural competence.

The results of the *Presence* and *Realism* questionnaires confirmed previous research findings that I-VR is a realistic, immersive, engaging, and interesting learning environment, has a high degree of usability, and impacts IC, particularly cultivating interest and emotions. More investigation and analyses should examine whether realism and presence predict the effects of I-VR experience on the IC scale and its relationship with emotional empathy. Prior studies (e.g., Gorini et al., 2012) suggest that a high level of presence experienced by participants can be related to increased emotional reactions. The results of the narrative responses showed qualitative changes in language, perspective, beliefs, and assumptions about intercultural differences. The qualitative data also provided interesting insights into how the learners' language, perception, and assumptions improved. The findings offer insights into the design of I-VR learning content and teaching resources. They could guide researchers in further investigating IC development with the applications of innovative and immersive technologies. Future research should explore whether the impact of the intervention on participants' cultural competence was merely due to the implicit technical affordance of the 3-D learning environment or highly impacted by the design of the intervention.

The study's findings are based on the responses of 20 participants. A small sample size limits the generalizability of the results. Furthermore, participants volunteered for the study, which may have introduced self-selection bias. Without a control group, it is hard to attribute understanding, empathy, and emotional changes solely to the VR intervention. Future researchers should consider a larger sample size and incorporate control groups to isolate the effects of VR interventions better.

REFERENCES

Akdere, M., Acheson-Clair, K., & Jiang, Y. (2021). An examination of the effectiveness of virtual reality technology for intercultural competence development. *International Journal of Intercultural Relations* 82: pp. 109–120.

Bennett, J. M. (1993). Toward Ethnorelativism: A Developmental Model of Intercultural Sensitivity. In R. M. Paige (Ed.), Education for the Intercultural Experience (pp. 21-71). Yarmouth, ME: Intercultural Press.

Blyth, C. (2018). Immersive technologies and language learning. *Foreign Language Annals*, 51(1), 225–232. https://doi.org/10.1111/flan.12327.

Chen, G. M., & Starosta, W. J. (2000). The development and validation of the Intercultural Sensitivity Scale, *Human Communication*, 3, 3–14- Available at Digital Commons@URI: https://digitalcommons.uri.edu/com_facpubs/36

Chen, G. M., & Starosta, W. J. (1997). A review of the concept of intercultural sensitivity. *Human Communication*, 1, 1-16.

Daniela, L., Lytras, M.D. (2019). Editorial: themed issue on enhanced educational experience in virtual and augmented reality. *Virtual Reality* 23, 325–327. https://doi.org/10.1007/s10055-019-00383-z

Deardorff, D.K. (2006). Identification and assessment of intercultural competence as a student outcome of internationalization. *Journal of Studies in International Education* 10(3): 241–66.

Freina, L., & Ott, M. (2015, April). A literature review on immersive virtual reality in education: state of the art and perspectives. In *The international scientific conference e-learning and software for education*, Vol. 1, No. 133, pp. 10-1007).

Gao, L., Wan a, B., Liua, G., Xiea, S., Huanga, J., & Mengb, G. (2021). Investigating the Effectiveness of Virtual Reality for Culture Learning, *International Journal of Human–Computer Interaction*, 37(18), 1771–1781. https://doi.org/10.1080/10447318.2021.1913858

Gorini, A., Capideville, C. S. De Leo, G. Mantovani, F. & Riva, G. (2011). The role of immersion and narrative in mediated presence: the virtual hospital experience. *Cyberpsychology, Behavior, and Social Networking*, 14(3):99–105, doi: 10.1089/cyber.2010.0100

Hammer, M. R. (2011). Additional cross-cultural validity testing of the intercultural development inventory. *International Journal of Intercultural Relations*, 35, 474e487. https://doi.org/10.1016/j.ijintrel.2011.02.014.

Huang, Y., Richter, E., Kleickmann, T., Wiepke, A., & Richter, D. (2021). Classroom complexity affects student teachers' behavior in a VR classroom. *Computers & Education*, 163, 104100. https://doi.org/10.1016/j.compedu.2020.104100

Li, C., Lo Kon, A. L., & Shing Ip, H. H. (2022). Use Virtual Reality to Enhance Intercultural Sensitivity: A Randomized Parallel Longitudinal Study. *IEEE transactions on visualization and computer graphics*, *28*(11), 3673–3683. https://doi.org/10.1109/TVCG.2022.3203091.

Li, C., S. Ip, H. H., Wong, Y. M., & Lam, W. S. (2020). An empirical study on using virtual reality for enhancing the youth's intercultural sensitivity in Hong Kong. *Journal of Computer Assisted Learning*, *36*(5), 625-635. https://doi.org/10.1111/jcal.12432

Lipp N., Sterna R., Dużmańska-Misiarczyk N., Strojny A., Poeschl-Guenther S., & Strojny P. (2021). VR Realism Scale—Revalidation of contemporary VR headsets on a Polish sample. *PLoS ONE* 16(12): e0261507. https://doi.org/10.1371/journal. pone.0261507.

McGarr, O. (2020). The use of virtual simulations in teacher education to develop pre-service teachers' behavior and classroom management skills: Implications for reflective practice. *Journal of Education for Teaching*, 46(2), 159–169. https://doi.org/10.1080/02607476.2020.1724654

Shadiev, R., Wang, X., & Huang, Y. M. (2023). Promoting intercultural competence in a learning activity supported by virtual reality technology. *International Review of Research in Open and Distributed Learning*, 21(3), 157-174. DOI: https://doi.org/10.19173/irrodl.v21i3.4752

Stafford, J.R., Bowman, R., Ewing, T., Hanna, J., & Lopez-De Fede, A. (1997). *Building Culture Bridges*. Bloomington, IN: National Educational Service.

Witmer, B. G., Jerome, C. J., & Singer, M. J. (2005). The Factor Structure of the Presence Questionnaire. *Presence: Teleoperators and Virtual Environments*, 14 (3): 298–312. doi: https://doi.org/10.1162/105474605323384654

GENERATING EXPLANATORY TEXTS ON RELATIONSHIPS BETWEEN SUBJECTS AND THEIR POSITIONS IN A CURRICULUM USING GENERATIVE AI

Ryusei Munemura[1], Fumiya Okubo[2], Tsubasa Minematsu[3], Yuta Taniguchi[4] and Atsushi Shimada[2]
[1]Graduate School of Information Science and Electrical Engineering, Kyushu University, 744, Motooka, Nishi-ku, Fukuoka 819-0395, Japan
[2]Faculty of Information Science and Electrical Engineering, Kyushu University, 744, Motooka, Nishi-ku, Fukuoka 819-0395, Japan
[3]Promotion Office for Data-Driven Innovation, Kyushu University, 744, Motooka, Nishi-ku, Fukuoka 819-0395, Japan
[4]Section of Educational Information Research Institute for Information Technology, Kyushu University, 744, Motooka, Nishi-ku, Fukuoka 819-0395, Japan

ABSTRACT

Course planning is essential for academic success and the achievement of personal goals. Although universities provide course syllabi and curriculum maps for course planning, integrating and understanding these resources by the learners themselves for effective course planning is time-consuming and difficult. To address this issue, this study proposes a method that uses generative AI to classify relationships between subjects and generate explanatory texts describing the connections of subjects and positions of subjects within the curriculum based on subject and curriculum information. An evaluation experiment involving learners demonstrated a classification accuracy of approximately 70% for inter-subject relationships. Furthermore, our experimental results confirm that that the generated explanatory texts significantly enhance the understanding of relationships between subjects, and are thus effective for course planning.

KEYWORDS

Course Planning, Syllabus, Curriculum, Generative AI, Classification of Course Relationships, Text Generation

1. INTRODUCTION

Course planning, which involves the selection of subjects from a wide range of options based on one's interests and concerns, is important because it facilitates personal achievement for the learner. As the number of subjects that students can take in higher education has been increasing, students may find it more complex to decide on courses that align with their goals and interests (Farzan and Brusilovsky, 2007). Furthermore, it has been suggested that similar course titles can lead to different career paths, making it essential to grasp the content and objectives of the courses in the course planning process.

To mitigate these challenges, higher educational institutions such as universities provide information on subjects and curricula. For instance, detailed information on each subject is recorded in the syllabus, whereas curricular structures – including learning outcomes, learning opportunities, assessments, and teaching methods – are visualized on a curriculum map (Harden, 2001). However, integrating and understanding multiple educational resources by the learners themselves for appropriate course selection is tedious (Apaza et al., 2014). Additionally, because the curriculum map does not contain subject details, it must be cross-referenced with the syllabus to understand the educational relationships between subjects and curricula. Thus, providing explicit inter-subject information is meaningful from the perspective of supporting course planning.

Moreover, course planning is also important from the perspective of self-regulated learning (SRL). SRL refers to learners' abilities to plan, monitor, evaluate, and adjust their learning processes as needed to acquire academic skills or achieve personal goals, leading to a more effective and efficient learning experience (Zimmerman, 1998). Research shows that students with SRL skills tend to improve their academic performance, as well as maintain self-efficacy and motivation, throughout the learning process (Zimmerman, 2002). By planning their coursework, these students find it easier to achieve their academic goals (Cho, Tao,

Yeomans, Tingley, and Kizilcec, 2024). Moreover, it has been reported that planning is positively associated to course completion and other personal learning objectives (Kizilcec, Pérez-Sanagustín and Maldonado, 2017). Thus, course planning represents an important activity in the context of SRL. However, many learners are yet to acquire sufficient SRL skills. In fact, approximately 75% of students were found to be undecided about career choices at the time of entering university (Cuseo, 2003).

To address these issues, this study proposes a method that uses generative AI to classify relationships between subjects and generate explanatory texts for these relationships. Specific types of relationships can provide useful information to foster a clearer perception of the subjects for learners, while explanatory texts vividly express the connections between subjects. Overall, this information can enable learners to understand connections with future subjects while reflecting on their current course enrollment status, thereby supporting learners with course planning and self-regulation.

2. RELATED WORK

2.1 Course Recommendation

Course recommendation has been widely researched as a common approach to academic planning, including methods using Latent Dirichlet Allocation (LDA) and regression models based on past academic performance (Apaza et al., 2014). LDA extracts latent topics from students' course histories and inputs them into a regression model to recommend the most suitable courses for individual students. This approach allows for more personalized recommendations by considering students' past performance patterns.

In addition, there are methods that create ontologies based on course information, such as syllabi, and use these ontologies to recommend courses (Jing and Tang, 2017; Ibrahim et al., 2018). Ontologies help clarify the relationships and prerequisites associated with courses, effectively aiding in the recommendation of courses that align with students' academic goals and interests. This makes it easier for students to select courses that are optimal for their educational objectives, while also facilitating smooth academic progress.

2.2 Syllabi and Curriculum Analysis

MIMA Search is a system that targets syllabi to search for and structure curricula, calculating subject similarities according to terms in syllabus documents and structured knowledge (MIMA, 2006). The processes of visualizing curricular structures and searching syllabi based on relatedness support course planning. The Curriculum Information System integrates subject information and learning management systems into a curriculum map to support inter-subject understanding, displaying keywords and links based on subject similarities (Yamamoto et al., 2021).

Some methods have been proposed to represent the relationships between subjects, or those between subjects and the curricula using graphs and keywords. However, these methods often fail to provide a detailed understanding of relationships and points of connection. Therefore, the present study was conducted to increase the specificity of inter-subject relationships and thus promote inter-subject understanding. The method proposed herein uses generative AI to classify inter-subject relationships into specific categories and explain these relationships in text form.

3. PROPOSED METHOD

The overall structure of the proposed method is illustrated in Figure 1, following the outlined steps.

(1) Collect subject and curriculum information from web syllabi and curriculum maps.
(2) Extract learning terms from subject information and calculate subject feature vectors using TF-IDF, then determine inter-subject similarities via cosine similarity.
(3) Use GPT to classify inter-subject relationships, as well as generate explanatory texts on these. relationships and the positioning of selected subjects within the curriculum.

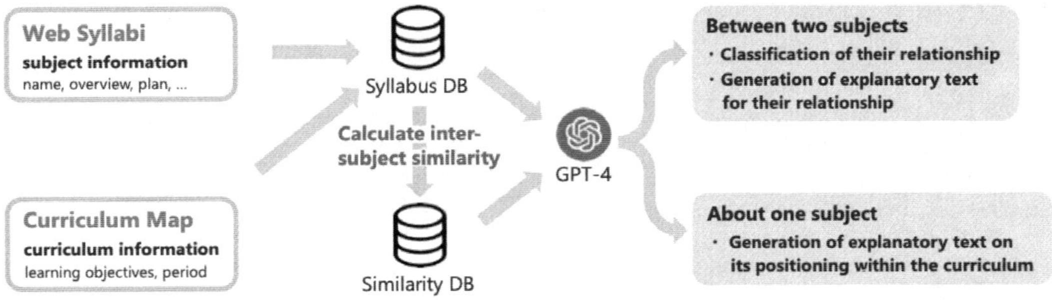

Figure 1. Overall workflow of proposed method

3.1 Collecting Subject and Curriculum Information

First, subject information was collected from Kyushu University's web syllabi, which contain basic information such as subject names and instructors, as well as subject descriptions and plans. Subject information was extracted from these syllabi to create a syllabus database. The curriculum map at our university visualizes the structure of the curriculum, direction and purpose of educational content, and learning objectives for each subject. We specifically collected the learning objectives and added them to the database.

3.2 Extracting Keywords and Calculating Inter-Subject Similarity

To capture the degrees of content-related relationships between subjects, the inter-subject similarity is calculated based on subject information. Initially, learning terms are extracted by analyzing the descriptions in the "subject description" and "subject plan" sections of the syllabus database. In the proposed system, text segmentation and morphological analysis are applied to extract only nouns and proper nouns as learning terms. Next, the TF-IDF (Ramos, 2003) values are calculated for each learning term. Feature vectors are created for each subject by arranging TF-IDF values for all terms represented in the subject information. Cosine similarity is then calculated between the feature vectors to determine inter-subject similarity. Similarity calculations are performed for all subject pairs, and the results are stored in a similarity database.

3.3 Classifying Inter-Subject Relationships and Generating Explanatory Texts

An overview of inter-subject relationship classification and explanatory text generation using GPT-4 is shown in Figure 2. Explanatory texts are generated using the following steps:

(1) Subject and curriculum information is described for two given subjects in the GPT prompt, including the overall ranking of inter-subject similarities. The types of relationships are defined in the prompt, enabling the GPT to select the appropriate relationship type.

(2) Based on the selected relationship type, a description is added to the prompt, and the subject information, curriculum information, and similarity ranking are re-entered to the prompt. Using this information, the GPT provides a detailed explanation of the relationship between the two subjects.

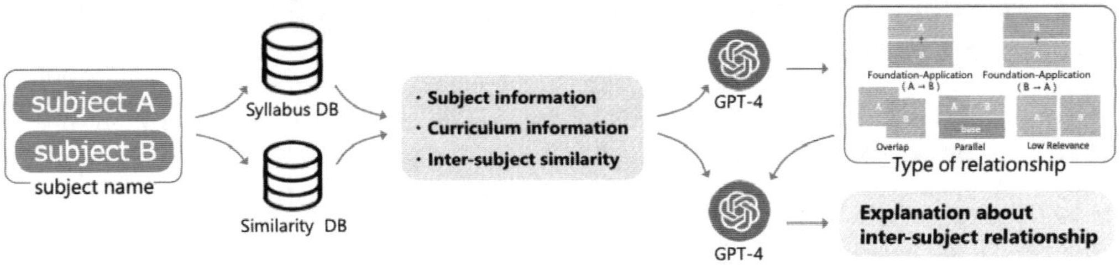

Figure 2. Overview chart of classifying inter-subject relationships and generating explanatory texts

3.3.1 Classifying Inter-Subject Relationships

First, the GPT is used to determine the types of relationships between two subjects. If the relationship type can be automatically determined, it will enhance the resolution of the generated text and potentially leads to a further examination of syllabi. The types of relationships between two subjects are defined as follows:

- Foundation-Application (A → B): Subject A is foundational, and Subject B is an application of Subject A.
- Foundation-Application (B → A): Subject B is foundational, and Subject A is an application of Subject B.
- Overlap: Both subjects cover the same content but are not in a foundational-application relationship.
- Parallel: Both subjects belong to the same field but have little direct connection.
- Low-Relevance: The two subjects have little direct connection.

The descriptions and plans of two subjects and learning objectives are extracted from the syllabus database and included in the GPT prompt. The ranking of their inter-subject similarity from the similarity database is also included. The defined relationship types and their definitions are entered into the prompt, and the GPT generates the appropriate relationship type and reason in JSON format.

3.3.2 Generating Explanatory Texts on Inter-Subject Relationships

Next, based on the relationship type and reason obtained in the previous step, the descriptions of the two subjects, curriculum plans, learning objectives, and similarity ranking are included in the GPT prompt, which describes the selected relationship type and corresponding reasoning. The GPT then provides a detailed explanation of the relationship between the two subjects that encompasses their mutual commonalities, differences, overall relationships, and application techniques. Text generation follows a one-shot approach, wherein a template is provided to guide the text structure. An example of the explanatory text is presented in Figure 3.

共通点
オペレーティングシステムＩと分散システムの講義は、両方とも情報工学の一部であり、コンピュータシステムの運用に関する知識を提供します。具体的には、両方の講義でプロセス管理、通信処理、同期処理などのトピックをカバーしています。また、学修目標も共通しており、実験や数値実験を適切に設計し、得られたデータを解釈して結論を導く能力や、電気情報工学分野における理論的、実験的、数値的な解析とモデリングの方法を理解し実行する能力を育成することを目指しています。

相違点
オペレーティングシステムＩは、計算機を動作させる基盤ソフトウェアであるオペレーティングシステムの基本的な機能や構造に焦点を当てています。一方、分散システムは、IoTやクラウドサービスの基本となる分散処理の基本構成と要素技術について学びます。つまり、オペレーティングシステムＩは一つのコンピュータシステムに焦点を当て、分散システムは複数のコンピュータシステムが連携して動作するシステムに焦点を当てています。

総合的な関連性
オペレーティングシステムＩと分散システムの講義は「**基礎応用関係**」にあります。オペレーティングシステムＩで学んだ知識は、分散システムの講義で学ぶ分散処理の基本構成や要素技術を理解するための基礎となります。例えば、オペレーティングシステムＩで学んだプロセス管理や通信処理、同期処理などの知識は、分散システムで学ぶ分散処理の理解に直接役立ちます。したがって、オペレーティングシステムＩは基礎となる講義であり、分散システムはその応用となる講義と言えます。

応用技術
例えば、オペレーティングシステムＩで学んだプロセス管理の知識は、分散システムでの複数のコンピュータ間でのプロセスの分散管理に応用されます。また、通信処理や同期処理の知識は、分散システムでのコンピュータ間の通信や同期の管理に直接応用されます。これらの知識を組み合わせることで、効率的な分散システムの設計や運用が可能となります。

Commonalities
The courses "Operating Systems I" and "Distributed Systems" are both part of information engineering and provide knowledge about the operation of computer systems. Specifically, both courses cover topics such as process management, communication processing, and synchronization. They also share common learning objectives, aiming to develop the ability to design appropriate experiments and numerical experiments, interpret the obtained data to draw conclusions, and understand and execute theoretical, experimental, and numerical analysis and modeling methods in the field of electrical and information engineering.

Differences
"Operating Systems I" focuses on the basic functions and structures of operating systems, which are the foundational software that operate computers. In contrast, "Distributed Systems" focuses on the basic configuration and elemental technologies of distributed processing, which are fundamental to IoT and cloud services. In other words, "Operating Systems I" focuses on a single computer system, whereas "Distributed Systems" focuses on systems where multiple computer systems work together.

Overall Relationship
The courses "Operating Systems I" and "Distributed Systems" have a "fundamental and applied relationship." The knowledge learned in "Operating Systems I" forms the foundation for understanding the basic configuration and elemental technologies of distributed processing taught in "Distributed Systems." For example, knowledge of process management, communication processing, and synchronization learned in "Operating Systems I" is directly useful in understanding distributed processing in "Distributed Systems." Therefore, "Operating Systems I" can be considered a foundational course, while "Distributed Systems" can be seen as an applied course.

Applied Technologies
For instance, the knowledge of process management learned in "Operating Systems I" can be applied to the distributed management of processes across multiple computers in "Distributed Systems." Additionally, knowledge of communication processing and synchronization can be directly applied to the management of communication and synchronization between computers in "Distributed Systems." Combining this knowledge allows for the efficient design and operation of distributed systems.

Figure 3. Sample explanatory texts on inter-subject relationships. Left: Japanese original, Right: English translation

3.4 Generating Explanatory Texts on the Positioning of a Selected Subject Within the Curriculum

The generation of generating explanatory texts for the positioning of a selected subject within a curriculum is outlined in Figure 4. First, the year and the selected subject are given. Based on the year, the three subjects with the highest similarity are extracted from the similarity database and assumed to be related, representing a previously taken, currently taken, and future subject. Descriptions of the selected subject, as well as nine additional related subjects, are extracted from the syllabus database and included in the GPT prompt. By providing a prompt template and adopting a one-shot approach, the GPT generates explanations of relationships between the selected and related subjects, the flow of coursework, and the positioning of selected subject within the curriculum.

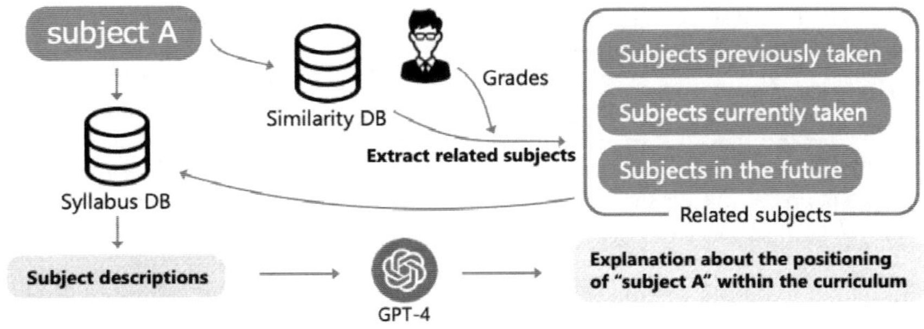

Figure 4. Overview of explanatory text generation on positioning within the curriculum

4. EXPERIMENTAL RESULTS & DISCUSSION

Experiments were conducted to evaluate the proposed method using subjects from the Computer Engineering Course of the Department of Electrical and Information Engineering at Kyushu University. The evaluation involved 43 third- and fourth-year students and course graduates. The evaluation aimed to determine the accuracy of classifying inter-subject relationships (Section 4.1), the effectiveness of generated explanatory texts in enhancing learners' understanding of these relationships (Section 4.2), and learners' preference for texts including the chronological positioning of subjects (Section 4.3).

4.1 Classification Accuracy of Inter-Subject Relationships

An evaluation questionnaire was administered to assess the classification accuracy of the five relationship types defined in Section 3.3.1. The evaluation targeted the eight subjects from the CM course curriculum listed in Table 1, with relationship types generated for the 28 pairs of subjects. Participants were presented with the "subject description" and "subject plan" from the syllabi, and asked to compare the learning content and select one relationship type for each subject pair. Based on the participants' responses, the most frequent relationship type selected for each subject pair was considered to be the ground truth.

Table 1. Courses to be evaluated for inter-subject relationships

Category	Subject name
system design	Operating system Ⅰ
	Computer system Ⅱ A
	Distributed system
signal processing	Digital signal processing
	Signals and Systems Ⅰ
foundation	Complex function theory
	Electro-informatics mathematics Ⅰ
exercises	Experiments in electrical and information engineering Ⅲ

Based on the ground-truth data obtained from the student responses, the accuracy of relationship classification was evaluated using the method described in Section 3.3.1. Because the GPT may generate somewhat inconsistent results, the classification of relationship types was performed 10 times for each of the 28 subject pairs, resulting in 280 classifications. The accuracy of these classifications was verified, and the results are presented in Table 2. The weighted average, which is the average of the product of each evaluation value and the amount of correct data, showed an accuracy of approximately 70%. Moreover, it was found that including the ranking of the subject similarity in the prompt improved accuracy for most metrics, demonstrating that the GPT can effectively consider the degree of relevance. Overall, these results confirm that the classification of inter-subject relationships can be performed with a reasonable level of accuracy.

Table 2. The evaluation of classification of relationship types

Type of relationships	Number in correct data	without inter-subject similarity				with inter-subject similarity			
		precision	recall	f1-score	accuracy	precision	recall	f1-score	accuracy
Foundation-Application(A → B)	30	0.52	0.77	0.62	0.77	0.52	**0.83**	**0.64**	**0.83**
Foundation-Application(B → A)	40	0.00	0.00	0.00	0.00	**0.25**	**0.07**	**0.12**	**0.07**
Overlap	30	0.28	0.37	0.31	0.37	0.28	0.37	0.31	0.37
Parallel	20	0.00	0.00	0.00	0.00	**0.30**	**0.15**	**0.20**	**0.15**
Low-Relevance	160	0.84	**0.98**	0.91	**0.98**	**0.88**	0.94	0.91	0.94
Weighted average	280	0.57	0.68	0.62	0.68	**0.65**	**0.69**	**0.65**	**0.69**

4.2 Evaluation of Explanatory Texts on Inter-Subject Relationships

We evaluated the explanatory texts generated for inter-subject relationships generated using the method described in Section 3.3.2 was conducted. Thurstone's paired comparison method (Thurstone, 1927) was adopted to assess the inclusion of subject information, response templates, learning objectives, and relationship types. Additionally, a five-point scale was used to determine whether the texts provided useful information to the students. The subjects targeted here were Operating system I, Distributed system, Signals and Systems I, and Electro-informatics mathematics I from Table 1.

4.2.1 Pair Comparison Method

The details of the paired comparison method used in this study are described here. This questionnaire was designed to analyze students' preferences for texts generated from five types of prompts.

Prompt A: Subject Description + Subject Plan

Prompt B: Subject Description + Subject Plan + Response Template

Prompt C: Subject Description + Subject Plan + Response Template + Learning Objectives

Prompt D: Subject Description + Subject Plan + Response Template + Relationship Type

Prompt E (Proposed Method): Subject Description + Subject Plan + Response Template + Learning Objectives + Relationship Type

For paired comparisons, students were shown all ten combinations of generated texts from the five prompts and asked to select the text they preferred. The questionnaire targeted four subjects, and six pairs of subjects were selected. Students compared 60 pairs in total, ensuring a random order and placement to avoid bias.

Responses from the paired comparisons were subjected to a consistency test. Combined with the agreement test described in the next section, the Bonferroni method was used to adjust the significance level from 5% to 2.5%, with responses not rejected at a 2.5% significance level considered inconsistent and excluded from further analysis. The percentage of inconsistent responses ranged from 21% to 42%.

For students whose responses were deemed consistent, an agreement test was conducted to verify whether their judgments of the generated texts were sufficiently consistent. If the judgments were found to be probabilistically consistent, the total rankings derived from these judgments were considered meaningful. The test results showed that for all subject pairs, the hypothesis stating that the students' judgments were consistent was supported at a significance level of 1.0%. Thus, low variability was observed in the ranking of generated sentences that students found desirable, and the calculated scale values can be considered reliable.

4.2.2 Scaling Preferences for Generated Texts:

The students' preferences for the generated texts were scaled using Thurstone's method, which calculates interval scale values from relative frequencies by applying a standard normal distribution to the data. The average scale values for the texts generated from the five prompts are listed in Table 3. Prompt E, the proposed method, was most preferred. This validates the proposed method, confirming that including subject description, plan, response template, learning objectives, and relationship type in explanatory texts is most effective.

Based on the proposed method, students rated a randomly selected description on a five-point scale. As described in Table 4, all students understood the relationship between the two subjects. Additionally, more 70% of the participants found the information useful for course planning. Thus, this method was found to effectively enhance inter-subject comprehension.

Table 3. Means of scaled preference values for generative sentences.

Prompt	A	B	C	D	E (Proposed method)
Average	-0.747	0.266	-0.041	0.202	0.320

Table 4. Ratings of the generated sentences explaining relationship between the two subjects (unit: %).
5: very much agree, 4: agree, 3: undecided, 2: disagree, 1: not at all agree

Evaluation item	Evaluation value				
	5	4	3	2	1
The relevance of the two subjects can be ascertained.	44.2	55.8	0.0	0.0	0.0
The information is useful for course planning.	23.3	53.5	16.3	7.0	0.0

4.3 Evaluation of Explanatory Texts on the Positioning of a Selected Subject

This evaluation targeted the explanatory texts generated using the method described in Section 3.4. Students assessed their text preferences using the subjects from Section 4.2, comparing texts with and without chronological context, with the results shown in Table 5. The proportion of texts generated by the proposed method ranged from approximately 40% to 80%. When the proposed method's texts did not clearly explain the relationships between subjects, texts without chronological context were generally preferred. Overall, considering the total percentage of responses, it was found that approximately 60% of students preferred the texts generated by the proposed method, indicating a preference for understanding subject positioning in line with the chronological order of their coursework. Moreover, Table 6 shows that more than 80% of participants found the randomly selected text useful for understanding subject relationships and positioning.

Table 5. Which generative statement is better for the selected one course and related courses (unit: %)

Subject name	Only related subject	Proposed method
Operating system Ⅰ	37.2	62.8
Computer system Ⅱ A	20.9	79.1
Distributed system	53.5	46.5
Digital signal processing	60.5	39.5
Signals and Systems Ⅰ	30.2	69.8
Complex function theory	44.2	55.8
Electro-informatics mathematics Ⅰ	37.2	62.8
Experiments in electrical and information engineering Ⅲ	34.9	65.1
Total Percentage of Responses	39.8	60.2

Table 6. Ratings of generative statements describing the position of one selected subject in the curriculum (unit: %).
5: very much agree, 4: agree, 3: undecided, 2: disagree, 1: not at all agree

Evaluation item	Evaluation value				
	5	4	3	2	1
Understand the relationship between courses already taken.	53.5	44.2	2.3	0.0	0.0
Understand the relationship between the course and the subject under study.	39.5	44.2	11.6	4.7	0.0
Understand the relationship between the course and future courses.	51.2	41.9	7.0	0.0	0.0
Understand the position of the subject in the curriculum.	44.2	44.2	9.3	2.3	0.0
The information is useful for course planning.	34.9	46.5	16.3	2.3	0.0

5. CONCLUSION & FUTURE WORK

We aim to support learners' course planning by clarifying relationships between subjects based on subject and curriculum information, using GPT-4. Our method involves three primary approaches. Firstly, relationships between pairs of subjects are classified to elucidate their connections and foster clearer perceptions of subjects, achieving an accuracy of approximately 70%. Second, explanatory texts are generated to help learners understand inter-subject relationships more concretely. The experimental results confirm that our method is most preferred through paired comparison, as it helps learners understand these relationships. Third, explanatory texts are generated to position a selected subject in the curriculum, allowing learners to understand its position in the curriculum. The results indicates that students generally prefer to understand the positioning of subjects in line with the chronological order of their coursework. Through these approaches, learners can understand connections with future subjects while reflecting on their current course enrollment status.

However, this study has several limitations. First, we used a one-shot approach without testing few-shot, leaving its reliability unverified. Second, we only used GPT-4, lacking comparisons with other models. Lastly, focusing on Computer Engineering Courses excluded humanities, leaving interdisciplinary use untested.

In future studies, we must verify the validity of the types of relationships defined between subjects. Furthermore, learners may have different evaluation criteria and information requirements, making it necessary to improve the system to present individually optimized information to learners, thereby enhancing interactivity.

ACKNOWLEDGEMENT

This work was supported by JST CREST Grant Number JPMJCR22D1, JSPS KAKENHI Grand Number JP22H00551 and JP22K19835, and Initiative for Life Design Innovation, Osaka University, Japan.

REFERENCES

Apaza, R. G., Cervantes, E. V., Quispe, L. V., and Luna, J. E. (2014). Online Courses Recommendation based on LDA. *Symposium on Information Management and Big Data.*

Cho, J. Y., Tao, Y., Yeomans, M., Tingley, D., and Kizilcec, R. F. (2024). Which Planning Tactics Predict Online Course Completion? *In Proceedings of the 14th Learning Analytics and Knowledge Conference (LAK '24). Association for Computing Machinery*, New York, NY, USA, pp. 360-370.

Cuseo, J. (2003). Academic advisement and student retention: Empirical connections and systemic interventions. *National Academic Advising Association*, pp. 2019-01.

Farzan, R. and Brusilovsky, P. (2006). Social Navigation Support in a Course Recommendation System. *International Conference on Adaptive Hypermedia and Adaptive Web-Based Systems*. Berlin, Germany, pp. 91-100.

Harden, R. M. (2001). AMEE Guide No. 21: Curriculum mapping: a tool for transparent and authentic teaching and learning. *Medical teacher*, 23(2), pp. 123-137.

Ibrahim, M. E., Yang, Y., Ndzi, D. L., Yang, G., and Al-Maliki, M. (2018). Ontology-based personalized course recommendation framework. *IEEE Access*, vol.7, pp. 5180-5199.

Jing, X. and Tang, J. (2017). Guess you like: course recommendation in MOOCs. *Proceedings of the international conference on web intelligence*. New York, USA, pp. 783-789.

Kizilcec, R. F., Pérez-Sanagustín, M., and Maldonado, J. J. (2017). Self-regulated learning strategies predict learner behavior and goal attainment in Massive Open Online Courses. *Computers & education*, vol.104, pp. 18-33.

Mima, H. (2006). MIMA search: a structuring knowledge system towards innovation for engineering education. *Proceedings of the COLING/ACL 2006 Interactive Presentation Sessions*. Sydney, Australia, pp. 21-24.

Ramos, J. (2003). Using tf-idf to determine word relevance in document queries, *Proceedings of the first instructional conference on machine learning*, Vol. 242, No. 1, pp. 29-48.

Thurstone, L. L. (1927). A Law of Comparative Judgement, *Psychological Review*, Vol. 34, pp. 278-286.

Yamamoto, Y. [山本雄介], Minematsu, T. [峰松翼], Naganuma, S. [長沼祥太郎], Taniguchi, Y. [谷口雄太], Okubo, F. [大久保文哉], and Shimada, A. [島田敬士] (2021). Kamoku no kanrenseijouhou wo hukashita karikyuramujouhou etsurannsisutemu no kaihatsu [科目の関連性情報を付加したカリキュラム情報閲覧システムの開発. Development of a curriculum information browsing system with subject relevance information], *IPSJ SIG Technical Report*, Vol. 2021, No. 9, pp. 1-8.

Zimmerman, B. J. (1998). Developing self-fulfilling cycles of academic regulation: An analysis of exemplary instructional models. In: Schunk, D. H., and Zimmerman, B. J. (eds.), *Self-Regulated Learning: From Teaching to Self-Reflective Practice, Guilford Press*, New York, USA.

Zimmerman, B. J. (2002). Becoming a Self-Regulated Learner: An Overview, *Theory into Practic*e, Vol. 41, No. 2, pp. 64-70.

PROPOSAL FOR AN APPROACH TO PROCESSING MEDIA OBJECTS USING AI AND METADATA: A MACHINE LEARNING-BASED APPROACH

Khalifa Sylla[1], Mama Amar[1] and Samuel Ouya[2]
[1]Cheikh Hamidou Kane Digital University of Senegal Un-CHK (ex-UVS), Cité du Savoir, Diamniadio, 15126 Dakar-Fann, Senegal
[2]LITA Laboratory, Polytechnic High School, Cheikh Anta Diop University of Senegal, Senegal

ABSTRACT

The paper must have an abstract. The abstract should be self-contained and understandable by a general reader outside the context of the paper. The use of artificial intelligence (AI) has revolutionized the organization and management of data in particular educational content on digital university platforms.
The combination of AI and metadata can facilitate the management and access to educational resources and allow personalized learning experiences tailored to learners' needs. Based on the possibilities offered by AI and metadata, we propose, in this paper, a model for processing media objects using AI and metadata. Our approach is based on the use of machine learning to enrich media objects with original and extracted metadata and efficiently process media objects (images, videos, etc.) using both raw media data and associated metadata.
In this study, we base use the pedagogical resources of the Cheikh Hamidou Kane Digital University's training courses.
The proposed model enables us to extract contextual information, classify metadata and categorize multimedia objects for future use.
The application of our model makes it possible to classify educational data by category or activity (consultation, TD, TP, project) according to pedagogical objectives; to automatically add metadata to a media object using the model; to manually annotate a media object by pedagogical actors; and finally, to create a search engine based on metadata.

KEYWORDS

Metadata, IA, Machine Learning, Multimedia, Annotations, Process

1. INTRODUCTION

The development of computing power and storage capacity encourages the multiplication of the production of multimedia documents. Thus, we are observing more and more creation of multimedia content in all sectors and in the field of education. Today, several digital universities are created (MOOC platforms, Digital Universities, e-learning systems, etc.). Since media objects are not structured, their exploitation generates a certain complexity.

In addition, we note that metadata offers additional information which can, through their exploitation, enrich multimedia objects and help in their exploitation. However, extracting and leveraging this metadata can be costly and time-consuming for organizations. Indeed, faced with the exponential growth of multimedia production, the various players in this sector are faced with numerous problems regarding the storage, annotation and extraction of multimedia objects. Thus, the international standards organization (ISO) and other multimedia communities have developed standards such as MPEG-7 (Sikora, 2001), Dublin Core for the description of the content of multimedia objects. However, these standards are not widely used because it is difficult to manually annotate multimedia objects.

On the other hand, artificial intelligence has seen significant development over the past decade. It now offers advanced capabilities for exploiting large volumes of data. These capabilities enable analysis and extraction of relevant information at a scale and speed previously impossible. As a result, the use of machine learning will make it even easier to automate the production of metadata to help find, filter and organize information, particularly multimedia type information.

In this article, we explore the possibilities offered by artificial intelligence and metadata associated with multimedia objects for optimal management of media objects. This will include developing machine learning models to extract contextual information, classify metadata and classify media objects for future exploitation. In this study, we base ourselves on the training content at the Cheikh Hamidou Kane Digital University (formally Virtual university of Senegal) (Ouya et al., 2015).

This paper will be organized as follows: we will start with the state of the art. Next, we will present our approach. Additionally, we will outline our proposed machine learning models. We will continue with the presentation of the implementation concept, then we will present the results of our experiments. Finally, we will end with the conclusion and perspectives.

2. STATE OF THE ART ON MEDIA OBJECTS MANAGEMENT MODELS

2.1 Multimedia Metadata

2.1.1 Metadata

A metadata is a data or information used to describe other data. There are several standards used to describe or classify media data using metadata. In the context of a library, metadata traditionally refers to elements such as bibliographic information about the collection's holdings and physical items; however, the current definition of metadata has evolved to include information about electronic or digital data, rather than primarily describing physical data elements.

Metadata can be classified by type to facilitate their management and organization. Thus, in our work, we have chosen the following types of metadata that are adapted to our use case, which will be presented in the following sections. However, our model allows for the definition of other types of metadata as well. We have identified below metadata types (Amar, 2012):

- ***Descriptive metadata*** include the metadata used to describe media objects (MOs) (Kogalovsky, 2013) and allow for the search and identification of an MO. Examples: title, author, location.
- ***Technical metadata*** describe the technical characteristics of media objects that will be used to classify the MOs. Examples: file format, size, dimensions.
- ***Administrative metadata*** represent the administrative information of the MOs and can be used in the management and archiving of an MO. Examples: archive date, rights information, archive profile, version.

2.1.2 Multimedia Metadata Standards

Metadata standards allow for the formalization of a metadata model that describes the semantics and value lists of the description elements as well as the links between the description elements. In the literature, we find several metadata standards, including:

Dublin Core (Underwood, 2020), which was developed to describe electronic text documents but has been extended to cover media objects.

It proposes a generic metadata schema that allows for the description of digital or physical resources based on a set of elements.

MPEG-7 (Multimedia Content Description Interface) (Burnett et al., 2003)(Morgan, 2012) is an international standard for describing multimedia objects recognized by the ISO/IEC consortium and developed by MPEG (Moving Picture Experts Group). The standard focuses on the semantically rich description of multimedia content. MPEG-7 allows the localization, filtering, management, and processing of desired multimedia files by tagging them with information about their content and origin.

MPEG-21 (Burnett et al., 2003) was developed to ensure the interoperability of multimedia objects. It is based on two essential concepts: the Digital Item, which represents the basic component of the standard, and the concept of Users interacting with the Digital Item. The Digital Item is a structured object with a standardized representation that includes multimedia content, associated metadata, and a set of syntax elements that describe the relationships between the media objects and their metadata. The user concept represents any entity interacting with the MPEG-21 environment or the Digital Item.

SMPTE Standard (Morgan, 2012) is a metadata dictionary standardized by the Society of Motion Picture and Television Engineers (SMPTE). SMPTE offers a list of structured metadata elements. A metadata dictionary is used to define the keys, the length of the values, and the semantics of these elements. The current structure defines classes of elements as follows: identification, administration, interpretation, parametric, process, relational, and spatio-temporal.

2.2 Metadata and ML for Multimedia Objects Processing

In this section, we will analyze a set of articles that use machine learning and metadata, selected based on their publication date (recency), the AI techniques used, and the concepts employed.

Studies on the use of metadata and AI for the management of media objects discuss a method for automatic classification of MOOC video topics using transcription features and convolutional neural networks (CNNs) (Chatbri et al., 2017). The method involves generating video transcripts using a speech recognition tool and converting the transcripts into images using a statistical co-occurrence transformation. The CNN (Sun et al., 2020) is then used to produce video category labels for the transcript image input. The method is evaluated using a Khan Academy dataset, which contains 2,545 videos labeled with one or two of 13 categories. The results show that the proposed method outperforms a baseline algorithm that uses superficial features, demonstrating its effectiveness in automatic video classification.

This method does not use video metadata, which could provide more information to facilitate the classification of course videos.

S. Bharitkar presents a method for classifying multimedia content using synthetic metadata and machine learning (Bharitkar, 2019). Synthetic metadata is used to train a neural network to classify multimedia content, achieving high accuracy with low latency. Synthetic metadata improves classification accuracy by providing additional features that complement the original content.

3. PROPOSAL OF A MODEL

The model we propose is based on the extraction, annotation, storage, and archiving of media objects. This approach aims to enable optimal archiving and utilization of media objects.

The model allows for the extraction and classification of metadata, annotation of media objects, utilization, and archiving after a certain period. This approach leverages the metadata associated with these objects to facilitate the organization, storage, archiving, and retrieval of these objects.

We also present the application that served as the framework for our approach. This approach is based on existing tools and provides solutions to address the problems or shortcomings of these tools.

3.1 Presentation of Our Approach

Our approach is based on a process that covers all stages of the life cycle of a media object (MO), from creation to archiving, and on the metadata associated with these objects. Throughout the MO's life cycle, additional metadata can be created and linked to the object. This metadata provides more information about the MO, thereby facilitating search, management, and archiving. This approach, while presenting specific features compared to existing approaches, incorporates some of their basic functionalities.

3.2 Use Case Definition

Our model is applied to course videos used in the teachings at UN-CHK. Our objective is to enable better utilization of resources (videos, syllabi, courses, supplementary documentation) by students and teachers by allowing them to:

- Classify by category or activity (consultation, tutorial, lab, project) based on educational objectives.
- Automatically add metadata to a media object by the model.

- Manually annotate a media object by the educational stakeholders.
- Use a search engine based on metadata.

3.3 Description of our Approach

The model we propose is based on a process composed of the following phases: Collection of media objects, media preprocessing, processing and extraction of metadata, annotation of media objects, and classification of media objects for future use.

- **Collection and Storage of Media Objects:** This phase involves gathering and importing educational data from various sources to apply our approach for metadata extraction. Once the media objects have been collected, they are stored in a database or file system associated with metadata for quick search and access.
- **Media Preprocessing:** This phase involves standardizing and normalizing the media objects to ensure they are understandable by our system.
- **Processing and Extraction of Metadata:** This phase involves extracting information that allows the description and classification of media data. During this phase, only the metadata that comes with the media object at its creation is extracted. The extracted metadata will be classified according to predefined categories.
- **Annotation of Media Objects:** This phase involves adding new metadata to be used effectively. There are two methods of annotation: the first involves manually adding metadata to the media object, and the second uses a machine learning algorithm to extract metadata from the media object and classify it according to predefined categories.

4. DESIGN AND IMPLEMENTATION

4.1 Description of the Model

In this section, we will present the approach we propose. We will outline the design and development of our model based on metadata and machine learning.

The approach we propose uses machine learning to efficiently process media objects (images, videos, etc.) by utilizing both raw media data and associated metadata. The approach is based on the following phases:

Collection and Storage of Media Objects: This phase categorizes media objects based on their content. In this step, we will use media objects created in the context of educational activities at UN-CHK (Sylla et al., 2020).

Preprocessing of Media Objects: This phase analyzes and extracts relevant information (metadata) from the content and characteristics of the media objects, storing it in a database for future use with the media objects.

Processing and Extraction of Metadata: Media objects are processed to extract metadata, which is then stored and associated with the media objects for future use. Metadata is subsequently processed (normalizing values, managing missing data, and transforming categorical data into numerical format) to organize and clean it.

Classification of Media Objects: A classification algorithm is used to classify media objects according to their types and categories.

4.2 Architecture of the Model

Our architecture is largely inspired by the machine learning lifecycle diagram proposed by Amazon Web Services (AWS) (Wittig et al., 2023). Figure 1 below shows the different components of this lifecycle.

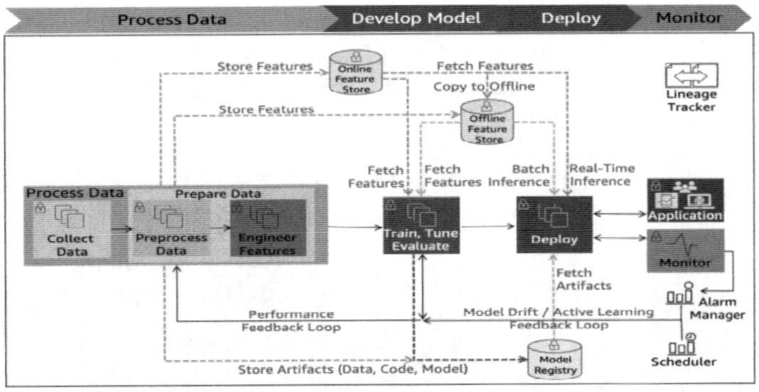

Figure 1. Different components of the lifecycle of ML models deployment

Thus, the architecture of the model we propose is structured around the following components:

- Data acquisition and processing: Data acquisition and processing involves collecting and preparing the data.
- Data preparation includes data preprocessing and feature engineering.
- Model development: Model development includes creating, training, tuning, and evaluating the model.
- Model deployment: After training, tuning, and evaluating our model, it will be deployed in production to be used with our production data.
- Model monitoring: The model monitoring system captures data, compares it with the model's training data, sets rules to detect issues, and sends alerts.

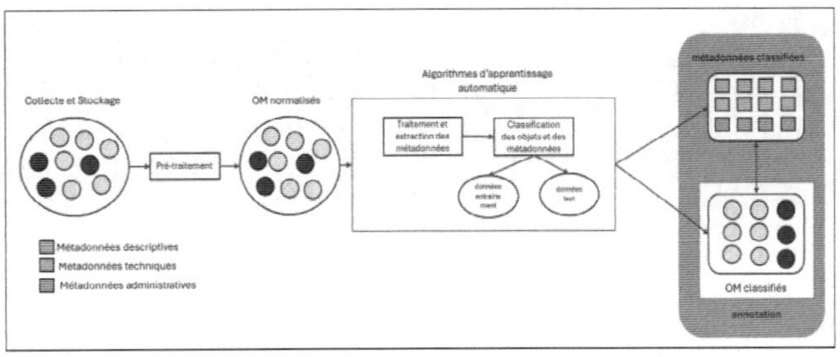

Figure 2. Architecture of the models of our solution

4.2.1 Data Collection and Preparation

The data to be used consists of a set of MOs (Media Objects) from online courses at UNCHK, including the MOs and their associated metadata. The data is cleaned to remove unnecessary or redundant information, handle missing data, and normalize the data if necessary.

4.2.2 Introduction to Algorithms in Our Model

In this stage of our process, we will perform data splitting. We will divide the dataset into two parts: training data and test data to evaluate the performance of the algorithms composed of the metadata extraction and classification algorithm, and the media object classification algorithm.

a) Metadata Processing Algorithm

For metadata processing, we have chosen to use the Convolutional Neural Network (CNN) algorithm. CNNs are commonly used to extract significant features from images and videos, making them suitable for extracting visual metadata such as objects, faces, and locations. CNNs can also be used for image classification tasks based on visual metadata.

The algorithm begins by examining each file in the training data directory to extract metadata. Once extracted, the algorithm classifies them into the predefined categories: Descriptive, Technical, and

Administrative. After classification, the metadata is stored in a DynamoDB database along with their links to the multimedia objects, ready for analysis or export in formats such as CSV.

While this algorithm focuses on metadata extraction and classification, it will also be integrated into the Machine Learning pipeline with the MO processing algorithm outlined in our approach for tasks such as content recommendation and multimedia data analysis.

The algorithm is designed to be adaptable based on specific user needs. The metadata extraction and classification functions can be customized by adding new features or adjusting classification criteria.

```
# Extraction des Métadonnées avec Apache Tika :
from tika import parser
import os
import pandas as pd
import csv


# Main function
def main():
    directory_path = './medias'  # directory of the media objects
    output_csv_filename = 'metadata_output.csv'
    metadata_list = []

    # Iterate through files in the directory
    for filename in os.listdir(directory_path):
        file_path = os.path.join(directory_path, filename)

        # Ensure it's a file (not a subdirectory)
        if os.path.isfile(file_path):
            metadata = extract_metadata(file_path)
            descriptive, technical, administrative =
classify_metadata(metadata)
            metadata_entry = {
                'File': filename,
                'Descriptive_Metadata': descriptive,
                'Technical_Metadata': technical,
                'Administrative_Metadata': administrative
            }
            metadata_list.append(metadata_entry)

    # Save metadata to CSV
    save_metadata_to_csv(metadata_list, output_csv_filename)
```

Figure 3. Metadata Extraction Algorithm

b) Media Object Processing Algorithm

For processing media objects, the Support Vector Machine (SVM) algorithm (Dai, 2018) has been chosen for the following reasons:

- SVMs are effective for binary or multi-class classification.
- They can be used to classify media objects based on their extracted metadata.
- SVMs are robust and perform well, especially with medium to large-sized datasets.

The multimedia data is preprocessed to be compatible with the SVM algorithm. This includes resizing, normalization, and extracting relevant features from the media.

The SVM model is trained on a labeled training dataset. Features extracted from the media objects and their associated metadata are used as input vectors, while class labels (types of media objects) are used as outputs.

Once trained, the SVM model is used to classify new media objects based on their predicted types. Classification is based on both media features and associated metadata.

The SVM model can be used to recommend relevant content to users based on their preferences and analysis of similar media objects.

c) Model Training and Validation

Our model is trained on a training dataset to adjust model parameters using extracted metadata as input and class labels as output. We evaluate the performance of our model using the accuracy metric to assess the quality of the classification.

5. RESULTS OF OUR SOLUTION

The results of our model can be presented according to the following components: Classification of Media Objects by Category and/or Activity Based on Educational Objectives.

Objective: Classify media objects (images, videos, audios) based on educational objectives, such as consultation, tutorials (TD), practical work (TP), and projects.

Results:

- Media objects are automatically classified into one of the educational categories (consultation, TD, TP, project).
- Improved organization of educational resources and easier access for students and teachers.

Addition of Metadata to a Media Object by the Machine Learning Model:

Objective: Enrich media objects with metadata automatically generated by the machine learning model.

Results:

- Media objects have richer and more accurate metadata, improving their descriptions and facilitating their search and use.
- Reduced time and effort required for manual annotation of media objects.

6. CONCLUSION

In this paper, we proposed an ML based solution that used metadata for efficient processing of media objects. The metadata makes it possible to enrich media objects and thus provide better processing of these unstructured data. With machine learning, our solution offers the possibility not only to process and classify metadata, but also to generate them automatically and use them to enrich media objects. In this work, we first defined a process composed of several steps which allow us to collect the OM, to pre-process the OM, to extract and process the metadata and to process and classify the OM using the metadata and machine learning.

To validate our approach, we experiment our solution using multimedia objects from eLearning files from UNCHK. The results of our approach showed the enrichment of media objects from original and extracted metadata from the media objects.

Our approach also improves the organization of educational resources and easier access to them for students and teachers.

As future work, we want to add more functionalities to our solution by allowing users to manually annotate multimedia objects. We also want to include a multimedia search engine that uses the metadata to our solution.

The approach that we proposed is generic and the solution can be applied to other use cases and domains. Thus, we want to use our solution for another use case. Ex: We want to use our approach to optimize the search for scientific articles in scientific article journals.

Furthermore, we would like to include a recommender system module in our solution to recommend e-learning videos to the students based on the related metadata.

We also want to experiment our solution with other machine learning models and perform comparisons to validate the performance of our model with different ML algorithms.

REFERENCES

Amar, M. (2012). *Métadonnées et processus pour l'archivage de données médiatiques* (Master's thesis). Université du Québec à Montréal, Montréal, Canada.

Burnett, I., Van de Walle, R., Hill, K., Bormans, J., & Pereira, F. (2003). MPEG-21: goals and achievements. *IEEE Multimedia*, 10, 60-70. https://doi.ieeecomputersociety.org/10.1109/MMUL.2003.1237551

Chatbri, H., McGuinness, K., Little, S., Zhou, J., Kameyama, K., Kwan, P., & O'Connor, N. E. (2017). Automatic MOOC video classification using transcript features and convolutional neural networks. In *Proceedings of the 2017 ACM Workshop on Multimedia-based Educational and Knowledge Technologies for Personalized and Social Online Training* (pp. 21-26). https://doi.org/10.1145/3132390.3132393

Dai, H. (2018). Research on SVM improved algorithm for large data classification. In *Proceedings of the IEEE 3rd International Conference on Big Data Analysis (ICBDA)*. https://doi.org/10.1109/ICBDA.2018.8367673

Kogalovsky, M. R. (2013). Metadata in computer systems. *Programming and Computer Software*, 39, 182-193. http://dx.doi.org/10.1134/S0361768813040038

Morgan, O. (2012). Structure and organization of metadata and the SMPTE metadata dictionary. In *File Interchange Handbook* (pp. 31-60). Routledge.

Ouya, S., Sylla, K., Sy, B., & Barry, M. (2015). Impact of integrating WebRTC in universities' e-learning platforms. In *Proceedings of the 2015 5th World Congress on Information and Communication Technologies (WICT)*. https://doi.org/10.1109/WICT.2015.7489664

Pereira, F. (2005). MPEG-21 standard: defining an open multimedia framework. In *Proceedings of the 47th International Symposium ELMAR*. Zadar, Croatia, pp. 5-8. https://doi.org/10.1109/ELMAR.2005.193627

Sikora, T. (2001). The MPEG-7 visual standard for content description-an overview. *IEEE Transactions on Circuits and Systems for Video Technology*, 11(6), 696-702. https://doi.org/10.1109/76.927422

Sun, Y., Xue, B., Zhang, M., & Yen, G. G. (2020). Automatically designing CNN architectures using the genetic algorithm for image classification. *IEEE Transactions on Cybernetics*, 50(9), 3840-3854. https://doi.org/10.1109/TCYB.2020.2983860

Sylla, K., Sy, B., Ouya, S., & Barry, M. (2020). Towards the use of a contact center for the socialization and capacity reinforcement of learners of African digital universities. In *Proceedings of the 22nd International Conference on Advanced Communication Technology (ICACT)*. https://doi.org/10.23919/ICACT48636.2020.9061548

Underwood, W. (2020). Automatic extraction of Dublin Core metadata from presidential e-records. In *Proceedings of the 2020 IEEE International Conference on Big Data (Big Data)*, pp. 1931-1938. https://doi.org/10.1109/BigData50022.2020.9377943

Wittig, A., & Wittig, M. (2023). *Amazon Web Services in Action: An in-depth guide to AWS*. Simon and Schuster.

INVESTIGATING STRATEGY IN A MENTAL ROTATION TASK USING EYE-TRACKING HEAT MAP ANALYSIS

Kabyashree Khanikar and Ritayan Mitra
Centre for Educational Technology
IIT Bombay, India

ABSTRACT

This study investigates the cognitive strategies employed during a mental rotation task through the integration of interview data and eye-tracking heat map analysis. A total of 20 interviews between 4 participants were analyzed independently by two coders to identify holistic and piecemeal rotation strategies and eye-tracking heat maps were examined in conjunction with interview data to reveal patterns of visual attention corresponding to these strategies. Preliminary results indicate that heat maps can effectively distinguish between holistic and piecemeal strategies, characterized by distinct visual attention patterns. Holistic strategies displayed uneven attention distribution with complementary focal points on the two orientations, while piecemeal strategies exhibited multiple focal points that were mirror images of each other. These findings suggest that heat maps could offer a robust method for identifying cognitive strategies in mental rotation tasks, paving the way for a visual analytical framework of spatial thinking studies.

KEYWORDS

Mental Rotation, Eye-Tracking Heat Maps, Holistic Strategy, Piecemeal Strategy, Visual Attention

1. INTRODUCTION

Spatial ability is a fundamental element of human cognition, playing a pivotal role in learning, problem-solving, and academic achievement, particularly in STEM fields (Uttal & Cohen, 2012). Mental rotation ability, the most extensively studied type of spatial ability, involves mentally manipulating two-dimensional (2D) or three-dimensional (3D) objects to envision their appearance after a specific angular rotation around a defined axis (Shepard & Metzler, 1971). This ability, which is intrinsic to spatial cognition, has been widely studied as an important dimension of intelligence (Carroll, 2009) and has been measured effectively using the Vandenberg Mental Rotation Test (Vandenberg & Kuse, 1978). Shepard and Metzler's work established the foundational understanding of how individuals manipulate spatial information, demonstrating a linear relationship between rotation degree and reaction time.

Shepard and Metzler's (1971) work on mental rotation established a link between response time (RT) and angular disparity, showing that larger rotations take longer. This led to two key models: holistic, where objects are rotated as whole units, and piecemeal, where objects are rotated part-by-part (Zhao & Della Sala, 2017). Folk and Luce (1987) expanded on piecemeal rotation, describing it as sequentially rotating image components. Research on individual differences in strategy use placed holistic and piecemeal approaches on a continuum (Paivio, 1971; Gluck & Fitting, 2003). Hegarty (2018) expanded on these strategies, noting that mental rotation tasks (MRTs) can be solved with both spatial and analytic strategies, such as cube counting and local shape comparisons. Differences in the strategies used in mental rotation tasks are crucial for examining individual variations in spatial thinking (Hegarty, 2010), as these strategies are amenable to training, supporting the idea that spatial intelligence is malleable (Uttal and Newcombe, 2013).

Various strategies, such as holistic rotation, piecemeal rotation, perspective-taking, local turns, counting cubes and global shape have been suggested as strategies that individuals employ to rotate an object mentally (Hegarty, 2018). Among these, past research has predominantly focused on a dichotomous framework contrasting holistic and piecemeal approaches. Shepard and Metzler (1971) introduced the concept of holistic mental rotation, emphasizing the mental manipulation of entire objects. This perspective was challenged by Just and Carpenter (1976) and later by Pylyshyn (1979), who proposed a piecemeal approach involving the analysis of individual object components. Heil and Jansen-Osmann (2008) argued that men perform better in mental rotation tasks due to a preference for holistic strategies. Further research by Khooshabeh, Hegarty, and Shipley (2010, 2012) indicated that proficient imagers adapt their strategies based on task demands, while less proficient imagers rigidly adhere to piecemeal strategies. Nazareth (2018) advanced this understanding by emphasizing that strategy flexibility, rather than the superiority of any single strategy, leads to better performance.

Research on the strategy debate in mental rotation has primarily utilized eye-tracking data, retrospective interviews, and think-aloud protocols. Eye-tracking metrics such as fixation count and saccades have lately been used to define a "strategy ratio" (SR), calculated as the number of fixations within the figure divided by the number of switches between figures. An SR of 1 indicates a holistic strategy, while a ratio greater than 1 indicates a piecemeal strategy (Khooshabeh and Hegarty, 2010). This assumes that good rotators using a holistic strategy look at the reference object once, encode and rotate it, then confirm with the other figure. This is grounded in the fundamental definitions of holistic and piecemeal strategies. In a holistic strategy, an individual rotates the entire mental image of an object. Conversely, a piecemeal strategy entails breaking down the image into segments, rotating one part to align with the comparison figure, and then applying the same rotation to the remaining parts to determine if they correspond (Just & Carpenter, 1985). Nazareth (2018) challenged the SR approach, noting that an SR of 1 could reflect different eye-tracking patterns and suggested including fixation duration as an additional metric to better differentiate strategies. Overall, there seems to be poor consensus about the usability of this ratio to differentiate piecemeal from holistic. Therefore, other than asking participants how they solved a mental rotation problem there is currently no good way to find out.

A rather visual and somewhat less utilized eye tracking analytics are heat maps, which shows the density gradient of fixations over the duration of problem solving for either an individual or a group. Heat maps are 2D graphical representation of data where the values of a variable are shown as colors, and the colors red, yellow and green are indicative of high, medium and low density visual attention, respectively (Bojko, A. 2009). Used extensively in consumer research, heat maps are more visual and less quantitative, hence ignored in many domains such as cognitive science. However, heat maps, when used correctly, can also reveal detailed patterns of visual attention and information processing, thereby offering a visually vivid summary of strategies and/or cognitive processes (Negi and Mitra, 2020).

In this ongoing study we propose to investigate whether heat maps can be used to differentiate between holistic and piecemeal strategies. Participants were asked to solve spatial thinking problems. They were then interviewed and the heatmaps were carefully examined to reveal patterns indicating either of the two strategies. Using these interviews and heatmaps we propose a tentative set of rules that can be used on heat maps to reveal underlying spatial strategies, namely, holistic and piecemeal. A more thorough and formal analysis is pending. In this study, we would like to report our preliminary results.

2. METHODOLOGY

This study uses data collected in a larger study on spatial thinking and multimodal analytics. The details of the study can be found in the paper by Ashwin T.S. et al. (under revision). The questions in the study were modeled after Peter and Battista library (2008). For the purpose of this study we have considered a subset of the main study and we have used 10 questions for our analysis, a sample question of which is shown in Figure 1.

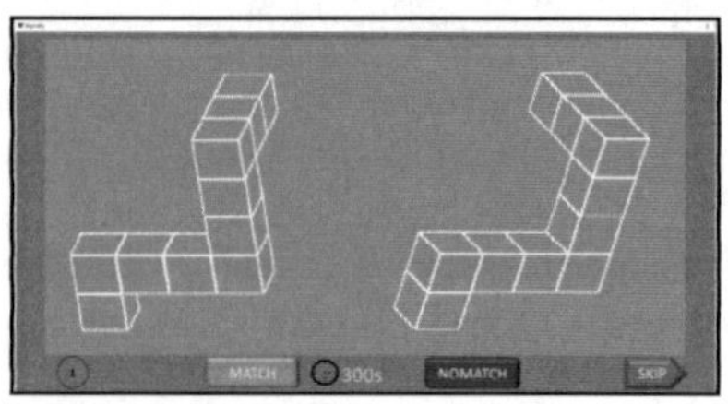

Figure 1. Screenshot of the sample question used for the study

After solving the questions the participants were interviewed and asked to reflect on what strategies they employed to answer the questions. A total of 20 interviews between 4 participants were analyzed for this study.

2.1 Interview Analysis

The interview data were analyzed independently by two coders, achieving an inter-rater reliability greater than 90%. Any discrepancies were resolved by a third rater and a coding scheme based on previous research by Hegarty (2018), was developed to identify holistic and piecemeal rotation strategies. For holistic rotation, we looked for keywords such as "rotate," "flip," "tilt," and "turn," and considered descriptions indicating that the participant mentally rotated the entire image while remaining stationary (Chu & Kita, 2011). Piecemeal rotation was identified through participants describing the process of breaking the image into parts to perform the rotation, without relying on a specific set of keywords. The interview analysis process is explained through Figure 2.

Although other strategies like local turn and cube counting were also identified, this study focused exclusively on holistic and piecemeal strategies. Only interviews explicitly stating the use of either holistic or piecemeal strategies were included in the analysis, ensuring a clear distinction between the two primary approaches.

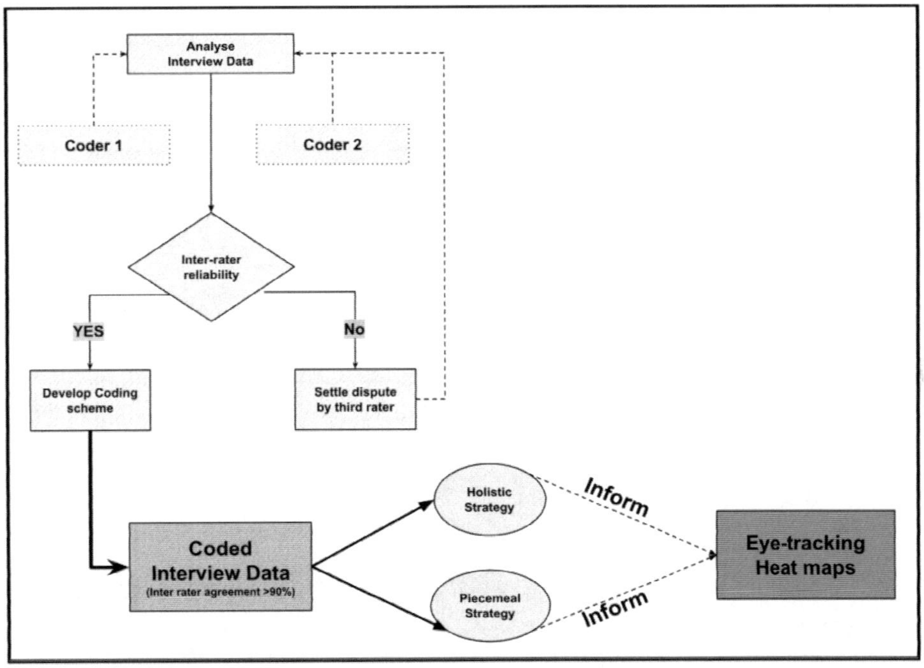

Figure 2. The Interview Analysis Process

2.2 Heat Map Analysis

The Tobii X3 sensor at a sampling rate of 120 Hz integrated with iMotions was used to collect the eye-tracking data. The data were analyzed using the I-VT (Interval Velocity Threshold) filter. The I-VT filter identifies fixations and saccades based on velocity thresholds, allowing for precise analysis of gaze patterns. Heat maps were then generated from the eye-tracking data, utilizing fixation counts to visualize areas of interest. The heat maps were then examined to see if any pattern emerged for holistic or piecemeal, as coded during the interviews.

3. RESULTS

3.1 Interview Analysis

We analyzed interviews from 4 participants for a total of 30 items, although there were initially 40 items (4 participants with 10 items each), as some participants could not recall the strategies they had used. Out of these 30 item-participant combinations, we discarded 10 items due to incorrect responses, as we surmised that analyzing incorrect responses could lead to misleading patterns of strategy use. Consequently, the final dataset for this study included 20 item-participant combinations. From these, we identified 10 holistic strategies, 9 piecemeal strategies, and 1 counting cubes strategy based on the interview coding.

Holistic rotations were evident from excerpts such as the following:

Interviewer: "How did you solve this problem? What strategies did you use?"
Participant 1: "....I rotated it..."
Interviewer: "Can you show me how you rotated it?"
Participant 1: "...I started mapping the right figure to the left figure..I noticed that if I flip the right image upward it will take the shape of the left figure..."
Interviewer: "Did you rotate the entire figure or did you rotate it in parts?"
Participant 1: "Yes...I rotated the entire figure...I realized that the figures are the same only in different directions...so if I rotate the right image by some degrees I will be able to get the left figure..."

In contrast to the above, piecemeal strategies were articulated quite differently in the interviews.

Interviewer: "How did you solve this problem? What strategies did you use?"
Participant 2: "I was mostly looking at the figures block by block, point by point and then compare it between the two figures..I first picked one figure as my reference figure, here the left figure was the reference figure..then I looked for an easy point i.e an anchor point so that I can find the corresponding point in the right figure..so I try to find an anchor point in the left figure and I try to find the exact anchor point in the right figure..then I try to find a sub-anchor point and match it with the relative position in the other figure.."

The participant clearly suggests that they investigated one of the figures 'block by block, point by point' and compared those with the other figure, indicating a piecemeal strategy.

3.2 Heat Map Analysis

The corresponding heat maps from those item-participant combinations (20) were subsequently investigated. Representative heat maps that typify holistic strategies as revealed by the interviews are shown in Figures 3-5. Similarly, piecemeal strategy heat maps are shown in Figures 6-8.

The heat maps were then examined to see if any pattern emerged for holistic or piecemeal, as coded during the interviews. Heat maps generated from participants employing a holistic strategy often displayed a pronounced focus in one figure. This is often evident as a single red area, most commonly not disjointed but may be of irregular shape (Figure 5), often on only one of the two figures (Figures 3 and 4) with some exceptions such as Figure 5 where we might get more than one such area between the two figures. More generally, the total attention between the two figures (all colors) often seem to be lopsided with one figure getting more attention than the other, as in Figure 4. Interestingly, however, we see that the areas of similar levels of attention (same color) between the two figures, mostly yellow and green (Figures 3 and 4) but also when red as in Figure 5, do not appear in corresponding parts of the figure. In fact, the areas seem to be complementary to each other. For example, in Figure 4, the middle two blocks seem to be covered more in the right side representation, whereas the two extreme parts of three and two blocks were in focus on the left. Similarly, in Figure 3 note the locations of the high attention areas in red in the both representations together make up the complete object. They appear on non-corresponding parts of the representations.

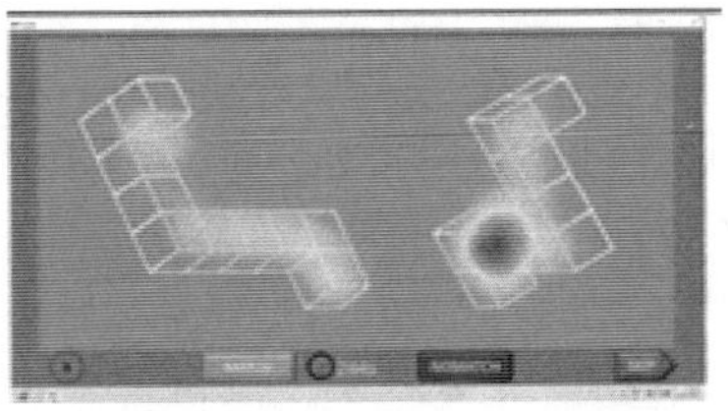

Figure 3. Heat map of participant 1

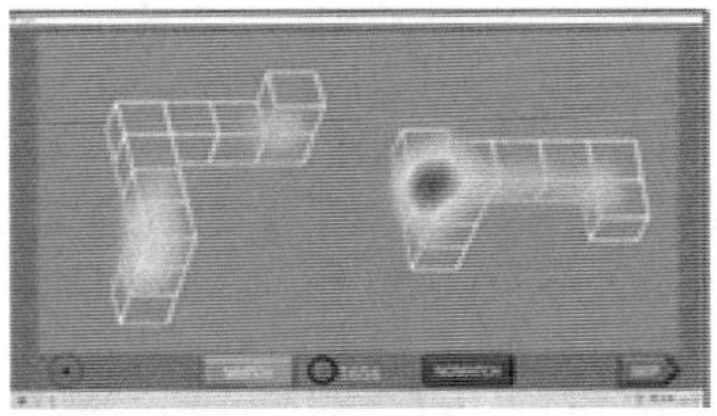

Figure 4. Heat map of participant 1

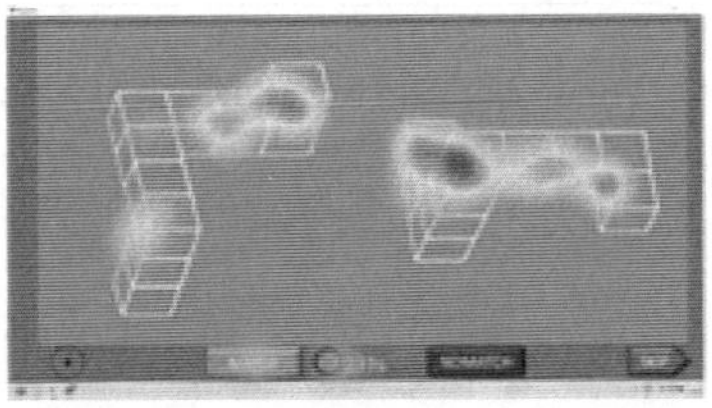

Figure 5. Heat map of participant 2

The heat maps that were coded as piecemeal through the interviews reveal starkly different patterns. Most importantly, unlike the holistic heat maps where we saw lopsided attention distribution between the two figures, the attention seems to be evenly distributed (Figure 7 and 8 but also Figure 6). Furthermore, the pattern in one figure seems to be a mirror-image of the other figure (Figures 5-8). Both of these are in stark contrast to what we observe for holistic items.

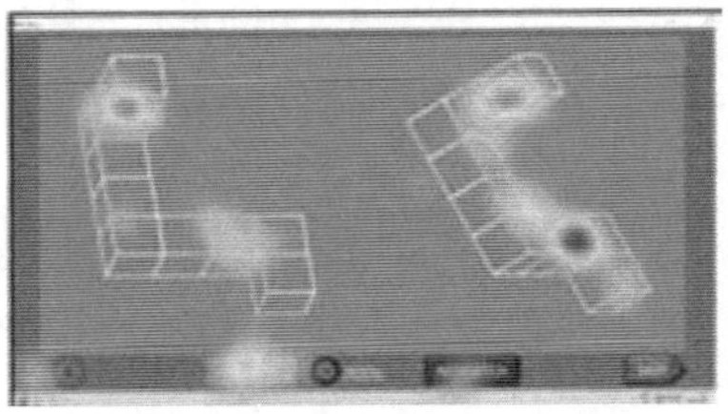

Figure 6. Heat map of participant 3

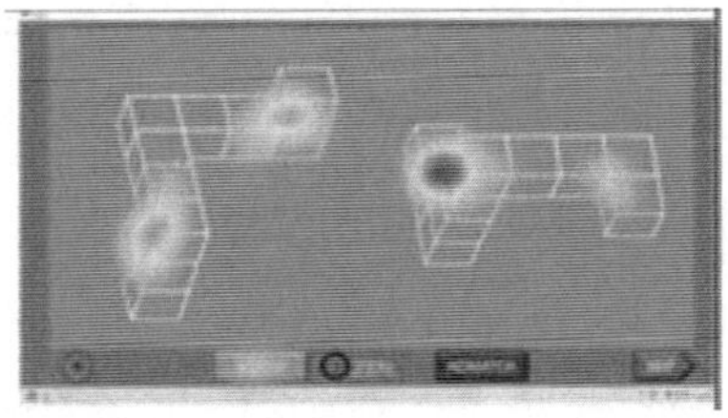

Figure 7. Heat map of participant 3

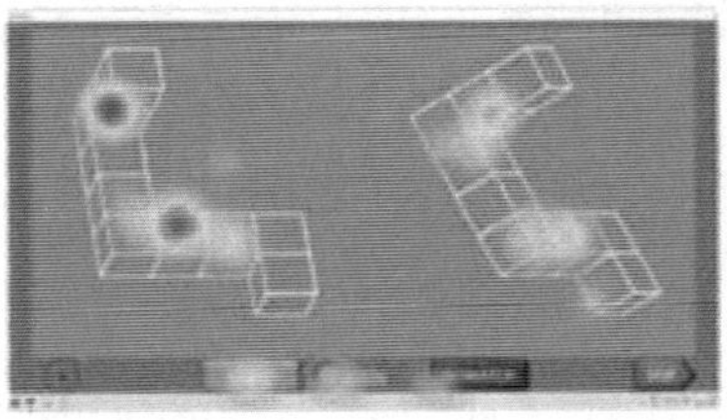

Figure 8. Heat map of participant 4

Out of the 20 item-participant combinations analyzed, we confirmed 8 as holistic and 7 as piecemeal strategies based on the heat map characteristics.

4. DISCUSSION

Eye-tracking heat maps are widely used in research to offer a visual representation of where users focus their gaze within an area of interest (AOI) (Kurzhals & Weiskopf, 2013). These maps provide a qualitative visualization by highlighting specific regions that attract the most attention during a task. A heat map typically uses color coding—such as red for areas of highest concentration and green for lesser focus—to illustrate gaze distribution, allowing researchers to see not just where people look, but also how long they fixate on certain parts of an image. According to Wooding, fixation map analysis primarily seeks to answer the question, "Where in the image did people tend to look?" and provides an objective way to assess the similarity between different eye-movement patterns, though research into such comparisons is still relatively rare.

By integrating eye-tracking heat maps with self-reported cognitive strategies, researchers gain deeper insights into spatial thinking, especially in tasks like the Mental Rotation Test (MRT). Distinct heat map patterns often correspond to different mental strategies employed during these tasks, making heat maps a critical tool for understanding how participants process visual information. A thorough analysis of these maps, paired with qualitative data from participant interviews, can provide clues about which cognitive strategies are at play during mental rotation. A more structured, rule-based approach could be developed to systematically interpret eye-tracking data in relation to specific mental strategies. However, despite the potential, research into quantifying the patterns found in heat maps to reveal mental rotation strategies remains limited.

Heat maps generated by participants using a holistic strategy typically show a concentrated focal point on one of the figures presented in the MRT. This focal point, often marked by a red "hot spot", signifies where the participants are focusing most of their attention. The intensity of this focus suggests longer fixation durations in this area, which implies that participants might be mentally rotating the figure in its entirety during these moments. The eye remains fixed on one part of the figure while the participant performs the mental rotation task in their mind. This reflects the holistic model of mental rotation, where the object is rotated as a whole, similar to physically rotating an object without breaking it into parts.

Additionally, participants using a holistic strategy often exhibit complementary attentional distribution between the two figures presented in the task. This means that their attention is shared between the two objects, absorbing information from both orientations to construct a unified mental representation. Essentially, participants are gathering information from both objects to create a single mental model that can be rotated. This balanced focus indicates that the entire object is being mentally manipulated, not just individual parts, and the participant is processing the two orientations as parts of the same whole.

In contrast, heat maps from participants employing a piecemeal strategy show distinct focal points scattered across the figure. Unlike the holistic approach, where attention is concentrated on one area, piecemeal strategies involve breaking the figure into smaller parts and rotating each part independently. The heat maps reveal multiple focal points, typically aligned with specific components of the object. These areas of concentrated gaze indicate that the participant is analyzing each part of the figure separately, rotating it mentally before moving on to the next section. This process is characteristic of the piecemeal model, where the rotation of the object happens incrementally, part by part.

Interestingly, the focal points in piecemeal heat maps often appear as mirror images between the two figures being compared. This suggests that participants are focusing on corresponding parts of each figure, aligning them mentally to check for similarities or differences. The mirrored focal points indicate that participants are likely rotating individual parts of the object independently, comparing them across both figures before reassembling them into a cohesive whole. This method of mental rotation is more analytical and involves detailed attention to the object's smaller components.

Heat maps are not only useful for revealing visual attention patterns but also provide crucial insights into cognitive strategies. By visualizing where and how long participants focus on different parts of a figure, heat maps can differentiate between individuals who use holistic strategies and those who prefer piecemeal approaches. This ability to map out strategy use is particularly valuable for understanding inter-individual differences—how different people approach the same task—and intra-individual differences, where the same person might switch strategies across different trials. These maps provide a qualitative window into participants' thought processes, allowing researchers to infer cognitive approaches based on gaze patterns.

In the context of the MRT, heat maps can be particularly powerful for uncovering individual and group differences in spatial reasoning strategies. They allow researchers to visualize how participants' attention is distributed across different areas of the task, offering a visual summary of where and how participants engage with the mental rotation task. This can help researchers understand not only how different cognitive strategies manifest in visual attention but also how effective these strategies are in solving mental rotation problems.

In conclusion, eye-tracking heat maps offer a rich source of data for studying mental rotation and spatial reasoning. By providing both qualitative and quantitative insights into visual attention patterns, they enable researchers to explore how different cognitive strategies unfold during tasks like the MRT. Whether used to examine individual differences or broader group trends, heat maps have the potential to significantly enhance our understanding of the mental processes underlying spatial thinking.

5. CONCLUSION AND FUTURE WORK

A preliminary analysis of the interviews and heat maps have revealed the following rules:

Holistic strategy heat map signature:

1. Uneven distribution of attention between two figures. This may appear as a single dominant focus area (red spot) in one figure.
2. Complementary attentional distributions between both the figures.

Piecemeal strategy heat map signature:

1. At least 2 disjoint focal points - indicating that the figure was broken up in at least two parts.
2. Attention to equivalent points in the two figures. This makes the heatmaps look like mirror images as opposed to complimentary in holistic.

We have come up with the above rules by comparing interviews that were coded separately with the heat maps. However, we need to undertake a thorough evaluation of the aforementioned rules by looking at the entire dataset covering all interviews and all heatmaps. Only then we would be able to establish valid and reliable ways of identifying mental rotation strategies with heat maps.

We have also conjectured certain things, such as mental rotation happening in areas of high attentional focus (red areas in lopsided holistic heat maps). However, we do not yet have any evidence for the same. Gaze patterns, where we can see the time evolution of attention, could indicate whether the focus is due to actual rotation or information gathering . For example, if the gaze pattern is stalling in the said area in the middle or later parts of the problem-solving process then it could be argued to be due to active mental rotation at that point in time. However, if the attention is largely happening in the beginning then that could be simply information processing or out of confusion. We believe gaze patterns that show time evolution of attention could play a significant role in building more nuanced and accurate models of visual signatures of mental rotations (RQRQ1Mitra and McNeal, 2017).

We also remain open to the possibility of other types of mental rotation strategies apart from holistic and piecemeal coming to light with a thorough and more detailed investigation of the interviews and heat maps together.

REFERENCES

Ashwin, T. S., Ranganath, S., Khanikar, K., Khan, K., Rajendran, R., & Mitra, R. (under review). A multisensor dataset of South Asian post-graduate students working on mental rotation tasks.

Bojko, A. (2009). Informative or Misleading? Heatmaps Deconstructed. In: Jacko, J.A. (eds) *Human-Computer Interaction. New Trends.* HCI 2009. Lecture Notes in Computer Science, vol 5610. Springer, Berlin, Heidelberg, 30-39.

Chu, M., & Kita, S. (2011). The nature of gestures' beneficial role in spatial problem solving. *Journal of Experimental Psychology: General, 140*(1), 102–116.

Hegarty, M. (2018). Ability and sex differences in spatial thinking: What does the mental rotation test really measure? *Psychonomic Bulletin & Review, 25*(4), 1212–1219.

Heil, M., & Jansen-Osmann, P. (2008). Sex differences in mental rotation with polygons of different complexity: Do men utilize holistic processes whereas women prefer piecemeal ones? *The Quarterly Journal of Experimental Psychology, 61*(5), 683–689.

Just, M. A., & Carpenter, P. A. (1976). Eye fixations and cognitive processes. *Cognitive Psychology*, *8*(4), 441–480.

Just, M. A., & Carpenter, P. A. (1985). Cognitive coordinate systems: Accounts of mental rotation and individual differences in spatial ability. *Psychological Review*, *92*(2), 137–172.

Khooshabeh, P., & Hegarty, M. (2010, March). Representations of shape during mental rotation. In *2010 AAAI spring symposium series*.

Khooshabeh, P., Hegarty, M., & Shipley, T. F. (2013). Individual differences in mental rotation. *Experimental Psychology*, *60*(3), 164–171.

Mitra, R., & Negi, S. (2020). Fixation duration and the learning process: An eye-tracking study with subtitled videos. *Journal of Eye Movement Research*, *13*(6), 1–11.

Nazareth, A., Killick, R., Dick, A. S., & Pruden, S. M. (2019). Strategy selection versus flexibility: Using eye-trackers to investigate strategy use during mental rotation. *Journal of Experimental Psychology: Learning, Memory, and Cognition*, *45*(2), 232–245.

Peters, M., & Battista, C. (2008). Applications of mental rotation figures of the Shepard and Metzler type and description of a mental rotation stimulus library. *Brain and Cognition*, *66*(3), 260–264.

Pylyshyn, Z. W. (1981). The imagery debate: Analogue media versus tacit knowledge. *Psychological Review*, *88*(1), 16–45.

Shepard, R. N., & Metzler, J. (1971). Mental rotation of three-dimensional objects. *Science*, *171*(3972), 701–703.

Uttal, D. H., & Cohen, C. A. (2012). Spatial thinking and STEM education: When, why, and how? In *Psychology of Learning and Motivation,* vol 57, Academic Press, 147-181.

Uttal, D. H., Meadow, N. G., Tipton, E., Hand, L. L., Alden, A. R., Warren, C., & Newcombe, N. S. (2013). The malleability of spatial skills: A meta-analysis of training studies. *Psychological Bulletin*, 139(2), 352–402.

Wooding, D.S. (2002). Fixation maps: Quantifying eye-movement traces. *In Proceedings of the symposium on Eye tracking research & applications—ETRA* '02, New Orleans, LA, USA, 25–27.

E-TUTORIAL USE AND STUDENTS' EPISTEMIC AND ACHIEVEMENT LEARNING EMOTIONS

Dirk Tempelaar
Maastricht University School of Business and Economics
Tongersestraat 53, 6211 LM Maastricht, The Netherlands

ABSTRACT

This study explores the effect of epistemic and achievement learning emotions on student engagement and performance in a foundational business and economics course. We focus on the interaction between epistemic emotions, e-tutorial trace data, and achievement emotions within the context of a compulsory introductory mathematics and statistics course. Epistemic emotions, such as curiosity, confusion, frustration, and surprise, are crucial for cognitive engagement and learning retention but are often overlooked compared to achievement emotions like anxiety, boredom, hopelessness, and enjoyment. By employing dispositional learning analytics and analysing data from six cohorts of first-year students in the Netherlands, we examine how these emotions explain students' engagement with e-tutorials and subsequent academic performance. Our findings highlight the significant role of epistemic emotions in shaping students' learning behaviours and achievement emotions, which in turn affect their overall performance. Achievement emotions were measured using the Achievement Emotions Questionnaire (AEQ) and the Epistemic Emotion Scales (EES). Statistical analyses, including ANOVA and path modelling, show that epistemic emotions and behavioural data from e-tutorials are strong predictors of students' achievement emotions and performance. This research advocates for a more balanced approach in studying learning emotions, emphasizing the importance of both epistemic and achievement emotions in educational settings to improve academic outcomes and student well-being.

KEYWORDS

Learning Analytics, Dispositional Learning Analytics, Learning Emotions, E-Tutorials, Epistemic Emotions

1. INTRODUCTION

In the higher education world, particularly in demanding subjects like mathematics and statistics, understanding the role of emotions in student learning is crucial for enhancing both academic performance and student well-being. This study examines the interplay between epistemic learning emotions, e-tutorial trace data, and achievement learning emotions in a foundational business and economics course. By analysing the interactions among these elements, we aim to shed light on the often-underestimated role of epistemic emotions in the learning process. Epistemic emotions, which include curiosity, confusion, frustration, and surprise, are directly related to the cognitive aspects of learning tasks. These emotions are pivotal as they influence how students engage with, process, and retain new information. Despite their importance, epistemic emotions have historically received less attention compared to achievement emotions—such as anxiety, boredom, hopelessness, and enjoyment—which are more commonly associated with overall academic performance and motivation.

Our study utilizes dispositional learning analytics to examine a compulsory introductory mathematics and statistics course at a university in the Netherlands. We collected data from six cohorts of first-year business and economics students, encompassing e-tutorial system trace data and survey data on learning dispositions, including epistemic and achievement learning emotions. By analysing the interplay between epistemic emotion data, behavioural logs from e-tutorials, achievement emotion data, and course performance data, we aim to highlight the critical role of epistemic emotions in shaping students' engagement with e-tutorials. This engagement, in turn, influences their achievement emotions and overall performance. Our ultimate goal is to advocate for a more balanced approach in learning emotion research, recognizing the importance of both epistemic and achievement emotions in the educational experience.

2. LEARNING EMOTIONS: EPISTEMIC AND ACHIEVEMENT TYPES

"Over the past several decades, considerable research has indicated that students' emotions play a vital role in learning by modulating cognitive and motivational processes in multiple ways" (D'Mello, Moulder, Jensen, 2024, p. 1). At the same time, most of that research shared a common focus. "An overwhelming proportion of existing studies on emotions in education focuses on achievement emotions. … Epistemic emotions have recently started to play a major role in research." (Goetz et al., 2023, p. 150). Achievement emotions stem from engaging in learning activities, such as completing homework, while epistemic emotions pertain to the cognitive aspects of the task itself. Examples of prototypical epistemic emotions include curiosity and confusion.

Achievement emotions are defined as emotions directly related to achievement activities or their outcomes. Two types of achievement emotions can be distinguished based on their focus: activity emotions, which relate to ongoing achievement-related activities, and outcome emotions, which relate to the results of these activities. According to the control-value theory of achievement emotions, students' cognitive appraisals of an achievement outcome or activity are the proximal antecedents of emotions experienced in achievement-related situations. Two groups of appraisals are particularly relevant for achievement emotions: subjective control over achievement activities and their outcomes (e.g., the belief that persistence in studying can be maintained and will lead to success) and the subjective value of these activities and outcomes (e.g., the perceived importance of success) (Pekrun, 2000, 2006). Subjective value appraisals can be intrinsic (e.g., finding a learning activity valuable in itself) or extrinsic (e.g., valuing a learning activity because of its outcome) (Goetz et al., 2024). Although empirical studies typically estimate linear versions of control-value models, the framework suggests that control and value appraisals jointly determine the intensity of the emotional experience, implying a multiplicative model (Goetz et al., 2023). An additional non-linear element in the theory are the under- and over-challenge effects related to the boredom achievement emotion, indicating a curvilinear relationship between boredom and control (Goetz et al., 2024). In this study, achievement emotions were measured with the Achievement Emotions Questionnaire (AEQ: Pekrun, Goetz, Frenzel, Barchfeld, & Perry, 2011).

Epistemic emotions do not refer to the learning activity, but to the cognitive aspects of learning knowledge. An example of a sequence of epistemic emotions when confronted with new knowledge incongruent with existing knowledge ranges from surprise to curiosity to confusion, anxiety and frustration when not successful, or enjoyment when successful (Goetz et al., 2023). In this study, epistemic emotions were measured with the Epistemic Emotion Scales (EES: Pekrun, Vogl, Muis, & Sinatra, 2017),

2.1 Dispositional Learning Analytics

Learning Analytics (LA, Ifenthaler, 2015) research primarily centred on constructing predictive models using data from institutional and digital learning platforms. The Dispositional Learning Analytics (DLA) infrastructure, introduced by Buckingham Shum and Deakin Crick (2012), combines learning data (trace data generated in logs of learning activities through technology-enhanced systems) with learner data (e.g., student dispositions, values, and attitudes measured through self-report surveys) (Tempelaar, 2024; Tempelaar, Rienties, & Giesbers, 2015). Learning dispositions represent individual differences that affect all learning processes and include affective, behavioural and cognitive facets (Rienties, Cross, & Zdrahal, 2017).

2.2 Research Aims

In this contribution, we aim to apply dispositional learning analytics to examine relationships between epistemic emotions, learning behaviours in the form of the use of e-tutorials, measuring both intensity and performance, as well as achievement emotions and course performance. In seeking better balance in the research community, this study emphasizes DLA over LA, and focuses on integrating epistemic emotions and achievement emotions. Our underlying hypothesis is that dispositions play a crucial role in LA studies, and epistemic emotions are essential in research on learning emotions. Additionally, since our data spans pre-pandemic, pandemic, and post-pandemic periods, a secondary objective is to explore the impact of the pandemic on students' learning emotions.

3. METHODS

3.1 Context and Setting

This research was conducted within an introductory mathematics and statistics course for first-year undergraduate students enrolled in a business and economics program in the Netherlands. The course demanded 20 hours of study per week over an eight-week period. It served as a compulsory foundational course, often proving challenging for students with limited mathematical aptitude. Employing a blended approach, the educational model followed the principles of flipped classroom design. The primary instructional method was Problem-Based Learning (PBL; Hmelo-Silver, 2004), conducted in small groups of 14 students each, guided by subject matter expert tutors. Attendance and participation in these tutorial groups were mandatory. Additionally, weekly lectures introduced fundamental concepts for that week's study. The remaining study hours were allocated for self-guided learning, facilitated by textbooks, along with access to two interactive e-tutorial platforms: Sowiso and MyStatLab, for mathematics and statistics, respectively. This educational framework emphasized student-centred learning, placing the responsibility for making educational choices primarily on the student. In student learning, we distinguish three phases. Phase 1 involved preparation for weekly tutorial sessions, where students engaged in discussions surrounding "advanced" mathematical and statistical problems. Successful participation in these discussions relied on prior self-study by the students. Phase 2 focused on preparing for bi-weekly quizzes, primarily serving as formative assessments to gauge students' comprehension of the weekly topics. Phase 3 encompassed preparation for the final exam in the eighth week, featuring formal, graded assessments. Consequently, students' study schedules were influenced by the varying demands of each phase, requiring different levels of preparation.

3.2 Participants

This study encompassed six cohorts of in total 6901 students spanning from the academic years 2018/2019 to 2023/2024. Within this sample, 38% were female, 62% were male, 18% possessed a Dutch high school diploma, while the remaining 82% were international students. Notably, among the international students, Germany (33%) and Belgium (20%) were well represented, with 7% of students from non-European countries. European high school systems exhibit significant variations in mathematics education, but all distinguish three tiers of math education in high school, tailored for sciences, social sciences, or humanities tracks. For admission to this international program, a background in mathematics geared towards social sciences is a prerequisite. Despite this, 37% of students pursued the highest academic track in high school, contributing to the diverse range of prior knowledge within the current sample. Given this diversity, the design of the first module for these students was pivotal. It necessitated flexibility, accommodating individual learning trajectories, and offering frequent, interactive feedback on students' learning strategies and tasks.

3.3 Data

In order to construct a longitudinal prediction model, our data is classified into six distinct time periods or intervals, as illustrated in Figure 1: demographic information obtained prior to the course commencement, epistemic emotions recorded during the initial week, e-tutorial trace data spanning the first four weeks, antecedents of achievement emotions along with the emotions themselves post the fourth week, and finally, course performance data at the conclusion of the course.

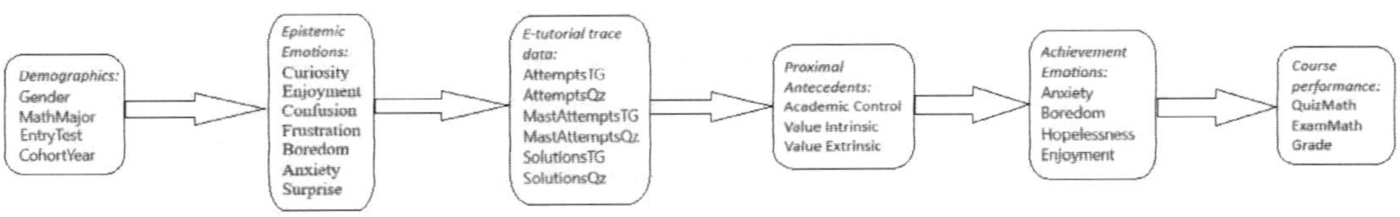

Figure 1. Data in this study, including temporal sequence

Demographics. This encompasses four key variables: Year indicator variables, Gender, indicating the gender of the student, MathMajor, indicating whether the student has previously studied mathematics at an advanced level, and EntryTest, which represents the score attained on a mathematics entry test.

Epistemic learning emotions. Epistemic emotions pertain to the cognitive facets of students' tasks. Characteristic epistemic emotions include curiosity and confusion. In this study, epistemic emotions were measured using the Epistemic Emotion Scales (EES) developed by Pekrun et al. (2017). The scales within the instrument can be categorized based on their valence (positive or negative) and activation component: either activating or deactivating. Positive, activating emotions comprise Curious and Excited, while negative, deactivating emotions encompass Confused, Frustrated, and Bored. Anxious represents a negative, activating emotion, while Surprised is classified as a neutral emotion.

E-tutorial log data were gathered from the Sowiso mathematics system, which is rooted in the instructional approach of mastery learning (Tempelaar et al., 2020). This methodology entails students progressively mastering mathematical concepts by successfully solving problems. Within Sowiso, students are provided with various scaffolding tools, including worked-out examples known as Solutions. The data includes information on Attempts, reflecting how many times a student has endeavoured to solve a problem, and Mastered Attempts, denoting the number of successful Attempts. In this study, we analyse trace data collected during the initial four weeks of the course. Specifically, this pertains to the recorded Attempts, Mastered Attempts, and Solutions during phase 1 learning (preparation for tutorial sessions, TG) for the first four weekly topics. Additionally, it includes data on Attempts, Mastered Attempts, and Solutions during phase 2 learning (preparation for quizzes, Qz) for the initial three weekly topics (with phase 3 extending beyond the fourth week).

Proximal antecedents of activity emotions. Academic Control, which reflects students' confidence in learning mathematics, was assessed using Perry, Hladkyj, Pekrun, & Pelletier's (2001) perceived Academic control scale. Value type of antecedents were determined using the SATS student attitudes toward learning quantitative topics questionnaire (Tempelaar, et al., 2007). Rooted in the expectancy-value theory proposed by Wigfield and Eccles (2000), this instrument incorporates two scales capturing the extrinsic and intrinsic aspects of valuing mathematics and statistics learning: Extrinsic Value assesses students' perceptions of the practical utility, while Intrinsic Value gauges their personal interest levels.

Learning Activity Emotions. The Control-Value Theory of Achievement Emotions (CVTAE), proposed by Pekrun (2000), asserts that emotions experienced during learning activities vary in terms of valence, focus, and activation. Emotional valence may be positive (e.g., enjoyment) or negative (e.g., anxiety). CVTAE delineates these emotions concerning an achievement activity (such as experiencing boredom while doing homework) or its outcome (such as feeling anxiety about an upcoming exam). The activation component characterizes emotions as either activating (prompting action, as in the case of anxiety) or deactivating (leading to disengagement, as with hopelessness). From the Achievement Emotions Questionnaire (AEQ) developed by Pekrun et al. (2011) to assess learning emotions, four scales were chosen: Enjoyment (LJO) representing a positive activating emotion, Anxiety (LAX) representing a negative activating emotion, and Boredom (LBO) and Hopelessness (LHL) representing negative deactivating emotions.

Course performance data. Student performance in the course is evaluated through three variables: QuizMath and ExamMath, which represent students' scores in mathematics quizzes and the final exam, respectively, and Grade, which encompasses scores from both mathematics and statistics exams and quizzes.

3.4 Procedure and Statistical Methods

Data collection occurred at various points in time, as depicted in Figure 1. Demographic information, along with epistemic emotions observed during the initial week of the very first university term, pertain to learning traits cultivated over six years of high school education. E-tutorial records were amassed within the first four weeks of the 8-weeks course, while achievement emotions and their proximal antecedents were assessed at the midpoint of the course, precisely four weeks into the course. In contrast to epistemic emotions, which focus on broader learning experiences, achievement emotions specifically target activities within the course, for clarification of the timing of data collection. Course performance data encompass the entirety of the course.

Statistical analyses were conducted using SPSS version 27 to compare groups through ANOVA, and MPlus version 8.11 for path modelling. In the path model, demographic factors and epistemic emotions act as exogeneous variables, e-tutorial trace data, achievement motivations and its antecedents, and course performance variables are endogenous. In line with previous studies into achievement emotions, we introduce quadratic and interaction terms in the estimation of activity emotions. Our goal is to develop a prediction model incrementally, aligned with the sequence of observations. Initially, exogenous demographic variables and epistemic emotions will predict learning activity. Next, control and value antecedents will be predicted using exogenous variables and learning activities as mediator. Following this, achievement emotions will be predicted by exogenous variables and both learning activity and control-value antecedents serving as mediators. Finally, in the fourth and final step, all these variables will be used to predict course performance.

4. RESULTS

4.1 Descriptives of Epistemic and Achievement Learning Emotions

Both epistemic and activity emotions demonstrate strong stability over years, as evidenced in Figure 2 and Table 1. Minor variations exist, with largest effect size for yearly differences being no more than 0.003.

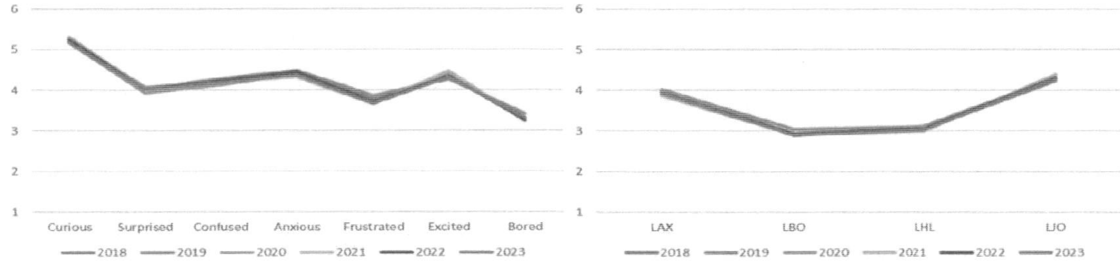

Figure 2. Yearly means of epistemic emotions, left panel, and achievement emotions, right panel

Table 1. Yearly means of epistemic emotions and achievement emotions

Year	Curious	Surprised	Confused	Anxious	Frustrated	Excited	Bored	LAX	LBO	LHL	LJO
18/19	5.24	4.06	4.22	4.4	3.78	4.35	3.27	3.96	2.89	3.05	4.24
19/20	5.18	4.03	4.27	4.47	3.85	4.27	3.42	4.02	3.05	3.11	4.29
20/21	5.18	3.93	4.13	4.4	3.68	4.38	3.26	4.01	2.94	3.12	4.31
21/22	5.31	4.04	4.20	4.33	3.66	4.46	3.24	3.87	2.91	3.00	4.38
22/23	5.25	4.02	4.23	4.44	3.70	4.34	3.27	3.95	2.93	3.06	4.31
23/24	5.17	4.02	4.18	4.37	3.68	4.31	3.32	3.93	2.92	3.02	4.28

Curiosity and Excitement, as epistemic emotions, consistently attain adaptive scores across all years, surpassing the neutral threshold of four. Conversely, negative epistemic emotions like Frustration and Boredom register scores below this neutral anchor, in accordance with adaptivity. However, both Confusion and Anxiety, also negative emotions, exhibit scores surpassing the neutral value, with Anxiety attaining the highest scores, the negative but activating emotion. The neutral emotion Surprise maintains neutral scores, displaying minor fluctuations around the neutral anchor.

Scores for achievement activity emotions tend to exhibit less deviation from the neutral anchor compared to epistemic emotion scores. Learning activity Anxiety (LAX) demonstrates minor fluctuation around the neutral anchor, while Boredom (LBO) and Hopelessness (LHL) consistently score below this neutral threshold. Conversely, Enjoyment (LJO) consistently registers scores above the neutral value.

4.2 Path Model

The scale and intricacy of the path model, in which the exogeneous variables, consisting of the demographic variables Year, Gender, MathMajor and EntryTest and the seven epistemic emotions Curiosity, Enjoyment, Confusion, Frustration, Boredom, Anxiety and Surprise explain the e-tutorial trace variables (Attempts, Mastered Attempts, Solutions, in first and second learning phase, registered in the first four weeks); trace variables together with exogeneous variables explain the proximal antecedents Academic control and Intrinsic and Extrinsic Value; all of these in turn explaining achievement emotions Anxiety, Boredom, Hopelessness and Enjoyment, and subsequently, all of these explaining the three course performance variables, prevents creating a diagram of the final path model. That final path model reaches adequate fit (χ^2 = 2570.735 with df = 268, CFI = 0.983, TLI = 0.973, RMSEA [90% CI] = 0.035 [0.034-0.037], and SRMR = 0.047). In the following paragraphs, instead of using a diagram, the estimates of the several explanatory equations will be discussed.

In the explanation of the e-tutorial trace variables (as well as course performance variables), discrepancies among cohorts are significant, stemming from variations in assignment content and timing. Consequently, year indicator variables are integrated into the explanatory equations. However, these indicator variables will not be explicitly specified in the reporting. Estimated coefficients in explanatory equations are standardized. Starring of coefficient estimates indicates statistical significance (*: $p<.05$; $^{**}p<.01$; $^{***}p<.001$).

AttemptsTG = 0.062***Surprise – 0.066***Confusion + 0.020***Frustration – 0.044***Boredom + 0.044***Female + 0.053***MathMajor + 0.037**EntryTest + YearIndicators; R^2 = 0.095

AttemptsQz = 0.032***Surprise + 0.030***Anxiety – 0.076***Boredom + 0.065***Female – 0.078***MathMajor – 0.029*EntryTest + YearIndicators; R^2 = 0.054

MasteredAttemptsTG = 0.053***Surprise – 0.062***Confusion – 0.046***Boredom + 0.073***Female + 0.088***MathMajor + 0.089**EntryTest + YearIndicators; R^2 = 0.139

MasteredAttemptsQz = 0.007**Curious – 0.079***Boredom + 0.121***Female + 0.071*EntryTest + YearIndicators; R^2 = 0.048

SolutionsTG = 0.063***Surprise – 0.059***Confusion + 0.038***Frustration – 0.037***Boredom - 0.033**EntryTest + YearIndicators; R^2 = 0.047

SolutionsQz = 0.045***Surprise + 0.043***Anxiety – 0.055***Boredom – 0.116***MathMajor - 0.093***EntryTest + YearIndicators; R^2 = 0.076

Between 4.7% and 13.9% of the variability in e-tutorial trace data can be accounted for by a combination of demographics and epistemic emotions. Regarding gender and previous education, we observe distinct patterns: students with greater prior knowledge (Math Major, high Entry Test score) engage in more preparation during the initial learning phase (Tutorial Group preparation), thus requiring less preparation during the subsequent learning phase (Quiz preparation). In contrast, coefficients for the Female indicator across all trace variables are positive, indicating that female students tend to prepare more intensively in both learning phases. Among epistemic emotions, Boredom consistently exerts a negative effect for all trace variables. Confusion plays a similar role but is specifically impactful on trace variables associated with learning during the initial phase, preparing tutorial group sessions. Anxiety confirms its status as a negative but activating emotion, but only for traces related to the learning in the second phase.

AcademicControl = 0.145***Curious – 0.074***Surprised – 0.111***Confused – 0.189***Anxious – 0.076***Frustrated – 0.050***Bored – 0.068***Female + 0.062***MathMajor + 0.074***EntryTest + 0.136***AttemptsQz + 0.041***MasteredAttemptsTG – 0.194***SolutionsQz; R^2 = 0.216

ExtrinsicValue = 0.246***Curious – 0.097***Confused – 0.142***Bored + 0.052***MathMajor + 0.057***EntryTest; R^2 = 0.156

IntrinsicValue = 0.369***Curious + 0.026***Surprised – 0.061***Confused + 0.053***Frustrated – 0.124***Bored + 0.131***Excited + 0.065***Female + 0.055***MathMajor + 0.041***EntryTest ; R^2 = 0.312

Epistemic emotions, particularly curiosity, are crucial in explaining the three proximal antecedents of achievement emotions. A consistent role is reserved for the two variables relating prior schooling, MathMajor and EntryTest. As anticipated, behavioural trace variables help explain Academic Control but not the two value constructs.

LAX, Anxiety = 0.440***Anxious + 0.079***Confused + 0.056***Frustrated + 0.122***Female – 0.175***AttemptsTG + 0.119***SolutionsTG – 0.310***AcademicControl – 0.049***AcademicControlSq; R^2 = 0.528

LBO, Boredom = 0.353***Bored – 0.097***Female + 0.033***MathMajor – 0.218***AttemptsTG + 0.138***SolutionsTG – 0.059***AttemptsQz – 0.229***AcademicControl – 0.031***AcademicControlSq – 0.060***ExtrinsicValue – 0.179***IntrinsicValue – 0.024***AcademicControlXIntrinsicValue; R^2 = 0.384

LHL, Hopelessness = 0.230***Anxious + 0.063***Confused + 0.085***Frustrated + 0.048***Bored + 0.062***Female – 0.033***EntryTest – 0.165***AttemptsTG + 0.127***SolutionsTG – 0.495***AcademicControl – 0.034***ExtrinsicValue – 0.056***IntrinsicValue; R^2 = 0.590

LJO, Enjoyment = 0.221^{***}Excited + 0.094^{***} Curious + 0.094^{***}Surprised – 0.066^{***}Bored + 0.085^{***}EntryTest + 0.068^{***}MasteredAttemptsTG + 0.161^{***}AcademicControl + 0.276^{***}IntrinsicValue + 0.039^{***} AcademicControlXIntrinsicValue; $R^2 = 0.427$

Both LAX and LBO are primarily explained not by the proximal antecedents from the CVTAE model but by their corresponding epistemic emotions: Anxious and Bored. LHL is best explained by a lack of Academic Control, while LJO is mainly explained by the epistemic emotion Excited, along with Academic Control and Intrinsic Value. Gender effects are evident in predicting Anxiety and Hopelessness. E-tutorial trace data follows a consistent pattern: students with more attempts during the initial learning phase (AttemptsTG) tend to have lower levels of negative achievement emotions, while students who only review worked examples during this phase (SolutionsTG) tend to have higher levels of negative achievement emotions. The quadratic term of Academic Control is significant only for explaining Anxiety, while the interaction between Academic Control and Intrinsic Value is significant for explaining both Boredom and Enjoyment.

MathExam = 0.153^{***}MathMajor + 0.074^{***}EntryTest + 0.235^{***}MasteredAttemptsTG + 0.364^{***}MasteredAttemptsQz – 0.298^{***}AttemptsQz + 0.073^{***}AcademicControl – 0.104^{***}LHL + YearIndicators; $R^2 = 0.460$
MathQz = 0.054^{***}MathMajor + 0.086^{***}EntryTest + 0.188^{***}MasteredAttemptsTG + 0.231^{***}MasteredAttemptsQz – 0.050^{***}SolutionsQz + 0.056^{***}AcademicControl – 0.036^{***}LHL + YearIndicators; $R^2 = 0.738$
Grade = 0.132^{***}MathMajor + 0.058^{***}EntryTest + 0.320^{***}MasteredAttemptsTG + 0.344^{***}MasteredAttemptsQz – 0.214^{***}SolutionsQz + 0.127^{***}AcademicControl – 0.122^{***}LHL – 0.014^{***}LBO – 0.053^{***}LJO + YearIndicators; $R^2 = 0.338$

E-tutorial trace data is the primary factor in explaining all three course performance measures. The key is the number of successful problem-solving attempts during the first two learning phases—Mastered Attempts to prepare for tutorial sessions and quizzes—adjusted for either the total number of attempts or the number of solution views. Achievement emotions play a minor role, with only LHL (Hopelessness) consistently appearing in all explanatory equations.

5. DISCUSSION AND CONCLUSIONS

Achievement emotions are crucial in any learning process, particularly for challenging subjects like mathematics and statistics in business and economics programs. Therefore, assessing and, where possible, influencing these emotions is important for both learning outcomes and student well-being. The control-value model is the most well-known theoretical framework for explaining levels of achievement emotions, focusing on three proximal antecedents: academic control, and extrinsic and intrinsic value. In this empirical study, we have shown that, beyond these proximal antecedents, distal antecedents in the form of epistemic emotions are equally important in understanding achievement emotions. For Anxiety and Boredom, these epistemic emotions, shaped by high school learning experiences, are even the dominant explanatory factors.

An additional note on control-value theory concerns the role of quadratic factors and interactions. The under- and over-challenge of students is expected to manifest in the negative emotion of Boredom. To demonstrate this, a quadratic term for Academic Control would be anticipated to have a positive coefficient. However, this term appears in the Anxiety and Boredom equations with a negative coefficient, indicating a levelling off at both high and low levels of academic control, in contrast to the hypothesis of under- and over-challenge. The interaction term between academic control and intrinsic value appears in the explanatory equations for two achievement emotions: Boredom and Enjoyment. The signs of the estimated coefficients are negative for Boredom and positive for Enjoyment, aligning with the control-value theory's assumption that strong achievement emotions develop when both control and value are high.

The most remarkable finding is however the interplay between epistemic emotions, students' e-tutorial activity, achievement emotions, and course performance. The only achievement emotion with a noticeable, though modest, effect on course performance is learning hopelessness. The primary factors explaining course performance are the counts of successful e-tutorial problem-solving attempts in the first and second learning phases, adjusted for unsuccessful attempts or simple solution views. These behavioural traces are in turn explained by epistemic emotions and demographics. Additionally, these same factors, along with trace variables, partially explain Hopelessness. This indicates that future research on learning emotions should prioritize epistemic emotions over achievement emotions. Moreover, it implies that educational practices should address maladaptive learning emotions that have emerged well before the class begins, rather than concentrating mainly on emotions that arise during in-class learning activities.

REFERENCES

Buckingham Shum, S., & Deakin Crick, R., 2012. Learning dispositions and transferable competencies: pedagogy, modelling and learning analytics. *Proceedings of the 2nd International Conference on Learning Analytics and Knowledge*, S. Buckingham Shum, D. Gasevic, and R. Ferguson (Eds.). ACM, New York, NY, USA, pp. 92-101. https://doi.org/10.1145/2330601.2330629

D'Mello, S. K., Moulder, R. G., Jensen, E., 2024. Momentary measures of emotions during technology-enhanced learning prospectively predict standardized test scores in two large samples. *Learning and Instruction*, Vol. 90, No. 101872, https://doi.org/10.1016/j.learninstruc.2023.101872

Goetz, T., Frenzel, A.C., Stockinger, K, Lipnevich, A.A., Stempfer, L, Pekrun, R., 2023. Emotions in education. R. J. Tierney, F. Rizvi, & K Ercikan (Eds.) *International Encyclopedia of Education* (Fourth Edition). Elsevier Science, pp. 149-161. https://doi.org/10.1016/B978-0-12-818630-5.14032-1

Hmelo-Silver, C. E., 2004. Problem-Based Learning: What and How Do Students Learn? *Educational Psychology Review*, Vol. 16, No. 3, pp. 235–266. https://doi.org/10.1023/B:EDPR.0000034022.16470.f3

Ifenthaler, D., 2015. Learning analytics. J. M. Spector (Ed.), *Encyclopedia of educational technology*, Vol. 2, pp. 447–451. Thousand Oaks, CA: Sage.

Loyens, S. M. M., Gijbels, D. Coertjens, L., & Coté, D. J., 2013. Students' Approaches to Learning in Problem-Based Learning: Taking into account Professional Behavior in the Tutorial Groups, Self-Study Time, and Different Assessment Aspects. *Studies in Educational Evaluation*, Vol. 39, No. 1, pp. 23–32. https://doi:10.1016/j.stueduc.2012.10.004

Pekrun, R., 2000. A social-cognitive, control-value theory of achievement emotions. J. Heckhausen (Ed), *Motivational Psychology of Human Development*, pp. 143-163. Elsevier.

Pekrun, R., 2006. The control-value theory of achievement emotions: Assumptions, corollaries, and implications for educational research and practice. *Educational Psychology Review*, Vol. 18, No. 4, pp. 315-341. https://doi.org/10.1007/s10648-006-9029-9

Pekrun, R., Goetz, T., Frenzel, A. C., Barchfeld, P., & Perry, R. P., 2011. Measuring emotions in students' learning and performance: The Achievement Emotions Questionnaire (AEQ). *Contemporary Educational Psychology*, Vol. 36, No. 1, pp. 36-48. https://doi.org/10.1016/j.cedpsych.2010.10.002

Pekrun, R., Vogl, E., Muis, K. R. & Sinatra, G. M., 2017. Measuring emotions during epistemic activities: the Epistemically-Related Emotion Scales. *Cognition and Emotion*, Vol. 31, No. 6, pp. 1268-1276, https://doi.org/10.1080/02699931.2016.120498

Perry, R. P., Hladkyj, S., Pekrun, R. H., & Pelletier, S. T., 2001. Academic control and action control in the achievement of college students: A longitudinal field study. *Journal of Educational Psychology*, Vol. 93, No. 4, pp. 776 –789. https://doi.org/10.1037/0022-0663.93.4.776

Rienties, B., Cross, S., & Zdrahal, Z., 2017. Implementing a Learning Analytics Intervention and Evaluation Framework: What Works? In B. Kei Daniel (Ed.), *Big data and learning analytics: Current theory and practice in higher education*, pp. 147–166. Cham: Springer International Publishing. https://doi.org/10.1007/978-3-319-06520-5_10

Tempelaar, D. T., 2024. Dispositional Learning Analytics to Comprehend Blended Learning. Sampson, D.G., Ifenthaler, D., & Isaías, P. (Eds.) *Smart Learning Environments in the Post Pandemic Era. Cognition and Exploratory Learning in the Digital Age*. Springer, Cham, pp. 207-226. https://doi.org/10.1007/978-3-031-54207-7_12

Tempelaar, D. T., Gijselaers, W. H., Schim van der Loeff, S., & Nijhuis, J. F. H., 2007. A structural equation model analyzing the relationship of student achievement motivations and personality factors in a range of academic subject-matter areas. *Contemporary Educational Psychology*, Vol. 32, No. 1, pp. 105-131. https://doi.org/10.1016/j.cedpsych.2006.10.004

Tempelaar, D. T., Rienties, B., & Giesbers, B., 2015. In search for the most informative data for feedback generation: Learning Analytics in a data-rich context. *Computers in Human Behavior*, Vol. 47, pp. 157-167. https://doi.org/10.1016/j.chb.2014.05.038

Tempelaar, D. T., Rienties, B., & Nguyen, Q., 2020. Individual differences in the preference for worked examples: Lessons from an application of dispositional learning analytics. *Applied Cognitive Psychology*, Vol. 34, No. 4, pp. 890-905. https://doi.org/10.1002/acp.3652

Wigfield, A. & Eccles, J. S., 2000. Expectancy -- Value Theory of Achievement Motivation. *Contemporary Educational Psychology*, Vol. 25, pp. 68-81. https://doi.org/10.1006/ceps.1999.1015

FOSTERING EXPLORATORY LEARNING IN A CRITICAL DIGITAL MEDIA UNDERGRADUATE COURSE AT A SOUTH AFRICAN UNIVERSITY

Lorenzo Dalvit
School of Journalism and Media Studies,
Rhodes University, South Africa

ABSTRACT

South Africa is characterised by persisting social inequalities, a vibrant civil society and one of the highest Internet penetrations on the African Continent. As in other parts of the World, digital media promised to revolutionise politics by giving a "voice to the voiceless", i.e., creating a space for silenced and marginalised opinions, positions and counter discourses. Recent local and international cases provide some sobering examples of how such voices may at times reflect fake news, conspiracy theories or hate speech. In this article I reflect on my experience teaching a third-year journalism and Media Studies course on radical discourses online at a small residential and historically privileged university in South Africa. By problematising the normative ideal of the Digital Public Sphere as a space for equal, unrestricted and rational deliberation through the notion of radical voices, the course seeks to provide students with the conceptual tools to identify and challenge the boundaries of what is acceptable, possible or even imaginable. After engaging with a set of key readings and a brief introduction to relevant methodologies, students engage in collecting and thematically analysing relevant online texts. My experience developing and teaching this course over a period of four years, including the moments of turmoil resulting from emergency remote teaching and learning, yielded some interesting insights in terms of teaching philosophy and practice.

KEYWORDS

South Africa, Digital Media, Situated Learning, Student-Directed Learning, Digital Public Sphere, Online Discourse

1. INTRODUCTION

Since 2018, I have been offering a module in "Radical Discourses Online and the South African Digital Public Sphere" as part of the third-year course in Journalism and Media Studies at a residential University in a small South african town. This offering responds to a need to teach Digital Media at undergraduate level in accordance with its increased importance in Journalism and Media, in academia and in society as a whole (Daniels, 2022). The focus on the Digital Public Sphere (Schäfer, 2015), an adaptation of Habermas' normative ideal, is aligned with my department's interest in Critical Theory and the intellectual legacy of the Frankfurt School. Engaging with a radical discourse, i.e., a claim, opinion or position which could be considered extreme or absurd (see Verhaar, 2016; Haugaard, 2022), serves several relevant purposes for a future journalist or media practitioner. First of all, it introduces the idea of a discourse, i.e., a construction of reality through media texts (Prinsloo, 2009). Secondly, it prompts students to reflect on their own perspective by having to explain why they feel something is radical and therefore realising that this often depends on one's context. Thirdly, it highlights specific social media phenomena such as echo chambers, siloses, conspiracy theories, the decrease of symbolic efficiency, the trap of endless reflexivity etc (Boczkowski and Papacharissi, 2018; Dean, 2019). Finally, it Problematises digital and social media as the voice of the voiceless by showing that such "voice" is not necessarily a positive or progressive one (Dalvit, 2021). As the end of a regular review cycle approaches, university policies recommend reflecting on and possibly updating the course. The aim of the present paper is to outline and problematise such reflections to inform future curriculum development.

2. BACKGROUND

The module seeks to foster situated and student-directed learning through an exploratory and reflexive approach. Situated learning stems from Lev Vygotsky's social development theory in which learning is viewed as "the appropriation of socially-derived forms of knowledge; which are constructed through the exchange between persons and social and cultural circumstances" (Billet 1996:263). Consistent with Vygotsky's views, learning activities provide the content and context for a zone of proximal development where students can move from what they already know to what they can potentially learn through interaction with teachers and peers. All students bring rich personal, educational and professional experiences to the classroom and as such need to be recognised as a peer with the potential to make a contribution and shape their own learning path. Student-directed learning takes place either within or outside formal settings and processes. Bandura (1971: 2001) conceptualises the idea that learning takes place through direct experience and observational experience. Direct experience is learning through one's own trial and error and often plays a key role in enquiry-based learning (Deignan, 2009). For example, when performing a Google search, students may make several unsuccessful attempts before discovering the combination of keywords and settings which yields relevant results (Khoo et al, 2018). Observational experience is learning from others either deliberately or inadvertently (Bandura, 1971; 2001). As an example, a lecturer who "thinks out loud" in class may model meta-cognitive practices for students to emulate (Hartman, 2001; Herreid, 2004). Individual differences play a significant role in terms of progressing through the four stages of learning identified by Bandura, i.e. attention, retention, reproduction and motivation. Rager (2009) also emphasises the role of emotions in self-directed learning, either as motivators or as barriers.

Current research findings in the field of e-learning and m-learning as well as Higher Education teaching in general support the choice of situated and student-directed learning as teaching approaches. Situated learning has the potential to foster motivation, interactivity and the acquisition of contextualised knowledge (Altomonte et al. 2016). Experiences from a Global South context (see Sun et al. 2023) support these findings and emphasise the need for clear goals in self-directed online learning. (Research into tutor assessment and feedback (Orsmond and Merry 2017) suggests that a situated learning approach reveals the need to consider and support independent learning outside the overt curriculum. The discussion of situated and student-directed activities in the present paper is based on my own reflections as well as on regular student evaluations. The combination of the two is recognised as an established tool to improve teaching (Tucker et al., 2003). However, though often a formal requirement, student evaluations may be viewed with skepticism (Spiller and Ferguson, 2011) or even suspicion and overt hostility (Davidovich and Eckhaus, 2019). For this reason, comments about the course are reported verbatim and the tone of the article is deliberately descriptive rather than interpretative. Individual students are anonymised as RDO [Year of Study][Identification Nr], e.g., RDO2021_5 indicates a student attending the course in 2021 whose evaluation was the fifth to be captured. In 2022 and 2023 I was on academic leave so the data for the corresponding years are not included. The module attracts approximately 100 students every year. It runs in the third year and is worth 7.5 NQF credits, equivalent to 75 notional hours. It can be divided into three phases, as discussed below.

3. TEACHING AND LEARNING ACTIVITIES

In the first phase students are introduced to the course and to key concepts and readings. In an introductory session, I explain the course outline and assessment. Feedback in earlier years, such as "[we would have needed] more clarification about the course from the beginning. It was a bit vague at first" (RDO2018_1) and "I do think that the class was struggling to understand what the course was about for a long time, and it took [the lecturer] too long to notice that." (RDO2018_12) prompted me to provide an extensive and detailed explanation of the rationale and focus of the course at the initial stage. Comments in subsequent years suggest things were clearer, albeit with some exceptions such as student RDO2021_5 who wrote:" "Although I learnt a great deal, I still am not entirely sure of what exactly we were supposed to take away from this course". The two statements might seem contradictory at first but I believe they make sense in the context of teaching within my department. As I discuss in more detail below, some students taking JMS as a major are primarily interested in Media Production and there is a general belief that some such students struggle with and do not see the point of the more theoretical Media studies modules. Learning activities consist mainly of engaging with key resources and define key terms from such resources in advance, to prepare for frontal lessons and class discussion. Resources include both academic texts and YouTube videos by reputable scholars and intellectuals such as Chimamanda Ngozi Adichie, Manuel Castells, Hayes Mabweazara, Wendy Willems etc. In earlier iterations, comments such as the ones by student RDO2018_7, who suggested that I "Add more South African readings regarding concepts we did for Assignment 1 or rather how they are used in the African context. [...] Add more videos, those were helpful." prompted me to maintain videos as educational tools (see Albó et al, 2015; Chintalapati and Daruri, 2017; Noetel et al 2021) and ensure balance between international and local scholars in the syllabus. Consistent with calls for decolonisation in Higher education (see Swart, Meda and Mashiyi, 2020) I made sure to include resources by local authors of both European and African descent.

The requirement to prepare a short definition of a key term from the recommended resources in preparation for each lesson ensures that students familiarise themselves with the content before class, thus coming to lessons prepared for discussion. This is consistent with a flipped classroom approach (Ozdamli and Asiksoy, 2016; Bognar et al, 2019) and is intended to encourage students to try and learn by themselves through engagement with the resources. Students recognised the value of this strategy, e.g., by commenting that "I also found that the continuous dictionary assignments were helpful in that they forced us to grapple with the readings. "RDO2019_7). Learning key terms is also an important step in mastering scientific and technological discourses, as familiar words like ubiquity or Public Sphere acquire a new specialised meaning (see Halliday and Martin, 2003). Addressing the comment by student RDO2021_5 that "The summaries we wrote each week were helpful for learning purposes, but they would have worked better if we covered a week's worth of work and then had to write a summary on the topic that had just been discussed "would not ensure engagement with the readings before class. The assignment requires students to write five submissions of between 50- and 100-words explaining concepts in their own words and linking them to key readings and additional resources. Only one of the five submissions (randomly chosen by me) for each student is actually assessed. Some students share the sentiments expressed by student RDO2019_2 who suggested: "I'd remove the mini assignments that we had to do weekly. Yes, it was helpful in doing our readings but the fact that only 1 gets marked is annoying.". This concern was also raised by a colleague who received similar feedback when marking only one of multiple submissions. I attribute such concerns to the fact that, as noted by Brown (2001) for students only what is assessed and contributes to their mark constitutes the actual curriculum. If this is the case, students' concerns reflect an extrinsic motivation which, though understandable, is at odds with some of the ideas (e.g. self-directed learning) which inform my practice. I try to address these concerns by explaining the rationale for marking only one of the five submissions during the introductory lesson. First of all, I bring to the students' attention that it is not unusual for an assessment task (e.g., multiple choice questions) to assess only a portion of what has been taught and learnt. Secondly, if they produce work of consistent quality all submissions are likely to receive similar marks. Thirdly, at the end of each lesson I show and discuss one successful and one problematic example of past years' submissions for each definition. The anonymised examples provide an opportunity to receive indirect feedback on the work they have submitted by exposing them to "good" assignments and by pointing out problematic areas ranging from language issues to going off topic. Students (e.g., RDO2019_7) seemed to appreciate having access to such examples. Finally, the amount of unmarked work (totalling at most 400 words) and the mark allocation (10%) are relatively small, especially if students consider they have to engage with the readings and master the key terms anyway to prepare for lessons. Student RDO2021_1 felt that "the weighting of assignment 1 the short responses were undervalued in comparison to the work put in." so I am considering increasing the mark allocation slightly in future.

In the second phase students identify a suitable topic for investigation through a small-scale enquiry using social media texts. Following a heutagogical model (see Cochraine et al., 2012), digital technology is thus instrumented as part of enquiry-based learning (Deignan, 2009). My role is mainly to scaffold the development of individual projects through probing questions which students are reminded of and encouraged to discuss at the beginning of each lesson, e.g. "Search online for one or more interesting issues or topics. It must be something open to contestation and, ideally, hotly contested. As a tip, try and identify a claim or statement which seems outlandish, absurd, despicable etc." I emphasise that although each project is different, several students may share similar doubts as to what constitutes radical in the context of this course, how to find and collect relevant social media texts, how many texts to collect, how to analyse them etc. Comments such as "I asked a lot of questions from other students and that gave me more clarity" (RDO2018_5) suggest the emergence of collaborative learning through interactions within a community of practice, one of the outcomes of situated learning (Altomonte et al. 2016). At least some of the topics are new to me every year so our contact sessions become opportunities for me to "think out loud" (see Herreid, 2004) as a way to model the critical thinking process I expect students to engage with when reflecting on their choice. Following the suggestion of student RDO2018_9, i.e. "I would change the scope of the course to focus on a more specific range of topics" would stifle some of the freedom and opportunities for learning (including for me). The last frontal lesson of the module takes place in this phase. While for the first three years feedback by the external moderator was almost unconditionally positive, in 2021 a new external moderator commented that the teaching of research methodology should include more detail. In 2022 this was addressed by allocating a double slot to it.

Each student develops and submits a mini-proposal of what they intend to do. The relatively low amount of marks allocated to it (30%) makes this a low-stakes exercise which serves a mainly formative purpose (Knight, 2001). Marks are allocated to preliminary work done, relevance of the topic, engagement with recommended and additional readings, an independently sourced reading and style/ formatting. Marks are deducted for each grammatical mistake, missing cover page or plagiarism declaration, late submissions or exceeding the word count. The threat of these penalties is intended to encourage students to proof read their work, follow instructions and submit timeously. These can be considered elements of the hidden curriculum (Sambell and McDowell, 1998; Jay, 2003), i.e. the set of habits, assumptions and values successful students need to subscribe to in order to succeed. In the past, students could choose between different formats (written, video, audio etc) in accordance with their specialisation in the production component of their degree. Comments such as "It is very nice having the options for the different formats of Assignment 2, even if they weren't used too widely, I appreciate that they were there" (RDO2019_2) indicate that students appreciated this possibility. Unfortunately, in 2020 and 2021 some students did not have access to equipment and editing software so all submissions were in written format. Students (e.g., 2021_4) appreciated writing a shorter assignment as a "pilot" on which they received feedback for the longer essay. Commenting on an initial draft is an established practice which appears to particularly benefit students from marginalised backgrounds (Gulley, 2012).

The third phase comprises mainly student-directed learning. Students work on collecting and analysing data which they report on in essay format for Assignment 3. Those who performed poorly in the second phase (based on their mark or any other emerging issue) are required to meet and discuss with me individually. I also make additional slots available for those who wish to discuss their topic, progress or challenges they face. Beyond the written feedback they receive for Assignment 2, these meetings represent an additional form of commenting on an initial draft (see Gulley, 2012). This strategy proved particularly beneficial during remote teaching and learning (e.g., RDO2020_39 commented that "The lecturer made time to meet on a one-on-one basis for feedback and this really aided my learning and success in the course.") at least for those who had connectivity. The choice of an essay instead of a sit-in exam was motivated by an emphasis on authenticity over memorisation and performance under controlled conditions (see More, 2018; Bengtsson, 2019). For many students this is the last exam before entering a journalistic or media profession in which the ability to produce relatively long texts has become increasingly important (Kartveit, 2020). The essay counts for 60% of the final mark. I provide very detailed requirements in terms of content and mark allocation for each section, style and formatting, minimum and maximum word count etc. Many students feel the maximum length of Assignment 3 (1200 words) is insufficient. Quoting Cicero, who wrote ""If I had more time, I would have written a shorter letter", I explain to the students every year that the rationale for such a draconian limit is precisely to force them to be concise and avoid repetitions. Capturing the incrementality and alignment of different assignments in the module, student RDO2021_6 commented that "I liked the small definition assignments, the proposal and essay. I think each assignment prepared us for the next."

4. EVALUATION AND DISCUSSION

Consistent with the digital focus of this module, digital technology and digital media play a key role as teaching and learning tools. First of all, resources are available and assignments are submitted exclusively via a Learning Management System. At the time of writing JMS3 students can safely be expected to be thoroughly familiar with such system as it is used extensively in their earlier modules and courses. Secondly, learning resources include both written texts (e.g., academic articles or book chapters) and YouTube videos by reputable scholars and intellectuals. This caters for students' different modes of learning and capitalises on the recognised potential of videos to support learning in Higher education (Albó et al, 2015; Chintalapati and Daruri, 2017; Noetel et al 2020). Thirdly, I use PowerPoint slides in lessons. The 2018 module evaluation conveyed through a report by the class representative states that "Students find slides to be "skinny". Students would like more detailed slides. [...] students have to try and jot down what is said as fast as possible in order to gain more detail, which can distract from actively listening and engaging with the lecture." Comments about slides and class discussion are repeated every year, e.g. "I found the lectures interesting but the slides were very plain and unhelpful." (RDO2021_5). Some feedback collected in 2019 directly contradicts these views, e.g. "[The lecturer's] slides were informative both in class and on [the LMS]. He did not read off of the slides in class but he taught us and the slides just helped put everything together." (RDO2019_4) and "I enjoyed class discussions and thought these catalysed some interesting examples. The PowerPoints were also laid out in a simple yet effective manner which was helpful." (RDO2019_7). I believe these contradictions reflect different learning styles and personal preferences among students. The use I envisaged for PowerPoint, i.e., to complement rather than replace lessons, was captured by the comment "The slides had limited information which forced me to listen to the lecture content, which I found engaged me and I didn't get distracted. (RDO2021_4).

During the COVID pandemic, I recorded my presentations and made them available to students in different formats (notes, audio and audio-video). This enabled me to implement a truly flipped learning approach ((see Bognar et al, 2019). Students could consult the material before class and make use of our time together for discussions. Zoom sessions during the allocated lecture times are an opportunity to discuss the readings, answer questions, summarise the slides presentation etc. These sessions are recorded and made available for download through RUconnected. Students could also ask questions via Discord, email or WhatsApp and have them answered in the following Zoom recorded session. Comments such as "we are able to ask for help when we need one, for example the RDO Has created a cord platform where we asked questions that we were uncertain about, and we were answered" (RDO2020_55) suggest that students found these channels of communication useful. The experience of remote teaching and learning during 2020 and 2021 revealed profound digital inequalities among our students.

This module consistently received positive reviews by students from the start. Since 2018, I offer this course every year. At the end of each iteration, I run a comparable set of questions including open ended and Likert-scale-type questions, which enables some comparison across years. The overall rating of the course increased from 3.3 in 2018 to 3.5 in 2019 and 4.6 in 2021. The improvement remains substantial even when I consider only the top scores to account for the smaller number of respondents in 2021 (6) compared to 2019 (8) or 2018 (16). Moreover, one might have expected less favourable ratings of recent iterations which were ran online compared to traditional face-to-face ones (Rovai, Ponton, Derrick and Davis, 2006). An open-ended question on what students felt they had learnt highlighted some differences between those interested in theoretical as opposed to practical aspects. The fact that we cater for these two rather different types of students is consistent with the nature of different scholarly traditions in the field. It is part of the reason for long-standing discussions about possibly having separate majors for Journalism and for Media Studies in my department. The views of students with a predominantly practical orientation are exemplified by comments such as, "I'm not quite sure I see value in the course for me as an individual per se because I do not want to specialise in media studies but overall, there is value." (RDO2018_13) or: "as I am not an activist journalist, and look merely to report on the world as it is, instead of trying to make an active change, I feel like the course was not the most useful to me." (RDO2018_9). Students interested in Media studies felt that they learnt a lot from the module, e.g.: This course has been different to any other during my time at [the University]. It has challenged me to think very critically and in a way that I haven't ever done before." (RDO2018_1). "After three years of Journalism at [the University], after this course I feel like a finally understand what as discourse is. I learnt to look at the media in a different way, not simply consuming news but analysing why there are these actions and reactions." (RDO2019_2). The comments above are consistent with a remark by student RDO2021_2 that "The style of learning was different to other courses but the constant submissions kept me engaged and interested". Comments such as "I realised just how much I don't notice and how entrench/naturalised things become." by student RDO2021_4 suggest evidence of increased critical awareness.

Students generally comment positively on me as a lecturer, highlighting some strong points. The first one seems to be clarity, as suggested by comments such as "[The lecturer]'s explanations of the topics covered were extremely clear and managed to help clarify issues I had been having with a few media terms for years" (RDO2019_2). The second strong point seems to be providing inspiration and engagement by fostering different learning strategies, as confirmed by comments such as, "[He] was an engaged lecturer and I do believe he inspired the students. The promotion of broad learning strategies was encouraged and I feel this was through the versatile assignments. (RDO2021_1). The 2020 evaluations confirm generally positive experiences of module content, structure and communication during remote teaching and learning, sometimes through favourable comparisons with other modules, e.g. "I felt that both the Digital Self-Representation and Radical Discourses courses took full advantage of online mediums in order to achieve their educational goals, but MLE did not. "(RDO2020_10). Another student describes me as "Absolutely great on all fronts. I can't think of anything that could improve." (RDO2021_4). While it is obviously pleasing that students recognise the effort I put into developing and teaching this module, critical feedback and suggestions for improvement, discussed above, remain the real point of course evaluation (Rovai et al, 2006; Thomas et al, 2014; see Bognar et al, 2019).

5. CONCLUSIONS

In this paper I discussed how course design reflects a situated and student-directed learning approach. Consistent with an understanding of curriculum development as a continuous process rather than a final product, the course evolved in response to the feedback received. For example, when 2018 and 2019 students mentioned that the purpose of the module should be made clearer from the beginning, that local examples and readings by African authors would be useful and that the word limit for the last assignment was too low, I responded by dedicating particular attention to explaining the purpose and focus of the course in the introductory session, by including local examples in my lessons and more African scholars in the syllabus and by explaining the rationale for the relatively low word count for the final essay. Once the COVID-19 pandemic ended, there was a tendency to revert to tried and tested models of teaching as a contact university. Positive evaluations and feedback for my course during that period support more recent calls for the appreciation of the potential of digital technology to foster flexible and independent learning. While the discussion above seems to warrant only minimal changes in the teaching plan, recent developments in artificial intelligence prompted the inclusion of a fourth activity in which students reflect on AI-generated texts. Initial exploration indicates that machine learning, algorythmic bias and anti-discrimination policies may pose some challenges in producing radical media texts. .

REFERENCES

Albó, L., Hernández-Leo, D., Barcelo, J., & Sanabria-Russo, L. (2015, June). Video-based learning in higher education: the flipped or the hands-on classroom? In *EDEN Conference Proceedings* (No. 1, pp. 400-408).

Altomonte, S., Logan, B., Feisst, M., Rutherford, P. and Wilson, R., 2016. Interactive and situated learning in education for sustainability. International Journal of Sustainability in Higher Education, 17(3), pp.417-443.

Bengtsson, L. (2019). Take-home exams in higher education: A systematic review. *Education Sciences, 9*(4), 267.

Boczkowski, P. J., & Papacharissi, Z. (Eds.). (2018). *Trump and the Media*. MIT Press.

Bognar, B., Sablić, M., & Škugor, A. (2019). Flipped learning and online discussion in higher education teaching. In V. Wang (Ed.), *Didactics of smart pedagogy: Smart pedagogy for technology enhanced learning* (pp. 371-392). Springer.

Brown, G. (2001). *Assessment: A Guide for Lecturers*. LTSN Generic Centre.

Chintalapati, N., & Daruri, V. S. K. (2017). Examining the use of YouTube as a learning resource in higher education: Scale development and validation of TAM model. *Telematics and Informatics, 34*(6), 853-860.

Cochrane, T., Sissons, H., Mulrennan, D., & Pamatatau, R. (2012). Journalism 2.0: exploring the impact of mobile and social media on journalism education. In *Proceedings of the IADIS International Conference on Mobile Learning* (pp. 165-172).

Dalvit, L. (2021). The voice of the voiceless? Decoloniality and online radical discourses in South Africa. In C. Ufuoma & C. Awino (Eds.), *Decolonising political communication in Africa* (pp. 207-223). Routledge.

Daniels, G. (2022). Decolonising curricula: Unravelling the master signifier in students' discourse from their demands during the #FeesMustFall protest in South Africa. In M. Ogunyemi (Ed.), *Decolonizing communication studies* (pp. 1-20). Cambridge Scholars Publishing.

Davidovich, N., & Eckhaus, E. (2019). Student evaluation of lecturers—What do faculty members think about the damage caused by teaching surveys? *Higher Education Studies, 9*(3), 12-21.

Dean, J. (2019). Communicative capitalism: This is what democracy looks like. *Revista de Comunicação e Linguagens*, (51).

Deignan, T. (2009). Enquiry-based learning: Perspectives on practice. *Teaching in Higher Education, 14*(1), 13-28.

Gulley, B. (2012). Feedback on developmental writing students' first drafts. *Journal of Developmental Education, 36*(1), 16.

Halliday, M. A. K., & Martin, J. R. (2003). *Writing science: Literacy and discursive power*. Taylor & Francis.

Haugaard, M. (2022). Reverse versus radical discourse: A qualified critique of Butler and Foucault, with an alternative interactive theorisation. *Global Society, 36*(3), 368-390.

Herreid, C. F. (2004). Can case studies be used to teach critical thinking? *Journal of College Science Teaching, 33*(6), 12-14.

Jay, M. (2003). Critical race theory, multicultural education, and the hidden curriculum of hegemony. *Multicultural Perspectives: An Official Journal of the National Association for Multicultural Education, 5*(4), 3-9.

Kartveit, K. (2020). How do they do it? Multimedia journalism and perceptions of the practice. *Journalism, 21*(10), 1468-1485.

Knight, P. (2001). A briefing on key concepts. Formative and summative, criterion & norm-referenced assessment. *LTSN Generic Centre*.

Noetel, M., Griffith, S., Delaney, O., Sanders, T., Parker, P., del Pozo Cruz, B., & Lonsdale, C. (2021). Video improves learning in higher education: A systematic review. *Review of Educational Research, 91*(2), 204-236.

Orsmond, P. and Merry, S., 2017. Tutors' assessment practices and students' situated learning in higher education: chalk and cheese. Assessment & Evaluation in Higher Education, 42(2), pp.289-303.

Ozdamli, F., & Asiksoy, G. (2016). Flipped classroom approach. *World Journal on Educational Technology: Current Issues, 8*(2), 98-105.

Prinsloo, J. (2009). Theorising news mediations of the Zuma rape trial—Citizens and subjects in collision. *Critical Discourse Studies, 6*(2), 81-96.

Rovai, A. P., Ponton, M. K., Derrick, M. G., & Davis, J. M. (2006). Student evaluation of teaching in the virtual and traditional classrooms: A comparative analysis. *The Internet and Higher Education, 9*(1), 23-35.

Sambell, K., & McDowell, L. (1998). The construction of the hidden curriculum: Messages and meanings in the assessment of student learning. *Assessment & Evaluation in Higher Education, 23*(4), 391-402.

Schäfer, M. S. (2015). Digital public sphere. In *The international encyclopedia of political communication* (pp. 1-7). Wiley.

Spiller, D., & Ferguson, P. B. (2011). Student evaluations: Do lecturers value them and use them to engage with student learning needs? *Journal of Higher Education Policy and Management, 33*(1), 57-67.

Sun, W., Hong, J.C., Dong, Y., Huang, Y. and Fu, Q., 2023. Self-directed learning predicts online learning engagement in higher education mediated by perceived value of knowing learning goals. The Asia-Pacific Education Researcher, 32(3), pp.307-316.

Swart, A., Meda, L., & Mashiyi, N. F. (2020). Lecturer conceptions of and approaches to decolonisation of curricula in higher education. *South African Journal of Higher Education, 34*(2), 146-168.

Thomas, S., Chie, Q. T., Abraham, M., Jalarajan Raj, S., & Beh, L. S. (2014). A qualitative review of literature on peer review of teaching in higher education: An application of the SWOT framework. *Review of Educational Research, 84*(1), 112-159.

Tucker, B., Jones, S., Straker, L., & Cole, J. (2003). Course evaluation on the web: Facilitating student and teacher reflection to improve learning. *New Directions for Teaching and Learning, 2003*(96), 81-93.

Verhaar, P. (2016). Radical Reddits: Into the minds of online radicalised communities (Master's thesis). *University of Amsterdam*.

Vygotsky, L. S. (1978). Interaction between learning and development. In M. Cole, V. John-Steiner, S. Scribner, & E. Souberman (Eds.), *Mind in society: The development of higher psychological processes* (pp. 79-91). Harvard University Press.

Welch, T., & Gultig, J. (2002, July). Becoming competent: Initiatives for the improvement of teacher education in South Africa 1995-2002. In *Proceedings of the Pan-Commonwealth Conference*. Durban.

AI-ASSISTED ENHANCING OF GENDER AWARENESS THROUGH READING COMPREHENSION IN HISTORY AND LITERATURE COURSES OF ANGLOPHONE CULTURES

Ivana Pondelíková and Jana Luprichová
Department of British and American Studies, Faculty of Arts,
University of Ss. Cyril and Methodius in Trnava
Námestie J. Herdu 2, Trnava, 917 01, Slovakia

ABSTRACT

The study investigates the pilot verification of the role of AI-powered tools like ChatGPT, Perplexity, and Gemini in enhancing reading comprehension and critical thinking skills among students in history and literature courses focused on Anglophone cultures. These tools provide personalized explanations and foster diverse text analysis, increasing awareness of gender biases and inequalities in canonical works. The research, based on workshops employing the design thinking principles (Plattner – Meinel – Leiffel, 2011), aims to engage Generation Z students, also known as the Homeland Generation (Carter, 2018). Zeers are often considered a "non-reading" generation as they address their digital preferences. Design thinking principles are employed to facilitate students' active participation in content creation. The workshops emphasize the dual roles of AI tools and educators, with teachers guiding students to navigate potential AI biases while promoting independent critical thinking skills. The methodology includes AI-assisted reading exercises, literary analysis, and searching for historical facts, encouraging students to engage with gender and transgender themes. The authors highlight the neurological risks of passive AI tool use, referencing Stranský (2023), stressing the importance of maintaining cognitive engagement. Preliminary findings indicate improved vocabulary and writing style among a third of participants, though grammar improvement remains limited. Therefore, it is crucial to form Zeers and raise Alphas and upcoming Betas to prevent generational degeneration. As these generations are digital natives, avoiding technology is impractical. Consequently, teachers must guide them on how to use AI tools wisely and integrate them effectively into the educational process. Careful integration of AI-assisted activities alongside traditional instructional methods can empower students to engage more deeply with course materials and recognize gender as a crucial lens for interpreting literary and historical narratives.

KEYWORDS

Reading Literacy, Reading Comprehension, History, Literature, Anglophone Cultures, AI Tools, Design Thinking, Gen Z, Gen Alpha

1. INTRODUCTION TO AI-ASSISTED GENDER AWARENESS IN READING COMPREHENSION

The advent of artificial intelligence (AI) tools in education marks a significant shift in how students engage with and comprehend course materials. AI-powered applications like ChatGPT, Perplexity, and Gemini offer personalized explanations and foster critical thinking skills in history and literature courses focusing on Anglophone cultures. These tools help students analyze texts from diverse perspectives, enhancing their awareness of gender biases and inequalities embedded in canonical works. This research explores the integration of AI tools in educational workshops aimed at improving reading comprehension and gender awareness among Generation Z, often labeled a "non-reading" generation due to their preference for digital content over traditional reading.

Recent studies, such as those by Alderson (2000), emphasize that reading comprehension is not merely a passive receptive skill but a complex cognitive process. Engaging Generation Z requires an educational approach that accommodates their digital nativeness while promoting critical literacy skills. Teachers must adopt roles as mentors, guiding students through the potential biases of AI systems and emphasizing the development of independent critical thinking. The work of neurologist Stranský (2023) underscores the importance of active engagement with AI tools to prevent cognitive decline.

The workshops organized by the authors applied design thinking principles to engage students actively. This method prioritizes understanding the needs of the user(s). By incorporating AI tools in these workshops, students are encouraged to contribute to their educational content, enhancing their reading comprehension and critical thinking skills. The workshops address gender and transgender questions by fostering open discussions and analyzing both literary works and historical events.

The integration of AI in education offers a multifaceted approach to addressing reading comprehension challenges and enhancing student engagement. By leveraging AI tools and methodologies, educators can create more inclusive and effective learning environments that cater to the diverse needs of students.

2. THEORETICAL FRAMEWORK: READING COMPREHENSION AND GENDER AWARENESS

2.1 Understanding Reading Comprehension Skills

English has become a prominent global language, especially in fields such as technology, economics, commerce, and science. Reading is a vital skill for processing this information, enabling students to understand various texts and acquire knowledge effectively. Schools usually categorize language skills into receptive (listening and reading) and productive (speaking and writing) skills. Reading, in particular, serves as a means of communication through written texts, allowing individuals to gather information across different aspects of life, including science and technology. It is essential for anyone seeking knowledge, as it helps individuals absorb a wealth of information. Moreover, the higher education environment necessitates the development of advanced reading skills, encouraging students to engage with both general and specialised texts to enhance their comprehension and analytical abilities (Kováčiková – Kráľová, 2021).

For English learners, reading enhances overall language skills, aids in thinking in English, expands vocabulary, improves writing, and introduces new ideas and experiences. This, in turn, deepens students' understanding of English (Mickulecky – Jeffries, 2004; Harmer, 2003). However, teaching reading skills presents several challenges. Understanding a text depends on students' background knowledge, cultural context, and familiarity with different text types. Without these, comprehension can be difficult (Alderson, 2002). Insufficient vocabulary, including technical terms and words with multiple meanings, further hinders text comprehension (Paren, 1996 in Harmer, 2003). Additionally, long, multi-clause sentences are harder to understand than shorter ones.

Language, as a tool for communication, is deeply connected to social contexts and individual identity. It conveys personal thoughts, cultural beliefs, and practices of communities. Language also distinguishes humans from animals, serving as a complex system of words and meanings (Haerazi et al., 2018). Unlike content-based subjects like science and mathematics, language (in our case English) encompasses four sub-skills: listening, writing, speaking, and reading.

Nowadays, technology plays a crucial role in enhancing learning processes, including reading comprehension. Reading comprehension is an interactive process involving the reader, the text, and the context, aiming to derive meaning from written words (Silliman – Wilkinson, 2007). Effective comprehension involves understanding simple terms, the author's intent, content evaluation, and adaptable reading speed. Silent reading is often the most effective activity for developing comprehension skills, as it allows for the interpretation of material read (Lestari et al., 2022). This interactive nature of reading underscores its complexity, involving visual activities and the process of translating written symbols into spoken words. It engages cognitive functions like word recognition, literal comprehension, interpretation, critical reading, and creative comprehension. Hafner and Pun (2020) categorize comprehension into literal understanding, interpretation, and critical reaction, ensuring that readers grasp the text's content.

Interestingly, Carlson et al. (2014) note that speed and comprehension are not necessarily correlated; fast readers often comprehend better because they view words in the context of whole sentences, rather than in isolation. This approach allows for quicker and more effective reading.

One modern technique to improve reading skills is through artificial intelligence (AI). AI technologies interact humanely with thought processes like learning, reasoning, and self-correction, offering a significant edge in language learning (Rasouli – Ahmadi, 2021). Before AI, students typically used other media to enhance their listening and reading skills. Integrating AI into reading instruction can provide personalized learning experiences, making the acquisition of reading skills more effective and engaging.

2.2 Addressing Gender and Transgender Issues in Literature

Given the rapid pace of societal change, it is crucial to foster open discussions about gender and transgender identity to create a more accepting environment for transgender individuals, women, and people of colour. Unfortunately, human society's foundations are built on ancient theories that prioritize white, cisgender men, perpetuating false beliefs about the inferiority of women and fostering harmful intolerance towards homosexuality and transgender identities. Despite significant progress in racial and gender equality, much work remains to ensure that everyone, particularly members of minority groups, can live in a safe and inclusive environment. Education is one of the keys to the reduction of gender disparities. To achieve gender equality, the curriculum should be designed to meet the needs and expectations of all social groups, and teachers must be trained to address gender-related issues and apply the curriculum impartially. Additionally, the community must be sensitized and involved in promoting gender equality and opposing any acts or policies that hinder community development. Implementing these resolutions requires significant resources, as well as the supervision and evaluation of various programs to assess their effectiveness and identify areas for improvement. Redesigning curriculum and pedagogy is a promising approach to achieving gender equality (Aikman et al., 2005). Literature has long served as a profound reflection of life, giving voice to various topics.

In recent times, modern and postmodern literary ideas have transformed the literary landscape. Writers worldwide have tackled the most urgent issues of their times, including gender inequality. These writers have actively championed social reform, tirelessly advocating for the marginalized and working towards meaningful societal change (Akhter, 2020). The exploration of gender and transgender issues in literature spans multiple genres and periods, reflecting societal changes and the evolving understanding of identity. Early literature often reinforced binary gender norms and marginalized non-conforming identities. In the 19th century, novels like George Eliot's *Middlemarch* (1871) and Thomas Hardy's *Jude the Obscure* (1895) depicted gender roles within the constraints of societal expectations. However, hidden within these works were subtle critiques of rigid gender norms, laying the groundwork for more explicit explorations of gender fluidity in later years. The 20th century marked significant progress in the representation of gender and transgender identities. Virginia Woolf's *Orlando* (1928) is a seminal work, presenting a protagonist who changes gender over centuries, challenging the fixed nature of gender identity. Woolf's narrative was revolutionary, highlighting gender as a fluid and dynamic construct. James Baldwin's *Giovanni's Room* (1956) further pushed the boundaries by addressing complex issues of sexuality and gender identity. The latter part of the 20th century and the early 21st century saw a surge in literature specifically focusing on transgender experiences. Leslie Feinberg's *Stone Butch Blues* (1993) is a cornerstone in transgender literature, offering an autobiographical account of growing up gender non-conforming. Among the more recent stories are Michal Cunningham's *The Hours* (1998) and David Ebershoff's *The Danish Girl* (2000). Both texts explore the complex nuances of gender identity and the societal limitations placed on individuals, providing profound insights into the characters' lived experiences. *Detransition, Baby* is a 2021 novel by American author Torrey Peters, made history as the first novel written by a trans woman to be included on the Women's Prize for Fiction list.

The discussion of gender inequality has gained notable traction in academic and scientific circles. Akhter (2020) examines all the elements of gender inequality, the agony, and the pain suffered by these members around the globe through the lenses of fiction. In 1997, Luise von Flotow published *Translation and Gender: Translating in the Era of Feminism*, a work that delves into feminist perspectives on gender as a cultural construct and examines translation as a form of cultural transfer. Sandra Lipsitz Bem's *The Lenses of Gender: Transforming the Debate on Sexual Inequality* (1993) re-examines traditional perspectives on gender and sexual inequality through a new theoretical lens. Bem, a prominent feminist psychologist, presents a groundbreaking analysis that challenges conventional views and offers fresh insights into the nature of gender inequality. Susan Stryker is a leading voice in transgender studies, offering a comprehensive overview of the history and social issues affecting transgender individuals. Her work *Transgender History* (2008) explores the representation of transgender lives in literature and media. In addition to these key figures, interdisciplinary approaches involving sociology, psychology, and cultural studies have enriched the study of gender and transgender literature. Scholars from these fields often collaborate with literary critics to offer a more comprehensive understanding of how gender and transgender issues are represented and perceived in literature. The work of these scholars and authors continues to shape the field, offering new perspectives and challenging existing norms, thereby advancing the study of gender and transgender literature.

3. WORKSHOP METHODOLOGY: APPLYING DESIGN THINKING PRINCIPLES WITH USING AI TOOLS

Design thinking is crucial in today's fast-paced environment, allowing organizations to innovate effectively. By prioritizing user's needs and fostering a culture of experimentation, businesses can develop solutions that not only meet market demands but also enhance customer satisfaction and loyalty (McKinsey, 2023). Companies like Google, Apple, and Airbnb have successfully employed design thinking to drive innovation and create user-friendly products and services (Interaction Design). Design thinking is a dynamic approach and mindset employed to explore innovative and creative solutions to a wide range of challenges (Pondelíková, 2023). It aims to meet three essential criteria: desirability, feasibility, and viability. Desirability addresses what people truly want and need. Feasibility considers whether it is technically possible to build the solution. Viability examines if the solution can be profitable for the company. The current generation of college students (Gen Z) and high school students (Generation Alpha) have specific expectations from their education. This is why design thinking, as an optimal teaching method, has increasingly been integrated into educational process. The potential of design thinking extends beyond stimulating creative thinking, teamwork, and problem-solving; it also plays a crucial role in developing foreign language competence, enhancing intercultural communication, and improving reading comprehension skills. This connection to cultural intelligence and communication competence is highlighted by Dančišinová and Kozárová (2021). Design thinking involves a shift from traditional didactic teaching methods to more interactive and collaborative approaches. This approach better equips students to navigate the complexities of real-world business environments (Wrigley et al., 2020). From a psychological perspective, design thinking is based on four core principles: observing and noticing, framing and reframing, imagining and designing, and making and experimenting. These principles align with social-psychological phenomena, indicating that design thinking aids individuals in overcoming cognitive biases and promotes innovative thinking (Thompson – Schonthal, 2020).

The authors of the text designed the workshops on enhancing gender awareness through reading comprehension in the history and literature of Anglophone cultures by following Plattner, Meinel, and Leiffel's (2011) four key principles of design thinking, which are the human rule, the ambiguity rule, the re-design rule, and the tangibility rule. In *An Introduction to Design Thinking*, Plattner (2010) explains that understanding the target group is essential for defining problems and seeking optimal solutions, which are subsequently tested and validated. The design thinking process involves the following phases, which were incorporated into the workshop:

1. Empathize: understand the needs of the target group through conversations and observations;
2. Define: identify and articulate a specific problem based on insights from the empathize phase;
3. Ideate: generate a wide range of creative solutions without aiming for the most optimal answer immediately;
4. Prototype: develop simple solutions to the identified problem, allowing for user interaction and refinement; and
5. Test: present prototypes to users, and collect feedback on usability and areas for improvement.

Each workshop was limited to 25 participants, organized into small groups of five to encourage communication and personalized attention. We conducted two pilot workshops, "Writing Texts with ChatGPT," targeting third-year students preparing their bachelor's theses. Of the 45 students, 7 were men, 37 women, and 1 identified as other, with ages ranging from 19 to 24, and 37% being 21 years old. Paying close attention to group size, participant age, and interactive elements was crucial for maximizing the workshop's effectiveness. We then assessed its impact by collecting student feedback through an online questionnaire.

In the introductory part of the workshop, students selected their topics, such as "The Question of Transgender Identity in *The Danish Girl* by David Ebershoff" or "The Gender Question in *The Hours* by Michael Cunningham". As for historical topics, students could choose a topic based on their preferences, for instance, "Tudor Monarchs: Royal Drama!", or "The Victorian Era: Empire, Industry and Social Changes". Once topics were chosen, participants followed the design thinking process by identifying their key strengths to contribute effectively to the team. They then assigned roles based on these strengths, such as writer, researcher, proofreader, and verifier. They then brainstormed their existing knowledge about the selected topics and used AI tools like ChatGPT or Gemini to gather additional information. After acquiring sufficient information, the ideation phase began, and they started developing their content, utilizing AI tools to enhance style and structure. The final version, refined and polished, reflected the quality expected of university students. This process required extensive reading comprehension and critical thinking, which were the main goals of the workshop. In the final phase of the workshop, participants engaged in peer feedback, assessing each other's work, offering constructive criticism, and suggesting ways to enhance the final product. As these were pilot workshops, no formal grading took place. Instead, the teachers' role was to summarize all the comments, highlight positive features, and point out potential improvements in working with ChatGPT.

The application of design thinking principles in the educational process enables continuous monitoring and adaptation to students' needs, fostering a more personalized and effective learning experience. By engaging students as users and utilizing iterative feedback, educators can develop innovative and customized educational solutions that meet the specific needs of their target group. Moreover, teachers can use design thinking to create more interactive reading assignments that engage students and improve their understanding and critical thinking.

The adequacy of the selected method concerning the goal is crucial and essential for effective education (Sirotová, 2022). Selecting the most fitting teaching methods ensures that the essence of the educational process aligns with the desired outcomes. One such versatile approach is design thinking, applicable not only to designers but to all innovators. It can be used in literature (Pondelíková, 2022; Brooks, 2022), foreign language teaching to engage students with the target language and cultures (Sperling, 2022), art where it is transforming into art thinking (Robins, 2018). Additionally, it enhances cognitive strategies in translation and interpreting (Bohušová, 2017) and improves translators' competencies (Welnitzová, 2023). Design thinking is also applied in music (Badizadegan, 2019), and prominently in science, industry, engineering, and business. Its primary objective is to uncover unconventional strategies and solutions beyond initial understanding.

While design thinking has shown great potential in enhancing educational outcomes, its implementation is not without challenges. A systematic literature review identified several obstacles faced by educators and students, including the need for continuous adaptation and the development of design thinking skills (Wrigley – Straker, 2015). Despite these challenges, the potential benefits of design thinking in education, such as the development of 21st-century competencies and increased student engagement, make it a valuable approach to be applied.

4. PRACTICAL OUTCOMES: ENHANCING GENDER AWARENESS AND READING COMPREHENSION

Reading and comprehending text is a fundamental skill crucial for academic success and lifelong learning, including in online environments, which also demand additional digital competencies. Students who struggle with reading comprehension encounter significant challenges, such as limited access to information, fewer academic opportunities, and diminished earning potential over their lifetimes (Kirsch et al., 2011). Therefore, identifying effective strategies to help students improve their reading comprehension skills is essential. Recent research highlights the effectiveness of personalized and adaptive learning strategies in enhancing reading comprehension (Fisher – Frey, 2020) and underscores the role of technology in addressing diverse learning needs.

Design thinking presents both opportunities and challenges in this context. While it fosters creative solutions and personalized learning experiences, it can also face limitations such as potential biases in understanding user needs, difficulty in addressing complex issues comprehensively, and the need for iterative testing and feedback (Brown, 2009). This approach can be particularly effective in increasing awareness of gender issues and developing critical thinking skills by encouraging students to deeply engage with diverse perspectives and real-world problems.

Literature and history courses offer valuable opportunities to delve into a range of topics, including contemporary issues like gender, through both literary analysis and historical context. The workshop conducted for students at the University of St. Cyril and Methodius in Trnava, Slovakia, aimed to raise awareness of this issue by integrating reading comprehension techniques with the use of artificial intelligence tools. The objective was to compose a book review of up to 250 words for the literary section, focusing on key facts and information related to gender and transgender identity, along with recommendations for further reading or viewing. The students were tasked with having ChatGPT restyle their text to reflect a more academic tone. Given that the students were enrolled in an American literature course, they had background knowledge about the work under discussion. The design thinking process started with brainstorming ideas and subsequently continued with developing students' version of the book review for *The Danish Girl* by David Ebershoff.

Students' version:
David Ebershoff's most successful novel published in 2000. Fiction love story based on true story of the first person who undergoes gender change surgery. Story about a married couple. Einar was a successful painter, but Gerda is still trying to make her name. Gerda who needed a female model for her portrait, and used Einar because she didn't have anyone else to use. Einar found out he liked being in women's clothes. They developed an alter ego for him – Lili as a game. But slowly Einar felt more like himself as Lili. At some point, Einar realized he wanted to become a real woman. Unfortunately, the surgery didn't go as planned and Einar passes away after being turned into a woman. We highly recommend to watch the movie or read the novel as it was very inspiring.

The student version straightforwardly provides basic information but lacks cohesion and is read like a series of disjointed statements. Although important details are included, they are not elaborated well. The narrative is fragmented, more like a list of facts than a coherent story. It briefly mentions Einar's realization of his interest in women's clothing and his desire to become a woman but does not explore the complexities of gender identity in depth. The tone is informal and conversational, making it less suitable for academic purposes. The limited complexity and depth do not challenge the reader's ability to understand. Some details, such as Einar's evolving identity as Lili, are unclear or poorly explained. Furthermore, the recommendation to read or watch the adaptation is not well integrated into the narrative.

ChatGPT version:
David Ebershoff's most acclaimed novel The Danish Girl, published in 2000, is a fictional love story grounded in the true narrative of the first individual to undergo gender reassignment surgery. The story centres on a married couple, Einar and Gerda. Einar is depicted as a successful painter, whereas Gerda is portrayed as an artist still striving to establish her reputation. The narrative begins with Gerda's need for a female model, leading her to use Einar in the absence of other options. This experience ignites Einar's realization of his affinity for women's clothing, resulting in the creation of an alter ego named Lili, initially conceived as a playful experiment. Gradually, Einar increasingly identifies with Lili, eventually recognizing a profound desire to live as a woman. The novel poignantly details Einar's decision to undergo gender reassignment surgery. Tragically, the procedure does not succeed, and Einar passes away after the transition. This compelling and inspirational story is highly recommended for those interested in exploring the novel or its film adaptation.

The ChatGPT version provides a cohesive and structured narrative, adding specificity by including the book's title, The Danish Girl. The tone is more formal and academic, with varied sentence lengths that improve readability and flow. The narrative is more engaging and descriptive, using sophisticated language and vocabulary, which distinguishes it from student writing. This version delves deeper into Einar's transformation into Lili, providing a clearer and more detailed account. The tragic outcome and inspirational aspects are compellingly highlighted and offer a comprehensive and clear portrayal of the whole story.

Final version:
David Ebershoff's successful novel The Danish Girl, published in 2000, delves into a captivating love story inspired by the true account of the first individual to undergo sexual reassignment surgery. The narrative focuses on the lives of Danish painters Einar and Gerda Wegener. Einar, a prosperous artist, and Gerda striving for recognition, embark on a journey of self-discovery when she employs Einar as a female model. What begins as a playful game with the alter ego Lili transforms into a profound realization for Einar to become a woman. Tragically, the procedure does not succeed, and Einar passes away after the transition. Ebershoff's narrative and its film adaptation provide an inspiring and thought-provoking experience, highly recommended for those

seeking a profound literary exploration of the human experience, particularly through the lenses of identity and transgender issues.

The final version maintains the structure and detail of the ChatGPT version while refining the narrative description to focus more on the Wegener couple's journey. Key points are integrated more smoothly, enhancing coherence. The formal and academic tone is retained and further polished, with more sophisticated language and phrasing. This version engages the reader with a more compelling and apt narrative, effectively emphasizing the journey of self-discovery and identity. The tragic outcome is covered briefly without losing its impact. Themes of gender and transgender identity are highlighted more effectively, providing a deeper understanding of the human experience, which was the main goal of the workshop. The recommendation is seamlessly incorporated, linking the narrative covering the key topic.

The revisions from the students' version to the ChatGPT version resulted in significant enhancements in cohesion and flow, delivering a more detailed and engaging narrative with an academic tone and clarity. Further improvements from the ChatGPT version to the final version polished the language and structure, offering a more sophisticated and nuanced presentation. The final version places a clearer emphasis on a key theme which is gender/transgender identity, providing the most comprehensive and engaging analysis. This demonstrates a notable improvement in developing reading comprehension skills, critical thinking, and a deeper understanding of this complex theme.

The historical exercise aimed to explore and gather facts about the chosen topic, guiding students to decide on the presentation style for their final versions. Students could select among journalistic, tabloid, or academic styles. Similarly to the literary section, students engaged in the design thinking process by brainstorming their understanding of the chosen topic and identifying key concepts. After ideating, they used these insights to compose their own paragraphs. Finally, they were tasked with using ChatGPT to refine the style of their text. The following example illustrates the work of a group of students who selected the topic "Tudor Monarchs: Royal Drama!"

Students' version: "Progress and Reform: Queen Victoria's Victorian Era"

The Victorian era begins with the ascend of Victoria, daughter of King William IV, to the British throne on 20th June 1837. This era is defined as an era of great progress, jumpstarted by the industrial revolution and the trade and geopolitical influence the colonialism era brought to the country. The progress in industry lead to major changes in the lifestyle of the British citizens, as the rural areas were deserted in favor of cities under the promise of higher pay and climbing the socioeconomic ladder. As times were tough, poverty was rising in the overpopulated cities. With poverty rose crime and disease, and many children were also forced to work in manufactories, as there were no worker rights written in law yet. Some of these issues changed thanks to queen Victoria, who along with her parliament and the first ever prime minister, Robert Walpole, managed to write some protections for citizens into law – namely – opening the first women's colleges, ensuring mandatory school attendance up to 10 years, abolishing slavery in the British empire, passing the first public health act to combat diseases like cholera and even allowing the construction of the world's first metro and revolutionizing trade between the colonies by opening trhe Suez canal. The era ends with queen Victoria´s death at 81 years of age, in 1901, after a 63 year successful reign.

The students' version accurately describes the Victorian era's beginning with Queen Victoria's ascension on June 20, 1837, highlighting significant progress driven by the Industrial Revolution and colonialism, although it mistakenly identifies Robert Walpole as a prime minister during her reign. It discusses urban migration, resulting in poverty, crime, disease, and child labour due to the lack of worker rights, and mentions key reforms such as women's colleges, compulsory education, the abolition of slavery, public health acts, the first metro, and the Suez Canal. The grammar is generally sound, but there are minor errors and awkward phrasings.

ChatGPT version: "Queen V's Reign: A Humorous Journey through the Victorian Era"

Ah, the Victorian era! It all kicked off when that bonny lass Victoria snagged the throne from her old man, King William IV, on June 20th, 1837. This period was a real hoot, filled to the brim with progress, thanks to the industrial revolution and the whole colonialism shebang that gave Britain a bit of a boost. Life was a whirlwind for the Brits back then! Rural areas became ghost towns as everyone scrambled to the cities for that sweet promise of more cash and a step up the ol' social ladder. But let me tell ya, it wasn't all sunshine and rainbows. Poverty skyrocketed in those overcrowded city streets, bringing along its pals crime and disease. And talk about child labor! Kids were toiling away in factories left and right because, well, nobody had bothered to jot down any worker rights yet. But fear not, for Queen Vicky swooped in like a hero with her trusty sidekicks Parliament and Prime Minister Robert Walpole. They whipped up some laws to protect the common folk, like opening women's colleges, making school mandatory for ten years (good luck getting out of math class, kiddos), and even putting the kibosh on slavery in the British Empire! And let's not forget the cherry on top: the world's first subway and the Suez Canal, making trade between colonies a breeze. Queen Victoria may have shuffled off this mortal coil in 1901 at a ripe old age of 81, but she left behind a legacy that'll have history buffs chuckling for centuries to come. Cheers to you, Queen V.

The ChatGPT version maintains factual accuracy without addressing or correcting the original version's errors but employs an overly informal and humorous tone. While this approach makes history engaging, it can also trivialize significant events. The version correctly integrates historical facts with engaging humour but is unsuitable for academic contexts due to its conversational style. It appears that ChatGPT responded to the students' directive to restyle their original text in a more humorous or tabloid manner. However, the issue arises from the students' oversight in not instructing ChatGPT to verify and correct any factual inaccuracies, resulting in unaddressed factual errors in their submission.

Final version: "Victoria's Legacy: Progress and Reform in the Victorian Era"

The Victorian era commenced on June 20th, 1837, with the ascension of Queen Victoria to the British throne, succeeding her father, King William IV. This era marked a period of significant progress, spurred by the industrial revolution and the economic and geopolitical impacts of colonialism. The rapid industrialization led to a mass migration from rural areas to urban centers, driven by promises of better pay and social advancement. However, this influx resulted in burgeoning poverty, crime, and disease in overcrowded cities, exacerbated by the lack of worker rights legislation, leading to child labor exploitation. Queen Victoria, along with Parliament and Prime Minister Robert Walpole, addressed these societal challenges by enacting various reforms. These included the establishment of women's colleges, compulsory education up to ten years, the abolition of slavery within the British Empire, and the implementation of the first public health act to combat diseases such as cholera. Additionally, groundbreaking infrastructural projects, such as the world's first subway and the construction of the Suez Canal, revolutionized trade between colonies. Despite the era's hardships, Queen Victoria's reign, spanning 63 years until her death at the age of 81 in 1901, left a lasting legacy of progress and reform. Her efforts, alongside the contributions of Parliament and Prime Minister Walpole, significantly improved the lives of British citizens and shaped the course of history for centuries to come. And with a dash of humor and wit, the tale of Queen Vicky's reign continues to entertain and educate history enthusiasts worldwide.

The final version combines the students' factual foundation (still with factual errors) with the engaging elements of ChatGPT's style, maintaining a balanced mix of formal and engaging tones. It accurately describes Queen Victoria's reign, industrialisation, urban migration, resulting societal issues, and key reforms without the earlier factual error, presenting a polished, academically appropriate account with a slightly humorous touch. The final version demonstrates the students' ability to refine and balance content and style, making it the best choice. Unfortunately, it also maintains factual (in)accuracy and academic integrity while incorporating elements of engagement, showing that students effectively synthesised their own work and the suggestions from ChatGPT.

It is recommended that educators closely monitor the commands students provide to ChatGPT, as the effectiveness of the tool in reformulating text heavily depends on the accuracy and specificity of these commands. Ensuring that students include instructions for fact-checking and correcting inaccuracies is crucial, as demonstrated in this instance.

The design thinking approach, particularly in the context of Generation Z, must adapt to their digital fluency and preference for interactive, multimedia content. The contemporary generation of university students and Alphas are deeply embedded in social media and the digital world. They share everything on social networks, prefer watching videos over reading, take photos of everything, and communicate more through pictures than words or text (Miština et al., 2022). In the academic environment, critical thinking and reading comprehension skills enable both students and teachers to find quality information sources, organize them hierarchically, identify plagiarism, and verify authors' authority (Javorčíková – Badinská, 2021). Consequently, educational strategies must align with these preferences by incorporating technology and interactive elements that resonate with this demographic. The pilot workshops, though preliminary, suggest that AI tools and personalized learning platforms can significantly enhance students' reading comprehension and critical thinking skills, provided they are used thoughtfully and with attention to the evolving needs of digital-native learners. Therefore, it is important to organize workshops where students learn to work with data correctly, evaluate them, improve their reading skills, and avoid future plagiarism. Considering that these were pilot workshops and AI tools have not been used for a long time in our university, we currently have only preliminary data indicating improvements in various skills. Based on feedback gained from the online questionnaire, one-third of students (33%) who attended the workshop and used ChatGPT extensively enhanced their vocabulary and writing style, although they did not see significant improvement in their grammar. Research has shown that personalized learning platforms and practical workshops can significantly enhance students' reading comprehension skills (Liu et al., 2020; Iwata et al., 2020; Akiba et al., 2020; Khan – Mutawa, 2021; Hidayat, 2024). Integrating AI tools and personalized learning platforms holds significant promise for transforming reading education and offering effective solutions for students experiencing difficulties with reading comprehension.

5. CONCLUSION AND FUTURE DIRECTIONS

The integration of AI tools like ChatGPT, Perplexity, and Gemini in educational settings has shown significant potential in enhancing reading comprehension and critical thinking among students. These tools, by offering personalized explanations and encouraging analysis from diverse perspectives, address the challenges faced by Generation Z, often characterized as a "non-reading" generation due to their preference for digital content. The workshops conducted in this research demonstrated how AI tools could effectively raise awareness of gender biases and inequalities in literature and history courses focused on Anglophone cultures.

The application of design thinking principles in these workshops has proven to be a valuable approach to engaging students actively. By following the phases of empathizing, defining problems, ideating, prototyping, and testing, students were able to contribute to their educational content and improve their reading comprehension skills. The workshops emphasized the importance of critical thinking and the need for teachers to guide students in understanding the limitations of AI systems and the societal biases they may reflect.

Preliminary data from these workshops indicate that one-third of students who extensively used AI tools showed significant improvements in their vocabulary and writing style, though grammar improvements were less pronounced. This suggests that while AI tools can enhance certain aspects of language learning, continuous guidance, and adaptation are necessary to address all areas comprehensively.

In conclusion, the integration of AI tools in reading comprehension and the application of design thinking in educational processes hold significant promise. They not only enhance students' engagement and comprehension skills but also promote a deeper understanding of gender issues in literature and history. The careful combination of traditional instructional methods with AI-assisted activities can create a more inclusive and critically engaged learning environment, preparing students to navigate and contribute to the evolving digital landscape effectively.

ACKNOWLEDGEMENT

This paper was created within the project KEGA No. 012UCM-4/2024 Women in science and technology – raising the awareness of male and female students in the field of gender equality.

REFERENCES

Aikman, S. and Unterhalter, E., and Challender, C. 2005. The education MDGs: achieving gender equality through curriculum and pedagogy change. *In C. Sweetman (Ed.), Gender and the Millennium Development Goals*. Oxford, Oxfam, UK.

Akhter, T. 2020. Gender Inequality and Literature: A Contemporary Issue. *In Advances in Social Science, Education and Humanities Research*, Vol. 51. Retrieved from file:///C:/Users/200700/Downloads/125949674.pdf

Akiba, M. et al. 2020. An AI-based reading comprehension support system for middle school students. *In Journal of Educational Technology Development and Exchange*, Vol. 13, No. 2, pp. 87-98.

Alderson, J. C. 2000. *Assessing Reading.* Cambridge, Cambridge University Press, UK.

Badizadegan, D. 2019. *Design Thinking for Musicians: An Introduction.* Retrieved from https://medium.com/swlh/designthinking-for-musicians-an-introduction-fe8451f6b8fe

Bem, S. L. 1993. *The Lenses of Gender: Transforming the Debate on Sexual Inequality*. New Haven, Yale University Press, USA.

Bohušová, Z. The cognition of interpreting and neutralization. *In Voprosy kognitivnoj lingvistiki = Issues of Cognitive Linguistics*, Vol. 13, No. 4, pp. 58-68.

Brooks, Ch. 2022. Incorporating Design Thinking in the Study of Literature. *In Edutopia*. Retrieved from https://www.edutopia.org/article/incorporating-design-thinking-study-literature/

Brown, T. 2008. Design Thinking. *In Harvard Business Review*. Retrieved from https://readings.design/PDF/Tim%20Brown,%20Design%20Thinking.pdf

Carlson, S. and Seipel, B. and Mcmaster, K. 2014. Development of a new reading comprehension assessment: Identifying comprehension differences among readers. *In Learning and Individual Differences*, Vol. 32, pp. 40-53.

Carter, T. 2018. Preparing Generation Z for the Teaching Profession. *In SRATE Journal*, Vol. 27, No. 1, pp. 1-8.

Dančišinová, L. and Kozárová, I. 2021. *Globalizácia, kultúra, interkultúrna komunikácia a kultúrna inteligencia vo vzájomných súvislostiach: dosahy pre interkultúrny manažment*. Prešov, Vydavateľstvo Prešovskej university, Slovakia.

Fisher, D. and Frey, N. 2020. *The distance learning playbook, grades K-12: Teaching for engagement and impact in any setting.* California, Corwin, USA.

Haerazi, et al. 2018. Incorporating Intercultural Competences in Developing English Materials for Writing Classes. *In Journal of Language Teaching and Research*, Vol. 9, No. 3, pp. 540-547.

Hafner, C. A., and Pun, J. 2020. Editorial: Introduction to this Special Issue: English for Academic and Professional Purposes in the Digital Era. *In RELC Journal*, Vol 51, No. 1. pp. 3-13.

Harmer, J. 2003. *How to teach English*. London, Longman, UK.

Hidayat, M. T. 2024. Effectiveness of AI-Based Personalised Reading Platforms in Enhancing Reading Comprehension. *In Journal of Learning for Development*, Vol. 11, No. 1, pp 115–125.

Iwata, Y. et al. 2020. An AI-based writing feedback system for improving reading comprehension skills. *In Educational Technology Research and Development*, Vol. 68, No. 4, pp. 1739-1759.

Javorčíková, J. and Badinská, M. 2021. Reading and Critical Thinking Skills of Undergraduate Students: A Quantitative Analysis. In *The Journal of Teaching English for Specific and Academic Purposes*, Vol. 9. No. 4. pp. 655-666.

Khan, A. and Mutawa, M. 2021. Enhancing reading comprehension skills of Arab EFL learners using an AI-based personalised reading platform. *In International Journal of Emerging Technologies in Learning*, Vol. 16, No. 6, pp. 119-136.

Kirsch, I. et al. 1993. *Adult literacy in America: A first look at the results of the National Adult Literacy Survey.* New Jersey, U.S. Department of Education. Office of Educational Research and Improvement, USA.

Kováčiková, E. and Kráľová, Z. 2021. Positive Views and Challenges of Using Project Work in ESP Lessons. *In Journal of Teaching English for Specific and Academic Purposes*, Vol. 9, No. 1. pp. 31-41.

Lestari, S. and Usadiati, W. and Misrita, M. 2022. The Correlation between Students' Artificial Intelligence and their English Reading Skills Achievement. *In Bahasa: Jurnal Keilmuan Pendidikan Bahasa dan Sastra Indonesia*, Vol. 3, No. 2. pp. 103-111.

Liu, Y. et al. 2020. An AI-based personalised reading platform for Chinese primary school students. *In Journal of Educational Technology Development and Exchange*, Vol. 13, No. 1, pp 1-16.

Mikulecky, B. S. and Jeffries, J. 2004. *More Reading Power. Reading for Pleasure, Comprehension Skills, Thinking Skills, Reading Faster.* New York, Longman, USA.

Miština, J. et al. The Impact of the Pandemic Crisis on Technology Standard of Traditional University Education. *In Mobility for Smart Cities and Regional Development - Challenges for Higher Education. ICL 2021. Lecture Notes in Networks and Systems*, Vol. 390, pp 187–198.

Plattner, H. et al. 2011. *Design Thinking. Understand – Improve – Apply*. Heidelberg, Springer, Germany.

Pondelíková, I. 2022. Design thinking ako moderný spôsob výučby interkultúrnej komunikácie. *In Interkultúrna komunikácia vo výučbe odborného cudzieho jazyka.* pp. 95–104.

Pondelíková, I. 2023. Design Thinking for Specific Purposes. Comparative Study of Design Thinking Technique to Enhance Educational Process for Students of English and Teachers of Various Academic Fields. *In The Journal of Teaching English for Specific and Academic Purposes*, Vol. 11, No. 3, pp. 633-650.

Rasouli, F. and Ahmadi, O. 2021. The Motivational Impact of Enhancing Reading Comprehension through Pictorial Fictions on the Involvement of Iranian EFL Students in Writing Activities. *In Cihan University-Erbil Journal of Humanities and Social Sciences*, Vol. 5, No. 1, pp. 82-87.

Robinson, K. 2011. *Out of Our Minds: Learning to be Creative*. Mankato, Capstone. USA.

Sirotová, M. 2022. *Efektívne učenie vo vysokoškolskej edukácii*. Trnava: Univerzita Sv. Cyrila a Metoda v Trnave, Slovakia.

Sperling, R. 2022. Design Thinking in the Second Language Classroom. *In CASLT.* 2022. Retrieved from https://www.caslt.org/en/blog-design-thinking/

Stranský, M. 2023. Jak nástup digitální technologie negativně ovlivňuje mysl a budoucnost našich dětí. *In blog.aktualne.cz.* Retrieved from https://blog.aktualne.cz/blogy/martin-jan-stransky.php?itemid=46117

Stryker, S. 2008. *Transgender History*. New York, Seal Press, USA.

Thompson, L. and Schonthal, D. 2020. The Social Psychology of Design Thinking. *In California Management Review*, Vol. 62, No. 2, pp. 84 - 99.

von Flotow, L. 1997. *Translation and Gender: Translating in the Era of Feminism*. Ottawa, University of Ottawa Press, Canada.

Welnitzová, K. 2023. *Chybovosť strojového prekladu*. Praha, Verbum, Czech Republic.

What is Design Thinking (DT)? *In Interaction Design Foundation.* Retrieved from https://www.interaction-design.org/literature/topics/design-thinking

What is design thinking? 2023. *In McKinsey & Company.* Retrieved from https://www.mckinsey.com/featured-insights/mckinsey-explainers/what-is-design-thinking

Wilkinson, L. and Silliman, E. 2007. *Language and Literacy Learning in Schools*. New York, Guilford Press, USA.

Wrigley, C. and Straker, K. 2015. Design Thinking pedagogy: the Educational Design Ladder. *In Innovations in Education and Teaching International*, Vol. 54, No. 4, pp. 374-385.

Wrigley, C. et al. 2020. Implementing Design Thinking: Understanding Organizational Conditions. *In California Management Review*, Vol. 62, No. 2, pp. 125-143.

ASSESSING THE DYNAMICS OF MIDDLE SCHOOL STUDENTS' JUDGMENT OF LEARNING (JOL) IN MATHEMATICS: A STUDY IN KENYA

Nisumba Soodhani K[1], Antony Prakash[1], Daevesh Singh[1], Rumana Pathan[1], Amit Mishra[2], Swati Shelar[2], Anand Sharma[2] and Ramkumar Rajendran[1]
[1]Indian Institute of Technology Bombay, India
[2]Radics Education, India

ABSTRACT

Monitoring one's learning activities is integral to self-regulated learning (SRL) and contributes significantly to successful learning outcomes. Judgments of learning (JOL), a crucial component of SRL, involve metacognitive assessments where individuals gauge their ability to recall learned material on future tests. While prior research underscores the link between accurate JOL and enhanced performance, there is a paucity of literature that studies JOL in resource-constrained countries and its temporal nature. Our study touches upon this gap by investigating the relationship between JOL and mathematics task performance while also examining the evolution of JOL over time among middle school learners from Kenya. Leveraging data from 317 students, our findings reveal that a majority of learners exhibit mostly accurate JOL (64.87%), with notable proportions being overestimated (31.33%) and a few students underestimated (3.80%). Moreover, learners initially demonstrating accurate JOL (62.73%) predominantly transition to correct JOL (60.39%), with a significant subset overestimating (31.68%) and a small subset underestimating (2.87%) their performance. Our research sheds light on the JOL variations in a different demography and highlights the stability in the temporal nature of JOL thus enriching our understanding of metacognitive processes, and informing the development of targeted interventions to enhance learning outcomes worldwide.

KEYWORDS

Judgement of Learning, JOL, Kenya, Temporal Analysis, SRL

1. INTRODUCTION

Understanding students' abilities to accurately predict their academic performance is crucial for learning outcomes and instructional strategies. Particularly in mathematics, where problem-solving skills are highly valued, assessing students' judgment of learning (JOL) becomes crucial for identifying strengths, weaknesses, and effective learning strategies. This paper delves into the relationship between middle school students' JOL and their actual performance in mathematics, as well as the temporal changes in JOL over time. Judgment of learning (JOL) is a fundamental aspect of students' metacognitive abilities, enabling them to evaluate their learning outcomes and make informed decisions about their learning process. It involves assessing one's estimate and the likelihood of recalling information or performing well on assessments during a learning task (Metcalfe & Finn, 2008). Studies have highlighted the importance of JOL in predicting learners' actual performance and shaping their study behaviours, such as material selection and study duration.

While JOL plays a crucial role in academic success, research on JOL has demonstrated considerable variability in the accuracy of JOL among students. Ericsson and Heit found that both undergraduate and high-school students often exhibited significant overestimations in predicting their performance in problem-solving contexts (Erickson & Heit, 2015). However, Anstead observed undergraduate students to predict their performance accurately, particularly in less complex mathematical problems (Anstead, 2022). Complexity also influences judgment of learning (JOL), as Baars et al. noted learners' increased accuracy in retrospective judgments for simpler problems (Baars et al., 2017). In middle school students, Oudman, van de Pol & van Gog uncovered substantial differences in JOL accuracy between high and low-performing students, with the latter often overestimating their performance (Oudman, van de Pol & Gog, 2022). Despite the extensive research in middle and high-income countries, there remains a gap in understanding JOL among students in low-income countries. Moreover, the existing literature has not sufficiently explored the temporal nature of JOL and its potential fluctuations over time. This study addresses these gaps by examining JOL among middle school students in Kenya and investigating how it changes over time.

To achieve this objective, a longitudinal study design was employed, tracking students' JOL and performance in mathematics over five weeks. Statistical analysis, including chi-square tests, was conducted to explore the relationship between JOL and math task scores. In addition to it, temporal nature of JOL was analyzed. On further investigating the temporal nature of JOL, the distribution of accurate JOL predictors, over estimators and under estimators remained constant on average over the 9 instances.

In the next section, we briefly describe JOL and related work. Section 3 explains the research methodology, including the study design and motivation behind the research questions. The results are discussed in Section 4, followed by further discussion in Section 5. Finally, the article concludes in Section 6.

2. BACKGROUND

In this section, we briefly describe JOL from the literature review and its importance in learning. Later, we discuss the existing literature on JOL's impact on math learning.

2.1 Judgement of Learning

Consider a student preparing for a mathematical problem-solving exam. After solving a problem, the student carefully evaluates whether their answer is correct or incorrect based on their past experiences to gauge their expected level of success. Will this prediction turn out to be accurate? What factors contribute to this prediction? Furthermore, how does having a more accurate prediction of outcomes help students perform better on the exam? These questions have been explored for the past 50 years through inquiries into predictions of future memory performance, known as judgments of learning (Rhodes, 2016). While studied extensively, judgments of learning (JOL) have gained significance as a crucial aspect of metacognitive activities with the advancement of self-regulated learning (SRL) theories and frameworks (Pintrich, 2000) (Zimmerman & Schunk, 2011). There are various types of JOL activities, each manifested differently. For example, learners may recognize when they encounter material they do not understand or when they are progressing through material too quickly or slowly relative to their objectives (Pintrich, 2000) (Pathan, Murthy & Rajendran, 2021). Additionally, JOLs can occur when learners assess their readiness to take a test on recently studied material or evaluate their ability to recall lecture information for future assessments (Myers, Rhodes & Hausman, 2020).

2.2 Importance of JOL

Numerous studies highlight the significance of JOLs in the learning process. For instance, research has consistently shown that JOLs made after a delay are more predictive of learners' actual performance compared to those made immediately after studying the material (Dunlosky & Nelson, 1992) (Nelson & Dunlosky, 1991) (Senkova & Otani, 2021). Moreover, JOLs are linked to study behaviors that influence the selection of study material and the duration of study sessions (Metcalfe & Heit, 2015). Similarly, Van Gog and colleagues found that making prospective judgments of learning enhances learning outcomes, particularly when learners anticipate engaging in the learning activity (Van Gog, Hoogerheide & Van Harsel, 2020). Additionally, providing learners with a standard, such as the correct answer or solution procedure, improves the accuracy of their JOLs, thereby aiding in more precise self-assessment (Baars et al., 2017). This precision in JOL affects the selection of cognitive and metacognitive strategies and skills, which are crucial for the learning task and subsequently academic performance (Tamayo Alzate, Herrera Florez & Romero Villegas, 2023). Consequently, existing research suggests that JOLs are integral to self-regulated learning behaviors and play a crucial role in metacognitive monitoring (Nelson & Narens, 1994).

2.3 Literature Review on JOL in Math Domain

Mathematical problem-solving skills are increasingly valued by both employers and higher education institutions because they foster critical thinking, and logical reasoning, and enhance career opportunities (Moore, 2020). As mentioned earlier, evaluating one's mathematical skills is crucial for recognizing strengths and weaknesses, setting goals, and determining appropriate metacognitive strategies to achieve those goals, ultimately improving problem-solving performance. However, assessing mathematical problem-solving abilities is more challenging than assessing factual knowledge (Black et al., 2012). In a study by Ericsson and Heit, both undergraduate and highschool students demonstrated significant overestimate in predicting their performance in mathematical problem-solving contexts (Erickson & Heit, 2015). Conversely, Anstead found that undergraduate students were able to predict their performance quite accurately, neither over nor underestimating their abilities (Anstead, 2022). Additionally, Anstead observed that predictions were more accurate for less complex mathematical problems compared to more complex ones (e.g., equations with two terms versus four terms). Similarly, Baars and colleagues noted that the complexity of the problem influenced the judgment of learning (JOL), with learners making more accurate retrospective judgments on simpler problems compared to more complex ones (Baars, 2017). Furthermore, a study by Oudman, van de Pol & van Gog on middle school students revealed significant differences in the accuracy of JOL between high and low-performing students (Van Gog, Hoogerheide & Van Harsel, 2020). Particularly, high-performing students demonstrated greater accuracy in judgments both before and after self-assessment in a mathematical activity compared to low-performing students. Another study found that low-performing students tended to overestimate their performance in mathematical tasks, both before and after testing (Erickson & Heit, 2015). This suggests that students lacking proficiency in a subject may also lack awareness of the standards against which their performance should be evaluated, leading to an overestimate of their abilities (Erickson & Heit, 2015). Therefore, it is crucial to identify students with poor judgment of learning skills so that appropriate support and scaffolding can be provided.

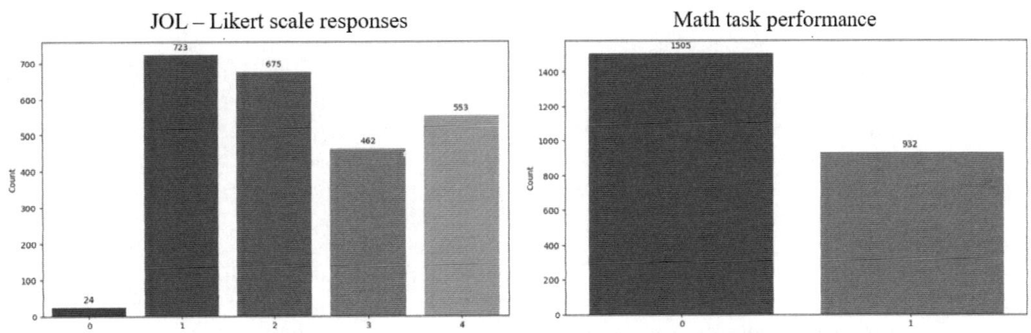

Figure 1. Frequency of JOL as per Likert scale responses and Math task performance

2.4 Research Gap

Despite the well-established recognition of learners' JOLs as often inaccurate, particularly among low-scoring learners, there is a gap in understanding its role in under-represented regions such as Kenya. Furthermore, while JOL research spans over 50 years (Rhodes, 2016), recently it has been increasingly recognized as a critical aspect of metacognition in SRL research, with a focus on its temporal nature (Sobocinski et al., 2024). However, limited research has explored how learners' JOLs change over time. Wang et al. conducted one such study using epistemic network analyses, revealing that learners who acted as cognitive knowledge builders exhibited higher accuracy in JOLs compared to those who were either cognitively loaded with the task or overloaded (Wang et al., 2023). Nevertheless, this research was conducted within the context of medical students interacting with an Intelligent Tutoring System. Notably, there is a dearth of studies investigating the temporal aspect of JOLs in mathematics education. Given these research gaps, we are motivated to explore the following research questions:

• RQ1: How does Judgments of Learning (JOL) relate to the math task performance of middle school learners?

• RQ2: How does Judgments of Learning (JOL) evolve during math tasks among middle school learners?

3. METHODOLOGY

To address the research questions, we designed and conducted a study. In this section, we describe the participants' details, the study design, the data collected, and the instrument used to collect. We chose the Metacognitive Performance Assessment (MPA) to formatively assess a student's metacognitive performance when engaged in a problem-solving task (Magno, 2009). MPA covers factors for both knowledge and regulation of cognition as shown in Table 1.

Table 1. Metacognitive performance assessment component description

Components	Sub-process	Description
Knowledge of cognition	Declarative knowledge	Knowledge about one's skills, intellectual resources and abilities as a learner
	Procedural knowledge	Knowledge about how to implement learning procedures (strategies)
	Conditional knowledge	Knowledge about when and why to use learning procedures
Regulation of cognition	Prediction	Assumed outcome of performance
	Planning	Planning goal setting and allocating resources before learning
	Monitoring	Assessing one's learning or strategy use
	Evaluation	Analysis of performance and strategy effectiveness after learning episodes

The final assessment device consisted of one math problem and eight metacognition measurement items, structured around student answers to the given math problem. The metacognition assessment items were a set of mixed items, including computational, short answer type, multiple choice, matching and a scale. In the component 'Regulation of Cognition' the sub-process 'Prediction' is Judgement of Learning (JOL). The study was conducted with 317 students from Kenya who took the adapted MPA assessment with an embedded math problem. Of these 317 students, 136 were females, and 181 were male. All students were aged between 9-16 years and were enrolled in Grades 4 to 8, from 8 low-fee private schools across Nairobi. We collected pre-survey datasets that included student demographics (name, age, gender) as well as their current math mastery level as per existing school academic records. Informed consent was obtained from the school leaders on behalf of students and teachers. No monetary compensation was given to the students. At the start of the study, a procedural protocol was implemented to facilitate the informed engagement of school leaders, students and teachers. In line with consent protocols of school authorities, the research aims were explained via in-person workshops to the school leaders. They were then given 10 days to either accept or reject the terms of participation mentioned in the consent form. For all participating schools, we received the consent forms signed by school leaders, thereby confirming the voluntary agreement of and on behalf of students and teachers from their respective schools to participate in this study.

After completing pre-study data collection, teachers administered the adapted MPA assessments to the students during school hours. All students took the assessments directly, with minimal support from teachers. The assessment schedule is outlined in Table 2, where I1 to I9 represent instances 1 to 9. Math problems of varying difficulty levels were chosen to mitigate response biases, resulting in 9 observations per student over five weeks. The responses to Math problems were scored '0' indicating Fail and '1' indicating Pass. For RQ1, we analyzed pre-test scores, JOL, and Math task. For RQ2, which examines the temporal nature of JOL, we focused on students who responded to all nine instances. Among them, 161 students responded to all nine instances, yielding 1449 unique responses.

Table 2. Instances of data collected

Week 1	Week 2	Week 3	Week 4	Week 5
I1, I2, I3	NA	I4, I5, I6	NA	I7, I8, I9

4. RESULTS

4.1 Judgement of Learning and Math Performance

To answer RQ1: How does Judgments of Learning (JOL) relate to the math task performance of middle school learners? We have used the JOL and math task scores over the nine instances, which accumulates to 2437 unique responses. Descriptive statics plots of JOL, math task performance and pre-test scores are given in figure 1. To check if there is a relationship between pre-test and cumulative math task scores, Pearson's correlation was performed. The correlation coefficient between the variables was $r = 0.24$, $p = 0.002$. Although this indicates a positive correlation, the relationship between the variables is weak (the closer the value is to zero, the weaker the relationship). The coefficient of determination (R^2) was 0.060, suggesting that approximately 6% of the variance in one variable is explained by the other variable.

Table 3. JOL and prediction categorization

JOL (Likert scale)	JOL (classification)	Math Task score	Prediction categorization
1	Low	0	Correct prediction
2		1	Underestimation
3	Medium	0	Overestimation
		1	Underestimation
4	High	0	Overestimation
5		1	Correct prediction

We performed a Chi-square test of independence to investigate the relationship between Judgement of Learning (JOL) scores and math task score. This analysis is detailed in Table 4. The results of the test revealed a statistically significant association between JOL and math task scores, with a Chi-square statistic χ^2 (4, N=2437) = 1505, of and a p-value of less than 0.001. This finding indicates a robust relationship between students' self-assessment of their learning and their actual performance on the math task.

The significance of this association suggests that students' JOL scores are meaningfully related to their performance in math, underscoring the potential role of JOL in predicting academic outcomes. Given these results, we next turn our attention to analysing the temporality of JOL. This further analysis aims to explore how the timing and progression of JOL assessments may impact or correlate with changes in math performance over time.

Table 4. Chi-square test: JOL and math performance

	Value	df	p - value
χ^2	1505	4	<0.001
N	2437		

4.2 Temporal Analysis of JOL

To answer RQ2: How do Judgments of Learning (JOL) evolve during math tasks among middle school learners? We categorized JOL Likert scale into Low, Mid, and High. Specifically, responses 1 and 2 fall into the Low category, response 3 into Mid, and responses 4 and 5 into the High. We considered nine instances of self-reporting, as mentioned in the study design. For this analysis, we identified the students who responded for all nine instances that is three instances per week. 161 students responded to all nine instances, leading to 1449 unique responses throughout the study. As shown in Table 5, on average 64.87% reported correct JOL, which means their judgement and their math score match. For example, students marking "High" in JOL and scoring "1" in math task and also students marking "Low" in JOL and scoring "0" in math task. 31.33% of students reported being overestimated, meaning students marked "High" or "Medium" in JOL and scored "0" in math task. 3.80% of students reported being underestimated, meaning they marked "Low" or "Medium" in

JOL and scored correctly in math task. Of 161 students 21 students reported correct JOL across all nine instances.

Table 5. Categories of JOL

Instances	Correct JOL	Over estimators	Under estimators
I1	62.73%	31.05%	6.21%
I2	63.35%	33.54%	3.10%
I3	59.62%	31.05%	9.31%
I4	78.26%	17.39%	4.35%
I5	71.43%	26.71%	1.86%
I6	62.73%	34.78%	2.48%
I7	72.67%	25.47%	1.86%
I8	56.52%	42.86%	0.62%
I9	56.52%	39.13%	4.35%
Average	64.87%	31.33%	3.80%

We then analysed the change in JOL based on the students' JOL reported on the first instance. The observations are:

- If the students reported correct JOL in the first instance (101) ie., Week1 Instance1, in the second instance
  - 60.39% of them continue to judge their learning correctly
  - 31.68% of report overestimate JOL
  - only 2.97% of them report underestimate JOL
- If 50 instances of overestimate were reported in the first instance, in the second instance
  - 62% of them reported correct JOL
  - 38% of continued reporting overestimate JOL
- Only 10 students reported an underestimate in the first instance. In the second instance
  - 50% of them gave a correct JOL
  - 30% of them report overestimate JOL
  - 20% of them continue to report underestimate JOL

However, as the weeks progressed, there was a positive shift in Judgment of Learning (JOL). In Week 1, Instance 3, the overestimated responses were reduced by six instances out of the initial 50. By Week 3, Instance 1, the overestimated responses further decreased to 1 out of the 50 instances. This trend indicates an improvement in JOL over the weeks, suggesting a learning curve and a growing alignment between self-assessment and actual performance. Regarding the underestimation of JOL by students, by the third instance, 2 out of the 10 instances changed to correct JOL, and the rest shifted to overestimate by Week 3. This indicates a dynamic shift in students' perceptions, with some initially underestimated students adapting to more accurate self-assessments or even transitioning to overestimating by the third week.

When analysing continuous reporting of Judgment of Learning (JOL) over two consecutive instances, it was observed that when students provided correct responses in the first two instances during the second week, subsequent data consisting of 462 unique responses demonstrated a noteworthy trend. Only 11 instances were reported as underestimated, whereas, 108 instances were reported as overestimated. This observation highlights a potential pattern of increased estimate among students who initially reported correct JOL in the early stages of assessment.

5. DISCUSSION

The assessment schedule (I1 to I9) spanned five weeks, featuring math problems of varying difficulty levels to ensure unbiased responses. Students' responses were scored '0' for Fail and '1' for Pass, resulting in 317 participants from Kenya. For RQ1, the analysis included pre-test scores, JOL, and math task scores. RQ2, focusing on the temporal nature of JOL, involved 161 students who responded to all nine instances, generating 1449 unique responses.

The study found a significant correlation between JOL predictions and math task scores, despite the lack of correlation between pre-test scores and math task scores. This finding supports existing literature, emphasizing the importance of JOL as a predictor of performance within low-income countries also. The findings from RQ2 reveal that in Kenya, learners' JOLs were predominantly accurate, with approximately 64.87% of JOLs being reported as such. Overestimators were observed in about 31.33% of cases, while underestimators were relatively low at 3.80%. Additionally, the analysis revealed a higher incidence of overestimated learners compared to underestimated ones, mirroring a common trend among middle school learners as per previous studies. Previous studies have highlighted a prevalence of overestimated JOLs among middle school students. One possible reason for this is that high-performing students, with their robust problem-solving skills and understanding of assessment criteria, can predict their performance accurately. On the other hand, low-performing students often overestimate their abilities due to overconfidence and a superficial grasp of the subject matter. This highlights the need for targeted strategies to address overconfidence and enhance JOL accuracy among students. Some common ways of addressing it are: providing regular feedback helps students calibrate their self-assessments; teaching metacognitive skills enhances their ability to evaluate their learning accurately; frequent formative assessments and encouraging self-reflection can further support this calibration; peer assessment and clear rubrics offer additional perspectives and standards, aiding in more precise JOLs.

In the initial instance, 101 reported instances by learners showed accurate JOL. Among these instances, the majority (66) maintained this accuracy in the subsequent instance, while 32 shifted towards overestimates. Conversely, only 3 showed a tendency towards underestimates. Among instances where learners initially overestimated their JOL (50), 31 adjusted towards accuracy in the subsequent instance, with 19 persisting in overestimates. Notably, none underestimated their JOL in the following instance. Regarding instances where learners initially underestimated their JOL (10), 5 transitioned to accuracy in the subsequent instance. Additionally, 3 became overestimated, and 2 remained underestimated.

These results indicate that the majority of learners maintained stable accuracy in their JOL, while some exhibited overestimates in the second instance, potentially influenced by successful recall from the initial assessment. Moreover, a significant number of learners who initially overestimated their abilities adjusted their judgments, indicating a degree of metacognitive awareness or improvement in calibration. Similarly, half of the learners who initially underestimated their abilities adjusted their judgments towards greater accuracy, suggesting an enhanced understanding of their learning process. The findings suggest implications for student support services and future research. Student support services can tailor interventions for learners exhibiting overestimates or underestimates, providing targeted support based on individual JOL patterns. Additionally, the study highlights the need for further research into the factors influencing JOL accuracy and the effectiveness of interventions designed to improve metacognitive skills, including the exploration of cultural differences and their impact on learning outcomes.

6. CONCLUSION

In this study, we explored how middle school students in Kenya assess their learning (JOL) about their performance in mathematics and how these assessments change over time. Analyzing data from 317 students, we found that most students (64.87%) accurately judged their learning, while 31.33% tended to overestimate and 2.87% tended to underestimate. Our statistical analysis revealed a significant connection between JOL and math task scores, but not between pre-test scores and math task scores. Additionally, we observed that students who initially had accurate JOL tended to maintain this accuracy over time, with few underestimating but a notable subset (31.68%) overestimating.

This research makes significant contributions by investigating JOL in the context of math performance among middle schoolers in under-resourced countries like Kenya, addressing a gap in the existing literature. Furthermore, our examination of the temporal aspect of JOL provides valuable insights into how metacognitive awareness evolves, influencing learning outcomes.

Despite these important findings, our study has limitations. Firstly, our focus on middle school students in Kenya limits the generalizability of our results to other contexts or student populations. Additionally, potential limitations related to the instruments used for data collection may have influenced the accuracy and depth of our findings.

Our future endeavour involves delving deeper into the underlying factors contributing to the Judgments of Learning (JOL) among Kenyan students and the stability observed in their JOL over time. One promising avenue for further exploration is the qualitative investigation of students' perceptions, beliefs, and learning experiences through interviews. Conducting such interviews can provide valuable insights into the cultural, educational, and contextual factors that influence students' metacognitive processes and JOL accuracy. Such research efforts would not only enrich our understanding of JOL in under-resourced contexts but also inform the development of targeted interventions to enhance metacognitive skills and improve learning outcomes among diverse student populations.

REFERENCES

Anstead, N. (2022). Judgments of Learning in the Context of Worked Mathematics Questions in College Students.

Baars, M., Van Gog, T., de Bruin, A. and Paas, F. (2017). Effects of problem solving after worked example study on secondary school children's monitoring accuracy. *Educational Psychology*, *37*(7), pp. 810-834.

Black, P., Burkhardt, H., Daro, P., Jones, I., Lappan, G., Pead, D. and Stephens, M. (2012). Educational Designer.

Dunlosky, J. and Nelson, T.O. (1992). Importance of the kind of cue for judgments of learning (JOL) and the delayed-JOL effect. *Memory & cognition*, *20*, pp. 374-380.

Erickson, S. and Heit, E. (2015). Metacognition and confidence: Comparing math to other academic subjects. *Frontiers in psychology*, *6*, p. 742.

Magno, C. (2009). Assessing grade school students metacognition in solving mathematical problem. *The Assessment Handbook*, pp. 1-22.

Metcalfe, J. and Finn, B. (2008). Evidence that judgments of learning are causally related to study choice. *Psychonomic Bulletin & Review*, *15*(1), pp. 174-179.

Moore, T. (2020). Mathematics: The Key to Empowering Tomorrow's Workforce. *Notices of the American Mathematical Society*, *67*(2).

Myers, S.J., Rhodes, M.G. and Hausman, H.E. (2020). Judgments of learning (JOLs) selectively improve memory depending on the type of test. *Memory & Cognition*, *48*, pp. 745-758.

Nelson, T.O. and Dunlosky, J. (1991). When people's judgments of learning (JOLs) are extremely accurate at predicting subsequent recall: The "delayed-JOL effect". *Psychological Science*, *2*(4), pp. 267-271.

Nelson, T.O. and Narens, L. (1994). Why investigate metacognition?

Oudman, S., van de Pol, J. and van Gog, T. (2022). Effects of self-scoring their math problem solutions on primary school students' monitoring and regulation. *Metacognition and Learning*, *17*(1), pp. 213-239.

Pathan, R., Murthy, S. and Rajendran, R. (2021). A coding mechanism for analysis of SRL processes in an open-ended learning environment. In *29th International Conference on Computers in Education Conference, ICCE*.

Pintrich, P.R. (2000). The role of goal orientation in self-regulated learning. In *Handbook of self-regulation* (pp. 451-502). Academic Press.

Rhodes, M.G. (2016). Judgments of learning: Methods, data, and theory. *The Oxford handbook of metamemory*, *1*, pp. 65-80.

Senkova, O. and Otani, H. (2021). Making judgments of learning enhances memory by inducing item-specific processing. *Memory & Cognition*, *49*, pp. 955-967.

Sobocinski, M., Dever, D., Wiedbusch, M., Mubarak, F., Azevedo, R. and Järvelä, S. (2024). Capturing self-regulated learning processes in virtual reality: Causal sequencing of multimodal data. *British Journal of Educational Technology*, *55*(4), pp. 1486-1506.

Tamayo Alzate, O.E., Herrera Flórez, P.A. and Romero Villegas, C. (2023). Metacognitive judgements in the learning of cellular theory in elementary school students. *Journal of Biological Education*, pp. 1-24.

Van Gog, T., Hoogerheide, V. and Van Harsel, M. (2020). The role of mental effort in fostering self-regulated learning with problem-solving tasks. *Educational Psychology Review*, *32*(4), pp. 1055-1072.

Wang, T., Li, S., Tan, C., Zhang, J. and Lajoie, S.P. (2023). Cognitive load patterns affect temporal dynamics of self-regulated learning behaviors, metacognitive judgments, and learning achievements. *Computers & Education*, *207*, p. 104924.

Zimmerman, B.J. and Schunk, D.H. (2011). Self-regulated learning and performance: An introduction and an overview. *Handbook of self-regulation of learning and performance*, pp. 15-26.

HOW TO TEACH PRIVACY: ASSESSMENT OF INNOVATIVE LEARNING APPROACHES FOR UNDERGRADUATE STUDENTS

Renata Mekovec and Marija Kuštelega
University of Zagreb Faculty of Organization and Informatics
Pavlinska 2, Varaždin, Croatia

ABSTRACT

The demand for privacy specialists is expected to increase, but there is a shortage of them to meet market demands. Certain ICT skills and competencies are required for professionals who develop, manage, and protect data that drive the digital world. The current study explores undergraduate students' attitude about different teaching strategies utilized in a newly developed course Privacy and personal data. A study using the revised Bloom's taxonomy and semantic differential measurement technique found that students were generally satisfied with course design and used teaching strategies. Students preferred the activity evaluation of cookie policies the most, thereby they grant the highest marks in five adjectives: useful, necessary, adequate, motivating, and facilitates the subject's learning outcomes. The most challenging activity for them was the creation of project tasks, while the most interesting was looking for examples of privacy breaches. Complex tasks were considered more challenging, but students showed slightly less motivation in solving them.

KEYWORDS

Privacy, Perception, Methods, Course, Students, Bloom's Taxonomy

1. INTRODUCTION

Demand for individuals with complex privacy expertise is likely to outstrip supply, creating a global need for advanced experts in an already limited pool (PwC, n.d.). The number of cybersecurity job openings worldwide has increased from 1 million in 2013 to 3.5 million by 2021 (Cybersecurity Ventures, 2021) but the gap between demand and supply is expected to persist until at least 2025 (Morgan, 2023).

Since the profession of teaching privacy is still largely undefined, it is useful to research what kind of expertise and skills employers are looking for. The European Cybersecurity Skills Framework (ECSF) defines 12 profiles to develop a common understanding of the roles, competencies, skills, and knowledge for individuals, companies, and training providers (ENISA, 2022). The NIST Privacy Framework (NIST, 2020) outlines privacy practices for organizations, consisting of three components: Core, Profiles, and Implementation Tiers, where each element strengthens privacy risk management by linking organizational roles, responsibilities, and privacy protection actions. Future privacy specialists should comprehend psychology, ethics, and technology-related legal skills in addition to STEM knowledge (PwC, n.d.). Therefore, it is important to mention the E-Competence Framework (HRN EN 16234-1:2019, 2019) which introduces transferable skills that can be applied to any ICT competency. In the age of IoT, AI, and Industry 4.0, transfer skills are required in all ICT-related operations. The fact that two of the seven stated transversal factors are security and privacy demonstrate the significance of this expertise. The Skills Framework for the Information Age (SFIA) provides a list of skills that are most relevant to a variety of professional disciplines, industry topics, and complementary frameworks through several views (SFIA Foundation, n.d.). Information and cyber security is one point of view, which includes skills such as information security, enterprise and business architecture, governance, risk management, audit, information assurance, continuity management, vulnerability assessment, digital forensics, penetration testing, research, and personal data protection.

Given the growing demand for privacy professionals and the sophistication of modern cyber threats, it's imperative to establish robust educational programs that equip future experts with the skills and knowledge needed to combat these challenges. To guarantee that privacy professionals have the essential knowledge and abilities, educational programs must be carefully designed. Student motivation should be a central focus in the learning process to encourage active engagement. Effective educational program design requires careful consideration of teaching strategies and task complexity to foster active learning participation. The purpose of this research is to investigate how students view the learning approaches taken to teach privacy-related subjects. To address this issue, the study research questions were placed:

- Q1: What are students' perceptions of the methods used to teach privacy related topics?
- Q2: Is there a difference in the perception of methods depending on the complexity of the tasks?

2. LEARNING PROCESS

Bloom et al. (1956) proposed a taxonomy of learning objectives which should provide a classification of the goals of education systems. Learning encompasses the cognitive, affective, and psychomotor domains. The cognitive domain comprises learning objectives, which are concerned with the recall or recognition of knowledge, as well as the development of intellectual abilities and skills. The affective domain includes learning objectives that explain changes in interest, attitudes, and values. The third domain focuses on manipulative or motor skills. The original Taxonomy provided definitions for each of the six major categories in the cognitive domain. The categories were Knowledge, Comprehension, Application, Analysis, Synthesis, and Evaluation. The categories were ordered from simple to complex and from concrete to abstract. Cognitive domain includes activities like remembering and recalling knowledge, thinking, problem solving and creating.

Anderson and Krathwohl (2001) proposed revision of Bloom's cognitive domain (they proposed Bloom's Revised Taxonomy). Six categories were kept, although with some significant modifications. In order to better align with their usage in the objectives, three categories underwent renaming, two were rearranged in terms of order, and the titles of the remaining categories were converted to verbs. The original Knowledge category's verb aspect was retained, but it was renamed Remember. The second of the original categories, comprehending, was renamed Understanding. The terms Application, Analysis, and Evaluation were kept, but they were expressed as Apply, Analyze, and Evaluate in their verb forms. Synthesis was renamed Create and swapped positions with Evaluation.

In addition to adding action words to increase usability, Bloom's Revised Taxonomy also included a cognitive and knowledge matrix that listed four levels of knowledge or products that could be processed (Krathwohl, 2002):

- Factual: the basic concepts that students need to understand in order to solve problems or get familiar with a subject.
- Conceptual: The connections between the fundamental components of a bigger structure that allow them to work as a unit.
- Procedures: How to accomplish purposes, how to undertake research, and rules for applying skills, algorithms, techniques, and methods.
- Metacognitive: Awareness and understanding of one's own cognition in addition to generic cognition information.

Cognitive complexity provides a significant viewpoint on task complexity (Urgo et al., 2019). The cognitive complexity of a task is determined by the type (and diversity) of mental activity necessary to perform it.

Learning is a comprehensive model that defines the learning process thru five aspects/dimensions (Marzano and Pickering, 2011): (1) attitudes and perception, (2) acquire and integrate knowledge, (3) extend and refine knowledge, (4) use knowledge meaningfully, and (5) habits and mind. All learning occurs in the context of learners' attitudes and perceptions (Dimension 1), as well as the application (or lack thereof) of positive habits (Dimension 5). Students with unfavorable attitudes towards learning are less likely to learn well. Positive attitudes and beliefs lead to easier and more effective learning. Positive attitudes and habits of mind lead to more effective thinking in Dimensions 2 and 3, which include acquiring and integrating knowledge, extending and refining knowledge, and using knowledge meaningfully (Dimension 4).

2.1 Teaching Strategies

Teaching and learning have evolved over time as a consequence of the emergence of new forms of delivery, such as blended and hybrid learning, as well as innovative pedagogical approaches such as project-based learning (Guo et al., 2020), problem-based learning (Savery, 2006), work-based learning (Rienties et al. 2023), inquiry-based learning and utilizing artificial intelligence in education (Feng and Law, 2021). Since the student is the main focus of curriculum development and teaching in a modern learning approach, educators have a major responsibility to include appropriate teaching and learning strategies and meaningfully use technology to help students achieve learning outcomes. With the widespread use of computers and digital technologies, online information seeking is becoming more incorporated into students' learning experiences (Mao et al. 2022). Table 1 introduces teaching strategies according to Bloom's revised taxonomy (Anderson and Krathwohl, 2001).

Table 1. Teaching strategies according to Bloom's revised taxonomy (Anderson and Krathwohl, 2001)

	LOWER ORDER THINKING			HIGHER ORDER THINKING		
Bloom's taxonomy	Knowing or remembering	Comprehending or understanding	Applying	Analyzing	Synthesizing or evaluating	Creating
Teaching strategies	Examples, illustrations, visuals, lecture, video	Discussion, questions, review, test, reports, exercises	Demonstration, practice, presentations, projects, role play, micro-teach	Problem solving, case studies, critical incidents, discussion, questioning, test	Projects, problem solving, case studies, plan development, constructing, simulations	Simulations, critiques, complex case study, design or development, product generation, producing

Online information searching provides diverse knowledge, but it also increases cognitive strain due to the enormous amount of information available online. People search for information to help their learning and to suit their information demands, either by adding new knowledge or restructuring current knowledge (Wu et al., 2018). Consequently, these searches help them produce better learning outcomes, such as assignments, presentations, and discussions (Chen et al., 2022), however, it must be noted that learning is a crucial result of search (Urgo and Arguello, 2022). The phrase "search as learning" (SAL) emphasizes the learning part of exploratory search with the purpose of understanding, which may lead to knowledge growth (von Hoyer et al., 2022). With SAL activities, learners spend time in an open, constantly evolving digital information environment through which they must effectively navigate in order to learn without or with minimal instruction. Unlike some other kinds of searches (Roy et al., 2020), those searches are usually iterative and necessitate the user to scan, read, and process a big number of documents. However, prior study (Froyd and Simpson, 2018; Kyndt et al., 2011) on the student-centered learning strategy was not always positive, emphasizing that such learning is only effective if it is properly approached. To be effective Smith et al. (2022) argue that a search-centric learning system must model four key components: individual students (searcher factors), the educational domain (topic factors), academic assignments (task factors), and progress toward learning goals (the end-to-end system's objective function).

3. METHODOLOGY

The current study explores undergraduate students' perception about privacy teaching strategies utilized in a newly developed course. To find out how students taking the course Privacy and Personal Data felt about teaching strategies, a survey was given to them. Table 2 shows a description of the tasks completed during the laboratory exercises. Teaching strategies are assigned to each activity according to Bloom's revised taxonomy (Anderson and Krathwohl, 2001).

Table 2. Description of laboratory exercise activities and teaching strategies

Activity	Task description	Teaching strategies
Job description of a privacy expert	List the job titles, education, required skills and knowledge, demand and average salary for privacy experts.	**Search for examples**
Examples of privacy breach	Examine 5 examples of privacy breach at a specific company, focusing on the type of data taken, the amount stolen, and the damage done.	**Review examples**
Identification and categorization of personal data	Choose three services used through websites, mobile apps/platforms, and direct contact, and define the types of personal data processed and the category (ordinary or special) they belong.	**Problem solving**
Analysis of privacy policies	Analyze three privacy policies and assess whether or not are they well-made, according to the „Guide - How to create a privacy policy".	**Problem solving, review**
Privacy certification programs	Describe information about privacy certification programs for individuals, organizations and process.	**Review**
Thinking about punishments	Choose three laws of the Republic of Croatia that deal with any domain (health, education, etc.) and extract from each law the provisions related to the protection of personal data.	**Problem solving, review**
Request for exercising the rights	Assess the rationale behind the application of the two given requests for data access and right exercise (laws used), and give your opinion.	**Problem solving, critiques**
Organizational/technical protection measures	Recommendation of appropriate protection measure.	**Problem solving**
Correct/incorrect cookie policy examples	Evaluation of cookie policy.	**Problem solving**
Consent or approval	Comparation of various types of consent.	**Problem solving, critiques**
Project task	Design the campaign for raising privacy awareness.	**Design/development**

3.1 Data Collection and Data Analysis

A survey was conducted among 45 out of 50 students enrolled in the course Privacy and personal data during their third year of undergraduate studies. The survey included 20 questions grouped into four sections: (1) lecture organization, (2) laboratory exercise structure, (3) project assignment, and (4) student recommendations for improvement. The survey was available in Croatian and took approximately 10 minutes to complete. The research aimed to gather feedback on teaching strategies, the effectiveness of student knowledge assessment methods, and potential improvements in course content and teaching methods.

In order to determine respondents' attitudes regarding used teaching strategies, the semantic differential measurement technique was employed. The semantic differential scale is a rating scale that measures people's reactions towards a specific concept using contrasting adjectives at each end. It measures the perceived gap between opposite concepts to provide better insight into the attitudes of the respondents about the certain topic (Heise, 1970).

Students were asked to use a five-point scale to rate each activity used as a knowledge assessment method with respect to the following seven categories with contrasting adjectives:

- Useless | Useful,
- Unnecessary | Necessary,
- Inappropriate | Appropriate,
- Unchallenging | Challenging,
- Demotivating | Motivating,
- Boring | Interesting,
- Not Facilitating the subject's learning outcomes | Facilitates the subject's learning outcomes.

For example, on a created semantic differential scale, a student scoring one on a five-point scale for the category „Useless | Useful“ indicates that he finds these activities strongly useless, whereas a rating of five indicates that he/she finds them strongly useful, and so on. Based on the survey data, a semantic differential analysis was made for the laboratory exercises' activities. The aim was to see if there is a significant difference between the activities performed in the exercises.

4. RESULTS

Figure 1 displays the results of the semantic differential measurement technique based on averaged evaluation score of contrasting adjectives for teaching strategies applied in laboratory exercises.

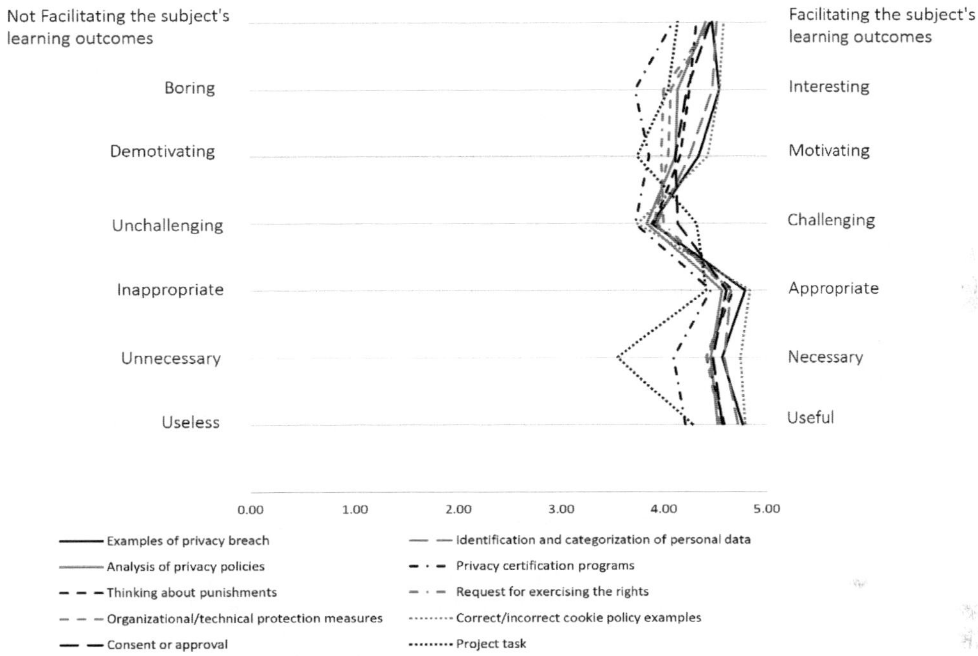

Figure 1. Results of semantic differential measurement technique for laboratory exercise activities

It can be seen that the curves are shifted to the right, with average grades ranging between 3.5 and 4.8 for observed attributes. This indicates very high ratings for the laboratory exercise activities that were carried out, showing that students were generally satisfied with the structure of laboratory exercises. The point that pops up is related to the “Project task” activity which the students thought was somewhat less necessary and useful for the successful acquisition of knowledge and skills in the subject, but on the other hand student marked this strategy as the most challenging.

Mostly all the activities were rated with very high grades, only a slight shift towards a lower rating can be seen in the aspect of challengingness of the tasks. It is interesting to notice that the students preferred the activity „Correct/incorrect cookie policy examples“ the most, thereby achieving the highest marks in five adjectives: useful (M=4.80), necessary (M=4.75), adequate (M=4.84), motivating (M=4.43), and facilitates the subject's learning outcomes (M=4.59). The most challenging activity for them was the creation of project tasks (M=4.32), while the most interesting (M=4.55) was looking for examples of privacy breaches.

The activity that received the lowest marks according to the criteria of useful (M=4.20), interesting (M=3.73) and facilitating the learning outcomes of the subject (M=4.09) is related to the task of searching information about privacy certification programs. The students rated the creation of the project assignment as less necessary (M=3.55) and adequate (M=4.41) for achieving the learning goals, and as it was an activity at the end of the semester, it was rated somewhat less motivating (M=3.75). The least challenging (M=3.66) activity for them was searching for a job description of a privacy expert.

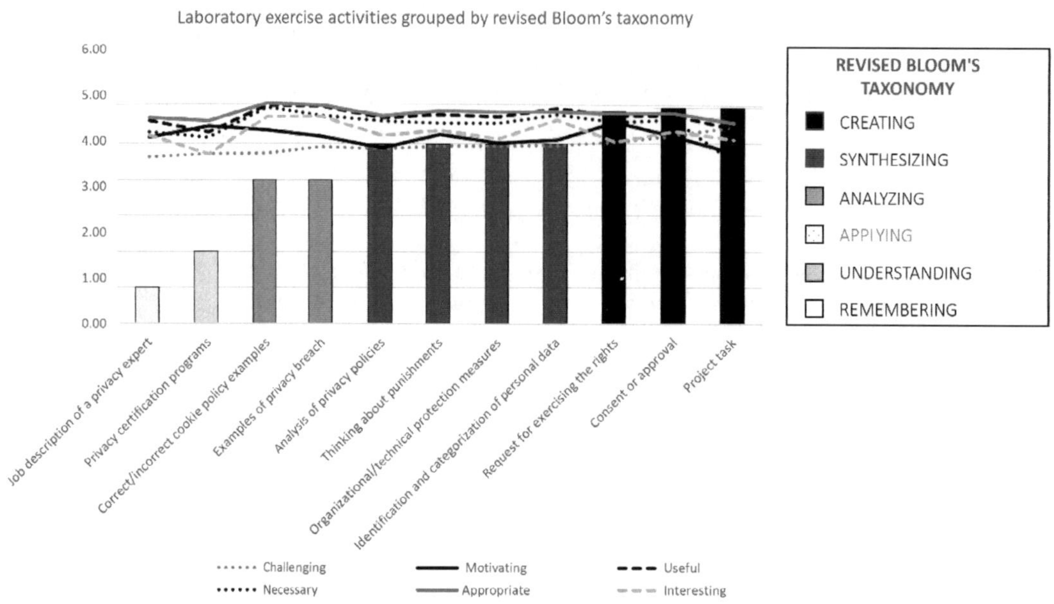

Figure 2. Results of semantic differential measurement technique with activities grouped by revised Bloom's taxonomy

Result presented in Figure 2 demonstrate that there was no difference of perception of activities regarding to complexity of utilized teaching strategy (by revised Bloom's taxonomy), although the perception of activity challenge is slightly raising with complicity of teaching strategy (project task is the most challenging). Also, it can be concluded that student's motivation is constantly high regardless of teaching strategy complexity.

5. DISCUSSION AND CONCLUSION

In today's digital world, where personal data has become a valuable asset, the problem of privacy is becoming increasingly important. Privacy has an unbreakable connection with our safety and well-being. By protecting our privacy, we can create a more secure and fair society. Protecting personal data safeguards us against identity theft, fraud, and other cybercrimes that can have fatal consequences. To properly address these difficulties, it is critical to understand how privacy is learned and efficiently promoted among individuals.

Teaching privacy is crucial in today's technology-driven world for protecting students' personal information, promoting safe online behavior, preparing them for the workplace, encouraging critical thinking, and empowering them (Sharma, 2022). Course design should focus on teaching strategies that foster students' critical reflection on the covered topics, keeping in mind that the quality of student learning is influenced by a complex interplay of factors, including student and teacher attributes, the educational setting, and educational regulations (Sánchez-Cabrero et al., 2021).

The degree to which a student perceives a task to be difficult influences how they will approach it. In terms of self-regulated learning, students' perceptions of task complexity can either motivate them to use existing knowledge to solve the problem or discourage them from trying (Winne, 2018; Mangos and Steele-Johnson, 2001). Our research shows that there was no variation in perception of activities based on the complexity of the used teaching strategy, although the impression of activity challenge increased slightly with teaching strategy complicity. The mentioned conclusions can be related to earlier studies which implicate that task difficulty increases when a student perceives the task as unfamiliar (Garcia-Ponce et al., 2022) or too complex to solve (Nawaz et al., 2020). Another crucial component is students' prior knowledge, as students with stronger self-regulated learning skills are better at recognizing and solving complicated problems (Koivuniemi et al., 2017). Awwad (2019) demonstrated that students are capable of categorizing more challenging tasks as more difficult.

In terms of future privacy education, privacy challenges brought by rapidly evolving technologies cannot be addressed by traditional methods alone; novel approaches must be used (Anastopoulo and Gressette, 2010). Our research can be related with Sharma (2022) proposition that most effective ways to teach students digital privacy are: (1) interactive workshops, (2) online resources that can be accessed any time, (3) role-playing exercises to practice privacy techniques, (4) guest speakers to share real-world knowledge, and (5) collaborative learning to develop recommendations for privacy protection. Indeed, our study demonstrated that promoting student discussion and employing engaging resources and content had a major impact on students' willingness to learn. Our course design which includes teaching strategies like search for examples, review examples, critiques, problem solving and design/development is perceived by students as good model to learn privacy.

We have a lack of people capable of creating organizational methods to secure users' privacy and collected information where most personnel in charge lack the requisite expertise. The practical implications of our study suggest that effective teaching approaches can be achieved by creating engaging and interesting tasks while balancing different complexity levels. Teaching and learning are dynamic processes that require ongoing adaptation to new possibilities and difficulties therefore our study can present model that can be used in teaching complex domain like privacy which must include also other domains like technology, legal rules, and safeguarding specific user rights. Our research can significantly contribute to the improvement of higher education in this field. The results can be used to adapt curricula, develop new teaching materials and methods, and better understand the learning process. To effectively promote privacy education, it is essential to consider the social, cultural, and technological contexts in which young people learn. Future research should focus on developing effective teaching strategies and assessing the long-term impact of privacy education programs.

This study is limited by the relatively small sample size and its homogeneity (students from one faculty). While the results showed interesting trends, caution should be exercised when generalizing the findings to a larger population. Future research should include a larger and more representative sample to confirm the results of this study, also it would be interesting to compare the results of the perception of students from different faculties.

REFERENCES

Anderson, L. W., & Krathwohl, D. R. (2001). *A taxonomy for learning, teaching, and assessing: A revision of Bloom's taxonomy of educational objectives: complete edition*. Addison Wesley Longman, Inc..

Anastopoulo, C., & Gressette Jr, T. P. (2010). Teaching Privacy in the Age of Octomom: Enhancing Case/Socratic Method with Structured Class Discussion. *Valparaiso University Law Review, 44*(2), 391-422.

Awwad, A. (2019). L2 learners' and professionals' perceptions of cognitive task complexity: Towards developing an index of task difficulty. In *Journal of Asia TEFL*, 16(2), 468.

Bloom, B. S. et al. (1956). *Taxonomy of Educational Objectives: The Classification of Educational Goals*. New York: Longman

Chen, Y. et al. (2022). The Effects of Topic Familiarity on College Students' Learning Search Process. In *Aslib Journal of Information Management* 74(6): 1151–73.

Cybersecurity Ventures (2021). *Cybersecurity Jobs Report: 3.5 Million Openings Through 2025*. Retrieved June 4, 2024, from: https://www.einpresswire.com/article/556075599/cybersecurity-jobs-report-3-5-million-openings-through-2025

ENISA (2022). European Cybersecurity Skills Framework Draft v0.5 Work In Progress APRIL 2022.

Feng, S., & Law, N. (2021). Mapping artificial intelligence in education research: A network-based keyword analysis. In *International Journal of Artificial Intelligence in Education*, 31(2), 277-303.

Froyd, J. and Simpson, N. (2008). Student-centered learning addressing faculty questions about student centered learning. In *Course, curriculum, labor, and improvement conference*, Vol. 30, No. 11, pp. 1-11.

Garcia-Ponce, E. E. et al. (2022). Role of EFL learners' perceptions of task difficulty in complexity, accuracy and fluency: An exploratory case study. In *Porta Linguarum: revista internacional de didáctica de las lenguas extranjeras*, (37), 123-142.

Guo, P. et al. (2020). A review of project-based learning in higher education: Student outcomes and measures. In *International journal of educational research*, 102, 101586.

Heise, D. R. (1970). The semantic differential and attitude research. In *Attitude measurement*, 4, pp. 235-253

HRN EN 16234-1:2019 (2019). E-Competence Framework (e-CF) - A Common European Framework for ICT Professionals in All Sectors - Part 1: Framework.

Koivuniemi, M. et al. (2017). Higher education students' learning challenges and regulatory skills in different learning situations/Desafíos de aprendizaje y habilidades de regulación en distintas situaciones de aprendizaje en estudiantes de educación superior. In *Infancia y Aprendizaje*, 40(1), 19–55. https://doi.org/10.1080/02103702.2016.1272874.

Krathwohl, D. R. (2002). *A Revision of Bloom's Taxonomy: An Overview. Theory Into Practice*, 41(4), 212–218. https://doi.org/10.1207/s15430421tip4104_2

Kyndt, E. et al. (2011). The perception of workload and task complexity and its influence on students' approaches to learning: A study in higher education. In *European journal of psychology of education*, 26, 393-415.

Mangos, P. M. and Steele-Johnson, D. (2001). The role of subjective task complexity in goal orientation, self-efficacy, and performance relations. In *Human performance*, 14(2), 169-185. https://doi.org/10.1207/S15327043HUP1402_03

Mao, S. et al. (2022). Students' online information searching strategies and their creative question generation: The moderating effect of their need for cognitive closure. In *Frontiers in Psychology*, 13, 877061.

Marzano, R. J., and Pickering, D. J. (2011). *Dimensions of Learning: Teacher's Manual*. ASCD.

Morgan, S. (2023). *Cybersecurity Jobs Report: 3.5 Million Unfilled Positions In 2025*. Retrieved April 4, 2024, from: https://cybersecurityventures.com/jobs/

Nawaz, S. et al. (2020). Analysis of task difficulty sequences in a simulation-based POE environment. In *Artificial Intelligence in Education: 21st International Conference, AIED 2020, Ifrane, Morocco, July 6–10, 2020, Proceedings, Part I 21*, pp. 423-436.

NIST (2020). NIST PRIVACY FRAMEWORK: A TOOL FOR IMPROVING PRIVACY THROUGH ENTERPRISE RISK MANAGEMENT, VERSION 1.0. https://doi.org/10.6028/NIST.CSWP.01162020 (June 1, 2022).

PwC (n.d.). *Privacy megatrend: Privacy engineering talent shortage*. Retrieved April 4, 2024, from: https://www.pwc.com/us/en/services/consulting/cybersecurity-risk-regulatory/library/seven-privacy-megatrends/privacy-engineering-talent-shortage.html

Rienties, B. et al. (2023). Online work-based learning: A systematic literature review. In *International review of education*, 69(4), 551-570.

Roy, N. et al (2020). Exploring Users' Learning Gains within Search Sessions. *Proceedings of the 2020 Conference on Human Information Interaction and Retrieval,* pp. 432–36.

Sánchez-Cabrero, R. et al. (2021). Models on teaching effectiveness in current scientific literature. In *Education Sciences*, 11(8), 409.

Savery, J. R. (2006). Overview of Problem-based Learning: Definitions and Distinctions. In *Interdisciplinary Journal of Problem-Based Learning*, 1(1), 9-20. https://doi.org/10.7771/1541-5015.1002

SFIA Foundation (n.d). *SFIA view - Information and cyber security*. Retrieved September 2, 2024, from: https://sfia-online.org/en/tools-and-resources/sfia-views/sfia-view-information-cyber-security

Sharma, A. (2022). Teaching Digital Privacy: Navigating the Intersection of Technology, Education, and Privacy. *International Journal of humanities,Law and Social Sciences 9 (*2), 154-162

Smith, C. et al (2022). Learner, Assignment, and Domain: Contextualizing Search for Comprehension. *Proceedings of the 2022 Conference on Human Information Interaction and Retrieval*, pp. 191–201.

Urgo, K. and Arguello, J. (2022). Learning Assessments in Search-as-Learning: A Survey of Prior Work and Opportunities for Future Research. In *Information Processing and Management* 59(2), 102821.

Urgo, K. et al (2019). Anderson and krathwohl's two-dimensional taxonomy applied to task creation and learning assessment. In *Proceedings of the 2019 ACM SIGIR International Conference on Theory of Information Retrieval*, pp. 117–124.

von Hoyer, J. et al. (2022). The Search as Learning Spaceship: Toward a Comprehensive Model of Psychological and Technological Facets of Search as Learning. In *Frontiers in Psychology* 13: 827748.

Winne, P. H. (2018). *Cognition and metacognition within self-regulated learning*. In Handbook of self-regulation of learning and performance (2nd ed., pp. 36–48). Routledge/Taylor & Francis Group. https://doi.org/10.4324/9781315697048-3.

Wu, D. et al. (2018). Collaborative Information Searching as Learning in Academic Group Work. In *Aslib Journal of Information Management* 70(1): 2–27.

SOCIALLY SHARED METACOGNITIVE REGULATION IN FACE-TO-FACE COLLABORATIVE PROBLEM-SOLVING: CYCLICAL PHASES, FOCI AND FUNCTIONS

Vishwas Badhe, Ramkumar Rajendran and Jyoti Shaha
Centre for Educational Technology
IIT Bombay, India

ABSTRACT

Collaborative problem-solving (CPS) is a vital 21st-century skill. Ill-structured problems demand effective shared regulation from teams to enhance CPS success. While socially shared metacognitive regulation (SSMR) is crucial in CPS, a deeper understanding of its nature is needed. This study investigates the detailed operationalization of SSMR in four teams (N=16), categorized as more successful outcome teams (MSOT) and less successful outcome teams (LSOT). The research spanned over 12 weeks, focusing on ill-structured tasks in a project-based Human-Computer Interaction course. We analyzed 35 hours of video data, capturing teams' verbalized interactions to identify SSMR episodes and coded them for cyclical phases, foci, and functions. Preliminary findings revealed differences between MSOT and LSOT in the number of SSMR episodes, cyclical phases, foci, and functions. Findings shows that achieving better outcomes in CPS requires combining both a cyclical phase in SSMR and a fundamental focus, along with appropriate strategy adaptations, to address internal task challenges effectively. A nuanced analysis of one comparison case (Team 1 vs. Team 4) highlighted the complementary nature of SSMR's function, focus, and cyclical phases and suggested its collective use. Further, a qualitative analysis provides more details about the cyclical phases, foci, and function of SSMR, enhancing the understanding of its nature in MSOT and LSOT. This study contributes to the contextual understanding of SSMR in CPS and underscores its importance for successful collaborative problem-solving.

KEYWORDS

Socially Shared Metacognitive Regulation (SSMR), Collaborative Problem-Solving (CPS), Project-Based Learning, Ill-Structured Problem-Solving, Cyclical phases of SSMR, Foci of SSMR, Function of SSMR

1. INTRODUCTION

A Collaborative problem solving (CPS) in the CSCL environment provides an opportunity to team members to apply their acquired skills and knowledge for a shared task at hand. As different learners are coming from diverse socio-cultural backgrounds, they bring diverse goals, approaches, attitudes, and experiences which become an important and dynamic element during CPS. While problem-solving in a collaborative environment looks attractive for facilitating collective knowledge construction, it's not easy to execute (Lobczowski et al., 2021). Handling the dynamic nature of the team and simultaneously achieving progress in a given problem/task needs many socially shared regulation strategies amongst the collaborating members (Järvelä et al., 2018). In collaborative problem-solving (CPS), team members regulate their cognition, metacognition, motivation, emotion, and behavior through shared metacognitive monitoring (Järvelä et al., 2013). However, cognitive and metacognitive issues may arise due to differences in task and content understanding or different interpretations of the task by team members (Sobocinski, Malmberg, Järvelä, 2022). Hence in CPS shared metacognition plays a vital role in collaboration by making members aware of challenges through shared monitoring processes and highlighting the need for regulation. Learners use different shared cognitive and metacognitive regulation strategies while working on a shared task and those strategies are related to monitoring, controlling, planning, or reflecting (Lobczowski et al., 2021).

Socially shared metacognitive regulation (SSMR) in particular, refers to regulation activities in which different students are simultaneously engaged when monitoring and controlling the group's cognition (Iiskala et al., 2015). SSMR is a crucial phenomenon in CPS as it ensures the appropriate direction of the groups' cognitive activity using constant monitoring and controlling of the cognitive process. This can refer to activities such as identifying task requirements and expectations (e.g. what has to be done); planning (e.g. time allocation); keeping track of the process and mindfully changing it if needed; monitoring comprehension (e.g. questioning the direction of the cognitive process) or evaluating the quality of the task outcome (Iiskala et al., 2015; Kerrigan et al., 2021). However, the shared regulation is not linear; it involves cyclical phases, making it important to show the detailed nature of the shared regulation (Järvelä, Järvenoja, Malmberg, 2019). This study has captured the cyclical phases and other characteristics of SSMR like foci (focus) and function.

Though there are comprehensive reviews of different forms of regulation (Järvelä et al., 2013) still the SSMR in collaborative processes is described in the general and empirical studies showing that micro-level unfolding of shared metacognitive processes is required (Iiskala et al., 2015). To gain a deeper understanding of the teams' SSMR, this study investigates the occurrences of cyclical phases, focus, and function of SSMR. In CPS, focus refers to the aspects that teams concentrate on during their tasks, which can be fundamental (essential aspects related to the task's goal), organizational (planning and managing task execution pragmatically), or surface (non-essential aspects) (Grau and Whitebread, 2012). The function of socially shared metacognition is to build a shared understanding of the problem by confirming agreed-upon ideas or activating processes to achieve consensus, and to control processes by inhibiting incorrect concepts and redirecting attention appropriately (Iiskala et al., 2011). However, detailed research on operationalizing metacognition in collaborative problem-solving remains limited. The evidence of the SSMR is scarce, and more knowledge is needed to understand what socially shared metacognition is, why it is important for CPS, and how it is operationalized (Vauras et al., 2021).

To investigate the characteristics of SSMR, the research question under investigation is: What are the differences between less and more successful outcome teams in cyclical phases, foci, and function of SSMR during CPS?

2. METHOD

To investigate the SSMR of teams, we chose an authentic semester-long course in Human-Computer Interaction for educational technology (HCI for ET). The course used a project-based learning pedagogy, which involved four milestones (see table 1) and many CPS tasks. Hence the study was conducted over 12 weeks in a graduate-level, face-to-face HCI for ET course in a collaborative classroom setting during Fall 2022. A total of twenty learners consisting of five Ph.D., two Master's learners, and thirteen bachelor's level students (Mean (age) =23.4 years, SD=4.09; 65% Male, 35% Female) participated in this study. None of the participants knew each other before the course and were divided into four teams consisting of 4 members each; each team consisted of Master's, Ph.D., and Bachelor's level learners. The course followed a project-based learning approach in which the following ill-structured problem (design challenge) was given to all the teams - "Design an intervention that supports special needs education (formal/informal) for speech and hearing impaired (DHH: Deaf or Hard of Hearing) students". All teams worked towards designing a solution for the given open-ended problem statement throughout the semester.

After basic orientation, the instructor announced the ill-structured design challenge in class. The semester-long course was divided into four major milestones (See table 3) leading to the final solution. Each task spanned approximately 3 weeks with predefined deliverables contributing to the final solution. For each week, learners were having two 1.5-hour-long in-class sessions. Each team was given the opportunity to collaborate and work on ill-structured problems for a total 8.5 hours in 7 weeks. Each session consisted of the following - (a) half an hour of instruction covering required concepts, tasks, deliverables, and resolving doubts, and (b) one hour for teamwork at the team's dedicated collaborative space (round table). During teamwork, learners discussed the design challenge and task strategies face-to-face and simultaneously documented their progress using the ConceptboardTM platform - a collaborative whiteboard enabling distributed teams to work together - and shared Google Document which contained their design journal. The instructor and TAs visited the teams at their tables whenever needed during teamwork. The course readings corresponding to each week and task were shared with the learners a week prior to the instruction. Learners were briefed about the tasks, associated activities, and deliverables each week as per the weekly course plan.

At the start and end of each milestone, team members were asked to do collective planning and evaluation. This facilitated metacognitive regulation opportunities for the teams while working collaboratively in each milestone. At the end of each milestone, teams were asked to present their team progress to the entire class. They were instructed to log their progress in shared group journals asynchronously (reflecting groups' status and individual contribution).

Table 1. Set of milestones and subtasks given for teams in project-based learning HCI course

Milestone	Task Name
1	Understanding problem & user needs using concept mapping, literature review Data gathering using interviews (on-field task) Problem definition using a fishbone diagram Analysis of user needs using empathy maps and user persona
2	Ideation for the design solution Study of existing systems Finalizing one idea using a decision matrix
3	Developing low-fidelity prototype Mapping prototype with the problem statement and theories Checking adherence to learned design principles with prototype
4	Evaluation of prototype with testing matrix and heuristics Refinement of prototype based on evaluation

2.1 Data Collection

The data was collected for the four teams and prior consent was taken. The verbal interaction of collaborating team members was video recorded, and the milestone-wise deliverable (performance) was evaluated using the rubric. Learners also worked synchronously and asynchronously outside regular class times, but that part was not recorded. ConceptboardTM board activity screenshots and shared group journals for teams were also collected. However, the solution they have developed, their write ups in group journals, written responses in planning, and evaluation should have been factored in the data analysis.

2.2 Data Analysis

We evaluated the team performance associated with each task using a rubric. All teams were first evaluated task-wise, then the total score was calculated by summing up the task-wise scores. The tasks were grouped logically into different milestones. While doing the task-wise evaluations using a rubric, we have also considered the team's ConceptboardTM screenshots and their shared group journal to validate the work done. This rubric had been shared with all the teams ahead of time. Out of four teams, two teams were placed in a more successful outcome team (MSOT), and two were placed in a less successful outcome team (LSOT). The MSOT (Team 1 and Team 3) scored 9 and 8.14 out of 10, respectively, whereas the LSOT teams (Team 2 and 4) scored 5 and 5.28 out of 10 respectively. We then sampled video data of the first two milestones (first seven weeks) of all four teams. In the first two milestones, various opportunities were given to all teams to decide problem statements and decide probable solution ideas, which were more challenging and involved substantial amounts of brainstorming and decision-making. The first two milestones allowed learners to put forward their thought processes more openly. To investigate the cyclical phases of SSMR and focus on those contrasting teams, we analyzed the video data (of thirty-five hours) from a synchronous face-to-face classroom interaction.

All four teams have chosen the problem statements around the proposed themes. The content analysis approach (Mayring, 2015, p. 95) was followed to analyze students' verbalized interactions during collaborative work. The verbal interactions during CPS were video recorded and transcribed for data analysis. The start points of conversational segments marked by shared metacognitive experiences were identified as trigger events. The endpoint was marked by the last conversational turn on the topic or the emergence of a new trigger (Iiskala et al., 2011). Segments were considered SSMR episodes if they included verbalizations of monitoring and controlling cognitive processes (De Backer et al., 2022). Each episode contained multiple conversational turns by team members. After identifying SSMR episodes from the video data, we coded the cyclical phases, focus, and function of each SSMR episode using the coding scheme shown in table 2. The reliability of data coding was established using Cronbach's Alpha, the inter-rater reliability method. The deductive coding method is used to code all 103 episodes for four teams. Inter-rater of the coding procedure is done by two educational technology researchers independently in the first round and by discussing and establishing agreement in the second round. We have used 20% samples of each Cyclical Phases, Focus , and Function of SSMR episodes.

Both independent researchers were well-versed in concepts related to metacognition and collaborative problem solving (CPS). Cronbach's Alpha for phases of SSMR is observed as 0.85, for the focus of SSMR is observed as 0.9, and for Function of SSMR is observed as 0.85, which lie between good to excellent band and establishes the reliability of the coding procedure.

Table 2. Deductive coding scheme followed while analyzing SSMR and the degree of transactivity for both teams

Particular	Subtype	Definition
Phases of Metacognitive regulation (De Backer et al., (2015)	Orienting	Students engage in task analysis, which might result in becoming aware of one's task perceptions or activating one's prior knowledge
	Planning	Encompasses selecting and sequencing problem-solving strategies and developing action plans.
	Monitoring	Involves learners' self-judgment upon completion of problem-solving. This can be directed at the learning outcomes, the problem-solving process, or the group members' collaboration.
	Evaluating	Involves quality control of one's learning or problem-solving, aimed at identifying inconsistencies and at optimizing task execution. It also involves monitoring for comprehension, progress, and collaboration.
Focus (Grau and Whitebread, 2012)	Fundamental	Refers to essential aspects discussed to solve the task. It is always related to the final goal of the task. it could include or not include discussions about knowledge.
	Organizational	Students Plan, monitor, change, and evaluate the organization of the task at a pragmatic level.
	Surface	Refers to non-essential aspects of the task, such as time management, choice of resources, etc. They are relevant to complete the task; however, the way this is done does not have a great influence on the quality of the outcomes.
Function (Iiskala, 2011; De Backer, 2022)	Facilitate-Activate	Activating a new direction for ongoing interaction or a new way of thinking in line with and building upon previous activity
	Facilitate-Confirm	Confirm ongoing interaction, eliciting a continuation of previous activity in the same direction
	Inhibit-Change	Changing the flow of collaborative learning, implying ongoing interaction is challenged and current activities are questioned and rethought to the extent that an alternate direction is taken

2.3 Descriptive Statistics

Table 3 presents descriptive statistics for SSMR episodes across four teams, revealing diverse patterns in metacognitive regulation.

Table 3. Descriptive Data showing information about team wise total episodes

	Team 1	**Team 2**	**Team 3**	**Team 4**
Number of Episodes (103)	27	17	32	27
Total Episode Duration	52.43	49.35	78.2	79.45
Min	0.24	0.11	0.17	0.15
Max	8.56	8.7	11.1	10.27
Mean	1.85	2.94	2.32	2.76
SD	2.16	2.5	2.6	2.66

(All data is in Minutes)

The 103 total episodes varied significantly among teams (17 to 32), with notable differences in total duration and average episode length. Episode lengths ranged from 0.11 to 11.1 minutes, with high standard deviations indicating substantial within-team variation. These findings highlight diverse SSMR engagement patterns in terms of frequency, duration, and consistency during collaborative problem-solving.

Table 4 gives team-wise information on different characteristics of the SSMR episodes (such as cyclical phases, foci, and function). Further descriptive statistics are shown in the following table 4, which shows the instances of SSMR episodes, cyclical phases in SSMR, the focus of SSMR episodes, and the function of SSMR episodes. The table 4 grouped teams 1 and 3 as more successful outcome teams (MSOT) and teams 2 and 4 as less successful outcome teams (LSOT), with the last column showing percentage differences based on effect size measures. These measures compare the number of SSMR episodes and key characteristics (cyclical phases, focus, and function) between MSOT and LSOT.

Table 4. Descriptive data analysis for coding team-wise episodes (Showing team-wise cyclical phases, focus, and function of the SSMR)

		Team 1	**Team 2**	**Team 3**	**Team 4**	**MSOT (Team 1 & 3)**	**LSOT (Team 2 & 4)**	**Percentage Difference based on effect size measure (MSOT Vs. LSOT)**
Number of Episodes		27	17	32	27	59	44	34.10%
Number of Cyclical SSMR Processes in episodes. (ex: Mon-Plan or Mon-Eval-Plan)		16	10	28	19	44	36	22.20%
Focus	Fundamental	15	4	25	12	40	16	150%
	Organizational	9	7	7	13	16	20	-20%
	Surface	3	6	0	2	3	8	-62.50%
Function	Activate	8	4	10	19	18	23	-21.70%
	Confirm	6	9	7	0	13	9	44.40%
	Change	13	3	15	8	28	11	154.50%

3. FINDINGS AND DISCUSSION

The differences between MSOT and LSOT concerning their cyclical phases, foci, and functions of SSMR are represented in quantitative and qualitative ways. The contrasting cases allowed us to capture and understand the team-level SSMR processes.

3.1 Data-Driven Distinction: MSOT vs. LSOT

The data shown in Table 4 indicate the measurable differences in the instances of the number of SSMR episodes and the characteristics observed for those episodes in LSOT and MSOT. The percentage difference based on the effect size measure shown in Table 4 reveals that MSOT had 34% more episodes than LSOT. This finding highlights that the identification of critical moments and the formation of regulation responses lead to the occurrence of SSMR episodes, allowing teams to identify the internal challenges of the task (Dindar, Järvelä, & Järvenoja, 2020). The higher number of episodes by MSOT shows that teams 1 and 3 exhibited more regulation behavior than LSOT during CPS. The lower number of SSMR episodes highlights the less frequent engagement in regulatory behaviors during collaborative problem-solving. Overall, MSOT exhibited a higher number of SSMR episodes, aligning with Iiskala (2015), Badhe, Priyadarshini, Dasgupta (2022), and Dindar, Järvelä, Järvenoja (2020).

Furthermore, regarding the phases of SSMR, MSOT had 22% more cyclical phases in SSMR than LSOT. The increased occurrences of cyclical phases in SSMR of MSOT indicate the process of identifying critical moments and becoming aware of discrepancies through shared monitoring. This finding is aligned with

Sobocinski, Malmberg, & Järvelä (2022) and Järvelä, Järvenoja, Malmberg (2019) while underlining that enhanced awareness of gaps in the metacognitive strategy or understanding leads to subsequent planning or evaluation.

The percentage differences shown in Table 4 highlight that the fundamental focus adopted by MSOT was 150% higher than that of LSOT, the organizational focus adopted by MSOT was 20% lower than that of LSOT, and the surface-level focus adopted by MSOT was 63% lower than that of LSOT. The fundamental focus is desirable as it allows teams to understand the essential aspects required to solve the task, whereas organizational and surface-level focuses are not desirable as they involve pragmatic or non-essential components of the task (Iiskala et al., 2011; Grau & Whitebread, 2012). Additionally, regarding the function of SSMR episodes, it was found that MSOT activated 22% fewer new task strategies than LSOT, reevaluated and confirmed the current task strategy 44% more than LSOT, and adapted and changed the current task strategy 154% more than LSOT. This finding related to the function of SSMR indicates that teams should prioritize gaining a fundamental focus while re-evaluating and adapting their existing metacognitive strategies instead of initiating new strategies for each challenge/critical moment (De Backer, 2022).

3.2 Nuanced Analysis: Comparing MSOT (Team 1) with LSOT (Team 4)

We delve into a detailed comparison that reveals the complexities of effective SSMR in collaborative problem-solving. This analysis challenges the simplistic view that more SSMR activity always leads to better outcomes. By comparing Team 1 (from MSOT) and Team 4 (from LSOT), we observed similar numbers of episodes and cyclical processes, with only slight differences in focus. However, the key distinction emerges in the function of SSMR, where Team 1 demonstrates a more balanced and adaptive approach to strategy management. This suggests that having a fundamental focus is important, but it needs to be coupled with the appropriate functions of SSMR to be truly adaptive. While Team 4 frequently activates new strategies, Team 1 shows higher rates of confirming and changing existing strategies, indicating a more reflective and adaptive regulatory process. This comparison underscores that effective SSMR is not about individual metrics but about the interaction and combined use of fundamental focus, and adaptive strategy management (Iiskala et al., 2015), and cyclical phases of regulation. It highlights that successful SSMR requires a blend of persistence in strategy use and flexibility in strategy adaptation, rather than merely increasing the quantity of regulatory activities. This nuanced understanding of SSMR emphasizes the importance of how teams apply metacognitive regulation, rather than simply whether or how much they apply it.

3.3 Contextual Regulatory Distinction: MSOT vs. LSOT

The differences in the SSMR episode level are shown in this section with the help of episodes. This will provide insights into the SSMR process along with contextual information about SSMR in CPS. Shared regulation responses by team 1 (MSOT) and team 2 (LSOT) varied during similar types of tasks. These episodes were captured while all teams were evaluating their work and strategies. The difference in the SSMR is visible in the above episodes of both teams (table 5). In team 1, at the L6, the response given by M3 shows that they all contribute to the discussion and thoughts by individuals also discussed in the group. The next response at L7 by M2 shows the common understanding by team members about how they handle contradictions/conflicts in their opinions and how they get on the same page to achieve a shared goal. Whereas in team 2, at L1 M3 expressed his difficulty with group coordination and not meeting asynchronously if they miss class. As a response to that M1 at L2 has expressed that if you all become particular about a task then group coordination will become better. Here we can say that Team 1 was regulating the challenges regarding tasks being on the same page and Team 2 was regulating group coordination-related challenges having scattered opinions. Team 1 ended up with a fundamental focus whereas Team 2 ended up with an organizational focus.

Team 1 has shown process evaluation MRS in the task performance strategy along with fundamental focus, whereas Team 2 has shown monitoring progress & strategic planning with an organizational focus. De Backer (2022) suggests that diverse responses to similar critical moments or challenging conditions can lead to varying degrees of facilitation for SSMR, which supports this finding. The above findings indicate that teams should gain a fundamental focus while re-evaluating and adapting their current metacognitive strategies rather than activating new strategies for each challenge. Team members need to see the linkages between sequential actions during task performance and optimize their strategies accordingly. Additionally, teams should aim to gain a fundamental focus while optimizing metacognitive strategies, as merely optimizing strategies with an organizational or surface-level focus will not yield better outcomes in CPS (Iiskala et al., 2015; De Backer, 2022).

Table 5. The difference in phase of SSMR and focus is given for more and less successful outcome teams

Team 1 (MSOT)	Team 2 (LSOT)
(L1) M2- Do we detect and correct errors? (L2) M1- Did we detect something? (L3) M3- and what would be the errors? (L4) M1- Yeah. (L5) M4- Error means it was just an improvement. (L6) M3- I mean we discuss individual thoughts on what we want to do and based on the discussion we decide. (L7) M2- In our group even if we had contradictions still (after making a consensus) we built upon ideas so we didn't reject anyone's idea, (L8) M1- But what to mark here? Neutral..! we are not sure. (L8) All- Yeah. Neutral	(L1) M3- We also don't meet if we miss the class, and to catch up and update the absent person.. (L2) M1- See.. you people (who miss class frequently) have to become more particular, just I have done my part on time, but you people were doing it very late at night, I was observing that live on Document.. but you didn't inform.. (L3) M1- Just like, see, M2 has also not done their respective part.. now I can't fill their columns in this sheet right.. (Unpleasant Feeling of (low) satisfaction). and I have prepared a whole structured sheet for us, and just thought let me take up that responsibility and do it. but you people have to at least put your ideas in it... (L4) M3 - Hmm (Yes) (L5) M1- If you want to meet then just schedule and fix the meeting, let's work. just don't say that we don't meet.. this doesn't work..
Analysis codes: Phase of SSMR: Process Evaluation Focus: Fundamental Function: Confirm	*Analysis codes:* Phase of SSMR: - Monitoring Progress - Strategic planning Focus: Organizational Function: Confirm

Team members negotiated, gathered perceptions about working in a team, and took control of tasks in various ways (Malmberg et al., 2015). For the given RQ, our findings showed that during critical moments in CPS, MSOT, and LSOT responded with different SSMR behaviors, illustrating the differentiated nature of SSMR in CPS. Our findings revealed that MSOT and LSOT differ in terms of cyclical phases, focus, and function of SSMR in different tasks. The data-driven distinction between MSOT and LSOT highlights that, instead of focusing solely on whether a team is applying metacognitive regulation, it is crucial to understand how they apply it. The "how" involves examining the cyclical phases, foci, and functions of SSMR collectively. A cyclical phase in SSMR along with a fundamental focus does not guarantee better outcomes in collaborative problem-solving (CPS), nor do mere adaptations in strategies alone. Both focus and function must be combined to address the internal challenges of the task and facilitate better-regulating opportunities during CPS.

4. CONCLUSION, LIMITATIONS AND FUTURE WORK

This study examined SSMR behavior in collaborative problem-solving tasks among four teams in an HCI course, categorized as MSOT and LSOT based on their performance. These two contrasting groups allow us to capture and understand the team-level SSMR processes in which team members (learners) negotiated, gathered perceptions about working in a team, and took control of the tasks in various ways. Findings reveal distinct SSMR patterns between these groups. LSOT demonstrated insufficient regulatory engagement, focusing more on surface-level aspects and showing inefficient strategy management. In contrast, MSOT exhibited more effective identification of critical moments and formation of regulation responses. We have presented sample episodes (table 5) to show the contextual regulatory distinction between MSOT and LSOT, which enhances the detailed understanding of SSMR behavior in these two groups. We also examined a comparison case of MSOT (Team 1) and LSOT (Team 4), which revealed critical differences in their SSMR behavior, despite having similar numbers. This examination provided a nuanced understanding of SSMR in collaborative problem-solving. While both teams exhibit similar numbers of episodes and cyclical processes, the key difference lies in the function of SSMR. Team 1 showed a more balanced and adaptive approach to strategy management, emphasizing the importance of not just the frequency but the nature of SSMR activities. These findings contribute to a nuanced understanding of SSMR's role in enhancing collaborative problem-solving effectiveness. This study also advances the understanding of SSMR in CPS by detailing its operationalization and unfolding processes. By identifying cyclical phases, foci, and functions of SSMR, our findings provide a premise for developing targeted support strategies to enhance SSMR in CPS contexts.

While this study adds valuable insights into metacognition in collaborative settings, it has limitations. Some teams may have worked outside the classroom, and their fieldwork was not recorded. Future research can consider capturing asynchronous interactions and include more data sources for comprehensive analysis. The small number of participants and potential confounding variables like individual motivation and task interest may impact SSMR. Increasing participant numbers and ensuring diverse samples will enhance the generalizability of findings. Replicating the study in various educational contexts will test the findings' applicability.

REFERENCES

Badhe, V., Priyadarshini, R., & Dasgupta, C. (2022). Understanding SSRL Strategies and Its Impact on Group Performance in a CSCL Environment: A Case Study From a Project-Based Learning Course in India. In Proceedings of the 15th International Conference on Computer-Supported Collaborative Learning-CSCL 2022, pp. 187-194.

De Backer, L., Van Keer, H., & Valcke, M. (2015). Exploring evolutions in reciprocal peer tutoring groups' socially shared metacognitive regulation and identifying its metacognitive correlates. Learning and Instruction, 38, 63-78.

De Backer, L., Van Keer, H., & Valcke, M. (2022). The functions of shared metacognitive regulation and their differential relation with collaborative learners' understanding of the learning content. Learning and Instruction, 77, 101527.

Dindar, M., Järvelä, S., & Järvenoja, H. (2020). Interplay of metacognitive experiences and performance in collaborative problem solving. Computers & Education, 154, 103922.

Grau, V., & Whitebread, D. (2012). Self and social regulation of learning during collaborative activities in the classroom: The interplay of individual and group cognition. Learning and Instruction, 22(6), 401-412.

Iiskala, T., Vauras, M., Lehtinen, E., & Salonen, P. (2011). Socially shared metacognition of dyads of pupils in collaborative mathematical problem-solving processes. Learning and instruction, 21(3), 379-393.

Iiskala, T., Volet, S., Lehtinen, E., & Vauras, M. (2015). Socially shared metacognitive regulation in asynchronous CSCL in science: Functions, evolution and participation. Frontline Learning Research, 3(1), 78-111.

Järvelä, S., Järvenoja, H., Malmberg, J., & Hadwin, A. F. (2013). Exploring socially shared regulation in the context of collaboration. Journal of Cognitive Education and Psychology, 12(3), 267-286.

Järvelä, S., Järvenoja, H., & Malmberg, J. (2019). Capturing the dynamic and cyclical nature of regulation: Methodological Progress in understanding socially shared regulation in learning. International journal of computer-supported collaborative learning, 14, 425-441.

Lobczowski, N. G., Lyons, K., Greene, J. A., & McLaughlin, J. E. (2021). Socially shared metacognition in a project-based learning environment: A comparative case study. Learning, Culture and Social Interaction, 30, 100543.

Mayring, P. (2015). Qualitative content analysis: Theoretical background and procedures. Approaches to qualitative research in mathematics education: Examples of methodology and methods, 365-380.

Sobocinski, M., Malmberg, J., & Järvelä, S. (2022). Exploring adaptation in socially-shared regulation of learning using video and heart rate data. Technology, Knowledge and Learning, 27(2), 385-404.

Kerrigan, S., Feng, S., Vuthaluru, R., Ifenthaler, D., Gibson, D. (2021). Network Analytics of Collaborative Problem-Solving. In: Ifenthaler, D., Sampson, D.G., Isaías, P. (eds) Balancing the Tension between Digital Technologies and Learning Sciences. Cognition and Exploratory Learning in the Digital Age. Springer, Cham.

Vauras, M., Volet, S., & Iiskala, T. (2021). Socially-shared metacognitive regulation in collaborative science learning. Trends and prospects in metacognition research across the life span: A tribute to Anastasia Efklides, 83-102.

Wei, Li., Lu, Lei., Peihan, Zhang. (2023). Collaborative programming based on social shared regulation: An approach to improving students' programming achievements and group metacognition. Journal of Computer Assisted Learning, doi: 10.1111/jcal.12828

DYNAMICS OF STUDENTS' AFFECTIVE STATES AND VIDEO INTERACTIONS WHILE WATCHING EDUCATIONAL VIDEOS

Burçak Aydın[1], Gökhan Akçapınar[1], Vildan Özeke[2] and Mohammad Nehal Hasnine[3]
[1]Department of Computer Education and Instructional Technology, Hacettepe University, Turkey
[2]Department of Computer Education and Instructional Technology, Tokat Gaziosmanpaşa University, Turkey
[3]Research Center for Computing and Multimedia Studies, Hosei University, Japan

ABSTRACT

This study explores the relationship between students' affective states and their interactions with educational videos. While video-based learning has become increasingly popular, it is important to understand the emotional and behavioral dynamics that influence learning outcomes. Using a qualitative content analysis approach, data were collected from 34 students enrolled in a Physical Programming course. The students' self-reported data after interacting with 15 educational videos were analyzed, focusing on behaviors such as pausing, seeking backward, seeking forward, or speeding up the videos. Additionally, their affective states, including engagement, boredom, confusion, and frustration, were examined. The findings reveal that students frequently pause and seek backward in videos when they encounter difficulty or need clarification, while seeking forward is often used to skip over familiar content. Boredom typically arises due to content density or presentation style, leading to early termination of video viewing. Conversely, engagement is fostered when students find the topic interesting or engage in practice activities, resulting in a more continuous viewing experience. The study highlights the need to consider both behavioral and affective factors when designing educational videos to optimize student engagement and learning. By providing insights into the connections between video interactions and emotional responses, this research contributes to improving the design of educational video materials and offers implications for enhancing video-based learning experiences.

KEYWORDS

Online Learning, Video Interactions, Emotion, Affect, Engagement, Boredom, Frustration, Confusion

1. INTRODUCTION

The integration of digital technologies in education has led to significant changes in teaching and learning processes. Educational videos are becoming an increasingly popular tool for learning, necessitating a deep exploration into how students interact with this medium and the impacts these interactions have on their learning experiences. Educational videos are reshaping how students explore, understand, and apply knowledge (Mayer, 2009). Videos are tools that facilitate learning by allowing learners to reflect and develop their understanding (Pérez-Torregrosa et al., 2017). Video-based learning is also found to be highly effective in capturing and disseminating information (Sablić et al., 2021), and educational videos offer opportunities to overcome the practical limitations of the real world and explore the vast possibilities of digital spaces (Giannakos et al., 2014). Videos can be used to teach various subjects, including academic topics, professional skills, and personal development (Hatch et al., 2016). Video-based learning can be effective because it is engaging, informative, and accessible (Santagata & Taylor, 2018). Students often process and remember images more efficiently than text or audio alone (Shorter & Dean, 1994). Video lessons also provide students with the ability to revisit course materials repeatedly, offering additional time to understand classroom content fully (Brecht & Ogilby, 2008). Dolan (2015) also found that students learning through video-based instruction performed significantly better in exams than those learning through traditional methods. Another study conducted on medical students revealed that students who watched video lessons performed better on exams than those who just read the contents (Dolmans et al., 1996).

On the other hand, students' affective states have significant effects on their learning processes. For example, Dillon et al. (2016) examined the affective states experienced by students based on self-reports in the context of Massive Open Online Courses (MOOCs). The results of their research show that feelings of anxiety, confusion, and frustration are significantly related to the likelihood of students dropping out of courses. These findings underscore the significant impact of affective states on students' abilities to cope with challenges in online learning environments. Video materials have the potential to offer a wide range of preferences and rich learning experiences for students. However, to make the most effective use of these materials, it is emphasized that the affective states of students must be considered (Brame, 2016). Studies show that the emotions students experience while watching video materials are directly related to their learning performance (D'Mello & Graesser, 2012). When videos successfully capture students' interest, this enhances focus on learning and consequently leads to more effective learning (Schwan & Riempp, 2004; Mayer, 2009). Conversely, if videos are confusing or boring for students, they can negatively impact learning performance (Kalyuga et al., 1999). Therefore, during the design phase of video materials, students' affective states should be considered a significant factor; videos should be both engaging and comprehensible, and suited to the students' level of difficulty. Additionally, designing videos to collect student feedback can better tailor these materials to student needs, thereby making learning through online video materials more effective and efficient (Kay et al., 2013).

The pervasive use of videos in educational settings necessitates a deeper understanding of student interactions with this medium. While existing data-driven studies have analyzed interaction logs to identify patterns, they often overlook the reasons behind these behaviors. This study also aims to establish the relationship between the affective states students experience while watching videos and the interactions they engage in, based on these underlying reasons. Through this focus, the following research questions were explored:

1. What are the reasons for students' specific video interactions such as pausing, seeking backward, seeking forward, or speeding up the videos?
2. What causes students to experience affective states such as boredom, frustration, or confusion while watching course videos?
3. What is the relationship between the affective states experienced by students and their video interactions?

2. BACKGROUND

2.1 Video Interactions in Education

Behaviors such as seeking forward, seeking backward, and speeding up the videos reflect students' need to control their learning pace, emphasizing the importance of personalized learning paths (Chen & Caropreso, 2004). Mayer (2014) explains that allowing students to determine their learning pace supports cognitive processes. Baker et al. (2021) investigated students' participation and perceptions of video lessons in an undergraduate course. The findings revealed that students tend to rewatch videos, particularly in sections considered important by educators. Merkt et al. (2022) analyzed students' pausing behaviors in educational videos. Researchers observed that students tend to pause videos when encountering difficulty or during meaningful breakpoints in the content. The findings indicate that students' pausing behaviors are significantly influenced by their perceptions of difficulty and meaningful breakpoints in the video.

Akçapınar and Bayazıt (2018) compared the video-watching behaviors of deep and surface learners in terms of interactions like play, pause, seek forward, and seek backward. The findings showed that students with a surface approach were statistically significantly more likely to seek forward while watching videos than students using a deep learning approach. Seo et al. (2021) examined how students' video interactions changed over a semester. A developed multilevel model revealed that students enrolled in online courses watched videos strategically. For example, they observed a decrease in *reflecting* and *searching* activities throughout the semester. However, during exam weeks and rewatching sessions, there was a significant increase in *searching* activities.

2.2 Affects and Learning

Educational research underscores the significant impact of students' affective states on learning outcomes (Andres et al., 2019; Harley et al., 2017). In psychological terms, 'emotion' and 'affect' are distinct yet often conflated in academic discourse along with 'feeling' and 'mood' (Feidakis et al., 2014; Öztüre et al., 2021; Baker et al., 2010). Emotions encompass physiological, behavioral, and cognitive changes, usually triggered by specific events, influencing thoughts and behaviors (APA, 2024). 'Affect' refers broadly to emotional experiences from pain to joy and includes complex and pathological responses (Aydin et al., 2011; Parrott, 2001). The term 'affective state' in e-learning captures this spectrum of emotional and cognitive experiences relevant to learning, with specific states such as engagement, confusion, frustration, and boredom identified as crucial for educational outcomes.

Engagement and flow describe an optimal experiential state achieved through intense participation in enjoyable activities, leading to deep immersion and a loss of self-consciousness and time awareness (APA, 2024; Csikszentmihalyi, 1990). Engagement in learning, as described by Heflin et al. (2017), entails students' dedicated time and effort in educational activities, involving three key components: behavioral, cognitive, and affective engagement. Behavioral engagement reflects participation in both academic and non-academic activities, cognitive engagement involves deep intellectual involvement and self-regulation in learning, and affective engagement relates to students' emotional responses towards the educational environment (Fredricks et al., 2005; Jung & Lee, 2018). These dimensions collectively influence learning performance and success in educational settings (Phan et al., 2016). Confusion is a psychological state or emotion characterized by a lack of understanding or clarity (APA, 2024). Students become confused when they have difficulty understanding the topic and are unsure of how to proceed (D'Mello & Graesser, 2014). Frustration is a negative affective state that occurs when a person's goal-oriented behavior is inhibited. It is often accompanied by feelings of anger, resentment, and helplessness (APA, 2024). Students experience frustration when they repeatedly make mistakes, get stuck, or have their important goals thwarted (Kapoor et al., 2007). Boredom is defined as a mental state marked by an absence of interest or stimulation, often resulting in a feeling of fatigue or ennui due to insufficient environmental engagement (APA, 2024). The consequences of boredom are substantial, potentially resulting in decreased productivity, increased stress, and diminished creativity (Eastwood et al., 2012).

This study aims to identify the reasons behind the affective states students experience and the interactions they engage in while watching course videos, and to establish a relationship between these interactions and affective states based on these reasons.

3. METHOD

Utilizing a content analysis approach—a qualitative research method—the data were systematically examined. The participants comprised 34 students from the Department of Educational Technology at a state university in Turkey, all enrolled in a Physical Programming course. Data were gathered through a questionnaire with 10 open-ended questions, designed to elicit detailed responses about their interactions, such as pausing, seeking backward, seeking forward, or speeding up the videos, as well as their affective states like engagement, confusion, frustration, and boredom. A questionnaire was administered face-to-face to students in a classroom setting at the end of the semester, focusing on their engagement with 15 course videos, each averaging 10 to 15 minutes in length. Before completing the questionnaire, students were briefed on interaction types and affective states addressed in the questions. For data analysis, the qualitative content analysis method was utilized, following Creswell's (2007) recommended steps and incorporating definitions of coding by Saldaña (2015). Initially, responses to open-ended questions were coded independently by an expert and GPT-4 Large Language Model (LLM). Then, discrepancies were reviewed by two additional experts. Interrater reliability between the expert and the LLM was calculated using Cohen's Kappa. This process highlighted the utility of LLMs like GPT-4 in capturing the nuances of human emotional and interactive experiences (Martínez-Pernía et al., 2024). The study analyzed frequency and commonality of codes across responses to explore interaction and affective states, aiding in answering the research questions through quantitative and visual data interpretations.

4. RESULTS

As a result of the analysis, the Cohen's Kappa reliability coefficient, which shows the agreement between the human expert and the GPT-4 LLM, was found to be 0.81 in the first round. This result indicates that the agreement between the human expert and LLM is high (Cohen, 1960). The codes were then reviewed and modified by two experts until full consensus was reached.

For the first aspect of the study, which explored students' reasons for specific video interactions, the findings showed that the reasons and percentage of students performing the "Pause" behavior while watching the videos as follows: Most students reported pausing the video for "Taking Notes" (32.35%) and "Not Understanding" (32.35%). Another significant reason mentioned was "Distraction" (14.71%). The most frequently reported reason for "Seeking Forward" was "Knowledge Mastery" (61.76%), meaning students skipped topics they were already familiar with. Other reasons, mentioned by a smaller number of students, included "Time Management" (8.82%), "Seeking Specific Information" (8.82%), and "Avoiding Details" (8.82%). Students reported that the most frequent reason for "Seeking Backward" was "Not Understanding" a part of the video (64.71%). The second most common reason was for "Reviewing" (14.71%). "Time Management" (38.24%) and "Teaching Style" (26.47%) were the most frequently mentioned reasons for students to "Speed Up" videos. A significant portion of the students (32.35%) reported watching the videos without any interaction, indicating "No Interaction" for "Focus." Additionally, 29.41% of the students stated that they did not watch continuously. Some students reported watching continuously due to "Passive Monitoring" (14.71%) and "Boredom" (11.76%). A considerable proportion of the students (29.41%) reported closing the video before it ended once they felt they had "Understood the Topic." Additionally, "Boredom" (17.65%) and "Finding the Information" they were searching for (14.71%) were cited as other significant reasons for stopping the video early.

When examining the factors contributing to students' affective states, the data revealed that students generally experienced feelings of "Boredom" due to "Topic Difficulty" (23.53%) and "Presentation Style" (17.65%) in the videos. "Not Understanding" was identified as the primary factor associated with "Frustration" (44.12%). Students expressed "Frustration" when there was "Missing Content" (26.47%). They reported experiencing a sense of "Flow/Engagement" most often when the topic was interesting (50.00%) and during practice (26.47%). Additionally, "Not Understanding" (29.41%) and "Lack of Prior Knowledge" (20.59%) were cited as the main reasons for "Confusion."

Finally, to investigate the link between students' affective states and their video interactions, a network graph presented in Figure 1 was developed. In the graph, interactions are represented by blue circles, affective states are shown as purple squares, and the reasons expressed by students are denoted by pink triangles. Lines connecting the symbols represent the relationships, with numerals indicating the frequency of cited reasons. The highest frequencies are represented by red dotted lines, while frequencies of less than three have been removed from the figure to enhance clarity. The connections illustrated in Figure 1 indicate significant findings. For example, the reason "Not Understanding" is a common challenge students face and is linked to various interactions and affective states. Students reported using actions like "Seek Backward" and "Pause" to better grasp concepts they did not understand. Additionally, "Not Understanding" was cited by students as a cause for feelings of "Confusion" and "Frustration." For "Time Management," students indicated performing video interactions such as "Speed Up," "No Interactions", "Seek Forward," and "Stop Before Finishing." "Mastery of Knowledge" was expressed by students as a reason for "Speed Up" and "Seek Forward" actions. They noted a tendency to speed up and skip through videos in parts they were already familiar with, for time management purposes. The "Presentation Style" was identified by students as a reason for "Boredom". Students who felt bored expressed a tendency to watch the video at an increased speed. Students reported experiencing a state of "Flow/Engagement" when they were "Focusing" or "Practicing". When "Focusing", they tended to watch without any interactions, and when "Practicing," they tended to "Pause" the video. "Distraction" emerged as a common factor intersecting with affective states like "Boredom," "Frustration," and "Confusion." When distracted, students indicated performing video interactions such as "Pause," "Seek Backward", and "Seek Forward."

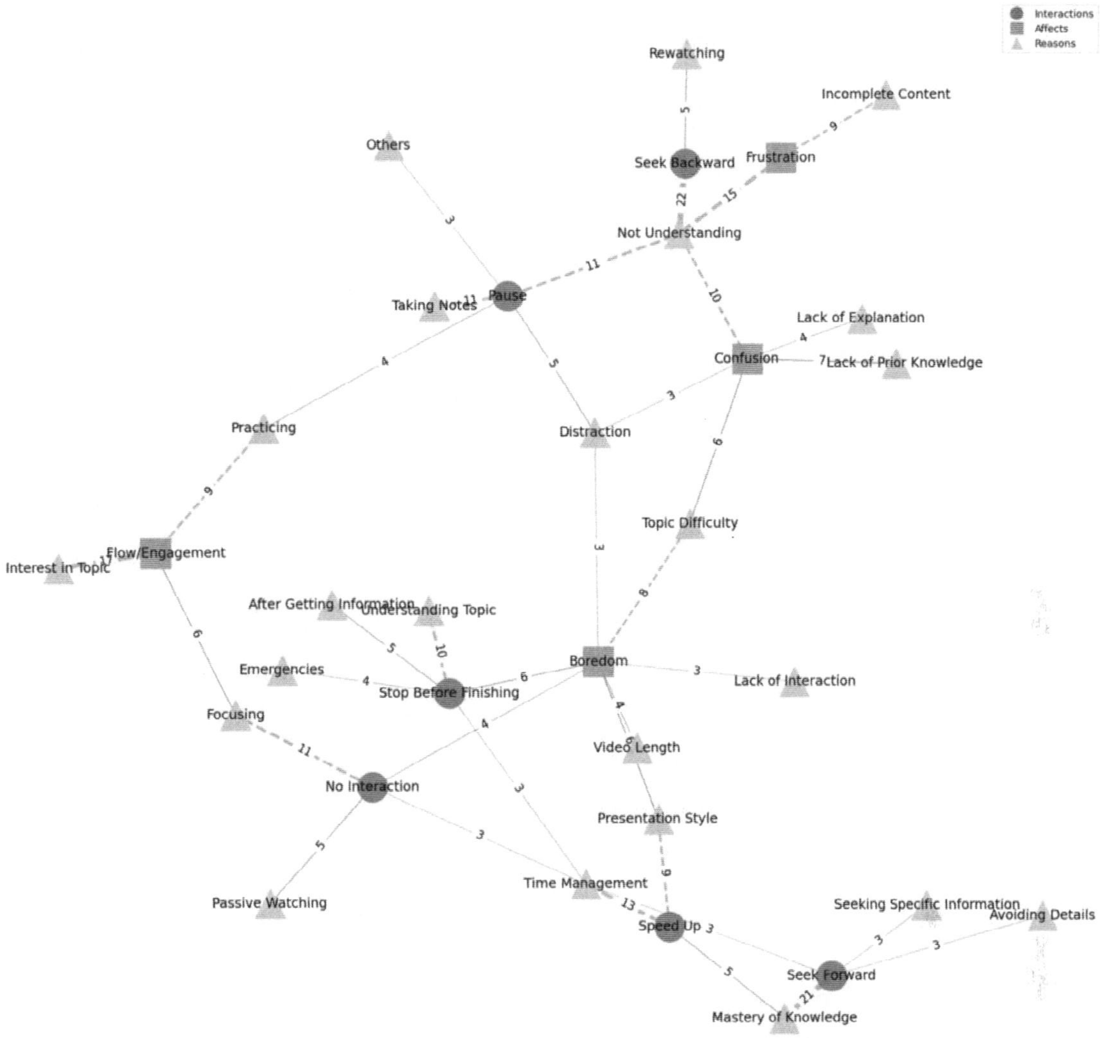

Figure 1. Relationships between Video Interactions and Affective States

5. DISCUSSION AND CONCLUSION

This study aims to investigate the reasons behind students' interactions and the affective states they experience while watching video materials. The findings can be used to relate the emotional states students experience to their video interactions, based on the reasons they expressed. For instance, students generally reported experiencing "Boredom" due to "Topic Difficulty" (23.53%) and "Presentation Style" (17.65%). They also indicated that these reasons led them to stop viewing the video before finishing it. Therefore, the "Stop Before Finishing" interaction can be linked to "Boredom." Previous studies have also shown that "Boredom" has a negative impact on learning (Craig et al., 2004; Graesser et al., 2008; Karumbaiah et al., 2022; Zambrano et al., 2024). "Frustration" was mostly associated with "Not Understanding" (44.12%) by students. Additionally, students expressed frustration when the information they expected was missing or the content was insufficient (26.47%). They also indicated that these reasons led them to pause or seek backward in the video.

The factors that increased students' feelings of flow/engagement while watching the course videos were "Interest in Topic" (50.00%), "Practicing" (26.47%), and "Focusing" (17.65%). These reasons were mostly associated with watching videos without any interaction. In other words, students stated that when they are engaged, they continue watching without interruption. However, previous studies have linked behaviors such as pausing, seeking forward, and seeking backward to more effective engagement with learning materials (Kay & Kletskin, 2012). Seeking forward behavior has been associated with information search (Yoon et al., 2021; Seo et al., 2021); however, in this study, only 3 students cited "Seeking Specific Information" as the reason for seeking forward. "Not Understanding" (29.41%) and "Lack of Prior Knowledge" (20.59%) were identified as the primary causes of "Confusion," which negatively impacts students' engagement and learning processes. Sweller (1988) highlighted that comprehension difficulties can demotivate students. Additionally, some students cited "Video Length" (11.76%) as a factor contributing to "Boredom." Hughes et al. (2019) observed that lengthy and complex videos can reduce attention.

In conclusion, the findings reveal clear links between students' affective states and their video interactions. Students often resort to actions like seeking backward and pausing in sections they find difficult, experiencing frustration and confusion in these moments. These actions may indicate that students are actively trying to comprehend challenging material and are engaging in self-regulated learning strategies (Kim et al., 2014). Conversely, boredom often stems from the complexity of the video content or its presentation style, leading to disengagement. When students find the material uninteresting or overly complex, they are less likely to maintain attention and may disengage from the learning process (Pekrun et al., 2002; Brame, 2017). Bored students are more likely to stop watching the video before it ends, and early dropouts correlate with low engagement levels, underscoring the importance of maintaining student interest throughout the video (Guo et al., 2014; Schroeder & Adesope, 2020; Yürüm et al., 2023).

Additionally, students display signs of flow and engagement when they are actively practicing or concentrating on the content. They typically pause during practice segments and watch continuously when fully focused. This state of deep engagement enhances learning outcomes and reflects optimal learning experiences (Csikszentmihalyi, 1990). These results have significant implications for the design and use of educational videos, emphasizing the need to consider students' affective states. Incorporating emotional factors into video content can enhance engagement and improve learning effectiveness (Calvo & D'Mello, 2010; Loderer et al., 2020).

REFERENCES

Akçapınar, G., & Bayazıt, A. (2018). Investigating video viewing behaviors of students with different learning approaches using video analytics. The Turkish Online Journal of Distance Education, 19(4), 116–125. https://doi.org/10.17718/tojde.471907.

American Psychological Association. (2024). Frustration. In the Dictionary of Psychology (5th ed., pp. 459-460). Washington, DC: American Psychological Association.

Andres, J. M. A. L., Paquette, L., Ocumpaugh, J., Jiang, Y., Baker, R. S., Karumbaiah, S., et al. (2019). Affect sequences and learning in Betty's brain. In Proceedings of the 9th International Conference on Learning Analytics & Knowledge (pp. 383–390). ACM International Conference Proceeding Series. https://doi.org/10.1145/3303772.3303785

Aydın, A., Araz, A., & Asan, A. (2011). Görsel Analog Ölçeği ve Duygu Kafesi: Kültürümüze Uyarlama Çalışması. Turk Psikoloji Yazilari, 14(27), 1.

Baker, R. S., D'Mello, S. K., Rodrigo, M. M. T., & Graesser, A. C. (2010). Better to be frustrated than bored: The incidence, persistence, and impact of learners' cognitive-affective states during interactions with three different computer-based learning environments. International Journal of Human-Computer Studies, 68(4), 223–241.https://doi.org/10.1016/j.ijhcs.2009.12.003

Baker, S., Field, C., Saintilan, N., & Lee, J. S. (2021). Supporting students' academic literacies in post-covid-19 times: Developing digital videos to develop students' critical academic reading practices. Journal of University Teaching and Learning Practice, 18(4), 35–49. https://doi.org/10.53761/1.18.4.5

Brame, C. J. (2017). Effective educational videos: Principles and guidelines for maximizing student learning from video content. CBE—Life Sciences Education, 15(4), es6. https://doi.org/10.1187/cbe.16-03-0125

Brecht, H. D., & Ogilby, S. M. (2008). Enabling a comprehensive teaching strategy: Video lectures. Journal of Information Technology Education, 7, 71e86. https://doi.org/10.28945/207.

Calvo, R. A., & D'Mello, S. (2010). Affect detection: An interdisciplinary review of models, methods, and their applications. *IEEE Transactions on Affective Computing*, 1(1), 18-37.

Chen, D., & Caropreso, E. J. (2004). Influence of personality on online discussion. Journal of Interactive Online Learning, 3(2), 1-19.

Cohen, J. (1960). A coefficient of agreement for nominal scales. Educational and Psychological Measurement, 20(1), 37-46. https://doi.org/10.1177/001316446002000104

Craig, S., Graesser, A., Sullins, J., & Gholson, B. (2004). Affect and learning: an exploratory look into the role of affect in learning with AutoTutor. Journal of educational media, 29(3), 241-250.

Creswell, J. W. (2007). Qualitative inquiry and research design: Choosing among five approaches (2nd ed.). Sage Publications.

Csikszentmihalyi, M. (1990). Flow: The Psychology of Optimal Experience. Harper & Row.

Dillon, J., Bosch, N., Chetlur, M., Wanigasekara, N., Ambrose, G. A., Sengupta, B., & D'Mello, S. K. (2016). Student emotion, co-occurrence, and dropout in a MOOC context. International Educational Data Mining Society.

D'Mello, S. K., & Graesser, A. (2012). Dynamics of affective states during complex learning. Learning and Instruction, 22(2), 145-157. https://doi.org/10.1016/j.learninstruc.2011.10.001

Schwan, S., & Riempp, R. (2004). The cognitive benefits of interactive videos: Learning to tie nautical knots. Learning and Instruction, 14(3), 293-305. https://doi.org/10.1016/j.learninstruc.2004.06.005

D'Mello, S. K., & Graesser, A. C. (2014). Confusion. In the International handbook of emotions in education (pp. 299-320). Routledge.

Dolan, J. (2015). The effectiveness of video-based instruction. Journal of Educational Psychology, 107(4), 852-863. https://doi.org/10.1037/edu0000023

Dolmans, D. H. J., van Merriënboer, J. J. G., & Schmidt, H. G. (1996). The use of worked examples in a multimedia learning environment. Journal of Educational Psychology, 88(2), 329. https://doi.org/10.1037/0022-0663.88.2.329

Eastwood, J. D., Frischen, A., Fenske, M. J., & Smilek, D. (2012). The unengaged mind: Defining boredom in terms of attention. Perspectives on Psychological Science, 7(5), 482-495. https://doi.org/10.1177/1745691612447303

Feidakis, M., Daradoumis, T., CaballÃ, S., & Conesa, J. (2014). Embedding emotion awareness into e-learning environments. International Journal of Emerging Technologies in Learning, 9(7), 39-46. https://doi.org/10.18608/hla17.023

Fredricks, J. A., Blumenfeld, P. C., & Paris, A. H. (2004). School engagement: Potential of the concept, state of the evidence. Review of educational research, 74(1), 59-109. https://doi.org/10.3102/00346543074001059

Giannakos, M. N., Chorianopoulos, K., Ronchetti, M., Szegedi, P., & Teasley, S. D. (2014). Video-based learning and open online courses. iJET, 9(1). https://doi.org/10.3991/ijet.v9i1.3354

Graesser, A. C., Rus, V., D'Mello, S., & Jackson, G. T. (2008). AutoTutor: Learning through natural language dialogue that adapts to the cognitive and affective states of the learner. In D. H. Robinson & G. Schraw (Eds.), Current Perspectives on Cognition, Learning, and Instruction: Recent Innovations in Educational Technology that Facilitate Student Learning (pp. 95–125). Information Age Publishing.

Guo, P. J., Kim, J., & Rubin, R. (2014). How video production affects student engagement: An empirical study of MOOC videos. In M. Sahami (Chair), L@S 2014: First (2014) ACM Conference on Learning @ Scale, Atlanta, Georgia, USA, March 4–5, 2014 (pp. 41–50). Association for Computing Machinery. https://doi.org/10.1145/2556325.2566239

Harley, J. M., Lajoie, S. P., Frasson, C., & Hall, N. C. (2017). Developing emotion-aware, advanced learning technologies: A taxonomy of approaches and features. International Journal of Artificial Intelligence in Education, 27, 268-297.

Hatch, T., Shuttleworth, J., Jaffee, A. T., & Marri, A. (2016). Videos, pairs, and peers: What connects theory and practice in teacher education?. Teaching and Teacher Education, 59, 274-284.

Heflin, H., Shewmaker, J., & Nguyen, J. (2017). Impact of mobile technology on student attitudes, engagement, and learning. Computers & Education, 107, 91–99. https://doi.org/10.1016/j.compedu.2017.01.006

Hughes, C., Costley, J., & Lange, C. (2019). The effects of multimedia video lectures on extraneous load. Distance Education, 40(1), 54–75. https://doi.org/10.1080/01587919.2018.1553559

Jung, Y., & Lee, J. (2018). Learning engagement and persistence in massive open online courses (MOOCS). Computers & Education, 122, 9–22. https://doi.org/10.1016/j.compedu.2018.02.013

Kalyuga, S. (2007). Enhancing instructional efficiency of interactive e-learning environments: A cognitive load perspective. Educational Psychology Review, 19(3), 387-399. https://doi.org/10.1007/s10648-007-9051-6

Kapoor, A., Burleson, B., & Picard, R. (2007). Automatic prediction of frustration. International Journal of Human-Computer Studies, 65, 724–736. https://doi.org/10.1016/j.ijhcs.2007.02.003

Karumbaiah, S., Baker, R., Tao, Y. and Liu, Z. 2022. How Does Students' Affect in Virtual Learning Relate to Their Outcomes? A Systematic Review Challenging the Positive- Negative Dichotomy. LAK22: 12th International Learning Analytics and Knowledge Conference (New York, NY, USA, 2022), 24–33. https://doi.org/10.1145/3506860.3506861

Kay, R. H., & Kletskin, I. (2012). Evaluating the use of problem-based video podcasts to teach mathematics in higher education. Computers & Education, 59(2), 619-627. https://doi.org/10.1016/j.compedu.2012.03.007

Kay, J., Reimann, P., Diebold, E., & Kummerfeld, B. (2013). MOOCs: So many learners, so much potential... IEEE Intelligent systems, 28(3), 70-77. https://doi.org/10.1109/MIS.2013.66

Kim, J., Guo, P. J., Seaton, D., Mitros, P., Gajos, K. Z., & Miller, R. C. (2014). Understanding in-video dropouts and interaction peaks in online lecture videos. In *Proceedings of the first ACM conference on Learning@ scale conference* (pp. 31-40).

Loderer, K., Pekrun, R., & Lester, J. C. (2020). Beyond cold technology: A systematic review and meta-analysis on emotions in technology-based learning environments. *Learning and instruction*, *70*, 101162.

Love, B., Hodge, A., Grandgenett, N., & Swift, A. W. (2014). Student learning and perceptions in a flipped linear algebra course. International Journal of Mathematical Education in Science and Technology, 45(3), 317–324. https://doi.org/10.1080/0020739X.2013.822582

Martínez-Pernía, D., Troncoso, A., Chaigneau, S., Marchant, N., Zepeda, A., & Blanco, K. (2024). A new horizon in mixed-method studies: ChatGPT-assisted qualitative analysis. https://doi.org/10.31234/osf.io/5xpn9

Mayer, R. E. (2009). Multimedia learning (2nd ed.). Cambridge University Press.

Mayer, R. E. (2014). Incorporating motivation into multimedia learning. Learning and Instruction, 29, 171-173. https://doi.org/10.1016/j.learninstruc.2013.04.003

Merkt, M., Hoppe, A., Bruns, G., Ewerth, R., & Huff, M. (2022). Pushing the button: Why do learners pause online videos? Computers & Education, 176, Article 104355. https://doi.org/10.1016/j.compedu.2021.104355

Öztüre, G., Fidan, A., Bakir, E., Uslu, N. A., & Usluel, Y. (2021). A systematic mapping study on technology and emotion studies in educational context: Definitions, theories, future directions. Educational Technology Theory and Practice, 11(1), 20-47. https://doi.org/10.17943/etku.745236

Parrott, W. G. (Ed.). (2001). Emotions in social psychology: Essential readings. psychology press.

Pekrun, R., Goetz, T., Titz, W., & Perry, R. P. (2002). Academic emotions in students' self-regulated learning and achievement: A program of qualitative and quantitative research. *Educational Psychologist*, 37(2), 91-105.

Pérez-Torregrosa, A. B., Díaz-Martín, C., & Ibáñez-Cubillas, P. (2017). The use of Video annotation tools in teacher training. Procedia-Social and Behavioral Sciences, 237, 458–464.

Phan, T., McNeil, S. G., & Robin, B. R. (2016). Students' patterns of engagement and course performance in a massive open online course. Computers & Education, 95, 36–44. https://doi.org/10.1016/j.compedu.2015.11.015

Sablić, M., Mirosavljević, A., & Škugor, A. (2021). Video-based learning (VBL)—past, present and future: An overview of the research published from 2008 to 2019. Technology, Knowledge and Learning, 26(4), 1061-1077.

Saldaña, J. (2015). The Coding Manual for Qualitative Researchers. Sage.

Santagata, R., & Taylor, K. (2018). Novice teachers' use of student thinking and learning as evidence of teaching effectiveness: A longitudinal study of video-enhanced teacher preparation. Contemporary Issues in Technology and Teacher Education, 18(1), 11-28.

Seo, K., Dodson, S., Harandi, N. M., Roberson, N., Fels, S., & Roll, I. (2021). Active learning with online video: The impact of learning context on engagement. Computers & Education, 165, 104132. https://doi.org/10.1016/j.compedu.2021.104132

Shorter, J., & Dean, R. (1994). Computing in collegiate schools of business: are mainframes & stand-alone microcomputers still good enough? Journal of Systems Management, 45(7), 36e41. https://doi.org/10.1080/07399019408960952

Schroeder, N. L., & Adesope, O. O. (2014). A systematic review of pedagogical agents' persona, motivation, and cognitive load implications for learners. Journal of Research on Technology in Education, 46(3), 229-251. https://doi.org/10.1080/15391523.2014.888272

Sweller, J. (1988). Cognitive load during problem solving: Effects on learning. Cognitive Science, 12(2), 257-285. https://doi.org/10.1207/s15516709cog1202_4

Yoon, M., Lee, J., & Jo, I.-H. (2021). Video learning analytics: Investigating behavioral patterns and learner clusters in video-based online learning. The Internet and Higher Education, 50, Article 100806. https://doi.org/10.1016/j.iheduc.2021.100806.

Yürüm, O. R., Yıldırım, S., & Taşkaya-Temizel, T. (2023). An intervention framework for developing interactive video lectures based on video clickstream behavior: a quasi-experimental evaluation. Interactive Learning Environments, 31(10), 6611-6626. https://doi.org/10.1007/s10758-023-09697-z

INVESTIGATING THE FUNCTIONALITY OF METACOGNITIVE PROMPT DURING THE CIRCUIT ANALYSIS PROBLEM-SOLVING

Jyoti Shaha, Vishwas Badhe and Ramkumar Rajendran
Indian Institute of Technology Bombay, India

ABSTRACT

Metacognitive strategies play a crucial role in Computer-Based Learning Environments (CBLEs). However, students often struggle to apply these strategies spontaneously during learning. Research demonstrates that metacognitive prompts can effectively guide students' awareness and help them monitor their learning progress, leading to improved outcomes. While studies have shown the benefits of metacognitive prompting in various domains such as clinical reasoning, biology, educational psychology, and social science, most focus on reading and writing tasks. There is limited research on problem-solving tasks, particularly in the engineering domain. To address this gap, we developed MetaGuru, a learning environment designed to stimulate learners' metacognitive strategies using prompts in electrical engineering circuit analysis problem-solving. In this paper we investigate the functionality of metacognitive prompts in engineering problem-solving with five participants. Participants solved circuit analysis problems within MetaGuru. We examined the functionality of prompts by collecting screen recordings and conducting semi-structured interviews. The findings reveal that while the orientation and planning prompts were effective, the monitoring and evaluation prompts showed limited effectiveness, highlighting the need for improvement in these areas.

KEYWORDS

Metacognition, Metacognitive Prompts, Engineering Problem-Solving, Computer-Based Learning Environment, Electrical Engineering

1. INTRODUCTION

Computer-based learning environments (CBLEs) are designed for instructional purposes and to support learners in achieving goals across various disciplines (Lajoie, S.P., Naismith, L. 2012, Aballe, K. S., et al. 2022)). Most CBLEs provide learning content through multimedia, text, images, animation, simulations, graphs, and Audio-video representation with tools (Fielding I. Winters, 2008, Jeffrey A. 2011). In CBLE, learners are allowed to follow their instructional path and have access to multiple representations of information and opportunities to manipulate them (Fielding I. Winters 2008). To access such information-rich environments, learners must make decisions and make an effective plan for spending their time and accessing the information, constantly identify relevant information, track progress toward the goal and sub goals, and make judgments of their learning (Jeffrey A. 2011). This highlights the importance of metacognitive skills for decision-making during learning and using strategic learning approaches (E Pieger, M Bannert 2018). Metacognitive skills refer to the planning, monitoring, control, and evaluation processes involved in learning and problem-solving (P Güner 2021, Jumari, N. F. 2022). Where planning refers to choosing appropriate strategies for the task, monitoring is an awareness of an individual's performance. Control and evaluation mean reviewing the process (Ochilova, V. R. 2021).

The underlying assumption is that learners know metacognitive skills. Still, they often struggle to recall or execute them spontaneously in a specific learning context. This phenomenon, a production deficit, can result in poorer learning outcomes (K Engelmann 2021). Educators often employ metacognitive prompting as an effective instructional strategy to address production deficits and promote self-regulated learning in CBLEs (M. Bannert. 2015; K Engelmann, 2021). Several Researchers have demonstrated that metacognitive prompts effectively guide students' awareness and facilitate self-monitoring during learning activities. This not only improves learners' metacognitive skills but also contributes to better overall learning outcomes (E Pieger, M

Bannert 2018, K Engelmann, M Bannert, N Melzner 2021, M. Bannert, C Sonnenberg, C Mengelkamp, E Pieger 2015, L Guo 2022).

Although extensive research has examined the effects of metacognitive prompts in computer-based learning environments (CBLEs) within social science and science domains, there remains a notable gap in the engineering domain. Also, current studies on metacognitive prompts have largely focused on reading and writing tasks, neglecting the realm of problem-solving. This research gap emphasizes a need for further exploration and empirical studies evaluating metacognitive prompts' impact and effectiveness within engineering domains' problem-solving contexts.

Problem-solving is the most essential factor for engineering graduates in the 21st century (Khairiyah Mohd-Yusof 2014). However, students enrolled in basic electrical engineering courses face difficulties while solving circuit analysis problems (Niebler, C. 2023). Due to a lack of metacognitive abilities, students may struggle to reach the correct answer despite having the necessary knowledge and formulas while solving circuit analysis problems (Murata, A., Ohta, Y., & Hayami, T. (2013). Students must develop and enhance their metacognitive skills to improve performance in basic electrical circuit problem-solving (Murata, A., Ohta, Y., & Hayami, T. (2013).

Hence, we designed and developed a learning environment named MetaGuru to support learners in basic electrical circuits' problem-solving. In this environment, metacognitive prompts are embedded to stimulate metacognitive skills while learners interact with the learning environment.

The primary objective of this paper is to analyze the functionality of metacognitive prompting during problem-solving process in MetaGuru. through learners' initial responses to them. To achieve this goal, we conducted a pilot study involving five participants interacting with MetaGuru. Our data collection methods included computer-generated trace data, screen recording, and semi-structured interviews, providing a comprehensive view of learners' interactions and experiences.

The following research questions are addressed in the present study:

RQ 1. What are the learners' initial responses to the metacognitive prompts in the circuit analysis problem-solving?

RQ 2. How well do learners understand the meaning of the metacognitive prompts in circuit analysis problem-solving?

The following sections will describe the theoretical framework (section 2), MetaGuru context, and embedded metacognitive prompts, followed by the learner interactions captured (section 3). Further, we describe the research goal, study design, and data collection for analyzing the functionality of metacognitive prompting (section 4). Finally, we report results and discussion (section 5), followed by a conclusion and future work (section 6).

2. THEORETICAL FRAMEWORK

2.1 Metacognition and Problem-Solving

Flavell introduced the concept of metacognition in the 1970s. Flavell (1979) proposed a model of metacognition comprising four interacting classes, i.e., goals, experiences, knowledge, and Strategies. Schraw proposed that metacognition includes two distinct components: knowledge of cognition and regulation of cognition. Knowledge of cognition encompasses three types of metacognitive awareness: declarative knowledge, procedural knowledge, and conditional knowledge. Regulation of cognition involves three key processes: planning, monitoring, and evaluation (Schraw, G., & Moshman, D. 1995). Desoete (2008) conceptualized metacognition as consisting of metacognitive knowledge and skills. There are four metacognitive skills: prediction, planning, monitoring, and evaluation. Whereas Efklides proposed that metacognition is a multifaceted phenomenon, Metacognitive Experience (ME), Metacognitive knowledge (MK), and Metacognitive skills (MS) are the three facets (Efklides 2008). Metacognitive knowledge (MK) is defined as knowledge of self and others, knowledge of tasks, and knowledge of multiple strategies. Metacognitive knowledge is continuously enriched, updated, and differentiated. Metacognitive Experience (ME) is what a person is aware of and can easily feel when across a task and processing related information, feeling of knowing, familiarity, and confidence, how a person feels in the context of problem-solving, i.e.,

Judgement of learning, an estimate of effort expenditure, an estimate of time needed or spent, an estimate of solution correctness, where metacognitive skills (MS)/strategies comprise orientation, strategy planning, regulation of cognitive processing, monitoring the execution of planned activities, and evaluation of the outcome of task processing (Efklides 2008).

Metacognition plays an important role in problem-solving (Flavell J. 1979). Metacognitive skills support learners in regulating the problem-solving process and deciding when and how to use knowledge and cognitive resources (Güner, P. & Erbay, H. N. 2021). Polya (1985) defines four phases of problem-solving. These phases are parallel to the skills in metacognition (Ader, 2019; Whitebread et al., 2009).

Table 1. Problem-solving phases mapping to the metacognitive skills (Güner, P. & Erbay, H. N. 2021)

Four phases of problem-solving (Polya 1985)	Metacognitive skills (Ader, 2019; Whitebread et al., 2009)
Understanding the problem	Planning
Making a plan	Monitoring
Carrying out the plan	Monitoring
Checking out the solution	Evaluation

2.2 Metacognitive Prompting

To address production deficit and stimulate metacognitive skills, metacognitive prompting is an effective instructional strategy in CBLE (M. Bannert. 2015; K Engelmann, 2021). Several studies have explored prompting use in CBLEs. For example, MetaTutor is a hypermedia-based intelligent tutoring system that incorporates virtual agents to assist students in developing effective learning strategies and metacognitive monitoring skills in biology. (Azevedo et al., 2018). BioWorld, a CBLE designed to support medical students in clinical problem-solving, provides conceptual, strategic, and metacognitive scaffolding during problem-solving tasks (Lajoie et al., 2013). Bannert and colleagues developed a hypermedia learning environment focusing on educational psychology topics. The learning environment involves reading and writing tasks to analyze the impact of metacognitive prompts on learning outcomes (Bannert et al., 2009; Bannert & Mengelkamp, 2013; Azevedo et al., 2018). These studies demonstrate the growing interest in implementing prompting strategies within diverse digital learning contexts to enhance metacognitive skills and learning outcomes.

3. METAGURU: LEARNING ENVIRONMENT

The following section introduces MetaGuru, a computer-based learning environment designed to assist students in solving problems in electrical engineering circuit analysis.

3.1 MetaGuru: Learning Environment

Freshman students in introductory electrical engineering courses often encounter difficulties when solving circuit analysis problems (Niebler, 2023). Despite possessing the necessary knowledge and formulas, students may struggle to arrive at correct solutions due to underdeveloped metacognitive abilities (Murata et al., 2013).

To address this challenge and the research gap outlined in the introduction, we developed MetaGuru. The primary objectives of MetaGuru are:

1. To stimulate learners' metacognitive strategies during circuit analysis problem-solving tasks.
2. To collect log data of learners' interactions with the learning environment.
3. To analyze the impact of metacognitive prompts on problem-solving performance.

MetaGuru's theoretical foundation is rooted in the instructional design framework for computer-based interactive content, as Zhang (2022) and David (1997) proposed. This framework guides the design of metacognitive scaffolds specifically tailored for problem-solving instruction. By incorporating these principles, MetaGuru aims to provide effective metacognitive support within the context of circuit analysis problem-solving. Figure 1 shows the screenshot of the MetaGuru earning environment.

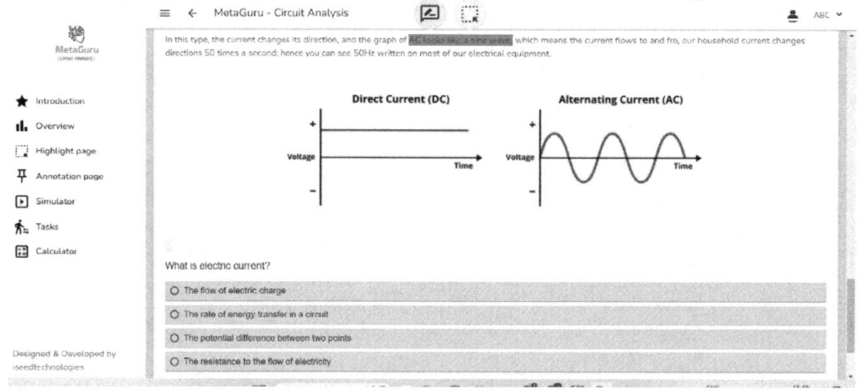

Figure 1. Screenshot of MetaGuru: Computer-based learning Environment

MetaGuru's learning materials encompass core topics in circuit analysis, including basic Concepts, DC circuits, and Circuit Theorems. These materials are presented through diverse media formats: Text, Videos, Pictures, and Solved examples. To promote self-assessment and comprehension, each sub-topic concludes with an assessment question that includes feedback. Additionally, assessment questions are integrated into the video content, reinforcing learning throughout the material. MetaGuru equipped users with a range of tools to support their learning. A countdown timer displays the remaining study time and begins to blink during the final ten minutes of the allocated period. This feature is designed to assist learners in efficiently managing their time during problem-solving tasks. The annotation tool enables learners to write interpretations of text by selecting specific passages. It allows them to enhance their comprehension by highlighting key points and appending their interpretations. The highlighter tool allows learners to emphasize text content by selecting specific passages and changing their background color. A MetaGuru incorporates a user-friendly circuit simulator called 'circuitjs1,' which allows learners to design and simulate electrical circuits. Learners can evaluate their solutions by comparing the simulated current with their calculated values. Metaguru allows learners navigation options to facilitate seamless movement through the learning content. By integrating these features, MetaGuru creates a comprehensive learning environment that addresses multiple facets of cognitive and metacognitive processes in circuit analysis problem-solving.

3.2 Metacognitive Prompts

Analyzing the existing literature, we curated a comprehensive list of metacognitive prompts that we integrated into our learning environment. The MetaGuru System employed a series of prompts strategically placed throughout the problem-solving journey. These prompts guided users towards effective strategies at each stage, enhancing their metacognitive strategies and problem-solving abilities.

Table 2 details the metacognitive prompts used in the MetaGuru and where they are placed. It shows the different steps of problem-solving mapped with metacognitive strategies and metacognitive prompts. Our system is structured around these five distinct prompts, each tailored to stimulate individuals through the orientation, planning, execution, and reflection phases of problem-solving

3.3 Log Data

This section describes the details of the interaction log data. The interaction log data of students using the MetaGuru provides a comprehensive overview of their engagement and activities within the system. This data captures a range of actions that detail how learners interact with different features and resources available in MetaGuru. Table 3 provides the details of the actions captured.

Table 2. Metacognitive prompts

Problem-solving process	Metacognitive skill	Metacognitive Prompts	Where they are placed
Represent Problem	Orientation	Think and write what specific concepts or techniques are needed to solve this problem successfully. (Q. Zang 2022)	On task page
Generate solution	Planning	What concepts or techniques do you think you need to revise or revisit to solve this problem? (Q. Zang 2022)	On task page
Generate solution	Monitoring	The information you are reading, is it relevant to solve this problem successfully? If yes, then write a summary of your understanding of the content you read. (Azevedo 2009)	On Every reading page
Present and evaluate	Evaluation	While working on your solution, have you thought about using a simulator to validate and confirm the accuracy of your answer? Think and write how you use a simulator to verify your answer.	On Solution page Before submitting solution
Reflect	Reflection	What did you gain as you worked through this problem? Write your understanding	On the solution page, after submitting the solution

Table 3. Problem-solving phases mapping to the metacognitive skills (Güner, P. & Erbay, H. N. 2021)

Actions captured	Metacognitive skill
System_access	Log in and log out to MetaGuru
Read	Course material is read
Video	Information about the video is played, paused, and seek
Highlight	Highlighting feature is used
Annotate	Highlighting feature is used
Highlight_View	The page where highlights are saved is viewed
Annotate_view	The page where annotations are saved is viewed
Calculator	Accessing calculator
Self_assessment_Question	Self-assessment question in video and text content is attempted
Prompt_Question	Metacognitive Prompt question is attempted
Simulator	Interacting with Simulator

4. METHODOLOGY

4.1 Study Design

Five learners (3 male, 2 female) first year of Engineering participated in the study voluntarily. The Institute Research Board (IRB) approved the study, and an informed consent form was obtained from all students. No monetary compensation was given to the students. The study was conducted in a lab setup to control the conditions wherein individual learners interacted with the MetaGuru for 120 min.

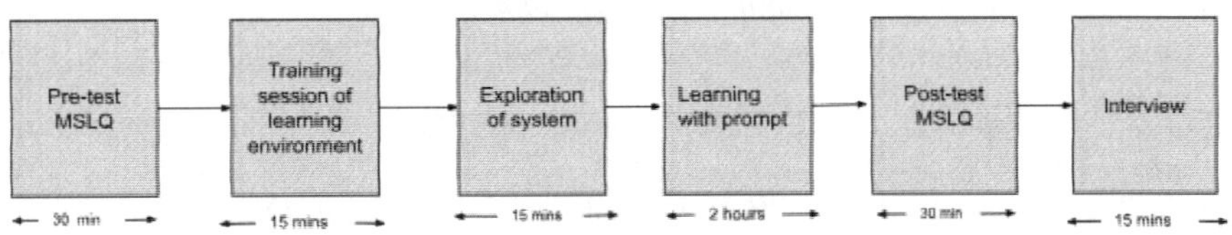

Figure 2. Design and procedure of research study

Figure 2 illustrates the study's detailed procedure. The learning activity took place over 2 hours, during which students interacted with the MetaGuru learning environment to solve three problems related to Thevenin's theorem. Students analyzed the circuits to find Thevenin's equivalent circuits, with the difficulty level increasing by the third problem. Students received different metacognitive prompts throughout this period to guide their problem-solving process.

4.2 Data Collection

Our study design incorporated three types of data collection methods to evaluate the overall experience with MetaGuru and the functionality of prompts. We collected interaction log data, screen recording, and semi-structured interview data. We captured interaction log data to investigate whether learners attempted the prompt. The screen recording is captured to analyze the learners' responses to the prompt. The final phase of the study involved individual interviews with the students, each lasting approximately 15 minutes. These semi-structured interviews aimed to gather students' perceptions of the MetaGuru learning environment and the prompts provided during the problem-solving session.

5. RESULT

This pilot study aimed to analyze learners' initial responses to the metacognitive prompts and the functionality of prompts through initial learner responses. We analyzed the initial response through log data and screen recording data.

Log data analysis revealed the following patterns in prompt attempts. The orientation prompt was attempted by 4 out of 5 learners. The reflection prompt was attempted by 3 out of 5 learners. The evaluation prompt was attempted by 2 out of 5 learners.

Screen recording analysis provided insights into learners' understanding and responses. 3 learners demonstrated understanding by providing expected answers to the orientation Prompt. These learners correctly outlined the steps to solve Thevenin's problem. Learner S1 correctly understood the evaluation Prompt and identified the use of the simulator for answer evaluation but did not use the simulator. Learner S2 suggested checking formulas and steps as an evaluation method. 3 out of 5 learners attempted the reflection prompt. These learners provided written reflections on their understanding of the problem-solving process.

To address RQ 2, first, we analyzed screen recording data capturing students' initial responses to the prompts. Second, we conducted semi-structured interviews to gather additional insights. Our analysis focused on assessing the functionality of the prompts.

Prompt functionality: We evaluated how well each prompt performed its intended metacognitive role. By combining data from screen recordings and interviews, we gained a comprehensive understanding of how students interacted with the prompts initially and how these interactions reflected the prompts' functionality. This approach allowed us to identify the strengths and potential areas for improvement in the MetaGuru system's metacognitive scaffolding.

To analyse the understanding of prompts, students were asked, "So this question is about prompts. Was the prompt helpful? How? Can you give an example?"

S5: "*The planning prompt was helpful to know how to solve the problem. Yes, after reading the prompt question, I started thinking of the answer that I have to do this, what will be the first step? What will be the second step? Before, I had an idea that yes we have to solve problems, But after this prompt question, I had a different idea that I have to go step-wise. Which step do we have to do first in the evidence Vth, Rth, Rl is the first one, So we solve it like that after reading the evaluation prompt.*"

The response of student S3 to the interview question: *"Planning prompt, writing steps on how to solve of the first task was helpful, the steps are helped in next tasks."*

The response of student S2 to the interview question: "*Orientation prompt attempted, It helps in writing the steps needed to solve the task.*"

The response of student S1 to the interview question: *"Monitoring prompt, questions were helpful but very repetitive. Like one question was repeated throughout a lot, so it was very tiring to answer the same questions again and again."*

S5 understood the evaluation prompt he reported *"I verified the answer, Whether the formulas were right or not, And Did I take any wrong steps. Not using a simulator to evaluate."*

S1 understood the evaluation prompt and reported, *"There was no time for me to go to the stimulator and check my answer. But yeah, I understood the prompt."*

Table 4. Overall functionality of prompts

Prompts	Overall Functionality of Prompt
Orientation	Effective for 4 out of 5 students
Planning	Effective, though ignored by S3
Monitoring	Needs improvement. All students ignored
Evaluation	Effective for some, but terminology (simulator) issues
Reflection	Effective though ignored by 2

Findings from the interview analysis shows that orientation and planning prompts generally worked well in helping students outline their steps for solving Thevenin's theorem, although there were cases of misunderstanding or ignoring. The monitoring prompt did not function as effectively as the others. All students ignored. There is need of improvement. The evaluation prompt helped some students verify their answer, but confusion about using a simulator. Needs Improvement. The reflection prompt worked well, encouraged students to think about their learning. Though two students ignored.

6. LIMITATIONS AND FUTURE PLAN

The limitation of this pilot study was the small sample size. Our next study aims to evaluate the revised MetaGuru version with a larger sample. Based on the insights from this pilot study, the future plan involves refining the prompts and the overall system to address the identified issues. Additionally, a more extensive study will be conducted to analyze the impact of these refined prompts on students' learning outcomes and metacognitive strategies.

7. CONCLUSION

This pilot study aimed to evaluate learners' initial responses to the metacognitive prompt and the functionality of prompts while problem-solving tasks. The findings reveal that the overall experience with MetaGuru was positive, with students, they attempted the prompts effectively. The effectiveness of the prompts varied significantly among participants. The planning and reflection prompts were generally well-received and provided valuable guidance in structuring the problem-solving process. Overall, the interactive and user-friendly nature of MetaGuru, coupled with well-designed planning and reflection prompts, can significantly enhance the learning experience. The prompts influenced the students' problem-solving strategies. However, prompt clarity, relevance, and design improvements are necessary to maximize their effectiveness. Based on the insights from this pilot study, the future plan involves refining the prompts and the overall system to address the identified issues. Additionally, a more extensive study will be conducted to analyze the impact of these refined prompts on students' learning outcomes and metacognitive strategies.

REFERENCES

Azevedo, R. et al. (2022). *Lessons Learned and Future Directions of MetaTutor: Leveraging Multichannel Data to Scaffold Self-Regulated Learning With an Intelligent Tutoring System. Frontiers in Psychology*, 13, p. 813632.

Bannert, M. and Reimann, P. (2012). *Supporting self-regulated hypermedia learning through prompts. Instructional Science*, 40, pp. 193-211.

Bannert, M. et al. (2015). *Short- and long-term effects of learners' self-directed metacognitive prompts on navigation behavior and learning performance*. Computers in Human Behavior, 52, pp. 293-306.

Brown, A.L. (1978). *Knowing when, where, and how to remember: A problem of metacognition. In: R. Glaser, ed. Advances in instructional psychology*. Erlbaum, Hillsdale, USA, pp. 77-165.

Efklides, A. (2008). *Metacognition: Defining its facets and levels of functioning in relation to self-regulation and co-regulation.* European Psychologist, 13(4), pp. 277-287.

Engelmann, K. et al. (2021). *Do self-created metacognitive prompts promote short- and long-term effects in computer-based learning environments? Research and Practice in Technology Enhanced Learning*, 16(1), p. 3.

Flavell, J. (1979). *Metacognition and Cognitive Monitoring A New Area of Cognitive—Developmental Inquiry*. American Psychologist, 34(10), p. 906.

Greene, J. et al. (2011). *Self-Regulation of Learning with Computer-Based Learning Environments. New directions for teaching and learning*, [online] Available at: https://doi.org/10.1002/tl449 [Accessed Date].

Guo, L. (2022). *Using metacognitive prompts to enhance self-regulated learning and learning outcomes: A meta-analysis of experimental studies in computer-based learning environments*. Journal of Computer Assisted Learning, 38(3), pp. 811-832.

Güner, P. and Erbay, H.N. (2021). *Metacognitive Skills and Problem-solving. International Journal of Research in Education and Science*, 7(3), pp. 715-734.

Hannafin, M. et al. (1999). *Open learning environments: Foundations, methods, and models. In: C. Reigeluth, ed. Instructional-Design Theories and Models: A New Paradigm of Instructional Theory. Lawrence Erlbaum Associates, Mahwah, USA, pp. 115-140.*

Jonassen, D.H. (1997). *Instructional Design Models for Well-Structured and Ill-Structured Problem-Solving Learning Outcomes*. Educational technology research and development, 45(1), pp. 65-94.

Jumari, N.F. et al. (2022). *Success factors in developing metacognitive skills among engineering students. In: AIP Conference Proceedings. AIP Publishing, 2433(1).*

Kim, Y.R. et al. (2013). *Multiple levels of metacognition and their elicitation through complex problem-solving tasks. The Journal of Mathematical Behavior, 32(3), pp. 377-396.*

Marra, R.M. et al. (2022). *Metacognition and the development of self-directed learning in a problem-based engineering curriculum.* Journal of Engineering Education, 111(1), pp. 137-161.

Mayer, C.W. et al. (2023). *Analysing domain-specific problem-solving processes within authentic computer-based learning and training environments by using eye-tracking: a scoping review.* Empirical Research in Vocational Education and Training, 15(1), p. 2.

Murata, A. et al. (2013). *Role of metacognition in basic electric circuit problem solving process*. In: HCI International 2013-Posters' Extended Abstracts: International Conference, HCI International 2013, Las Vegas, NV, USA, July 21-26, 2013, Proceedings, Part I 15. Springer Berlin Heidelberg, Berlin, Germany, pp. 442-446.

Niebler, C. (2023). *Overcome learning obstacles in circuit network analysis with flowcharts*. In: 2023 32nd Annual Conference of the European Association for Education in Electrical and Information Engineering (EAEEIE). IEEE, pp. 1-6.

Pieger, E. and Bannert, M. (2018). *Differential Effects of learners' self-directed metacognitive prompts. Computers in Human Behavior*, 86, pp. 165-173.

Schraw, G. and Dennison, R.S. (1994). *Assessing metacognitive awareness*. Contemporary educational psychology, 19(4), pp. 460-475.

Schraw, G. and Moshman, D. (1995). *Metacognitive theories. Educational psychology review*, 7, pp. 351-371.

Sun, L. et al. (2024). Review Flow: *Intelligent Scaffolding to Support Academic Peer Reviewing*. In: Proceedings of the 29th International Conference on Intelligent User Interfaces. pp. 120-137.

Van Der Graaf, J. et al. (2021). *Do Instrumentation Tools Capture SelfRegulated Learning?* In: LAK21: 11th International Learning Analytics and Knowledge Conference.

Wang, T. et al. (2023). *Computer-based scaffoldings influence learners' metacognitive monitoring and problem-solving efficiency in an intelligent tutoring system.* Journal of Computer Assisted Learning, 39(5), pp. 1652-1665.

Zhang, Q. and Lockee, B. (2022). *Designing a Framework to Facilitate Metacognitive Strategy Development in Computer-Mediated Problem-Solving Instruction*. Journal of Formative Design in Learning, 6, pp. 127-143.

Zheng, J. et al. (2023). *Supporting self-regulated learning in clinical problem-solving with a computer-based learning environment: the effectiveness of scaffolds*. Metacognition and Learning, 18(3), pp. 693-709.

UNDERSTANDING THE INFLUENCE OF PROGRAM OF STUDY AND AGE ON SHARED METACOGNITION WITHIN THE COMMUNITY OF INQUIRY IN STEM EDUCATION

Larisa Olesova[1], Ayesha Sadaf[2], Mihai Boicu[3], Harry J. Foxwell[3], Tram Leo Bao Pham[3] and Ioulia Rytikova[3]
[1]*University of Florida*
0502G Norman Hall, PO Box 117048 Gainesville, FL 32611, USA
[2]*University of North Carolina Charlotte*
9201 University City Boulevard Charlotte, NC 2822, USA
[3]*George Mason University*
MS#1G8 4511 Patriot Cir, Fairfax, VA 22030, USA

ABSTRACT

Graduate STEM students need to cultivate transferable skills for effective research before entering the workforce. This study examined the influence of STEM students' program of study (study (MS Data Analytics Engineering -DAEN, MS Applied Information Technology -AIT, PhD Information Technology - IT, MS INFS, and Accelerated MS Applied Information Technology -AIT) and age on their perceived shared metacognition (individual and group) within the Community of Inquiry (CoI) that consists of three presences–teaching, social and cognitive. 149 STEM students participated in the pre-developed inquiry-based research learning modules across different courses and course instructors during one semester. This study found that the program of study can influence cognitive presence (p=0.01) while age influences teaching presence (p=0.02) among three CoI presences. We did not find any influences for the shared metacognition based on the program of study or age. Students had similar perceptions of shared metacognition independent of their age group or the program of study. The findings will help others who are interested in shared metacognition for graduate STEM students.

KEYWORDS

Community of Inquiry, Shared Metacognition, STEM Education

1. INTRODUCTION

Current trends in Science, Technology, Engineering, and Math (STEM) Education dictate the need for more innovative learning approaches to equip a new generation of students with purposeful workforce-related skills. Inquiry-Based Learning (IBL) stands out as one of the most effective and promising instructional strategies to help STEM students develop a range of transferable skills, such as critical thinking, problem-solving, decision-making, and collaborative skills. These are the examples that industry, government, and other employment sectors expect current graduates to demonstrate, along with in-depth content-specific knowledge, by the time of their employment in the rapidly changing landscape of the STEM jobs market (Denecke et al., 2017). As educators actively look for innovative ideas to design IBL, learning that is designed based on the principles of the Community of Inquiry (CoI) shows good promise in its ability to support STEM students with the development of those needed transferrable skills. This design can help promote inquiry skills through collaboration where students learn from each other. CoI admits that IBL occurs at the intersection of the three presences: 1) social presence (SP); 2) teaching presence (TP); and 3) cognitive presence (CP). CP is the construction of meaning through reflection and discourse; SP is the ability to project oneself as an actual person both socially and emotionally in a learning environment; and TP is the design, facilitation, and direction of CP and SP (Garrison et al., 2001). The CoI requires collaborative learning where STEM students not only develop transferrable skills for their future workforce but also develop shared metacognitive skills. Shared metacognition is a cognitive ability to achieve meaningful learning that can be viewed from individual and collaborative perspectives. When shared metacognition is facilitated within the CoI, it can help regulate the cognitive processes of self and others within collaborative learning activities (Garrison & Akyol, 2015).

From an educational approach, knowledge of shared metacognition can guide the implementation of effective facilitation techniques in the collaborative IBL and realize meaningful learning outcomes. In the long term, shared metacognition is the key to understanding how to learn in a collaborative IBL. In our previous studies, we found that more than 80% of the participants who were enrolled in the IBL reported positive perceived shared metacognition across delivery methods (on-site and online) and students' status (domestic in the USA and international) (Olesova et al., 2023, 2024). We also found that international students perceived higher shared metacognition than domestic students. Similarly, on-site students perceived shared metacognition higher than online students. These findings are consistent across all the exploratory studies we have been collecting from Fall 2022 until Spring 2024. While the findings show consistency across the students' status and course delivery mode, our other findings haven't still revealed any consistent patterns on how STEM students' program of study (MS Data Analytics Engineering -DAEN, MS Applied Information Technology -AIT, PhD Information Technology - IT, MS INFS, and Accelerated MS Applied Information Technology -AIT) and age can influence shared metacognition when they are enrolled in the IBL. Arbaugh et al. (2010) found that the program of study influences the students' perceptions of SP, TP, and CP within the CoI in the applied disciplines. The hard, applied disciplines such as engineering and nursing have an emphasis on problem-solving while soft, applied disciplines such as health sciences emphasize transferrable skills for reflective practice and lifelong learning. CP is higher among health disciplines than engineering and nursing. Shea and Bidjerano (2009) found that the program of study can influence how students perceive SP and CP differently while students' academic level can influence the TP. However, Garrison et al. (2010) did not find differences in how the program of study can influence CP. Previous studies on how age influences CoI did not reveal significant differences (Horzum, 2015; Shea & Bidjerano, 2009). However, Akyol et al. (2010) found that young people between the ages of 18 and 22, and elderly between the ages of 48 and 62, perceived CP and TP as the same element of learning. Therefore, our study is an attempt to understand the influence of STEM students' program of study and their age on their perceived shared metacognition within the CoI when students participated in IBL. The research questions were: 1) What is the influence of the STEM students' program of study on the perceived shared metacognition within the CoI in IBL? and 2) What is the influence of the STEM students' age on the perceived shared metacognition within the CoI in IBL?

2. METHODS

This exploratory study used quantitative research methods to examine the influence of the program of study and age on students' perceptions of shared metacognition within the CoI. STEM students were enrolled in IBL courses that were offered both on-site and online in the spring of 2024. The IBL courses in STEM used pre-developed three generic research learning modules and were implemented into three domain-specific courses. The research modules were implemented across different courses and instructors with one common learning goal to introduce students to research activities gradually, consistently, and systematically. The research modules were implemented into the following courses: 1) Algorithms and Data Structures Essentials through a project-based approach intended to put the basis of quantitative research by analyzing various sorting and searching methods on different data samples and comparing their efficiency; 2) Database Management Systems through a research paper to support students in developing and applying research skills to explore and produce creative solutions to relevant industry problems of their choice in data science fundamental knowledge and core data analytics technologies; and 3) Analytics: Big Data to Information through a hands-on, project-based approach to understanding and practicing the nature of data and data analytics, with a focus on the tools and methods of data exploration, statistical summarization, and effective visualization. The final project is prepared and presented in the form of a traditional research report. Three learning modules follow real-world research processes (identifying questions, conducting literature reviews, and performing research). Each module is based on a generic template that includes the following sections: 1)

Selected and annotated learning materials of textbooks, papers, and videos. All materials are grouped into three categories: (a) required: to build a strong foundation in scientific knowledge and understanding, (b) recommended: to provide additional examples and illustrations on the topics covered in the required section, (c) optional: to support students interested in going beyond the required level; 2) Knowledge tests include tests to assess mastery, featuring 10 randomized questions from a large pool of questions in multiple-choice, true/false, and fill-in-the-blank formats. These tests can be retaken as needed, with only the highest score counting towards the final grade; 3) Discussion boards facilitate engagement by having students post drafts and provide meaningful feedback on peers' work; 4) Self-reflection is based on the collaborative assignment where students summarize their experience on the discussion board, present and provide an explanation of one suggestion to improve their assignment or one aspect that they learned or was challenging related to the assignment; and 5) A written assignment aims at organizing their findings, making connections, elaborating ideas, and constructing an argument based on the research they have conducted.

2.1 Participants

A purposefully self-selected sample of 149 graduate STEM students were enrolled in five sections of the three selected Applied Information Technology (AIT) courses that participated in this study in the spring of 2024. All participants were from a public university in the Mid-Atlantic area of the USA. The majority (44.30%, n=66) were from other STEM areas while 39 (26.17%) were from computer science, 38(25.50%) were from information technology, and only six (4.03%) were non-STEM students. Out of 149 students, 87 participants were from MS DAEN; 43 from MS AIT; 10 from PhD IT, 5 from MS INFS, and 4 from Accelerated MS AIT (Figure 1). From this, more than double were taught on-site (n=102/68.46%) compared with online (n=47/31.54%). The sample was 46 (30.87%) domestic students in the USA and 103 (69.13%) international students outside of the USA. Most of the participants were male (60.14%, n = 89) while there were 59 females (39.86%) and approximately half (68.24%, n = 101) of them were 24 or below years old (Figure 2).

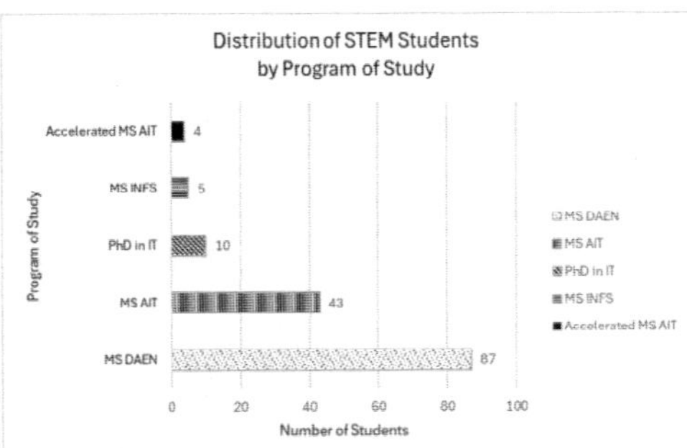

Figure 1. By the program of study (n=149)

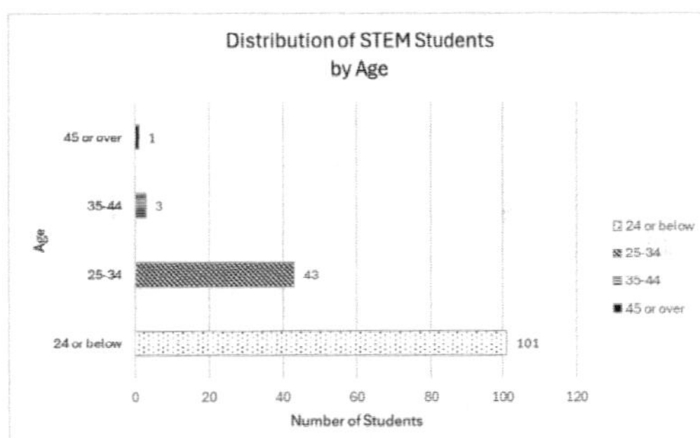

Figure 2. By age (n=149)

2.2 Data Collection and Analysis

The data were collected from the end-of-the-semester anonymous survey based on the 24 shared metacognition items constructed by Garrison and Akyol (2015) at the five-point Likert scale anchored by "Strongly Disagree" and "Strongly Agree." To analyze the CoI, we used the 16 CoI survey items on a five-point Likert scale where five is "Extremely Agree" and one is "Extremely Disagree." The CoI survey was validated with Cronbach's Alpha and yielded internal consistencies equal to 0.94 for TP, 0.91 for SP, and 0.95 for CP (Arbaugh et al., 2008). For this study, to examine shared metacognition, we adjusted the original 16 CoI items for the context of our study. We used the five-point Likert scale anchored by "Very Dissatisfied" and "Very Satisfied." All students were contacted via announcements and asked to complete the survey for bonus points. The collected survey data were analyzed by descriptive statistics to understand the overall patterns across all the sections and track descriptive differences between STEM students by their age and the program of study. Then, we ran a t-test to understand the statistical differences between the age and the program of study. Finally, we applied ANOVA to understand statistical differences across the programs of study.

3. RESULTS AND DISCUSSION

3.1 By the Program of Study

To see if there is a significant difference between the answers based on their program of study, we performed ANOVA tests for each of the categories. The answers to all the questions in a category were averaged per each student and then a single factor ANOVA test was applied for these averages. For instance, for the individual shared metacognition the results are presented in the table below.

Table 1. ANOVA single factor summary by the program of study (n=149)

	Count	Sum	Average	SD
Accelerated MS AIT	4	16.38	4.10	0.62
MS AIT	43	188.54	4.38	0.80
MS DAEN	87	382.60	4.40	0.77
MS INFS	5	21.85	4.37	1.09
PhD in IT	10	41.38	4.14	0.77

Table 2. ANOVA single factor results for the program of study

	SS	df	MS	F	p-value	F crit
Between Groups	0.91	4	0.23	0.37	0.83	2.43
Within Groups	89.35	144	0.62			
Total	90.26	148				

The results indicate that students had similar individual shared metacognition perception in all programs of study (p=0.83). Similar global results were obtained for the other criteria except for CP for which the means were reported as different (p=0.045). For CP, the ANOVA single factor test indicated that there is a difference between groups by the program of study (p=0.045<0.05). Further, to get a clearer image of the differences between the two most representative groups (MS DAEN and MS AIT) we performed t-tests for each of the questions and the cumulative results. All the answers were similar except for the following questions (for the first three the results of the t-test are included). It is important to remark that in all these situations the average results of the MS AIT were lower than the average of MS DAEN.

Table 3. T-test results for shared metacognition differences by the program of study (n=149)

Shared Metacognition Survey Items	MS DEAN	MS AIT	t-test p-value
Item 8: When I am engaged in the learning process as a member of a GROUP in the Discussion Boards in the Research Modules [I request information from others.]	M=4.34 SD=0.90	M=3.91 SD=1.23	p=0.013
Item 10: When I am engaged in the learning process as a member of a GROUP in the Discussion Boards in the Research Modules [I help the learning of others.]	M=4.41 SD=0.92	M=4.09 SD=1.06	p=0.039
Item 11: When I am engaged in the learning process as a member of a GROUP in the Discussion Boards in the Research Modules [I monitor the learning of others.]	M=4.23 SD=1.04	M=3.84 SD=1.35	p=0.035

Table 4. T-test results for the CoI differences by the program of study (n=149)

CoI Survey Items	MS DEAN	MS AIT	t-test p-value
The instructor communicated important course goals (TP).	M=4.68 SD=0.66	M=4.40, SD=1.00	*p*=0.02
The instructor helped to keep course participants engaged and participating in productive dialogue (TP).	M=4.65 SD=0.62	M=4.40, SD=1.11	*p*=0.05
Getting to know other course participants gave me a sense of belonging in the course (SP).	M=4.43 SD=0.71	M=4.00, SD=1.31	*p*=0.01
I felt comfortable interacting with other course participants (SP).	M=4.49 SD=0.73	M=4.20, SD=1.08	*p*=0.03
Research module activities enhanced my curiosity (CP).	M=4.45 SD=0.76	M=4.05, SD=1.29	*p*=0.01
I felt motivated to explore course content-related questions (CP).	M=4.51 SD=0.66	M=4.02, SD=1.14	*p*=0.00
I utilized a variety of provided information sources to explore the topics in research modules (CP).	M=4.49 SD=0.70	M=4.23, SD=0.95	*p*=0.04
Research learning activities helped me construct explanations/solutions about my selected research topic (CP).	M=4.55 SD=0.61	M=4.21, SD=1.08	*p*=0.04
Reflection on research module content and discussions helped me understand fundamental concepts in this class (CP).	M=4.53 SD=0.61	M=4.21, SD=1.08	*p*=0.02
I can describe ways to test and apply the research knowledge created in this course (CP).	M=4.52 SD=0.70	M=4.16, SD=1.11	*p*=0.01
Based on my research experience, I can describe ways to test and apply the domain knowledge created in this course (CP).	M=4.52 SD=0.71	M=4.07, SD=1.20	*p*=0.00
In my research activities, I have developed solutions to course problems that can be applied in practice (CP).	M=4.52 SD=0.71	M=4.05, SD=1.20	*p*=0.00
Based on my research activities, I can develop solutions to problems that can be applied in practice (CP).	M=4.53, SD=0.71	M=4.07, SD=1.26	*p*=0.00
I can apply the research knowledge created in this course to my work or other non-class related activities (CP).	M=4.48, SD=0.76	M=4.16, SD=1.02	*p*=0.02
CP Overall	M=4.49, SD=0.62	M=4.17, SD=0.98	*p*=0.01

3.2 By Age

To see if there is a significant difference based on their age, we performed ANOVA tests for each of the categories. The answers to all the questions in a category were averaged per each student and then a single factor ANOVA test was applied for these averages. For instance, for the individual shared metacognition the results are presented in Tables 5-6 below.

Table 5. ANOVA single factor summary by the STEM students' age (n=149)

	Count	Sum	Average	Variance	t-test p-value
24 or below	101	446.35	4.42	0.52	0.60
25-34	43	181.94	4.23	0.87	
35-44	3	13	4.33	0.33	0.39

Table 6. ANOVA single factor results by the STEM students' age (n=149)

	SS	df	MS	F	p-value	F crit
Between Groups	1.07	2	0.54	0.87	0.42	3.06
Within Groups	88.78	144	0.62			
Total	89.85	146				

The results indicate that students had similar individual shared metacognition perception independent of their age group (p=0.42). Similar global results were obtained for the other criteria. Further, to get a clearer image of the differences between the most representative two groups (24 or below and 25-34), we performed t-tests for each of the questions and the cumulative results. All the answers were similar except for the following questions below. It is important to remark that in all these situations the average results of the 25-34 were lower than 24 or below (Tables 7-8).

Table 7. T-test results for shared metacognition differences by the STEM students' age (n=149)

Shared Metacognition Survey Items	24 or below	25-34	t-test
I am aware of my level of motivation.	M=4.50, SD=0.81	M=4.21, SD=1.05	p=0.038
I question my thoughts.	M=4.31, SD=0.93	M=3.95, SD=1.15	p=0.028
I observe how others are doing.	M=4.39, SD=0.95	M=4.07, SD=1.08	p=0.04

Table 8. T-test results for the CoI differences by the STEM students' age (n=149)

CoI Survey Items	24 or below	25-34	t-test
The instructor provided clear instructions on how to participate in course learning activities (TP).	M=4.66 SD=0.62	M=4.42 SD=0.93	p=0.03
The instructor communicated important due dates/time frames for learning activities (TP).	M=4.69 SD=0.66	M=4.44 SD=1.02	p=0.04
The instructor helped identify areas of agreement and disagreement on course topics that helped me to learn (TP).	M=4.64 SD=0.66	M=4.35 SD=1.02	p=0.02
The instructor helped to keep course participants engaged and participating in productive dialogue (TP).	M=4.64 SD=0.64	M=4.33 SD=1.06	p=0.01
The instructor helped keep the course participants on task in a way that helped me to learn (TP).	M=4.64 SD=0.64	M=4.30 SD=1.01	p=0.01
The instructor encouraged course participants to explore new concepts in this course (TP).	M=4.66 SD=0.66	M=4.26 SD=1.07	p=0.00
Instructor actions reinforced the development of a sense of community among course participants (TP).	M=4.61 SD=0.69	M=4.37 SD=0.95	p=0.05
The instructor helped to focus the discussion on relevant issues in a way that helped me to learn (TP).	M=4.60 SD=0.68	M=4.37 SD=0.93	p=0.05
The instructor provided feedback that helped me understand my strengths and weaknesses relative to the course goals and objectives (TP).	M=4.59 SD=0.69	M=4.30 SD=1.01	p=0.02
The instructor provided feedback in a timely fashion (TP).	M=4.63 SD=0.67	M=4.35 SD=0.95	p=0.02
TP Overall	**M=4.64 SD=0.60**	**M=4.37 SD=0.91**	**p=0.02**
Research module activities enhanced my curiosity (CP)	M=4.40 SD=0.68	M=4.12 SD=1.12	p=0.05
I utilized a variety of provided information sources to explore the topics in research modules.	M=4.46 SD=0.73	M=4.21 SD=0.94	p=0.04
Based on my research experience, I can describe ways to test and apply the domain knowledge created in this course (CP).	M=4.48 SD=0.79	M=4.09 SD=0.99	p=0.01
In my research activities, I have developed solutions to course problems that can be applied in practice (CP).	M=4.46 SD=0.79	M=4.14 SD=0.99	p=0.02
Based on my research activities, I can develop solutions to problems that can be applied in practice (CP).	M=4.49 SD=0.79	M=4.12 SD=1.05	p=0.01

4. DISCUSSION

Our findings indicate that although students exhibited similar perceptions of individual shared metacognition across all programs of study, global results demonstrated significant influences on CP related to the program of study. Additionally, we observed that age shows noticeable differences in TP and CP across different age groups within the CoI framework.

4.1 Influence of Program of Study

Our analysis revealed that students enrolled in different STEM programs demonstrated varying levels of CP, with a notable difference between the MS DAEN and MS in AIT programs. Similarly to Arbaugh et al. (2010), we can assume how hard, applied disciplines can influence the CP to compare with soft, applied disciplines where reflection and transferrable skills are emphasized. More analysis should be completed to understand this phenomenon in more detail. However, this variation could be explained, to some extent, by the different curricular emphases and admission criteria of the two programs. For instance, the DAEN program, with its strong focus on data science and analytics, specifically enhances CP through rigorous statistical analysis and data-driven decision-making. This approach aligns with the findings of Garrison et al. (2001), who identified CP as a crucial element for meaningful learning. Conversely, the MS AIT program, while also fostering complex problem-solving, offers a comprehensive curriculum that extends beyond the focused technical training of programs like MS DAEN, covering a broader spectrum of IT topics. The observed differences between MS DAEN and MS AIT students indicate that cognitive engagement is not uniformly experienced even within STEM disciplines. This finding reinforces that curriculum design, rather than merely discipline, plays a crucial role in shaping cognition and metacognitive skills (Al-Gaseen et al., 2020). This shows that cognitive engagement in STEM is not solely dependent on individual students' capabilities but also on how the curriculum demands critical reflection, analysis, and integration of knowledge. It places a strong emphasis on practical implementation, equipping students with the necessary skills to oversee and guide IT operations within organizations.

4.2 Age and Its Effects on Teaching Presence

Our results indicate that perceptions of shared metacognition among STEM students do not significantly differ based on age, revealing no strong age-related trends. This finding reinforces prior research by Al-Gaseen et al. (2020), who also found that STEM students' metacognitive skills weren't different in gender and class standing. This suggests that educational approaches to developing metacognition could be universally effective across different age groups. However, a closer examination through t-tests of two key age groups, those 24 or below and those between 25-34, reveals subtle variances in specific aspects, with the latter group consistently scoring lower. Aligning with the findings of Akyol et al. (2010), our study suggests that while the overall perception of metacognitive practices may not vary, the depth and way these practices are engaged could differ slightly between younger and older students. This is consistent with observations by Akyol et al. (2010) that different age groups may perceive learning objectives and the educational process differently, potentially influencing their engagement and the outcomes of their learning experiences. These findings reinforce the necessity of adopting more personalized educational strategies that effectively support the unique cognitive needs of different age groups to optimize learning outcomes. This study aligns with Kovanović et al. (2015), who advocate for a more refined course design approach that considers the specific cognitive challenges presented by different STEM disciplines.

5. FUTURE RESEARCH

More research on STEM students' demographic background, such as age and program study is needed. Specifically, how hard applied programs of study influence overall students' perception of CP and TP when they are enrolled in IBL courses. In addition, while this study focused on perceived shared metacognition, future studies could explore objective measures of shared metacognition, such as the quality of group discussions or performance outcomes. This would offer a more comprehensive understanding of how metacognitive awareness manifests in IBL and its direct impact on STEM students' learning outcomes. Additionally, expanding this research to include a broader range of STEM disciplines could provide further insights into how instructional design and program characteristics shape shared metacognition.

6. CONCLUSION

This exploratory study's findings significantly contributed to the field of teaching and learning in IBL environments, specifically in STEM Education. Moreover, this study's findings revealed that more attention needs to be provided to how the program of study and students' age can influence shared metacognition within the CoI. While the influence of the program of study on CP and age on TP highlights the varied ways in which students engage with the learning process, the lack of a significant relationship between either program or age and shared metacognition suggests that the development of metacognitive skills occurs independently of these factors. This finding is crucial for educators and curriculum designers, as it indicates that shared metacognition can be cultivated across diverse student populations, regardless of their academic program or age group.

REFERENCES

Akyol, Z. et al. (2010). The Relationship Between Course Socio-Epistemological Orientations and Student Perceptions of Community of Inquiry. *Internet and Higher Education,* Vol. 13, No.1-2, pp. 66-68.

Al-Gaseem, M. et al. (2020). Metacognitive Thinking Skills Among Talented Science Education Students. *Journal for the Education of Gifted Young Scientists*, Vol. 8, No. 2, pp 897–904. https://doi.org/10.17478/jegys.707205

Arbaugh, J. et al. (2010). Subject Matter Effects and the Community of Inquiry (CoI) Framework: An Exploratory Study. *The Internet and Higher Education,* Vol. 13, No.1–2, pp. 37–44.

Denecke, D. et al. (2017). *Professional Development: Shaping Effective Programs for STEM Graduate Students.* Council of Graduate Schools.

Garrison, D. R. and Akyol, Z. (2015). Toward the Development of a Metacognition Construct for the Community of Inquiry Framework. *Internet and Higher Education,* Vol. 24, pp. 66–71.

Garrison, D. R. et al. (2001). Critical Thinking, Cognitive Presence, and Computer Conferencing in Distance Education. *American Journal of Distance Education,* Vol. 15, No.1, pp. 7-23.

Garrison, D. R. et al. (2010). Exploring Causal Relationships Between Teaching, Cognitive and Social Presence: Student Perceptions of the Community of Inquiry Framework. *The Internet and Higher Education,* Vol. 13, No. 1-2, pp. 31-36.

Horzum, M. B. (2015). Online Learning students` perceptions of the community of inquiry based on learning outcomes and demographic variables. *Croatian Journal of Education,* Vol. 17, No. 2, pp. 535-567.

Kovanović, V. et al. (2015). Analytics of Communities of Inquiry: Effects of Learning Technology Use on Cognitive Presence in Asynchronous Online Discussions. *The Internet and Higher Education*, Vol. 27, pp. 74-89.

Olesova, L. et al. (2024). Transforming STEM Education Through Inquiry-Based Collaborative Approach: Examination of Metacognition and Cognitive Presence. *The American Society for Engineering Education Southeastern Section Meeting.* Marietta, USA.

Olesova, L. et al. (2023). Metacognition in Graduate Engineering Courses. *The 2023 American Society for Engineering Education Annual Conference & Exposition.* Baltimore, USA.

Shea, P. and Bidjerano, T. (2009). Community of Inquiry as a Theoretical Framework to Foster ''Epistemic Engagement" and ''Cognitive Presence" in Online Education. *Computers & Education,* Vol. 52, No.3, pp. 543-553.

DEVELOPMENT AND VALIDATION OF THE 3S-T E-LEARNING EDUCATIONAL MODEL TO MEASURE EDUCATIONAL ICT USAGE AND THE IMPACT OF COVID-19 PANDEMIC ON HIGHER EDUCATION. MODERATING CROSS CULTURAL TENDENCIES

Mónica Martínez Gómez[1*], Eliseo Bustamante García[1] and César Berna Escriche[1, 2]
[1]*Departamento de Estadística, Investigación Operativa Aplicadas y Calidad, Universtitat Politècnica de Valencia (UPV), Camino de Vera s/n, Building 7-A, 46022 Valencia, Spain, Tel. +34 963877490 / Fax. +34 963877499*
[2]*Instituto de Ingeniería Energética, Universtitat Politècnica de Valencia (UPV), Camino de Vera s/n, Building 8-E, 46022 Valencia, Spain, Tel. +34 963879245*

ABSTRACT

E-learning was a vital tool for education during the global lockdown, as it was the only alternative for billions of students worldwide to continue learning amid the COVID-19 crisis. However, despite the importance and relevance of E-learning, there is a significant lack of studies that examine E-learning success under heterogeneity effects, such as gender, cross-cultural, or level of education. A clear and comprehensive framework that encompasses all necessary e-learning services is crucial to ensure their effective implementation, use, and impact on student learning and achievement. For this purpose, we used a new version of the original 3S-T model that measured the E-learning success based on self-student assessment through a survey study with 136 students from the Universitat Politècnica de València (Spain) and 81 from the Central University of Ecuador (Ecuador). This model that expands the existing theoretical framework of models related to E-Learning (Technology Acceptance Model (TAM), Extensions of TAM model, and Information Systems Success Model (ISSM) identifies a broad range of success predictors that help to achieve success, such as learning and academic outcomes. The success predictors include factors related to the surrounding conditions, the system features, the tutor's development, the student's performance, accessibility, interactivity, content quality, assessment methods, learning outcomes, and student engagement. This conference paper uses a multigroup Analysis (MGA) using Partial Least Squares (PLS-SEM) to evaluate moderation across both countries over the depurate 3S-T model, including the assessment measurement invariance of composite models (MICOM) procedure.

KEYWORDS

3S-T model, E-learning Methodology, Student Self-Assessment, Multigroup Analysis (MGA), PLS-SEM

1. INTRODUCTION

Information and Communication Technologies (ICT) have undergone significant advancements in recent decades, leading to numerous changes across various disciplines (Zhao et al., 2022). Specifically, the COVID-19 pandemic forced changes in the educational response, involving the intensive use of ICT, among other interventions. The rapid development of new technologies has led to the creation of new products, markets, processes, and services. Education is one field that has been greatly impacted by these technologies, giving rise to significant changes. The use of these new technologies on a global scale has introduced new learning paradigms such as E-Learning and mobile learning, replacing the traditional face-to-face classroom. E-Learning has proven to be a crucial resource, enabling learning to continue during the COVID-19 lockdown (Baber, 2021).

* Corresponding Author
ORCID: 0000-0003-2401-9403
e-mail corresponding author: momargo@eio.upv.es

Following the description in the previous paragraph, e-learning has proven to be the most utilized method for accessing remote educational resources with the aid of computers, laptops, tablets, internal networks, and any other current technological device. This utilization of the latest technologies provides an additional advantage in an ever-changing field such as education, where the teaching-learning process must remain dynamic. Unlike traditional forms of learning, E-Learning has many advantages, among which quick and smooth communication can be mentioned, allowing greater access to educational material and greatly facilitating the possibility of academic collaboration between students and teachers. In summary, E-Learning systems should be considered a major advancement, as these systems can even compensate for the weaknesses of traditional learning methods, in addition to offering the possibility of extending knowledge to a greater number of students, since even when located on the other side of the world, the student-teacher relationship can continue without major impediments. Therefore, leveraging all these possibilities offered by new technologies provides great opportunities for young people and anyone seeking to learn about any field of knowledge. However, once E-Learning has been implemented, in order to assess whether its implementation truly represents an improvement over traditional classroom-based education, it is essential to have tools to measure the degree of success achieved. In order to obtain information about the added value provided, the effect of management operations, and the return on investment, this measurement/estimation of the success of E-Learning initiatives has been widely researched since the early years of distance education. Among the studies related to this evaluation of E-Learning success, a recent model, the 3S-T model (Martínez-Gómez et al., 2022) based on different theoretical frameworks, has been validated with a sample of high school students to assess student satisfaction and E-Learning performance. The 3S-T model builds upon various previous models, such as the Technology Acceptance Model (TAM) (Davis, 1989), the revised D&M model (Venkatesh and Davis, 2000) and the Information Systems Success or D&M Model (Delone and McLean, 2003).

The TAM suggests that three particular beliefs, PU, PEOU, and PE, are the primary drivers for explaining and predicting user acceptance of IS (Sánchez and Hueros, 2010). PU is defined as 'the degree to which a person believes that using a particular system would enhance their job performance,' and PEOU is defined as 'the degree to which a person believes that using a particular system would be free from physical and mental effort' (Davis et al., 1989). The revised D&M model includes six dimensions: (1) information quality, (2) system quality, (3) service quality, (4) use/intention to use, (5) user satisfaction, and (6) net benefits (Delone and McLean, 1992 and 2003). After the completion of the D&M Model, many researchers argued that the D&M model was incomplete; and many additional measures have been proposed and used to capture the system quality construct in its entirety (del Barrio-García et al., 2015; Adetimirin, 2015).

This conference paper presents the capability of the 3S-T model for measuring the performance of E-learning systems based on students' academic achievements and learning outcomes. Its primary purpose is to evaluate the validation of this 3S-T model in higher education students, which was also proposed by the current authors (Martínez-Gómez et al., 2022), and to assess the moderating effect of cross-cultural tendencies. This model provides a quantifiable tool to better understand the factors influencing students' E-learning, and not only this, but also to estimate the importance of each of them. In this regard, the current model is not only capable of conducting the measurement of importance for each validated construct, but also the relationships between the measurement model and the structural model were determined. Therefore, the objective of this research is to examine the acceptance of E-learning among university students from different nationalities, so that conclusions can be drawn about the differences and similarities between them. It should be noted that the 3S-T model was validated in a previous study only with high school students, subsequently in further studies on students from a single university, so within the framework of this study, it has been extended to university students from two countries on different continents, although presenting certain similar cultural traits, namely Spain and Ecuador.

2. THEORETICAL FRAMEWORK

E-learning is a contemporary educational method that uses technology to access resources remotely, offering advantages over traditional learning. It saves time and money, enhances retention, provides accessibility to teaching material, and facilitates fast communication and academic collaboration.

Authors vary in their definitions, with some considering it the delivery of learning content and activities, while others perceive it as an information system integrating various educational resources and tools.

Assessing the success of an e-learning system involves multiple models, such as the Information Systems Success Model (ISSM), TAM, User Satisfaction Model (USM), and E-Learning Quality (ELQ) models.

This study incorporates insights from various theories and acceptance models in the literature to establish a comprehensive and inclusive definition of E-learning and assess its success. In this context, the authors introduced a novel model, the 3S-T model, which enhances and integrates aspects of the ISSM, TAM, USM, and ELQ. This model underwent development and testing based on analyzing approximately 300 questionnaires from secondary school students (Martínez-Gómez et al., 2022). The current study extends this evaluation to university students of two countries, testing the 3S-T model's capabilities and assessing its performance. The aim of this work is twofold. On the one hand, to validate the 3S-T model in higher students of Ecuador and secondly, to capture the distinct characteristics of both cross-cultural universities for a better understanding of the model's effectiveness.

3. CONCEPTUAL ANALISIS

In our study, a version of the validated 3S-T model has been used to identify the major dimensions that significantly impact E-learning achievements, which also considers the four most widely used approaches for evaluating E-learning over the past decades. These dimensions include Social aspects, Student factors, System factors, and Tutor's capabilities. We further divided the student's factors into three sub-factors: individual factors, user beliefs, technology acceptance, and the student's performance. Student satisfaction has consistently emerged as a robust indicator for measuring the success of E-learning implementations (Kerzic et al., 2021; Sun et al., 2008; Eom et al., 2006; Gray & DiLoreto, 2016; Marks et al., 2005) and Student Learning Achievements (SSA) have been extensively employed as an evaluation mechanism in the field of education (León et al., 2021; Ganji, 2017). SSA emerges as a potent tool for assessing the effectiveness of E-learning strategies in higher education. Hence, it becomes imperative to employ group comparison analysis to assess the moderating effect of individual-level cultural values on users' acceptance of E-learning in different countries that help education authorities and institutions review and rethink their particular strategies.

The version of 3S-T model comprises five independent constructs: technical system quality, information quality, self-efficacy, subjective norm, and tutor quality and preserves the nine dependent constructs: perceived satisfaction, perceived usefulness, use as sustainability, student satisfaction, engagement, strategy student satisfaction, students' self-assessment, and student learning achievements, as we can see in Figure 1. A description of each construct that includes some variables related to the COVID-19 pandemic, along with the indicators utilized to represent them, supported by relevant studies, can be found in Martínez-Gómez et al. (2022).

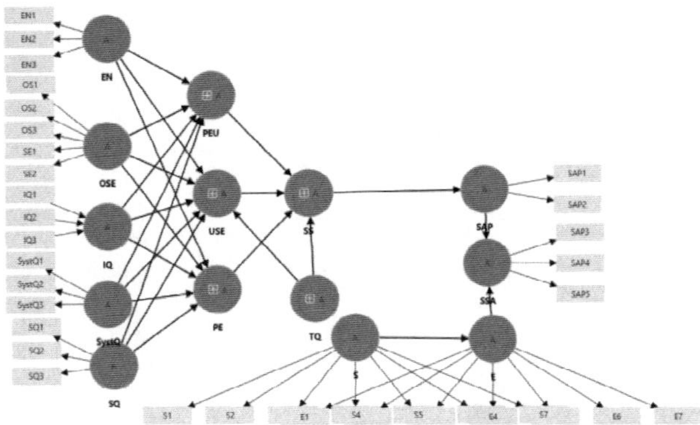

Figure 1. Validated 3S-T model version used in this study.
Note: OLE, Online Learning Environment; OLSE Online learning self-efficacy; OSE, One-Self Efficacy; PE, Perceived Enjoyment; PEU, Perceived Usefulness; S, Strategy; SAP, Student Academic Performance; SN, Subjective Norm; SEQ; Service Quality; SQ, System Quality; SS, Student Satisfaction; SSA, Student Self-Assessment

4. RESEARCH METHOD

In this study, we performed a two-step analysis. In the first step, a confirmatory analysis (CFA) with structural equation modeling using partial least squares SEM (PLS-SEM) was used to examine the measurement model and structural model (x items and x constructs) of the new version of the 3S-T model, based on composites factors formulated as type A. This technique was preferred for its ability to simultaneously examine a series of dependence relationships, especially when the model has first-order and second-order latent variables (Hair et al., 1998).

The model was measured and evaluated through data computation in SmartPLS 4. The measurement model evaluates the relationship between indicators reflecting each construct and tests the reliability and validity of measures. Assessment criteria included:

1. Indicator Reliability: Indicators should have outer loadings ≥ 0.70 (Hair et al., 2010).

2. Internal Consistency Reliability: Assessed via Cronbach's alpha (α) and Composite reliability (CR), with a cutoff of ≥ 0.70 for both tests (Urbach & Ahlemann, 2010).

Three conditions must be assessed:

a. Validity:

b. Convergent Validity: Average Variance Extracted (AVE) should be ≥ 0.50 (Fornell & Larcker, 1981).

c. Discriminant Validity: Assessed through the Fornell-Larcker criterion, cross-loadings, and Heterotrait-Monotrait ratio (HTMT) (Henseler et al., 2015).

Structural models describe relationships among constructs. The assessment criteria proposed by Hair et al. (2011) include:

- Collinearity Issues: Evaluated using Variance Inflation Factor (VIF) < 5;
- Significance and Relevance of Structural Relationships: $p < 0.05$;
- R^2 Levels: Categorized as weak (0.190), moderate (0.333), or substantial (0.670);
- Q^2 Levels: Should be more significant than zero;
- Model Fit: Assessed using Standardized Root Mean Square Residual (SRMR) ≤ 0.08 and Root Mean Square Error of Approximation (RMSEA) ≤ 0.12.

In the second step, a multigroup analysis (MGA) was developed. MGA is used to evaluate differences across groups defined by a categorical moderate variable. In our research, we develop the three-step of Measurement Invariance of Composite Models MICOM procedure, based on a non-parametric test that involves the assessment of configural invariance (i.e. equal parameterization and way of estimation), compositional invariance (i.e. equal indicator weights), and the equality of a composite's mean value and variance across groups. Configural invariance is the most important step and is a precondition for compositional invariance, which is again a precondition for significantly assessing the equality of composite mean values and variance. If configuration and compositional invariance are stablished, it can be confirmed that partial measurement invariance and it can be compared to the standardized path coefficients of structural relationships across the groups.

5. RESULTS

The instrument used to measure the variables of this research was structured in two parts. The first one deals with general issues relating to age or center of study. The second part focuses on factors related to Students Performance and Students Satisfaction including perceived usefulness, perceived ease of use, tutor quality, strategy, subjective norm, self-efficacy, information quality, system quality, service quality and intention of use.

A total of 81 students of the Central University of Ecuador (UCE) (Ecuador) with 38 males and 43 females and 137 students of the Universitat Politècnica de València (UPV) (Spain) with 85 males and 52 females, from different degrees and masters, participated in this study. The sample size is in line to other contemporary works in this purpose (Zobeidi et al., 2023; Wu, 2024)

This study performs three-step approaches: assessment measurement model, structural model, and multigroup analysis (MGA) (Hair et al., 2019).

5.1 Measurement Model

5.1.1 Outer Loading, Internal Consistency and Reliability

To examine the reliability of each item, we assess the loadings of the indicators in both groups following the suggestion of Hair et al. (2010), which states that:
- If the external loading is lower than 0.4, remove the indicator.
- If the external load is above 0.7, keep the indicator.
- If the external load is between 0.4 and 0.7, assess the impact of dropping the indicator on the Extracted Variance (AVE) and Composite Reliability (CR). Table 1 shows these statistics, in both groups.

Table 1. Measures of Internal Consistency Reliability and Validity of Both Groups

	UPV Student			UCE Student		
	Cronbach's alpha	Composite reliability (rho_a)	Average variance extracted (AVE)	Cronbach's alpha	Composite reliability (rho_a)	Average variance extracted (AVE)
E	0,833	0,907	0,559	0,933	0,940	0,721
EUS	0,701	0,711	0,623	0,905	0,924	0,839
OSE	0,829	0,850	0,596	0,895	0,915	0,705
PE	0,805	0,814	0,718	0,936	0,937	0,888
PEU	0,899	0,900	0,833	0,936	0,937	0,887
S	0,710	0,782	0,627	0,784	0,816	0,693
SAP	0,853	0,859	0,872	0,943	0,944	0,946
SystQ	0,861	0,869	0,783	0,943	0,943	0,878
SQ	0,568	0,724	0,683	0,853	0,855	0,871
SS	0,889	0,890	0,900	0,862	0,863	0,879
SSA	0,860	0,862	0,781	0,962	0,963	0,930
TQ	0,910	0,941	0,692	0,948	0,956	0,796

5.1.2 Discriminant Validity

Discriminant validity is the extent to which a construct is different from other constructs. The Fornell-Lacher criterion indicates a satisfactory level of discriminant validity for both groups, and we also evaluated the Heterotrait-Monotrait ratio (HTMT) following the recommendation of Henseler et al. 2015. Again, in both cases, the value does not exceed the threshold (values ≤ 0.9 are accepted); we can conclude that the study's measurement parameters provide sufficient evidence of reliability and convergent and discriminant validity for both groups.

5.1.3 Significance of Outer Loading

The bootstrapping algorithm with samples 50000 to estimate the t and p values to test the significance of the outer loadings with a 5 % probability of error has been used. The results indicate that all outer values are significant, with p-values lower than 0.05.

5.2 Structural Model

The path coefficients (β values) of the relationships between constructs and constructs are shown in Figure 2 and Figure 3. It can be appreciated that the coefficients differ in some of the relationships according to the university, for example, there is a notable effect of the tutor's role in UCE students on strategy and engagement, which has a positive effect on SAP, but this is not so higher in UPV students. All path coefficients were significant using the bootstrapping algorithm (p-values lower than 0.05).

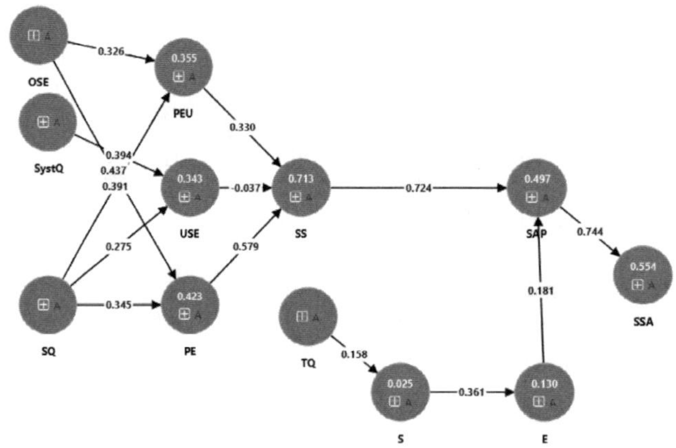

Figure 2. Structural Model Path Coefficients for UPV students

The coefficient of determination (R^2) of the endogenous variables can be interpreted as the predictive accuracy of the proposed model are shown in Figures 2 and Figure 3. Hair et al. (2010) stated that values of 0.75 are substantial, 0.5 moderate and 0.25 weak. In both cases, the results of R^2 show a sufficient level of this measure.

Finally, we assess the predictive relevance, denoted as Q^2. If the model performs a predictive relevance (values of Q^2 higher than 0), a study will show accuracy in predicting data points of items (Hair et al., 2019). Accordingly, Hair et al., 2019, Q^2 value of 0.02 denotes low predictive relevance, a value of 0.15 indicates medium relevance and a value of 0.35 denotes high predictive relevance. In our research, in UCE Students except S (Q^2=0.277) all factors have values of relevance predictive higher than 0.35 which means high relevance predictive. However, in UPV students, the value of Q^2 is less than 0.15 in Strategy (S) and Engagement (E).

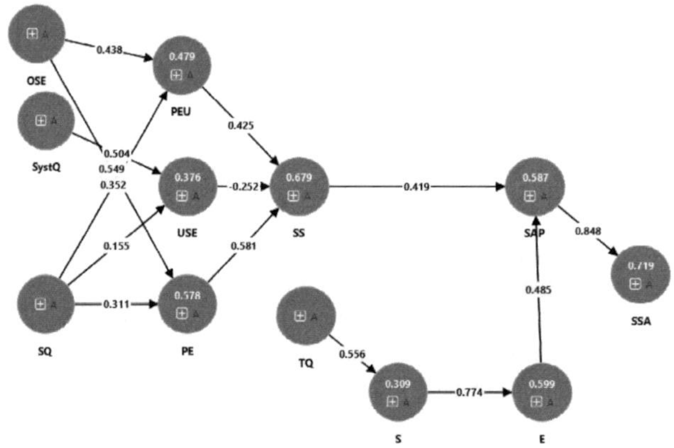

Figure 3. Structural Model Path Coefficients for UCE students

5.3 Multigroup Analysis

Finally, we perform an MGA. As established Henseler et al. (2016) to develop a MGA, it is necessary to confirm that differences between the two groups are due to differences in the structural model and not in the measurement model. The results of MICOM analysis for University confirm that partial invariance can be established, hence the moderating role is confirmed.

We can state that the tutor role, the strategy, and the engagement have a higher influence on Student's Academic Achievement and Performance and that USE, PEU and PE are most affected by on-line self-efficacy and System Quality UCE students. On the other hand, the path coefficient of the relationship between Student Satisfaction and Student academic performance is higher in UPV Students.

These differences in results can be partially attributed to the respective countries and their cultural dimensions similarly the results of Jorgji et al., 2023.

6. CONCLUSIONS

The Covid pandemic accelerated the E-learning process, where billions of students around the world were locked up receiving this teaching system. In this conference paper, we evaluate the success of E-learning using a 3S-T model already tested with secondary school students, but now testing its performance with university students (UCE students from Ecuador and UPV students from Spain). This 3S-T model was based on models in the existing specific literature (TAM, extensions of TAM, ISSM, SERVQUAL). Through this 3S-T model, we are validating E-learning success and gaining a better understanding of the factors that influence students' E-learning. Our research methodology consisted of two steps: (i) a confirmatory analysis (CFA), with structural equation modeling using partial least squares SEM (PLS-SEM), to examine the measurement model and the structural model and (ii), a multigroup analysis (MGA) to analyze the invariance. Through this procedure, we obtained results in two spheres, general issues related to age or center of study and factors related to Student Performance and Student Satisfaction including perceived usefulness, perceived ease of use, tutor quality, strategy, subjective norm, self-efficacy, information quality, system quality, service quality and intention of use. According to the results of CFA and PLS-SEM, a notable effect of the tutor's role in UCE students on strategy and engagement but not so high in UPV students has been found. Based on the results of MICOM analysis it has been found that the tutor role, the strategy, and the engagement have a higher influence on Students' Academic Achievement and Performance in UCE students; on the other hand, the path coefficient of the relationship between Student's Satisfaction and Student's academic performance is higher in UPV students than in those of UCE. In this sense, the discrepancies in results are due more to investments in digital infrastructure, economic disparity, accessibility and connectivity than to the cultural dimension (Ecuador and Spain share Hispanic culture). In UCE (Ecuador) these variables related to technological infrastructure are worse than in UPV (Spain) and even more so during the Covid-19 pandemic. Starting with this conference paper, we will expand the sample with more university students from other Hispanic countries and study additional cultural frameworks to analyze the cultural dimension in more depth.

FUNDING

This paper has been written with financial support from the Project of the Universitat Politècnica de València (PAID-06-23), "*Support through Data Science, Social Media and Innovation to Enhance Digital Divide and Sustainability with a gender approach: An International Study (DIVIDataSci)*".

ACKNOWLEDGEMENT

We thank to all students who participated in this study and invested their time in completing the research questionnaire.

REFERENCES

Adetimirin, A. *An empirical study of online discussion forums by library and information science postgraduate students using technology acceptance model 3*. Journal of Information Technology Education: Research **2015**, 14, 257-269. Retrieved from http://www.jite.org/documents/Vol14/JITEv14ResearchP257- 269Adetimirin1854.pdf.

Baber, H. *Modelling the acceptance of e-learning during the pandemic of COVID-19-A study of South Korea*. The International Journal of Management Education. **2021**, 19, 100503.

Davis, F.D. *Perceived usefulness, perceived ease of use, and user acceptance of information technology*. MIS Quarterly **1989**, 13, 319–340.

Davis, F.D., Bagozzi, R.P., Warshaw, P.R. *User acceptance of computer technology: a comparison of two theoretical models*. Management Science **1989**, 35, 982–1003.

Del Barrio-García, S, Arquero, J.L., Esteban, R-F. *Personal learning environments acceptance model: The role of need for cognition, e-learning satisfaction and students' perceptions*. Educational Technology & Society **2015**, 18(3), 129- 141. Retrieved from http://www.jstor.org/stable/jeductechsoci.18.3.129.

Delone, W. H. and McLean, E. R. *The Delone and McLean Model of Information Systems Success: A Ten-Year Update*. Journal of Management Information Systems **2003**, 19 (4), 9-30. DOI: 10.1080/07421222.2003.11045748.

Eom, S.B., Wen, H.J., Ashill N. *The determinants of students' perceived learning outcomes and satisfaction in university online education: An empirical investigation*. Decision Sciences of Journal Innovative **2006**, *4(2)*, 215–235. https://doi.org/10.1111/j.1540-4609.2006.00114.x.

Fornell, C.; Larcker, D. F. *Evaluating structural equation models with unobservable variables and measurement error.* Journal of Marketing Research **1981**, 18(1), 39–50. https://doi.org/10.2307/3151312.

Ganji Arjenaki, B. *Surveying the quality of electronic tests in the student satisfaction*. Education Strategies in Medical Science **2017**, 10(3), 180–188.

Gray J.A., DiLoreto M. *The effects of student engagement, student satisfaction, and perceived learning in online learning environments.* International Journal of Educational Leadership Preparation **2016**, 11 (1). Available online: https://files.eric.ed.gov/fulltext/EJ1103654.pdf. (Accessed on May 19, 2024).

Hair, J.F., Black, W.C., Babin, B.J., Anderson, R.E. *Multivariate Data Analysis.* **2010** 7th Edition, Pearson, New York.

Hair, J. F., Sarstedt, M., Ringle, C. M., Gudergan, S. P. *Advanced issues in partial least squares structural equation modeling (PLS-SEM)* **2017**. Thousand Oaks: Sage.

Hair, J.F., Risher, J.J., Sarstedt, M., Ringle, C.M. *When to use and how to report the results of PLS-SEM.* European Business Review **2019**, 31(1), 2-24. https://doi.org/10.1108/EBR-11-2018-0203

Henseler, J., Sarstedt, M. *Goodness-of-Fit Indices for Partial Least Squares Path Modeling*. Computational Statistics **2013,** 28, 565-580. DOI 10.1007/s00180-012-0317-

Henseler, J., Ringle, C., Sarstedt, M. *A New Criterion for Assessing Discriminant Validity in Variance-based Structural Equation Modeling*. Journal of Academic Marketing Science **2015**, 43, 115-135. DOI 10.1007/s11747-014-0403-8.

Jorgji, S., Davletova, A., Sandugash, A., Susimenko, E., Kulikova, E., Kosov, M., Vlasova, E., Shcherbatykh, L., Saddhono, K., Dudnik, O. *A cross-cultural study of university students' e-learning adoption.* Emerging Science Journal **2023**, 8(3), 1060-1074.

Kerzic, D. *Academic student satisfaction and perceived performance in the e-learning environment during the COVID-19 pandemic: Evidence across ten countries*. PLOS ONE **2021**. https://doi.org/10.1371/journal.pone.0258807.

León, S.P.; Augusto-Landa, J.M.; García-Martínez, I. *Moderating Factors in University Students' Self-Evaluation for Sustainability.* Sustainability **2021**, 13, 4199. https://doi.org/10.3390/su13084199.

Marks, R.B., Sibley, S.D., Arbaugh, J.B. *A structural equation model of predictors for effective online learning.* Organizational Behavior Teaching Review **2005**, 29(4), 531–563. https://doi.org/10.1177/1052562904271199.

Martínez-Gómez, M.; Bustamante, E.; Berna-Escriche, C. *Development and Validation of an E-Learning Education Model in the COVID-19 Pandemic: A Case Study in Secondary Education.* Sustainability **2022**, 14, 13261. ttps://doi.org/10.3390/su142013261.

Sánchez, R. A., Hueros, A. D. *Motivational factors that influence the acceptance of Moodle using TAM.* Computers in Human Behaviour **2010**, 26(6), 1632-1640. DOI 10.1016/j.chb.2010.06.011.

Sun, P.C., Tsai, R.J., Finger, G., Chen, Y.Y., Yeh, D. What drives a successful e-Learning: *An empirical investigation of the critical factors influencing learner satisfaction.* Computers & Education **2008**, 50(4), 1183–1202 https://doi.org/10.1016/j.compedu.2006.11.007.

Urbach, N., Ahlemann, F. *Structural equation modeling in information systems research using Partial Least Squares.* Journal of Information Technology Theory and Application **2010**, 11, 5-40. Available online: https://aisel.aisnet.org/jitta/vol11/iss2/2 . (Accessed on May 19, 2024).

Venkatesh, V., Davis, F.D. *A theoretical extension of the technology acceptance model: four longitudinal field studies*. Management Science **2000**, 46 (2), 186-204.

Zhao, L., Cao, C., Li, Y., Li, Y. *Determinants of the digital outcome divide in E-learning between rural and urban students: Empirical evidence from the COVID-19 pandemic based on capital theory.* Computers in Human Behavior **2022**, 130(3), 107–177.

Zobeidi, T., Homayoon, S.B., Yazdanpanah, M., Komendantova, N., Warner, L.A. *Employing the TAM in predicting the use of online learning during and beyond the COVID-19 pandemic.* Frontiers in Psychology, **2023**, 14. https://doi.org/10.3389/fpsyg.2023.1104653

EVALUATION OF THE EFFECTIVENESS OF READING ALOUD A PROGRAM CODE IN LEARNING PROGRAMMING BASED ON BRAIN-ACTIVITY MEASUREMENTS

Tetsuo Tanaka[1], Ryo Horiuchi[1] and Mari Ueda[2]
[1]*Dept. of Information and Computer Sciences, Faculty of Information Technology, Kanagawa Institute of Technology*
1030 Shimo-ogino, Atsugi, Kanagawa, 243-0292, Japan
[2]*Dept. of Information Media, Faculty of Information Technology, Kanagawa Institute of Technology*
1030 Shimo-ogino, Atsugi, Kanagawa, 243-0292, Japan

ABSTRACT

We evaluate the effectiveness of reading aloud a program code in learning programming from a neuroscientific perspective by measuring brain activity using a near-infrared spectroscopy device. The results show that when reading aloud and then reading silently, brain activity increases during reading aloud; a similar trend is observed when the reading order is reversed. In addition, written tests, such as C-language fill-in-the-blank questions, result in higher scores when the participants read aloud than when they read silently. Furthermore, no characteristic differences in brain activity were found between students with good programming skills and those without. Significant differences were found for students with average programming skills. In a future study, we will increase the number of participants to verify the above results and clarify the relation between brain activity and the difficulty level of the program code, reading speed, subvocalization during silent reading, and other factors. Our aim is to establish an efficient learning programming method by employing the reading-aloud technique.

KEYWORDS

Brain-Activity, Programming, Learning, Reading Aloud, NIRS

1. INTRODUCTION

Reading aloud can be an effective method for learning programming learning as well as natural language learning [Li J., 2020, Huimin W. et al., 2021]. A reading system for learning C language has been developed by the authors [Ueda M., et al., 2022] and its effectiveness was verified for University students. Additionally, reading aloud was found to be more effective for beginners in programming than silent reading or "shakyo" (sutra copying learning, learning programming by transcribing sample code) [Okamoto M., et al., 2010, Ueda M., et al., 2023]. Experiments involving elementary school students have also shown that reading a program code aloud contributes to improving syntax memorization and code comprehension [Swidan A., et al., 2019].

However, the verification of the effectiveness of the reading-aloud technique in previous studies was based on comparisons of scores obtained from task experiments and subjective evaluations through questionnaires, making it difficult to objectively evaluate the benefits of learning programming. Inspired by the research conducted on the effectiveness of reading aloud in learning natural languages [Takeuchi H., et al., 2021], we evaluate the effectiveness of the reading-aloud technique more objectively than previously evaluated by conducting neuroscientific experiments.

It has already been reported that the reading-aloud technique increases brain activity compared with the reading-silently technique [Kawashima R., et al., 2005, Chiarenza A. G., et al., 2014]. The brain activity during programming has also been reported [Hermans F., 2021]. For example, the use of near-infrared spectroscopy (NIRS) to measure a person's mental workload during software development has been described in [Nakagawa T., et al., 2014]. The effect of programming with (or without) music on the electromagnetic waves in the brain of software developers has been reported in [Thapaliya A., 2021]. In [Thapaliya A., 2020], it was verified that pair programming leads results to a higher concentration level than solo programming.

However, the effectiveness of the reading-aloud technique in learning programming has not been reported in the literature. In this study, we conduct NIRS experiments to measure the brain activity of persons while they read a program code. The aim is to objectively verify the effectiveness of the reading-aloud technique in learning programming. We also investigate the differences in programming ability and the relation between programming ability and brain activity during reading aloud and reading silently.

In Section II, we explain the NIRS measurement procedure of brain activity. In Section III, we evaluate the effectiveness of the reading-aloud technique in learning programming through a C-language test. In Section IV, we discuss the relation between test scores and brain activity. Section V concludes the paper.

2. MEASUREMENT OF BRAIN ACTIVITY

2.1 Experiment Overview

In this study, we focused on brain (frontal lobe) activity to assess the effectiveness of reading aloud a program code in learning programming. We measured changes in the cerebral blood flow using a 2-channel NIRS device, which is used for measuring work efficiency.

For this purpose, we employed NIRS to measure the brain activity of 19 students of the Faculty of Information Technology, Kanagawa Institute of Technology, when they read a program code aloud and silently. A portable brain-activity measurement device (HOT-2000, NeU, Tokyo, Japan) was used for NIRS measurements. The output values obtained from the HOT-2000 device provide a brain-activity indicator based on changes in the blood flow (hemoglobin concentration) in the frontal lobe of the brain. Since these values are not absolute values, we investigated the changes in brain activity starting from a certain point in time.

After a brief explanation of the measurement procedure, each participant read two program codes aloud and silently while wearing the HOT-2000 device. Table 1. summarizes the measurement procedure. The numbers in parentheses indicate the time in seconds).

Table 1. Measurement procedure

Code1	Rest(10)	Reading Aloud(60)	Rest(25)	Reading Silently(60)	Rest(10)
Code2	Rest(25)	Reading Silently(60)	Rest(25)	Reading Aloud(60)	Rest(10)

2.2 Results and Discussion

HOT-2000 is a 2-channel device featuring two sensors, left and right. Figure 1 shows the measurement results obtained from a participant. The blue and green graphs represent changes in the values obtained from the right and left sensors, respectively. The left sensor values correspond to the brain's left hemisphere, which controls language; therefore, in this measurement, we used the values obtained from the left sensor.

To investigate the overall trend, we divided a 60-s reading into 6 parts and calculated the average value for each 10-s period for each participant. The results are shown in Figure 2. The brain activity indicator values increase during Reading Aloud1 and decrease during Reading Silently1; they remain relatively stable during Reading Silently2 and increase during Reading Aloud2.

To verify this trend, we conducted a paired two-sample t-test to evaluate the amount of change between the start and end of the reading-aloud process and that between the start and end of the silent reading process, as shown in Figure 3.

For Code1, the brain-activity indicator values increase during Reading Aloud1 and decrease during Reading Silently1. These two processes are significantly different ($p = 0.015$). Regarding brain activity from Reading Silently2 to Reading Aloud2 for Code 2, the change in the brain activity indicator values was slightly larger in Reading Aloud 2, but the variance was large and no statistically significant difference was observed.

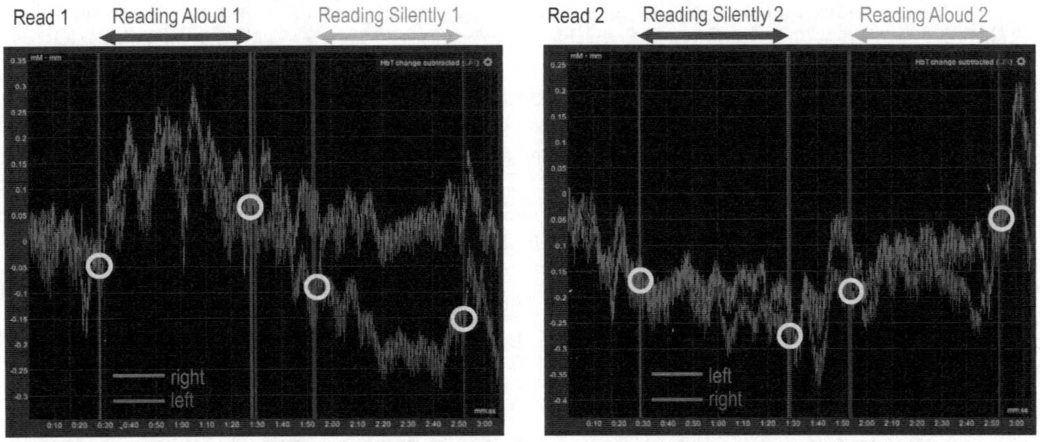

Figure 1. Example of graphing experimental results

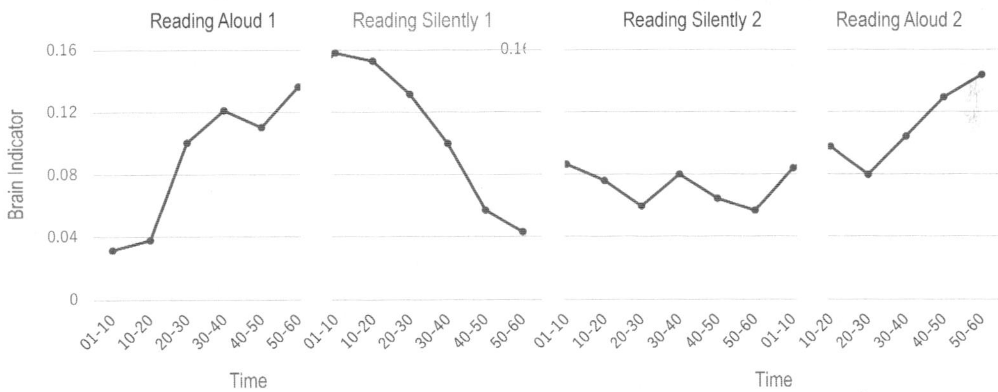

Figure 2. Line graph of 10 s average of left brain indicators

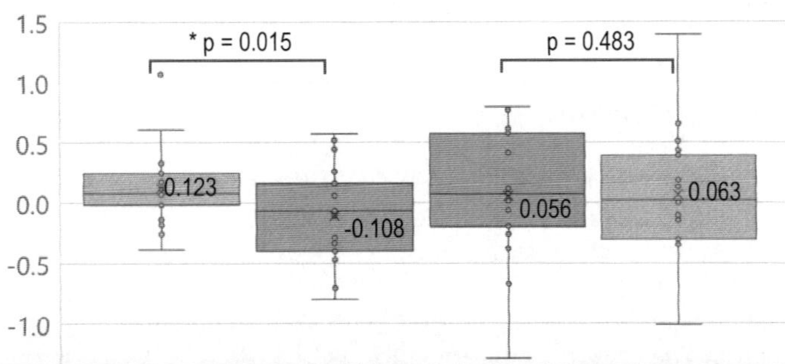

	code1		code2	
	aloud1	silently1	silently2	aloud2
μ	0.123	-0.108	0.056	0.063
σ^2	0.105	0.150	0.268	0.248

Figure 3. Boxplot of changes in left brain indicators (N=19)

Looking at individual data, for some participants, the change in the brain activity indicator values was significantly in the direction opposite to the overall trend. There are various possible reasons for this. Specifically, brain activity increases because the participants have difficulties in understanding the source code, the code is long, the participants perform subvocalization (internal vocalization) when reading silently, and other reasons.

Therefore, to verify the effectiveness of the reading-aloud technique in learning programming, it is necessary to collect and analyze more data and to examine their relation with brain activity indicators. The difficulty and length of the source code used in the measurements, the voice volume when reading aloud, the presence or absence of subvocalization during silent reading, and the participant's programming skills must be considered.

Furthermore, it is possible that the initial Reading Aloud1 process affected brain activity during the subsequent Reading Silently1, Reading Silently2, and Reading Aloud2 processes. The reading speed could also affect brain activity. Therefore, we need to employ measurement procedures that eliminate these problems.

3. INVESTIGATION OF THE EFFECTIVENESS OF THE READING-ALOUD TECHNIQUE ON LEARNING PROGRAMMING USING A WRITTEN TEST

We investigated the differences in programming ability and the relation between programming ability and brain activity when reading aloud and silently.

3.1 Experiment Overview

In this experiment, students participated in two written C-language tests (Test 1 and Test 2) with 10 questions each. The questions included the prediction of the program results and answering the blanks based on the program with blanks and the execution results. Each problem was based on five programs (branches, loops, structures, pointers, functions) of 10–20 lines for beginners in the C language.

The participants were 18 undergraduate and graduate students in their early 20s. Seventeen of them were the same students who participated in the brain activity measurement experiment, and one was a new participant. The 18 participants were divided into two groups of 9 people each: Group 1 and Group 2. Each Group 1 participant answered Test 1 by reading the program code aloud three times and Test 2 by reading the source code silently three times before answering. Conversely, each Group 2 participant, read the program code silently during Test 1 and aloud during Test 2.

3.2 Results and Discussion

Table 2. shows the score results of Tests 1 and 2 for the 18 participants (the maximum score was 10 points), the total scores, and the score difference between Tests 1 and 2. A boxplot of the test scores is shown in Figure 4. (1) is based on data obtained from all participants, (2) is based on data obtained from Group 1, and (3) is based on data obtained from Group 2.

On average, the participants scored 1.2 points higher in test 2 than test 1. As shown in Figure 4. (1), there is a significant difference between them, indicating that Test 2 was easier than Test 1. Furthermore, for both Group 1 participants, who read aloud during Test 1, and Group 2 participants, who read aloud during Test 2, the difference in the mean scores for Tests 1 and 2 was 1.2. Based on the average scores, we cannot say that reading aloud is effective. However, Figure 4. (2) and (3) show no significant difference among Group 1 participants but a significant difference among Group 2 participants. This indicates that in Group 1, the easiness of Test 2 was offset by reading aloud during Test 1. In Group 2, the effect of reading aloud appeared in addition to the easiness of Test 2, indicating the effectiveness of reading aloud.

Table 2. Test score

participants	group	test1	test2	sum	difference
a	1	7	7	14	0
b	1	5	8	13	3
c	1	6	7	13	1
d	1	6	7	13	1
e	1	4	6	10	2
f	1	5	5	10	0
g	1	1	6	7	5
h	1	5	1	6	-4
i	1	1	4	5	3
j	2	8	7	15	-1
k	2	5	7	12	2
l	2	5	6	11	1
m	2	4	7	11	3
n	2	4	4	8	0
o	2	3	5	8	2
p	2	4	4	8	0
q	2	2	6	8	4
r	2	3	3	6	0
average		4.3	5.6	9.9	1.2

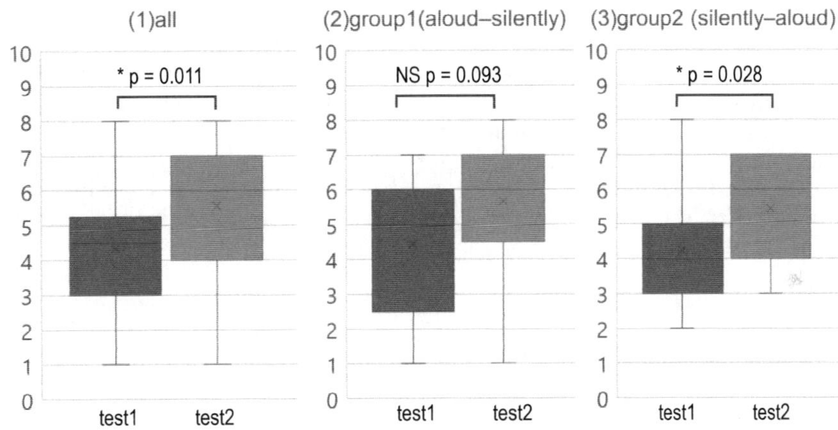

Figure 4. Boxplot of test score (N=18)

4. RELATION BETWEEN TEST SCORES AND BRAIN ACTIVITY

To identify possible differences in brain activity depending on the test performance, in Table 3, we summarize the test scores and brain-activity indicator values of 17 students, who participated in both the brain-activity measurement experiment and the C-language writing test.

We sorted the sums of Tests 1 and 2 in descending order. The following observations can be made:

(1) No significant changes in the amount of brain activity for the two participants with good programming skills (total test scores of 14 points or higher). This can be attributed to the fact that their brain was not overloaded with simple problems.

(2) For the 12 participants with average programming skills (total test scores between 8 and 13 points), their brain activity increased when reading aloud and decreased when reading silently. This confirms the results reported in [Ueda M., et al., 2023] (namely, that reading aloud is effective in learning programming).

(3) The three participants with poor programming skills (total test scores of 7 points or less) exhibited active brain activity, even when reading silently. This is probably because they were trying to read the code carefully, even when reading silently. This confirms the results reported in [Ueda M., 2023] (i.e., reading aloud is not effective in a programming course that incorporates the reading-aloud technique for students with poor programming skills).

Table 3. Test score and brain activity

subject	test sum	aloud1	silently1	silently2	aloud2
j	15	-0.016	-0.058	-0.189	-0.106
a	14	0.065	0.258	0.074	-0.0004
b	13	0.015	-0.801	-0.674	0.033
c	13	-0.39	0.057	-1.294	0.653
d	13	0.074	-0.472	-0.382	-0.329
k	12	-0.018	-0.29	0.582	-1.009
l	11	0.176	-0.708	0.098	0.187
m	11	0.248	-0.339	-0.262	-0.148
e	10	0.201	0.164	0.113	0.392
f	10	0.35	-0.401	0.016	-0.305
p	8	0.085	-0.058	-0.065	0.134
o	8	0.115	-0.459	-0.199	-0.338
n	8	0.099	-0.266	0.614	1.391
q	8	-0.138	-0.03	0.014	-0.351
g	7	-0.182	0.517	0.769	0.02
h	6	0.009	-0.109	0.792	-0.101
r	6	1.064	0.572	0.574	0.51

We verified observation (2) using the brain-activity data presented in Section 2. Figure 5 shows a boxplot of the amount of brain activity during Aloud1 and Aloud2, Silently 1 and 2, and the results of a paired two-sample t-test. The left side is based on the data obtained from all 17 participants, and the right side is based on the data obtained from the middle 12 participants.

Although no significant difference was observed between reading aloud and reading silently for all participants, a significant difference ($p = 0.032$) was observed in the middle group of 12 participants, confirming that reading the program aloud activated brain activity.

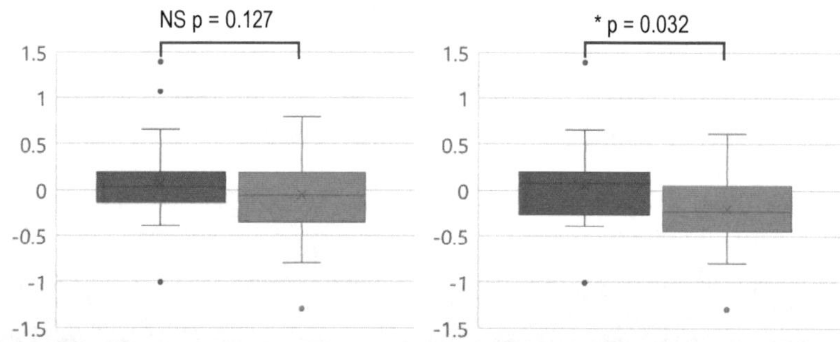

	All aloud (N = 34)	All silently (N = 34)	8-13 aloud (N = 24)	8-13 silently (N = 24)
μ	0.070	-0.054	0.047	-0.210
σ^2	0.176	0.222	0.193	0.279

Figure 5. Brain activity during reading aloud and silently
(all participants and participants with test scores of 8 to 13 points)

5. CONCLUSION

We used NIRS to measure the brain activity of participants when they read a source code aloud to investigate the effectiveness of the reading-aloud technique in learning programming from a neuroscientific perspective.

We found that the brain-activity indicator values increase during reading aloud and decrease during reading silently when participants read silently after reading aloud. A similar trend was observed when the reading order was reversed. In addition, a written C-language test conducted when the participants read aloud indicated that reading aloud improved test scores. Furthermore, there was no characteristic difference in brain activity between reading aloud and reading silently between the participants with good programming skills and those with bad programming skills. However, a significant difference was observed for participants with average programming skills.

In the future, we will increase the number of participants to verify the above results. We also analyzed the relation between brain-activity indicator values and the difficulty and length of the source code, reading speed, volume of voice when reading aloud, presence of subvocalization, and programming skills of the participants. Thus, we established an efficient programming learning method employing the reading-aloud technique.

ACKNOWLEDGEMENT

This work was supported by JSPS KAKENHI, Grant Number JP23K02747. We are grateful to Mr. Tomura and Mr. Hasegawa of NeU Co., Ltd., for their help in analyzing the NIRS data.

REFERENCES

Li J. (2020). An Empirical Study on Reading Aloud and Learning English by the Use of the Reading Assistant SRS, *Int. J. Emerg. Technol. Learn. (iJET)*, 15, 103–117

Huimin W. et al. (2021). Application of Reading Aloud in Middle School Oral English Teaching, *Studies in Literature and Language*, 22, June 30

Ueda M., et al. (2022). A Proposal of Programming Learning System with Reading Aloud "ONDOKU", *IIAI AAI 2022 Proc.*, pp. 260–263

Okamoto M., et al. (2010). Computer Programming Course Materials for Self-Learning Novices, *Proceedings of ED-MEDIA 2010*, 2855–2861

Ueda M., et al. (2023). Basic study on the effectiveness of reading aloud in learning programming languages, *Acoustical Science and Technology*, Vol. 44, No. 1, pp. 33-35

Swidan A., et al. (2019). The Effect of Reading Code Aloud on Comprehension: An Empirical Study with School Students, *Proc. of the ACM Conference on Global Computing Education*, pp. 178–184

Takeuchi H., et al. (2021). Effects of Training of Shadowing and Reading Aloud of Second Language on Working Memory and Neural Systems, *Brain Imaging and Behavior*, Vol. 15, pp. 1253–1269

Kawashima R., et al. (2005). Reading Aloud and Arithmetic Calculation Improve Frontal Function of People with Dementia, *The Journals of Gerontology: Series A*, Vol. 60, No. 3, pp. 380–384

Chiarenza A. G., et al. (2014). The Psychophysiology of Reading, *International Journal of Psychophysiology*, Vol. 94, pp. 111-119

Hermans F. (2021). The Programmer's Brain: What every programmer needs to know about cognition, Manning

Nakagawa T., et al. (2014). Quantifying programmers' mental workload during program comprehension based on cerebral blood flow measurement: a controlled experiment. *In Companion Proceedings of the 36th International Conference on Software Engineering (ICSE Companion 2014)*, pp. 448–451

Thapaliya A. (2021). Effect on brain activity while programming with (without) music, *In Companion Proceedings of the 43th International Conference on Software Engineering (ICSE Companion 2021)*, pp. 93–95

Thapaliya A. (2020). Evaluation of brain activity while Pair Programming, *In Companion Proceedings of the 42th International Conference on Software Engineering (ICSE Companion 2020)*, pp. 104-106

Ueda M. (2023). Trial of programming education for athletic students, *JUCE Educational Innovation Conference*, 2 pages (in Japanese)

BRAIN WAVES AND LEARNING IN CHILDREN WITH ADHD: IMPACT OF EDUCATIONAL VIDEO GAMES VS TRADITIONAL METHODS

Cristina Rebollo, Anna Tonda, Cristina Sorlí and Inmaculada Remolar
Institute of New Imaging Technologies, Universitat Jaume I, 12071 – Castellón, Spain

ABSTRACT

The traditional learning method can be a challenging activity if the students are children with ADHD. There are studies that indicate that educational video games enhance the learning process in children. To objectively validate the aforementioned claim, this study aims to analyze and compare the brain waves activity of children with ADHD while learning scientific concepts through traditional methods and educational video games. To do this, the activity is monitored with an EEG headset while they learn. A pilot study has been conducted with 7 children aged 7 to 9 to evaluate the learning effectiveness of using video games versus traditional learning. The results support that playing educational video games makes the learning process more enjoyable and engaging for children with ADHD, thereby improving their study skills and knowledge acquisition.

KEYWORDS

ADHD, Learning, Serious Games, Brain Waves, Cognitive Engagement

1. INTRODUCTION

Attention Deficit Hyperactivity Disorder (ADHD) is a mental health problem that is typically identified during childhood and is categorized as a neurodevelopmental disorder. Approximately 3-5% of school-aged children worldwide have ADHD (Rief, 2012). According to (Brito et al, 1995), ADHD causes disruptions in behavioral, cognitive, academic and social functioning. Children diagnosed with ADHD exhibit a range of behavioral and cognitive difficulties, including inattention, impulsivity, difficulty concentrating and memory problems that hinder the acquisition and retention of knowledge in both the short and long term. These children are unable to complete activities to a satisfactory standard and become bored easily (Wagner, 2000). There are studies that have further explored the importance of improving cognitive engagement (attention and concentration, mental effort, persistence, learning strategies, interest, and motivation in educational activities) as a means of overcoming these deficiencies (Lorch et al, 2006). Students who are cognitively engaged tend to perform better, have a deeper understanding of the material, and have a greater ability to apply what they have learned in different contexts (Fredricks et al, 2004).

Serious games (SGs), those that have targets different from only fun (Gee, 2003), have gained popularity in non-entertainment domains as they make tasks more engaging and appealing (Furió et al, 2013). This kind of game possesses significant educational potential, benefiting cognitive processes, executive functions, social skills, and the inclusion of students with specific educational support needs, especially with ADHD children (García-Redondo et al, 2019).

Electroencephalography (EEG) is a method used to evaluate brain waves. These are divided into multiple frequency bands: the δ-band, dominant in children during sleep, is linked to linguistic acquisition (Penolazzi et al, 2008); the θ-band predominates during drowsy states; the α-band indicates relaxation; the β-band is associated with fast activities; and the γ-band is related to problem-solving and memory (Wang et al, 2010). These measurements are made using devices that capture real-time data on brain activity, providing relevant information about cognitive processes and their response to different educational approaches. Studying brain waves will allow the identification of characteristic patterns during learning activities, evaluation of their effectiveness, and assessment of student participation.

Taking into account the above and aiming to quantify and contrast the brain waves measurements of children diagnosed with ADHD while learning with traditional educational methods and video games, this work proposes: to analyze and compare children's brain waves while learning with traditional methods and video games to explore differences in cognitive engagement between these approaches and assessing knowledge acquisition in both learning methods.

To this purpose, three objectives (O) were established:

- O1: Evaluate, by recording and analyzing brain waves, if video games offer ADHD students a more motivating learning method than traditional learning.
- O2: Identify brain waves patterns in ADHD children during traditional and GBL.
- O3: To assess knowledge acquisition in both learning methods.

Knowledge tests and brain waves measurements were used, and six research questions (RQs) were defined:

- RQ1: How does Game-Based Learning (GBL) impact the Attention levels of children with ADHD compared to traditional learning methods?
- RQ2: Does GBL promote higher levels of Appreciation and Enjoyment in children with ADHD compared to traditional learning methods?
- RQ3: How does GBL affect the Ease of Use and resulting stress levels for children with ADHD during learning activities compared to traditional methods?
- RQ4: How does the overall Quality of learning, reflected in Attention, Engagement, and Relaxation, compare between GBL and traditional methods?
- RQ5: Does GBL improve Cognitive Engagement more effectively than traditional learning methods for children with ADHD?
- RQ6: Is more knowledge acquired in the same period of time with GBL than compared to traditional methods?

RQs 1, 2, 3, 4, and 5 are aimed at supporting Objectives 1 and 2, while RQ6 is focused on supporting O3.

The paper is structured as follows: Section 2 reviews publications that serve as a starting point for this research: Section 3 outlines the process from objective setting to experimental design. Section 4 evaluates the effectiveness of GBL versus traditional learning for ADHD children. Sections 5 and 6 present the conclusions and future work.

2. PREVIOUS WORK

In the search for more effective educational methods, educators and researchers have become increasingly interested in Game Based Learning (GBL) methodologies (Boyle et al, 2015), which have been shown to have a high potential to increase student motivation (Hussein et al, 2019) (Rebollo et al, 2022). In the context of ADHD, the use of Serious Games (SGs), has emerged as a methodology for the increase of motivation, the retention of knowledge in educational contexts (Manero et al, 2016). In (Avila-Pesantez et al, 2018), results showed improved concentration in children who used ATHYNOS educational video game. In this sense, the comparison between learning through SGs and traditional learning is an aspect of considerable importance. The results of the work of (López-Fernández et al, 2021) show that GBL was as effective as traditional teaching for knowledge acquisition but was especially successful in increasing student motivation, preferring GBL over traditional teaching.

The brain characteristics of ADHD most often cited in the literature include an excess of θ-band, which are associated with sleep and decreased alertness, and a deficit of β-band, which are related to concentration (Moriyama et al, 2012). The study by (Juiter et al, 2021) aimed to measure the impact of music tones on the behavior of ADHD children aged 7 to 9 years, focusing on attention (θ-band), relaxation (α-band), and concentration (β-band). The results indicated that music tones had a significant impact on the behavior of ADHD children, as evidenced by significant changes in their brain waves scores across the three types of brain waves studied. Besides, various studies examine brain waves to enhance cognitive skills such as memory and attention while playing video games (Liu et al, 2014), (Alchalabi et al, 2018). In (Muñoz et al, 2015), neurophysiological signals in children with ADHD are monitored while playing a serious game to reinforce waiting ability, planning ability, ability to follow instructions, and ability to achieve goals. This work can discriminate between children with and without ADHD, aiding diagnosis.

Based on this literature review, it is valuable to explore the benefits of serious games in educational settings with children with ADHD, alongside analyzing their brain waves status as they learn.

3. USER EXPERIENCE DESIGN

Prior to the experiment, essential tasks were conducted to ensure optimal conditions and precise implementation: Criteria for population inclusion, selection of the EEG headband meeting research requirements, selection of experimental games, material selection and procedure.

3.1 Criteria for Population Inclusion

Considering that ADHD is typically identified during childhood, children in early schooling stages were included. Selection was based on the criteria in Table 1, communicated orally to the families.

Table 1. Inclusion criteria

Description	Sample
Children - diagnosed with TDAH - IQ (intelligence quotient) indices were normal. - aged 6 to 9 years - willingness to engage in both paper-based learning and gaming activities - were unaware of the knowledge they would acquire	7 (1 girl, 6 boys) 7-9 years old (M = 8.71; SD =0.70)

3.2 Selection of the EEG Headband Meeting Research Requirements

The selection of the headband is critical for the success of the research, especially when involving children with ADHD. Five EEG devices were evaluated: Emotiv Insight, Neurohead Band, NeuroSky, Muse 2 and Macrotellect BrainLink Pro. The choice of the Macrotellect BrainLink Pro headband was based on its ability to record and analyze brain waves, providing an effective platform for real-time monitoring of users' mental states. Its ergonomic design ensures user comfort during extended usage sessions, maintaining the quality of brain waves measurements. They are suitable for use with children. Its compatibility with various devices and platforms allows seamless integration with different operating systems and applications, enhancing its usability in diverse study and clinical contexts. Their advanced algorithms offer accurate feedback on the user's mental state, making it a comprehensive and user-friendly tool. Additionally, it provides high functionality and ease of use at an affordable cost.

3.3 Selection of Experimental Games

To select the suitable video games for the experiment, the Kokoro Kids commercial app was used, offering more than 200 games designed to enhance school activities and foster children's mental and cognitive skills. In 2024, Kokoro Kids received the PlayForAll award from the LEGO Foundation, recognizing solutions that facilitate learning through play, especially for neurodivergent children with ASD and ADHD. The selected games needed to provide educational content and enable the assessment of cognitive functioning, attention, and concentration.

Independent expert evaluators selected the games "*Flying through the Continents*" (FC) and "*Flying through the Solar System*" (FSS) (Figure 1). These enable the assessment of brain waves behavior during the learning of continent and planet names and locations. They help children locate these on a world or solar system map, guide them in navigating from one continent or planet to another by following instructions, and enable quick and efficient recognition of all continents and planets.

3.4 Material Selection

The following materials were used in the experiment:

Traditional Learning (Figure 2):
- A printed sheet depicting the planets of the solar system, each labeled with its respective name.
- A printed map showing the continents, each labeled with its respective name.

Learning with Video Games (Figure 1):
- A video game designed to teach the continents and their names.
- A video game designed to teach the planets and their names.

Evaluation Instruments:
- An EGG device for recording brain waves (Macrotellect BrainLink Pro headband).
- A printed sheet of the solar system's planets with white labels for their names.
- A printed map of the continents with white labels for their names.

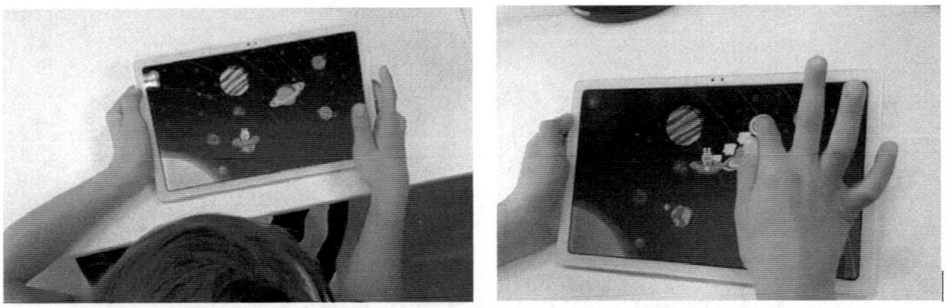

Figure 1. *"Fly solar system"* game from Kokoro Kids app (left) and child playing the game (right)

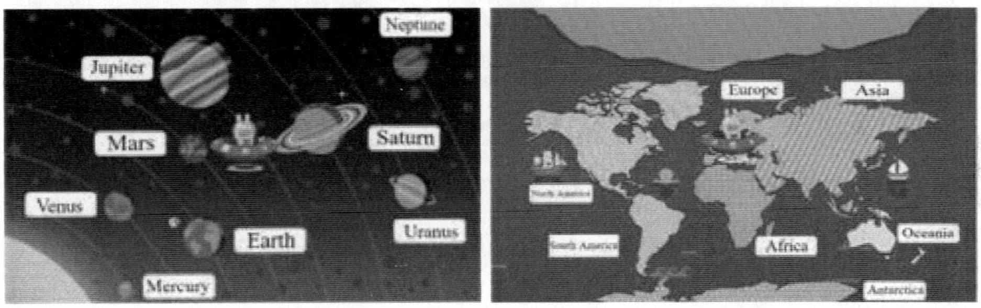

Figure 2. Printed sheets depicting the planets (left) and the continents (right)

3.5 Procedure

The research adhered to the 1964 Declaration of Helsinki and its subsequent amendments, approved by the Deontological Commission of Jaume I University under file number "CEISH/143/2023". Parents or legal guardians of participating children provided written informed consent after receiving an information sheet detailing the research objectives and participation specifics. The sessions were conducted in a quiet environment at Jaume I University. Age, gender, IQ and education level were collected through personal communication. Participant anonymity was ensured by assigning a Unique Identification Number (ID#) where "#" corresponds to the order number of the experience execution.

During the learning experience, each participant wore a Macrotellect BrainLink Pro headband to record EEG signals. Brain waves were continuously recorded throughout the learning process.

The experiment follows a structured format for each participant (Figure 3):
- **Paper-Based Learning Task:** Participants engage in traditional learning studying the contents using customized educational materials.

- **Game-Based Learning Task:** Participants switch topics; those who studied planets traditionally will learn continents through gameplay, and vice versa.
- **Knowledge Test:** Before and after each learning task, participants undergo a test to assess their knowledge. The tests involve identifying images and completing the names of planets or continents.
- **Gaming Task:** Participants play the game corresponding to their traditional learning topic, allowing for the measurement and analysis of brain waves activity for all games and children.

Each experiment lasted approximately two hours and it was divided as follows:

- 5 min. for a preliminary phase to understand both the traditional learning activity and the games' instructions and practice.
- 5 min. to complete the knowledge pre-test.
- 10 min. for the traditional learning task + 5 min. to respond to the learned concepts questionnaire.
- 5 min. to complete the knowledge post-test.
- 10 min. for the GBL task (game 1) + 5 min. to respond to the learned concepts questionnaire.
- 5 min. to complete the knowledge test.
- 10 min. to play the game 2.
- A 3-5 min. break was taken between each of the activities.

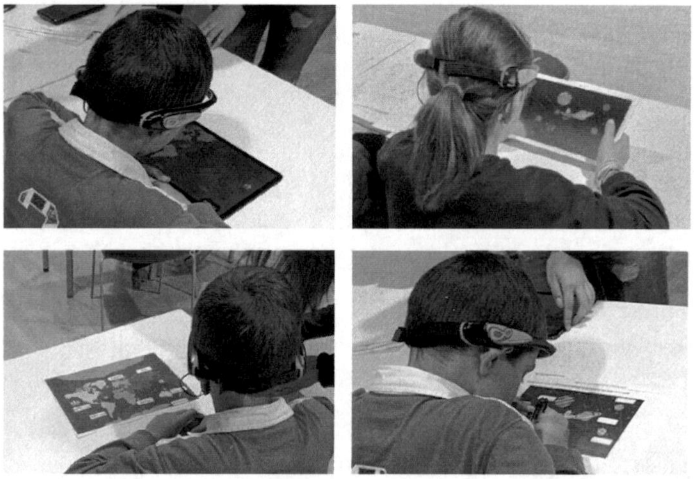

Figure 3. Learning the planets (top left) and continents (top right) using video games. Learning the planets using a traditional method (bottom left). Completing the knowledge test (bottom right)

4. EVALUATION

To assess the effectiveness and experience of game-based vs traditional learning for ADHD children, this section evaluates both methods. Two studies are conducted: the first analyzes brain waves in both methods, and the second evaluates the knowledge acquired. A quantitative, comparative, cross-sectional design (Ato et al, 2013) is used for this exploratory study.

4.1 Analysis & Findings

This section describes the data collection process.

4.1.1 Brain Waves: Traditional vs. Game-Based Learning

The data collected comprise cognitive metric measurements from children aged 7 to 9 while engaging in activities such as studying planets on paper (PP), continents on paper (PC), or playing "Fly the Solar System" (FSS) or "Fly the Continents" (FC) games. These measurements encompass five main metrics: *Attention* (Att.), *Relaxation* (Rel), *Appreciation* (App), *Mental Effort* (ME), and *Familiarity* (Fam.). A summary of the mean, maximum, and minimum values of these key variables is presented in Table 2.

Table 2. Means, Maximum, and Minimum Values of Key Variables.

	Mean				Maximums' means				Minimums' means			
	FSS	FC	PP	PC	FSS	FC	PP	PC	FSS	FC	PP	PC
Att.	44	49	45	48	82.1428	83	77	83,6667	18,4285	17	13	17
Rel.	51	56	57	59	75.2857	88	95.5	94,6667	13,1428	23	16,25	14,6667
App.	2	2	1	1	2.8571	3	2	2	0,5714	1	0	0
ME	18	15	13	3	40.8571	42	36.25	29,3333	-22,4285	-19	-38,5	14,6667
Fam.	-2	-7	-5	5	18.5714	13	23	33	-25,5714	-39	-32,5	-17,3333

These data provide an overview of how each group of children responded in terms of the measured variables while studying on paper and while playing. The values of the variables correspond to a scale varying between a minimum and maximum value as indicated Table 3.

Table 3. Scale of the maximum and minimum values for each of the variables measured,

Var.	Scala	Meaning
Att.	**0-100**	The higher the value, the greater the mental concentration.
Rel.	**0-100**	The higher the value, the greater the level of calmness and relaxation. The lower the value, the higher the level of stress.
App.	**0-4**	The higher the value, the greater the appreciation for the visual or auditory activity, while a lower value indicates neutrality.
ME	**-100-100**	The higher the value, the greater mental effort experienced during the activity.
Fam.	**-100-100**	The higher the value, the greater the learning progress during the activity. The lower the value, the less familiarity with the task.

4.1.2 Knowledge Acquisition: Traditional vs. Game-Based Learning

Before and after each learning task, participants undergo a test to assess their knowledge. The tests involve identifying images and completing the names of 8 planets or 7 continents and their positions, as depicted in Figure 2. Each test is labeled with the child's identifier. (ID#). Table 4 presents the results from pre- and post-tests for each of the learning activities.

Table 4. Results from pre- and post-tests for each learning activity. Note: '-' indicates that the participant was not required to complete that part of the test

	Pre-test				Post-test			
	Game		Paper		Game		Paper	
	FSS	FC	FSS	FC	FSS	FC	FSS	FC
1#	-	4	3	-	-	7	8	-
2#	2	-	-	1	6	-	-	4
3#	-	0	2	-	-	3	6	-
4#	2	-	-	3	7	-	-	4
5#	-	0	1	-	-	0	3	-
6#	-	2	4	-	-	5	8	-
7#	2	-	-	2	8	-	-	7

It is important to note the crossover design of the study: if a participant learned about the continents using traditional methods, they would learn about the planets through a video game, and vice versa. This approach ensured that each child experienced both types of learning methods, allowing for a direct comparison of their effectiveness.

4.2 Discussions

The analysis of the data collected for both experiments is given below.

4.2.1 Comparative Brain Waves Analysis: Traditional vs. Game-Based Learning

At first glance, the analysis of brain waves (Table 2) reveals an intriguing pattern: individuals who performed well in the paper-based learning mode also excelled in GBL, and vice versa. While initially suggesting similarities between the results of paper-based and GBL activities, further examination of the collected data uncovers nuanced differences in cognitive responses. These subtle yet significant variations warrant deeper investigation, as developed below.

Considering the dichotomy between relaxation and engagement, while paper-based learning appears to foster a slightly more relaxed learning environment, characterized by moments of tranquility and calm, gameplay shows an aura of heightened arousal and engagement. This heightened state of arousal during gameplay may signify a deeper level of cognitive stimulation, where learners are actively immersed in dynamic problem-solving scenarios.

Moreover, the differential responses in *Appreciation* underscore the profound impact of experiential learning on children's perceptions and attitudes towards educational content. GBL activities seem to evoke a deeper sense of appreciation and enjoyment, transforming learning from a passive endeavor into an enriching and enjoyable experience.

Finally, descriptive statistics were calculated for the brain wave measurements (Table 2). The analysis unveiled significant differences in brain activity during each game. Figures 4, 5, 6, 7 and 8 display the analysis results, comparing brain waves metrics across the two games and illustrating variations in attention, familiarity, and relaxation levels. These results indicate that:

- Both games showed similar mean appreciation levels (Figure 4), which aligns with the children's positive feedback. The higher variability for the FC game might suggest that individual preferences varied more for this game.
- Attention levels (Figure 5) were consistently higher for the FC game, suggesting that children were more engaged and attentive during this game.
- Familiarity levels (Figure 6) were higher and more variable for FSS, indicating that while some children learned with the game, others did not.
- Levels of mental effort (Figure 7) were similar between the two games, with the FSS game showing slightly higher effort levels, possibly indicating greater engagement or complexity.
- Relaxation levels (Figure 8) were slightly higher and less variable for the FC game, suggesting a more consistently relaxing experience, indicating that the FC game may have been perceived as less stressful or more relaxing.

The comparison between "F*lying through the Solar System*" (FSS) and "*Flying through the Continents*" (FC) is crucial to assess how different learning contexts impact the brain waves of children with ADHD. While both games are designed to teach names and locations, their unique contexts may affect attention, relaxation and other cognitive aspects differently. Evaluating both allows for a broader understanding of how different types of educational content influence learning and cognitive engagement in these children.

Overall, the evaluation of brain waves data reveals that both games were well-received and enjoyable. FC games required more attention and were more consistently relaxing, while FSS games showed more variability in *Appreciation* and *Familiarity*, suggesting different learning curves. Both games were generally easy to understand, with the FSS game requiring slightly more mental effort.

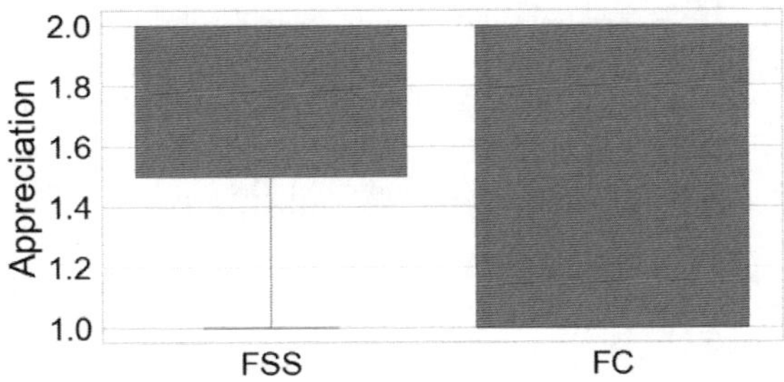

Figure 4. Appreciation Levels by Game

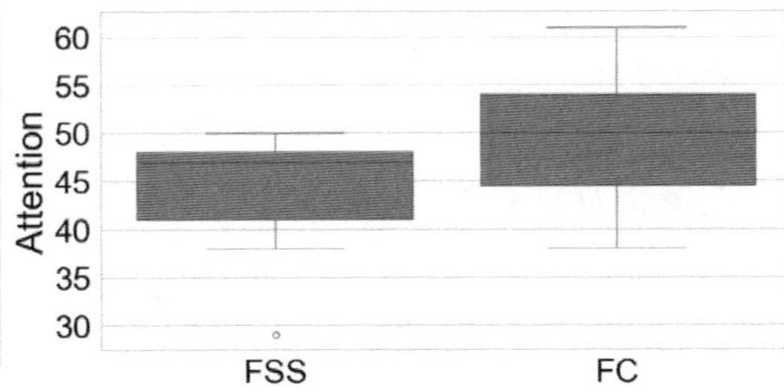

Figure 5. Attention Levels by Game

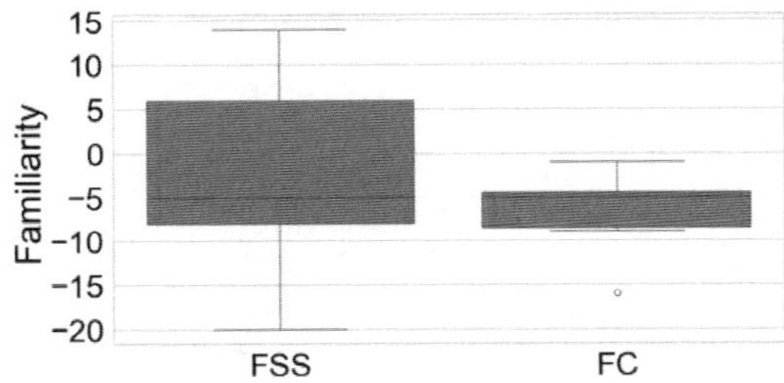

Figure 6. Familiarity Levels by Game

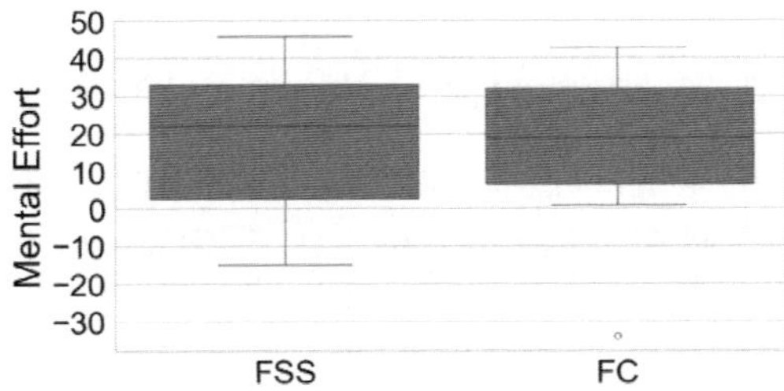

Figure 7. Mental effort Levels by Game

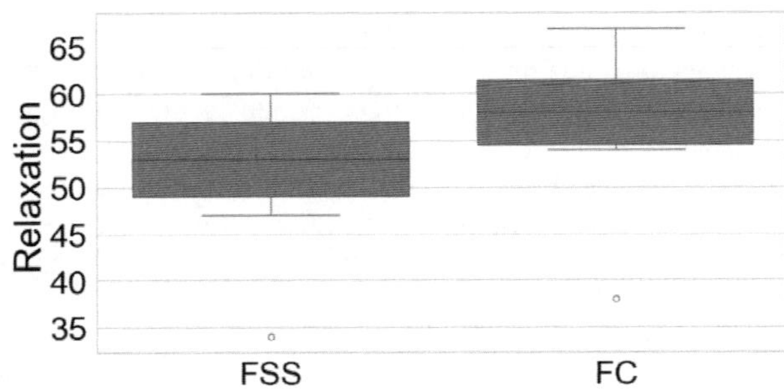

Figure 8. Relaxation Level by Game

4.2.2 Knowledge Acquisition Analysis: Traditional vs. Game-Based Learning

The data shown in Table 4 were merged using each child's unique identifier (ID#), enabling the integration of the results from the pre- and post-tests. This enabled an analysis of the extent to which children learned with each of the methods.

The results indicate substantial improvements in post-test scores for both learning methods (GBL and traditional). However, most participants showed greater progress when using the "*Flying through the Solar System*" (FSS) game. This game not only captured the children's attention more effectively but also promoted greater appreciation and mental effort, suggesting a more interactive and stimulating learning environment. Specifically, the data showed that attention levels were consistently higher during the FSS game, which indicates that this type of content may be more effective in keeping children focused. Moreover, the variability in familiarity suggests that while some children quickly adapted and learned effectively with FSS, others performed better with traditional methods, underscoring the importance of tailoring educational strategies to the individual needs of each student. This finding highlights that while FSS can significantly enhance learning for many students, traditional methods still hold value for others, emphasizing the need for a diverse approach in educational practices.

Interestingly, the effectiveness of each method varied among participants. Some children showed remarkable progress with GBL, while others achieved similar or even better results with paper-based methods. For instance, while some participants using the "*Flying through the Solar System*" (FSS) game saw substantial score improvements, others using the traditional method (PP) also showed significant gains. This underscores the importance of tailoring the learning medium to the individual preferences and strengths of each student.

5. CONCLUSIONS

The purpose of this section is to present the conclusions derived from comparing the cognitive and emotional engagement of children during traditional paper-based learning and GBL.

5.1 Effectiveness and Brain Patterns in Learning Methods

After thorough analysis, we conclude that the study successfully achieved its objectives. The data provides clear evidence regarding the effectiveness and motivational aspects of GBL (O1) and reveals distinct patterns in brain waves behaviors among children with ADHD (O2):

- **O1:** The results indicate that educational video games enhance the learning experience for children with ADHD. Brain waves analysis revealed higher levels of engagement during GBL compared to traditional methods. The *Familiarity* values obtained confirm that, for the most part, children acquire more knowledge in a shorter period of time with GBL.
- **O2:** The EEG data analysis showed distinct brain waves patterns between traditional and GBL methods. GBL resulted in higher mean and maximum values of *Attention* and *Relaxation*, suggesting enhanced focus compared to traditional methods. *Appreciation* and *Mental Effort* were also higher in GBL, indicating that children found the games more engaging. While some children experienced occasional higher stress levels during GBL overall, the data suggests this method creates a more stimulating environment for ADHD children.

Regarding the Research Questions (RQ1, RQ2, RQ3, RQ4, and RQ5) that support these objectives (O1 and O2), we can confirm that all of them are met, as demonstrated below. We can conclude that the results indicate that the playability of GBL is well accepted by children with ADHD, showing higher levels of attention and engagement during gameplay (**RQ1**). The brain waves data demonstrated greater appreciation and enjoyment during GBL, indicating positive sympathy and enjoyment factors (**RQ2**). The consistent concentration and low stress levels observed during gameplay suggest that the ease of use of these video games is positive (**RQ3**). Higher overall quality, reflected in better attention, engagement, and relaxation, suggests that the percentage accuracy quality factor of these video games is high (**RQ4**). Brain waves data showed higher cognitive engagement during GBL compared to traditional methods, suggesting that video games do improve cognitive engagement (**RQ5**).

In summary, GBL shows advantages over traditional methods in sustaining children's attention and engagement. The higher levels of appreciation suggest that GBL offers a more enjoyable and less stressful learning environment.

5.2 Knowledge Acquisition in Learning Methods

We can conclude that the study successfully achieved assess knowledge acquisition in both traditional and GBL methods (O3):

O3: The results in Table 4 indicate significant post-test score improvements for both methods.

Regarding the Research Question (RQ6) supporting objective (O3), the results show that GBL often led to greater knowledge acquisition within the same period of time compared to traditional methods for many participants. However, traditional learning also resulted in substantial improvements. This indicates that both methods can be effective in facilitating knowledge acquisition, depending on the individual learner's needs and preferences. Furthermore, the *Familiarity* variable evaluated, closely related to RQ6, reflects the learning curve. The analyzed data indicates that children became proficient more quickly with GBL, suggesting greater knowledge acquisition within the same timeframe. However, as mentioned earlier, the effectiveness of each method varies based on individual preferences and learning styles.

As a general reflection from this research, it can be said that this study provides compelling evidence that GBL offers significant benefits over traditional methods, enhancing an effective and motivating learning environment. Additionally, the distinct brain wave patterns observed during GBL suggest it is more cognitively stimulating. In conclusion, GBL can serve as a valuable supplement to traditional educational methods, providing personalized and engaging content that addresses the unique learning needs of children with ADHD. By leveraging the strengths of both approaches, educators can create a more inclusive and effective learning environment that fosters academic success and holistic development.

6. FUTURE WORK

Given the small sample size of seven children aged 7 to 9, future studies should expand the sample to improve the reliability and generalizability of findings.

Subsequent research will involve including non-ADHD children and diverse serious video games targeting cognitive skills like attention and memory. This approach aims to identify brain wave activity patterns in children with ADHD compared to typically developing children, across various game-related abilities. These patterns could potentially serve as diagnostic markers, enhancing clinicians' ability to diagnose ADHD more effectively.

ACKNOWLEDGEMENT

Authors would like to APADAHCAS (Association of Parents of People with Attention Deficit and Hyperactivity Disorder in the province of Castellón) for the participation of their children and to the staff of Lernin Games, S.L., developers of the Kokoro Kids app, for their collaboration in this research.

This work has been partially funded by the e-DIPLOMA, project number 101061424 and by the OSCAR project number 101132432, both funded by the European Union (EU). Views and opinions expressed are, however, those of the authors only and do not necessarily reflect those of the EU or the European Research Executive Agency (REA). Neither the EU nor the granting authority can be held responsible for them.

REFERENCES

Alchalabi, A. E., Shirmohammadi, S., Eddin, A. N., & Elsharnouby, M. (2018). FOCUS: Detecting ADHD patients by an EEG-based serious game. *IEEE transactions on instrumentation and measurement*, *67*(7), 1512–1520. https://doi.org/10.1109/tim.2018.2838158

Ato, M., López-García, J. J., & Benavente, A. (2013). Un sistema de clasificación de los diseños de investigación en psicología. *Anales de psicología*, *29*(3), 1038–1059. https://doi.org/10.6018/analesps.29.3.178511

Avila-Pesantez, D., Rivera, L. A., Vaca-Cardenas, L., Aguayo, S., & Zuniga, L. (2018). Towards the improvement of ADHD children through augmented reality serious games: Preliminary results. *2018 IEEE Global Engineering Education Conference (EDUCON)*, 843–848.

Boyle, E. A., Hainey, T., Connolly, T. M., Gray, G., Earp, J., Ott, M., Lim, T., Ninaus, M., Ribeiro, C., & Pereira, J. (2016). An update to the systematic literature review of empirical evidence of the impacts and outcomes of computer games and serious games. *Computers & Education*, *94*, 178–192. https://doi.org/10.1016/j.compedu.2015.11.003

Brito, G. N. O., Pinto, R. C. A., & Lins, M. F. C. (1995). A behavioral assessment scale for attention deficit disorder in brazilian children based on DSM-IIIR criteria. *Journal of Abnormal Child Psychology*, *23*(4), 509–520. https://doi.org/10.1007/bf01447211

Fredricks, J. A., Blumenfeld, P. C., & Paris, A. H. (2004). School engagement: Potential of the concept, state of the evidence. *Review of Educational Research*, *74*(1), 59–109. https://doi.org/10.3102/00346543074001059

Furió, D., González-Gancedo, S., Juan, M.-C., Seguí, I., & Rando, N. (2013). Evaluation of learning outcomes using an educational iPhone game vs. traditional game. *Computers & Education*, *64*, 1–23. https://doi.org/10.1016/j.compedu.2012.12.001

García-Redondo, P., García, T., Areces, D., Núñez, J. C., & Rodríguez, C. (2019). Serious games and their effect improving attention in students with learning disabilities. *International Journal of Environmental Research and Public Health*, *16*(14), 2480. https://doi.org/10.3390/ijerph16142480

Hussein, M. H., Ow, S. H., Cheong, L. S., Thong, M.-K., & Ale Ebrahim, N. (2019). Effects of digital game-based learning on elementary science learning: A systematic review. *IEEE access: practical innovations, open solutions*, *7*, 62465–62478. https://doi.org/10.1109/access.2019.2916324

Juiter, C., & Wu, K.-C. (2021). The analysis of brainwaves to measuring music tone impact on behavior of ADHD children. En *Universal Access in Human-Computer Interaction. Design Methods and User Experience* (pp. 555–566). Springer International Publishing.

Liu, Y., Sourina, O., & Hou, X. (2014). Neurofeedback games to improve cognitive abilities. *2014 International Conference on Cyberworlds*.

Lopez-Fernandez, D., Gordillo, A., Alarcon, P. P., & Tovar, E. (2021). Comparing traditional teaching and game-based learning using teacher-authored games on computer science education. *IEEE transactions on education*, *64*(4), 367–373. https://doi.org/10.1109/te.2021.3057849

Lorch, E. P., Milich, R., Astrin, C. C., & Berthiaume, K. S. (2006). Cognitive engagement and story comprehension in typically developing children and children with ADHD from preschool through elementary school. *Developmental Psychology*, *42*(6), 1206–1219. https://doi.org/10.1037/0012-1649.42.6.1206

Manero, B., Torrente, J., Fernandez-Vara, C., & Fernandez-Manjon, B. (2017). Investigating the impact of gaming habits, gender, and age on the effectiveness of an educational video game: An exploratory study. *IEEE transactions on learning technologies*, *10*(2), 236–246. https://doi.org/10.1109/tlt.2016.2572702

Moriyama, T. S., Polanczyk, G., Caye, A., Banaschewski, T., Brandeis, D., & Rohde, L. A. (2012). Evidence-based information on the clinical use of neurofeedback for ADHD. *Neurotherapeutics: The Journal of the American Society for Experimental NeuroTherapeutics*, *9*(3), 588–598. https://doi.org/10.1007/s13311-012-0136-7

Munoz, J. E., Lopez, D. S., Lopez, J. F., & Lopez, A. (2015). Design and creation of a BCI videogame to train sustained attention in children with ADHD. *2015 10th Computing Colombian Conference (10CCC)*.

Penolazzi, B., Spironelli, C., & Angrilli, A. (2008). Delta EEG activity as a marker of dysfunctional linguistic processing in developmental dyslexia. *Psychophysiology*, *45*(6), 1025–1033. https://doi.org/10.1111/j.1469-8986.2008.00709.x

Rebollo, C., Remolar, I., Rossano, V., & Lanzilotti, R. (2022). Multimedia augmented reality game for learning math. *Multimedia Tools and Applications*, *81*(11), 14851–14868. https://doi.org/10.1007/s11042-021-10821-3

Rief, S. F. (2012). *How to reach and teach children with ADD / ADHD: Practical techniques, strategies, and interventions*. John Wiley & Sons.

Wagner, B. J. (2000). Attention deficit hyperactivity disorder: current concepts and underlying mechanisms. *Journal of Child and Adolescent Psychiatric Nursing: Official Publication of the Association of Child and Adolescent Psychiatric Nurses, Inc*, *13*(3), 113–124. https://doi.org/10.1111/j.1744-6171.2000.tb00088.x

Wang, Q., Sourina, O., & Nguyen, M. K. (2010). EEG-based "serious" games design for medical applications. *2010 International Conference on Cyberworlds*, 270–276.

THE ROLE OF PEER SUPPORT IN STRENGTHENING COMMUNITY VALUES, SOCIAL SKILLS AND EDUCATION IN SUB-SAHARAN AFRICA

Ibolya Tomory
Óbuda University, Ágoston Trefort Centre for Engineering Teacher Education, Hungary

ABSTRACT

In social sciences and in pedagogy, the role of peers, peer groups and social relationships in successful learning and belonging is not unknown. This often refers to small group or pair learning and its positive effects.
This paper addresses the topic from the perspective of African traditions, community values and their transmission in traditional education. It also provides insights into some concrete contemporary examples and programmes in which peer support/peer learning is consciously applied. This is a less discussed aspect of the resources on education in Sub-Saharan Africa, although the role of peers, the contribution of local knowledge and community in one way or another, contributes to the development and learning of the individual in both traditional and contemporary education. Mutual support for each other is one of the traditional values of African communities, along with other areas that are today referred to and emphasised as soft skills. This social skill reflects the collectivist approach of Black African cultures, in which learning is both a personal and shared value. The support received from peers is passed on as part of community belonging today and can be understood as a contribution to learning success. The paper summarises its current forms and characteristics, highlighting the importance of the role of peers in local knowledge and contemporary educational expectations, with the aim to identifying opportunities and challenges for support. It lists examples of programmes that can serve as models for peer support and highlights its role in strengthening communities and addressing various social problems.

KEYWORDS

Peer Support, Traditional Education in Africa, African Societies, Soft Skills in Africa

1. INTRODUCTION

Contemporary helping and teaching each other is not unknown in the history of pedagogy, with examples from antiquity to the present day. Its importance has grown steadily as practical experience and scientific perspectives have complemented each other to shape the disciplines of education. Some authors even see contemporary influences as promoting health (Feith-Falus, 2019; Turner and Shepherd, 1999)

The motivational impact of the learning environment is a well-known factor, where peer support is one of the most effective forces in learning, and also determines behaviour and attitudes towards others and learning. It is particularly important to bear this in mind from adolescence onwards, when peers take over from adults as reference persons. In modern pedagogy, the use of peer activities, small group work and methods is therefore recommended as a means of mediating educational and pedagogical goals. A characteristic of indirect effects management is that the sources of educational effects are tasks, roles and peers, i.e. the teacher indirectly achieves the goals set by providing joint activities and tasks. (Bábosik, 2004) This creates opportunities for experience from which independent thinking, conclusions and lessons can be drawn. In this way, peer support becomes a mutually supportive tool for both learning and expected behaviour. Carl Rogers (1983) also attributes the importance of peer support to self-evaluation and peer evaluation.

In terms of contexts and influences, some authors focus on peers and motivation, others on classroom contexts and learning communities (Ryan, 2000; Meyer-Turner, 2006; Langerné, 2019). Other sources place it in sociocultural and socioeconomic contexts (Lew-Levy et al., 2023).

One of the approaches focuses on how intergenerational and peer relationships play a major role in teaching people to think. While knowledge sharing across varying skill levels is often said to be a matter of greater knowledge, it is often said that learners with greater knowledge do not benefit adequately, while slower learners find it difficult to keep up with faster progress. However, several good practices report on solutions that are effective in this case, including the author's and similar cooperative exercises, such as the one Berzsenyi reported in a lecture. The starting point is that everybody can be good at something and have weaknesses (subject, topic, type of task). Pairing the best and the hardest learners, even in understanding a single unit of learning, a single mosaic, often results in a rebalancing, not to mention an increase in self-confidence, motivation and social skills. This is the basis of cooperative learning methods (Kagan-Kagan, 2009; Berzsenyi, 2015).

The contemporary influences approach to education has become more widely known and accepted as cooperative pair and group approaches have spread, and its geographical reach has expanded to include different countries around the world. (Parkin and McKeganey, 2000; Sugai,2006) In Black Africa, it is also more frequently emerging from the perspectives of learning success, catching up and equal opportunities (Bannink et al, 2016; Takyi-Amoako - Lumumba, 2018)

The approach of this study is different in that it considers contemporary support as a given, inherited from traditional education in Sub-Saharan Africa, which is also part of the soft skills that are highlighted today. To some extent it is already present in today's public education and higher education systems, but it can be more consciously integrated and made a methodological part of daily practice.

The author will list examples of this alongside a peer support/learning-focused presentation of traditional education. In previous publications, in agreement with some other sources, she refers to the tension between Western-style education and African traditional education, and links peer support to the potential of soft skills (missing links, etc.) and the African understanding of collectivism as a way of understanding peer support as a boundary between community values and cohesion, social skills and education (Mitchell, 2023; Serpell 2011; Serpell-Adomson-Holley, 2017).

2. APPROACH AND METHODOLOGICAL BACKGROUND

This study is based on a combination of qualitative and quantitative data collection, using both social science and ethnographic-anthropological approaches. The world of local society, which we need to understand in terms of local characteristics of regions or small units of a continent, cannot be divided into quantitative indicators or 'soft' data or intuitions. The two ways of collecting and interpreting data can be used as a complement to each other, without any specific conditions and with prior knowledge.

The research thus draws on existing literature and summarises peer support as a pedagogical phenomenon and its African contexts. It reviews the existing sources and looks at its place in the framework of traditional education and addresses its emergence embedded in socio-cultural contexts and education, and contemporary examples of its applicability in school and community settings in sub-Saharan Africa. It identifies the place, role and functions of peer collaboration, reflecting on indigenous values and practices and their potential for educational innovation today.

The other side of data collection is qualitative, on-the-spot observation and the additional research possibilities that this offers, such as interviews. One of the author's fields of study is cultural anthropology, which is part phenomenology and part history and history of knowledge, and participatory fieldwork is an effective way of gaining insights and understanding of the situation. In the anthropological approach, the subject is presented as a consciously filtered field, the engagement sometimes being limited to an example, a single site. However, this can provide a mosaic-like picture, similar to historical detail, and is therefore useful and used in a wide variety of research. (Kottak, 2021; Berzsenyi, 2024) In this way, the study of historical, social, cultural and religious interactions as a whole, both through source processing and through the classical anthropological-ethnographic approach, mixing both, leads to valuable results in research, whether looking back to the past or to the present, not to mention the articulation of sensitive issues, such as the history and interpretation of disability, or the subject of this study.

Data collection is more structured in terms of collecting, selecting, reading and interpreting the content of the sources, a quantitative approach. More qualitative, less structured, observing and questioning in a field-adapted way, it focuses on what is important locally, in line with the anthropological approach (A. Gergely, 1996; Berzsenyi, 2020)

The present study does not aim to shed light on the topic in its entirety, but to provide an overview and draw attention to the less ummarized aspects and opportunities that currently exist, so that practitioners can be better prepared to launch a development programme, design training and undertake further research. The resource analysis in the introduction and later sections provides the theoretical background and leads through to the examples listed. The fieldwork will take place in East Africa, Kenya, Tanzania, Uganda and Ethiopia.

Overall and in essence:

The aim of the study: Identify opportunities and challenges for support. Raising awareness of the valuable potential of traditional education in contemporary schools and learning. To help find the links between local values and modern, European-style education, and to fill in the so-called missing links. To present programmes that are examples of how peer support can be an effective tool for strengthening communities and addressing various social problems in sub-Saharan Africa.

Research question:

Are there elements of traditional knowledge and education that can be used in today's education and development programmes? What are they?

How does peer support support the preservation of community values, the development of important skills and the success of learning-to-teach?

Research method: a combination of two research methods will be implemented.

One: using a quantitative approach to study sources and ummariz their essential elements. Some of the sources are ethnographic-anthropological descriptions of ethnic groups, others are about peer support and its emergence.

The other: qualitative research using the methods of anthropological observation and participant observation in the field. This means that different ethnic groups, different types of settlements and schools were visited by the author, and the characteristics of traditional and contemporary education and communities, their ways of thinking and the role and meanings of peer support in these. She recorded the data collected in a fieldwork diary and on images and video, analysed them to find elements relevant to the topic, discussed them in comparison with information from literature sources and supplemented them with her own experiences.

Together, they formed the content of the article and the author's position.

3. THE ROLE OF PEERS IN TRADITIONAL EDUCATION SYSTEMS IN SUB-SAHARAN AFRICA

Peer support is deeply rooted in the community and collective learning culture of Black Africa and is reflected in traditional education. Indigenous education systems often rely on the community and the family to transmit knowledge and preserve social values. The concept in an African perspective refers to individuals helping and supporting each other in similar life situations or challenges. This practice is rooted in Black Africa and deeply embedded in the lives of different communities. It not only provides personal support, but also strengthens community ties and contributes to knowledge transfer and sharing (Sifuna, 1990; Jukes et al, 2018). The importance of peer support is reflected in the community and family linkages and its location in the indigenous education system, but the changes also pose challenges to its contemporary relevance. Perspectives on this are ummarized in Table 1.

Table 1. Place and role of peer support in the community and in traditional education systems

	Perspective, interpretationt	Impact
Community		
Community-based support	Community cohesion and support are traditionally strong in Black African societies. In this sense, peer support is a natural part of everyday life, where people help each other solve problems and provide each other with advice. The rites belonging to the life of the community connect the members and families.	Fostering community spirit and collective learning, where everyone plays a role in sharing and maintaining knowledge.
Family and friendship relationships	Family and friendship ties are also so important that peer support often appears in these relationships as well, for example advice from older family members and help between friends. Learning often takes place within the family unit.	It is here that the transmission of life skills, culture, traditions and moral values begins, often with older brothers and sisters teaching younger brothers and sisters and practising different roles to support each other.
Education		
Learning groups, community learning and rituals	Indigenous education systems often rely on community learning and study groups. In these groups, students help each other, share their knowledge and experiences, which strengthens the knowledge base of the entire community. rituals and ceremonies play an important role in the transmission of knowledge. These events provide community learning opportunities.	Peer support happens naturally here, as older children and young people help the younger ones to learn and develop.
Master-student relations	Master-apprentice relationships are common in indigenous cultures, where more experienced individuals mentor younger ones. This includes not only professional but also life coaching.	The pattern of peer support here is that of master-mentor relationships and cooperation with other learners, embedded in learning from older, more experienced learners.
Challenges and opportunities		
Modernization and changes	Globalisation and modernisation are also changing traditional support systems. It has been difficult to preserve traditions in Western forms of education. Today, there is an effort to re-harness the strengths of peer support and adapt to new challenges.	Peer learning and support efforts are necessary and useful in terms of flexibility and adaptation to changes.
Peer Tutoring and Mentoring	In the school system, peer tutoring and mentoring are also used in more formal settings. Older or better-performing students help younger or lower-performing peers with their learning, often in organised groups or individual sessions.	Learning outcomes and academic performance improve, while social support and cooperation between students is strengthened.
Learning Groups and Collaborative/Cooperative Learning	The use of cooperative learning and learning groups is also widespread in schools. In these groups, students work together on projects, share knowledge and support each other in the learning process.	Critical thinking, problem-solving skills and teamwork are developed, and the sense of community is strengthened.

Community and family learning and its more organized forms in traditional education systems are not far from the ideas of important skill areas to be developed, which are considered of utmost importance today. Such is the field of soft skills, the elements of which are implicit in the collective functioning of the community, in the relationship of people to each other and in its educational formations. Of course, the contents of the table only comprehensively show some commonly found elements and cannot give a complete picture of the countries of Africa and the various ethnic groups. In Table 2, we see some examples of how peer support appears in traditional education, many of which were experienced by the author himself during fieldwork and are also shown in the sources. (Sifuna, 1990; Omolewa, 2007; Funteh, 2015)

Table 2. Some examples of peer support in the community and African traditional education systems

Country	Ethnicity	Cultural element, practice	Peer support
Kenya	**Maasai**	**Maasai Moran Initiation Rites:** moran (warrior) initiation rites are an important part of young men's coming of age. These ceremonies take place in groups, and the older Morans teach and support the younger ones, sharing their martial skills, cultural knowledge and community norms. (Sankan, 1995)	Young Morans develop a strong peer support network to help them through initiation ceremonies and everyday challenges.
	Kikuyu	**Kikuyu Peer Teaccing:** older children traditionally teach younger children about roles, farming, crafts and other life skills. This transmission of knowledge often takes place in informal settings, such as at home or in the fields (Kenyatta, 1962).	The older children are involved and are gradually introduced to responsibility, they participate in the teaching and mentoring of the younger ones, strengthening community bonds.
Tanzania			
	Chagga	**Chagga Dancing and Storytelling Groups:** dance and storytelling play an important role in the transmission of cultural knowledge. Older children and young people lead dance groups and storytelling sessions where younger children participate and learn (Mosha, 1999).	These groups provide community experiences where younger people learn from older people and are supported in strengthening their cultural identity.
	Hadza	**Hadza Foraging and Hunting Education:** lead a hunter-gatherer lifestyle, with older children teaching younger children the art of hunting and gathering. Knowledge is often passed on in groups, where younger children watch and learn from older ones (Lew-Levy, 2019).	The role of older children in teaching and mentoring is important and strengthens community cohesion and survival skills.
Uganda			
	Baganda	**Baganda Clan Education System:** clans play an important role in education and the transmission of social norms. Older clan members teach younger members about traditions, history and moral values (Beattie, 2002).	The older children within the clan help and mentor the younger ones, ensuring a continuous transfer of cultural knowledge.
	Gisu	**Community values, ritual learning-teaching:** by gradually introducing older people to community practices and rituals, they set an example of knowledge sharing. They teach about important aspects of life and activities through initiation ceremonies. During Inemba, for example, initiates have three days to get to know their peers and share their experiences. Master-disciple relationships are also important. More experienced farmers mentor younger ones and help them learn the skills of farming and the rules of community life (Makwa, 2010).	Study groups are often set up, where young people have to share their knowledge, teach and help each other. This practice not only helps to transfer professional knowledge but also strengthens community ties.
Ethiopia			
	Amhara	**Amhara Traditional Schools (Chewa Bet)**: in traditional schools (chewa bet), older students often help younger students with their studies, especially in memorising religious texts and learning liturgical chants (Chali et al, 2022)	Mentoring and supporting older students helps younger ones to achieve academic success and preserve religious traditions.
	Oromo	**Gadaa System**: Gadaa is a traditional social, political and cultural system that ensures the transmission of knowledge across generations. Grouped by age, older generations teach younger generations the rules, history and practices of Gadaa (Tomory, 2010).	Peer support and mentoring among younger people helps to maintain the system and strengthen community identity.

The information in Tables 1 and 2 shows that children and young people are involved in economic and social activities and that involvement from an early age ensures the acquisition of social and community skills and techniques in a practice-oriented environment. This participation also provides opportunities to practise other skills such as metacognition, psychomotor skills, cooperating with others. They will experience how to deal with different situations, conflicts and how to communicate their emotions, thoughts and reflect on events, behaviour, etc. around them.

These examples reinforce the author's view that peer support is not new in African education, and that it is therefore not only possible to incorporate it into today's school settings, but that it can be built on existing foundations. What is more questionable is what role it is intended to play, what is expected of it and how it is reflected in the level of burden and responsibility of the learner, and how compatible it is with the expectations of formal education.

4. PEER SUPPORT IN CONTEMPORARY AFRICA

Peer support and peer learning are increasingly becoming recognized tools in education and community development programs in sub-Saharan Africa. These approaches enable communities to mobilize internal resources and achieve sustainable development outcomes. Programs using such peer support:

- Health Initiatives: peer support is a widely used method in the treatment of HIV/AIDS and other chronic diseases. For example, peer groups in Tanzania and Kenya help patients access treatment, provide emotional support and overcome stigma.
- Mental Health: in the field of mental health, in Uganda, for example, programs have been launched in which people with mental health problems help their peers to recover.
- Women and Girls: there are many programs aimed at supporting women and girls, especially in the areas of education, health and economic development. For example, peer mentoring programs in Malawi help girls stay in school and avoid early marriage.

The author came across the following specific programs, which are good examples of the importance of peer support and peer learning in East Africa.

Kenya
TAP (Tegemeza Adherence Program)

- TAP is a peer support programme that helps HIV-positive people adhere to treatment. The programme includes trained peer mentors who help participants to adhere to medication adherence, provide social support and manage stigma.
- Impact: Improved treatment adherence and overall health of patients and reduced HIV-related stigma.

Champion Community Initiative

- This health programme in Kenya uses a community-based approach to tackle various health problems such as malaria, HIV/AIDS and tuberculosis. Under the programme, community leaders and trained peer educators help local residents to raise health awareness and disseminate preventive practices.
- Impact: Improved access to health services and health outcomes.

Tanzánia
Kizazi Kipya Project:

- This project focuses on supporting orphans and vulnerable children in Tanzania. Peer support groups help children and young people access education and health services and provide emotional support.
- Impact: The project improved the quality of life and future opportunities of the children and young people involved.

Tanzanian Youth Alliance (TAYOA):

- TAYOA is a youth organization that provides contemporary support and health education for young people, especially in the field of HIV/AIDS prevention. Within the framework of the program, trained peer educators hold sessions and consultations to help their peers develop a healthy lifestyle.
- Effect: It increased the health awareness of young people and reduced the number of HIV infections.

Uganda

StrongMinds Uganda:

- This program focuses on the treatment of depression among Ugandan women. Peer support groups are created where participants can share experiences and develop strategies to improve their mental health.
- Effect: The participants' mental health and quality of life improved, and the incidence of depression decreased.

Uganda Youth Development Link (UYDEL):

- UYDEL is a youth organization that offers different programs to fight poverty and social exclusion. Peer support groups help young people develop employment skills and provide social support.
- Impact: The economic situation and social integration of young people improved.

Etiópia

Integrated Family Health Program (IFHP):

- IFHP provides family planning and health services, with a focus on rural areas. Peer educators trained as part of the program help community members to increase health awareness and use health services.
- Impact: Increased the use of health services and improved the health status of communities.

Network of Networks of HIV Positives in Ethiopia (NEP+):

- This programme supports HIV-positive people in Ethiopia. Peer support networks help participants manage the disease, provide social support and overcome stigma.
- Impact: Improved quality of life and access to treatment for HIV-positive people.

Other programmes that have proven effective in integrating peer support in different areas of Sub-Saharan Africa.

Health Initiatives

Mothers2Mothers (m2m):

- m2m is a program that creates mentoring groups of HIV-positive mothers. These Mentor Mothers are trained to provide support to other HIV-positive mothers, helping them with treatment, prevention and combating stigma.
- Countries: Many sub-Saharan countries, including Kenya, Uganda, Malawi and South Africa.
- Impact: The m2m program helped significantly reduce mother-to-child transmission of HIV and improved access to treatment and patient information.

Zvandiri Program:

- The Zvandiri Program (which means "this is me") supports young HIV-positive people. The program trains youth "Child Adherence Counselors" to support other youth in adhering to antiretroviral therapy and maintaining mental health.
- Country: Zimbabwe.
- Impact: The program achieved significant results in increasing treatment adherence and improving mental health.

Mental Health

BasicNeeds Program:

- BasicNeeds is a program that supports people with mental health problems. Within the framework of the program, peer support groups are created where members can share their experiences and work together on recovery.
- Impact: The program improved access to mental health services and reduced stigma.

Education and Youth Development
Camfed (Campaign for Female Education):

- Camfed is an organization that supports girls' education. In the program, alumnae serve as mentors, helping current students stay in school and achieve academic success.
- Countries: Zimbabwe, Zambia, Ghana, Tanzania, Malawi.
- Impact: The program significantly increased girls' school participation and performance.
-

Economic Development
BRAC Uganda's Empowerment and Livelihood for Adolescents (ELA) Program:

- The goal of the BRAC ELA program is to improve the economic and social situation of adolescents. As part of the program, peer support groups are created, in which young people receive training in business knowledge and financial awareness, as well as support each other in taking advantage of economic opportunities.
- Country: Uganda.
- Impact: The program increased the economic independence of young people and improved their quality of life.

These programmes all show that peer support can be an effective tool for strengthening communities and addressing various social problems in Sub-Saharan Africa.

5. TRADITIONAL ELEMENTS AND PEER SUPPORT OPPORTUNITIES IN EDUCATION

The impact of modernisation and globalisation is also being felt in African countries. Urbanisation and technological development are bringing changes in traditional ways of life and education. An important question is how these communities can preserve their cultural identity and traditions while adapting to the challenges of the modern world. One option is to incorporate them into today's educational frameworks. From a pedagogical perspective, peer learning programmes have long been developed at all levels of education, such as:

- **Public education**: peer learning is increasingly popular as it promotes active participation and ownership of the learning process by students. In Nigeria and Ghana, peer learning groups are being set up in which students teach and support each other, and many countries are making similar conscious efforts.
- **Adult education:** peer learning methods are used in all fields, but particularly in the agricultural sector. In Uganda and Kenya, for example, farmers learn from each other about sustainable agricultural practices and new technologies.
- **Community development**: in community development projects, peer learning helps local people to share knowledge and experience and to solve local problems together. This is particularly important for reducing poverty and increasing community resilience.

In East African countries, there are several successful educational development programmes and good practices that the author has encountered during fieldwork. Here are some concrete examples and initiatives from Kenya, Tanzania, Uganda and Ethiopia where peer support and peer learning are consciously integrated and central:

Kenya
Digital Learning Programme (DLP)

- A programme launched by the Kenyan government to provide laptops to primary school pupils. The programme aims to develop digital skills and make learning more interactive.
- **Peer Learning**: students learn together and help each other to use technology, encouraging group work and collaborative learning.

Young African Leadership Initiative (YALI)

- A USAID-supported program that develops young African leaders, including in the education sector. Program participants mentor each other and share their experiences.
- **Peer Support**: Participants form networks and work together on projects, supporting each other in developing leadership skills and implementing educational innovations

Tanzania

Tanzania Beyond Tomorrow (TBT)

- A non-profit organization focused on training teachers and educating students. The aim of the program is to introduce modern pedagogical methods and support peer learning.
- **Peer Learning**: During teacher training, emphasis is placed on cooperative learning techniques, which are then applied in the classroom.

BridgeIT Tanzania

- A project supported by USAID and Nokia that uses mobile technology to improve education. The program provides students with interactive learning materials and videos.
- **Peer Support:** Students watch videos and work on assignments together, encouraging group learning and social support.

Uganda

Educate!

- A non-profit organization that provides entrepreneurship and leadership training in secondary schools in Uganda. The aim of the program is to develop students' practical skills.
- **Peer Support:** Students mentor each other and work together on projects, strengthening teamwork and leadership skills.

Strengthening Education Systems for Improved Learning (SESIL)

- A program launched by the Ugandan government and its partners to improve learning outcomes. Among other things, the program focuses on teacher training and the introduction of peer learning methods.
- **Peer Learning:** Cooperative learning techniques introduced in schools, where students work together and support each other in the learning process.

Ethiopia

General Education Quality Improvement Program (GEQIP)

- A program financed by the Ethiopian government and the World Bank, which aims to improve the quality of primary and secondary education. As part of the program, teachers are trained and peer learning methods are introduced.
- **Peer Learning**: In teacher training, emphasis is placed on cooperative learning and social support between students.

Digital School in a Box

- A new initiative to provide portable digital learning tools to rural schools. The aim of the program is to improve access to technology and increase digital learning opportunities.
- **Peer Learning:** Students use digital tools together, help each other master the technology and the learning process.

These examples give a taste of how peer support and peer learning methods are used in modern education in East Africa, both by integrating traditional values and introducing new pedagogical methods. These programs contribute to improving learning outcomes, strengthening cooperation between students and preserving community values.

6. LOCAL PRACTICES AND CHALLENGES OF FORMAL EDUCATION

In many African societies, in the local enculturation-socialization-education system, the cultural meaning systems, especially in rural communities, differ from those that determine the pedagogical practices of public schools.

"The African traditional practice of assigning social responsibility to young people from an early age is highly compatible with contemporary goals of education in Africa and elsewhere. At best, it can serve as a context for learning about health and nutrition, as well as fostering the values of cooperation and nurturant support of others, contributing to peaceful coexistence in society. Participation by children in family work is construed in many African societies as priming for social responsibility, an important dimension of intelligence. Work and play are better understood as complementary dimensions of activity than as discrete alternatives. Cooperation with peers can be mobilized as a resource for co-constructive learning. Strategic opportunities for countering systemic bias in educational systems include generative curriculum development, teacher sensitization to psychosocial dimensions of learners' development, and legitimizing local community impact as a criterion of educational success." (Serpell-Adamson-Holly, 2017:20)

From the examples listed above, in addition to the positive side, it can also be seen that the dimensions of responsibility, social and individual responsibility are clearly inherent in traditional community cohesion and education. This can be interpreted as a heavy burden, but above all, it must be taken into account that the sociocultural background factors of peer support in formal education are completely different and receive a different interpretation. In Western education, this phenomenon is primarily used in a cooperative methodological environment with the aim of improving learning success and the results of individual subjects, or, similar to the previously mentioned example, as a solution to a given topic or deadlock by consciously organizing pairs of better learners and students with difficulty.

The tension between the two approaches cannot be separated from the gap between collectivist local and Western-type thinking coming from outside. In traditional education, goals, methods and content were intertwined in the principle of permanence and a holistic approach to learning, learning was simultaneously multi-purpose and prepared for a thorough knowledge of certain specializations, but always in a life-like environment, through life-like and comprehensible contents and activities. Theory was less and more understandable than in Western-style education. In tribal education, the content of learning was related to the social content in which people had to live and the individual became a cultural being, a community member and a craftsman at the same time. (Tomory, 2019) In my opinion, this is difficult to reconcile with the technique-oriented approach of Western-style schools that focus on the cognitive side, on mere knowledge. The conservation and preservation of traditional practices can be attributed to efforts to preserve culture.

From this perspective, it must also be difficult to understand the peer support function, which perhaps places a great deal of responsibility on the fitalos. While agreeing that a child or young person should not be burdened with what they are not yet mature enough to do, the author's view is that it is certainly necessary to set the boundaries of peer support/learning responsibilities, but at the same time it cannot be taken out of the cultural embeddedness as if it were not part of a system.

Serpell (2017) argues that the social responsibility traditionally conferred on young people from a young age is largely compatible with the contemporary goals of education, both in Africa and elsewhere in the world.

In this light, the common ground between formal formal education and traditional African principles and practices may be the design and implementation of peer support in education and headship programmes, based on community values but taking into account age and present life circumstances.

7. CONCLUSION AND RECOMMENDATION

Based on the examples taken from the traditional education presented and from today's programs, it can be said that there are similar elements and, overall, the aforementioned ethnic groups incorporate the practices of peer support and traditional education into their daily lives in a similar way, thus strengthening their community cohesion and passing on their knowledge to the next generations.

Today's developments and programs indicate that it is a traditional practice in Africa to involve young people in assuming social responsibility and that this is compatible with contemporary goals and the goals of education.

We take the position that cooperation with peers is best realized in the context of learning, but it is not always necessary to follow patterns rooted in imported formal education. The source analysis and on-site empirical research experiences also point to the fact that, instead of external approaches and models and practices, learning about and including African enculturation values and non-formal educational practices in the various programs is a feasible and effective solution.

The basic principle of the proposal is that the success and reliability of all development and innovation is based on an understanding of local needs, knowledge and values, and that all support requires a participatory approach and understanding of these. Incorporating local knowledge, community belonging and the educational traditions that go with it, from planning and needs assessment to professional principles and implementation steps, must be adapted to community and societal needs, variables and changes, because they can only be understood in the context in which they are rooted and exist today.

The traditional African practice of giving young people social responsibilities from early childhood onwards is largely compatible with contemporary goals and objectives of education in Africa and elsewhere. At its best, it can serve as a context for learning. promoting the values of health and nutrition and cooperation and collaboration. education in cooperation and collaboration, and education in supporting others, which contributes to peaceful social coexistence.

Agreeing with Mitchell (2023): while peer learning cannot solve disadvantage, difficult economic circumstances, poverty and access to school, it can make a significant contribution to individual learning progress and the development of social competence.

REFERENCES

Babosik, I., (2004). *Neveléselmélet. Nevelés az Európai Unióban.* Osiris tankönyvek, Budapest

Bannink, F.et al, (2016). "I Like to Play with My Friends": Children with Spina Bifida and Belonging in Uganda. In Social Inclusion 4 (1), pp 127–141.

Beattie, J., (2002). Bunyoro: An African Kingdom. Mason, OH: Cengage Learning

Berzsenyi, E., (2015). Papság és szerzetesség az etióp zsidóság hagyományos rendjé ben. In: Gér, A. et al (ed.) „Hiszek, hogy megértsem"! Doktoranduszok Országos Szövetsége Hittudományi Osztály Fiatal Kutatók és Doktoranduszok IV. Nemzetközi Teológuskonferenciája. 463 p. L'Harmattan Ki-adó, Károli Gáspár Református Egyetem, pp. 87-94.

Berzsenyi, E., (2020). *Kiválasztott vagy megbélyegzett? Tanítások a fogyatékosságról: a zsidóság, a kereszténység és az iszlám szent könyvei szerint.* Eötvös József Kiadó, Budapest

Berzsenyi, E., (2024). *Bűnös vagy ártatlan? Az európai középkor fogyatékosságtörténete*. Eötvös József Kiadó, Budapest

Chali, G. T. et al, (2022). Education in Ethiopia. Afrika Focus. 34 (2), pp 343–359.

Feith, H.J.- Falus, A. (ed.), (2019). *Egészségfejlesztés és nevelés A kortársoktatás pedagógiai módszertana elméletben és gyakorlatban.* Akadémiai Kiadó, Budapest

Funteh, M. B., (2015). Dimensioning Indigenous African Educational System: A Critical Theory Divide Discourse. *In International Journal of Humanities and Social Science* Vol. 5, No. 4., pp 139-150.

Jukes, M. C. H., (2018). "Respect is an Investment": Community perceptions of social and emotional competencies in early childhood from Mtwara, Tanzania. *In Global Education Review*, 5 (2), pp 160–188.

Kagan, S. – Kagan,M., (2009). Kagan kooperatív tanulás. Önkonet szolgáltató és tan. Kft., Budapest

Kenyatta, J., (1962). *Facing Mount Kenya.* Vintage Publisher

Kottak, C., (2021). *Cultural Anthropology*. McGraw-Hill Education

Langerné, B.J. (2019). A tanulás új útjai: a tanulóközösségek. In Új Pedagógiai Szemle, 2019/5-6., pp 49-65.

Lew-Levy, S. et al (2023). Peer learning and cultural evolution. Child Development Perspectives, 2023;17, pp 97–105.

Lew-Levy, S., (2019). *Children learning from each other in hunter-gatherer societies promotes collaborative problem-solving and can help us rethink approaches to child development.* https://childandfamilyblog.com/children-learning-from-each-other/

Makwa D. B., D., (2010). *Musicking and Dancing Imbalu Circumcison Rituals (Khushina Imbalu): Performing Gender Among the Bagisu of Eastern Uganda.* Dissertation. Makerere University, Kampala

Meyer, D., K. – Turner, J. (2006). Re-conceptualizing Emotion and Motivation to Learn in Classroom Contexts. *In Educational Psychology Review* 18(4), pp 377-390.

Mitchell, R., (2023). Peer support in sub-Saharan Africa: A critical interpretive synthesis of school-based research. *In International Journal of Educational Development* Vol. 96 (2023) 102686, Elsevier, pp 1-9.

Mosha, R.S., (1999). *The Heartbeat of Indigenous Africa: A Study of the Chagga Educational System.* Routledge

Omolewa, M., (2007). Traditional African modes of education: their relevance in the modern world. In International Review of Education, Volume 53, pp 593–612.

Parkin, S. és McKeganey, N., (2000). The Rise and the Rise of Peer Education Approaches. *In Drugs, Education Prevention and Policy*, 7. 3. sz., pp 293–310.

Rogers, C., (1983) *Freedom to Learn for the 80's* (2 nd edition). Ohio, Merrill

Ryan, A.M. (2000). Peer Groups as a Context for the Socialization of Adolescents' Motivation, Engagement, and Achievement in School. *In Educational Psychology*, 35, pp 101-112.

Sankan, S.S., (1995). The maasai. Kenya Literature Bureu, Nairobi

Serpell, R. (2011). Social Responsibility as a Dimension of Intelli gence, and as an Educational Goal: Insights from Programmatic Research in an African Society. *In Child Development Perspectives*, 5(2), 126–133. https://doi.org/10.1111/j.1750–8606.2011.00167.x

Serpell, R., Adamson-Holley, D., (2017). African socialization values and nonformal educational practices: child development, parental beliefs, and educational innovation in rural Zambia. In: (ed.) Abebe, T. et al: Labouring and Learning. Springer., pp 19-43.

Sifuna, D., (1990). Development of education in Africa, The Kennyan experience. Initiatives Ltd., Nairobi, Kenya

Sugai, G. és Horner, R. R., (2006). A promising approach for expanding and sustaining school-wide positive behavior support. *In School Psychology Review*, 35. 2. sz., pp 245–259.

Tabulawa, R., (2013). *Teaching and Learning in Context: Why Pedagogical Reforms Fail in Sub-Saharan Afric*a. CODESRIA. African Books Collective

Takyi-Amoako, E.J - Assi´e-Lumumba, N.T., (2018). *Re-Visioning Education in. Africa: Ubuntu-Inspired Education for Humanity*. Springer

Tomory, I., (2010). Etiópia „többségi kisebbsége", az oromók és egy demokratikus oktatási és társadalmi rendszer: a gadaa. *In Belvedere Meridionale,* 22-1-2., pp 22-35.

Tomory, I., (2019). The Cultural Context of Adaptation Western Education in East-Africa: Paradoxons and Missing Links. *In West East Journal of Social Sciences.* vol.8.-2019., pp 133-145.

Turner G, Shepherd J. (1999). A method in search of a theory: Peer education and health promotion. *In Health Education Research*. 1999;14(2), pp 235–247.

RELATIONSHIP BETWEEN MATHEMATICAL PROBLEM-SOLVING SKILLS AND ASYNCHRONOUS COLLABORATION IN DIGITAL LEARNING ENVIRONMENTS

Alice Barana, Marina Marchisio Conte and Sara Omegna
Department of Molecular Biotechnology and Health Sciences, University of Turin, Piazza Nizza 44, 10153 Torino, Italy

ABSTRACT

This study investigates the relationship between students' problem-solving skills in solving mathematical problems and asynchronous collaboration in digital learning environments. The research focuses on the Digital Math Training (DMT) project, designed by the DELTA research group at the University of Turin, which aims to enhance students' digital mathematics skills and problem-solving abilities. Through a detailed analysis of student participation and performance data, including responses to a final questionnaire on the perceived benefits of asynchronous collaboration, the study identifies significant relationships between students' problem-solving abilities and the effectiveness of their collaborative activities. The findings highlight the benefits of asynchronous forums in fostering a sense of community, collaboration and reflective thinking among students, ultimately contributing to improved mathematical competence. The study's results underline the importance of integrating asynchronous collaborative tools into digital learning environments to support students' academic growth and prepare them for future challenges.

KEYWORDS

Asynchronous Collaboration, Digital Learning Environment, Problem Solving, Mathematics Education, Student Performance, Collaborative Learning

1. INTRODUCTION

Collaborative Learning is defined as a group of learners working together by sharing ideas, solving problems, or pursuing common goals (Lahann & Lambdin 2014). Although traditionally developed in the classroom through peer-to-peer discussions, technological advances have allowed for innovations such as access to transcripts of previous discussions, expanding opportunities for collaboration (Hammond 2017). Technology-enabled asynchronous discussions encourage the articulation of ideas, feedback, problem solving, and reflection on the opinions of others. This has led to talking about Computer Supported Collaborative Learning, a pedagogical approach that uses computing devices to enhance learning through social interaction and by offering new tools such as simulations and visualisations to improve students' conceptual understanding (Ludvigsen & Arnseth 2017). Technological innovations in education have also had a significant impact on how problem-solving skills in Mathematics are developed. For example, asynchronous online discussions, such as forums, allow students to engage in reflective thinking and knowledge construction. These platforms allow students to articulate their ideas and receive feedback, thus fostering a deeper understanding of mathematical concepts and the development of critical thinking. The aim of this research is to examine the relationship between achievement of problem-solving skills in mathematics and asynchronous collaboration in digital learning environments.

2. THEORETICAL FRAMEWORK

In the literature, problem solving is defined by (Martinez 1998) as "the process of moving toward a goal when the path to that goal is uncertain." It elaborates that problem solving occurs every time we achieve something without knowing beforehand how to do it. This encompasses both simple, everyday challenges and more complex, ill-defined problems that require navigating uncertain paths and making decisions step by step (Martinez 1998). It is the basis for creative thinking, new inventions, evolution, continuous improvement, communication, and learning. These skills are therefore essential for every citizen of the world, not only for their careers but also for their everyday life outside work. In this context, mathematics plays a crucial role in enhancing problem-solving skills, particularly in higher education (Fissore et al. 2021).

With the advent of technology in education, we started to talk about Digital Learning Environment (DLE), which is composed by a human component (the learning community), the technological component and the interrelations among the two (Barana & Marchisio 2022). The technological component of a DLE is based on a Learning Management System, through which it is possible to evaluate learning objectives, keep track of the progress of the students involved, and collect data to supervise the learning process (Barana, Marchisio & Miori 2019). Furthermore, within a DLE, online and asynchronous learning modes can be developed; for example, online discussion forums stimulate critical evaluation and thinking skills, as well as reflection on the ideas presented by other participants (Thomas 2002). This leads to the construction of personal meaning, which is not individual but a product of interaction between learners. This tool is asynchronous, non-hierarchical and reciprocal: instead of a mere a transfer of declarative knowledge, the construction of complex knowledge structures is now promoted. Indeed, each participant has the opportunity to be exposed to a variety of different perspectives, to engage in critical reflection, and to change his or her own perspective (Thomas 2002).

Asynchronous discussion groups are one of the best tools to promote interaction and learning, especially when facilitated by new technologies (Lucas, Gunawardena & Moreira, 2014). Indeed, they allow the automatic recording of discussions or messages, which can be consulted by students for reflection or by teachers to assess the level of knowledge achieved by students. This mode of interaction is often used because it has several advantages, such as allowing time to think, reflect, and search for information before participating in the discussion, thus avoiding off-topic messages or misunderstandings, equal opportunities for interaction and participation, and the development of learning communities and networks, where knowledge is the result of discussions, shared practices and collaboration (Lucas, Gunawardena & Moreira 2014).

Before going into the details of this research, we would like to focus on three studies in the literature.

The first study (Jacob & Sam 2008) is a pilot study exploring the promotion of critical thinking among first-year university mathematics students through asynchronous discussions. The problem-solving sessions activated through online discussion forums in these classes were examined. 46 participants were involved with the aim of adapting a model to assess critical thinking at the individual level in mathematical problem-solving sessions in online discussion forums; examining the relationship between mathematical achievement, as measured by final exam grades, and critical thinking in online discussion forums; testing whether there was a progression in critical thinking skills based on discussion forum posts in week 3 and week 11. The results showed an increase in the number of posts in the second forum compared to the first one, but the lower stage of critical thinking (clarification and evaluation) was prevalent in most posts, while the higher stages (inference and strategies) occurred for only a few students.

The second study (Jacob 2012) examines the relationship between critical thinking (CT) skills and student performance in an engineering mathematics course. Specifically, participation in asynchronous discussion forums (ADFs) was measured to assess CT skills using the CAIS model, which assigns a weighted CT score to each student. The ADFs were integrated into the course to encourage collaborative problem solving and critical thinking among students. Mathematical performance was measured by final exam scores, while initial mathematical ability was assessed by an initial test. This analysis showed that CT skills, when properly encouraged through structured and moderated ADF sessions, can improve students' mathematical success. For instance, students engaged in ADFs exhibited a notable improvement in their CT scores between the two problem-solving sessions, reflecting their enhanced ability to analyse, infer, and strategize effectively. This highlights the importance of encouraging CT skills in engineering students to improve their mathematical success. It also suggests that further research into the use of online discussion forums to facilitate CT could be useful for educators and researchers both in mathematics and other disciplines.

The third study (Alshaye, Tasir & Jumaat, 2023) involved 120 eleventh grade students from two secondary schools in Riyadh, equally divided into a control group and an experimental group. The research aimed to investigate the effectiveness of online problem-based learning (PBL) tasks in improving students' problem-solving ability (PSA) and programming skills. In particular, the experimental group engaged in complex programming tasks through asynchronous collaboration in Facebook groups, which allowed them to reflect and contribute to problem solving at their own pace, fostering a more critical and in-depth approach to learning. The study concluded that online PBL significantly improved both students' problem-solving and programming skills, promoting more autonomous and effective learning.

3. RESEARCH METHOD

3.1 The Digital Math Training Project

The context of this study is the Digital Math Training (DMT) project, designed and managed by the DELTA - Digital Education for Learning and Teaching Advances research group at the University of Turin. The DMT project aims to improve the mathematical, digital, and problem-solving skills of the participating students in grades 10, 11 and 12 (when students are between 16 and 18 years old), in order to prepare them to understand the processes of social transformation of which they must be an active and conscious part (Barana & Marchisio 2016). The DMT project offers optional extra-curricular activities, open to different schools each year, which can be recognised as part of the PCTO (Pathways for Transversal Skills and Orientation), which combines theoretical and practical learning to prepare students for the labour market. The aim is to use the mathematical skills learnt at school to solve real-world problems, thereby reducing the gap between theory and practice and between school and work. Specifically, students work in a DLE based on a dedicated Moodle platform and solve problems every ten days, submitting their solutions for assessment. These problems, open to different solution strategies, encourage asynchronous collaboration through forums; for each relevant intervention, points can be earned that contribute to a final ranking, thus motivating active participation (Barana et al. 2023; Floris et al. 2024). This platform is integrated with an Advanced Computing Environment (ACE), a system that allows students to do mathematics by performing numerical calculations, symbolic computations, graphical visualisations in two or three dimensions, and programming embedded components such as sliders, buttons, and boxes through a simple programming language (Barana et al. 2020). During the DMT project, the difficulty of the proposed problems gradually increases. Initial problems are simpler and allow students to familiarise with the use of the ACE, while subsequent problems become progressively more complex, focusing on developing problem-solving strategies. The problems are related to school topics to enhance the understanding of the subject outside school. The problems are divided into sequential and open-ended prompts: the former ones help to understand, explore, and identify a solution model, while the latter ones require generalisation using the interactive components of ACE, which can be programmed to perform calculations and provide numerical or graphical results (Barana et al. 2020).

Each problem is evaluated by the tutors according to a specifically designed assessment rubric containing five indicators: 1. understanding of the problem, 2. identification of a solution strategy, 3. development of the solution process, 4. argumentation, 5. use of Maple. For each of these, the tutor must indicate the level of competence achieved (from one to four), identified by descriptors, and the corresponding score, which can vary from 1 to 100 for each problem. In particular, the first four indicators are taken from the (Polya 1945) model and refer to the four phases of solving a problem, while the fifth indicator refers to the use of ACE.

3.2 Data Collection

The sample considered in this study is composed of 172 grade 11 participants (i.e. 17 years old) in the school year 2021/22. The data analysed to understand if there is a relationship between the achievement of problem-solving skills and asynchronous collaboration are the following:

- The number of messages sent by each student in the forums throughout the project to measure their level of active engagement in asynchronous collaboration;
- The total score, i.e., the sum of the scores obtained by the students in solving the eight problems of the online training, which we considered an index of the development of problem-solving skills achieved by each of them through the project (Barana et al. 2023);
- The students' answers to specific questions concerning their perception of the usefulness of asynchronous collaboration included in the final questionnaire given to all the participants at the end of the project via the platform.

The questions, asked on a Likert scale from 1 (not at all) to 5 (very much), are the following:

1. I felt part of a community;
2. The forums allowed me to collaborate with other students to solve problems;
3. The atmosphere on the platform was positive;
4. The interventions in the forums were helpful in solving problems;
5. I felt competitive with other participants;
6. I felt helped;
7. I posted on the forums to get points;
8. This kind of online collaboration could be useful for my future work;
9. I found answers to my questions on the forums.

3.3 The Research Process

Before carrying out the analyses, all participants who did not take part in the survey were eliminated from the data set, leaving 131 participants, or approximately 76% of the participating students. For each student, the score obtained from the sum of the results for each delivery and in all project activities was calculated, and the number of messages posted in the discussion forums for each proposed problem was identified.

The first step was to divide the students into classes according to the final score obtained. A histogram was created using R-studio to describe qualitatively the frequency distribution of the total scores and to calculate the empirical density, approximating the theoretical density. In this way, it was possible to divide the students into two classes using a classification based on a mixture of normals. Next, the correlation between the total score and the number of posts was examined to see if there is a relationship between problem-solving skills and participation in asynchronous discussions in discussion forums. Lastly, a comparison was then made between the score means for each class into which we divided the students, using the bootstrap technique, analysing the relative p-values to understand which questions were influenced by the total scores. In particular, we expect the mean of the class characterised by having achieved higher problem-solving skills to be greater than or equal to the mean of the other class.

4. RESULTS

The first step in the analysis was to create a histogram (see Figure 1a), representing the distribution of scores, with the total score on the abscissa and the frequency of occurrence of these scores on the ordinate.

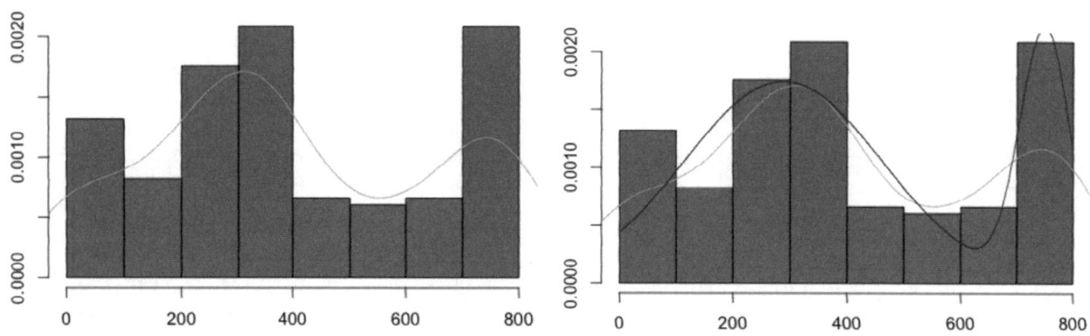

Figure 1a. Histogram of scores; Figure 1b. Histogram with BIC method estimation

The green curve of Figure 1a is the non-parametric estimate of the density function and it allowed us to assume that the whole group of students could be divided into two classes, represented by the two 'peaks', based on the score obtained; an attempt has therefore been made to estimate this curve. In particular, looking at the shape of the empirical density, it could be assumed that the two groups, taken individually, are distributed as normals. Therefore, we used an algorithm included in Mclust, which employs an iterative method, known as the E-M algorithm. It aims to find the mean variance and probability values that maximised the maximum likelihood function. In addition, in order to find the ideal number of classes, we used the Bayesian Information

Criterion (BIC), which removed values from the maximum likelihood function as the number of classes increased. This is because, as the number of classes increased, it became easier to describe the data due to the increased degrees of freedom. In this way, a balance was struck between the number of classes used and the quality of data modelling. As we expected, the most likely situation was one with two classes, where the blue curve in Figure 1b represents the estimate resulting from the BIC method.

Conclusions about the two classes could be drawn from the graph shown in Figure 2, where the dots represent the students, positioned alphabetically along the x-axis and according to their scores on the y-axis.

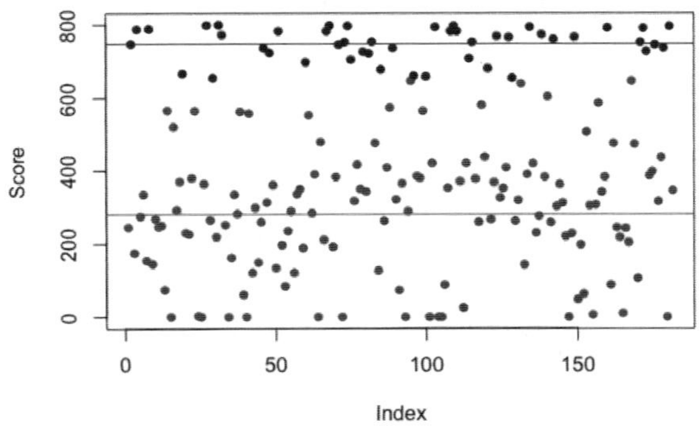

Figure 2. Scatterplot on the division of students into classes according to score

The graph shows that those belonging to the first normal, represented by the red dots, were the students with the lowest scores and were clearly separated from those in the other class, represented by the blue colour. In the following, these classes have been referred to as "lower achieving" and "higher achieving" respectively. Figure 3 shows a scatterplot where each dot represents a student, positioned alphabetically on the x-axis and according to their scores on the y-axis, with colours indicating their group: red for "lower achieving" and blue for "higher achieving."

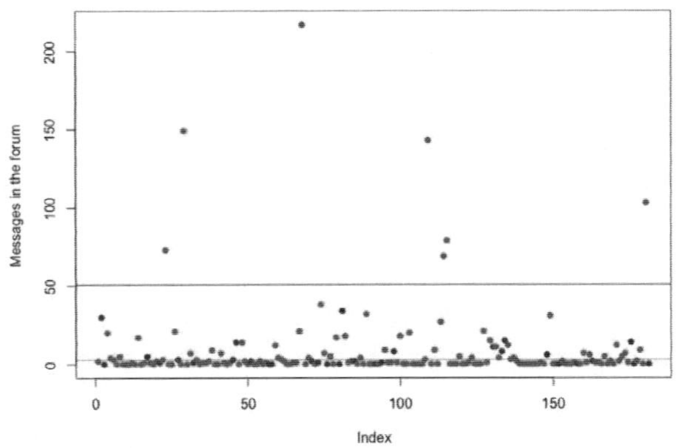

Figure 3. Scatterplot of the messages sent by each participant, where the colour indicates whether the participant belongs to the "lower achieving" (red) or "higher achieving" (blue) class

From the graph, it can be observed that students with higher scores generally sent, on average, a greater number of messages. The mean of messages sent by each class was represented by a line, red for the former and blue for the latter. In addition, the correlation index between the total score and the number of messages sent is 0.369, which is slightly above the significance level commonly accepted in educational research. This allows us to state that there is a relationship between the two variables considered.

At this point, we investigated whether this division into classes was related to the answers to the questions. The graphs in Figure 4 display each student's answers, with their indices on the x-axis and responses on the y-axis, color-coded according to the previous classification. Specifically, red represents students in the first class, while blue represents students in the second class, i.e. those who scored higher by solving the problems. In particular, Table 1 shows the means for each class and the relative p-value for each question.

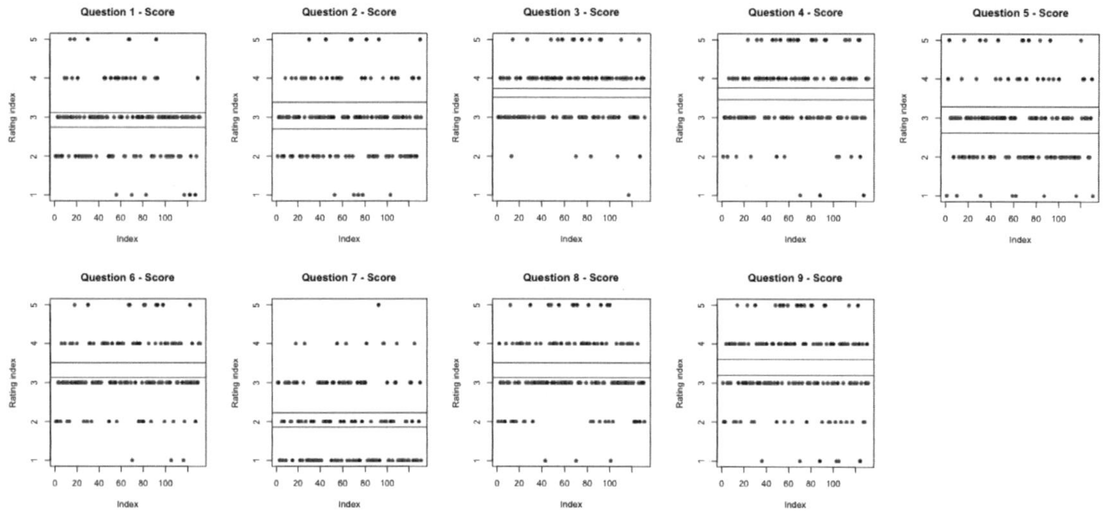

Figure 4. Analysis of the answers according to the classification given by the scores obtained by solving the problems

Table 1. Mean of the answers divided into the two classes obtained from the scores obtained by solving the problems and study of the p-Value

Question	"Lower achieving" class	"Higher achieving" class	p-value
I felt part of a community.	2.732558	3.111111	0.0210
The forums allowed me to collaborate with other students to solve problems.	2.697674	3.377778	0.0000
The atmosphere on the platform was positive.	3.511628	3.733333	0.0582
The interventions in the forur were helpful in solving problems.	3.465116	3.755556	0.0812
I felt competitive with other participants.	2.616279	3.288889	0.0000
I felt helped.	3.127907	3.511111	0.0100
I posted on the forums to get points.	1.860465	2.222222	0.0260
This kind of online collaboration could be useful for my future work.	3.127907	3.511111	0.0172
I found answers to my questions on the forums.	3.197674	3.600000	0.0326

We can reject the assumption that the means of the two groups are equal if the p-value is less than 0.05 using a one-tailed test (since we expect the mean of the class "Higher achieving" to be greater than or equal to the mean of the class "Lower achieving"). In this case, our initial hypothesis is correct: the mean of the class "Higher achieving" (shown in blue in Figure 4) is greater than the mean of the class "Lower achieving" (shown in red in Figure 4). However, the results vary according to the question. Specifically, we reject the hypothesis in the following cases: *I felt part of a community*; *the forums allowed me to collaborate with other students to solve problems*; *I felt competitive with other participants; I felt helped*; *I posted on the forums to get points*; *this kind of online collaboration could be useful for my future work* and *I found answers to my questions on the forums*. However, the hypothesis was not rejected in the following cases: *the atmosphere on the platform was positive* and *the interventions in the forums were helpful in solving problems*.

5. DISCUSSION AND CONCLUSION

From the analysis of the correlation between the total score and the number of messages sent by each student, we were able to observe a relationship between the perception of asynchronous collaboration and the problem-solving skills developed: in fact, greater collaboration is associated with higher levels of problem-solving ability. Furthermore, by examining the p-values, we observed a relationship between the problem-solving skills achieved by each student and the answers to the self-assessment questions on the perceived usefulness of asynchronous collaboration. When the p-value was less than 0.05, it indicated that belonging to a particular class, i.e. possessing certain problem-solving abilities, influenced the perception of specific aspects. In particular, this relationship was evident in the following statements:

- I felt competitive with other participants;
- I posted on the forums to get points.

These elements highlight the more competitive side of the project: each student earns points for each forum intervention, and accumulating a lot of points is essential to win. This competitive feature undoubtedly encourages students to engage more actively in the forum; however, it may serve as an initial incentive for some students to view the forum differently, i.e. as an opportunity to solve problems in a better way through interaction with other participants. In addition, influences were observed in the following questions:

- I felt part of a community;
- The forums allowed me to collaborate with other students to solve problems;
- I felt helped;
- This kind of online collaboration could be useful for my future work;
- I found answers to my questions on the forums.

Students who achieved higher levels of problem-solving skills at the end of the project also exhibited greater engagement with asynchronous collaboration, actively using the forum to post questions and answers. These students perceived the DLE as collaborative and supportive, suggesting that asynchronous collaboration facilitated the formation of a learning community. These results indicate that the competitive side of the project did not undermine the development of a community where participants, by sharing their opinions, both assist others and open themselves to feedback and validation.

Notably, no significant difference was found between the two classes in the answers to the statements "The atmosphere on the platform was positive" and "The interventions in the forums were helpful in solving problems". These are also the items that received the highest scores. This indicates that both the positive climate and the perceived usefulness of asynchronous collaboration were recognised by students with lower problem-solving skills as well as those with higher skills.

Our research has proven the existence of a relationship between students' final grades, reflecting their problem-solving skills in mathematics and their engagement with asynchronous collaboration, including their perceptions of its usefulness. Notably, we found a significant connection between the students' sense of competition and their motivation to contribute to forums for points. Additionally, students' views on asynchronous collaboration highlighted a strong sense of community and the value of working together to solve problems. Many students, regardless of their final point totals, reported feeling supported and believed that this form of collaboration would benefit their future work. This suggests that, beyond its cognitive advantages, asynchronous collaboration can positively impact community building and socio-emotional learning by fostering a supportive environment that promotes active participation and knowledge sharing. When conducting this discussion, however, it is important to keep in mind the research context in which the results were obtained: the project aims to stimulate and enhance mathematical and computational skills. At the same time, participants are in a competitive atmosphere due to the final ranking, feature that has undoubtedly influenced their behaviour.

In conclusion, the studies reviewed, together with our empirical observations, indicate the existence of a relationship between students' mathematical problem-solving skills and the perception of asynchronous collaboration in digital learning environments. These results are significant, as online learning continues to grow in popularity: it is therefore necessary to continue researching and optimising these tools to maximise their educational potential. In this analysis, we only took into account grade 11 students (when they are 17 years old); future research could extend the sample to include other classes participating in the DMT project to determine if similar results are observed across different age groups. Additionally, it could be interesting to differentiate between students participating for the first time and those with prior experience in the project, examining how their perceptions of asynchronous collaboration evolve over time and to extend this study to other skills, such as programming, to explore the full potential of asynchronous collaboration in improving different academic skills.

ACKNOWLEDGEMENT

The research was carried out within INDAM - Istituto Nazionale Di Alta Matematica "Francesco Severi" and the Diderot Program funded by the Bank Foundation "Cassa di Risparmio di Torino" (Fondazione CRT). The authors would like to thank the Fondazione CRT for funding the DMT project. Moreover, the authors would like to thank all the students, tutors, and teachers who participated in the project.

REFERENCES

Alshaye, I. A., Tasir, Z., and Jumaat, N. F. (2023). The Effectiveness of Online Problem-Based Learning Tasks on Riyadh's Secondary School Students' Problem-Solving Ability and Programming Skills. *Open Education Studies*, Vol. *5*, No. 1, 20220208.

Barana, A. et al. (2020). The Creation of Animated Graphs to Develop Computational Thinking and Support STEM Education. *In Maple in Mathematics Education and Research*, Springer, Cham, pp. 189–204. https://doi.org/10.1007/978-3-030-41258-6_14

Barana, A. et al. (2023). Assessment of Digital and Mathematical Problem-Solving Competences Development. *Proceedings of the 15th International Conference on Computer Supported Education (CSEDU 2023)*, Vol. 2, pp. 318-329.

Barana, A., and Marchisio, M. (2022). A model for the analysis of the interactions in a digital learning environment during mathematical activities. *In Computer Supported Education*, Springer, Cham, pp. 429-448.

Barana, A., and Marchisio, M. (2016). From digital mate training experience to alternating school work activities. *Mondo Digitale*, Vol. 15, No. 64, pp. 63–82.

Barana, A., Marchisio, M., and Miori, R. (2019). MATE-BOOSTER: Design of an e-Learning Course to Boost Mathematical Competence. *Proceedings of the 11th International Conference on Computer Supported Education (CSEDU 2019)*, Vol. 1, pp. 280–291.

Fissore, C. et al. (2021). Development of problem solving skills with Maple in Higher Education. *In Maple in Mathematics Education and Research: 4th Maple Conference*, pp. 219-233.

Floris, F. et al. (2023). Design Gamification Strategies in a Digital Learning Environment: The Impact on Students. *In International Conference on Games and Learning Alliance*, pp. 464-469.

Hammond, M. (2017). Online collaboration and cooperation: The recurring importance of evidence, rationale and viability. Education and Information Technologies, Vol. 22, No.3, pp.1005–1024.

Jacob, S. M. (2012). Mathematical achievement and critical thinking skills in asynchronous discussion forums. *In Procedia-Social and Behavioral Sciences*, Vol. 31, pp. 800-804.

Jacob, S. M., and Sam, H. K. (2008). Critical thinking skills in online mathematics discussion forums and mathematical achievement. *In Proceedings of the 13th Asian Technology Conference in Mathematics*, pp. 15-19.

Lahann, P., and Lambdin, D. V. (2020). Collaborative learning in mathematics education. *Encyclopedia of mathematics education*, pp. 94-95.

Lucas, M., Gunawardena, C., and Moreira, A. (2014). Assessing social construction of knowledge online: A critique of the interaction analysis model. *Computers in Human Behavior*, Vol. 30, pp. 574-582.

Ludvigsen, S., and Arnseth, H. C. (2017). Computer-supported collaborative learning, *Technology enhanced learning: Research themes*, pp. 47-58.

Martinez, M. E. (1998). What is problem solving?. *The Phi Delta Kappan*, Vol. 79, No. 8, pp. 605-609.

Polya, G. (1945). *How to Solve It*, Princeton University Press

Thomas, M. J. (2002). Learning within incoherent structures: The space of online discussion forums. *Journal of Computer Assisted Learning*, Vol. 18, No.3, pp. 351-366.

ROBOTICS EDUCATION THROUGH CROSS-AGE PEER TUTORING: EVALUATING THE LEARNING OUTCOMES FOR TUTORS AND TUTEES

Vaso Anastasiou, Yiota H. Diakou and Charoula Angeli
University of Cyprus, Cyprus

ABSTRACT

This study examines the impact of educational robotics and cross-age peer tutoring in primary education and focuses explicitly on the outcomes for tutors and tutees. Forty students from a public school in a European country participated, with fifth graders as tutors and fourth graders as tutees. Using the LEGO Education SPIKE Prime Set, both groups showed significant improvement in computational thinking after nine hours of learning with educational robotics activities. A quasi-experiment research procedure was followed to collect quantitative and qualitative data. The results indicate that peer tutoring was effectively used as a learning strategy to promote computational thinking through educational robotics activities. Implications for future research are provided.

KEYWORDS

Educational Robotics, Cross-Age Peer Tutoring, Computational Thinking Primary Education

1. INTRODUCTION

Educational robotics (ER) activities in classrooms are on the rise, aimed at developing 21st-century skills (Chevalier, 2020). ER promotes learning through engaging pedagogical activities that include active robot participation (Angel-Fernandez & Vincze, 2018) and holds significant promise for enhancing Computational Thinking (CT) in primary school children (Ching & Hsu, 2023).

Peer tutoring (PT) is a structured learning strategy in which one student tutors another, aiming at mutual benefits (Topping, 2000). Due to their recent experiences and relatable communication styles, students often mediate learning more effectively than adults (Alegre et al., 2019). PT has shown academic and non-academic advantages across various educational levels (Ain et al., 2023). It has been applied in subjects like Language (Thurston et al., 2021; Xu et al., 2008), Mathematics (Thurston et al., 2020; Alegre et al., 2019), Music (Fernández-Barros et al., 2023), Sciences (Zeneli & Tymms, 2015), and education for minority students (Barahona et al., 2023). The benefits of PT include improved academic performance, self-esteem, social skills, and positive student relationships (Alegre et al., 2019; Ain et al., 2023; Barahona et al., 2023; Thurston et al., 2021). While positive impacts on both tutees' and tutors' academic performance have been observed (Alegre et al., 2019), there is no unanimous agreement. Research by Thurston et al. (2021) suggests more significant benefits for tutors, indicating a need for further study. The literature review reveals further gaps in the research. Alegre et al. (2019) note that most PT studies focus on same-age groups and academic performance, with less emphasis on other forms. Additionally, there is a lack of research on using PT to develop CT using ER, thus presenting an opportunity for future research.

This study aims to evaluate the effectiveness of peer tutoring in the context of robotics education in primary education and examines the outcomes for both tutors and tutees. The research questions are:

1. Does student performance in computational thinking tests differ according to their role (tutors or tutees) in educational robotics activities using peer tutoring?
2. What benefits do tutors and tutees perceive they gain from participating in educational robotics activities with peer tutoring?

The lack of research on using PT in ER to develop CT highlights the importance and necessity of this study. Practically, the study offers guidelines and advice for cost-effective implementation of ER in elementary schools using PT. Theoretically, it investigates the effects of PT in ER courses, providing data to address current research gaps related to the teaching and development of CT.

2. LITERATURE

2.1 Educational Robotics and Computational Thinking

ER activities are connected to Papert's constructionist theory and the concept of learning by making (Papert & Harel, 1991). Robots are cognitive tools that facilitate practical, interactive learning, allowing students to test hypotheses, receive immediate feedback, and better understand abstract concepts and problem solving (Chevalier et al., 2020).

It is reported that ER is increasingly utilized in primary classrooms to cultivate CT (Chevalier et al., 2021). Wing (2006) defines CT as solving problems, designing systems, and understanding human behavior through computer science principles. Wing (2006) emphasizes that CT is an essential skill for everyone and should be included in primary education. CT encompasses abstraction, generalization, decomposition, algorithmic thinking, and debugging (Angeli, 2022). Abstraction focuses on identifying the essential features of an object, generalization involves creating solutions applicable to various problems, decomposition breaks down problems into smaller parts, algorithmic thinking involves writing step-by-step instructions, and debugging entails identifying and correcting errors (Piedade & Dorotea, 2023). Additionally, critical elements of CT include the algorithmic concepts of sequencing (writing an algorithm) and flow of control (Angeli, 2022).

In the context of primary education students, it is critical to avoid student frustration often caused from challenging hardware and software (Ching & Hsu, 2023). Thus, it is of utmost importance to use age-appropriate robotics kits in the context of systematic interventions to avoid trial-and-error attempts and allow the maximization of learning and CT development for all learners (Chevalier et al., 2020).

2.2 Peer Tutoring: from Theory to Practice

PT goes beyond traditional knowledge transfer, aligning with theoretical frameworks that emphasize social interaction, active learning, and the social construction of knowledge. Vygotsky's theory (1978), particularly the Zone of Proximal Development, underscores cognitive development through interactions with more knowledgeable peers (Akpan et al., 2020).

The Theory of Social Interdependence (Johnson & Johnson, 2013) focuses on structured group activities where learning and success hinge on collaborative efforts. By just grouping students, it does not guarantee effective collaboration; it requires more than just grouping such as setting common goals and cooperative actions. Johnson and Johnson (2013) identified five essential elements for successful cooperative learning: positive interdependence, where group members depend on each other to achieve their goals; individual and group accountability, ensuring personal and collective responsibility; promotive interaction, where members encourage and support each other; the appropriate use of social skills, including effective communication and teamwork; and group processing, which involves reflecting on group performance to enhance future outcomes.

PT can be implemented in various formats depending on the roles of the students. They can act as tutors or tutees with fixed or reciprocal roles. The implementation can vary based on the students' ages and abilities, including same-age groups, similar abilities, or cross-age tutoring where older students serve as tutors for younger students (Thurston et al., 2020; ul Ain et al., 2023). The latter was the focus of this study.

3. METHODOLOGY

3.1 Participants

The study included 40 students from a public elementary school in a European country. Twenty-two fifth graders, all 11 years old, acted as tutors, while eighteen fourth graders, aged 10, were the tutees. The fifth-grade students participated in learning activities guided by their classroom teacher. None of the participants had prior knowledge of educational robotics.

Tutor-tutee pairs were created based on academic performance in Mathematics and Language lessons, with students ranked from highest to lowest in each grade and paired with same ability students. Due to the difference in grade sizes, four groups consisted of one tutee and two tutors. Once formed, these groups remained consistent throughout the intervention to maximize interactions and benefits (Thurston et al., 2021).

3.2 Data Collection Methods

3.2.1 Computational Thinking Test

The same test was administered before and after the intervention to assess CT skills. The test includes a series of exercises designed to measure CT skills. Exercises 1A and 1B require students to number the steps for baking cookies or assembling a toy, thus measuring algorithmic skills (sequencing). Exercises 2A and 2B ask students to provide directional instructions for a taxi, assessing algorithmic thinking (flow of control) and decomposition. Exercises 3A and 3B involve selecting a dress or drawing based on specific attributes and evaluates pattern recognition, abstraction, and generalization skills. In Exercises 4A and 4B, students identify and repeat a dance pattern or guide a robot using repeated movements, measuring pattern recognition, decomposition, and generalization. Exercises 5A and 5B require students to confirm the sequence of steps for dressing as a pirate or to evaluate and correct taxi directions, thus testing algorithmic thinking, decomposition, and debugging skills. Finally, Exercises 6A and 6B involve completing or extending a pattern, assessing pattern recognition, abstraction, and generalization skills. Exercise 4B was excluded from the overall results due to student-expressed confusion.

The Intraclass Correlation Coefficient (ICC) and Cronbach's Alpha were calculated to assess interrater reliability. The ICC values for pretest and posttest scores were 0.985 and 0.995, respectively, indicating excellent agreement between raters. Additionally, the Cronbach's Alpha values for pretest and posttest scores were 0.995 and 0.997, respectively, demonstrating very high internal consistency of the ratings. These results confirm the reliability and consistency of the evaluations, supporting their use in assessing intervention outcomes.

3.2.2 Interviews

Eight pairs of tutors and tutees with varying academic performances were chosen for the interviews, making a total of 16 children. This maximum variation sampling was intended to encompass a wide range of cases for the study. Semi-structured interviews were conducted with the 16 children in the sample. Using a question guide with predefined questions, the interviews were adapted and guided by the children's responses, following suggestions from the literature (Gibson, 2012). The interviews included questions about each child's behavior, opinions, and feelings during the intervention. All interviews were conducted by the tutors' teacher, who, with her knowledge of child development and personal experience with the children, ensured the use of child-friendly language and created a trusting atmosphere. The interview protocols can be found in Appendix, Tables 3 and 4.

3.3 Digital Tools

The LEGO Education SPIKE Prime Set, suitable for ages ten and up, was used. The set includes Lego bricks, axles, a hub, motors, and various sensors. The children followed the building instructions in the Lego Spike app and used a drag-and-drop programming language based on Scratch to code the computer programs.

3.4 Research Procedures

A quasi-experimental design was used for the purposes of this study. Older students acted as tutors, and younger students as the tutees. As shown in Figure 1, the research procedure began with a 45-minute pretest to measure CT. The second phase included 14 forty-minute ER lessons for fifth graders over six days in three weeks, targeting different CT sub-skills with increasing difficulty and four worksheets for basic software commands. More details of each lesson are shown in Table 1. A forty-minute session explained the tutor's role. In the third phase, fifth graders tutored fourth graders using the same activities and worksheets over 14 forty-minute sessions. In the final phase, the interviews were conducted.

Figure 1. Research Procedure

Table 1. Robotics Course Content

	Course topic	Time	Programming	CT sub-skill
1	Introduction to educational robotics: What robots are and examples of robot use in our daily lives. Acquaintance with the Lego Spike educational robotics package and its software.	80’		algorithmic thinking
2	Assembling the Break Dancer robotic construction by following the build instructions in the software. Complete worksheet 1.	120’	Motors, light, events	algorithmic thinking debugging
3	Programming the Break Dancer robot. Complete worksheet 2.	80’	Use of color sensors When the color is, wait and repeat	abstract skill
4	Assembling the Robotic Construction Driving Base. Complete worksheet 3.	120’	The use of distance (when closure than) and pressure (when pressed) sensors, events – broadcast a message	generalization
5	Programming the Driving Base robot with color sensors. Complete worksheet 4.	80’	Use of color sensors When color is, events – Broadcast a message	decomposition
6	Robotic challenge: Children are asked to program a robot that moves around a city on a mat, avoiding obstacles, and responding accordingly when encountering traffic lights.	80’	All of the above	all

3.5 Data Analysis

To determine the improvement in students' computational thinking, statistical tests were conducted using SPSS. T-tests examined differences between tutors' and tutees' performances, and ANCOVA was conducted to examine the effect of role.

All interview data underwent qualitative content analysis to interpret students' participation during the intervention. After an initial reading, the researcher performed open coding, followed by axial coding to organize the codes into categories. Finally, selective coding was used to identify the most significant and frequent categories. The analysis employed an abductive approach, expanding conceptual schemas from the theoretical framework of Johnson and Johnson (2013), which identifies five essential elements for successful cooperative learning: positive interdependence, individual and group accountability, promotive interaction, appropriate use of social skills, and group processing. The interrater reliability was found to be .91.

4. RESULTS

4.1 Statistical Analyses

Descriptive statistics indicate an improvement in performance for both tutors and tutees after the intervention (Table 2). For tutors, the post-test score (M=83.5, SD=16.06) was higher than the pre-test (M = 77.95, SD = 11.60). The paired t-test confirmed that the difference was statistically significant ($t = -2.49$, $df = 21$, $p < 0.02$) suggesting that the intervention had a significant effect on the tutors' performance. Cohen's D was approximately 0.53, indicating a moderate effect size. For tutees, the post-test score (M=69.11, SD=16.3) was higher than the pre-test (M = 62.22, SD = 14.11). The paired t-test confirmed that the difference was statistically significant ($t = -3.19$, $df = 17$, $p < 0.005$) suggesting that the intervention had a significant effect on the tutees' performance. Cohen's D was approximately 0.75, indicating a moderate effect size.

Table 2. Tutors and Tutees Performance

	Test	M	SD	t	df	p
Tutors	Pre-test	77.95	11.60	-2.49	21	0.02
	Post-test	83.50	12.89			
Tutees	Pre-test	62.22	14.11	-3.19	17	0.005
	Post-test	69.11	16.30			

An ANCOVA was conducted to examine the effect of role (tutor vs. tutee) on posttest scores while controlling for pretest scores. Levene's test confirmed the assumption of equal variances ($p = 0.672$). The analysis showed no significant difference in posttest scores between tutors and tutees after adjusting for pretest scores ($F(1, 37) = 0.088$, $p = 0.768$). This suggests that the intervention had a similar effect on students regardless of their role as a tutor or tutee.

4.2 Qualitative Analyses

Both tutors and tutees stated that they benefited from the learning experience in various ways. Interviewees described it as a positive learning experience by using words like "nice," "creative," "perfect," and "fantastic." They appreciated the novel experience and the opportunity for collaborative learning. For example, tutee T4 stated, "I liked working with others. Collaboration is better when one person has one idea, and another has a different one."

All participants highlighted academic benefits, emphasizing the positive interdependence developed for achieving common goals. Tutees noted gaining new knowledge about robotics, while tutors mentioned reinforcing their existing knowledge, saying that teaching helped them learn it better.

The robotics activities encouraged tutors and tutees to engage in interactive learning activities and felt motivated and assisted each other in completing tasks and reaching group objectives. As stated in the interviews, all tutors asked questions to encourage tutees to think out loud. Tutees found tutors clear and compelling in their explanations and instructions, judging them as good teachers. For example, tutees said the tutors "explained everything like a game," "explained everything in detail," and "explained everything thoroughly and did not get tired of explaining." T4 tutee mentioned, "I understood everything as my tutor explained it." Many tutees revealed that they felt more comfortable asking questions to students rather than teachers, stating that a peer can explain things multiple times, making it easier to understand.

Tutors expressed pride and satisfaction from helping others and successfully teaching robotics activities, indicating individual accountability. Both tutors and tutees had responsibilities, reflecting on their own and their peer's performance at the end of each session. Tutors showed concern for the tutees' learning and asked questions to evaluate their understanding. Tutor TU2 mentioned, "I would ask if he understood certain things, and if he said OK, we would continue."

A significant finding was the creation of new acquaintances and friendships. Students noted that the robotics activities allowed them to meet new classmates and develop closer relationships, enhancing their social skills. Reflecting on the relationships between tutors and tutees, some children initially felt uncomfortable because they did not know their partner well. However, this changed over time. As the children got to know each other better, they reported that this familiarity helped the activities to proceed more smoothly and in a more enjoyable atmosphere. One tutor described the tutees as 'Teacher friends.'

Several students mentioned challenges they faced, indicating group processing. They discussed their actions when making mistakes and efforts to coordinate their work better, resulting in improved performance and outcomes. From the tutees' perspective, mistakes were not seen negatively by their peers and did not negatively impact their perception of their tutors. They believed that everyone learns from mistakes.

One issue highlighted in the interviews was the concern of some tutors during the teaching phase about providing more space for autonomy to the tutees. Tutor TU1 stated, 'Basically, it is difficult to know when to stop and when to leave him alone. That was a bit challenging for me.' Another tutor (TU8) mentioned that it was important for the tutees to do things on their own since 'That's how they'll learn. '

Another issue that emerged was almost all the tutees' preference for being taught by a peer rather than a teacher. They explained their preference by stating that it allowed for personalized instruction, more attention, and greater comfort in asking questions.

5. DISCUSSION

This study demonstrated that PT effectively develops students' CT, confirming its value in educational settings including ER activities. PT improves understanding and skills and offers a cost-effective solution by utilizing existing student resources without needing additional materials or staff (Alegre et al., 2019; Ain et al., 2023).

Statistical analyses showed no significant difference in post-test scores between tutors and tutees when controlling for pretest scores. The analysis confirmed that cross-age PT benefited tutors and tutees and was an effective instructional approach to close the gap between tutors' and tutees' initial differences in CT, consistent with other studies (Alegre et al., 2019).

Qualitative analyses supported the Theory of Social Interdependence (Johnson & Johnson, 2013), highlighting the multifaceted benefits for both tutors and tutees. Students reported about a positive learning environment and engaging in enriching learning experiences. Beyond acquiring ER knowledge and skills, students developed social and interpersonal skills. The robotics activities also facilitated new friendships and social networks, further enhancing social skills and fostering a supportive learning community. Tutors also honed their mentoring skills, boosted their self-confidence, and experienced a deep sense of satisfaction from helping others. Similar findings were observed in related research on various subjects (Willis et al., 2012) and studies showing positive impacts on all participants, regardless of their role (Ain et al., 2023; Parker et al., 2023).

In conclusion, the study highlights the value of peer tutoring in educational robotics, showing significant improvements in computational thinking skills and promoting a collaborative learning environment in line with Social Interdependence Theory.

5.1 Future Suggestions and Limitations

Some tutors recognized the importance of learners actively confirming their understanding to regulate learning. They used targeted questions to encourage critical thinking and reflection, aiding self-regulation. These tutors displayed metacognitive skills essential for managing cognitive processes (Flavell, 1979). The link between

PT and metacognitive skill development needs more research, as Ain et al. (2023) noted, highlighting an area for future study.

Additionally, many tutees' preference for PT over adult educators reflects Bandura's social learning theory of learning through observation, imitation, and modeling (McLeod, 2011). Even when making mistakes, peer tutors serve as relatable role models, providing accessible examples. Positive feedback and rewards for successful tasks enhance learning, consistent with Bandura's theory that reinforcement and social rewards are crucial. Future research could explore the connection between social learning theory and peer tutoring.

This research is subject to limitations that should be acknowledged. The data collected do not support broad generalizations due to the small sample size. Further work is required to explore these patterns in more detail and determine whether they can be generalized to a larger sample of students. Future research should also explore long-term impacts and variations in PT to optimize educational outcomes further. Nevertheless, the current study provides baseline data for the effectiveness of PT in CT development through educational robotics activities.

REFERENCES

Akpan, V. I., Igwe, U. A., Mpamah, I. B. I., & Okoro, C. O. (2020). Social constructivism: Implications on teaching and learning. *British Journal of Education*, 8(8), 49-56.

Alegre, F., Moliner, L., Maroto, A., & Lorenzo-Valentin, G. (2019). Peer tutoring in mathematics in primary education: A systematic review. *Educational Review*, 71(6), 767-791.

Angel-Fernandez, J. M., & Vincze, M. (2018). Towards a definition of educational robotics. *In Austrian Robotics Workshop 2018* (Vol. 37).

Angeli, C. (2022). The effects of scaffolded programming scripts on pre-service teachers' computational thinking: Developing algorithmic thinking through programming robots. *International Journal of Child-Computer Interaction*, 31, 100329.

Barahona, E., Padrón, Y. N., & Waxman, H. C. (2023). Classroom observations of a cross-age peer tutoring mathematics program in elementary and middle schools. *European Journal of Science and Mathematics Education*, 11(3), 515-532.

Chevalier, M., Giang, C., Piatti, A., & Mondada, F. (2020). Fostering computational thinking through educational robotics: A model for creative computational problem-solving. *International Journal of STEM Education*, 7, 1-18.

Ching, Y. H., & Hsu, Y. C. (2023). Educational robotics for developing computational thinking in young learners: A systematic review. *TechTrends*, pp. 1-12.

Fernández-Barros, A., Duran, D., & Viladot, L. (2023). Peer tutoring in music education: A literature review. *International Journal of Music Education*, 41(1), 129-140.

Flavell, J. H. (1979). Metacognition and cognitive monitoring: A new area of cognitive-developmental inquiry. *American psychologist*, 34(10), 906.

Gibson, J. E. (2012). Interviews and focus groups with children: Methods that match children's developing competencies. *Journal of Family Theory & Review*, 4(2), 148–159.

Johnson, D. W., & Johnson, R. T. (2013). Cooperation and the use of technology. *In Handbook of research on educational communications and technology* (pp. 777–803). Routledge.

McLeod, S. (2011). Albert Bandura's social learning theory. *Simply Psychology*. London.

Papert, S., & Harel, I. (1991). Situating constructionism. *constructionism*, 36(2), 1-11.

Parker, E., Tariq, A., & Smith, A. (2023). Exploring the Effectiveness of Peer Tutoring in English Language Learning Among Young Learners. *Research Studies in English Language Teaching and Learning*, 1(2). https://doi.org/10.62583/rseltl.v1i2.13

Piedade, J., & Dorotea, N. (2023). Effects of Scratch-based activities on 4th-grade students' computational thinking skills. *Informatics in Education*, 22(3), 499-523.

Thurston, A., Roseth, C., Chiang, T. H., Burns, V., & Topping, K. J. (2020). The influence of social relationships on outcomes in mathematics when using peer tutoring in elementary school. I*nternational Journal of Educational Research Open*, 1, 100004.

Thurston, A., Cockerill, M., & Chiang, T. H. (2021). Assessing the differential effects of peer tutoring for tutors and tutees. *Education Sciences*, 11(3), 97.

Topping, K. (2000). *Tutoring.* Educational Practices Series; 5.

ul Ain, Q., Thurston, A., MacKenzie, A., & Ozkaya, C. (2023). What does previous research tell us about the effects of peer tutoring on metacognition in primary and secondary schools? *International Journal of Educational Research Open*, 4, 100248.

Vygotsky, L. (1978). *Mind in society: The development of higher psychological processes.* Cambridge, MA: Harvard University Press.

Xu, Y., Gelfer, J. I., Sileo, N., Filler, J., & Perkins, P. G. (2008). Effects of peer tutoring on young children's social interactions. *Early Child Development and Care*, 178(6), 617-635.

Willis, P., Bland, R., Manka, L., & Craft, C. (2012). The ABC of peer mentoring–what secondary students have to say about cross-age peer mentoring in a regional Australian school. *Educational Research and Evaluation*, 18(2), 173-185.

Wing, J. M. (2006). Computational thinking. *Communications of the ACM*, 49(3), 33-35

Zeneli, M., & Tymms, P. (2015). A review of peer tutoring interventions and social interdependence characteristics. *International Journal for Cross-Disciplinary Subjects in Education*, 5(2), 2504-2510.

APPENDIX

Table 3. Interview Protocol for Tutors

	Questions and Probes
1	Today we did robotics with our class along with the 4th-grade students. How did you find the activity we did? What did you like? What didn't you like?
2	Did you previously know (name)with whom you collaborated in robotics activities? Describe the relationship you had until now.
3	You had the role of tutor, which means you had to teach a student at our school some robotics exercises. How did you find this role? What did you like? What didn't you like?
4	Did you encounter any difficulties teaching your tutee? What was the most challenging for you? What did you do to solve this problem?
5	How did you do in the end?
6	How important is your role in this collaboration?
7	What benefit did you gain?
8	Do you want to continue the robotics lessons?
9	What would you like to keep the same and what would you like to change?

Table 4. Interview Protocol for Tutees

	Questions and Probes
1	Today we did robotics with the 5th-grade students. How did you find the activity we did? What did you like? What didn't you like?
2	Did you previously know (name)with whom you collaborated in robotics activities? Describe the relationship you had until now.
3	Today you had a student at our school as your tutor. How did you find this role? What did you like? What didn't you like?
4	Did you encounter any difficulties having a student as your tutor? What was the most challenging for you? What did you do to solve this problem?
5	How clear were the instructions from your tutor?
6	How did you do in the end?
7	How important is your role in this collaboration?
8	If you had the choice to be taught by a teacher like me or a student of the school, what would you choose?
9	What benefit did you gain?
10	Do you want to continue the robotics lessons?
11	What would you like to keep the same and what would you like to change?

THE EFFECTS OF POLITENESS IN SHAPING DISCOURSE IN ONLINE DEBATES

Allan Jeong[1] and Ming Ming Chiu[2]
[1]*Florida State University*
Tallahassee, Florida, USA
[2]*The Education University of Hong Kong*
Ting Kok, Hong Kong

ABSTRACT

Computer-supported collaborative argumentation is an online activity that can engage students in deep discussion and analysis of complex problems. Given the potentially confrontational nature of argumentation, using polite language becomes a strategic approach to prevent breakdowns in group communication and nurture productive dialogues. This study aims to understand how politeness and argumentation moves influence subsequent conversation dynamics in online debates. Student postings in threaded discussions (from 20 online debates containing 2,008 messages posted by students across five semesters of a graduate-level course on distance education) were coded and scored on politeness and impoliteness using natural language processing software. The scored postings were examined to determine how impoliteness and politeness impact students' proclivity to engage in and produce more sustained argumentative exchanges to evaluate presented claims thoroughly. The findings from this study reveal the possible effects of specific behaviors on how students engage in argumentation and provide guidance on what behavioral standards to emphasize when students participate in group debates. Moreover, the findings lay the groundwork for establishing behavioral standards with clearer definitions of specific linguistic markers. Future iterations of netiquette guidelines can draw upon the findings from this study and future studies to furnish students with concrete examples that illustrate the practical application of each behavioral norm.

KEYWORDS

Computer-Mediated Communication, Argumentation, Politeness, Critical Thinking, Interaction Analysis

1. INTRODUCTION

Online group discussion is a fundamental instructional strategy in online learning, providing opportunities for students to interact with course content, peers, and instructors and helping increase student engagement. These discussions are primarily asynchronous, allowing for virtual participation and fostering collaborative learning that adds a rich dimension to the learning experience. Online discussions promote learner interaction, supplement content delivery, offer opportunities to apply the knowledge practically and meaningfully, and provide opportunities for in-depth, thoughtful reflection and responses. Most of all, online discussions can enhance cognitive and exploratory learning, empower students, and promote active engagement with course content. Overall, online discussions can play a crucial role in facilitating a sense of community and promoting critical thinking to help increase the depth of learning and understanding in online courses. Critical thinking is a process of purposeful, self-regulatory judgment that involves interpreting, analyzing, evaluating, and reasoning about information and ideas in a reflective and systematic manner. Critical thinking is essential in online learning as it enables students to engage with course content deeply and meaningfully, leading to a more thorough understanding of the material. It also fosters the development of essential skills such as problem-solving, decision-making, and effective communication, which are highly valuable in academic and professional contexts. Moreover, critical thinking encourages students to question assumptions, consider alternative perspectives, and make well-informed judgments, ultimately leading to a more enriching and intellectually stimulating learning experience.

One type of discussion activity where students engage in critical thinking and defend their reasoning is group debates. In group debates, students engage in dialogue with others to construct, evaluate, and justify claims based on evidence and reasoning, plays a crucial role in supporting student learning in online courses (Chen, Zhai, Zhu, and Li, 2022; Rapanta & Felton, 2022). Research has shown that collaborative argumentation can foster critical thinking, creativity, communication, and problem-solving skills, which are essential for online learning environments (Asterhan & Schwarz, 2016; Baker, Andriessen, & Schwarz, 2019). However, collaborative argumentation can also pose some challenges, such as managing social conflicts (Chiu et al., 2021; Chiu & Khoo, 2003; Li et al., 2023) and other less desired social behaviors. Social conflicts in online discussions can disrupt effective communication and create socially polarized environments, impacting the quality of dialogue and collaboration (Chiu & Koo, 2003; Lu, Chiu, & Law, 2010).

To foster an environment where students feel safe to engage critically with one another, guidelines for online conduct, known as netiquette, can be invaluable (McMurdo, 1995; Scheuermann & Taylor, 1997). Netiquette sets forth accepted norms of behavior, stressing the importance of maintaining respect, courtesy, and professionalism, while discouraging personal attacks and disruptive behavior. Adhering to these standards, such as acknowledging others, speaking kindly, respecting differing opinions, refraining from personal inquiries, offering sincere apologies, and being considerate, can significantly reduce the likelihood of misunderstandings, conflicts, and disruptions during online discussions (Mistretta, 2021). However, prior research on the impact of applying netiquette in online discussion is limited by their differing definitions of netiquette (and specific behavioral standards) and methods used to measure its impact on discussions (Soler-Costa, Lafarga-Ostáriz, Mauri-Medrano, and Moreno-Guerrero, 2021). Danescu-Niculescu-Mizil et al. (2013) identified specific behaviors that are perceived to be polite (e.g., expressing gratitude, deference, greetings, apologizing) while also identifying the specific behaviors that can be perceived to be impolite (e.g., asking a direct question, stating things as a matter of fact, and directing a statement to another starting with the "you").

Developing clearer netiquette guidelines requires a closer examination of how specific polite and impolite linguistic markers impact the emergence and management of social conflicts in online discussions (Levy et al., 2022). Politeness theory (Brown & Levinson, 1987) characterizes "face" as the positive social value individuals claim for themselves, encompassing interpersonal needs such as appreciation, belonging, and autonomy. In small group discussions, students face threats by critiquing peers' contributions, admitting their own mistakes, or suggesting specific behaviors, all considered face-threatening acts (Brummernhenrich et al., 2021). Face threats can impede productive discussions, but individuals often mitigate them using politeness strategies, such as hedging contributions, indirect speech, or solidarity markers (Brown & Levinson, 1987; Holtgraves, 1997). Prior studies that politeness strategies can facilitate smooth communication, maintain relationships, and reduce interpersonal friction in group discussions (Chiu, Oh, Kim, & Cionea, 2022; Holtgraves, 1997). Holtgraves (1997) described linguistic mechanisms people use when engaging in disagreements with one another, highlighting the use of positive politeness in conversation arguments. However, they also highlight potential drawbacks, such as inhibiting critical feedback and fostering superficial communication. In online debates, polite disagreement tactics can influence democratic discussions (Chiu, Oh, Kim, & Cionea, 2022).

Deeper investigations into the role of politeness strategies can be conducted using natural language processing (NLP) tools (Chang et al., 2020). NLP techniques can be used to analyze the types of language students produce in online debates that are perceived to be impolite, identify patterns of impolite language use, detect emotional intensity changes over a conversation, and predict conflict based on user characteristics and conversational dynamics. For example, the Convokit:politeness tool in the ConvoKit open-source toolkit was developed to enable more researchers to apply natural language processing to analyze conversations and the social interactions embedded within conversations (Chang et al., 2020). The tool has been used in research on politeness to study the use of politeness strategies in conversations, including online discussions. One of the findings from the research is that the tool can be applied to understand the use of politeness strategies in conversations that have gone awry on platforms such as Wikipedia. The tool provides a framework for characterizing utterances and terms based on their expected politeness, allowing for analyzing politeness and impoliteness in conversational data.

The purpose of this study was to use the Convokit politeness tool to identify the potential impact of contextual factors, such as the use of politeness across different types of dialog moves in online debates and how politeness and impoliteness in one dialog move influence subsequent dialog within conversational threads as students participate in argumentation. As a result, the following research questions were addressed in this study:

(1) Which polite and impolite linguistic markers are used in students' online debates? Where and when do they occur in dialog moves and discussion threads?
(2) How do polite and impolite markers in specific dialog moves impact the way the opposition responds to the dialog move?
(3) When a student's argument is challenged by the opposition, how do polite and impolite markers in the challenge impact how to what extent the student responds to the challenge in the ensuing discussion thread?

2. METHOD

2.1 Participants

A total of 87 master's students (53 females and 34 males, between the ages of 20 to 50 years) enrolled in a 15-week, fully asynchronous, online course titled "Introduction to Distance Education" in a master's program at a major university in the southeastern United States from the spring of 2005 through the fall of 2007 semesters.

2.2 Procedure

Each student participated in four team debates (each one week in duration) using asynchronous threaded discussion forums in a course management system. Each debate aimed to help students critically examine design issues, concepts, and principles regarding distance learning. For each debate, students were randomly assigned to one of two to either support or oppose the assigned claim and were required to post a minimum of four posts per debate. The instructor presented Toulmin's (1958) model of argumentation to the students before and during the debates to help them identify premises (labeled ARG) to either support or oppose the given claim (warrants), present evidence (EVID) to support a premise (facts), give explanations (EXPL, backing), or pose challenges (BUT, rebuttals). Students classified each of their postings into one of the four categories by adding the corresponding label to the subject heading of each post, restricting the content of each message to address only that one category, and identified which side they were assigned to debate by prefacing each label with "-" for the opposing team or "+" for the supporting team (e.g., +ARG, ARG). Following each message tag, students added one sentence to convey the main idea presented in the message. At the end of each debate, students completed an online poll to reveal their personal conclusions and positions on the debate proposition and submitted a written explanation for their conclusions. Participation in the debates and all other class activities contributed to 20% of a student's course grade and were conducted under netiquette guidelines presented in the course syllabus. The guidelines consisted of 10 core rules of netiquette (Shea & Shea, 1994): 1) remember the human; 2) adhere to the same standards of behavior online that you follow in real life; 3) know where you are in cyberspace; 4) respect other people's time and bandwidth; 5) make yourself look good online; 6) share expert knowledge; 7) help keep flame wars under control; 8) respect other people's privacy; 9) don't abuse your power; and 10) be forgiving of other people's mistakes.

2.3 Data Preparation

In the 2,008 total messages posted in the online debates, the students' labels they assigned to their messages were downloaded to identify each message as an argument (ARG, n = 391), challenge (BUT n = 955), explanation (EXPL, n = 368), or evidence (EVID, n = 294). One debate from each course was randomly selected and coded to test for errors in students' message labels. Based on the codes of 157 messages consisting of 42 arguments, 17 supporting evidence, 81 critiques, and 17 explanations, overall agreement between the students and the researcher's codes was 91% with excellent inter-rater reliability (Cohen's kappa = .86). The mean number of words per posting was 80 words (*SD* = 29 words).

2.4 Coding Postings on Politeness and Impoliteness

To measure the degree of politeness and impoliteness expressed in each student's posting, the Convokit:politeness software was used to automatically create variables from each student's posting. Danescu-Niculescu-Mizil et al. (2013) created this software by annotating over 10,000 requests posted by the Wikipedia editors community and by the Stack Exchange question-and-answer community. Crowdsourcing the efforts of 431 total workers on Amazon Mechanical Turk, each request was rated on level of politeness (from "very impolite" to "very polite") by five annotators. The annotators also scored each request by the discomfort or stress they experienced when reading each request (while asked to imagine themselves performing the role of an editor in Wikipedia). The Stanford Dependency Parser (de Marneffe et al., 2006) extracted the politeness markers and created a specialized set of lexicons from this annotated data. These lexicons were then used to create the Convokit:politeness software to identify words or phrases that reveal 15 forms of politeness (positive ratings) and 6 forms of impoliteness (negative ratings), summarized in Table 1. The software was used to score each posting in the debates on the 21 forms of politeness/impoliteness (as a 0 or 1) and to score each posting on the stress level exhibited in each posting.

Table 1. Debate postings scored on the following forms of politeness and impoliteness identified by the Convokit: politeness software

Markers	Politeness Rating	Example from Wikipedia*
Gratitude	0.87	I appreciate that you've done them.
Deference	0.78	Nice work so far on your rewrite.
Greeting	0.43	Hey, I just tried to...
Positive lexicon	0.12	Wow! This is a great way to deal...
Negative lexicon	-0.13	If you're going to accuse me...
Apologizing	0.36	Sorry to bother you...
Please	0.49	Could you please say more...
Please start	-0.30	Please do not remove warnings...
Indirect (btw)	0.63	By the way, where did you find...
Direct question	-0.27	What is your native language?
Direct start	-0.43	So can you retrieve it or not?
Counterfactual modal	0.47	Could/Would you...
Indicative modal	0.09	Can/Will you...
1st person start	0.12	I have just put the article...
1st person pl.	0.08	Could we find a less complex name...
1st person	0.08	It is my view that...
2nd person	0.05	But do you have in mind?
2nd person start	-0.30	You explain that...
Hedges	0.14	It might be true some of the time...
Factuality	-0.38	In fact you did link...

**Source*: Danescu-Niculescu-Mizil et al. (2013)

3. RESULTS

3.1 When Polite/Impolite Markers are used in the Debates

The most common polite markers used in the debates were positive lexicon, followed by first-person and hedges. At the same time, the remaining politeness strategies (e.g., gratitude, deference, greeting, apologies) occurred at very low frequencies overall. Among the six impolite markers examined in this study, negative lexicon and factuality were used most frequently. In contrast, the use of direct questions and direct start was used in moderate numbers. Polite markers were most frequent in challenges (about 44% times more so than in presented ARGs) among the four dialog moves, with moderate effects size (d = .28). Likewise, the presence of impolite markers was highest in challenges (about 32% times more so than in presented ARGs) among the four dialog moves, with overall effect size was small (d = .16). The frequency of polite markers was not statistically different between BUT, EXPL, and EVID. In contrast, the frequency of impolite markers was significantly higher in BUT than in EXPL and EVID. Of the 955 challenges posted in the debates, 663, or 69.5% of challenges contained impolite markers, and the remaining challenges (30.5%) possessed no impolite markers. More than half of all postings contained both polite and impolite markers, while a third contained only polite markers, with few containing only impolite markers or no markers at all.

As to when the markers appear within discussion threads, the ANOVA on the observed frequencies of all polite markers posted in thread levels 1 through 6 showed significant differences in mean number of polite markers between levels (increasing by 139% from level 1 through 6, $F(6,2001) = 61.13$ p =.000). A significant difference was also found in the mean number of impolite markers between levels 1 through 7, $F(6, 2001) = 10.39$, p = .000, increasing by as much 84% from level 1 through 7. In contrast, 0%, 1%, 0%, and 9% of all posts at thread levels 2, 3, 6, and 8 contained apologies that convey politeness. In general, the use of positive lexicon remained relatively stable from early to later posts in threads, whereas the use of negative lexicon increased in frequency at higher thread levels.

Comparing the frequency distributions of the six impolite markers across thread levels 1 through 11 produced a Chi-square test that was statistically significant, X^2 (df = 50) = 103.68, p = .0000. The use of negative lexicon, direct questions, second person, and factuality increased as discussions progressed, while the use of please start and direct starts remain largely constant from early to late in discussion threads. When comparing the frequency distributions of the 14 polite markers across thread levels 1 through 11, the Chi-square test was statistically significant, X^2 (df = 120) = 299.18, p =.0000. This finding indicates that as discussions progressed, students used progressively more gratitude, positive lexicon, 1st person starts, 1st person pl, 1st person, 2nd person, and hedges. Politeness markers that showed no change in usage from early to later in the threads (and were rarely used in students' postings) were deference, greetings, apologies, please, indirect, counterfactual, and indicative modal.

3.2 How Politeness Impact Responses to Opposing Team Posts

The Discussion Analysis Tool or DAT (Jeong, 2005a) was used to sequentially analyze (Bakeman & Gottman, 1997; Jeong, 2005b) the threaded discussions by: a) determining the frequencies and relative frequencies (or transitional probabilities) of each transition from one dialog move to another dialog move (e.g., -ARG→+BUT, +BUT→-EXPL); b) applying z-score tests (critical p-value at .05) to determine if each observed probability was significantly higher than the expected probability based on chance alone; and c) creating transitional state diagrams to reveal and compare response patterns that emerged from posts with versus without polite and impolite linguistic markers. The transitional state diagrams showed that the way the opposition replied to posts with polite markers only (P) vs. impolite markers only (I) vs. with both polite and impolite markers (B) were largely similar. Overall, the response patterns to posts with P and to posts with B were nearly identical. Three notable differences in response patterns can be found when comparing the behavior patterns between the four state diagrams. For example, arguments posted with P, I, and B were more likely to elicit challenges from the opposition while arguments with N were less likely to elicit challenges (BUT) from the opposition (and in turn) are more likely to elicit counterevidence from the opposition. Challenges (BUT) with N were more likely to elicit counterchallenges from the opposition than challenges with P, I, and B. Evidence presented with I was more likely to elicit no responses from the opposition than evidence presented with P, B, and N.

3.3 How Students Respond to Challenges Presented with Polite & Impolite Markers

The correlation between the number of polite and impolite markers in each posting was significant, $r = .349$ ($n = 2027$), $p = .000$. This finding suggests that students used more polite language when presenting ideas (particularly ideas that convey disagreement) that others could perceive to be contentious and/or impolite in tone. No significant difference was found in the number of responses students posted in the ensuing discussions following the initial rebuttal posted in response to challenges with polite markers only ($M = 1.55$, $STD = 1.23$, $n = 20$) versus with both polite and impolite markers ($M = 1.17$, $STD = .90$, $n = 46$), $t(19, 45) = 1.38$ at $p = .085$ with a one-tailed test and the assumption that students feel more comfortable and are more engaged when the tone of the discussion is more positive than negative. Though not significant, the overall trend in findings indicates that students might post more responses when challenges to their arguments are posted with more polite language and less impolite language.

No significant difference was found in the number of turns into the conversation (the response posted at the highest thread level) students posted in the ensuing discussions following the initial rebuttal posted in response to challenges with polite markers only ($M = 3.55$, STD = 1.28, $n = 20$) versus with both polite and impolite markers ($M = 3.37$, $STD = 1.16$, n = 46), $t(19, 45) = .562$ at $p = .287$ using a one-tailed test under the same assumption describe above. Though not significant, the overall trend in the findings shows students might post responses deeper into the discussions when challenges to their arguments are posted with more polite and less impolite language.

A significant difference was found in the average levels of stress exhibited across all responses students posted in the ensuing discussions following challenges with polite markers only ($M = -1.84$, $STD = .88$, $n = 20$) versus with both polite and impolite markers ($M = -2.30$, $STD = .95$, $n = 46$), $t(19, 45) = 1.86$ at $p = .033$ using a one-tailed test under the previously stated assumption. This finding shows that students can feel more discomfort when responding to challenges with more impolite than polite language.

4. DISCUSSION

Online discussions are vital for interactive learning, and emphasis on critical thinking in online environments promotes deep engagement, problem-solving, decision-making, and effective communication skills. Group debates, a form of collaborative argumentation, support student learning by fostering critical thinking, creativity, and problem-solving. However, social conflicts in online discussions can disrupt effective communication, impacting dialogue quality. Linguistic and interactional features influence social conflicts in online discussions. Politeness theory highlights the role of politeness strategies in mitigating face threats during argumentative interactions, and prior studies show how politeness can facilitate and inhibit argumentation. To gain a deeper understanding of the impact of politeness on how students engage in argumentation, this study utilized a natural language processing tool to analyze a large corpus of postings from online debates to determine what politeness markers were used in the debates, where and when they are used in the debates, what impact they have on student responses to posts from the opposition.

The findings show that positive lexicon, first person, and hedges were used most frequently among the 14 polite makers examined in this study and that polite markers were used most frequently when presenting arguments in the debate. In contrast, negative lexicon and factuality were the most frequent impolite markers, and these and other impolite markers were used most often when students presented challenges. When impolite markers were used in postings in general, students almost always included polite markers. Furthermore, students used increasingly more polite markers in posts as the frequency of impolite markers increased in posts made later in discussion threads. These two findings suggest that students in the debates tried to soften the tone of their oppositional posting (and potentially reduce the perception of impoliteness and social conflict) by including polite language.

The sequential analysis of how posts with markers impact how students in the opposition respond to posts revealed the unexpected finding that arguments with N were less likely to elicit challenges from the opposition. This finding suggests that polite markers can help invite or elicit responses from the opposition and that students from the opposition are less likely to post a response when they are absent. In theory, the absence of impolite markers in arguments can help increase students' willingness to respond to arguments with challenges, but the findings show the opposite. One possible explanation for this unexpected finding is that the students posted arguments in response to the debate prompt (not in direct response to another student's posting) and, as a result, had no reason to use direct questions, direct starts, and 2nd person starts. Also, the specific arguments with N may have been weak arguments that lacked supporting facts or were arguments posted supporting the proposition under debate. In contrast, arguments with I elicited more challenges than expected, possibly because many of these arguments were posted to oppose the debated proposition.

In determining how students respond to challenges presented with polite and impolite markers, the sequential analysis revealed that challenges with N revealed a higher-than-expected tendency to elicit counterchallenges from the opposition than challenges with P, I, and B. This finding is partly expected given that the absence of impolite markers in a challenge (when challenges are already contentious) can help reduce students' inhibitions from posting a counterchallenge. It is possible that this specific dynamic prevailed over the potentially negative impact caused by the absence of politeness in the posted challenges. Overall, these findings above emphasize the importance of examining the impact of politeness markers in context to the specific dialog moves in which they are used. Most of all, the findings highlight the importance of politeness when presenting arguments for critical review and discussion.

In examining how responses with specific markers that challenge presented arguments impact discussions, this study found no significant difference in the number of responses students posted following challenges with polite markers only versus challenges with polite and impolite markers. Nevertheless, the data reveal a trend that suggests that students might post more responses when challenges are framed with more polite language and less impolite language. Similarly, no significant difference was found in the number of turns (depth of engagement) in the conversation following challenges with polite markers compared to challenges with polite and impolite markers. Yet, the trend in the data suggests that students might post responses deeper into the discussions when challenges are presented more politely and less impolitely. Also, a significant difference was found in students' average stress levels in response to challenges with P versus B. The postings exhibited more discomfort when responding to challenges framed with more impolite than polite language. As a result, these findings suggest a nuanced relationship between politeness, impoliteness, and student engagement in online discussions, and the significant difference in stress levels highlights the discomfort students can potentially feel when responding to challenges framed with impolite language, emphasizing the importance of maintaining a polite tone in online discussions.

The study's findings regarding the limited impact of politeness on both the frequency and depth of engagement in responses can be partially attributed to several factors. Firstly, the need to focus on a smaller subset of data, specifically responses from individual students who countered challenges to their arguments, may have influenced the observed outcomes. Additionally, challengers' occasional use of polite markers could have moderated the effects of impolite markers, whether intentional or not. Moreover, members of each debate team comprising 12 or more students per side could contribute additional rebuttals to challenges, reinforcing the initial arguments. Combined with the requirement that each student post a minimum of for postings per debate, this ample team size likely motivated students to participate more frequently and contribute to ongoing discussion threads. Finally, certain behaviors that might be perceived as impolite, such as using a negative lexicon, were inherent to the nature of argumentation and were possibly accepted by the students within the context of the debate.

Regarding the instructional implications, this study's findings provide valuable information for shaping and improving netiquette standards. These standards cover behavioral expectations such as showing acknowledgment, using respectful language, embracing diverse opinions, avoiding personal questions, offering sincere apologies, and demonstrating consideration. Adhering to these norms can reduce confusion, conflicts, and interruptions in online interactions. The study underscores the importance of these norms, especially in contexts where students face challenges and engage in deeper discourse over the merits of a specific argument. Additionally, it identifies impolite behaviors that may emerge in such debates, which instructors can work to discourage.

The findings from this study also uncover the potential impact of specific behaviors on how and to what extent students engage in argumentation, guiding instructors on which behavioral standards to emphasize when students participate in group debates. Moreover, examining polite and impolite markers in the study lays the groundwork for establishing behavioral standards with clearer definitions of specific linguistic markers. Future iterations of netiquette guidelines (developed by researchers and instructors) can draw upon these findings and those of similar studies to furnish students with concrete examples that illustrate the practical application of each behavioral norm.

In conclusion, the tools and methods presented in this study provide one approach that researchers can use in the future to measure and achieve deeper insights into the use and the impact of politeness markers on student participation and engagement in online discussions, with a specific focus on how they can influence the level and quality of critical thinking in group discussions. Using the described tools and methods, this study's findings give researchers and instructors a clearer understanding of the underlying dynamics and interplay between social and cognitive presence in online learning. Applying the findings produced with these methods and reported in this study may help improve student engagement, increase the quality and depth of group discussions in online courses, and, most of all, help students improve learning and understanding.

REFERENCES

Asterhan, C. S., & Schwarz, B. B., 2016. Argumentation for learning: Well-trodden paths and unexplored territories. Educational Psychologist, Vol. 51. No. 2, pp. 164–187.

Bakeman, R. & Gottman, J., 1997). *Observing interaction: An introduction to sequential analysis*. Cambridge University Press.

Baker, M. J., Andriessen, J., & Schwarz, B. B., 2019. *Collaborative argumentation-based learning. The Routledge International Handbook of Research on Dialogic Education*, pp. 76-88.

Brummernhenrich B., Baker M. J., Bietti L. M., Détienne F., Jucks R., 2021. Being (Un)safe Together: Student Group Dynamics, Facework and Argumentation. In F. Maine, & M. Vrikki (Eds.), *Dialogue for Intercultural Understanding (*pp. 119–134). Springer, Cham.

Chang, J.P., Chiam, C., Fu, L., Wang, A., Zhang, J., and Danescu-Niculescu-Mizil, C., 2020. ConvoKit: A toolkit for the analysis of conversations. In *Proceedings of the 21st Annual Meeting of the Special Interest Group on Discourse and Dialogue*, pp. 57–60, Association for Computational Linguistics, 1st virtual meeting.

Chen, X., Zhai, X., Zhu, Y., & Li, Y., 2022. Exploring debaters and audiences' depth of critical thinking and its relationship with their participation in debate activities. *Thinking Skills and Creativity*, 44.

Chiu, M. M., & Khoo, L., 2003. Impoliteness and status effects during group problem solving: Do they bias evaluations and reduce the likelihood of correct solutions? *Journal of Educational Psychology*, Vol. 95, No. 3, 506.

Chiu, M. M., Oh, Y. W., Kim, J. N., & Cionea, I. A., 2022. Serving the greater social good for personal gain: effects of polite disagreements in online debates. *Communication Research*, Vol. 49, No. 3, pp. 451-473.

Holtgraves, T., 1997. Yes, but... positive politeness in conversation arguments. *Journal of Language and Social Psychology*, Vol. 16, No. 2, pp, 222-239.

Jeong, A., 2005a. A guide to analyzing message-response sequences and group interaction patterns in computer-mediated communication. *Distance Education*, Vol. 26, No. 3, pp. 367–383.

Jeong, A. (2005b). *Discussion analysis tool.* Retrieved July 19, 2024 from https://myweb.fsu.edu/ajeong/dat

Lu, J., Chiu, M. M., & Law, N., 2010. Effects of on-line collaborative argumentation processes on justifications. In Gomez, K., Lyons, L., & Radinsky, J. (Eds.), *Learning in the Disciplines: Proceedings of the 9th International Conference of the Learning Sciences (ICLS 2010)*, Volume 1, Full Papers (pp. 207-214). International Society of the Learning Sciences.

McMurdo, G., 1995. Netiquettes for networkers. *Journal of Information Science*, Vol. 21, pp. 305–318.

Mistretta, S., 2021. The new netiquette: Choosing civility in an age of online teaching and learning. *International Journal on E-Learning*, Vol. 20, No. 3, pp. 323-345.

Rapanta, C., & Felton, M. K., 2022. Learning to argue through dialogue: A review of instructional approaches. *Educational Psychology Review*, pp. 1-33.

Scheuermann, L., & Taylor, G. (1997). Netiquette. *International Research*, Vol. 7, pp. 269–273.

Shea, V., & Shea, C., 1994. *Netiquette.* Albion Books.

Soler-Costa, R., Lafarga-Ostáriz, P., Mauri-Medrano, M., & Moreno-Guerrero, A. J., 2021. Netiquette: Ethic, education, and behavior on internet—a systematic literature review. *International Journal of Environmental Research and Public Health*, Vol. 18, No. 3, pp. 1212.

Wikle, J. S., & West, R. E., 2019. An analysis of discussion forum participation and student learning outcomes. *International Journal on E-Learning*, Vol. 18, No. 2, pp. 205-228.

EDUCATIONAL BOARD GAME FOR IMPROVING EMPATHETIC MIND AND COMMUNICATION

Samoekan Sophonhiranrak, Putthachat Angnakoon, Sarunwit Promsaka Na Sakonnakron, Yada Atanan and Tida Tubpun
Thammasat University
Pathumthani, Thailand

ABSTRACT

The Friedrich Naumann Foundation and the King Prajadhipok's Institute in Thailand created the educational board game PeaceSoCracy, based on the online game available on the Tabletopia platform. The purpose of this board game is to encourage non-violent communication and an empathetic mind. Each process in the game play delivers more than just communication skills. Furthermore, playing educational board games means more than just following the rules; it also gives players the opportunity to experience and learn various lessons and skills. This research study examined players' learning experiences, decision-making skills, opinions, attitude, perspective, social skills, and communication skills that came from playing the PeaceSoCracy board game both online and offline. The research methodology employed qualitative research, which involved interviewing participants about their opinions and observations during the play session. In this study, 18 undergraduate students participated in face-to-face (F2F) sessions, and five undergraduate students played both F2F and online platforms. The observation and interview phases employed thematic analysis. The results indicated that the participants reported distinct differences in their experiences when playing in face-to-face (f2f) sessions compared to the online platform (via Tabletopia), especially the emotional engagement and interpersonal interaction. Moreover, players utilized a variety of skills in each phase, including creative thinking, problem solving, and communication, while the facilitators could potentially influence the play session by providing encouragement, guidelines, rules, and monitoring questions and answers. Furthermore, the players understood each other through communication and had an empathy mindset.

KEYWORDS

Educational Board Game, Communication Skill, Undergraduate Students, Empathetic Mind

1. INTRODUCTION

The Friedrich Naumann Foundation and King Prajadhipok's Institute designed PeaceSoCracy, a board game, to foster communication skills in the face of social conflict, as part of their "Promotion of Peaceful Society" statement (Sukumal Surichamorn et al., n.d.-b, n.d.-a). There were fifteen stories from three clusters or levels: family, society, and country (Sukumal Surichamorn et al., n.d.-a, n.d.-b). These stories would encourage awareness of nonviolent communication and judgment without bias.

Conflicts of communication and emotion that caused various problems, particularly in negotiations and meetings, sometimes came from "assertiveness" (Dzaferovic, 2012) and thought under inadequate resources (Oetzel & Ting-Toomey, 2013). These conflicts were caused by differences in beliefs, opinions, and feelings, miscommunication, and unfair power. We could categorize them into five types: data conflict, structural conflict, interest conflict, value conflict, and relationship conflict (Moore, 2014). Therefore, there is a need for tools or methods to alleviate the conflict. Communication is one of the most critical elements of conflict resolution, resulting in the theoretical innovation of diverse communication techniques. Among those well-known concepts, nonviolent communication (NVC) gains practitioners' attention to solve these conflicting problems.

Nonviolent communication (NVC), or compassionate communication (Rosenberg, 2015), is a communication skill that includes listening and speaking to understand and connect the mind of a speaker to a listener deeply (Lasater & Lasater, 2022; MacNair & Psychologist for Social Responsibility, 2006; Martin & Varney, 2003; Rosenberg, 2015). However, NVC was not only a communication technique but also concentration with the thoughtful topic (Rosenberg, 2015) and the appropriate words that were chosen for talking with anyone (Lasater & Lasater, 2022). Furthermore, one of the key factors in NVC was empathy and a lack of judgment were key factors in NVC, which supported successful communication (Juncadella & Blackmore, 2013; Koopman & Seliga, 2021).

Owing to the meaning and connotation of words and phrases, each conversation really shows the thoughts of the speaker, awareness, and understanding of the situation, culture, and listeners' minds (Lasater & Lasater, 2022). This concept also reminds the speakers to be aware of using words and gestures before expressing each dialogue (Lasater & Lasater, 2022). Upon the concern of the empathetic conversation, NVC absolutely reduces conflict and increases peace in the community (MacNair & Psychologist for Social Responsibility, 2006) through regenerating positive dialogue and solutions (Dzaferovic, 2012). Applying NVC in real life may decrease stress, anxiety (Zandkarimi et al., 2019), anger, and heart healing from bad situations (Roy, 2019). Furthermore, NVC could be a tool for leveraging the emotional well-being of family members (Cheung et al., 2023).

NVC is not only the communication process or language usage; it also integrates observation and understanding the feelings, needs, and requirements of others (Museux et al., 2016; Rosenberg, 2015). There are four crucial elements of NVC that contribute to communication without judgement or discussion about emotion (Koopman & Seliga, 2021; Zandkarimi et al., 2019). Firstly, observation without judgment (Museux et al., 2016) focuses on not only words in the conversation but also nonverbal communication using gestures, postures, or facial expressions (Jung et al., 2023; Sung & Kweon, 2022). Secondly, Museux et al. (2016) emphasize the importance of accepting others' feelings, while Sung & Kweon (2022) emphasizes the importance of comprehending and connecting these feelings to needs. Some researchers applied tools such as word charts of feelings and needs to increase comprehension (Jung et al., 2023; Koopman & Seliga, 2021; Sung & Kweon, 2022), pictures, or situations (Baesler & Lauricella, 2014; Jung et al., 2023). Thirdly, signal comprehension happened after a long conversation, involving both feelings and needs (Museux et al., 2016). The last one asks for generating effective and tangible action (Museux et al., 2016). Nevertheless, these skills cannot be articulated without training; the instructor needs to nurture and encourage the practitioners to have them. Experiencing listening, thinking, and speaking was a powerful method to enhance nonviolent communication skills (Koopman & Seliga, 2021; Lasater & Lasater, 2022) that was related to playing a board game as a simulation, such as the PeaceSoCracy board game.

In a gaming session, the gameplay unfolds through observation and interaction between participants, which leads to the development of communication skills (Museux et al., 2016). Additionally, integrated activities, feeling cards, and other media could support communication skills (Jung et al., 2023).

"Game" is one play tool that is applied in learning activities to encourage learners' knowledge and skill (Plass et al., 2019; Thomas & Brown, 2011); consequently, applying games in education was called an educational game that was different from only "game." Educational games were designed to enhance learning with elements in the game and instructional steps in the game dynamic to gain knowledge along with play to debrief (Garris et al., 2002).

Generally, instructions for game-based learning consist of three main steps (Figure 1), including input, process, and output (Garris et al., 2002). The first step is to provide 1) academic content and 2) game factors. The second one was the game cycle, which consisted of 1) user judgment or reaction happening in the game, such as joy, happiness, and attraction; 2) user behavior; and 3) system feedback. This second step shows that engagement in content and game flow is a key to encouraging motivation and constructing knowledge through games by themselves. Owing to the process in the second step, it was aligned with experiential learning theory (ELT), which focused on learning in practical context and creating knowledge by themselves (Kolb & Kolb, 2009; Kolb, 2014). Furthermore, the third step was the debriefing and learning outcomes, which were meaningful because there was a relation between game cycle and achievement (Eisenack, 2013; Pivec & Dziabenko, 2004).

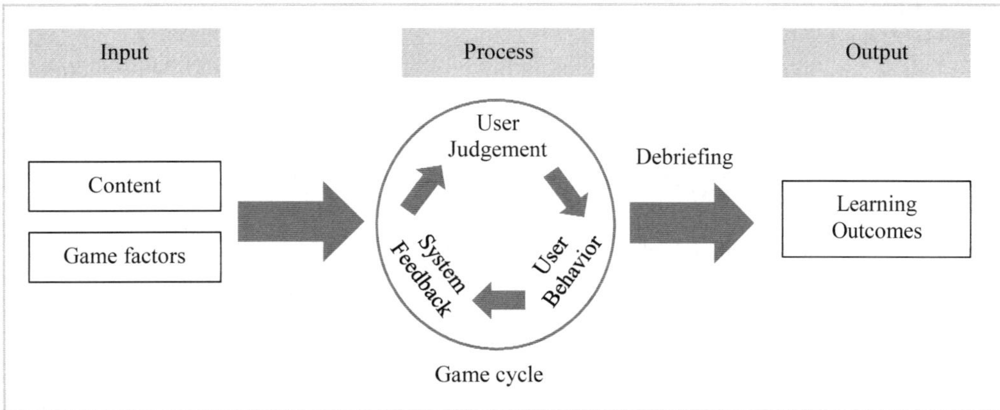

Figure 1. Input-Process-Output Game Model (Garris et al., 2002)

Board game was applied as a learning tool that encouraged participation (Eisenack, 2013; Fjællingsdal & Klöckner, 2020) in class and cooperativeness, especially, 'incorporating board game' could improve problem solving skills, critical thinking, system thinking, and communication skills (Hinebaugh, 2009). Consequently, a board game that could encourage skills and knowledge about a specific topic might have various dynamics, such as remembering or sorting for increasing memorizing skills or answering the question for approving understanding skills. The first type of board game, such as a memory board game, was a board game that helped players understand the concept of a specific topic in an easy way, increasing learning engagement in the classroom (Normalita et al., 2023). Whereas there were other types, such as complex board games that consisted of strategies, rules, roles, materials, and dynamics, players had to plan strategies for reaching the goal of the game (Gobet et al., 2004).

Owing to various types of board games, the instructors tried to apply both commercial board games, gamification, and educational board games in learning sessions, not only in class but also after class (Gobet et al., 2004; Hinebaugh, 2009). Although educational board games would have to focus on education and learning, enjoyment and engagement were still key points in this context (Booker & MItchell, 2021). Applying subjects or learning topics to a board game during a learning session practically enhanced learners' participation and attention in lessons (Normalita et al., 2023). Some studies demonstrated that learners discussed and focused on the instruction much more than without game playing (Normalita et al., 2023).

Online board games such as the Tabletopia platform are open to long-distance players. This platform made the board game that had to be played offline an online game (Jensen et al., 2023). Playing on an online platform encouraged the possibility of learning and upskilling from playing board games that were once limited to face-to-face sessions. This platform could help, especially not only players but also developers, initiate board games in the COVID-19 period (Almeida et al., 2021). As a PeaceSoCracy board game that was translated into English and converted to an online board game on the Tabletopia platform. There were both Thai and English versions that could play as individual (Solo function) and group (Hotseat).

However, both board games and online board games still had a well-planned lesson, including an introduction, monitoring, and reflection session with organized questions and skilled facilitators for effective playing board games. Accordingly, this research study was conducted to explore the steps in learning activities that were designed, the opinions about games and learning experiences from games, and the skills that participants acquired from playing this game.

1.1 Research Objectives

The objectives of this research were threefold. First of all, the researchers aimed to explore the learning activities and experiences that emerge during gameplay. Second, the study sought to examine the specific skills that participants develop from playing the PeaceSoCracy board game. Finally, this research will compare the differences between playing the game with friends in an on-site setting and playing it on an online platform.

2. METHOD

This research study was conducted with qualitative research that consisted of observation and interviewing the participants.

2.1 Sample

After signing the research consent form, we recruited 23 undergraduate students from public and private universities in Thailand through volunteer applications. Grantors and faculty published recruitment details and application links on their social media pages. The registration process gathered basic information and sorted the games based on participant preference. The project coordinator, who managed the activities, described the activity details to each participant before confirming their decision to join the playing session and the activity date.

Before the play session on the activity date, the researchers informed the participants about the purpose and process of the activity, the research study, and the data collection process, giving them the option to withdraw at any time.

For the play session, two facilitators, experienced in non-violent communication and PeacSoCracy board games, divided the 18 undergraduate students into two groups. Following the play session, ten undergraduate students agreed to participate in interviews. Five undergraduate students engaged in both on-site and online gaming through the Tabletopia platform.

2.2 Research Tools

To explore the action and skills that occur during game play, we used a recording observation note and a semi-structured interview form to gather context and reflection from the game. Firstly, the recording note consisted of 1) duration, 2) action, and 3) behaviors and/or words from players (as shown in Table 1).

Table 1. Observation note

Duration	Action/steps	Behavior/words
20 minutes	**Briefing**: Greetings and introduction to the PeaceSoCracy board game, with questions posed to the participants, such as Do you have any experience with conflict? And what's the solution? After that, the play coach would present the game rule, set up the game, and choose one scenario.	Participants would share experiences and ideas that led to educational goals, game goals, and rules. ***The researchers would record time, gestures, and conversation.***
45 minutes	**Playing**: the play coach would monitor, support, and encourage participants to ask the questions, collect the information, and share ideas.	***The researchers would record time, questions, and conversations.***
35 minutes	**Debriefing**: the participants would share their opinions and experiences from the playing session.	***The researchers would record shared messages.***

Based on the recorded information from the playing session, the researchers conducted an interview to gather more detailed information about the participants' thoughts, thinking processes, and opinions during playing times and reflection periods. The researchers interviewed the participants, who were two play coaches and three players after the game session, in a semi-structured interview. The interview consisted of three main topics: 1) the experiences from the game session; 2) the thinking skills that happened in the game; and 3) the impact on communication and conflict management.

2.3 Analysis

The researchers transcribed, decoded, and analyzed the information from observation and interview using the thematic analysis method. To verify the qualitative data, the researchers interpreted observation notes and keywords from interview transcripts, such as role play, reasoning, sharing ideas, questions, thinking, and others. These words represented the situations that occurred during the play session, as well as the reflections and perspectives on each case.

Thematic analysis was employed as the method to systematically decode the language from the interview transcripts. This entails interpreting the data by identifying patterns based on the research questions and pre-defined themes. The resulting themes or codes revealed key insights, which formed the core findings of the study (Clarke & Braun, 2017).

2.4 Research Ethics

Before commencing the play session, the participants would receive information about the research study, the voluntary process, registration, and orientation. The information included purpose and process of activity, brief of research study, collecting data process, participation agreement, and assurance of confidentiality. Moreover, the participants were able to withdraw anytime during the research study process.

3. RESULT

The PeaceSoCracy board game was not only a party game, but it also served as an educational tool, encouraging players to learn and understand other perspectives with empathy. To achieve the educational goal, the play coach will take the following five steps with the fellows: 1) introduction; 2) preparation (or setting up a game); 3) briefing; 4) playing; and 5) debriefing.

First, the play coach would have outlined the education goal and game goal by identifying objectives, followed by a brief description of empathetic communication and the game scenarios, categorized into three levels: family, society, and country. The most crucial aspect for all players to concentrate on was articulating the game goal, as they were required to begin by choosing a case from a selection of 15 cases across three levels: family, society, and nation. Secondly, the main elements of the game included the peace board, situation cards, inquiry cards, heart, and sandglass, while the personal elements included player cards, question examples, character cards, story cards, and other cards. After setting up the game session, the play coach guided the players by eliciting their conflict experiences and selecting one scenario from a selection of 15 cases based on the group's decision. Next, the coach assigns roles to the players, after which players A and B proceed to read the scenario. When all players understood the roles and rules of the game, they started to ask questions and collect information.

Due to the dynamic nature of the game, players were required to gather information by questioning the case owners and actively listening to their fellow players. These sessions required players to generate questions, engage with the case owner, review, and reflect on the information shared and persuaded by each party. Table 2 displays the details of each step.

Table 2. Process of playing board game

Steps	Role of play coach	Scope of reflection from interview and observation
Introduction (10 minutes)	1. Overview the objectives in game. 2. Give a concept of empathetic communication. 3. Explain three types of scenarios: family, society, and country.	- Prior knowledge about communication and empathy is reviewed and recalled. - Experiences, age, and academic level were factors in selecting types of scenarios.
Preparation (10 minutes)	1. Set up the game. 2. Deal cards and distribute other elements.	- Review cards on hand. - Understand the context of the card.
Brief (10 minutes)	1. Ask a question about the conflict situation. 2. Provide an example and a few instances of conflict in society. 3. Explain the education goal and the game goal (how to win). 4. Set roles for each player. 5. Describe the rules of the game: steps to play and point counting. 6. Play Turn No. 0 (Zero) as a simple turn.	- Create a set of questions and collect data. - Plan and set goals for collecting and analyzing information.
Play (60 minutes)	1. Guide players to follow the rules and role play. 2. Encourage players to ask, examine, and criticize the given information. 3. Monitor players to listen and be concise.	- Ask questions to collect information. - Communicate with other players and topic owners (players A and B). - Listen and judge without bias.
Debrief (30 minutes)	1. Reflect on deductive and inductive reasoning. 2. Connect the game with real life.	- Connect the play experience (that has just been done) and story with real life. - Share your opinion and discuss it with other players with reasons.

As a result of activities in three steps (brief, play, and debrief), players could improve various skills, especially communication skills, creative thinking, critical thinking, and listening skills. Player A reflected, "I had to persuade and improvise after reading the information on a card." "I had to make up a story based on my experiences." This message indicated that the players were required to understand the message on the cards, scrutinize the answers and information provided by the topic owners, establish connections between each answer, and formulate various questions to gather additional data and prepare their responses. These skill sets were always present during the play phase and the reflection phase (see Table 3).

Furthermore, some participants expressed that they would actively listen, gather, and analyze data during each turn to determine the final answer. According to the role in the game, the players reflected that they could practice listening and speaking skills without judgement because of the dynamic in the game that directed participants to listen to the story from both sides and ask questions to understand the feelings of each side. So, they did not focus on right or wrong; however, they concentrated on information and context in the situation.

Table 3. Detail and reflection in play session

Sub steps in play session	Skill sets	Reflection
Sharing information by topic owners 	- Communication skill - Persuasion - Creative thinking	*I had to persuade and improvise after reading up a story based on experience.* *(player A)*
Understanding information in a card 	- System thinking - Critical thinking - Communication skill - Interpretative skill	*I chose "question card", I would get more information and could interpret.* *(Player B)*
Collecting information 	- Listening skill - Analyze the information - Evaluate the data and collect more - Connect each information	*If I have a chance, I will choose only "Open 5 cards" and "3 questions" for gathering information and eliminating the choices.* *(player C)* *There are many questions and sometimes the same questions are asked, so I had to reply in other sentences under the given message* *(Player F)*
Asking and answering the questions 	- Problem solving - Creative thinking - Deep listening	*... I tried to ask the desire of the case owner, why they would like it that way, and how to reach the goals because the case owner could not share the desire directly.* *(Player I)* *I had to create questions for gathering more data and create an answer for giving more detail.* *(Player D)* *If I were a mediator, I would have been neutral and listened to both sides before deciding without bias.* *(Player E)* *I would concentrate on the keywords from the conversation that related to the case and focus on the repeated words about feeling and desire.* *(Player G)*
Assessing information and anticipating the targeted mindset 	- Critical thinking - System thinking	*I think the "eliminate choice" card could help me if I didn't know how to ask more questions.* *(Player H)* *The solution to everything should be based on data from communication and not on the bias of only one person. We synthesized all data.* *(Player J)*

In addition, participants reflected that they could learn the process to understand the complicated issue in society as follows: "*Board games helped learners understand the difficult social topics*" (Facilitator A) and "*I felt that communication in games increased awareness between two sides, and at the same time, the players could get more heart (~points) from discussion or answering questions*" (Player E). Because of the play steps in game dynamic, the answer of each case came from listening, asking, listening again, summarizing, matching the information with the prior data, deciding the feeling of case's owner, and answering the mission.

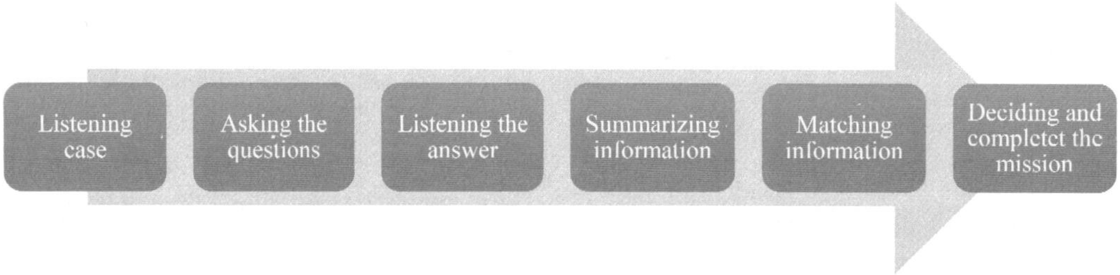

Figure 2. Process to achieve the mission

This process might run as a loop for criticizing the information that came from his/her turn and other players because each player in his/her turn would draw the different question card or action card. Each card brought to the new information that they collected and used for guesting the final answer as the player reflected that "*The solution of everything should base – on data from communication not from bias of only one person. We synthesized all data...*".

The online platform (Figure 2) offers three distinct types of play: solo, group, and online. According to the three different types, 1) Solo promotes one-player setup and solo play, 2) Hotseat offers multiplayer mode on the same desktop, and 3) Online mode allows players to play with other online users. Although there was an individual type, all players recommended that there should be four players per playing session. They could not play only one in a game like this communication game. However, the participant said that "*if they set the chatbot or integrate AI in the system, solo is possible because we can chat with computers*."

Figure 3. PeaceSoCracy in Tabletopia website: https://tabletopia.com/games/peacesocracy

Nevertheless, this game should have four players to make the situation clearer and participate in questioning. Most of them mentioned that they prefer to play on-site more than online because they can see facial expressions and chit-chat with their friends, although there are supporting tools in online sessions such as chatrooms or VDO conferencing.

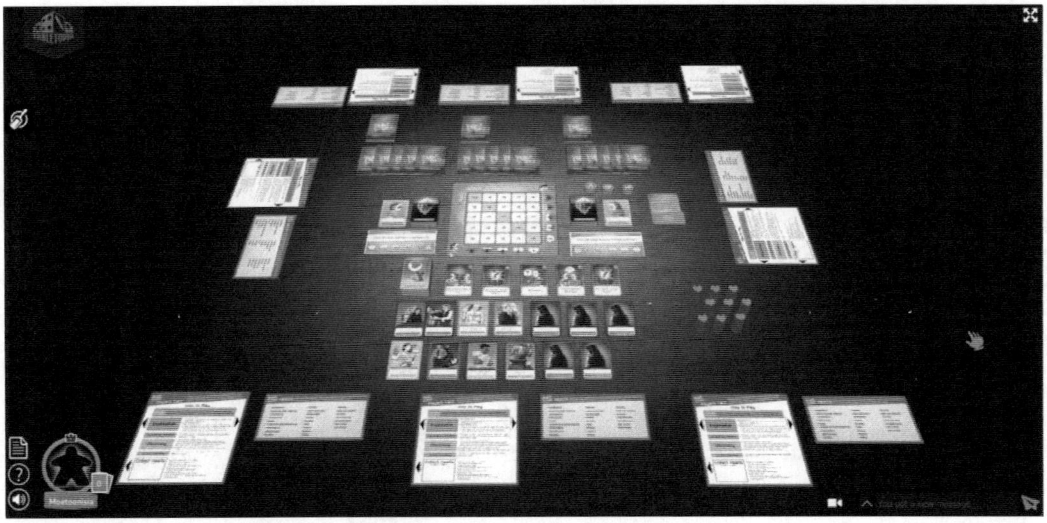

Figure 4. PeaceSoCracy online board game set up in Tabletopia

All participants mentioned the moderators who should have background in NVC or communication for more proficiency during the game. Furthermore, the moderators should prepare themselves in the game manual, cases, and questions in each card for solving or answering the questions.

In part, all participants said that "I prefer to play with an unknown person or stranger more than close friends because of avoiding bias and nervousness.

4. CONCLUSION

The PeaceSoCracy board game, both online and physical, successfully fosters empathy, critical thinking, and communication skills. It included five phrases: 1) introduction, 2) preparation, 3) briefing, 4) playing, and 5) debriefing—players engage with complex social scenarios, requiring them to actively listen, ask questions, analyze information, understand the situation, and answer the questions. These processes help develop crucial skills such as persuasion, creative thinking, and conflict resolution.

Participants highlighted the benefits of face-to-face gameplay that enhanced emotional engagement and interpersonal interaction compared to online play. While the online platform offered flexibility, most players recommended group play for better immersion. They suggested integrating AI for solo play.

Participants suggested that a background in communication or nonviolent conflict resolution was crucial for the moderator's role in effectively guiding the gameplay. Many also preferred playing with strangers to avoid bias and enhance open-mindedness.

5. DISCUSSION

This research study aimed to explore learning activities that happen in game play both online and offline, and examine skills that come from playing the PeaceSoCracy board game. According to the research objective, the study was conducted with qualitative methodology through interviews and observation. The research study was organized by implementing the PeaceSoCracy board game with undergraduate students and integrating debriefing sessions after playing the game. On the report of the implementation session, the moderator was the important person who regulated, monitored, and facilitated as a play coach. According to regulation for this kind of board game, the moderator should have experience and knowledge of NVC, the roles and rules of the game, and the persons who had to organize the NVC workshop because of the event in each session (Dzaferovic, 2012).

Situations that were classified into three levels: family/personal, community/society, and country/international topics were the meaningful cases for practicing listening, thinking, discussing, and expressing ideas (Koopman & Seliga, 2021). Each topic in each level could encourage the players to relate the gameplay experience to their real-world experiences. In common cases, the players would feel free to understand, ask questions, and discuss with other players.

Sometimes it was the emotional conversation that made it hard to empathize with the other in communication (Juncadella & Blackmore, 2013); nevertheless, the board game might decrease the complicated process and information through steps of talking and release people's feelings and needs. Because effective communication should begin with showing the intention, feeling, belief, or trust with a true discussion and deeply listening to another group (Sofer & Goldstein, 2018).

The game session's discussion and questioning encouraged the players to reflect, comprehend the information, and recognize the necessity and crisis of both sides in relation to the real-life situation (Eisenack, 2013). Additionally, the players who owned the topic had to use rhetoric and integrate it into communication ways to persuade the other players to trust their messages (Cattani, 2020; Gorsevski, 1999). The facilitators in the session have the potential to shape the atmosphere and engagement, mirroring the development of NVC. The facilitator should understand the concept of NVC at the very least and engage with the activity (Gill et al., 2022). Consequently, the facilitators who had different basic concepts, either game playing or nonviolent communication, might shape the tone, questions that happened, and discussion in game play. In an online platform, synchronous discussion via typing or talking supports effective communication; however, body language still plays a crucial role in perception(Ismail et al., 2021), who identified that a real-time conference with an open camera was the key.

Observation was another important skill in NVC because observers would collect more information from verbal and nonverbal communication, especially tone of voice, eyes, gestures, and patterns of conversation (Jung et al., 2023; Mayes, 2010; Sung & Kweon, 2022). Some players used the observation skill for both tone of voice, gesture, and facial expression.

Moreover, there were a set of words that helped players guess the feelings and/or needs of case owners and a set of questions to collect information and eliminate that guessing word. These tools could help players understand (Koopman & Seliga, 2021) and focus on the case and related information; furthermore, the empathetic mind was increased from listening sessions and conversations between players. According to empathizing with the case, the players had to ask various questions to collect sufficient information, which indicated the much more questions a conversation effected the message from the case's owner because the case's owner cannot sometimes say the direct message or requirement.

The players identified that the more they talked, the more they understood each other and got more points. Talking sessions were meaningful for increasing awareness among litigants (Mayes, 2010). This proved that board games could be a tool for encouraging learning and knowledge to do something (Taspinar et al., 2016), like the PeaceSoCracy board game, which showed the improvement of deep listening, communication skills, analysis thinking, and system thinking skills.

Consequently, an online platform might support communication and enhance the NVC skill through playing an online PeaceSoCracy board game because of the online environment that allowed the players to meet the various players and talk without bias (Antonijevic, 2008) via VDO conference (Ismail et al., 2021) or emoticons (Koh, 2022). These online tools were the supporting materials for enhancing an empathetic mind and comprehensive communication.

ACKNOWLEDGEMENT

The author gratefully acknowledges the financial support provided by the Friedrich Naumann Foundation Thailand. Through a research grant in 2023 that was used to conduct the study. Additionally, Thammasat University's Faculty of Learning Sciences & Education provided financial support for presenting the academic work.

REFERENCES

Antonijevic, S. (2008). From text to gesture online: A microethnographic analysis of nonverbal communication in the Second Life virtual environment. *Information Communication and Society*, *11*(2), 221–238. https://doi.org/10.1080/13691180801937290

Baesler, E. J., & Lauricella, S. (2014). Teach peace: Assessing instruction of the nonviolent communication and peace course. *Journal of Peace Education*, *11*(1), 46–63. https://doi.org/10.1080/17400201.2013.777899

Booker, K. L., & MItchell, A. W. (2021). From Boring to Board Game: The Effect of a Serious Game on Key Learning Outcomes. *Journal of Occupational Therapy Education*, *5*(4). https://doi.org/10.26681/jote.2021.050407

Cattani, A. (2020). Persuading and Convincing. *OSSA Conference Archive*. https://scholar.uwindsor.ca/ossaarchivehttps://scholar.uwindsor.ca/ossaarchive/OSSA12/Thursday/11

Cheung, C. T. Y., Cheng, C. M. H., Lam, S. K. K., Ling, H. W. H., Lau, K. L., Hung, S. L., & Fung, H. W. (2023). Reliability and Validity of a Novel Measure of Nonviolent Communication Behaviors. *Research on Social Work Practice*, *33*(7), 790–797. https://doi.org/10.1177/10497315221128595

Clarke, V., & Braun, V. (2017). Thematic analysis. In *Journal of Positive Psychology* (Vol. 12, Issue 3, pp. 297–298). Routledge. https://doi.org/10.1080/17439760.2016.1262613

de Almeida, L. G., Pasternak Taschner, N., & Lellis-Santos, C. (2021). Outbreak! an Online Board Game That Fosters Collaborative Learning of Viral Diseases. *Journal of Microbiology & Biology Education*, *22*(1). https://doi.org/10.1128/jmbe.v22i1.2539

Dzaferovic, M. (2012). Nonviolent Communication, Empathy and Assertion as Modern Strategies in the Study of Overcoming Conflicts. *Metodički Obzori*, *7*(1), 105–117.

Eisenack, K. (2013). A Climate Change Board Game for Interdisciplinary Communication and Education. *Simulation and Gaming*, *44*(2–3), 328–348. https://doi.org/10.1177/1046878112452639

Fjællingsdal, K. S., & Klöckner, C. A. (2020). Green Across the Board: Board Games as Tools for Dialogue and Simplified Environmental Communication. *Simulation and Gaming*, *51*(5), 632–652. https://doi.org/10.1177/1046878120925133

Garris, R., Ahlers, R., & Driskell, J. E. (2002). Games, motivation, and learning: A research and practice model. *Simulation and Gaming*, *33*(4), 441–467. https://doi.org/10.1177/1046878102238607

Gill, R., Leu, L., & Morin, J. (2022). *Nonviolent Communication Toolkit for Facilitators*. PuddleDancerPress.

Gobet, F., Retschitzki, J., & Voogt, A. de. (2004). *Moves in Mind: The Psychology of Board Games* (First). Psychology Press.

Gorsevski, E. W. (1999). Nonviolent Theory on Communication: The Implications for Theorizing a Nonviolent Rhetoric. *Peace & Change*, *24*(4), 445–475. https://doi.org/10.1111/0149-0508.00133

Hinebaugh, J. P. (2009). *A board game education*. R&L Education.

Ismail, N. A. S., Bujang, S. M., & Awang Besar, M. N. (2021). NON-VERBAL FEEDBACK FROM LECTURERS TO STUDENTS DURING SYNCHRONOUS ONLINE COMMUNICATION COURSE: WHAT CAN WE LEARN? *EDULEARN21 Proceedings*, *1*, 1783–1788. https://doi.org/10.21125/edulearn.2021.0416

Jensen, V. V., Lindholm Nørgaard, J., & Teli, M. (2023). *Digital Card Game Platforms for Digitalising Design Games*. https://prod-aaudxp-cms-001-app.azurewebsites.net/media/kpibxnt3/tech4sdt_report__digital_card_game_platforms.pdf

Juncadella, C. M., & Blackmore, C. (2013). *What is the impact of the application of the Nonviolent communication model on the development of empathy? Overview of research and outcomes.* University of Sheffield.

Jung, H., Lee, Y. H., & Park, J.-H. (2023). Effects of Customized Communication Training on Nonviolent Communication, Nonverbal Communication, and Self-Acceptance: Evidence from Korean Nursing Students. In *Iran J Public Health* (Vol. 52, Issue 9). https://creativecommons.org/licenses/by-nc/4.0/

Koh, J. (2022). The Role of Nonverbal Communication in Asynchronous Talk Channels. In *Journal of Open* (Vol. 26, Issue 2).

Kolb, A. Y., & Kolb, D. A. (2009). Experiential learning theory: A dynamic, holistic approach to management learning, education and development. *The SAGE Handbook of Management Learning, Education and Development*, 42–68.

Kolb, D. A. (2014). *Experiential Learning: Experience as the Source of Learning and Development* (second). Pearson FT Press.

Koopman, S., & Seliga, L. (2021). Teaching peace by using nonviolent communication for difficult conversations in the college classroom. *Peace and Conflict Studies*, *27*(3). https://doi.org/10.46743/1082-7307/2021.1692

Lasater, J. H., & Lasater, I. K. (2022). *What We Say Matters: Practicing Nonviolent Communication* (Second edition). Shambhala Publications.

MacNair, R. M., & Psychologist for Social Responsibility. (2006). *Working for Peace: A Handbook of Practical Psychology and Other Tools*. Impact Publishers.

Martin, B., & Varney, W. (2003). *Nonviolence speaks: communicating against repression.*

Mayes, I. (2010). Nonviolent Communication: Tools and Talking-Points for Practicing the Person-Centered Approach. *The Person-Centered Journal*, *17*(1), 90–99.

Moore, C. W. (2014). *The Mediation Process: Practical Strategies for Resolving Conflict* (Forth). Jossey-Bass.

Museux, A. C., Dumont, S., Careau, E., & Milot, É. (2016). Improving interprofessional collaboration: The effect of training in nonviolent communication. In *Social Work in Health Care* (Vol. 55, Issue 6, pp. 427–439). Routledge. https://doi.org/10.1080/00981389.2016.1164270

Normalita, E., Svonni, C., & Maluleka, P. (2023). Application of Discussion Methods and Memory Board Games to Increase Student Activity and Learning Outcomes in History Learning. *Indonesian Journal of Education Research (IJoER)*, *4*(6), 147–154. https://doi.org/10.37251/ijoer.v4i6.774

Oetzel, J. G., & Ting-Toomey, S. (2013). *The SAGE Handbook of Conflict Communication: Integrating Theory, Research, and Practice* (Second). Publisher SAGE Publications, Inc.

Pivec, M., & Dziabenko, O. (2004). Game-Based Learning in Universities and Lifelong Learning: "UniGame: Social Skills and Knowledge Training" Game Concept. *Journal of Universal Computer Scicence*, *10*(1), 14–26.

Plass, J. L., Mayer, R. E., & Homer, B. D. (2019). *Handbook of Game-Based Learning*. The Massachusetts Institute of Technology.

Rosenberg, M. B. (2015). *Nonviolent communication: A language of life: Life-changing tools for healthy relationships* (third). PaddleDancer Press.

Roy, S. (2019). Role of Nonviolent Communication in our Daily Life. *Pragyaan: Journal of Mass Communication*, *17* (1 & 2), 24–27.

Sofer, O. J., & Goldstein, J. (2018). *Say What You Mean: A Mindful Approach to Nonviolent Communication*. Shambhala.

Sukumal Surichamorn, Suthida chariyasuwan, & Panida Tancharoen. (n.d.-a). *PeaceSoCracy board game*.

Sukumal Surichamorn, Suthida chariyasuwan, & Panida Tancharoen. (n.d.-b). *PeaceSoCracy: Peaceful Society in Democracy*. Retrieved November 25, 2023, from https://tabletopia.com/games/peacesocracy

Sung, J., & Kweon, Y. (2022). Effects of a Nonviolent Communication-Based Empathy Education Program for Nursing Students: A Quasi-Experimental Pilot Study. *Nursing Reports*, *12*(4), 824–835. https://doi.org/10.3390/nursrep12040080

Taspinar, B., Schmidt, W., & Schuhbauer, H. (2016). Gamification in education: A board game approach to knowledge acquisition. *Procedia Computer Science*, *99*, 101–116. https://doi.org/10.1016/j.procs.2016.09.104

Thomas, D., & Brown, J. S. (2011). *A new culture of learning: Cultivating the imagination for a world of constant change*. CreateSpace.

Zandkarimi, G., Kamelifar, L., & Heshmati-Molaee, N. (2019). Nonviolence Communication to Reduce Stress, Anxiety and Depression in Young Iranian Women: A Randomized Experiment. *Child and Adolescent Social Work Journal*, *36*(5), 549–555. https://doi.org/10.1007/s10560-018-0584-y

VIDEO FOR NAVOICA, A POLISH MOOC PLATFORM

Krzysztof Gurba[1], Anna Ślósarz[1] and Eugenia Smyrnova-Trybulska[2]
[1]University of National Education Commission, Krakow
Podchorążych 2, 30-084 Krakow, Poland
[2]University of Silesia in Katowice
Bankowa 12, 40-007 Katowice, Poland

ABSTRACT

The content analysis included video lectures posted in 208 MOOCs on the Polish educational platform NAVOICA. The aim was to determine their subject matter and the methods of preparing video lectures. It turned out that video lectures were included in 57% of MOOCs, most often related to *Medical and health sciences* and *Humanities*. They appeared least frequently in MOOCs in the fields of *Engineering and technology* and *Natural sciences*, as they were replaced by recordings of screen scrolling and PowerPoint presentations, usually supplemented with commentaries and music. Video lectures were short, just a few minutes in length. Authors introduced the course and its modules, presented educational content by speaking to the camera, staged scenes illustrating the course issues, interviewed experts, conducted experiments, and presented and commented on events and phenomena such as landforms and water conditions. Videos downloaded from YouTube and Vimeo were also used. Some video lectures were produced as part of international projects. Implementation possibilities were limited by the COVID 19 pandemic, as more than 160 MOOCs were realized as part of a project launched in November 2019. Moreover, most universities did not have the technical conditions to produce high-quality films. The use of synthetic voiceovers limited the expression of comments. There is a need for organizational and technical support for lecturers and a systematic addition of high-quality video lectures to the NAVOICA platform resources.

KEYWORDS

Lecture, Postproduction, Recordings, Animation, Label, Interview

1. INTRODUCTION

A MOOC needs to be integrated into the user's communication habits. The development of the gaming industry has triggered the expectation of multimedia and visualization. Platform administrators take these habits into account. Videos have become the main elements of knowledge transfer in MOOCs (Stöhr et al., 2019, p. 166). They are standard components of MOOCs on the British FutureLearn platform, the American edX and Coursera, the Japanese Gacco and the Chinese XuetangX.

Videos are a more effective educational tool in the 21st century than printed materials (Armstrong et al., 2011). Watching video lectures is the primary activity of MOOC users and the most important way to transfer knowledge in MOOCs. Swedish students found video lectures more attractive than traditional ones, even in design-build-test project courses based on tutoring. They especially appreciated the availability of digital content during the project (Bhadani et al., 2017).

A strong correlation was observed between the number of videos watched in MOOCs and students' academic performance. Therefore, it was found that watching videos is an important element of online learning, and this is true for both specialists, dealing with the subject matter of the course and non-specialists (Stöhr et al., 2019, p. 166). Recent research confirms that participants more actively engaged in video lectures "could achieve better grades and higher course completion rates" (Wei et al., 2023, p. 3).

At the height of the development of MOOCs, when 2012 was declared the "Year of the MOOC", the use of videos in them developed. It turned out that educational videos watched online must be short and formally adapted for educational use. Australian experts (Glance et al., 2013) emphasized the need to make video descriptions more precise and to intersperse segments of the video with tests. To ensure that video viewing is not passive, Taiwanese experts (Lee et al., 2015) suggested displaying videos along with the chatrooms, where participants can exchange comments in real time and subsequent students can view previous recordings. In turn, an American team (Bonafini et al., 2017, p. 230) found a correlation between the degree of participants' engagement in watching videos and the likelihood of completing MOOCs, as well as a positive correlation between the number of videos watched and students' achievements. They recommended creating interactive videos: with content segmentation and inserting questions. Recently, a team of Chinese researchers, after analyzing logins and detailed records of students' interaction with videos, found that as much as 59.45% of their activity was watching videos (Hui et al., 2019, p. 6482).

However, users do not always maintain attention until the end of watching the video. Pausing, speed changes, and searching mainly occur in the first minute of the video and quickly decrease after 300 seconds (Hui et al., 2019, p. 6488). This may mean that after five minutes of watching, users are no longer focused on watching the video, perhaps even moving away from the screens. During this study, however, videos in MOOCs s on the Coursera platform usually lasted 10-15 minutes (Galán et al., 2019, p. 83). According to these Spanish authors, "new university training scenarios are moving towards a new model of mass education, open and free through a methodology based on video-simulation and collaborative work of the student" (p. 49).

It was found that there are cultural differences in the use of video, resulting from the collectivistic nature of Eastern cultures and the individualistic attitude of Western users (Ślósarz, 2024). MOOCs participants in South Asia watched videos willingly, and as the number of videos increased, their risk of dropping out decreased. They perceived the teacher on the screen as present in front of them. However, students of the Anglo-Saxon region and Germanic Europe reported aversion to instructional videos in FutureLearn MOOCs, complaining that they were slow, leading to loss of concentration. They substituted watching by reading transcripts in search of "knowledge in a nutshell". Consequently, the number of videos watched achieved a slight negative relationship with those learners' persistence in MOOCs (Rizvi et al., 2022, p. 108-109). “Participants from all around the world consistently raised a need for more interactive videos or videos with embedded quizzes.” – conclude authors (p. 112).

In the case of learning English, teacher talk videos that present the interpersonal functions of language play a key role (Halliday, 1975). Chinese researchers (Tang et al., 2022) studied for discourse analysis 11 short videos, totaling 43 minutes and 45 seconds, in the MOOC course “Critical English Writing” at Nankai University. They found that the use of mood, modality, personal pronouns, speed and syntax is necessary for learning to speak effectively during interactions (p. 182). Brazilian researchers (Fontana, & Leffa, 2018) presented suggestions of digital architecture for the design of a LMOOC within a communicative perspective, underlying the importance of using videos that stimulate students' motivation and involvement in language learning. In practice, language teaching in MOOCs focuses on grammar rather than communicative aspects and interactions. Meanwhile, video has powerful teaching effects (from Spanish *efeitos didáticos poderosos*, p. 465) – so verbal communication should be part of the interaction rather than a series of presentations.

Videos promoting MOOCs are the most carefully prepared. An analysis was made of 420, posted by 105 universities and educational centers on the Miríadax platform (Rajas-Fernández et al., 2021). They were found to contain information, teaching and advertising content. They use the aesthetics of audiovisual, advertising and television communication (staging, interviews, reports), 2D and 3D animations, photographs and graphics, texts superimposed on images, and music. They imitate classroom activities, but enrich the message narratively and aesthetically in order to capture the attention of the student-viewer, inform the characteristics of the classes, and offer valuable content.

The researchers’ findings influenced practice. For example, at Khan Academy, the lectures in front of the camera were replaced by videos lasting several minutes, showing, in addition to experts, maps, graphics, places with transcriptions, and user comments. There is even an opportunity to learn about a specific topic by watching selected videos from various courses (Khan Academy, n.d.).

2. METHODS

2.1 Aim, Methods, Instruments and Procedures

The aim was to find out whether video lectures are always posted in MOOCs on the NAVOICA platform and how they were prepared.

A quantitative method was used to determine the degree of participation of video lectures in MOOCs. A categorization key for the films was developed and the results were coded. Then they were analyzed using the content analysis method, which covers both the features of texts and the contexts of their occurrence, in order not only to describe the state of affairs, but also to explain its causes (Michalczyk, 2009, p. 97).

A video was defined as a sequence of events recorded by a camera as a set of moving images. Therefore, PowerPoint presentations and recordings of screen scrolling with sound were not included. Assuming that videos have become the main carrier of teaching content in e-learning, and most of the resources of the NAVOICA platform are the result of collective projects, a hypothesis was formulated: *the MOOCs posted on the NAVOICA platform contain video lectures in each unit of their content.*

Using the Firefox browser, all courses posted on the NAVOICA platform were logged in and their components were analyzed. A quantitative analysis was carried out: it was checked how many MOOC courses from each scientific discipline included video lectures. The data obtained were entered into an Excel spreadsheet, taking into account four categories of videos:

1. Introductory – when lecturers announce the content of the course, its purpose, and requirements. They are posted in course descriptions and on social media.
2. Video lectures – when instructors present the course content by addressing the camera. They most often follow the pattern of a talking head and a writing hand. They can be recorded in the field or laboratory, contain animations and embedded questions.
3. Interviews and reports – developing course content, presenting people, places, and phenomena.
4. Animations with audio narration, explaining key topics from the course.

Attention was paid to whether the video was accompanied by a transcription in the form of an stand-alone text placed below the recording and whether it was complemented by on-screen explanatory labels and drawings. If they appeared only once in the MOOC, their existence was noted, as was that of a single video lecture. Introductory videos were considered to be those posted at the beginning of the modules, excluding those posted at the beginning of the course. Videos included from YouTube were treated equally to those prepared by the MOOC creators. A quantitative analysis of the data obtained was developed in Excel sheets, followed by a qualitative analysis of video lectures. The strategies for the creation of the video lectures studied were established.

2.2 Research Material

The research material consisted of 208 MOOCs that were avaliable on the Polish educational platform NAVOICA on May 21-22, 2024. They were prepared by 29 universities and educational entities. The largest number of courses were prepared by: Białystok University of Technology (32), The University of Economics and Human Sciences in Warsaw (30), The West Pomeranian Business School Applied Sciences Academy (22), and Cracov University of Technology (14). The dominant MOOCs were in the fields of *Social sciences* (84 – 40%), and *Natural sciences* (46 – 22%). Less well represented were *Humanities* (39 – 19%, including 28 courses in the field of teaching foreign languages), *Engineering and technology* (25 – 12%), and *Medical and health sciences* (14 – 7%). Their equipment in video lectures is presented in Table 1.

Table 1. Video lectures in MOOCs from specific fields of science. Source: own work

	Natural sciences	Engineering and technology	Medical and health sciences	Social sciences	Humanities	Total
With video lecture	16	7	13	55	27	118
No video lecture	30	18	1	29	12	90

Video lectures were most frequently used in MOOCs related to *Medical and health sciences*, as they covered such attractive topics as dietetics and health, as well as in the MOOC *ELLIPSE Gatekeeper+ Course in Suicide Prevention*, presented in 7 languages. The smallest share of video lectures marked the MOOCs in the field of *Engineering and Technology*, as IT specialists most often replaced video lectures with recordings of screen scrolling.

The MOOC courses on the NAVOICA platform have a precise structure: MOOCs are divided into modules, these into lessons, and lessons into short units. Therefore, the videos were often followed by exercises or tests. Every video on the NAVOICA platform must be subtitled following the Web Content Accessibility Guidelines. In addition, the content of the video is sometimes provided in the form of a transcript below the recording, which allows MOOCs to be adapted to the needs of people with limited capabilities: those with hearing or visual impairments (Bolińska, & Gurba, 2022).

2.3 Results

The authors of most MOOCs include video lectures. Instead of them or in parallel, they used other ways to transfer knowledge. Table 2 compiles them.

Table 2. Video lectures in the context of other modes of knowledge transfer in in MOOCs

	Video lecture	Trans-cription below the recording	Video introdu-ction to module	Promo-tional video	Anima-tion	PowerPoint presenta-tion with sound	Screen recording with sound	Explana tory labels
With	118	27	45	68	65	83	42	89
None	90	181	163	140	143	125	166	119

Table 2 shows that recorded video lectures were most often not post-produced, so they did not include transcripts, animations, or explanatory labels. Video was rarely used as promotional material, with only 33% of MOOCs using it in this way. The video was used as an introduction to a module in 22% of all MOOCs. Video lectures were often replaced by PowerPoint presentations with audio and recordings of screen scrolling with audio. The universities that prepared the most MOOCs set up recording studios. They professionally prepared promotional videos and the opening sequences with which the video lectures were preceded. However, these foreheads disturb viewers when they present the university and last for several seconds or so, delaying the opening of the content. Users may also be discouraged by the inclusion of the same videos in different courses.

Over 43% of MOOCs authors did not use video lectures. The main reason for this phenomenon is external. The NAVOICA platform was launched in October 2018, and more than 160 courses were developed and published as part of the project announced in late 2019 by the Ministry of Science and Higher Education "Direction to the MOOCs" (Smyrnova-Trybulska et al., 2021). Thus, the implementation of most MOOCs was disrupted by the pandemic, which especially affected the recording of video lectures. They require prolonged and direct cooperation between instructors and developers, specialized equipment, software, and a studio. Meanwhile, the pandemic prevented or limited direct contact and made consultations, recordings, and film editing especially difficult. Videos were sometimes carried out in the unattractive convention of a remote lecture in an apartment. Many universities had equipment problems. A camera was sometimes purchased during the project implementation. As lecturers acted students, trying to faithfully read the text, but unable to convey scientific passion in front of the camera. The same limitation applies to the use of expressionless synthetic voice-overs.

The second reason for the lack of video lectures in over half of the MOOCs was that during the period of creating the NAVOICA platform resources, university employees, i.e. the authors of MOOCs, were overloaded with remote teaching. Preparing and sharing classes in digital form requires more time than conducting them in person. In addition, lecturers most often had to quickly master the necessary digital competence. Remote classes in real-time were not always conducted efficiently in technical terms, and students were often overloaded with factual material. As a result, the surveyed UKEN students (Długosz, 2021) complained of fatigue (64%), mental exhaustion (62%), mood swings (60%), and deterioration of relationships with peers and lecturers (52%). Recorded lectures are also exhausting for students from a neurodidactic point of view due to difficult concentration, lack of engagement, and low motivation, as well as the resulting fatigue (Romaniuk & Łukasiewicz-Wieleba 2021, 44).

Even some language courses lacked video lectures – 10 out of the 28 had none, and four were missing multimedia. MOOCs on the NAVOICA platform are not moderated, so there was also no interaction between teachers and users. That is, there was no communicative language teaching.

In case of implementation difficulties, video lectures were replaced or supplemented with PowerPoint and Prezi presentations (83) or recordings of screen scrollings (42) with sound. These were accompanied by clarifying animations (65), descriptive labels (89), and music. In some cases, videos from YouTube and Vimeo platforms were indicated as video lectures and analyzed.

Some courses were implemented as part of international projects. Those videos included contributions from foreign experts, as in the MOOC *ELLIPSE Gatekeeper+ course in suicide prevention* addressed for managers, doctors, social workers, journalism students, journalists, teachers, and further professionals responsible for other people (Pawelec et al., 2023). Authors this project, which included MOOCs in three languages, used the emotional song *I'm OK* by musician and psychologist, Filip Mizia in the introduction.

The most interesting video lectures turned out to be:

1. Filmed experiments, for example when the author conducts them in the field to examine the quality of surface water (Pełechaty, 2023).
2. Film reports showing MOOCs author explaining the terrain around him while being in the field (Jaśkiewicz, Kaczmarek & Lorenc, 2023).
3. Filmed activities, e.g. polymer testing equipment operating in the laboratory as a background for the statements of the MOOC authors (Mierzwiński et al., 2022).
4. A funny dialogue between a competent Karolina and an incompetent Krystian as the presentation of the content of the course *Taming Python III* (Wernikowski et al., 2022).
5. Statements of the MOOC authors to the camera, made in the studio, and later illustrated with labels with captions, animations, etc. (Białowąs, & Szyszka, 2024).

The third reason for the scarcity of video lectures may have been the insufficient technical skills of some of the MOOCs' authors. However, most courses were created in teams and with technical support. In addition, long-term projects have been implemented in Poland for years to improve the competence of lecturers (priority is often given to the oldest), teachers, and future teachers in the field of creating multimedia publications in video format, among others. (Smyrnova-Trybulska et al., 2022, p. 17-19).

3. CONCLUSION

MOOCs on the NAVOICA platform featured all categories of videos: introductions, video lectures, interviews, reports, and animations. Their diversity and modes of filmmaking testify to the high creative potential and ingenuity of the authors as well as the high technical competence of the developers. This optimistic conclusion from our study is an important guide for the organizers of subsequent MOOC competitions or for the administrators of the NAVOICA platform and similar ones.

However, the hypothesis that *MOOCs posted on the NAVOICA platform include video lectures in every unit of their content* has not been proven to be true. Text, graphics, photos, PowerPoint presentations, and recordings of screen scrolling were often used in place of video lectures as teaching content media. Instead of video lectures, MOOC authors often used text, graphics, photos, as well as sound-added PowerPoint presentations and recordings of screen scrolling. The main reasons for this were the reduction in cooperation due to the pandemic, the limited capacity of most universities to produce videos, and the habit of lecturers to use PowerPoint presentations and screen recordings – scrolling and static, not provided with sound.

The study results cannot be generalized. The resources of the NAVOICA platform were mostly created during the COVID-19 pandemic, were largely conditioned by PR mechanisms, and are still being updated. However, we believe that this study provides educational institutions, MOOC course authors, and platform administrators with guidelines and recommendations listed in the next chapter regarding the preparation and use of video lectures on MOOC platforms in Poland and other countries. International exchange of experiences and institutional support for this modern form of education as well as systemic solutions at national levels are necessary.

4. RECOMMENDATIONS

Based on our findings, practical strategies can be applied in video lecture organization, preparation, and design. First, the authors of MOOCs need technical support for video production and especially in the post-production stage. Recording studios and multimedia centers operating at some universities are a good solution. Implementation services could be provided to all Polish authors of MOOCs by the National Information Processing Institute as the administrator of the NAVOICA platform and creator of many MOOCs. Then the NAVOICA platform could contain more high-quality video lectures and disseminate good practices as a national educational asset. The use of video as the main medium for knowledge transfer should be perfected to add value to education through the use of sound, image, motion, color, music, etc. Recordings may be accompanied by questions, tests and discussions. However, it is worth limiting the use of sequences promoting universities and courses in video lectures. Providing users with the ability to download videos for later offline viewing is strongly needed.

Second, NAVOICA's and other MOOC platforms' resources should be systematically supplemented. However, organizing a large-scale project for this purpose proved to be ill-advised. A better result would be the creation of the scientific discipline *Educational technology* in Poland, which would allow researchers to devote more time to the creation of video lectures, MOOCs, research teams, and developing national and international cooperation.

However, knowledge transfer in MOOCs cannot be based solely on video lectures. Reading texts, graphics, screen recordings, and PowerPoint presentations should be offered in parallel. MOOCs without video lectures can also be attractive and have high content value.

DATA AVAILABILITY

The research data have been published in the RODBUK open database and are available at Ślósarz, A. (2024). *Elements of cognitivist and constructivist learning on Polish MOOC platform NAVOICA*. RODBUK (Repository of Open Research Data of Krakow Universities, V1) [data set]. University of the National Education Commission. https://doi.org/10.24917/UKEN/FNMAGC

ACKNOWLEDGEMENT

The study was supported by the Research Fund of the Discipline of Social Communication and Media Science at the University of the National Education Commission, Kraków.

REFERENCES

Armstrong, A.W. et al. (2011). Effects of video-based, online education on behavioral and knowledge outcomes in sunscreen use: a randomized controlled trail. *Patient Education and Counseling*, *83*, 273–277. https://doi.org.10.1016/j.pec.2010.04.033

Bhadani, K. et al. (2017). Student perspectives on video-based learning in CIDO-based project courses. Proceedings of the 13th International CDIO Conference, Calgary, Canada. http://www.cdio.org/knowledge-library/documents/students-perspectives-video-based-learning-cdio-based-project-courses

Bolińska, M., Gurba, K. (2022). MOOC courses on the Polish NAVOICA educational platform and their characteristics. In *2022 IEEE Learning With MOOCS (LWMOOCS)* (pp. 238-239). Antigua, Guatemala. https://doi.org.10.1109/LWMOOCS53067.2022.9927704

Bonafini, F.C. et al. (2017). How much does student engagement with videos and forums in a MOOC affect their achievement? *Online Learning, 21*(4), 223-240. https://doi.org/10.24059/olj.v21i4.1270

Długosz, P., & Foryś, G. (2021). *Zdalne nauczanie na Uniwersytecie Pedagogicznym im. Komisji Edukacji Narodowej w Krakowie z perspektywy studentów i wykładowców* [*Remote teaching at the Pedagogical University of Krakow from the perspective of students and lecturers*]. Kraków: Wydawnictwo Naukowe Uniwersytetu Pedagogicznego, https://rep.up.krakow.pl/xmlui/handle/11716/10085

Fontana, M.V.L., Leffa, V.J. (2018). LMOOCs: LMOOCs: Reflexões preliminaries para o desenvolvimento de MOOCs comunicativos [Preliminary reflections for the development of communicative MOOCS]. *Calidoscópio*, *16* (3), 460 - 468, https://doi.org/10.4013/cld.2018.163.10

Galán, J.G. et al. (2019). *MOOC courses and the future of higher education. A new pedagogical framework.* Gistrup: River Publisher. https://www.riverpublishers.com/book_details.php?book_id=695

Glance, D.G. et al. (2013). The pedagogical foundations of massive open online courses. *First Monday, 18*(5). https://doi.org/10.5210.fm.v18i5.4350

Halliday, M.A.K. (1975). *Learning how to mean: explorations in the development of language.* London: Edward Arnold.

Hui, H. et al. (2019). Big data analytics for MOOC video watching behavior based on Spark. *Neural Computing and Applications*, *32*, 6481-6489. https://doi.org.10.1007/s00521-018-03983-z

Khan Academy, n.d. https://www.khanacademy.org/search?referer=%2F&page_search_query=video

Lee, Y.-Ch. et al. (2015). Using time-anchored peer comments to enhance social interaction in online educational videos .*Chi '15: Proceedings of the 33rd Annual ACM Conference on Human Factors in Computing Systems*, 689-698. http://doi.org/10.1145/2702123.2702349

Michalczyk, S. (2009). *Uwagi o analizie zawartości mediów* [Notes on media content analysis]. *Rocznik Prasoznawczy*, *3*, 95-109.

Rajas-Fernández, M. et al. (2021). Knowledge in images and sounds: Informative, narrative and aesthetic analysis of the video for MOOC. *Publications*, *9*(3), https://doi.org/10.3390/publications9030032

Rizvi, S. et al. (2022). *Culturally adaptive learning design: a mixed-methods study of cross-cultural learning design preferences in MOOCs.* In B. Rientes, R. Hampel, E. Scanlon, & D. Whitelock (Eds.), *Open world learning. Research, innovation and the challenges of high-quality education*, pp. 103-115. Abingdon: Routledge.

Romaniuk, M.W., & Łukasiewicz-Wieleba, J. (2021). *Raport z badań. Zdalna edukacja kryzysowa w APS w okresie pandemii COVID-19. Z perspektywy rocznych doświadczeń* [*Research report. Remote crisis education in APS during the COVID-19 pandemic. From the perspective of one year of experience*]. Warszawa: Akademia Pedagogiki Specjalnej im. Marii Grzegorzewskiej. https://www.aps.edu.pl/media/2392732/raport-z-badania-zdalna-edukacja-kryzysowa-w-aps-w-okresie-pandemii-covid-19.pdf

Ślósarz, A. (2024). MOOCs: Global business goals and local educational strategies. *International Journal of Research in E-learning, 10*(1), 1-23. https://journals.us.edu.pl/index.php/IJREL/article/view/15879

Smyrnova-Trybulska E. et al. (2021). Preliminary analysis of the development and implementation of the MOOC project: A case study. In Smyrnova-Trybulska E. (Ed.), *E-learning in the time of COVID-19* (pp. 137-150). "E-learning" series vol. 13. Katowice-Cieszyn: STUDIO NOA for University of Silesia. https://rebus.us.edu.pl/bitstream/20.500.12128/22234/1/Smyrnova_Trybulska_preliminary_analysis_of_the_development.pdf

Smyrnova-Trybulska, E. et al. (2022). Evaluation of the MOOCs quality and its effectiveness for teachers' training in the field of digital competences and their use in education: a case study. *International Journal of Research in E-learning*, *8*(1), 1-34. https://doi.org/10.31261/IJREL.2022.8.1.03

Stöhr, Ch. et al. (2019). Videos as learning objects in MOOCs: A study of specialist and non-specialist participants' video activity in MOOCs. *British Journal of Educational Technology*, *50*(1), 166-176. https://doi.org/10.1111/bjet.12623

Tang, W. et al. (2022). An analysis of the characteristics of teacher talk on MOOCs based on interpersonal function: Take the "National Excellent Course" of English writing as an example. *ICEMT'22. Proceedings of the 6th International Conference on Education and Multimedia Technology, ACM International Conference Proceeding Series*, 182-189. https://doi.org/10.1145/3551708.3551714

Wei, X. et al. (2023). Do learners share the same perceived learning outcomes in MOOCs? Identyfying the role of motivation, perceived learning support, learning engagement, and self-regulated learning strategies. *The Internet and Higher Education*, *56*, 1-17. https://doi.org/10.1016/j.iheduc.2022.100880

MOOCs

Białowąs, S., & Szyszka, A. (2024). *Eksperyment – projekt, analiza statystyczna i raport APA* [*Experiment - design, statistical analysis and APA report*], Poznań University of Economics and Business, https://navoica.pl/courses/course-v1:UEP+POL002+2024_1/about

Jaśkiewicz, M. et al. (2023). *Czytanie rzeźby terenu* [*Reading the terrain*], Adam Mickiewicz University Poznań, https://navoica.pl/courses/course-v1:UAM+SEJ_K2+2023_E4/about

Mierzwiński, D. et al. (2022). *Geopolimery – nowoczesne i przyjazne środowisku materiały dla budownictwa* [*Geopolymers – modern and environmentally friendly materials for construction*], Cracow University of Technology, https://navoica.pl/courses/course-v1:PolitechnikaKrakowska+PK_WIMiF_Z5_01+2022_24/about

Pawelec, R. et al. (2023). *ELLIPSE Gatekeeper+ Course in suicide prevention*, Jagiellonian University, https://navoica.pl/courses/course-v1:JagiellonianUniversity+EG_A+2023_2_EN/about

Pełechaty, M. (2023). *Jakość wód powierzchniowych i jej ocena metodą bioindykacji* [*Surface water quality and its assessment by bioindication method*], Adam Mickiewicz University Poznań, https://navoica.pl/courses/course-v1:UAM+SEJ_K3+2023_E4/about

Studzinska, M.M. et al. (2023). *ELLIPSE Gatekeeper+ course in suicide prevention*, Jagiellonian University et al., https://navoica.pl/courses/course-v1:JagiellonianUniversity+EG_A+2023_2_EN/about

Wernikowski, S. et al. (2022). *Oswój Pythona III* [*Taming Python III*], West Pomeranian University of Technology in Szczecin, https://navoica.pl/courses/course-v1:ZUT+INF04+2022_S3/about

Short Papers

DESIGNING STRUCTURED REFLECTIONS FOR GUIDING LEARNERS' INTERACTIONS WITH GENERATIVE AI

Rwitajit Majumdar[1], Daevesh Singh[2] and Mei-Rong Alice Chen[3]
[1]*Research and Education Institute for Semiconductors and Informatics, Kumamoto University*
2-40-1, Kurokami, Chuo-ku, Kumamoto, 860-8555, Japan
[2]*Interdisciplinary Programme in Educational Technology (IDP-ET), Indian Institute of Technology (IIT) Bombay*
Powai, Mumbai 400 076, India
[3]*Department of English Language and Literature, Soochow University,*
Q114 No. 70 Linxsi Rd., Shilin, Taipei, 11102, Taiwan

ABSTRACT

Generative AI tools have opened up discussions in the education space and among its policymakers. While educators see opportunities, they also worry that students might only use them to produce their answers if they reflect on the content generated by those tools. In this work, we propose a micro-learning activity where structured reflections are designed as prompts to support comprehension of the learning content and reflection on the learning process. The context of this study is an undergraduate EFL students' reading class where they were allowed to use generative AI tools to comprehend academic research papers written in English. The structured reflection task was authored in a learning analytics-enhanced interactive learning environment that can also trace the learner's interactions. In this pilot study, we present the task design and focus on tracing learners' (n=22) on-task behavior, structured reflection, perceived effort, and judgment of learning from the log data. We present a descriptive analysis of the interactions with the Generative AI tool and the learner's effort and judgment related to the reading comprehension task.

KEYWORDS

Generative AI, Critical Thinking, Micro-learning Task, Learning Analytics, LAreflecT

1. INTRODUCTION

The advent of the Generative Artificial Intelligence (GenAI) chatbots has opened up opportunities as well as challenges within the higher educational landscape (Chan & Hu, 2023). GenAI potentially influences students' learning behaviors; however, its development speed makes research lag in exploring students' interaction behaviors and investigating how they impact students' perceived effort and judgment of learning. Implementing new tools like the GenAI chatbot also makes it essential to understand the implications of self-regulation of learning (Chen 2024 a, b).

In this study, we look at students' reading comprehension activity and support their GenAI interactions with structured reflection prompts. We present the activity design and then utilize the analytics-enabled platform to implement it. The pilot study collects multimodal data of interactions with the prompts, the artifacts generated, the conversation with the LLM, and the perception response of judgment of learning and effort required for the task.

The following two research objectives guide the work:

1. Designing structured reflection for supporting students' interactions with generative AI in the context of English as a foreign language reading comprehension task.
2. Exploratory multimodal data analysis to understand learning behaviors and perceptions related to the structure reflection activity.

2. DESIGNING AND EXECUTING STRUCTURED REFLECTIONS

Authoring Structured Reflection (SR) by the Educator: The educator begins by selecting appropriate reading material that aligns with the learning objectives and the topic of discussion for a particular class. They then create prompts for structured reflection. These prompts are divided into two categories: First is the SR on content, which includes eliciting basic understanding (Derry, 1987), critical analysis, interpretation, and reflection of the reading content (Harkin, 2005). The other category of the prompt is for SR on the process (Goupil & Kouider, 2019), which includes learners reflecting on their AI interaction, judgment of learning (Nelson, 1984), and effort perception (Zijlstra & Van Doorn, 1985) during the given task, in our case the reading comprehension activity.

Learners interact with the content through two primary methods. First, they use Generative AI tools to enhance their understanding and interactively engage with the material. Second, they participate in a Guided Reading activity, where one group of peers presents and discusses the reading material, facilitating collaborative learning and deeper comprehension. While engaging with the content and peers, learners respond to the SR prompts related to the content by answering questions and reflecting on their understanding, critical analysis, and interpretation of the reading material. This phase helps solidify their grasp of the content and encourages deeper cognitive processing. In the final phase, learners reflect on the learning process itself. They respond to SR prompts related to their interactions with the AI tools and peers. Additionally, they can check the learning dashboard, which provides insights into their learning interactions, such as time spent on each phase or steps of tasks. This phase helps learners develop metacognitive skills and enhances their overall learning experience. This workflow ensures a comprehensive and interactive approach to learning, combining structured reflection, technology, and peer interaction to achieve effective microlearning. Figure 1 provides an overview of the design and execution of the structured reflection.

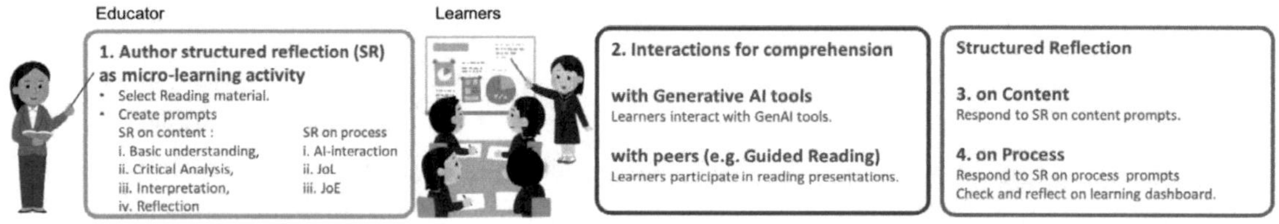

Figure 1. Workflow of the design and execution of the microlearning activity

For this study, we adopted the LAreflecT system (Majumdar et al., 2023). It integrates with a Learning Management System (LMS) like Moodle through the Learning Tool Interoperability (LTI) Protocol. The system consists of three main modules: Authoring, Viewing, and Dashboard. In the Authoring module, educators create and store learning activities in the Activity Database. Once the activity is published, the Viewing module allows learners to interact with these activities, generating logs that are captured through APIs and stored in the Learning Record Store (LRS). This data is then processed and visualized in the Dashboard, which pulls from the Dashboard Database to provide analytics and insights. Additionally, the system connects LLM-based tools through APIs. If a task has the ChatGPT element, learners' input text is augmented to the part of the portion set by the instructor and then parsed as a prompt through the ChatGPT API to receive a response. Artifacts such as the learner's prompts and responses from the LLM are also saved in the LRS. Figure 2 presents an overview of the modules and data flow in LAreflecT system.

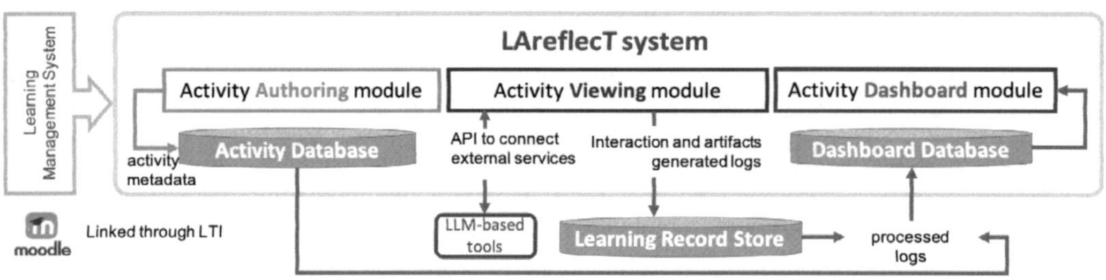

Figure 2. Modules and data flow in LAreflecT system

3. PILOT STUDY AND FINDINGS

A pilot study was conducted in a private university in an Asian country with undergraduate students as a part of their English as a Foreign Language course. The course was online, and the teacher shared the reading list at the beginning of the semester. For their reading task, the selected reading was Pretorius (2023). Students could interact with an LLM chatbot, ChatPDF, that provides restricted responses to the content of the reading. The particular session analyzed in this study had an in-class component where one participating group presented the assigned weekly paper in class. After the reading and presentation, the students posed a question related to the article and provided their judgment of learning and perceived effort of learning.

Figure 3 presents the particular instantiation of the current activity. The instructor used the authoring tool to design the activity and separated the content and process reflection prompts into two tasks for the reading activity. The user interface supported localization in different languages; the teacher used English in this study. Each task had interactive multimedia elements, like text input and pictures, that the students could use. In the Activity Viewer, learners interacted with the elements and responded to the prompts. In the process reflection task, they rated effort and judgment of learning and presented a question based on their comprehension. The Dashboard module offers comprehensive analytics, displaying overall activity metrics, detailed interaction timelines, social comparison insights, and self-comparison visualizations.

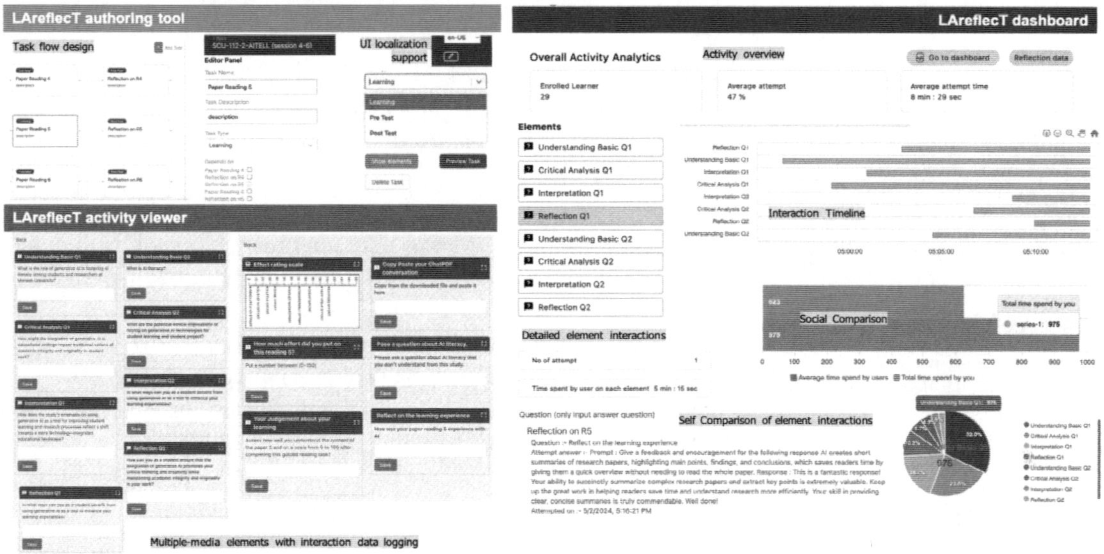

Figure 3. UI components of the LAreflecT system for the reading comprehension task with structured reflection prompts

Researchers could extract all the log data through the data export function in the dashboard. It included the system calculated time on task, effort rating, and judgment of learning by the students. A total of 30 registered students in the course comprised 19 females and 11 males. After screening absentees, we could consider 22 students' data logs in the system. Conducting an iSAT analysis (Majumdar & Iyer, 2016) helped to understand the transition of proportions of those students between high and low groups in terms of time on task, perceived efforts, and JoL. The groups were split based on the means for the time on task and JoL attributes, and for effort, a value above 80 was considered high. Figure 4 presents the iSAT visualization and the tabulated values of the different transition proportions. 24% of the students relatively used less time to respond and reflect on the prompts; they perceived higher effort required but had high judgment of learning. 2 students (10%) spent higher time but perceived lower effort required and had higher JoL.14% had low-low-high mostly indicating higher confidence in comprehension.

Analysis of 133 interaction logs with ChatPDF from 18 students found that the conversations majorly used the prompts directly (66%). Some used GenAI to translate the article and followed up in their native language (13.5%). Main follow-up prompts requested to shorten the earlier response generated by GenAI (18%); the remaining (2.5%) had self-created statements. The mode of the count of conversation was 8, implying the prompts focused on conversations with GenAI rather than the initially observed scenario of only one dialogue.

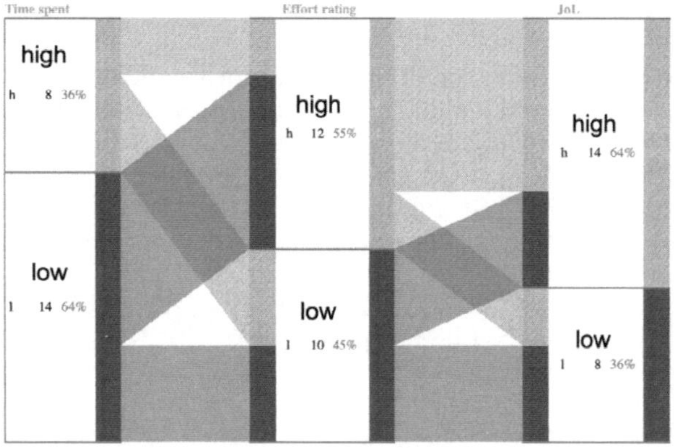

N = 22			Time spent (minutes)	Effort rating [1-150]	JoL [0-100]
Distribution (mean, sd)			69.8, 55.8	95.63, 26.27	78.5, 10.45
Pattern of Transition	n	% of N			
high-high-high	3	14%	38%	27%	23%
high-high-low	0	0%	0%	0%	0%
high-low-high	2	10%	25%	20%	15%
high-low-low	3	14%	38%	30%	38%
low-high-high	5	24%	38%	45%	38%
low-high-low	3	14%	23%	27%	38%
low-low-high	3	14%	23%	30%	23%
low-low-low	2	10%	15%	20%	25%

Figure 4. iSAT analysis of time spent on task, perceived effort and Judgement of Learning (JoL)

4. CONCLUSION

This study presents a theory-informed learning task design for supporting structured reflection while using GenAI to aid reading comprehension (research objective 1). Through this pilot study, we could implement a workflow using the LAreflecT platform. Currently, for research objective 2, the log data was analyzed to find transition cohorts of system use, perception of effort, and JoL for one reading activity. Highlighting differences in the proportion of cohorts might also provide further pointers of process reflection for the students, and it can be included in the peer comparison component of the dashboard. Future studies aim to implement a control design to understand the causal implications of learning with structured reflection while learners use GenAI.

ACKNOWLEDGEMENT

This study is supported in part by JSPS JP22H03902 and (TW) NSTC 111-2410-H-031-092-MY2; Soochow University (112160605-0009); “Empower Vocational Education Research Center” of NTUST, from the Featured Areas Research Center Program by the Ministry of Education (MOE) in Taiwan.

REFERENCES

Chan, C.K.Y. & Hu, W. (2023). Students’ voices on generative AI: Perceptions, benefits, and challenges in higher education. *International J. of Ed. Tech. in Higher Education*, *20*(1), 43. https://doi.org/10.1186/s41239-023-00411-8

Chen, M.R.A. (2024a).Metacognitive mastery: Transformative learning in EFL through a generative AI chatbot fueled by metalinguistic guidance. *J. of Edu. Tech. & Society, 27(3).* https://www.j-ets.net/collection/forthcoming-articles/27_3

Chen, M.R.A. (2024b).The AI chatbot interaction for semantic learning: a collaborative note-taking approach with EFL students. *Language Learning & Technology,28* (1) 1-24.

Derry, S. J. (1996). Cognitive schema theory in the constructivist debate. *Educational psychologist*, *31*(3-4), 163-174.

Goupil, L., & Kouider, S. (2019). Developing a reflective mind: From core metacognition to explicit self-reflection. *Current Directions in Psychological Science, 28*(4), 403-408.

Harkin, P. (2005). The reception of reader-response theory. *College Composition and Communication*, *56* (3), 410-425.

Majumdar, R., & Iyer, S. (2016). iSAT: A Visual Learning Analytics Tool for Instructors. *Research and practice in technology enhanced learning, 11*, 1-22.

Majumdar, R., Prasad, P., Kadam, K., Gatare, K. & Warriem, J.M. (2023). LA-ReflecT: A Platform Facilitating Micro-learning and Its Multimodal Learning Analytics. In *ECTEL* (pp. 731-735). Cham: Springer Nature Switzerland.

Nelson, T.O. (1984). A comparison of current measures of the accuracy of feeling-of-knowing predictions. *Psychological bulletin*, *95*(1), 109–133. https://doi.org/10.1037/0033-2909.95.1.109

Pretorius, L. (2023). Fostering AI literacy: A teaching practice reflection. *Journal of Academic Language & Learning*, *17*(1), T1-T8.

Zijlstra, F.R.H. & Van Doorn, L. (1985). The construction of a scale to measure perceived effort (Technical report). *Delft, the Netherlands: Delft University of Technology.*

IDENTIFYING INFLUENTIAL FACTORS IN STUDENT DROPOUT USING DECISION TREES

Daniel Plúa Morán[1], Mónica Martínez Gómez[2] and Víctor Yeste[2,3]
[1]Universidad Politécnica Salesiana, Ecuador
[2]Universitat Politècnica de València, Spain
[3]Universidad Europea de València, Spain

ABSTRACT

This document presents the development of a classification model to analyze the factors that influence a student at the Universidad Politécnica Salesiana to drop out of their degree program. This analysis is based on data provided by the university. The approach is based on classifications using decision trees. The methodology follows the Knowledge Discovery in Databases (KDD) process and consists of five steps: selection, processing, transformation, data mining, and evaluation. Using Python's Classification and Regression Tree (CART) algorithm, a tree with five levels and seventeen rules was created to identify potential dropouts. It concludes that factors such as the level of studies, academic performance, and the number of subjects taken by the student in a term are decisive in the decision to drop out.

KEYWORDS

Decision Tree, KDD, Student Dropout

1. INTRODUCTION

Nowadays, private companies need to ensure their income by preventing customers from ceasing to consume their services. This applies equally to the university sector (Poveda Velasco, Poveda Velasco and España Irala, 2020), particularly to the Universidad Politécnica Salesiana of Ecuador, which is the subject of this proposal, where there is a high rate of students dropping out of various programs (around 10%), especially in the first semesters (Villa-Murillo, Costa and Vásquez, 2024). This results in a significant amount of unearned income (Pehlivanova and Nedeva, 2021), as well as potential problems or factors that the university does not take into account (Nuñez-Naranjo, 2020; Mellizo-Soto, 2022), which can be crucial in improving its management.

This study aims to help the university by using machine learning techniques to identify the variables that influence a student to drop out. It will be able to develop different strategies based on the factors (Parra-Sánchez, Torres Pardo and Martínez De Merino, 2023) that genuinely influence student retention, achieving better results and steering towards a future-oriented university.

2. METHODOLOGY

The methodology follows the KDD process (Miranda and Guzmán, 2017) with five stages: selection, processing, transformation, data mining, and evaluation.

2.1 Selection

This study included 16,396 university students from the Universidad Politécnica Salesiana of Ecuador from 41 undergraduate programs. The university's technical data science secretariat provided information from 2021 to 2023, including students' academic information, socioeconomic information, and anonymized personal data to maintain confidentiality. Dropout is considered for students who have stopped studying for one semester.

2.2 Processing

The data were cleaned and processed using the Oracle database management system. Additionally, a function was created to identify whether a student has withdrawn from a program, defined as the student not enrolling in any courses at the subsequent academic level.

2.3 Transformation

The variables were adjusted using the Python programming language to be standardized, and missing values were handled using the 'median' strategy.

2.4 Data Mining

The study employs the decision tree technique to analyze student data (Casanova *et al.*, 2018).

Authors (Parra-Sánchez, Torres Pardo and Martínez De Merino, 2023; Villa-Murillo, Costa and Vásquez, 2024) discuss the classification technique based on decision trees to predict students who may drop out. Factors used include the level of studies, marital status, and physical problems, among others. From this, we selected the variable referring to the educational level the student is enrolled in. Additionally, dropout patterns (Parra-Sánchez, Torres Pardo and Martínez De Merino, 2023) were identified based on the average grades; hence, the variable referring to the student's average grades was used. Feature importance determined that the variable related to the number of subjects taken in a term also influences the relevance of the proposed decision tree model. The variables considered include:

- EPA_NIVEL_CURSA: Educational level the student is enrolled in.
- CANTIDAD_MATERIAS: Number of subjects taken by the student in a term.
- PROMEDIO_NOTAS: Average grades of the student.

The hyperparameters, split criterion (criterion), maximum depth (max_depth), maximum number of leaf nodes (max_leaf_nodes), and minimum number of samples required to split a node (min_samples_split) were optimized through a grid search method to enhance the overall model performance.

Table 1. Hyperparameters used in the model

Hyperparameter	Value
max_depth	7
criterion	"gini"
max_leaf_nodes	16
min_samples_split	5

The dataset was divided into training (70%) and testing (30%) sets to evaluate the model's accuracy. The primary evaluation metric was the model's accuracy on the test set, measured using the accuracy_score function.

2.5 Results

Using the decision tree model facilitated the identification of significant patterns in the data (Diaz Pedroza, Chindoy Chasoy and Rosado Gómez, 2019). The relevance of each variable was determined using the feature_importances_ attribute of the decision tree model in Python. This attribute quantifies each variable's contribution to reducing impurity across all decisions in the tree. Feature importances are normalized so that their total sum equals 100%. In this analysis, as shown in Table 2, it was found that the average grades variable was the most important, followed by the number of subjects and, finally, the educational level.

Table 2. Importance of each variable in the model

Variable	Importance
PROMEDIO_NOTAS	62.9 %
CANTIDAD_MATERIAS	34.5 %
EPA_NIVEL_CURSA	2.6 %

The generated decision tree, as shown in Figure 1, clearly represents the decision criteria used to predict outcomes based on various academic characteristics of the students. The decision tree analysis reveals that academic performance (measured by average grades), subject load, and course level are vital determinants of student retention and academic success.

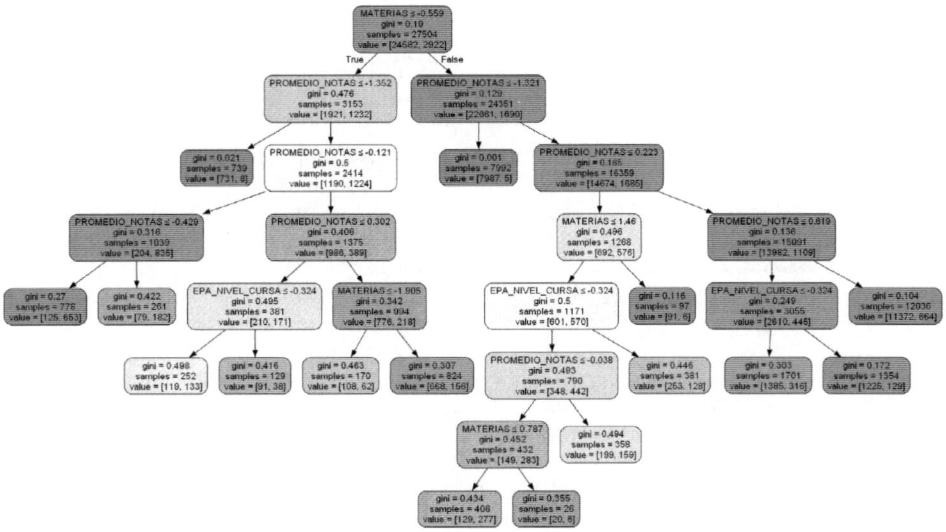

Figure 1. Generated decision tree

The model's accuracy with the data provided by the university was 92.4%, indicating a high predictive capability in identifying students at risk of dropping out.

3. DISCUSSION

This study reveals that the grade point average at a given level of study is the primary determinant of student attrition, followed by the number of courses taken and the academic level. With a predictive accuracy of 92.4%, the model highlights the importance of these variables, suggesting they should be the focus of interventions to reduce dropout rates. These findings emphasize the need for universities to concentrate their efforts on monitoring and supporting students' academic performance, as well as effectively managing course loads. Additionally, the early implementation of this predictive model could transform retention practices, allowing for proactive and personalized interventions

4. CONCLUSION

This study developed a predictive model based on decision trees to identify the factors that influence student desertion and academic performance at the Salesian Polytechnic University of Ecuador. The results reveal that the grade point average is the most critical factor in the dropout probability, followed by the number of subjects taken and the academic level. The decision tree generated provides a clear and understandable representation of these factors, allowing the university to identify and focus its efforts on the most critical areas.

For future research, other machine learning models, such as random forest models, gradient boosting, and neural networks, should be used, which could offer additional improvements in the accuracy and generalization of the model. In addition, more variables, such as psychological, social, and economic factors, which may also play a significant role in student dropout, are suggested.

ACKNOWLEDGEMENTS

We thank the Universidad Politécnica Salesiana del Ecuador and the research group GIIAR for the support and resources provided for this study.

REFERENCES

Casanova, J. *et al.* (2018) 'Factors that determine the persistence and dropout of university students', *Psicothema*, 30, pp. 408–414. Available at: https://doi.org/10.7334/psicothema2018.155.

Diaz Pedroza, K.Y., Chindoy Chasoy, B.Y. and Rosado Gómez, A.A. (2019) 'Review of techniques, tools, algorithms and attributes for data mining used in student desertion', *Journal of Physics: Conference Series*, 1409(1), p. 012003. Available at: https://doi.org/10.1088/1742-6596/1409/1/012003.

Mellizo-Soto, M.F. (2022) *Análisis del abandono de los estudiantes de grado en las universidades presenciales en España*. Ministerio de Universidades.

Miranda, M.A. and Guzmán, J. (2017) 'Análisis de la Deserción de Estudiantes Universitarios usando Técnicas de Minería de Datos', *Formación universitaria*, 10(3), pp. 61–68. Available at: https://doi.org/10.4067/S0718-50062017000300007.

Nuñez-Naranjo, A. (2020) 'Deserción y estrategias de retención: un análisis desde la universidad particular', *593 Digital Publisher CEIT*, 5–2(5), pp. 79–87. Available at: https://doi.org/10.33386/593dp.2020.5-2.306.

Parra-Sánchez, J.S., Torres Pardo, I.D. and Martínez De Merino, C.Y. (2023) 'Factores explicativos de la deserción universitaria abordados mediante inteligencia artificial', *Revista Electrónica de Investigación Educativa*, 25, pp. 1–17. Available at: https://doi.org/10.24320/redie.2023.25.e18.4455.

Pehlivanova, T.I. and Nedeva, V.I. (2021) 'Attributes selection using machine learning for analysing students' dropping out of university: a case study', *IOP Conference Series: Materials Science and Engineering*, 1031(1), p. 012055. Available at: https://doi.org/10.1088/1757-899X/1031/1/012055.

Poveda Velasco, J.C., Poveda Velasco, I.M. and España Irala, I.A. (2020) 'Análisis de la deserción estudiantil en una universidad pública de Bolivia', *Revista Iberoamericana de Educación*, 82(2), pp. 151–172. Available at: https://doi.org/10.35362/rie8223572.

Villa-Murillo, A., Costa, L. and Vásquez, C. (2024) 'A METHODOLOGICAL PROPOSAL TO ADDRESS THE ACADEMIC DROPOUT PHENOMENON BASED ON AN INTELLIGENT PREDICTION MODEL: A CASE STUDY', *Millenium: Journal of Education, Technologies, and Health*, 2(23). Available at: https://doi.org/10.29352/mill0223.31378.

A SYSTEMATIC REVIEW ON THE EFFECTIVENESS OF EDUCATIONAL TECHNOLOGIES IN WORKPLACE LEARNING

Xinjie Xing[1] and Dirk Ifenthaler[1, 2]
[1]*Learning, Design and Technology, University of Mannheim, Baden-Württemberg, Germany*
L 4, 1 - Room 401, 68161 Mannheim, Baden-Württemberg, Germany
[2]*UNESCO Co-Chair on Data Science in Higher Education Learning and Teaching, Curtin University, Australia*

ABSTRACT

This systematic review employs the 3-P Model (presage, process, and product) to evaluate the efficacy of three prominent educational technologies—adaptive learning, e-learning, and online learning—in facilitating workplace learning. Exhaustive research was conducted, analyzing 607 articles related to the three educational technologies, and extracted 29 articles with data published between 2000 and 2023. The findings support the positive impact of the 3-P Model related to educational technologies. This study offers valuable insights into the relative effectiveness and applicability of adaptive learning, e-learning, and online learning in enhancing workplace learning initiatives through systematic synthesis. Furthermore, a comparative analysis of educational technologies is presented, elucidating their respective strengths, limitations, and potential applications. The findings contribute to a deeper understanding of the role of educational technology in workplace education and inform decision-making processes regarding the adoption and implementation of technology-enhanced learning programs in organizational contexts.

KEYWORDS

Systematic Review, Adaptive Learning, E-learning, Online Learning, 3-P Model, Workplace Learning

1. INTRODUCTION

In the contemporary global business environment, the importance of workplace training in supporting employee performance and advancing organizational success has increased considerably (Odunayo and Fagbemide, 2024). The 3-P Model of workplace learning, as outlined by Tynjälä (2013), offers a framework delineating the interrelated components of learning within a professional setting. A current area of focus in workplace learning research is the growing role of educational technologies. This trend is indicative of the growing significance of online resources, learning platforms, and tools in enabling the development of professional competencies and the creation of knowledge within work environments (Ifenthaler, 2018). Prior research indicates that established educational technologies possess distinctive characteristics and prioritize disparate objectives for success in the workplace. For example, the feedback provided by adaptive learning technology support deeper understanding and advanced performance (Granito et al., 2014). E-learning is a method of education and training that is facilitated by information and communication technologies and is accessible to individuals anywhere, anytime (Šumak et al., 2011). Moreover, online learning can be defined as the construction of knowledge or skills that occur either wholly or partially through internet-based platforms, thereby allowing learners access to information without constraints related to time or location (Sun et al., 2008).

This systematic review examines the interrelationships between adaptive learning, e-learning, and online learning technologies and the presage, process, and product phases of workplace learning. It is therefore anticipated that an understanding of the factors related to educational technologies affecting learning in the workplace will facilitate the design and implementation of future workplace learning.

2. WORKPLACE LEARNING

The 3-P Model of learning proposed by Biggs consists of presage, process, and product phases of learning. A more sophisticated model was subsequently developed by Tynjälä (2013). It proposes a framework for anticipating the intentions of employees and the factors that influence their decisions. This model includes the interaction of intrinsic and extrinsic factors affecting the decision-making process between presage and process phases. The process phase includes workplace learning strategies, and the product phase involves workplace performance.

A trending theme in workplace learning research is an emphasis on educational technology. Accordingly, the intention towards workplace learning related to educational technologies in the presage phase includes the motivation, willingness, and acceptance to use these technologies. Intrinsic factors, including effort expectancy, attitudes, and anxiety, exerted a greater influence on employees' inclination toward using educational technologies in the workplace than extrinsic factors like performance expectancy, social influence, facilitating conditions, and the geographical location of the workplace learning providers. Nevertheless, the influence of intrinsic motivation serves to mediate the effects of extrinsic motivation (Yoo et al., 2012).

Moreover, the motivation of employees to engage in learning activities influences their perception of the utility and satisfaction derived from the use of educational technologies, which in turn enhances their performance in their respective tasks (Chen and Kao, 2012). The choice of learning providers and locations emerged as crucial determinants of employee's preference for learning with educational technologies (Haley, 2008). Fleming et al. (2017) emphasize the importance of factors like low complexity, authenticity, and technical support in predicting future use intentions. Thus, there is a consensus among scholars that the role of the three education technologies in workplace learning is significant. According to Kravčík et al. (2017), the use of personalization and adaptive methods in the context of video content represents a promising approach to the enhancement of informal learning in workplace settings. Furthermore, e-learning platforms, distinguished by their capacity to disseminate content at any given moment, in any location, on an array of electronic devices, and reusable materials, facilitate self-directed learning (Pashev et al., 2020). Further, Thorpe and Gordon (2012) proposed that online environments designed to facilitate workplace learning should focus on the socio-technical interaction network, with particular emphasis on the integration of social context throughout every phase of learning.

3. SYSTEMATIC REVIEW

This systematic review examines the existing evidence on the effectiveness of educational technology in facilitating workplace learning. The research questions are as follows:

1. How do the intrinsic and extrinsic factors of the 3-P model support the decision to engage in workplace learning?
2. How does the use of educational technologies related to the 3-P model impact the effectiveness of workplace learning?

We outlined a research protocol detailing search strategies, criteria of inclusion, and key terms of the search definitions. Several search strategies were executed to classify empirical studies on workplace learning. Initially, electronic searches were conducted in databases such as Psycnet, ERIC, psycArticles, psycINFO, PSYNDEX, ACM library, Web of Science, Science Direct, DBLP, Springer Link, and Semantic Scholar. Additionally, a manual search of the reference lists of selected relevant publications was conducted. These combined efforts resulted in the identification of $N = 607$ publications. The publication screening process is based on the Preferred Reporting Items for Systematic Reviews and Meta-Analyses theory (PRISMA). To begin with, Citavi and Zotero were utilized to eliminate duplicates and publications that were not published in academic journals automatically. Then, the remaining publications' titles, abstracts, and full texts were examined according to the sorting criteria created for publication screening. The initial step involves the categorization of participants based on their educational background, distinguishing between university and vocational school students. This delineation is crucial as it allows for a more focused analysis, with workers representing the sole participants in the selected papers. Furthermore, studies were excluded from the analysis due to the absence of quantitative data. Also, only studies published in the English language were included in the analysis. Finally, only studies published in a peer-reviewed journal were included, according to Hemmler and Ifenthaler (2024), peer-reviewed journal papers assures the quality of primary papers included. After a thorough screening process, 36 publications were deemed eligible for inclusion, including those with quantitative data suitable for conducting future meta-analyses. In conclusion, the systematic review encompassed a total of 29 key articles, with a total sample of 9,787 learners.

4. FINDINGS AND CONCLUSION

This systematic review is the inaugural investigation to contrast disparate educational technologies for workplace learning in accordance with the 3-P Model. The findings indicate that the presage and process phases are the most motivating factors for the use of educational technologies in workplace learning. This provides companies with a direction for enhancing intrinsic and extrinsic factors and for continuous improvement of educational technologies in the future.

A descriptive analysis is employed to respond to the two research questions. To respond to the initial research question, it is necessary to consider the 12 key articles that have been selected from the entire corpus of papers. These articles focus on the presage phase, emphasizing the influence of intrinsic and extrinsic factors on the act of engaging in workplace learning. A greater number of authors emphasize intrinsic factors than extrinsic factors. For example, Roca and Gagné (2008), as well as Teoh and Tan (2020) highlight that perceived usefulness influence the decision to engage in workplace learning. Park and Wentling (2007), Yoo and Huang (2016), and Yoo et al. (2012) suggest that the participant's attitude affects the decision. Cheng et al. (2011) point out that the intention to use the educational system matters. Chen and Kao (2012), Lantu et al. (2023), Ghosh et al. (2022), and Yoo et al. (2012) propose learning motivation, such as personal development needs, affect the decision to engage in workplace learning. A smaller number of papers address the extrinsic factor. For instance, Becker et al. (2013) emphasize that the barriers to e-learning adoption are decisive, while Kapo et al. (2021) and Yoo et al. (2015) state that social and environmental factors affect the adoption. Findings for research question one suggests different factors deeply influence an employee's choice to engage in workplace learning. Hence, organizations could use these factors to encourage participation in workplace learning.

Regarding the second question, we examined the factors that impact the effectiveness of each educational technology in seven related key articles. Pulakos et al. (2000) emphasize the taxonomy of adaptive performance because it is a multidimensional construct. Lee and Kim (2015) suggest that the user's preference for the educational technology matters because it can be conservative for a particular culture. Cheng and Chen (2015), Lee (2010), and Rodríguez-Santero et al. (2020) emphasize the importance of system quality and design of the system, while Reavley et al. (2018) and Reavley et al. (2021) consider the format of e-learning can impact the effectiveness of workplace learning. To summarize the result of research question two, the efficacy of workplace learning is contingent upon the presence of educational technologies and the motivation of the user to utilize educational technologies.

The relatively limited number of key articles related to adaptive learning indicates a need for further research and development to gain a deeper understanding of the ways in which adaptive learning systems support workplace learning. It is acknowledged that this systematic review may be biased due to the inclusion of only key articles written in English and published in peer-reviewed journals. A meta-analysis is currently being conducted for future research with the aim of strengthening the findings. To conclude, the systematic review emphasizes that workplace learning is essential for growth and development of organizations and highlights the positive relationship between workplace learning phases and educational technologies.

ACKNOWLEDGEMENT

We acknowledge the support of the China Scholarship Council (https://www.csc.edu.cn/).

REFERENCES

Becker, K. et al. (2013). A Learner Perspective on Barriers to E-Learning. *Australian Journal of Adult Learning*, Vol. 53, No. 2, pp. 211-233.

Chen, H. J. and Kao, C. H. (2012). Empirical Validation of the Importance of Employees' Learning Motivation for Workplace e-Learning in Taiwanese Organisations. *Australasian Journal of Educational Technology*, Vol. 28, No. 4, pp. 580-598.

Cheng, B. et al. (2011). Acceptance of Competency-Based Workplace e-Learning Systems: Effects of Individual and Peer Learning Support. *Computers & Education*, Vol 57, No. 1, pp. 1317–33.

Cheng, W. Y. T. and Chen, C. C. (2015). The Impact of E-Learning on Workplace on-the-Job Training. *International Journal of E-Education, e-Business, e-Management and e-Learning*, Vol. 5, No. 4, pp. 212-228.

Fleming, J. et al. (2017). Factors for Successful E-Learning: Does Age Matter? *Education + Training,* Vol. 59, No. 1, pp. 76–89.

Granito, A. et al. (2014). Adaptive Feedback Improving Learningful Conversations at Workplace. *Journal of E-Learning and Knowledge Society,* Vol. 10, No. 1, pp. 63-83.

Ghosh, N. et al. (2022). Technology Integrated Inclusive Learning Spaces for Industry 4.0 Adaptive Learners- Lur Model for Sustainable Competency Development. *ECS Transactions,* Vol. 107, No. 1, pp. 13823–13832.

Haley, C. K. (2008). Online Workplace Training in Libraries. *Information Technology and Libraries,* Vol. 27, No. 1, pp. 33–40.

Hemmler, Y.M. and Ifenthaler, D. (2024). Self-Regulated Learning Strategies in Continuing Education: A Systematic Review and Meta-Analysis. *Educational Research Review*, Vol. 42.

Ifenthaler, D. (2018). How We Learn at the Digital Workplace. *Digital Workplace Learning: Bridging Formal and Informal Learning with Digital Technologies.* Springer International Publishing, New York City, USA.

Kapo, A. et al. (2021). Continuous E-Learning at the Workplace: The Passport for the Future of Knowledge. *Information Technology & People,* Vol. 34, No. 5, pp. 1462–89.

Kravčík, M. et al. (2017). Adaptive Video Techniques for Informal Learning Support in Workplace Environments. *Emerging Technologies for Education. Rome, Italy,* pp. 533–543.

Lantu, D. C. et al. (2023). Workplace E-Learning Acceptance: Combining Symmetrical and Asymmetrical Perspectives. *Journal of Workplace Learning,* Vol. 35, No. 4, pp. 341–58.

Lee, J. (2010). Design of Blended Training for Transfer into the Workplace. *British Journal of Educational Technology,* Vol. 41, No. 2, pp. 181–98.

Lee, S. and Kim, B. G. (2015). Users' Preferential Factors in Web-Based e-Learning Systems for Ease of Workplace Learning in Korea. *Learning and Individual Differences* Vol. 39, pp. 96–104.

Odunayo, H. A. and Fagbemide, O. I. (2024). Workplace Training and Employee Effectiveness: A Case Study of Nigerian Banking Industry. *Acta Universitatis Danubius. ØEconomica,* Vol. 20, No. 1, pp. 88–106.

Park, J. H. and Wentling, T. (2007). Factors Associated with Transfer of Training in Workplace e–Learning. *Journal of Workplace Learning,* Vol. 19, No. 5, pp. 311–329.

Pashev, G. et al. (2020). Adaptive Workplace E-Learning Model. *TEM Journal*, Vol. 9, No. 2, pp. 613–618.

Pulakos, E. D. et al. (2000). Adaptability in the Workplace: Development of a Taxonomy of Adaptive Performance. *Journal of Applied Psychology,* Vol. 85, No. 4, pp. 612–624.

Reavley, N. J. et al. (2021). Longer-Term Effectiveness of eLearning and Blended Delivery of Mental Health First Aid Training in the Workplace: 2-Year Follow-up of a Randomised Controlled Trial. *Internet Interventions,* Vol. 25.

Reavley, N. J. et al. (2018). Effectiveness of eLearning and Blended Modes of Delivery of Mental Health First Aid Training in the Workplace: Randomised Controlled Trial. *BMC Psychiatry,* Vol. 18, No. 1.

Roca, J. C. and Gagné, M. (2008). Understanding E-Learning Continuance Intention in the Workplace: A Self-Determination Theory Perspective. *Computers in Human Behavior,* Vol. 24, No. 4, pp. 1585–1604.

Rodríguez-Santero, J. et al. (2020). Confirmatory Factor Analysis of a Questionnaire for Evaluating Online Training in the Workplace. *Sustainability,* Vol. 12, No. 11.

Šumak, B. et al. (2011). A Meta-Analysis of e-Learning Technology Acceptance: The Role of User Types and e-Learning Technology Types. *Computers in Human Behavior,* Vol. 27, No. 6, pp. 2067–2077.

Sun, P. C. et al. (2008). What Drives a Successful E-Learning? An Empirical Investigation of the Critical Factors Influencing Learner Satisfaction. *Computers & Education,* Vol. 50, No. 4, pp. 1183–1202.

Teoh, A. P. and Tan, Y. S. (2020). Predicting Behavioural Intention of Manufacturing Engineers in Malaysia to Use E-Learning in the Workplace. *The International Review of Research in Open and Distributed Learning,* Vol. 21, No. 4, pp. 20–38.

Thorpe, M. and Gordon, J. (2012). Online Learning in the Workplace: A Hybrid Model of Participation in Networked, Professional Learning. *Australasian Journal of Educational Technology,* Vol. 28, No. 8.

Tynjälä, P. (2013). Toward a 3-P Model of Workplace Learning: A Literature Review. *Vocations and Learning,* Vol. 6, No. 1, pp. 11–36.

Yoo, S. J. et al. (2015). Gender Still Matters: Employees' Acceptance Levels towards e-Learning in the Workplaces of South Korea. *Knowledge Management & E-Learning An International Journal*, Vol. 28, No. 8, pp. 1267-1282

Yoo, S. J. et al. (2012). The Roles of Intrinsic Motivators and Extrinsic Motivators in Promoting E-Learning in the Workplace: A Case from South Korea. *Computers in Human Behavior,* Vol. 28, No. 3, pp. 942–50.

Yoo, S. J. and Huang, W.D. (2016). Can E-learning System Enhance Learning Culture in the Workplace? A Comparison among Companies in S Outh K Orea. *British Journal of Educational Technology,* Vol. 47, No. 4, pp. 575–591.

MOBILE EDUCATION SYSTEM FOR ENHANCING THE EFFICIENCY OF PHYSICAL CIRCUIT CONSTRUCTION AND ITS APPLICATION TO LABORATORY EXPERIMENTS

Atsushi Takemura
Tokyo University of Agriculture and Technology
2-24-16, Naka-cho, Koganei-shi, Tokyo 184-8588, Japan

ABSTRACT

This study proposes a novel mobile education system that helps students to efficiently learn experiments that involve the design and construction of electronic circuits. Generally, teaching and learning circuit construction involves several inevitable problems, such as the large student-to-instructor ratio and the likelihood of accidents. To solve these problems, this study developed a new education system that enables students to efficiently learn the design and construction of circuits and to improve the completeness of the constructed circuits based on instruction from the system. The effectiveness of the proposed system was verified in actual classes of 40 undergraduates. The comparison tests between two groups of students who used or did not use the proposed system demonstrated the effectiveness of the system.

KEYWORDS

Mobile Education System, Experiment, Physical Circuit Construction

1. INTRODUCTION

Teaching about electronic circuits and learning about them are important to education in the field of science and technology. A comprehensive understanding of electronic circuits would cover theoretical analysis, design, construction, and experimentation, and it is imperative to building in-depth knowledge of related technologies (e.g., signal processing, machine control, and robotics). Recently, several education systems that would help students understand the theories and analysis of electronic circuits have been developed, such as education systems for the computer-based learning of theoretical analysis (Ortega-Alvarez, 2018) and simulator-aided reflective learning (Dickerson, 2022). To improve students' skill in electronic circuit experiments, several educational support systems have been developed. These include virtual circuit construction using 3-D printed models (Dominguez-Reyes, 2023), remote and virtual experiments on control system design (Lei, 2021), and a remote laboratory for project-based learning about digital electronics (Hayashi, 2023).

To improve students' comprehensive understanding of electronic circuits and their abilities in technological development, the teaching of physical circuit construction and experiments that use real laboratory equipment is essential. However, conventional systems are limited only in theoretical or virtual learning of circuits within a subject area. Thus, these systems are unable to teach real experiments that involve the construction of physical circuits. To address this shortcoming, this study developed a new system for experiments that involve the construction of physical circuits. The proposed system uses a new technique to automatically recognize inaccurate components and inappropriate parts in a physical circuit and to give instruction in correcting mistakes and in improving the completeness of the constructed circuit. The proposed system makes it possible to learn the design and construction of circuits efficiently. It also decreases the instructor's workload for confirming the numerous circuits with different layouts and compositions constructed by individual students and for preventing accidents (e.g., electric shock or fire).

2. TECHNICAL FEATURES OF THE PROPOSED SYSTEM

Conventional education systems for teaching electronic circuits have difficulty coping with the following situations, which occur in general laboratory education:

(1) The student-to-instructor ratio is usually quite high, and it is therefore difficult to ensure efficient individual instruction and to note the mistakes in the circuits constructed by individual students. An educational support system that can decrease the instructor's load for assessing the circuits constructed by students is needed.

(2) Circuits that are incorrectly constructed by students may cause serious accidents, such as electric shocks or fire. An education system must be developed that is able to detect the mistakes in the students' circuits and provide instruction to correct the mistakes.

(3) Even when students' circuits are correctly composed, the circuits frequently include inappropriate parts (e.g., unnecessary wirings and inappropriate ground connections), which can destabilize the operation of the circuit and should be rearranged. An education system is needed that instructs students on improving the completeness of the constructed circuits.

To solve these problems, this study develops a new technique based on the recognition of circuit images and proposes its application in a system that educates about experiments involving circuit construction. The technical novelties of the proposed system are listed below.

(1) The system recognizes the composition of circuits with different layouts constructed by individual students, and it detects errors in the circuits. If an error is detected, the system instructs the student in correcting the constructed circuit.

(2) The system evaluates the appropriateness of a circuit composition (e.g., the types and positions of connected devices and wirings). If an inappropriate part that requires improvement is detected, the system instructs the student in improving the constructed circuit.

Figure 1 schematizes the functions of the proposed system. This system allows students to carry out an experiment involving circuit construction using the two functions described in the Sections 2.1 and 2.2, which follow.

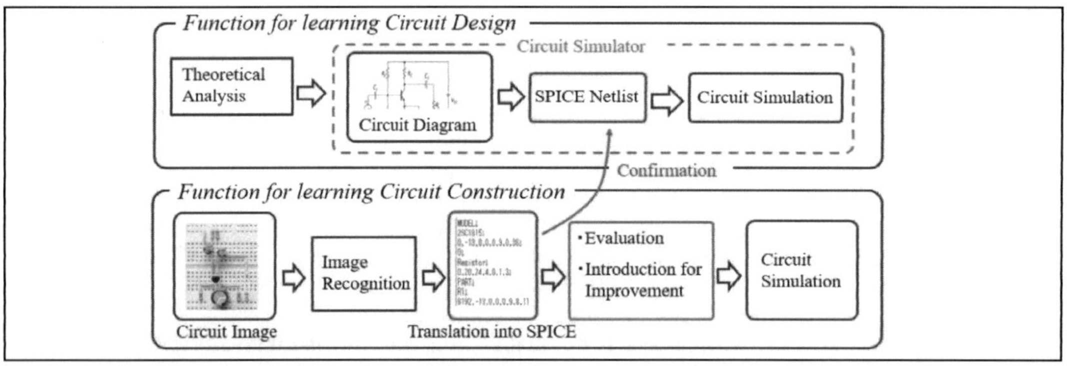

Figure 1. Schematic of the functions and workflow of the proposed system

2.1 Function for Learning Circuit Design

The function for circuit design was developed in a previous study (Takemura, 2023). This function allows individual students to use their mobile PCs and helps students to learn the theoretical analysis and design of electronic circuits and to understand the operation of circuits through circuit simulation. As shown in Figure 1, students use this function to prepare for circuit construction. Based on a SPICE netlist, which is a general circuit-description language and is obtained from a designed circuit, this system informs the student of the mistakes in the designed circuit. The system requires the students to check whether the simulated working of their designed circuit corresponds to the given specifications. If a designed circuit does not work according to the specifications, the student corrects the circuit.

2.2 Function for Learning Circuit Construction

The function for learning the construction of physical circuits in the proposed system is comprised the new technologies *A)* and *B)*, which are described as follows.

A) Circuit Recognition and Translation into SPICE

During the experiments, the individual students construct their circuits on breadboards, and then they transmit images of their constructed circuits to the system using mobile PCs. This function employs image processing techniques, such as segmentation and pattern recognition, on the circuit images to assess the compositions of the circuits. The image-recognition technique proposed in the previous study (Takemura, 2023) enables the system to recognize the following components of a constructed circuit: (1) connected devices and wirings, and (2) hazardous parts that should be corrected (e.g., cross-wiring using insulating cables).

By increasing the size of the training dataset and the number of components that can be recognized through circuit recognition, this study improved the image-recognition technique so that the following items (3)–(5) could be recognized: (3) equipotential nodes to be unified, (4) unnecessary or excessively long wiring to be rearranged, (5) inappropriate ground connections to be corrected. These items are frequently found in students' circuits and cause unstable or hazardous circuit operation. Here, the excessively long wiring in (4) was defined as a wiring longer than 1.5 times of required length.

Based on the information of the components discriminated by the circuit recognition process, the system translates the compositions of a physical circuit into a SPICE netlist. This circuit translation technique plays a vital role in giving instruction on correcting or improving the circuits to the individual students (described in *B)*).

B) Introduction for Improvement and Correction

In this study, a new technique for giving automated instruction to students to correct and improve the physical circuits they construct was developed. This function checks whether the SPICE netlist of a constructed circuit, which is obtained via the circuit translation technique, is consistent with that of the circuit designed at process (described in Section 2.1). It detects the erroneous and inappropriate parts of a circuit. If erroneous and inappropriate parts are detected, the system transmits instructional messages to correct and improve the physical circuit. Figure 2 shows examples of the system's performance. Figure 2(a) shows examples of messages for correcting and improving a constructed circuit by category. As shown in Figure 2(b) and (c), the system successively classifies the erroneous and inappropriate parts of a circuit constructed by students and indicates the parts in the circuit images based on the legend shown in Figure 2(a). Subsequently, the student corrected and improved the circuit according to the system's instruction (Figure 2(d)).

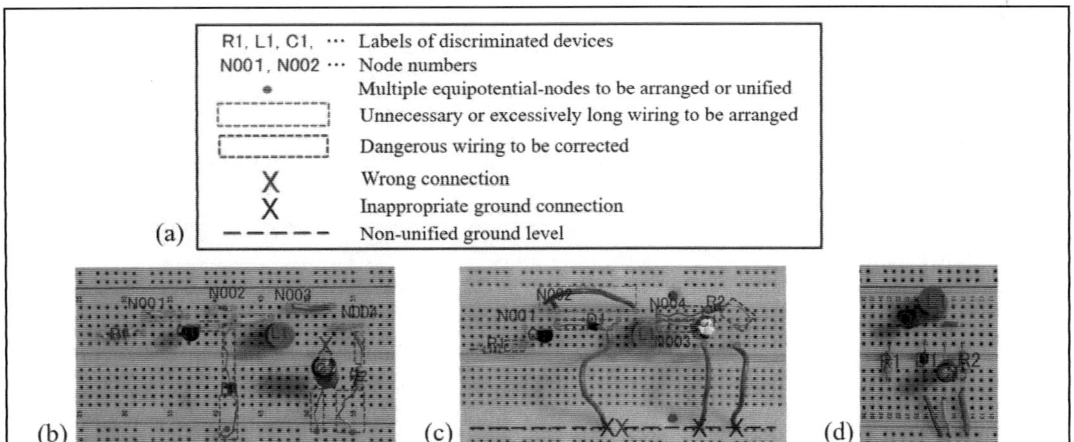

Figure 2. Example showing the performance of the proposed system: (a) instructional messages for correcting errors and improving inappropriate parts in a constructed circuit by category; (b) and (c) indication of the errors and inappropriate parts in a constructed circuit; and (d) circuit correctly constructed in accordance with the system's instruction

3. METHODOLOGY FOR EVALUATING THE PROPOSED SYSTEM

The effectiveness of the proposed system was evaluated with a comparative study that involved two distinct groups (Group-1 and Group-2) of students aged 19–21 years at the Tokyo University of Agriculture and Technology. Each group comprised 20 students who were tasked with the design and construction of three types of DC-DC converters: (1) buck converter, (2) boost converter, and (3) buck-boost converter. Figure 3 shows diagrams of these circuits. DC-DC converters are used in various electronic equipment (e.g., power-source and micro-controller); thus, learning about these circuits is essential to an education in the field of science and technology at the university level.

Group-1 performed the experiment involving the design and construction of the circuits according to the conventional method for conducting an experiment in 2022. Group-2 performed the same circuit design and construction as those in Group-1, but they used the new system and conducted the experiment in 2023. Prior to beginning the experiments, questionnaires were administered to determine each student's degree of experience with circuit construction. Based on their responses, the students were classified into the following two categories:

A: Experienced in circuit construction, in addition to practice exercises at school.

B: No experience in circuit construction, except for practice exercises at school.

Figure 4 shows the number of students in each experience category. The results show that the majority of the students were classified into category B.

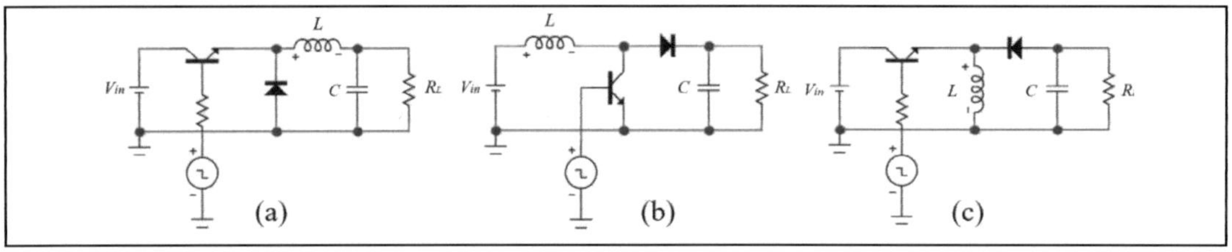

Figure 3. Diagrams of the circuits to be constructed in the experiments: (a) buck converter, (b) boost converter, and (c) buck-boost converter

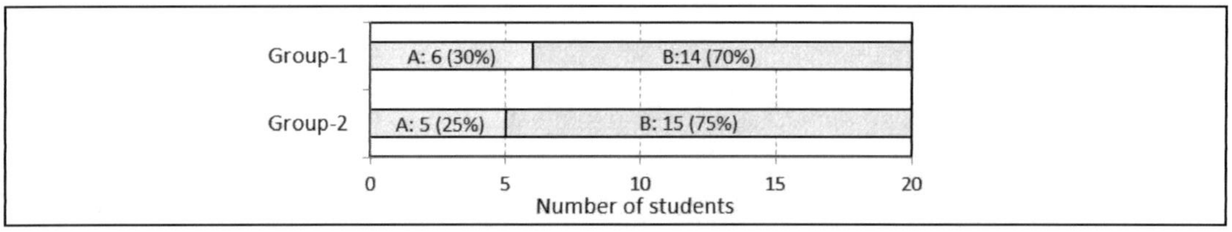

Figure 4. Grouping of students for the evaluation of the proposed system, and the proportion of students in each of the experience categories

The individual students in Group-1 were tasked with designing and constructing circuits based on the conventional method outlined in (T1)–(T5).

(T1) Lecture on the theory and method for constructing the circuits

(T2) Circuit design

(T3) The students submit the designed circuits to the instructor. The instructor examines the designs to ensure that they adhere to specifications. If an incorrect part is identified, the student corrects it under the instructor's guidance.

(T4) Circuit construction using the necessary components in the laboratory.

(T5) The students submit the constructed circuits to the instructor. The instructor inspects the constructed circuit. If an erroneous or inappropriate part is discovered, the student corrects it under the instructor's guidance.

The individual students in Group-2 were tasked with designing and constructing the same circuits as those in Group-1, but they used the newly proposed system in accordance with the following processes. Here, the tasks (T1), (T3), and (T5) were also carried out by Group-2, but the tasks (T2-G2) and (T4-G2) for circuit design and construction by Group-2 differed from those denoted as (T2) and (T4) for Group-1, as follows:

(T2-G2) Circuit design and confirmation of the characteristics of the designed circuits using the system's simulator.

(T4-G2) Circuit construction using the necessary components in the laboratory. Subsequently, the student uses his mobile PC to transmit an image of the constructed circuit to the system and then receives feedback from the system. If the system indicates erroneous or inappropriate parts in the circuit, the student corrects or improves the circuit based on the system's instruction. Moreover, the student assesses the characteristics of the constructed circuits by using the system's simulator. If the student's simulation results do not meet certain criteria, the student corrects the circuit accordingly.

4. RESULTS AND DISCUSSION

Figure 5 shows the test results for Group-1 and Group-2, which demonstrate the effect of the proposed system on the experiment described in Section 3. Figure 5(a) shows a circuit that has been correctly constructed by a student in Group-2. Figure 5(b) shows that the averages and ranges of the required time for circuit design and construction in Group-2 were less than those in Group-1. This result implies that the use of the circuit simulator decreases the time needed to complete the circuit design.

Figure 5(c) shows the frequency of errors in the designed circuits that were identified by instructors during the process (T3). As shown in this figure, six students in Group-1 (30% of students) had errors in their designed circuits that were observed by the instructor. In Group-2, there were no errors in the circuits designed by the students in Category A, but one student (7%) in Category B had errors. This result indicates that the check of the circuit's operation using the circuit simulator during the design process reduced the time needed to achieve accurate circuit design. However, errors were detected in the circuits that were designed by students in Group-1 and Group-2 who misunderstood the necessary circuit theory.

Figure 5(d) shows the frequency of errors and hazardous parts to be corrected in the constructed physical circuits, as discovered by the instructors during step (T5). This figure shows that seven students in Group-1 (35% of students) had constructed circuits with errors and hazardous parts that were observed by the instructor. Conversely, no errors or hazardous parts in the circuits constructed by the students in Group-2 were noted. This result demonstrates that the proposed system is effective in preventing errors in a constructed circuit, regardless of the student's experience with circuit construction.

Figure 5(e) shows the frequency of inappropriate parts in the constructed physical circuits that need to be improved, as discovered by instructors during step (T5). This figure shows that 11 students in Group-1 (55% of students) had unnecessary wirings or inconsistent ground connections that had to be unified, as observed by the instructor. In Group-2, the existence of unnecessary wirings was observed in the circuits constructed by two students (13% of students) in Category B. These students misunderstood the instruction from the system and were thus not able to repair their circuits. This result demonstrates that the instruction by the new system is effective in helping students improve or rearrange their circuits that are correctly composed but include inappropriate parts.

During the evaluation process, positive responses were obtained from the instructors, and it provided further validation of the effectiveness of the proposed system. Their comments highlighted the following key points:

- The new system is effective for decreasing the instructor's work to validate circuits having different layouts and compositions constructed by numerous students and for preventing the occurrence of accidents caused by operating inappropriate circuits.

Furthermore, the students in Group-2 gave positive responses relating to the usefulness of the proposed system. These included:

- The system's instruction relating to the incorrect or inappropriate parts of a constructed circuit helped the student to efficiently and safely complete the construction of the circuit without an instructor.

To improve the applicability and usefulness of the system, the following objectives should be pursued:

- Instruction for beginners that is more user-friendly and more detailed
- Enhancing the applicability to the construction of circuits on different types of circuit boards (e.g., universal circuit-boards and printed circuit boards)

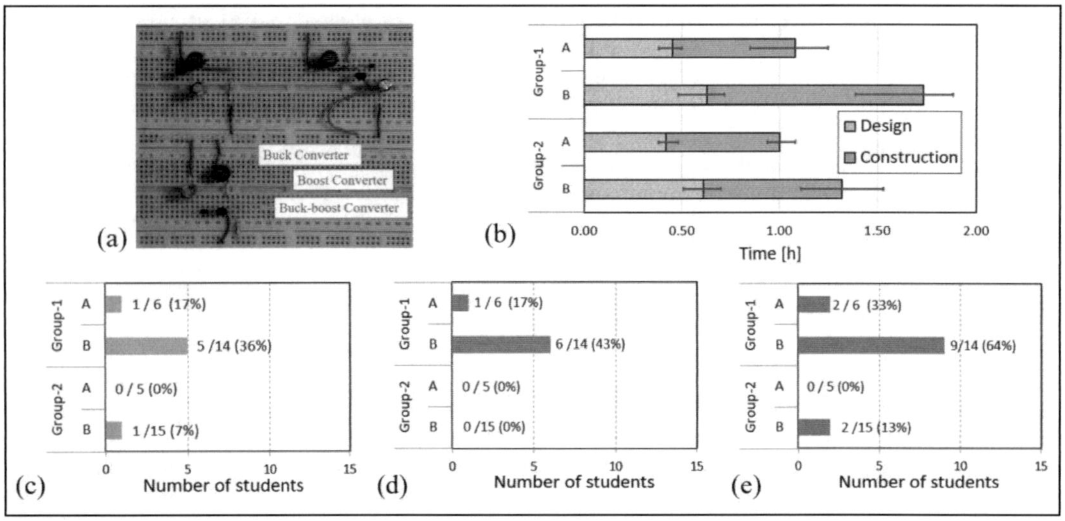

Figure 5. Results of the comparison test between Group-1 and Group-2: (a) correct circuit constructed by a student in Group-2, (b) average and range for the time required for the design and construction of circuits by group and degree of experience, (c) number of students whose designed circuits included errors, (d) number of students whose constructed circuits included errors and hazardous parts, and (e) number of students whose constructed circuits included inappropriate parts that had to be corrected

5. CONCLUSIONS

In this study, a novel mobile education system for the design and construction of DC-DC convertor circuits, which are essential to a university-level science and technology education, is demonstrated. The proposed system enables students to efficiently learn the design and construction of circuits and to improve any circuits that have errors or inappropriate parts in accordance with the system's instructions. The effectiveness of the proposed system is demonstrated by a test that compared two groups of university students. By enhancing the techniques of automated instruction for circuit construction, the system's usefulness could be greatly improved.

ACKNOWLEDGMENT

This study was partly supported by a Grant-in-Aid for Scientific Research (KAKENHI) 23K02629 from the Japan Society for the Promotion of Science.

REFERENCES

Dickerson, S. J., et al. (2022). Use of SPICE circuit simulation to guide written reflections and metacognition, *In IEEE Transactions on Education*, vol. 65, no. 3, pp. 471-480.

Dominguez-Reyes, R., et al. (2023). Modular 3-D-printed education tool for blind and visually impaired students oriented to net structures, *In IEEE Transactions on Education*, vol. 66, no. 1, pp. 55-61.

Hayashi, V. et al. (2023). Implementation of PjBL with remote lab enhances the professional skills of engineering students, *In IEEE Transactions on Education*, vol. 66, no. 4, pp. 369-378.

Lei, Z., et al. (2021). 3-d interactive control laboratory for classroom demonstration and online experimentation in engineering education, *In IEEE Transactions on Education*, vol. 64, no. 3, pp. 276-282.

Ortega-Alvarez, J. D., et al. (2018). Exploring undergraduate students – computational modeling abilities and conceptual understanding of electric circuits, *In IEEE Transactions on Education*, vol. 61, no. 3, pp. 204-213.

Takemura A. (2023). Mobile system for simulation of physical circuit operation and application to education involving circuit construction, *Proceedings of IADIS International Conference CELDA 2023*, pp. 433-438.

ENHANCING PERSONALIZED DIABETES TREATMENT WITH LARGE LANGUAGE MODELS AND CHAIN-OF-THOUGHT REASONING

Qi Sun[1], Xuekuan Fu[2] and Chenyang Zhou[3, 4]
[1]*Software Engineering Center, Chinese Academy of Sciences, China*
[2]*Rockford Christian School, Illinois, United States*
[3]*Beijing Aortic Disease Center, Beijing Anzhen Hospital, China*
[4]*Medical University, Beijing, China*

ABSTRACT

Diabetic patients often struggle to determine the appropriate dosage of short-acting insulin to effectively manage their blood glucose levels. Miscalculating the insulin dose can lead to serious complications, such as hypoglycemia or hyperglycemia. In this paper, we propose a novel approach for personalized insulin treatment using large language models (LLMs), dubbed L4DT (Large Language Models for Diabetes Treatment). This method can be divided into two phases. The first phase involves applying chain-of-thought reasoning for data augmentation, simulating so that L4DT could learn the step-by-step thought processes that human experts would use to determine optimal insulin dosages. The second phase focuses on training the LLM to obtain personalized insulin dosage recommendations. Our evaluation of the L4DT demonstrates its expertise in insulin dosage prediction. On the MIMIC-IV dataset, the L4DT model achieves a mean squared error of 4.55 and a mean absolute error of 2.01, outperforming existing approaches. This study not only enhances the application of exploratory learning approaches in complex medical domains but also assesses the impact of exploratory technologies like LLMs on diabetes treatment. The integration of technology and expertise in this model offers a reliable reference for clinicians and a platform for continuous learning and expertise development in the field of diabetes management.

KEYWORDS

Large Language Model, Chain-of-Thought, Diabetes Treatment, Data Augment

1. INTRODUCTION

In recent years, the emergence of large language models (LLMs) has demonstrated great potential in the medical field by revolutionizing medical education, enhancing learning experiences, and improving the overall quality of medical education through a wide range of applications (Abd-Alrazaq 2023). LLMs possess the capability to integrate data from various sources, such as patients' electronic health records and wearable devices, in order to generate personalized treatment recommendations. Furthermore, by incorporating chain-of-thought reasoning (Wei 2022), LLMs can effectively simulate the step-by-step reasoning process of humans.

This paper proposes a personalized short-acting insulin injection treatment method, dubbed the L4DT (Large Language Models for Diabetes Treatment), which is based on the integration of LLMs and chain-of-thought reasoning for diabetic patients. Through rigorous comparative experiments, we have verified that our L4DT method outperforms alternative approaches, including machine learning, deep neural networks, and GPT-3.5, in the task of predicting insulin dosage. Moreover, we have conducted comprehensive ablation studies to determine the key physiological characteristics that have the most significant impact on insulin dose prediction.

2. BACKGROUND AND RELATED WORK

The field of diabetic management has seen significant advancements with the integration of machine learning and artificial intelligence techniques. Several recent studies have explored the potential of these technologies to improve real-time clinical performance. Xiran Zheng investigated the application of various machine learning algorithms, including linear regression, decision trees, and neural networks, to predict inpatient glucose levels and insulin dosing using electronic health record (EHR) data (Liu, 2020). Further advancements have been made in the development of neural network-based approaches for predicting insulin dosage for diabetic patients, with a study by Zahran et al. (2016) demonstrating the ability of Artificial Neural Networks (ANNs) to effectively model the non-linear relationship between patient characteristics. Additionally, the use of reinforcement learning has emerged as a promising approach, as evidenced by a study by Miguel Tejedor in which the researchers developed a reinforcement learning-based system that leverages patient-specific data to provide personalized insulin dose recommendations for inpatients (Tejedor, 2008).

Recent studies have also explored the use of large language models (LLMs) in various medical applications, including clinical decision support, knowledge extraction, and medical education, with promising but mixed results, as evidenced by their performance on tasks like medical question answering, clinical note generation, and the United States Medical Licensing Examination (Thirunavukarasu et al., 2023; Yang, R., 2023; Lucas, 2024). A recent study by Yang et al. examined the use of a fine-tuned ChatGLM model integrated into a hospital's information system to generate personalized treatment recommendations, laboratory test suggestions, and medication prompts for diabetic patients, with the findings indicating the model's ability to provide reasonably accurate treatment recommendations but also noting certain limitations (Yang, H., 2023).

Building upon these existing studies, the proposed work on "Leveraging Medical Big Data and Large Language Models for Personalized Insulin Dosage Prediction in Diabetes Treatment" seeks to explore the potential of large language models to further improve the accuracy of insulin dosage predictions by integrating chain-of-thought reasoning with LLMs.

3. METHOD

In this section, we proposed a novel treatment approach for diabetic patients based on large language models.

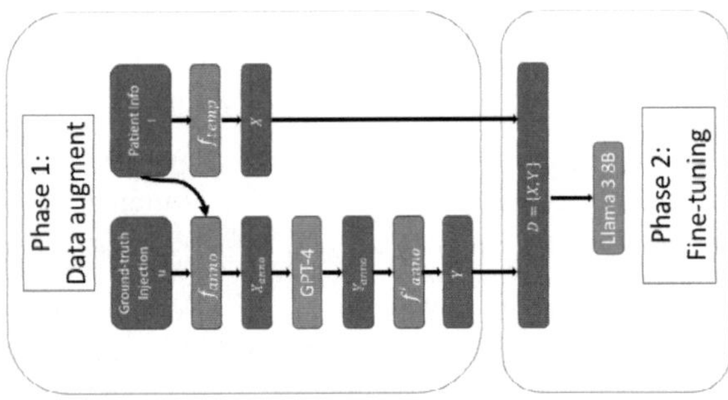

Figure 1. L4DT Pipeline

Figure 1 is a dedicated demonstration of the behind logic of the L4DT Pipeline. The L4DT consists of two phases, including data augment and Llama fine-tuning.

3.1 Data Augment

The purpose of data augment, which is based on chain-of-thought, is to convert the numeric input and output in the original dataset into natural language to leverage the powerful comprehension and reasoning capabilities of GPT-4 to annotate the data, as well as distill the knowledge from the GPT-4 model, which is difficult to train and deploy, into a Llama model that is more easily trainable and deployable.

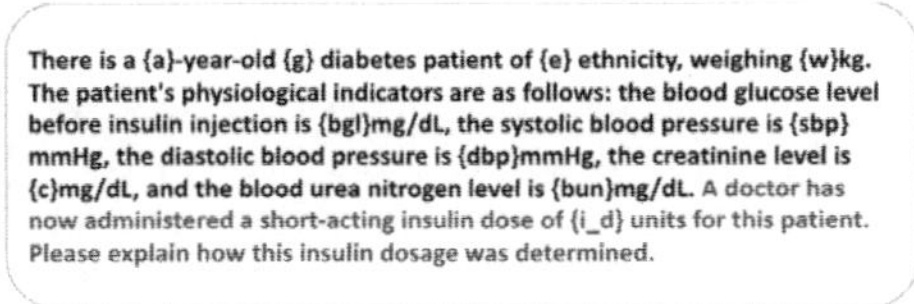
There is a {a}-year-old {g} diabetes patient of {e} ethnicity, weighing {w}kg. The patient's physiological indicators are as follows: the blood glucose level before insulin injection is {bgl}mg/dL, the systolic blood pressure is {sbp} mmHg, the diastolic blood pressure is {dbp}mmHg, the creatinine level is {c}mg/dL, and the blood urea nitrogen level is {bun}mg/dL. A doctor has now administered a short-acting insulin dose of {i_d} units for this patient. Please explain how this insulin dosage was determined.

Figure 2. f_{anno} template

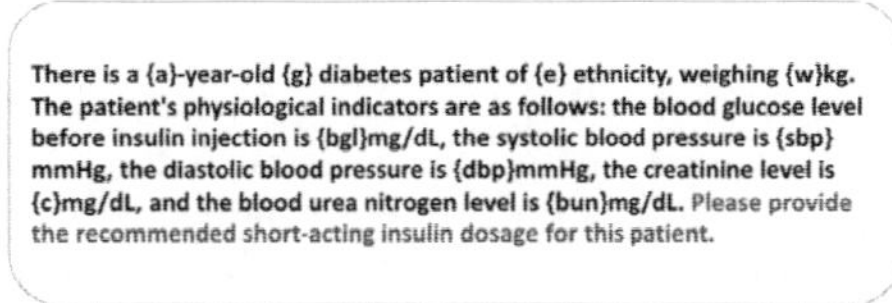
There is a {a}-year-old {g} diabetes patient of {e} ethnicity, weighing {w}kg. The patient's physiological indicators are as follows: the blood glucose level before insulin injection is {bgl}mg/dL, the systolic blood pressure is {sbp} mmHg, the diastolic blood pressure is {dbp}mmHg, the creatinine level is {c}mg/dL, and the blood urea nitrogen level is {bun}mg/dL. Please provide the recommended short-acting insulin dosage for this patient.

Figure 3. f_{temp} template

The input of the first column within phase I consists of two parts:

a) The patient's input information, dubbed I, include (gender, age, weight, ethnicity, creatinine, injected insulin dose, blood glucose, level before insulin injection, blood urine nitrogen, systolic blood pressure and diastolic blood pressure).

b) The current insulin dosage (marked as 'u') administered to the patient by a sophisticated physician.

$$I = (u, g, a, w, e, c, bun, sbp, dbp) \quad (1)$$

$$X_{anno} = f_{anno}(I)$$

By using Eq. (1), inputs(including basic information, physiological data and u) are transformed into a particular template in natural language so it can be understood by GPT-4. The f_{anno} template (Figure (2)) is constructed based on chain-of-thought reasoning. In this case, GPT-4 can provide us with more accurate outputs.

Table 1. Comparison of performance

Abbreviations	Data Item
g	gender
a	age
w	weight
e	ethnicity
c	creatinine
u	injected insulin dose
bgl	blood glucose level before insulin injection
bun	blood urine nitrogen
sbp	systolic blood pressure
dbp	diastolic blood pressure

All input data item abbreviative explanations can be find in Table 1.

Additionally, as depicted in Eq. (2), Y_{anno} is the generated descriptive treatment recommendation.

$$Y_{anno} = GPT - 4(X_{anno}) \quad (2)$$

Finally, to form accurate insulin dosage data and provide a standard for Llama 3 8B output, the function

$$Y = f'_{anno}(Y_{anno}, u) \quad (3)$$

is used to attached i_d at the end of Y_{anno} to get Y, which can be used as target label data of Llama 3 8B.

At the second column, inputs do not contain the dosage value u. Those inputs are then transformed into a particular template in natural language so it can be understood by Llama 3 8B, according to Eq. (4). The f_{temp} template in Fig. (3). then generates the input data item of Llama 3 8B.

$$X = f_{temp}(g, a, w, e, c, bun, sbp, dbp) \quad (4)$$

3.2 LLM Fine-Tuning

In phase II, we fine-tuned Llama 3 8B In order to facilitate training and deployment, we use a relatively smaller LLM, Llama, and fine-tune it on the dataset we have constructed. During fine-tuning of Llama 3 8B(phase II), we use two training objectives, which are max log-likelihood (MLE) loss and value-based reinforcement learning (VRL) loss. The MLE loss is widely adopted in the pre-training and fine-tuning of language models, which trains the model to maximize the probability of the ground-truth sentence, as shown in Eq. (5).

$$\mathcal{L}_{\mathcal{MLE}} = -\sum_{(X,Y)\in\mathcal{D}} \log p_\theta (Y|X) \tag{5}$$

However, the MLE loss cannot accurately measure the difference in insulin dosage value since it only models the literal difference instead of the value difference. To address this, we performed reinforcement learning to minimize the difference in value between the insulin dosage in the model-generated answer and the ground-truth insulin dosage. The training objective is shown in Eq. (6), where θ is the parameter of the LLM, π_θ denotes the wrapped insulin injection policy, $\tilde{u}$ is the insulin injection dosage sampled from π_θ, u is the ground-truth insulin injection. The corresponding loss function of training objective Eq. (6) can be represented as Eq. (7).

$$argmax_\theta \sum_{I} E_{\tilde{u}\sim\pi_\theta(\cdot|I)}[-(\tilde{u}-u)^2] \tag{6}$$

$$\mathcal{L}_{\mathcal{VRL}} = \sum_{(I)} E_{\tilde{u}\sim\pi_\theta}(\cdot\,|I)[(\tilde{u}-u)^2 \, log \, \pi_\theta \, (\tilde{u}|I)] \tag{7}$$

The final loss function is a linear combination of the MLE loss and the VRL loss, balanced by a hyperparameter λ, as shown in Eq. (8).

$$\mathcal{L} = (1-\lambda)\mathcal{L}_{\mathcal{MLE}} + \lambda\mathcal{L}_{\mathcal{VRL}} \tag{8}$$

Algorithm 1 : Training procedure of L4DT
Data: Composed dataset D, initial policy parameter $\theta^{(1)}$, training steps S
Result: The finally trained policy parameter $\theta^{(S)}$
For $i \in \{1,\cdots,S\}$ do
Sample $\{I, X, Y, u\}$ from dataset D;
Compute gradient: $\nabla_{\theta^{(i)}}\mathcal{L}_{\mathcal{MLE}} = -\nabla_{\theta^{(i)}} \log p_{\theta^{(i)}} Y|X)$
Sample an answer from LLM: $\tilde{Y} \sim p_{\theta^{(i)}}(\cdot\,|X)$;
Split the insulin injection dosage from the answer: $\tilde{u} = f_u(\tilde{Y})$;
Compute gradient: $\nabla_{\theta^{(i)}}\mathcal{L}_{\mathcal{VRL}} = -\nabla_{\theta^{(i)}}(\tilde{u}-u)^2 \log \pi_{\theta^{(i)}} (\tilde{u}|I)$;
Update parameter: $\theta^{(i+1)} \leftarrow \theta^{(i)} + (1-\lambda)\nabla_\theta\mathcal{L}_{\mathcal{MLE}} + \lambda\nabla_\theta\mathcal{L}_{\mathcal{VRL}}$;
End
Return ;

4. EXPERIMENT

The experimental data for this section is derived from the MIMIC-IV database, and the data processing steps are consistent with those used in the paper by Baoyu Tang (Tang 2024). Randomly select 80% of data and assign them to the training set and assign the rest 20% to the testing set.

In this section, we thoroughly validated the performance of the L4DT by comparing it with several other existing methods using Mean Squared Error (MSE) and Mean Absolute Error (MAE) metrics to demonstrate the strengths and weaknesses of our method relative to alternative approaches. Furthermore, we carried out a series of ablation experiments focusing on various physiological indicators by systematically removing each physiological indicator one at a time

4.1 Performance Comparison

As depicted in Table 2, we have compared the performance of the L4DT with not only the methods discussed in Yusra's paper—namely KNN (K-Nearest Neighbors), Decision Tree, and ANN (Artificial Neural Network)—but also with GPT-3.5. Our comparison revealed that the L4DT outperformed the others in terms of both MSE (Mean Squared Error) and MAE (Mean Absolute Error) metrics, achieving the most favorable results.

Table 2. Comparison of performance

Method	MSE	MAE
L4DT	**4.55**	2.01
KNN	6.47	2.33
ANN	5.79	2.12
Decision Tree	8.59	2.41
GPT-3.5	5.29	2.10

The L4DT's superiority is particularly evident when addressing the "hallucination" issue often encountered in GPT-3.5, where the model might generate responses that are coherent but factually incorrect or irrelevant due to the lack of contextual grounding. In contrast, our method incorporates structured medical knowledge and evidence-based constraints, effectively mitigating this problem and providing reliable insulin dosage recommendations.

Moreover, when compared to traditional machine learning approaches such as KNN, Decision Tree, and ANN, the L4DT offers a distinct advantage. It not only provides accurate dosage suggestions but also elucidates the rationale behind each recommendation. This transparency is crucial in a clinical setting, where healthcare providers must understand the basis for treatment decisions to ensure patient safety and trust.

Our method's ability to explain its recommendations stems from its design, which integrates interpretable features and logical reasoning pathways. This design enables the L4DT model to trace the decision-making process, making it an valuable tool for clinicians who require clear justifications for the proposed insulin dosages. Furthermore, the L4DT's performance was validated through rigorous testing and cross-validation procedures, ensuring robustness of our model is a testament to its potential for real-world application in healthcare settings.

4.2 The Ablation Study

Extensive medical research has indicated that a patient's weight, age, gender, blood pressure, heart rate, renal function, and other physiological indicators can significantly influence the clinical efficacy of rapid-acting insulin. However, the impact of these factors is typically limited to clinical observational and statistical studies. Clarifying the association between various physiological characteristics of patients and the efficacy of insulin is crucial for the clinical application of rapid-acting insulin. This not only helps to reveal the biological mechanisms related to insulin action and efficacy but also guides clinicians in making more precise personalized treatment decisions for patients. To investigate the relative importance of these patient characteristics, researchers conducted feature ablation experiments. They sequentially removed the seven characteristics involved in the study—patient weight, age, gender, ethnicity, creatinine, blood urea nitrogen, and blood pressure—from the input data and performed the prediction of insulin efficacy using the remaining six patient characteristics. The same preprocessing method was used to perform thought chain data augmentation on the dataset containing six features, and the ablation model with one input feature removed was trained in the same manner as before. By comparing these scores, the changes in the accuracy of the L4DT after feature removal were quantified and compared, thereby determining the relative importance and contribution of the seven input attributes to the accuracy of the insulin dosage prediction model.

Table 3 demonstrates the impact of different feature values.

Table 3. The Result of the Ablation Study

Method	MSE	MAE
L4DT	**4.55**	2.01
Gender	6.12	2.26
Age	5.79	2.19
Weight	6.52	2.36
Ethnicity	4.78	2.03
Creatinine	6.32	2.29
blood urine nitrogen	6.48	2.33
blood pressure	5.93	2.25

5. CONCLUSION

The L4DT method presents a significant advancement in personalized insulin treatment for diabetes patients. By leveraging large language models, chain-of-thought reasoning, and hybrid training objectives, the method is able to generate highly accurate and tailored insulin dosage recommendations for individual patients by simulating or learning actual clinical logic from clinicians. Additionally, the insights gained from the ablation studies provide valuable guidance to clinicians on prioritizing the most impactful physiological indicators when determining personalized insulin regimens. Overall, the L4DT approach showcases the transformative potential of integrating advanced language models and reasoning techniques to enhance personalized diabetes care and empower patients to better control their condition.

REFERENCES

Abd-Alrazaq, A., AlSaad, R., Alhuwail, D., Ahmed, A., Healy, P. M., Latifi, S., ... & Sheikh, J. (2023). Large language models in medical education: opportunities, challenges, and future directions. JMIR Medical Education, 9(1), e48291.

Liu, X., Jankovic, I., & Chen, J. H. (2020). Predicting inpatient glucose levels and insulin dosing by machine learning on electronic health records. medRxiv, 2020-03.

Lucas, H. C., Upperman, J. S., & Robinson, J. R. (2024). A systematic review of large language models and their implications in medical education. Medical Education.

Magoulas, G. D., & Prentza, A. (1999). Machine learning in medical applications. In Advanced course on artificial intelligence (pp. 300-307). Berlin, Heidelberg: Springer Berlin Heidelberg.

Tang, B., Yuan, Y., Yang, J., Qiu, L., Zhang, S., & Shi, J. (2022). Predicting Blood Glucose Concentration after Short-Acting Insulin Injection Using Discontinuous Injection Records. Sensors, 22(21), 8454.

Tejedor, M., Woldaregay, A. Z., & Godtliebsen, F. (2020). Reinforcement learning application in diabetes blood glucose control: A systematic review. Artificial intelligence in medicine, 104, 101836.

Thirunavukarasu, A. J., Ting, D. S. J., Elangovan, K., Gutierrez, L., Tan, T. F., & Ting, D. S. W. (2023). Large language models in medicine. Nature medicine, 29(8), 1930-1940.

Torlone, E., Pampanelli, S., Lalli, C., Sindaco, P. D., Vincenzo, A. D., Rambotti, A. M., ... & Bolli, G. (1996). Effects of the short-acting insulin analog [Lys (B28), Pro (B29)] on postprandial blood glucose control in IDDM. Diabetes Care, 19(9), 945-952.

Wang, Y. M., & Elhag, T. M. (2008). An adaptive neuro-fuzzy inference system for bridge risk assessment. Expert systems with applications, 34(4), 3099-3106.

Wei, J., Wang, X., Schuurmans, D., Bosma, M., Xia, F., Chi, E., ... & Zhou, D. (2022). Chain-of-thought prompting elicits reasoning in large language models. Advances in neural information processing systems, 35, 24824-24837.

Yang, H., Li, J., Liu, S., Du, L., Liu, X., Huang, Y., ... & Liu, J. (2023). Exploring the potential of large language models in personalized diabetes treatment strategies. medRxiv, 2023-06.

Yang, R., Tan, T. F., Lu, W., Thirunavukarasu, A. J., Ting, D. S. W., & Liu, N. (2023). Large language models in health care: Development, applications, and challenges. Health Care Science, 2(4), 255-263.

Zahran, B. (2016). A neural network model for predicting insulin dosage for diabetic patients. The International Journal of Computer Science and Information Security (IJCSIS), 14.

HUMAN CENTRED AI: SOCIAL AND COLLABORATIVE LEARNING WITH HUMANOID ROBOTS

Sanaz Fallahkhair[1], Bex Dagless[2] and Masoud Rahimpoor[2]
[1]Principal Lecturer in Human Centred AI and Interaction
University of Brighton, United Kingdom
[2]MSc User Experience Design Student
University of Brighton, United Kingdom

ABSTRACT

The integration of social robots into educational settings marks a significant paradigm shift in the application of technology to facilitate learning and education. Social robots, characterised by their ability to interact, engage, and communicate with humans, offer unprecedented opportunities for enhancing collaborative learning experiences. This paper explores the potential of social robots to address key questions, including: Will robotic solutions be useful and accepted by humans for educational applications? How can social robots be designed to enhance collaborative learning experiences? What guidelines should be devised to ensure human-centred AI development? By examining these questions, we present two case studies that seek to investigate and contribute towards the development of Human-Centred AI Design guidelines that prioritise the diverse needs of humans and enhance Human Robot Interactions (HRI).

KEYWORDS

Human-Centred AI, Collaborative Learning, Social Robots, Artificial Intelligence, Human Robot Interaction (HRI)

1. INTRODUCTION

The integration of social robots into educational settings marks a significant paradigm shift in the application of technology to facilitate learning and education. Social robots, characterised by their ability to interact, engage, and communicate with humans, offer unprecedented opportunities for enhancing collaborative learning experiences. As the educational landscape evolves, the adoption of these robotic solutions has become a focal point of research, raising critical questions about their utility, acceptance, and design in educational applications. This paper explores the potential of social robots to address key questions, including their usefulness and acceptance by humans, the design enhancements for collaborative learning experiences, and the establishment of Human Centred Artificial Intelligence (HCAI) and Human Robot Interaction (HRI) development guidelines. By examining these questions, we aim to contribute to the development of human centred AI design guidelines that prioritise the diverse needs of humans and enhance human-robot interactions.

In the following sections, we will review existing literature on social robots in education to present several case-studies that highlight lesson learnt into its implementations. The review aims to direct our project to develop and test further case-studies investigating a potential of humanoid robot for collaborative learning.

2. SOCIAL ROBOTS IN EDUCATION

The use of social robots in education has garnered considerable attention in recent years, driven by advancements in robotics and artificial intelligence. These robots, equipped with the ability to interact socially with humans, present unique opportunities for enhancing the educational experience. Research indicates that social robots can facilitate learning by providing personalised and engaging interactions, thereby improving students' motivation and participation (Belpaeme et al., 2018). Moreover, social robots can be programmed to adapt to the individual learning styles and needs of students, making them valuable tools for personalised education (Mubin et al., 2013).

Socially interactive robots are gaining increasing significance in collaborative experiences and learning. Hence, user experience plays a vital role in social robotics, directly influencing users' interaction, communication and trust levels when engaging with robots (Corrales-Paredes et al., 2023). Positive user experience is crucial for the long-term success of socially interactive robots, encompassing aspects like acceptance, usability, learnability, safety, trust, and credibility. While some of these facets receive considerable attention in human robot interaction research, others remain understudied (Alenljung et al., 2017). There is significant interest in introducing social features into robots to improve interaction experiences and promote long-term engagement. Designing successful social robots requires the involvement of end users throughout the design process and unravel about what are the value and metrics we would like to encompass to be incorporated as a core skill for collaborations.

Table 1 outlines a range of commercially available social robots which are predominantly used for research.

Table 1. Competitive analysis of social robots currently available on the market

Robot (Year)	**NAO (2008)** 	**Pepper (2014)** 	**RoboThespian (2006)** 	**Zenbo (2016)** 	**MiRo (2018)** 	**Ameca (2022)** 
Key features	Sensors, face recognition, voice interaction	Human emotion recognition, touch screen, sensors	Face tracking, LCD eyes, interactive touch screen	Social assistant, multimedia, reminders	Sensors, interactive learning, voice commands	AI-driven interactions, face recognition, robotics

Understanding the ecological and landscape of HCAI and collaborative learning experience requires us to review some related projects. One of the recent studies, by Georgieva-Tsaneva et al. (2023) looked at social robots in assisting vocabulary and language development to support skills such as articulation, speech rate control and storytelling to support learners in improving social skills. Robots used to learn and engage socially and emotionally with users through audio, visual, and tactile inputs. This makes them useful tools for supporting individuals with communication disorders or social anxiety (Rasouli et al., 2022). In another study, social robots have been tested if they could be used to reduce loneliness, reinforce interpersonal communication, enhance mood, and reduce stress, especially for older adults, with the potential to enhance healthcare and elderly care settings (Zöllick et al., 2022). The study revealed the results that social robots can provide companionship and support daily activities. Research signifies that using robots in educational settings can be useful, for example, it is proven that social robots increase the listening and speaking skills of children (Özkan & Toz, 2022). Chen et al., 2022 presented the development of a system using robots for training English-language tour guides, integrating AI and VR technologies. The study highlights the effectiveness of robot-assisted language learning (RALL) in increasing motivation, engagement, and providing an active learning experience for students.

In higher education, humanoid robots were used to facilitate collaborative research projects among university students. These robots acted as research assistants, helping students organise their work, conduct experiments, and analyse data. Study by Bechem & Backer (2022) presents the design of humanoid robot assisted learning scenario and the results of an exploratory study with 27 undergraduate students who participated in the robot experiment with the humanoid robot NAO in hybrid settings. The results of the study show that students positively assessed the NAO as an educational technology and perceived NAO as a friendly, likeable, funny, trustworthy and motivating anthropomorphic agent.

RoboThespian has been flagged and used as Robot teacher to make science fun and engage students (Verner et al., 2016) exploring school lesson mediated by a humanoid robot. The project aimed to investigate how students' outcomes, perceptions and attitudes are influenced. Total of 189 students from the ages of 11-13 years old. Learning outcomes were evaluated. The results of the quiz scores indicates that a majority learnt the subject successfully and many students had a positive attitude towards the lesson and robot teacher.

There are some other studies also highlights some drawbacks and potential pitfalls of using robotic solution in education. For example, Long-term field trials, however, revealed that commercially available co-existing robots failed to be sustainably integrated into people's everyday life (Weiss & Spiel, 2022). Furthermore, social robots have been used in educational settings; however, most studies have been investigating a short-term interaction. Learning takes place over extended period of times; therefore, it is imperative to evaluate the potential of educational robots over longer periods of time to investigate how they can be deployed in real life settings (Letendre & Gray, 2024). There are many challenges faced during long-term interaction with social robots, one of the key issues being the decline in user interest over time. There are multiple factors that contribute to the loss in interest, such as the user finding the robot or task failing to be fulfilling as well as a relationship of human to the robot failing to meet the expectations (Weiss & Spiel, 2022). Moreover, the use of social robots raises ethical concerns around privacy, data security, and the risk of over-dependence on non-human relationships (Rasouli et al., 2022).

In next section we discuss two case studies, that encompassed multiple methods to investigate the key questions: How do people perceive humanoid robot as an educational technology, how do they assess the interactions with humanoid robot, how humanoid robot should be designed to be acceptable, useful, and usable to use? First case study focuses on primary school children and the use of robot for communication and language learning, whilst the second case study is looking into adults' work-based learning in the domain architecture and façade engineering. We have used two totally distinct case studies to explore the educational potential of humanoid robot. These case studies are presented in the following section (3.1).

2.1 Case study I: Educational Robot for Language and Collaborative Learning in Primary School (Edbot)

The EdBot project integrates social robotics in education to enhance student engagement. We undertake Human Centred AI design principles, prototyping a tabletop social robot named "Edbot," which aims to provide a supportive, interactive learning experience to encourage communication and language learning. The visual design of Edbot was created using AI-based text-to-image generation, enabling rapid visualisation based on descriptive input. We gathered data from multiple methods, including surveys (Godspeed Questionnaire Series) and Embodiment Ranking (Weiss & Bartneck, 2015). The session began with participants watching a video of RoboThespian, where Will Jackson, founder of Engineered Arts, demonstrated the robot's interactive abilities in his TEDxTruro talk. The video highlighted the contrast between media portrayals of robots and their real-world capabilities, emphasising the challenges of achieving true robotic intelligence. This was followed by a demonstration of Figure robot's OpenAI speech-to-speech reasoning. We also explored the participants' preferences for different robot embodiments and their perceptions of robots' potential use in educational settings. Due to ethical considerations and lab limitations, the study could not be conducted with children, so we included adults instead.

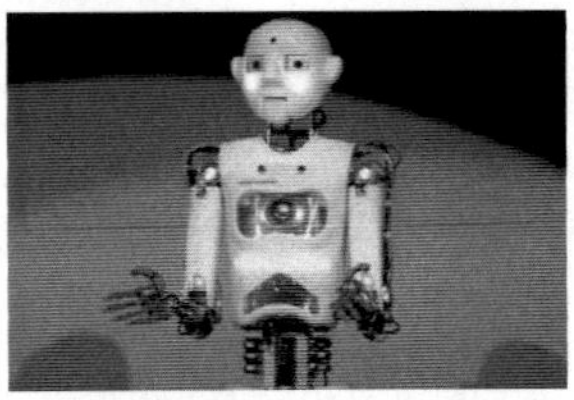

Figure 1. Screenshot from the video of RoboThespian

Figure 2. Screenshot from the video of OpenAI's Figure robot

Total 25 participants took part for Godspeed Questionnaire Series (GQS) survey and embodiment ranking. Participants age range include 18-35. All participants have been using technologies frequently. Results revealed an intriguing insight, that we have used in the design of our tabletop robot (Edbot). Embodiment Ranking. Participants were tasked with ranking various robot embodiments solely based on aesthetics. The options encompassed a range of choices including humanoid, machine-like, animal-like, hybrid, and more.

ID	Robot
A	Zenbo
B	RoboThespian
C	Paro
D	Pepper
E	Miro-E
F	Figure 01
G	Mesmer
H	Aibo
I	Ameca

Figure 3. Robot embodiment ranking task

The expectations individuals hold regarding the functionalities of a social robot are greatly influenced by its physical form (Mahdi et al., 2022). Robot A (Zenbo) emerged as the top choice in terms of accepting embodiment, with participants appreciating its "cute" appearance and the fact that it didn't attempt to mimic human features. On the other hand, Robot G (Mesmer) ranked the lowest, with 42% of participants ranking it as least favourite, with participants expressing discomfort and commenting on how the attempt at mimicking humans too closely contributed to its unsettling nature. It was intriguing to note that RoboThespian ended up second to last in the rankings, perceived less popular.

Godspeed Questionnaire. The Godspeed Questionnaire Series (GQS) is a tool used to assess how users perceive their interactions with both robots and humans (Weiss & Bartneck, 2015). GQS was used to measure human perceptions of robots. It evaluates five key dimensions: anthropomorphism, animacy, likeability, perceived intelligence, and perceived safety. Participants were shown a recently released video featuring OpenAI and Figure's social robot, referred to as Figure 01 (Figure, 2024). The video, played at speed 1.0x, depicted Figure 01 interacting with a human and demonstrating speech-to-speech reasoning capabilities. Participants then completed the Godspeed ranking survey, rating the robot across the five categories using a 1-5 scale. The results revealed overall score: anthropomorphism (2.51), animacy (2.91), likeability (3.51), perceived intelligence (2.91), and perceived safety (2.72). The Results from embodiment ranking and godspeed survey led to the redesign of a tabletop-sized social educational robot, shown in Figures 4 & 5. Participants preferred a non-humanoid, machine-like appearance, finding it more approachable and less unsettling than humanoid designs.

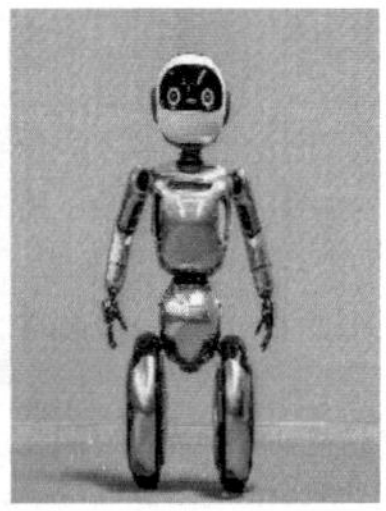

Figure 4 & 5. Edbot design for language and collaborative learning at Primary School

There are some limitations of this small-scale project, including sample size, and methods used, in which for the future of this research we are aiming to extend our sample size including primary school children and carry out further qualitative data collection, including contextual interview. From the results of this case study, we would like to devise the following guidelines:

- Design robots with a non-humanoid, machine-like appearance.
- Create user experiences and HRI that are engaging, safe, transparent and responsive. Incorporate multilingual conversational platforms, which have been highly praised.
- Design robots specifically to support collaborative learning and language development to encourage teamwork and enhance language skills through engaging activities and conversations.
- Incorporate adaptive personalise educational experiences based on individual student needs.

2.2 Case study II: Educational Robot for Work-based and Collaborative Learning - EduFaç

In the second case study, we aimed to explore and develop the potential of humanoid robots for work-based learning in the architecture and façade engineering domain to collaborate with engineers about training tasks, especially the hazards. We launched EduFaç, a robot specially created to aid team learning efforts and boost safety measures in demanding task scenarios. The motivation for this study is drawn from our research funding and we aspire to develop interdisciplinary projects that bring expertise from multiple disciplines. Figure 3 demonstrates our Robotic lab, using our RoboThespian, and our study participants interacting with the user interface kiosk-style screen. We have used the contextual interview method to collect data and to gather insights from architects and facades. Contextual interviews were conducted with 18 adult participants in the 20-55 age range, including architects, façade engineers and educators. We started our session with participants watching the video of RoboThespian features and interacting with its functionalities to get some insights into how humanoid robots look, feel, and communicate. Then, we interviewed them, asking semi-structured questions to investigate how they perceived the humanoid robots as educational technology, how they assessed their interactions with a humanoid robot, and how humanoid robots should be designed to be acceptable, helpful, and usable to use. The results from the interview helped us to inform the redesign for RoboThespian for Façade engineering with tools embedded within humanoid ideate the development of an educational robot for the Façade engineering field, EduFac robot hand depicted in Figure 6.

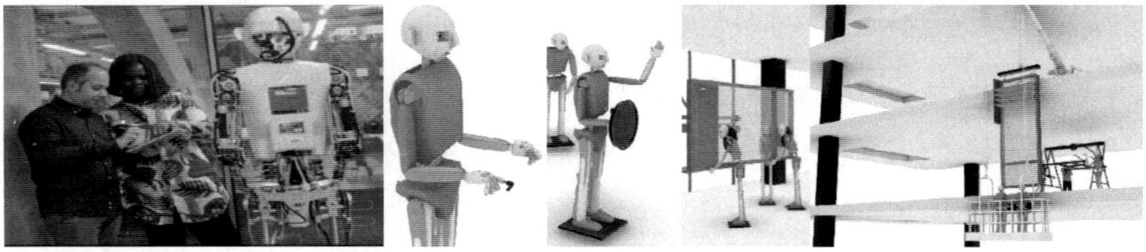

Figure 6. RoboThespian interacts with architectural and façade engineers and redesigns the robot (all the 3D models are generated in person with 3D Rhinoceros software)

From the results of our case study, we have devised the following guidelines:

- Design robots as machine-like assistants with complete human control, avoiding human-like appearances.
- Incorporate interactive, adaptive features to enhance collaborative learning.
- Create robots as mentors and trainers for high-risk tasks.
- Focus on task-specific cognition, avoiding full autonomy.
- Ensure precision, safety and responsiveness in HRI.
- Foster social collaboration and educational mentoring.

3. CONCLUSION AND FURTHER WORK

In this paper, we have presented a small-scale project that aimed to review the potential of humanoid robots for collaborative learning. We discussed two case studies (Edbot and EduFac) that tested a humanoid robot (RoboThespian) and provided design guidelines for humanoid robots to support collaborative learning, contributing to Human-Centred AI guidelines. These case studies further highlight the versatility and potential of social robots in educational settings. From primary school education to work-based learning, robots have been perceived as acceptable tools for enhancing collaborative experiences and fostering communication. Our participants viewed the robots as auxiliary machines, similar to mobile devices or home assistants, and did not prefer humanoid embodiments to resemble humans. These findings suggest that, with a robust and thoughtful analysis of human needs and an understanding of human-centred principles for designing AI and robotics, social robots can address diverse human needs, facilitate collaboration, and provide valuable support.

In our study, we also reviewed several methodological approaches that have been used to test, evaluate, and design robotic solutions. From the insights we gathered from the literature and our own studies, employing multiple methods such as Embodiment Ranking, the Godspeed Survey, and contextual interviews, we believe there is a gap in the literature for a methodological framework for human-centred AI and robotic design, particularly in educational domain. We aim to further our investigation in this field and contribute towards developing a novel methodological framework for human-centred AI and human-robot interaction. This framework will ensure that AI is integrated in ways that prioritise human needs and provide functionalities that support and enhance human cognition, collaboration, and strengths, rather than replacing humans.

REFERENCES

Alenljung, B., Lindblom, J., Andreasson, R. & Ziemke, T. (2017). User experience in social human-robot interaction. *International journal of ambient computing and intelligence,* 8, 12-31.

Belpaeme, T., Kennedy, J., Ramachandran, A., Scassellati, B., & Tanaka, F. (2018). Social robots for education: A review. *Science Robotics*, 3(21), eaat5954.

Benedek and T. Miner. (2010). Measuring desirability: New methods for evaluating desirability in a usability lab setting. *Proceedings of UPA 2002 Conference*

Buchem, I., Backer, N. (2022). Humanoid Robots in higher education: An exploratory study on applying the NAO Robot as an educational Technology in Business studies in hybrid setting. *Proceedings of 16th International Technology, Education and Development Conference.*

Chen, Y.-L., Hsu, C.-C., Lin, C.-Y., Hsu, H.-H. Robot-Assisted Language Learning: Integrating Artificial Intelligence and Virtual Reality into English Tour Guide Practice. *Educ. Sci.* (2022), *12*, 437. https://doi.org/10.3390/educsci12070437

Corrales-Paredes, A., Sanz, D. O., Terrón-López, M. J. & Egido-García, V. (2023). User Experience Design for Social Robots: A Case Study in Integrating Embodiment. *Sensors (Basel),* 23.

Diehl, J. J., Schmitt, L. M., Villano, M., & Crowell, C. R. (2012). The clinical use of robots for individuals with Autism Spectrum Disorders: A critical review. *Research in Autism Spectrum Disorders*, 6(1), 249-262.

Fernaeus Y, Hakansson M, Jacobsson M, Ljungblad S (2010) How do you play with a robotic toy animal? a long-term study of pleo. In: Proceedings of the 9th international Conference on interaction Design and Children, pp 39–48

Figure. (2024). *Figure* [Online]. Available: https://www.figure.ai/ [Accessed 21st March 2024].

Georgieva-Tsaneva G, Andreeva A, Tsvetkova P, Lekova A, Simonska M, Stancheva-Popkostadinova V, Dimitrov G, Rasheva-Yordanova K, Kostadinova I. Exploring the Potential of Social Robots for Speech and Language Therapy: A Review and Analysis of Interactive Scenarios. *Machines*. 2023; 11(7):693. https://doi.org/10.3390/machines11070693

Letendre, , K. G. & Gray, R. (2024). Social robots in a project-based learning environment: Adolescent understanding of robot–human interactions. *Journal of Computer Assisted Learning,* 40, 192-204.

Mahdi, H., Akgun, S. A., Saleh, S. & Dautenhahnh, K. (2022). A survey on the design and evolution of social robots — Past, present and future. *Robotics and autonomous systems,* 156, 104193.

Mubin, O, Stevens, C.J., Shahid, S. and Al-Mahmud, A. A review of applicability of robot in education. Journal of Education and Learning. DOI:10.2316/Journal.209.2013.1.209-0015

Obaid, M., Barendregt, W., Alves-Oliveira, P., & Paiva, A. (2016). Enhancing physical education with social robots. *International Journal of Social Robotics*, 8(2), 225-235.

Özkan, S. B. & Toz, M. (2022). A review study on the investigation of the effects of using robots in education on metacognitive behaviors. *Computer applications in engineering education,* 30, 1277-1288.

Steinke, G., LaBrie, R.C. and Sarkar, S. (2022). Recommendation for Continuous Ethical Analysis of AI Algorithms. *ACM Digital Library*. Available at: https://dx.doi.org/10.1145/3528580.3532996.

Tanaka, F., Cicourel, A., & Movellan, J. R. (2015). Socialization between toddlers and robots at an early childhood education center. *Proceedings of the National Academy of Sciences*, 104(46), 17954-17958

Tsiourti C, Pillinger A, Weiss A. (2020). Was vector a companion during shutdown? Insights from an ethnographic study in austria. In: Proceedings of the 8th International Conference on Human-Agent Interaction, HAI '20 Association for Computing Machinery, New York, USA, p 269–271. https://doi.org/10.1145/3406499.3418767

Verner, M. I., Polishuk, A. & Krayner, N. (2016). Science Class with RoboThespian: Using a Robot Teacher to Make Science Fun and Engage Students. *IEEE Robotics & Automation Magazine,* 23, 74-80.

Weiss, A. & Bartneck, C. (2015). Meta analysis of the usage of the Godspeed Questionnaire . IEEE International Symposium on Robot and Human Interactive Communication (RO-MAN) pp. 381-388. 10.1109/ROMAN.2015.7333568

Weiss, A., Spiel, K. Robots beyond Science Fiction: mutual learning in human–robot interaction on the way to participatory approaches. *AI & Soc* 37, 501–515 (2022). https://doi.org/10.1007/s00146-021-01209-w

Zöllick, J. C., Rössle, S., Kluy, L., Kuhlmey, A. & Blüher, S. (2022). [Potentials and challenges of social robots in relationships with older people: a rapid review of current debates]. *Z Gerontol Geriatr,* 55, 298-304.

HOW CAN GENERATIVE AI BE ADAPTED FOR LEARNING CONTEXT SUPPORT IN CONTEXTUAL VOCABULARY ACQUISITION?

Mohammad Nehal Hasnine[1], Mirai Yamada[1] and Gökhan Akçapınar[2]
[1]Research Center for Computing and Multimedia Studies, Hosei University, Japan
[2]Department of Computer Education and Instructional Technology, Hacettepe University, Turkey

ABSTRACT

Learning contexts play a crucial role in the acquisition of new vocabulary and its use in other contexts. Language learners use contextual clues, such as relevant expressions, small sentences, multimedia annotations, or images, to keep a learning context in memory. However, contextualizing vocabulary is exceedingly challenging even with multimedia contents, as learning contexts are very personal and involve learners making personal connections to the vocabulary. This paper explores how Generative Artificial Intelligence (GenAI) can foster learning context support for foreign language learners within multimedia-aided language learning frameworks. This paper introduces a new approach and a custom version of ChatGPT, Wordhyve-Glc, to assist language learners in constructing learning contexts for learning new vocabulary. Wordhyve-Glc also generates an image representing the learning context to be used as a contextual clue to memorize the learning context. Wordhyve-Glc will be integrated with Wordhyve, a multimedia-supported vocabulary learning app on Google Play, to foster contextual vocabulary acquisition.

KEYWORDS

AI-Assisted Vocabulary Learning, Contextual Vocabulary Acquisition, Generative AI, Image Generation, Sentence Construction and Error Correction

1. INTRODUCTION

Vocabulary acquisition is the key to foreign language learning. With a limited vocabulary, one could stop conversing or code-mixing while talking with others. Lack of insufficient vocabulary could be an obstacle for learners of any age.

Contextual vocabulary acquisition and contextualizing vocabulary are dynamic sub-fields of second or foreign language learning. Contextualizing vocabulary refers to how a learner infers the meaning of an unfamiliar word within a context or a sentence by using clues obtained from adjacent words. While contextual vocabulary acquisition is defined as deliberate acquisition of meaning for a word in a text by reasoning from textual clues and prior knowledge, including language knowledge and hypotheses developed from prior encounters with the word, but without external sources of help such as dictionaries or people (Rapaport, 2003). One example of contextual vocabulary acquisition is that a learner could take a self-described memo or draw a picture of something related to a word he/she encountered to help him/her remember the word. Hence, learning context is the key to contextualizing a vocabulary or contextual vocabulary acquisition. Nonetheless, the term 'context' could create confusion, as its meaning could vary depending on when and how it is used.

Vocabulary learning could be contextualized with sentence construction support. Contextual clues or associated words are essential for a learner to construct a sentence. In addition, an image to represent the word would help the learner to remember the context. Therefore, in this work, we aim to develop a learning system that could provide contextual vocabulary acquisition by providing sentence construction support, error detection in learner-described sentences, summarizing the errors a learner often makes, and image generation to describe a context. We leveraged the power of generative artificial intelligence (Generative AI) to accomplish the research objectives. Generative AI is an artificial intelligence technology that has shown great promise in human-like text and image generation. It has shown a significant impact in educational research but has yet to be explored in complex research, such as personalized learning context generation in foreign vocabulary acquisition.

The research questions are: (RQ1) Can learning effects be obtained by using generative AI, image-generative AI, and learning logs to recommend images and learning contexts that are differently recognized for each learner's nationality? (RQ2) Do similarities and differences in images and learning contexts created by generative AI, deep learning, or data-driven approaches affect learning outcomes for each learner? (RQ3) Can generative AI and image-generative AI be used to generate images and learning contexts appropriate for learning logs such as abstract nouns and adjectives? and (RQ4) Are the learning contexts recommended according to the learner's learning situation appropriate for the learner in terms of vocabulary level and content?

2. RELATED WORKS

In recent years, many chatbots and intelligent pedagogical agents are developed using generative artificial intelligence. @llegra is a chatbot developed by Oliver Bendel's team at FHNW University of Applied Sciences and Arts Northwestern Switzerland (Bendel & Jabou, 2024). It can process and output text and has voice output by which users can communicate in the Rhaeto-Romanic idiom, Vallader. They used GPT-3 and GPT-4 to build @llegra. Another study by the same team developed three custom GPTs namely Digital Learning Facilitator, Digital Learning Coach and Digital Learning Mentor for self-regulated learning in the corporate educational context (Hauske & Bendel, 2024). The first GPT, Digital Learning Facilitator can reply to learners' questions and correct misunderstandings. It can also work with learners in a collaborative dialogue to con-struct knowledge and improve comprehension and retention. The second GPT, Digital Learning Coach can enhance learners' metacognition skills by assisting in setting goals and effective strategies. The third GPT, Digital Learning Mentor helps in boosting learners' motivation. It provides constant feedback and acknowledges when learners accomplish something.

By now, Generative AI has not just been used for research-based applications. It has been used in building university-wide frameworks. One example is University of Michigan. At University of Michigan, a custom suite of generative AI tools to their staffs, faculties and students (https://genai.umich.edu) is developed. University of Michigan uses its generative AI-powered too U-M Maizey for multimedia contents generation and teacher assistant in the class.

The lead author and his rotating teams have been researching on vocabulary learning in mobile learning, ubiquitous learning and seamless learning context. We developed Wordhyve (Hasnine et al., 2023; Hasnine & Wu, 2021), a vocabulary learning app and released it on Google play in 2023. This app could be downloaded from Google play for free. Wordhyve uses various multimedia annotations such as text, audio and images in supporting vocabulary acquisition. The app can generate Smartly-generated Learning Contexts (SLC) to support learning contexts. However, the app has certain limitations. First, Wordhyve can generate Smartly-generated Learning Contexts (SLC) only if a learning log is created and supported by a picture. The app is not able to generate Smartly-generated Learning Contexts (SLC) without a picture. Second, there is a lack of support for sentence construction and error detection in Wordhyve. Third, it has limitations in comprehension and communication by allowing a learner to infer the meaning of unfamiliar words through contextual clues. Therefore, this work aims to address those problems with the help of generative AI, as this sophisticated technology can personalize context. In addition, generative AI-enabled vocabulary learning could foster learners' interests, generate learning content tuned to their interests and positively affect their learning motivations.

3. GENERATIVE AI TO SUPPORT CONTEXTUAL VOCABULARY ACQUISITION

In this paper, we developed a new approach and a custom version of ChatGPT called Wordhyve-Glc to explore generative AI to support the contextualization of vocabulary learning. In this section, we discuss the method first (in 3.1). Next, in 3.2, we provide a guideline on the GPT configuration of Wordhyve-Glc. Finally, in 3.3, we discuss how Wordhyve-Glc supports foreign language learners in learning vocabulary.

3.1 Method

Our proposed method to adapt Generative AI in contextualizing vocabulary acquisition is as follows:

1. The GPT of Wordhyve-Glc recommends multiple words in the target language.
2. Next, it lets the learner to choose one out of the given options.
3. Next, the model suggests three keywords associated to the vocabulary chosen by the learner.
4. Next, the learner is asked to construct sentences using those keywords to describe a context.
5. Once the sentence(s) is constructed, the model's AI checks whether there are any errors in the sentence(s) constructed by the learner.
6. Next, it corrects any errors found in the sentence.
7. Next, the model's AI provides the correct form of the sentence constructed by the learner.
8. Next, it points out the kind of errors (for example, grammatical errors) being made by the learner.
9. Lastly, the AI of the model generates an image describe the context. This generated image is named as, Context-specific Appropriate Image (CAI).

3.2 GPT Configuration

Wordhyve-Glc is created using OpenAI's GPT Builder (http://openai.com). Our GPT could be configured with prompt engineering by letting the GPT what the user expects. One example is (taken from the database): "I am teaching in Japanese university; and I need to teach courses in Japanese language. I know basic Japanese as I have acquired JLPT (Japanese Language Proficiency Test) N3 in 2018. Since then, I have not been practicing Japanese frequently. Sometimes I read Kanji books, mostly in the evening before going to bed. My weakness in language is reading and writing. To teach in Japanese, I need to learn more complex words than I know. I want to improve my Japanese vocabulary skills so that I can teach Computer Science-related course in Japanese language. I also want to learn vocabulary that are frequently used by Japanese students when they ask questions to the teacher". In addition, the user could tell the GPT on their demographic information. For example: Nationality: Bangladesh, Age: 38, Gender: Male, Native: Bengali, Target language: Japanese, Target language's level: Intermediate level of Japanese, and Profession: Faculty.

3.3 Vocabulary Acquisition using Wordhyve-Glc System

Wordhyve-Glc's target users are university students learning foreign languages. However, this application could be used by learners of any age, starting from junior high school.

In Wordhyve-Glc, the learning process begins with a screen showing learners different types of vocabulary. It provides direct instructions, shows the options, and offers a range of resources for further exploration. For the first-time user, the screen provides consistent guidance and fosters independence. Based on a learner's prior experiences with the target language, learning motivation, and expectations, Wordhyve-Glc suggests 5 words. Then, the learner chooses a word to learn. Next, Wordhyve-Glc recommends three keywords/words by which the learner could describe a context synonymously and construct sentence(s). Then, it checks the errors in the learner-constructed sentence(s), points out the type of errors made, such as grammatical errors, spelling mistakes, etc., and summarizes their errors. It also corrects the sentence. Finally, Wordhyve-Glc generates an image to describe the learning context. Figure 1 provides the user interfaces of the Wordhyve-Glc.

4. DISCUSSION

Learning vocabulary in context, or contextual vocabulary learning, is a popular strategy for improving the vocabulary of a foreign language. This strategy helps in improving reading skills and how much a learner understands by learning vocabulary in context. Therefore, computer-assisted, mobile-assisted and multimedia supported environments could support contextual vocabulary learning. In these environments, contextual clues, including examples, contrast, and a clue from an associated sentence, are often provided to the learners.

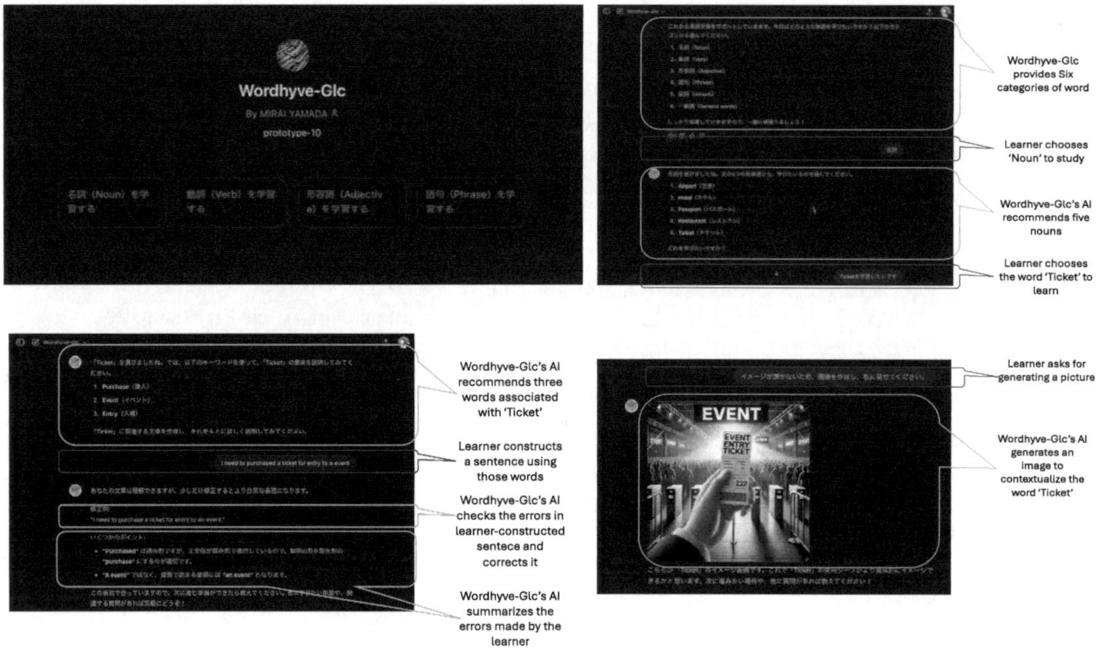

Figure 1. Wordhyve-Glc. (https://bit.ly/wordhyve)

However, it is difficult to automatically generate the learning context from the learner's contextual factors (such as situation and context). Using a large-scale language model (such as Meta's Llama-2) could better understand and analyze a learner's learning situation, including knowledge level, emotion, interaction information, etc.

In this paper, we introduce a GPT-enabled vocabulary acquisition system called Wordhyve-Glc that uses Generative AI to understand learners' expectations. Wordhyve-Glc can support a learner by providing contextual clues, sentence construction, error detection, and image generation.

ACKNOWLEDGEMENT

This work was supported by JSPS Grant-in-Aid for Early-Career Scientists Grant Number 24K16766.

REFERENCES

Bendel, O., & Jabou, D. (2024). @llegra: A chatbot for Vallader. International Journal of Information Technology, 16(4), 2035–2045. https://doi.org/10.1007/s41870-024-01779-0

Hasnine, M. N., & Wu, J. (2021). Wordhyve: A context-aware language learning app for vocabulary enhancement through images and learning contexts. Procedia Computer Science, 192, 3432–3439. https://doi.org/10.1016/j.procs.2021.09.116

Hasnine, M. N., Wu, J., & Ueda, H. (2023). Wordhyve: A MALL Innovation to Support Incidental Vocabulary Learning. In C. Stephanidis, M. Antona, S. Ntoa, & G. Salvendy (Eds.), HCI International 2023 Posters (pp. 246–250). Springer Nature Switzerland. https://doi.org/10.1007/978-3-031-35998-9_34

Hauske, S., & Bendel, O. (2024). How Can GenAI Foster Well-being in Self-regulated Learning? Proceedings of the AAAI Symposium Series, 3(1), 354–361. https://ojs.aaai.org/index.php/AAAI-SS/article/view/31234

Rapaport, W. J. (2003). What is the Context for Contextual Vocabulary Acquisition? Proceedings of the 4th Joint International Conference on Cognitive Science/7th Australasian Society for Cognitive Science Conference, 2, 547–552.

SELF-ASSESSMENT OF DIGITAL LITERACY-COURSES WITH PUPILS. INTERIM PROJECT REPORT *TEACHING-LEARNING-HUB: DIGITAL HISTORY*

Sophie-Luisa Hopf
Friedrich-Schiller-Universität Jena, Fürstengraben 1, 07743 Jena, Germany

ABSTRACT

According to the European DigComp framework, digital literacy is one of the eight competencies of lifelong learning and is therefore essential for navigating our increasingly digitalised society. In order to promote young people's digital skills outside the curriculum, numerous labs for school pupils have been established in Germany, most of which are based in the STEM subjects. In addition, such programmes often focus on university research topics and have little connection to the lifeworld and interests of the pupils.

The 'Teaching-Learning Hub: Digital History' project responds to the resulting gap in the promotion of digital skills among pupils in the context of humanities disciplines (especially digital humanities and digital cultural heritage). As part of the project, students are trained as tutors to run self-designed courses on digital history education with pupils. The aim of these courses is to strengthen the digital skills of pupils, particularly in dealing with historical topics such as local historical events and personalities. The focus of the teaching is on the ability to search for, process and present information.

The extent to which this goal has been achieved should be assessed with the help of partially standardised initial and final surveys. The results of the surveys should be used by the students to evaluate their courses on the one hand, and on the other hand provide points of reference for reflection and further development of the entire project. In addition, the results of the initial surveys should be used by the student tutors to check whether the pupils have the media and digital skills required for the course. So far, a total of 43 participants have been surveyed in each three courses of the first (2022/2023) and the second cohort (2023/2024).

Due to the individual preparation of the surveys, the autonomous realisation of these by the student tutors and the varying settings of the different courses, unforeseen difficulties appeared during and after the surveys, that made them hardly useful. To finally evaluate the courses' goal to raise the level of the pupils' media literacy, the surveys need to be more systematized.

This contribution to CELDA '24 uses the results of the "Learning history with Instagram" course as an example to reflect on the method of surveying pupils in hardly controllable survey settings. This article aims to increase the accuracy and informative value of the surveys so that they can be better compared in the overall evaluation of the project.

KEYWORDS

Self-Assessment, Surveys, Digital Literacy, Education, Digital History, Teaching

1. INTRODUCTION

The 2016 report by the German Kultusministerkonferenz states that digitalization in German schools also requires a redesign of teaching and learning processes (KMK, 2016). To promote this development for prospective teachers at the Friedrich-Schiller-University Jena, the project *Teaching-Learning-Hub: Digital History* was launched in 2022. The aim is to train students to design their own teaching concepts for digital history education and implement them with pupils. To this end, a block seminar with self-study units and individual coaching sessions has already been held with two cohorts, enabling students to design course concepts for digital history education and test it with pupils (Münster, 2023). The *Junior Professorship Digital Humanities* cooperates with cultural institutions such as schools, museums and youth centres. As of June 2024, two seminars have been held with students and then six courses with pupils.

During the course of the project, self-evaluation was an important part of quality assurance on the part of the project staff and student tutors. Not only were the students surveyed at the end of the block seminars, but surveys were also carried out with the pupils at the beginning and end of the student courses.

Feedback in the sense of self-assessment was obtained at each stage of the project, enabling both the project staff and the students to evaluate and further develop their teaching activities. The assessment of the 'Learning history with Instagram' course is presented below as a practical example for the latter.

2. METHOD

The 'Learning history with Instagram' course was held from January to April 2024 in cooperation with a community school in Jena. The participating pupils were to learn how to present historical figures in a short text they had researched themselves and to prepare an Instagram post from it with an AI-generated image. A 60-minute course was held every Tuesday. Ten pupils aged ten and eleven from grades five and six took part in the course and the surveys to test their digital literacy.

According to the European DigComp framework, digital literacy is understood as the ability to deal with digital media in a critical and goal-oriented manner (Ferrari, 2013). As media skills, such as text comprehension or source criticism, are prerequisites for digital literacy (Brandhofer & Wiesner, 2018), both areas must be covered in the surveys.

2.1 Design and Approach

The media and digital literacy surveys were designed in the sense of evaluation research. This is defined by Uwe Flick as a 'special sub-area of empirical research', which deals with the evaluation of the effectiveness of intervention programmes and other teaching-learning settings. The question is 'to what extent and with what effort goals (of an intervention, measure, person ...) are achieved and what undesirable side effects occur'. According to Flick, a distinction should be made between external evaluation and self-evaluation (Flick 2014). The evaluation of the results of the surveys presented here should enable the latter in a double sense; the self-evaluation of the courses created by the students and the self-evaluation of the project concept by the project staff.

In the first cohort of courses (2023), the project concept envisaged that the students would design, conduct and evaluate their own surveys for their courses – an initial survey for the beginning and a final survey for the end of the course. However, to make the analysis of the collected data useful not only for the students' self-reflection, but also for the evaluation of the overall project result, the surveys for the second cohort (2024) were designed by the project team in consultation with the students. This resulted in the following research interests:

Table 1.

Survey Level	Goal	
Initial Survey How high is the level of digital literacy of the pupils in the course?	1	Determination of needs for the detailed design of the courses on the part of the students
	2	General evaluation of the digital competencies of pupils of different ages (from different courses)
Initial Survey vs. Final Survey Has the level of the students' digital literacy changed because of our courses?	3	Feedback for students to reflect on their courses
	4	Checking the project objective 1 'digital literacy'

2.2 Instruments

For all courses of the Teaching-Learning-Hub, the surveys needed to be planned as quantitative questionnaires because of a small time-window during the courses. Only in the case of the 'Learning history with Instagram' course, the results of the questionnaires could be supplemented by observations and short conversations with the pupils, as a project employee was present in the course to support the tutor. This is why the results of the courses' surveys are used as example here to describe the possibilities and obstacles of digital literacy surveys with pupils. The mixture of quantitative and qualitative research methods allows to somewhat compensate the small time-window as well as the small sample size, which could not be selected at random (Lamnek & Krell, 2016).

The first part of the questionnaire consists of six questions, which are used for all courses. The second part of the questionnaire was designed by the student tutors to align the questions with their course content. The same questions were used at both points in time to ensure comparability between the initial and final surveys. The design of the courses and thus also the question catalogue are based on the European DigComp framework (Ferrari 2013).

3. RESULTS

The results of the initial surveys of the "Learning history with Instagram" course had a considerable influence on the course design. Most of the assumed media and digital skills were not developed to the expected extent, which is why tasks had to be formulated in more detail and more time had to be scheduled for them. In the following, questions 4a, 4b, 6, 8a and 8b of the survey are used to illustrate the effects their results had on the course concept, whether they indicate that the students' digital skills were increased by the course and what potential sources of error occurred during surveying.

In the course concept, it was assumed that the pupils, because of their school research activities, were already familiar with secure websites where they could find valid information. In question 4a[1], four pupils even stated that they were familiar with reliable websites. These four pupils also gave free text answers to 4b[2], although one answer was 'no idea' and the other three named 'Google' as a safe website. However, as *google.com* is primarily a search engine and therefore hardly provides any information of its own, none of the free text answers given indicate that the pupils actually know and use safe websites.

The course concept responded to this blank space by naming children's search engines that were supposed to support the pupils in their research but were hardly used. Instead, almost all pupils worked with *wikipedia.de*, which is also reflected in the final survey. In the free text responses, four mentions of 'Wikipedia' were added. This website was presented by the student tutor as a semi-safe source of information, where the original sources should always be checked. However, as this could not be done in the course, it was apparently wrongly conveyed that Wikipedia itself should be categorized as a reliable source. The answer 'tiktok' is even more thought-provoking, as this platform should by no means be categorized as a secure website with reliable information. In general, it seems that the concept of 'safe internet source' is not familiar to the pupils.

Question 6[3] showed that the self-assessment of the students' word processing skills at the beginning of the course varied greatly. Only three of the students stated that they were very good or good at searching a text for important information, a further three rated themselves as mediocre and another three as bad. The observations revealed that the pupils were not able to filter the most relevant information from a larger text without specific instructions. Here, too, the concept had to be specified (e.g. by specifically naming the relevant aspects of the text). Fortunately, this specified exercise seemed to have given the pupils more confidence in processing texts, as in the final survey seven pupils already rated themselves as very good or good at searching a text for important information.

Finally, questions 8a[4] and 8b[5] were intended to test the pupils' knowledge of artificial intelligence (AI), as AI-generated images were also created in the course. In the initial survey, almost all pupils stated that they had already heard something about AI. Two of them wanted to know (very) much about it, seven students rated their knowledge of AI as average, and one student stated that they knew little about it. In the final survey, the results shifted into positive territory: a total of four pupils now stated that they knew (very) much about AI, while the remaining six pupils rated their knowledge as average. However, this self-assessment is

---

[1] *(4a) Do you know any websites that are safe and where you can find reliable information? [Yes] [No]*
[2] *(4b) If yes: Which ones? [free text answer]*
[3] *(6) How good are you at searching a text for important information? [Very good] [Good] [Mediocre] [Poor] [Rather poor]*
[4] *(8a) Have you ever heard of artificial intelligence (AI)? [Yes] [No]*
[5] *(8b) If yes: How much do you already know about artificial intelligence? [Very much] [A lot] [Moderately] [A little] [Very little]*

not seen by the researchers as a positive development, but rather as the fundamental problem with this type of survey. Since only one AI tool (*perchance.org*) was used in the course and only rudimentary information was provided about how it works, it cannot be assumed that any of the students actually know 'very much' about AI - at least according to the researchers' definition. It is possible that the students assessed their knowledge in comparison to their classmates. This also suggests once again that the students were generally overwhelmed with this form of self-assessment and not prepared to rate their knowledge and skills like they were asked to.

In general, observation of the course setting revealed that the students were not always serious when completing the survey. A lack of concentration (due to the course taking place on a Tuesday afternoon), a lack of consequences for inactivity (as the student tutor is not part of everyday school life) and a lack of understanding of the usefulness of scientific surveys for the purpose of teaching innovation were identified as three further factors that may have led to distortions in the survey results. In addition, the questionnaire itself may have led to comprehension difficulties for the students.

In the case of the 'Learning history with Instagram' course, it cannot be said with certainty whether the level of digital literacy of the participating pupils was actually increased. Not only was the survey possibly distorted by the factors assumed above. In addition, the lack of media skills (e.g. text processing) and the lack of digital skills (e.g. safe internet searching) meant that further digital skills were difficult to teach. The content should have been more closely aligned with the existing skills of the pupils and should also have been organized in more detail. The latter is also the case for the surveys.

4. CONCLUSION

In theory, self-assessment of courses with students is a way of checking the prerequisites and objectives of learning units and thus optimizing teaching and learning in the digital age. In practice, however, there are various obstacles that distort the results of self-assessment surveys.

On the one hand, the non-controllable research environment requires a high degree of flexibility on the part of the researchers, and on the other hand, it must be borne in mind that pupils are generally not used to the process of self-assessment and may not be familiar with concepts that appear in the surveys.

Furthermore, the optimum balance must be found between the time frame and scope of the surveys and the survey setting must be understood as a communication process. To do this, student tutors should make the purpose of the surveys clear to students, e.g. by explaining how they can benefit from the curriculum changes after the initial surveys or that they are part of a wider research context along with the other Teaching-Learning-Hub courses.

For further project runs, it would be advisable to conduct the initial survey on the pupils' level of digital and media skills *before* starting to plan the course, so that it can serve as a basis for the development of the content to be taught. Moreover, the questionnaire should be revised again and the survey setting should be more closely integrated into the preparation.

REFERENCES

Brandhofer, G. and Wiesner, C. (2018). Medienbildung im Kontext der Digitalisierung. Ein integratives Modell für digitale Kompetenzen. *Online Journal for Research and Education*, No. 10, pp. 1-15.

Ferrari, A. (2013). *DIGCOMP: A Framework for Developing and Understanding Digital Competence in Europe*. European Commission, Seville, Spain.

Flick, U. (2014). *Sozialforschung: Methoden und Anwendungen*. Rowohlt Taschenbuch Verlag, Reinbek near Hamburg, Germany.

KMK. (2016). *Bildung in der digitalen Welt. Strategie der Kultusministerkonferenz.* Beschluss der Kultusministerkonferenz vom 08.12.2016 in der Fassung vom 07.12.2017, kmk.org.

Lamnek, S. and Krell, C. (2016). *Qualitative Sozialforschung*, 6th, revised edition, Beltz Verlag, Weinheim, Germany.

Münster, S. et al. (2023). Digital History Education For Pupils. First Steps Towards a Teaching Learning Lab. *The International Archives of the Photogrammetry, Remote Sensing and Spatial Information Sciences*, Vol. XLVIII-M-2-2023, pp. 1105-1111.

TWO-EYED SEEING: VR LEARNING WITH INDIGENOUS RELEVANCE

Twylla Soosay and Stella George
School of Computing and Informaiton Systems, Faculty of Science and Technology, Athabasca University
1, University Drive, Athabasca, Canada

ABSTRACT

Indigenous knowledge sharing is a vital part of community connection and strength. As many Indigenous communities are rural and widespread, sharing of knowledge within the community is becoming more difficult. Work and life off-reserve is often busy, leaving little community time. Consideration of technologies such as augmented reality (AR) and virtual reality (VR) to provide a more immersive connection with community knowledge than simply reading a pdf or web content. Embedding resources made with AR/VR technology in the community can strengthen community ties and provide connection points for dispersed community members on their own schedules. A first goal in the creation of a virtual space for learning in the community of one of the researchers has been to utilize a 360-degree camera as a virtual learning tool for a project to sew a traditional ribbon skirt. This research takes the perspective of a learner using "etuaptmumk" or two-eyed seeing to learn with the influence of both western and Indigenous epistemologies. This ongoing investigation considers the suitability of VR technology for this task, and what building a virtual space and learning environment will involve.

KEYWORDS

Virtual-Reality (VR), Cultural Knowledge Sharing, Two-Eyed Seeing, Rural Community

1. INTRODUCTION

The needs of Indigenous communities are now being considered more fully through the actions of decolonization and reconciliation activities across the globe, including in Australia, Canada, New Zealand and the USA. No matter the location Indigenous knowledge sharing is a vital part of community connection and strength. As many Indigenous communities are rural and widespread, and paid work and essential services are far from reserve communities, sharing of knowledge within communities has become more difficult. One of the authors has lived off and on Indigenous land in Canada. Her perspective on the current levels of Indigenous knowledge sharing have led to her proposing a technologically supported community sharing approach. Through *two-eyed seeing*, access to Indigenous knowledge sharing and learning can be provided via a range of technologies that support current community needs (Bolduc-Simpson. 2020). Her overall intention to create a virtual classroom for curation and learning about cultural skills in her community is an investigation whether approach this can alleviate time-based issues and keep some levels of connection to cultural knowledge active in her community. This paper describes the first steps in this overall development: aim to determine the potential of virtual reality (VR) technologies as learning tools for cultural knowledge sharing.

2. DEVELOPING A VR LEARNING ENVIRONMENT WITH INDIGENOUS RELEVANCE

> *"The core concepts in Indigenous educational philosophies are land, relationalism, and holism. These ideas are present in nearly all of the varied Indigenous educational philosophies from across what is now Canada. In addition to these three concepts, the ideas*

of circularity in education and experiential education are two of the most prominent methods of Indigenous educational practice." (Arney, 2021)

The primary purpose of the overall study is to investigate whether virtual learning can be used effectively as an innovative tool in learning cultural skills. Findings of the project contribute to furthering understanding of potential methods for supporting cultural learning and sharing. This first stage investigation considers the suitability (acceptability and efficacy) of VR technology for the cultural skill of making a ribbon skirt. Cultural skills are traditionally communicated orally and by following by example, an experiential process that is relational, holistic and land based. Here, exploration focusses on the use of VR in the capture of cultural skill, relationally and holsistically. As an educational tool, VR provides an experiential learning opportunity that is not solely place based but is connected to a specific land and community. Results are also expected to set the direction for further research lines of enquiry in this underdeveloped field of study.

Research questions are posed as to (1) what is involved in building a virtual learning space for Indigenous cultural knowledge sharing when VR technologies are employed; (2) what are the pros and cons of a virtual environment for learning compared to combinations of written, video and in person instruction.

2.1 Approach and Methodology

The research project's philosophy is guided by the perspective of learners viewing with *two-eyed seeing*. In Cree "Etuaptmumk", *two-eyed seeing*, means the influence of both western and Indigenous epistemologies are present in the learning experience (Smalley, 2022). The concept of *two-eyed seeing*, was proposed in 2004 by Mi'kmaq Elder Albert Marshall (2018 and http://www.integrativescience.ca/Principles/TwoEyedSeeing/), drawing upon the strengths of each Western Scientific way to look at the world and an Indigenous way to look at the world (Bartlett et al 2012; Wright et al 2019). Virtual learning plays an important role in education and skills development, it is a way to decolonize the western-centric form (instructor-learner) of educating, as well as giving the learner a unique way to learn a new skill. Being able to learn a culturally significant skill such as ribbon skirt making from a *two-eyed seeing* approach is unique.

VR is known for increasing memory, and knowledge retention. It creates interactive exploration when teaching new concepts, improves critical thinking skills, and helps with engaging the learner with new material (Johnes, 2023). This engagement helps boost the interest of the learner, simulating new experiences through experiential learning. It has been proven to build emotional intelligence, awareness and understanding (ibid). During Cultural Week 2024 at Maskwacis Cultural College, a cultural skill of ribbon skirt making was scheduled. Ribbon skirts symbolize a sacred symbol of women and traditions that can be worn during ceremonies and other events that have meaning to the community (Ash, 2023). Ribbon skirts are also worn in the powwow either in jingle dress, fancy dress or traditional dress, or as other ceremonial dress (https://www.rcmp-grc.gc.ca/en/news/2024/further-information-the-rcmps-inclusion-the-ribbon-skirt-the-approved-ceremonial-dress#). More and more women are making and wearing the ribbon skirt because it makes them feel they are honoring their culture and traditions.

In addition to the instructor-learner approach already scheduled, a VR-learning approach was selected as an additional mechanism to communicate cultural knowledge sharing and learning. Being able to incorporate the *two-eyed seeing* approach, learning to see from ways of knowing using these eyes together for the combined benefit (Wright et al 2019). Using the Oculus rift headset is similar to *two-eyed seeing* because each sight is equal in every sense, but stronger together. The ribbon skirt creation (Saddleback, 2023) and instruction was revised, improved (Mitchie et al, 2019, 2023; Cook et al 2019; Garin, 2020; Shi 2020, Katona, 2021; Flynn & Frost 2021; Green et al, 2021; Lynch 2021; Farrell et al 2022; Indeed 2023) and then captured using a 360-degree Ricoh Theta camera which has two lenses. This provides the ability to shoot in all directions, up, down, left, right, front, and back. Each lens has wide-angle with a field of view over 180 degrees (Rodgers, 2023). Software converts the spherical image from the lens of this camera into an omnidirectional planar (or equirectangular) image. The image is like a world map from a globe, unwrapped and flattened (Rowell, 2019). The videos created were then edited (Levine, 2022) and made available for free use on YouTube.

YouTube has been hosting 360 footage since 2015, including coverage of Indigenous content, for example:

- Our Worlds is an app that is available on Apple, (PBS SoCal, 2023), it captures immersive VR videos with the intent on preserving Indigenous traditions;

- Immersive Link (2024a, 2024b), multiple cultural VR content from making a drum, making deer hoof rattles, to various traditional dances and cultural/medicine picking walks.
- A worldwide project that is incorporating VR technology to teach Nisga'a culture and language (Johnson, 2020).
- Indigenous Language via VR (McDonald, 2023)

Participants receive seated instruction and view the video from a first-person perspective through the VR headset (figure 1). One controller is needed to select the video which delivers a visual learning experience, using multisensory elements – visual, audial, tactile, and kinesthetic. Participants can view the interactive 360 video on a computer screen if necessary.

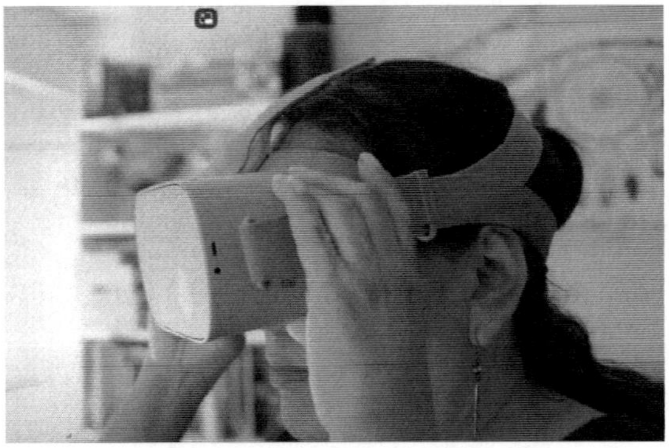

Figure 1. Wearing the VR headset

The Oculus Rift with two pairs of lenses its 1920x1080HD resolution but delivering 960x1080 display per eye, refresh rate of 60Hz and 100-degree horizontal field of view (Nield, 2016). Being able to use Head-Related Transfer Function (HRTF) technology, combined with the Rift's head tracking to create a true 3D audio spatialization, creating sounds in all directions (ibid). This immersive sound is used to include Cree drum and singing (cultural Cree songs from the Samson Cree Nation Pow-wow 2023 grand entry) to help immerse the learner into the environment further.This research is focused on the skills exploration aspects of cultural knowledge, incorporating not only the first-person perspective in the 360-degree video and sound, but also a focus to minimize the causes of VR sickness, a feeling of dizziness and/or nausea. Sickness can be reduced by limiting the field of view 180 degrees (Blue, 2021) and the introduction of multisensory use of sound (ibid). Additionally restriction of movement of the upper part of the body in short sessions are recommended. The full ribbon skirt creation instruction is available as four parts.

2.2 Participation

Participants were invited to be part of the study during cultural week at Maskwacis Cultural College in June 2024. Materials and instruction were provided for participants choice of written, instructional VR and/or in person instruction. There were no restrictions on the time to create the skirt. Unfortunately, the community college, which is a supporter of the project, was forced to close due to heavy rainfall collapsing the roof and exposing a mold problem. Classes at the college moved online, and the cultural week was cancelled. The in-person sewing moved into the community, within personal homes. Participants with good internet access could still view the VR video in the headset. To date, five participants have been recruited, more are sought.

A risk assessment was carried out to minimize the impact of VR sickness in the experimental phase of the project. A number of approaches were put in place and communicated to participants in advance of their VR participation. The video length is retricted to snippets between 2-5 minutes, the less time using the VR headset has shown to produce less VR sickness. Anyone experiencing VR sickness symtoms can stop headset use and work only with the video (no headset) or remove themselves from the study. We were concerned to build confidence and boost learner engagement through practice-centric visual learning experience/training. In time research will compare the outcomes of the learning approaches employed: (1) person to person, in front of class instruction; (2) recorded instruction via VR video created from a 360-degree camera showing the learner a first- person perspective, and (3) written only instructions on how to make a ribbon skirt.

Each participants completes a survey after their instruction. Contextual information regarding prior experiences of learning methods and preferences, was requested along with questions (Kovach, 2010) focused on:

- the quality of VR experience, visuals and soundscape connecting to relationalism and holistic nature of the instruction;
- any aspects of VR sickness or discomfort
- comparison of instructional methods
- the future of technology in learning for Indigenous communities

3. DISCUSSION AND CONCLUSIONS

In focusing on Indigenous adult learners this study integrates Equity, Diversity, and Inclusion (EDI) principles through several key approaches, ensuring the study is respectful, inclusive, and sensitive to the needs and perspectives of Indigenous adult learners.

- Cultural Sensitivity: It respects and incorporates Indigenous cultural practices, such as ribbon skirt making, to preserve and share cultural knowledge.
- Accessibility: Utilizes VR technology to overcome physical barriers, making cultural skill learning accessible regardless of location.
- Decolonization: Offers a non-Western-centric educational approach, empowering Indigenous learners to reclaim and celebrate their heritage.
- Diverse Representation: Ensures diversity within the sample by including participants from various Indigenous communities and backgrounds.
- Inclusive Methodology: Employs qualitative methods to capture the diverse experiences of Indigenous learners with VR instruction.
- Ethical Considerations: Prioritizes cultural sensitivity, respect for Indigenous knowledge, and participant confidentiality, with ongoing consultation with the Maskwacis community.

Sponsorship of the project by Maskwacis Cultural College was important in providing credibility of the study within the community and provided a base from which to recruit participants. Interest in the intent of the overall project demonstrates future thinking by the college about all forms of education for the community. The practical issues in the interactive experimentation part of this research were largely logistical. The community college closure and fragility of its infrastructure is not uncommon in rural and Indigenous communities. Although reliant on internet accessibility (which is also an issue in many communities) the availability of technological solutions to physical barriers can support community knowledge sharing.

The logistical issues faced by the research mean it is too early in the study to anlyse findings from the survey but we can indicate use of VR does appear to reduce distractions over traditional classroom instruction. When using a VR headset, distractions are minimized, allowing for a more focused learning experience. While an instructor provides their perspective and explanations, VR allows the learner to develop their own understanding and can be more engaging. Practical cultural skills such as sewing, drum and musical instrument making using written instructions alone can be ineffective. It is difficult to visualize the act of sewing from written instuction, whereas watching an instructor demonstrate or a youtube does provide more visual context. The VR's more immersive, first-person perspective, is one step further. The practicality of a watch-and-do synchronous approach is perhaps a limitation of this method over the use of video without headset, however, the nature of the initial place based learning inside a community can be one of observation before doing onself.

The study explores the potential of virtual reality (VR) technology for sharing Indigenous cultural knowledge, within a rural community. We position VR technology as acceptable for Indigenous community learning, the initial reception from the Maskwacis Cultural College appears to support this position. We also suggest it to be an enabler rather than a barrier to *two-eyed seeing*, again preliminary evidence indicates that technology has a place in communities with fragile instrastructure. Building a virtual learning space for Indigenous cultural knowledge sharing requires both digital infrastructure and community support to succeed.

The technological apsects of VR may be limited for learning by VR sickness for some participants, but the opportunity to dip-in and out of learning as the learner has opportunity is of value. It is too early in this ongoing study (due to logistical issues) to conclude pros and cons of a virtual environment for learning compared to combinations of written, video and in person instruction. There is no evidence to date that *two-eyed seeing* is not positively supported by a VR approach in an Indigenous community as proposed in the paper. The VR approach has the potential to enhance community connections and preserve cultural skills, such as ribbon skirt making, by creating a virtual classroom containing multisensory instruction on cultural skill development.

ACKNOWLEDGEMENT

The Maskwacis Cultural College, Elders and the Community provide permission and support for this research. Research was carried out under Athabasca University REB approval with participant informed consent. Our thanks go to the REB office for guidance. Thanks go to Athabasca University Graduate Student Research Fund for helping with equipment costs.

REFERENCES

Arney, N. (2021) Work-Integrated Learning and Indigenous Educational Philosophy: A Review of the Literature *Canadian Journal for New Scholars in Education* Vo12, No 2.

Ash, P. (2023). *History of the Ribbon Skirt.* Forsyth Independent Press. July 1, 2023.

https://www.independent-press.com/news/history-of-the-ribbon-skirt/article_3827a432-15ce-11ee-9f7c-4f3560741a48.html.

Bartlett, C. Marshall, M., & Marshall, A. (2012). Two-Eyed Seeing and other lessons learned within a co-learning journey of bringing together Indigenous and mainstream knowledges and ways of knowing. *Journal of Environmental Studies and Science*, 2(4), 331-340. http://doi.org/10.1007/s13412-012-0086-8

Blue. R. (2021). *How to stop VR sickness: the best ways to reduce VR motion sickness.* https://www.techradar.com/how-to/how-to-stop-vr-sickness-the-best-ways-to-reduce-vr-motion-sickness

Bolduc-Simpson, S., & Simpson, M. (2020, December 1). Social Places in Virtual Spaces: Creating a Social Learning Community in Online Courses. *Distance Learning,* 17(4), 83.

Cook, M., Lischer-Katz, Z., Hall, N., Hardesty, J., Johnson, J., McDonald, R., & Carlisle, T. (2019).

Challenges and Strategies for Educational Virtual Reality: Results of an Expert-led Forum on 3D/VR Technologies across Academic Institutions. *Information Technology and Libraries*, *38*(4), 25. https://doi.org/10.6017/ITAL.V38I4.11075

Elder Albert Marshall (2018) *Learning Together by Learning to Listen to Each Other.* https://www.edcan.ca/articles/learning-together-learning-listen/

Farrell, R., Cowan, P., Brown, M., Roulston, S., Taggart, S., Donlan, E., & Baldwin, M. (2022). Virtual Reality in Initial Teacher Education (VRITE): a reverse mentoring model of professional learning for learning leaders. *Irish Educational Studies*, 41(1), 245–256. https://doi.org/10.1080/03323315.2021.2021102

Flynn, C. and Frost, P. (2021). *Making VR a reality in the Classroom.* https://er.educause.edu/articles/2021/4/making-vr-a-reality-in-the-classroom

Garin, E. (2020). PDS and the Pandemic: Lessons Learned from Creating a Virtual Third Space. *School-University Partnerships*, 13(2), 77–81.

Greene, C. M., Broughan, J., Hanlon, A., Keane, S., Hanrahan, S., Kerr, S., & Rooney, B. (2021). Visual search in 3D: Effects of monoscopic and stereoscopic cues to depth on the validity of feature integration theory and perceptual load theory. *Frontiers in Psychology*, 12. https://doi.org/10.3389/fpsyg.2021.596511

Immersive Link (2024a). Reimagined education and training with the power of VR. https://immersivelink.ca/ Immersive Link (2024b). Making Deer Hoof Rattles. https://vimeo.com/916709089?share=copy

Indeed Editorial Team. *What Is Didactic Teaching?(Plus How It's Different From Pedagogy).* Indeed. (Jan 26, 2023) https://www.indeed.com/career-advice/career-development/didactic-teaching.

Johnes, S. (2023). *8 Impressive ways to Leverage Virtual Reality Technology in the classroom for Enhanced Learning Experiences.* https://scienceandliteracy.org/how-to-use-virtual-reality-in-the-classroom/?expand_article=1

Johnson, R. (2020). *Project to use virtual reality technology to teach Nisga'a culture and language.* https://www.cbc.ca/news/indigenous/nisga-a-vr-technology-language-culture-1.5846341

Katona, J., & Vezzetti, E. (2021). A Review of Human–Computer Interaction and Virtual Reality Research Fields in Cognitive InfoCommunications. *Applied Sciences* (2076-3417), 11(6), 2646. https://doi.org/10.3390/app11062646

Kovach, M. (2010). Conversation Method in Indigenous Research. *First Peoples Child & Family Review,* 5(1), 40–48. https://doi.org/https://doi.org/10.7202/1069060ar

Levine, J. (2022). *How to edit 360/VR Video in Premiere Pro CC 2017 (Monoscopic & Stereoscopic).* https://www.youtube.com/channel/UCtiKVxfHJx2VH9H5g5o-52A

Lynch, G. (2021). How to set up your room for VR. https://www.space.com/how-to-set-up-your-room-for-vr

McDonald, M. (2023). *Teaching and Learning an Indigenous Language in VR.* https://www.youtube.com/watch?v=OlgogmO7xJ4

Michie, M., Hogue, M. & Rioux, J.(2023) Two-Ways thinking and Two-Eyed Seeing as ways of implementing https://doi.org/10.1186/s43031-023-00084-3

Michie, M., Hogue, M. & Rioux, J. The Application of Both-Ways and Two-Eyed Seeing Pedagogy: Reflections on Engaging and Teaching Science to Post-secondary Indigenous Students. *Res Sci Educ* 48, 1205–1220 (2018). https://doi.org/10.1007/s11165-018-9775-y

Nield, D. (2016). *How Oculus Rift works: Everything you need to know about the VR sensation.* https://www.wareable.com/vr/how-oculus-rift-works

PBS SoCal. (2023). *This VR Project is Preserving Indigenous Traditions* | KCET. https://www.youtube.com/watch?v=sTvMkSEHUFI

Rodgers, S. (2023). *How does a 360 degree camera work? RICOH THETA and the equirectangular image format.* https://blog.ricoh360.com/en/8409

Rowell, M. (2019). *VR Video Formats Explained.* https://360labs.net/blog/vr-video-formats-explained

Royeyko, O. (2022) Why and How to Add AR/VR Experiences to Your LMS. https://agentestudio.com/blog/add-vr-ar-experiences-lms

Saddleback, M. (2023). Teachings making of the ribbon skirt – Interview/Instruction. Personal Communication.

Shi, H., & Niu, D. (2020). Application Research of Virtual Reality Technology in Ocean Environmental Art Design. *Journal of Coastal Research*, 104, 296–301. https://doi.org/10.2112/JCR-SI104-054.1

Smalley, S. (2022). *Expanding Perspectives: A Journey with Two-Eyed Seeing.*

VR Direct. (2021). VRdirect – The Platform. https://www.vrdirect.com/lp/get-started/

Wright, A. L., C. Gabel, M. Ballantyne, S. M. Jack, and O. Wahoush (2019) "Using Two-Eyed Seeing in Research With Indigenous People: An Integrative Review." International Journal of Qualitative Methods 18 (January 1, 2019): 1609406919869695. https://doi.org/10.1177/1609406919869695.

SENSORY PREREQUISITES FOR DIGITAL ENCOUNTERS: STATISTICAL LEARNING AND LANGUAGE OUTCOMES IN NORWEGIAN PRESCHOOLERS

Giulia Zantonello, Valentin Vulchanov and Mila Dimitrova Vulchanova
Language Acquisition and Language Processing Lab, Department of Language and Literature, Norwegian University of Science and Technology (NTNU), Trondheim, Norway

ABSTRACT

With the growing exposure to digital technology as a source of language input, it has become essential to gain a deeper understanding of the mechanisms that support learning in this modern context. Statistical learning (SL) is a sensory processing mechanism believed to play a significant role in various aspects of language acquisition. Differences in children's language development are thought to partly stem from variances in their ability to extract statistical information from the environment. The current study first aims to contribute new insights into the role of SL in language development across different domains. Behavioural and electroencephalography (EEG) measures were collected from 32 typically developing Norwegian preschoolers. Although the research is ongoing, the anticipated outcomes are expected to enhance the understanding of the processes underlying children's language processing. This knowledge could subsequently inform applied research, particularly in the development of digital educational tools and tailored interventions to better support children's language acquisition in digital contexts.

KEYWORDS

Statistical Learning, Language Development, Auditory Modality, Preschoolers, Digital Technology

1. INTRODUCTION

Given the increasing role of digital technology as a primary source of language input, understanding the complex processes involved in learning and acquisition within the digital landscape has become a priority. Insights into these mechanisms are expected to drive the development of innovative educational technologies tailored to individual learning styles and needs, fostering more effective language acquisition strategies.

Within this framework, statistical learning (SL), an intrinsic mechanism for detecting regularities in the environment, is believed to contribute to various aspects of language acquisition and development (Saffran et al., 1996b; Romberg & Saffran, 2010). Individual differences in the ability to extract statistical information may partly explain variability in language development (Batterink & Paller, 2017; Abreu et al., 2023). Observed across different age groups (Saffran et al., 1996a; Raviv & Arnon, 2018), SL has been described as both a broad cognitive mechanism operating across sensory modalities and domains, as well as input- or modality-specific (Saffran & Kirkham, 2018).

SL in the language domain is typically assessed through exposure to an artificial language, followed by implicit (e.g., eye movements, reaction times) or explicit post-exposure learning measures (e.g., forced-choice tasks, target detection, serial recall). Studies investigating SL and language competence have yielded mixed results, showing both positive correlations and null findings (Sjuls et al., 2023). Recently, Batterink and Paller (2017) proposed using an entrainment EEG-based measure, Inter-Trial Phase Coherence (ITPC), to monitor "online" the "word-identification" component of SL. This measure tracks neural activity alignment to the input phase, reflecting a segmentation process from syllable to word level through exposure. However, the role of neural entrainment as a pure assessment of SL learning remains debated (Sjuls et al., 2023).

The present study thus aims to first deepen our understanding of the functioning of statistical sensory processing and its potential links with language development by collecting combined behavioural and

EEG-based SL measurements from a group of Norwegian preschoolers, an age range particularly underrepresented in the literature. This research seeks to unravel the extent to which children's language skills across various domains are associated with SL abilities in the auditory modality and if these change with age. We anticipate observing correlations between auditory SL skills and preschoolers' lexical, phonological, morphological, or syntactic skills. Furthermore, this study aims to use the gathered evidence to form hypotheses and predictions about the growing impact of digital technology on language development and the consequences this ecology might have on child development. Gaining insights into these processing mechanisms and the potential associations with language domains could inform the design and development of digital tools and educational supports, optimizing learning experiences and interventions to meet children's specific needs within the digital context.

2. METHODS

PARTICIPANTS: 32 native monolingual Norwegian and typically developing children (16 female; mean age = 5.08 years; SD = 0.61; age range = 4.25 – 6.33) were recruited from local kindergartens. Parents provided written informed consent for participation in the study and completed a sociodemographic survey. The experimental protocol was approved by the National Centre for Research Data and the municipality. All participants visited the University Lab on two separate days. Currently, 32 participants have completed Session 1, and 25 children have completed Session 2.

BEHAVIOURAL MEASUREMENTS: Participants' phonological and working memory skills were assessed using an adapted version of the Children's Test of Nonword Repetition (Gathercole et al., 1994), in which a set of pseudowords curated to adhere to Norwegian were combined with a set of nonwords sourced from the Quasi-Universal Nonword Repetition Task (Boerma et al., 2015). To evaluate lexical skills, the Norwegian-validated version of the British Picture Vocabulary Scale, Second Edition (Lyster et al., 2010) was utilized, in a reduced version. Morphological skills were examined using the Morphological Awareness Test, adapted in Norwegian (Garcia Grande, 2010). Syntactic comprehension and production skills were measured with selected sections of the New Reynell Language Development Scales in Norwegian (Vulchanova et al., 2019). As a control measure for attention, the Picture Deletion Test for Preschoolers Revised (Byrne et al., 1998) was introduced in a reduced and revised version. Tests were consistently administered in the same sequence, a break was provided after every two tests, and the session typically lasted approximately 90 min, including breaks.

A newly designed questionnaire (Aldemir et al., 2024) was also administered to parents to capture important information about children's use and exposure to digital media, household composition, and language environments.

SL MEASUREMENTS: The EEG design of this study was child-adapted from the original adult paradigm by Batterink and Paller (2017). 24 speech syllables were generated in Norwegian using an online speech synthesizer (https://ttsmp3.com/; female natural voice) at a sampling rate of 44100 Hz. These were arranged into two structured streams consisting of four repeating trisyllabic "words": *tupiro, golabu, bidaku, padoti* (Set 1), and *meluga, rafinu, fudemi, bamoli* (Set 2). Word boundaries were indicated solely by transitional probabilities between syllables, which were higher within words (1.00) than between words (0.33). As a control, two additional random streams were created. Each stream consisted of 1200 syllables (400 "words"), each presented at a rate of 300 msec per syllable per condition, totalling 6 min, and divided into four blocks of 90 sec each, with breaks between each block. The assignment of syllable sets between structured and random conditions, as well as the stream presentation order, was counterbalanced across participants to mitigate any potential stimulus- or presentation-driven effect on the data.

After exposure, the Statistically Induced Chunking Recall (SICR) task was used as an offline measure of SL abilities. The current paradigm was adapted from Kidd (2020) and Isbilen and colleagues (2017). Following familiarization, participants were presented with 8 3-syllable and 16 6-syllable sequences (either a familiar sequence or a foil). They were instructed to immediately repeat each item after a cross appeared on the PC screen (500 msec after the item offset). The familiar sequences were generated from the "words" heard during the exposure task.

During the EEG Session, children sat either alone or on their parent's lap within a sound-attenuated, electrically shielded EEG booth in the Lab for 30 min, in front of a PC screen and two speakers placed at approximately 120 cm in front of them. While listening to the auditory streams, children viewed a static alien picture on a PC monitor in front of them. The whole experiment was conducted using Psychopy (version 2022.2.5; Peirce et al., 2019).

EEG neural activity was recorded using the actiCAP system by Brain Products GmbH from 32 active scalp electrodes (Fp1, Fp2, F7, F3, Fz, F4, F8, FC5, FC1, FC2, FC6, T7, C3, Cz, C4, T8, TP9, CP5, CP1, CP2, CP6, TP10, P7, P3, Pz, P4, P8, PO9, O1, Oz, O2, and PO10). The reference electrode was placed on the left mastoid, and TP10 served as the reference electrode on the right mastoid. EEG data were sampled at 1000 Hz with a high cutoff filter set at 1000 Hz and a 10-second time constant (low cutoff). Impedance was kept below 5 kOhm across all channels throughout the experiment.

PLANNED ANALYSES AND PREDICTIONS: Several analyses are planned for the different types of collected data. First, composite scores from both comprehension and production scales across various language domains will be derived from the behavioural tests. For each language test, statistical analyses will be conducted, also referencing normative data, to examine the developmental trajectories of children's performance, with age as a covariate. Concerning the EEG data, we aim to replicate and adapt the analyses performed in Batterink and Paller (2017), quantifying neural entrainment measures of SL at syllabic and word frequencies using the inter-trial coherence (ITC) and the Word Learning Index (WLI) measures to track participants' shift in sensitivity to the underlying structure in the speech stream. Added to this, we may explore the N400 ERP response, known as a robust measure of speech segmentation. The accuracy performance in the SICR task will be evaluated based on the methods in Isbilen and Kidd (2017; 2020). Several correlation analyses are also planned. We will first investigate whether EEG online neural entrainment measures of SL can predict performance in the SICR post-exposure learning task. Subsequently, correlations will be examined between each behavioural language measure and the EEG online neural entrainment measures of SL to establish to what extent neural entrainment is associated with language status. Next, we will evaluate responses to the questionnaire administered to parents about children's digital exposure, household composition, and language environments, and try to establish associations with the behavioural language measures.

We anticipate observing an increase in EEG phase entrainment from syllabic frequencies to word-level frequencies in the structured condition compared to the control random condition, indicating potential "online" tracking of SL as a function of stimulus exposure. Regarding the learning effect in the SICR offline task, we expect to see better recall accuracy for familiar sequences compared to foils, with significant correlations to the neurophysiological measure of SL. Additionally, we predict some level of correlation between individual EEG entrainment measures and children's behavioural language performance in domains beyond the largely investigated lexical skills. We expect to find some associations also in the phonology, morphology, or syntax domains which have been neglected to date.

3. PRELIMINARY RESULTS

Initial exploratory analyses were performed on the data collected through the administered questionnaire, focusing on participants' digital backgrounds and exposure. Two key measures provided noteworthy insights into our sample.

Firstly, we gathered information about the number of digital devices each family has at home, which revealed an average of 7.6 devices (SD = 3.4) per household. However, there was significant variation in the answers, with some families reporting very few devices and others many more.

Second, we examined participants' exposure to different types of digital media in terms of time spent using them. Overall, we found a trend of reduced digital technology use and exposure. TV usage is generally limited to 15-30 minutes per day, although some children watch it for 1 to 2 hours daily while others do not watch it at all. Regarding tablets and smartphones, which are among the most frequently used devices, the majority of parents reported that their children spent between 15 and 30 minutes per day on them, with occasional instances where tablet usage extended from 1 to 3 hours. In contrast, most children do not use laptops or game consoles at all.

This pattern may be attributed to parental control over media usage, cultural characteristics specific to the country, and the young age of the participants. Consequently, the reported exposure times may not be very representative or indicative of broader trends. Given this context and the limited use of certain technologies, we do not anticipate finding significant correlations with the language status of our sample.

4. CONCLUSION

In light of the increasing influence of digital technology on language development, behavioural and EEG-based measures were collected from a group of Norwegian preschoolers to shed light on the role that sensory mechanisms may play in language processing. While our research is currently ongoing, the ultimate goal of this study is to leverage this knowledge in applied research on digital technology, informing the design of personalized interventions tailored to children's individual needs and processing abilities.

Future research could benefit from a larger sample size and a longitudinal design, allowing for comparisons between different age groups and providing a clearer understanding of the time course of the SL mechanism in language development within the digital context.

ACKNOWLEDGEMENT

The study has received funding from the European Union's Horizon 2020 research and innovation programme under Marie Skłodowska-Curie Actions grant agreement No 857897. We thank Ingrid Bastøe Larssen, Sigurd Farstad Iversen, Anna Brandal, Elida Gjerde Thorvik, Lieke Neeleman, and Dina Sofie Vollen for their help in data collection.

REFERENCES

Abreu, R., et al. (2023). The association between statistical learning and language development during childhood: A scoping review. *In Heliyon*, Vol. 9, No. 8.

Aldemir, H., et al. (2024). Integrated Project 1: Gender and Population-level Variables in Language Learning and Use of Digital Tools. OSF. https://doi.org/10.17605/OSF.IO/JTZ9V.

Batterink, L. J., and Paller, K. A. (2017). Online neural monitoring of statistical learning. *In Cortex; a Journal Devoted to the Study of the Nervous System and Behavior*, Vol. 90, pp. 31–45.

Boerma, T., et al. (2015). A quasi-universal nonword repetition task as a diagnostic tool for bilingual children learning Dutch as a second language. *In Journal of Speech, Language, and Hearing Research*, Vol. 58, No. 6, pp. 1747–1760.

Byrne, J. M., et al. (1998). Clinical Assessment of Psychopharmacological Treatment of Preschoolers with ADHD. *In Journal of Clinical and Experimental Neuropsychology*, Vol. 20, No. 5, pp. 613–627.

Garcia Grande, G. (2018). Morphological Awareness in Norwegian Pre-schoolers [Master thesis].

Gathercole, S. E., et al. (1994). The children's test of nonword repetition: A test of phonological working memory. *In Memory*, Vol. 2, No. 2, pp. 103–127.

Isbilen, E. S., et al. (2017). Testing statistical learning implicitly: A novel chunk-based measure of statistical learning. *In The 39th Annual Conference of the Cognitive Science Society (CogSci 2017)*. London, UK, pp. 564-569.

Kidd, E., et al. (2020). Measuring children's auditory statistical learning via serial recall. *In Journal of Experimental Child Psychology*, Vol. 200.

Lyster, S.-A.H., et al. (2010). Ordforråd og ordforrådsutvikling hos norske barn og unge: Resultater fra en utprøving av British Picture Vocabulary Scale, second edition (BPVS-II). *In Spesialpedagogikk*, Vol. 9, pp. 35–43.

Peirce, J. W., et al. (2019). PsychoPy2: experiments in behavior made easy. Behavior Research Methods.

Raviv, L., and Arnon, I. (2018). The developmental trajectory of children's auditory and visual statistical learning abilities: Modality-based differences in the effect of age. *In Developmental Science*, Vol. 21, No. 4.

Romberg, A. R., and Saffran, J. R. (2010). Statistical learning and language acquisition. *In Wiley Interdisciplinary Reviews. Cognitive Science*, Vol. 1, No. 6, pp. 906–914.

Saffran, J. R., et al. (1996a). Statistical learning by 8-month-old infants. *In Science*, Vol. 274, No. 5294, pp. 1926–1928.

Saffran, J. R., and Kirkham, N. Z. (2018). Infant Statistical Learning. *In Annual Review of Psychology*, Vol. 69, pp. 181–203.

Saffran, J. R. et al. (1996b). Word segmentation: The role of distributional cues. *In Journal of Memory and Language*, Vol. 35, No. 4, pp. 606–621.

Sjuls, G. S. et al. (2023). The relationship between neural phase entrainment and statistical word-learning: A scoping review. *In Psychonomic Bulletin & Review*, pp. 1-21.

Vulchanova, M. D. et al. (2019). *NRDLS – The New Reynell Developmental Language Scales*. Hogrefe. Oslo, Norway.

ASSESSING YOUNG LEARNERS' INFORMAL LEARNING IN A ROBOTIC PROGRAM

Liyan Song, Qijie Cai, Suzhen Duan and Scot McNary
Towson University
8000 York Road, Towson MD 21252, U.S.A.

ABSTRACT

Investigating elementary students' learning experiences is a challenge due to their abilities and maturity to articulate their thought processes during interviews and self-evaluate their perceptions on survey instruments. Traditional research on elementary students' learning experiences has mostly utilized surveys and observations (Chiu, 2012). Occasionally, interviews are employed as an additional data collection method. However, there are fundamental concerns about using surveys for data collection, especially those with self-reported questions as they are often criticized for lacking validity due to their assumption of participants' ability to accurately report their knowledge and behaviors (Porter, 2011). Despite this weakness, surveys are popular tools for academic assessment because they can help collect data that are not easily obtainable otherwise (Porter, Rumann, & Pontius, 2011). The purpose of this paper is to report an evaluation study that aims to examine the cognitive, affective, and psychomotor domains of elementary students' learning in an informal robotics program by employing multiple data collection techniques that involve various stakeholders.

KEYWORDS

STEM Learning, Evaluation Research, Elementary Students' Learning

1. INTRODUCTION

Young learners' learning assessment is different from that of older children or adults in that young learners often engage in experiential and hands-on learning rather than abstract reasoning (Bredekamp & Copple 1997). Additionally, young learners, at their early stage of biological growth, may not be able to process and comprehend sophisticated information due to their maturity level (Piaget, 1960). Therefore, ssessing young learners' learning can be a challenge due to their abilities and maturity to articulate their thought processes during interviews and self-evaluate their perceptions when answering questions on a survey instrument.

Traditional research on elementary students' learning experiences has mostly utilized surveys and observations (Chiu, 2012). Occasionally, interviews are employed as an additional data collection method. However, there are fundamental concerns about using surveys for data collection, especially those with self-reported questions as they are often criticized for lacking validity due to their assumption of participants' ability to accurately report their knowledge and behaviors (Porter, 2011). Despite this weakness, surveys are popular tools for academic assessment because they can help collect data that are not easily obtainable otherwise (Porter, Rumann, & Pontius, 2011).

This is a free Saturday robotics program offered through a university to elementary students in grades 2 to 7. The program involves four university faculty (one project manager, and three researchers), four coaches (university students), and 12-17 elementary students. There are 6-7 sessions in each semester and the program is currently in its third implementation semester. Students in the robotics program learn to design and code Vex Go robots to solve a real-world challenge related to the theme of the semester (e.g., Mars exploration, protecting earth's resource).

The revised Bloom's Taxonomy (Anderson & Krathwohl, 2001; Krathwohl, Bloom, & Masia, 1964) served as the framework to guide the data collection process for the research. The revised Bloom's Taxonomy expanded from the original Taxonomy's focus on the cognitive domain to include the affective domain and psychomotor domain to evaluate the student's learning. The cognitive domain is focused on knowledge and processes (Anderson & Krathwohl, 2001). The affective domain includes emotions, interpersonal relationships, attitudes, and beliefs (Savic & Kashef, 2013). Social, emotional, and behavioral skills are promising predictors of students' positive development (Napolitano et al., 2021). The affective domain is especially important in a robotics program where students' collaboration is an integral part of the learning experience. The psychomotor domain refers to manual and physical skills (Zollman, 2012). This domain has traditionally been less of a focus in STEM learning than the cognitive and affective domains (Zollman, 2012). However, in a robotics program where they engage in hands-on building and coding of the robot, psychomotor skills are essential to students' learning success.

2. RESEARCH METHODOLOGY

The research study took place in an informal robotics program hosted on a university campus in the Mid-Atlantic region of the United States. The program aimed top offer free robotics design and build activities to students in grades 3-7 in the local community with priority given to underrepresented students.

To holistically evaluate the elementary students' learning experiences, we have utilized multiple data collection methods including student surveys, parent surveys, teachers interviews and reflections, classroom observations, researchers' reflections, and video clips to capture all three domains of student's learning.

2.1 Research Questions

The following research questions guided the data collection efforts:

- What is the impact of the robotics program on students' cognitive learning growth.
- What is the student's affective learning like in the robotics program?
- How do the students demonstrate their psychomotor skills when completing activities in the robotics program? the text here.

2.2 Research Instruments

The research utilized instruments that measured students' learning in cognitive, affective, and psychomotor domains. Bloom (1956) defined cognitive learning outcomes as the acquisition of knowledge and intellectual skills. Cognitive learning focuses on student's knowledge and experiences. In the specific context of the robotics program, the knowledge acquisition focuses on students' gained knowledge on computational thinking such as algorithm thinking. The intellectual skills include creative and critical thinking involved in solving design problems. To measure the cognitive domain of learning for the learners in the robotics program, we have implemented a student computation thinking survey with questions on algorithm thinking, creativity, and critical thinking. Researchers' non-participant observations of students' understanding of the algorithm or coding logic through their completion of the robot design and build activities. Students also completed exit tickets upon at the end of each session to report their gained knowledge and learning experiences during that session.

Bauer (2005) argued that researchers should examine student's affective learning beyond the "attitudes" level and include constructs such as interests, values, self-concept, and self-efficacy. For student's affective learning in this robotics program, we examined student's interest, satisfaction, values, and motivation through teacher reflections, non-participant observations, students' self-reported attitudes, interests, and satisfaction on their exit tickets. The students completed a Best Possible Self activity during each session, which students' attitudes and beliefs about their STEM identify. This activity asks the students to think about their best possible self in relation to their STEM identify through drawing and writing. We have also collected survey data from the parents on their perceptions of their children's interests in learning with and through robotics.

Psychomotor domain describes how students imitate, manipulate, and articulate to achieve precision and naturalization (Dave, 1975). For student's psychomotor learning outcomes, we observed through non-participant observation the student' competence in building and manipulating the robot and their assembling and dissembling the robot (imitate). Researchers and teachers also engaged in discussions of their observed students' behaviors through collaborative reflections after each session and at the end of the robotic program. Video clips of students' participation in session activities were analyzed for students' psychomotor skill development as well.

2.3 Participants

The data collection process involves all stakeholders including the students, the parents, the teachers, and the researchers. The students in the program completed a computational thinking survey (adapted from Korkmaz et al., 2017) before and after the robotics program. They also completed a Best Possible Self activity during each session and an exit ticket with questions about their learning experiences at the end of each session. Parents were asked to complete a survey at the end of the program to share their perspectives on the impact of the program on students' learning, their attitudes and interest related to STEM, and how the students felt about the program. At the end of program, the teachers were interviewed and asked to reflect on their observations of students' engagement and challenges with various design challenges. Two researchers conducted non-participant observations (DeWalt & DeWalt, 2002) where they have no interaction with the students. The project manager (also a researcher) and the coaches shared their observations of students' engagement during their interactions with the students. At the end of each instructional session, researchers shared their highlights from their observations and discussed how students were engaged or disengaged in the activities.

3. FINDINGS AND CONCLUSION

Overall, students demonstrated improved knowledge about computational thinking (CT survey), growth mindset about science and engineering (exit tickets), and improved STEM identify (BPS activities). Researchers' observations, teachers' reflections, and parents' survey data suggested that the students were actively engaged in the robotics activities and demonstrated their interests in and positive attitudes toward designing and building robot to solve problems. Vido clips showed students' competency in robot build and drive. The preliminary findings from the data analysis indicates that we are able to capture data for all three domains of student's learning. In addition, different data sources with different stakeholders help provide different perspectives on student's learning that one single source with one stakeholder might not be able to illustrate. The mixture of quantitative and qualitative data helps triangulate and provide various layers of interpretation of student's behaviors. We hope our evaluation approach helps offer an example to examine student's learning holistically.

REFERENCES

Anderson, L. W. et al. (2001). *A taxonomy for learning, teaching and assessing: A revision of Bloom's taxonomy of educational objectives.* Longman, New York, USA.

Bauer, c. et al. (2005). Beyond "student attitudes": Chemistry self-concept inventory for assessment of affective component of student learning. *Journal of Chemical Education,* Vol. 82, No. 12, pp. 1864-1870.

Berger, R. (2020). *Here's what's wrong with bloom's taxonomy: A deeper learning perspective (opinion)*. Education Week.

Bloom, B.S. (1956). *Taxonomy of educational objectives, Handbook: The cognitive domain*. David McKay, New York.

Bloom, B.S. et al. (1956). *Taxonomy of educational objectives: The classification of educational goals, by a committee of college and university examiners.* Longman, New York.

Bredekamp, S. et al. (1997). *Developmentally appropriate practice in early childhood programs* (revised ed.). NAEYC, Washington, DC.

Chiu, M.S. (2012). Identification and assessment of Taiwanese children's conceptions of learning mathematics. *International Journal of Science and Mathematics Education, Vol.10,* pp. 163-191.

DeWalt, K.M. et al. (2002). *Participant observation.* Altamira, New York.

Korkmaz, O. et al. (2017). A validity and reliability study of the computational thinking scales (CTS). *Computers in Human Behavior,* Vol. 72, pp 558-569.

Moffa, K. et al. (2021). The me and my school questionnaire: Examining the cross-cultural validity of a children's self-report mental health measure. *International Journal of School and Educational Psychology,* Vol. 9, No. 1, pp. 31-41.

Napolitano, C.M. et al. (2021). Social, emotional, and behavioral skills: An integrative model of the skills associated with success during adolescence and across the life span. *Frontiers in Education,* Vol. 2.

Piaget, J. (1960). Equilibration and the development of logical structures. In J. M. Tanner &B. Inhelder (Eds.), *Discussions on child development* (Vol. IV). Tavistock Publications, London.

Porter, S.R. (2011). Do college student surveys have any validity? *The Review of Higher Education,* Vol. 35, No. 1, pp. 45-76.

Porter, S.R. et al. (2011). The Validity of student engagement survey questions: Can we accurately measure academic challenge? *New Directions for Institutional Research,* Vol. 2011, pp87-98.

Savic, M. et al. (2013). Learning outcomes in affective domain within contemporary architectural curricula. *International Journal of Technology and Design Education,* Vol. 23, pp987-1004.

Zollman, A. (2012). Learning for STEM literacy: STEM literacy for learning. *School Science and Mathematics,* Vol. 112, No. 1, pp. 12-19.

FROM SCREENS TO WORDS: UNDERSTANDING THE ROLE OF MODALITY IN DIGITAL SECOND LANGUAGE VOCABULARY LEARNING

Paula Janjic and Kenny R. Coventry
University of East Anglia, United Kingdom

ABSTRACT

This study explores the influence of modality (picture-based vs. text-based) on second language vocabulary learning in relation to testing modality, translational ambiguity and word class. Conducted with 160 monolingual adults, the research investigated the effects of learning and testing modalities on learning of different types of words in the digital setting. Results revealed a significant impact of testing modality, with the picture-text combination between learning and testing outperforming congruent modality combinations. Additionally, text testing modality was found to be particularly advantageous for verbs and prepositions. These findings suggest that while pictures might enhance encoding, text cues may be more effective for retrieval in early second language learning stages and for certain word types. This research underscores the need for nuanced language teaching strategies and the development of more effective digital learning tools.

KEYWORDS

Second Language Learning, Vocabulary Learning, Multimodality, Digital Learning

1. INTRODUCTION

Vocabulary acquisition is a critical component of learning a second language, as it lays the foundation for more advanced language skills (Grabe, 2009). The success of second language (L2) vocabulary learning depends on numerous factors, yet the interactions between these factors remain poorly understood. Moreover, new digital learning technologies open questions about how these variables interact and how best to leverage them for effective vocabulary acquisition. Digital language learning introduces possibilities of multimodal learning that align well with well-established theories such as the Dual Code Theory (Paivio and Csapo, 1969) or Levels of Processing Theory (Craik and Lockhart, 1972), that suggest that combining verbal information with sensory experiences like pictures leads to deeper encoding, better retention, and faster retrieval. However, their application is not always straightforward.

Traditional methods are thought to create connections between first language and second language words, whereas newer approaches aim to link L2 words directly to their concept, thus forming stronger connections between the word and its meaning. There are arguments in support of both approaches. Some suggest that in the initial phases the benefit of multisensory input is limited because the form-meaning link is not yet created (Kroll & Stewart, 1994), whereas the evidence in support of the latter suggest that it helps in creation of stronger connections from the very beginning (Macedonia, 2019).

The lack of consistent results with regard to the learning modality (Butler, 2019), points to a need for further explanation of the underlying mechanisms and their interactions. This variability could stem from the differences in research designs used so far. While some studies use picture stimuli in addition to text-based conditions, others use either pictures or text. These variations introduce effects of working memory, processing speed, cognitive load, which can obscure the effects of modality (Boers, 2017). Likewise, the *modality of testing* can mask or enhance the effect of different learning modalities, since they draw on different cognitive resources and have already been found to lead to a difference between word naming times (de Bruin & Xu, 2023, Lotto & de Groot, 1998).

In addition to modalities, there are other variables affecting the learning outcomes, including *word properties* (Lotto & de Groot, 1998). Properties of words can shape the way we process and represent their meaning (Pulvermüller et al., 2010, Markostamou & Coventry, 2022), which might also lead to different strategies and outcomes during L2 learning. Despite that, the majority of studies were done on concrete nouns, thus missing important aspects of vocabulary, making it difficult to generalize results (Butler, 2019).

Finally, languages differ in how they describe concepts (Malt et al., 2003), leading to *translational ambiguity*. For example, the Dutch language will have three words that all mean different things, but translate to the English word "on", since the English language does not make the same distinctions. This makes it harder for the learner to learn the conditions under which particular words are used. This is found to occur more frequent in prepositions as a word class, making them more challenging to learn (Coventry et al., 2012). Because of these cross-linguistic differences, the learner's first language knowledge or world experience does not help (or might even mislead) in learning new vocabulary.

With all these factors in mind, the present study set to investigate whether pictures or text lead to better retention and recall of foreign vocabulary items, while accounting for different word types, word classes, and testing modalities. This research aims to clarify the modulating factors and resolve conflicting results from previous studies. Based on the previous findings, it was hypothesized that the advantage of pictures would vary with word class, word ambiguity, and testing modality, thus explaining the inconsistencies.

2. METHODOLOGY

2.1 Materials and Methods

2.1.1 Participants

The study involved 160 monolingual English-speaking adults aged 18 to 30, who had normal or corrected-to-normal vision, and no known learning disabilities or hearing issues. The recruitment took place via online recruitment platforms. Participants received credits or financial compensation for their participation.

2.1.2 Design and Procedure

Participants learned pseudowords in an online experimental setting. They were randomly assigned to either a picture modality or text modality group for learning, and each of these groups was further divided into picture or text modality for testing, creating four between-participant groups. Two variables were manipulated within participants: word class (nouns, verbs, prepositions) and ambiguity (translation ambiguous, translation unambiguous). The experiment took place over eight days. First two consecutive days involved a learning and a testing session. Third day occurred a week later, featuring a delayed testing session and additional verbal and visuospatial tests to control for individual differences.

During learning sessions, participants saw text showing the target pseudoword with an auditory presentation of the pseudoword and its English translation, followed by the pseudoword embedded in a short sentence (Figure 1). This sentence was read aloud by an artificial voice and paired with either text or a picture, depending on the condition.

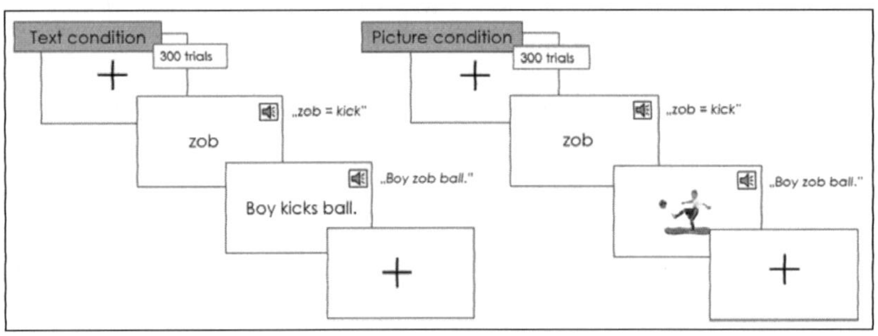

Figure 1. Figure is showing the sequence of trials comparing text and picture conditions

Each learning session lasted about 40 minutes, with each item presented for 6.5 seconds (2500ms for the word and translation, 4000ms for the word in a sentence) with breaks in between. Each word appeared five times in different sentences in a random order. The testing phase involved two tasks: a production task and a recognition task. In the production task, participants saw the context (picture or text) and a sentence missing the target word, which they typed into a bracket. In the recognition task, participants selected the correct pseudoword from four options.

3. RESULTS

Data was analyzed using generalized linear mixed-effects models with a logit link function and binomial distribution. Fixed effects included learning modality, task modality, word class, translation ambiguity, and their interactions, while random effects included words and participant intercepts to account for repeated observations. The outcome measure was accuracy score (correct/incorrect), with p-values significant at $\alpha < 0.05$. Four analyses were run, on immediate and delayed production and recognition data.

In the immediate recognition task a significant three-way interaction was found between learning modality, task modality, and ambiguity (X^2=26.28, p<0.001) (Figure 2). Post-hoc comparisons revealed that the picture-text group (M=0.796, SD=0.044) performed significantly better than both congruent modality groups (picture-picture (M=0.688, SD=0.057) and text-text (M=0.711, SD=0.055). The same three-way interaction was found in the delayed recognition (X2=51.480; p<.001), as well as in the immediate production task (X2=12.826; p<.001). This suggests that testing modality significantly impacts outcomes, with the picture-text group outperforming the picture-picture group, indicating that congruency does not drive the effect. The effects were observed only for unambiguous words.

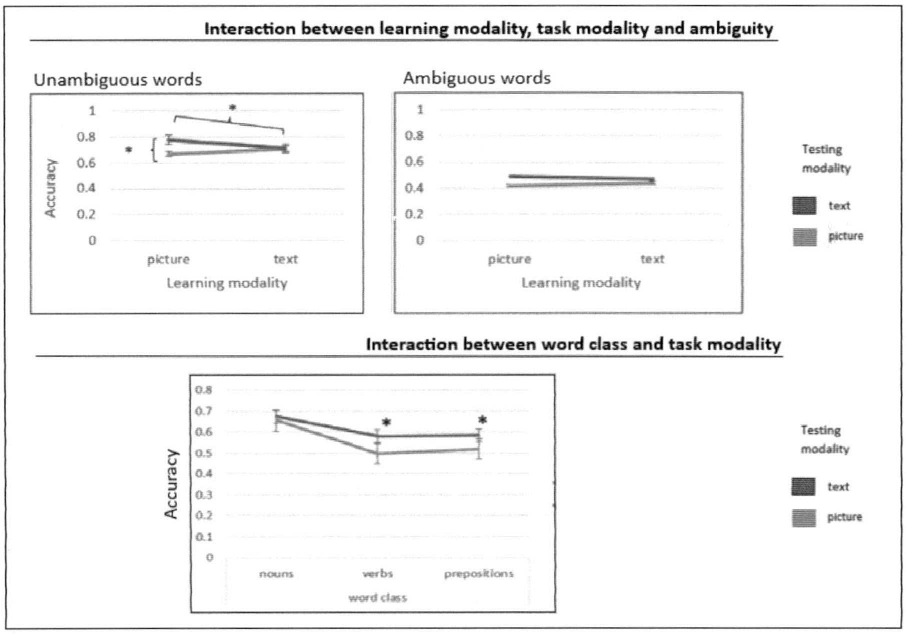

Figure 2. Figure showing significant interactions. Similar pattern was found both in the recognition and production tasks.

Additionally, a two-way interaction between testing modality and word class was found significant in the immediate recognition task (X^2=36.091, p<0.001; see Figure 2). Prepositions had higher scores when tested with text (M=0.585, SD=0.493) than with pictures (M=0.520, SD=0.500; β=0.681, p=0.005). Similarly, verbs tested with text (M=0.580, SD=0.494) scored higher than those tested with pictures (M=0.497, SD=0.500; β=0.639, p<0.001). The same two-way interactions were discovered in the delayed recognition task.

4. DISCUSSION AND CONCLUSION

This study provides valuable insights into the complex dynamics of second language vocabulary learning by focusing on often overlooked factors such as testing modality, word class, translational ambiguity, and research design. The findings particularly highlight the impact of testing modality and word class. The best learning outcomes were achieved with the combination of the picture learning modality and text testing modality. Unexpectedly, congruency between the learning and testing modalities did not bring an advantage. This could potentially mean that while pictures can work well as a tool to enhance encoding, in the very early stages of adult L2 learning they might not work well as a cue for retrieval. In this particular population retrieval might still be guided more strongly by the lexical connections, as proposed by the Revised Hierarchical model (Kroll & Stewart, 1994). Also, there was a positive effect of the text testing modality that was specific to verbs and particularly prepositions. This finding confirms the view that different word classes are processed in different ways (Markostamou & Coventry, 2022; Bultena et al., 2013) and that distributional learning might be particularly beneficial for prepositions as a word class (Coventry et al., 2012).

Taken together, these findings suggest that there are several important factors at play when it comes to initial second language vocabulary learning. By understanding the underlying processes, language teaching strategies and digital learning tool designs can be refined to enhance language learning outcomes.

ACKNOWLEDGEMENT

This work was supported by the European Union's Horizon 2020 research and innovation programme under the Marie Sklodowska-Curie Actions grant agreement No 857897.

REFERENCES

Boers, F., Warren, P., Grimshaw, G., and Siyanova-Chanturia, A. (2017). On the benefits of multimodal annotations for vocabulary uptake from reading. Computer Assisted Language Learning, 30(7), 709-725.

de Bruin, A., & Xu, T. (2023). Language switching in different contexts and modalities: Response-stimulus interval influences cued-naming but not voluntary-naming or comprehension language-switching costs. Bilingualism: Language and Cognition, 26(2), 402-415. https://doi.org/10.1017/S1366728922000554

Bultena, S., Dijkstra, T., & van Hell, J. G. (2013). Cognate and word class ambiguity effects in noun and verb processing. Language and Cognitive Processes, 28(9), 1350-1377. https://doi.org/10.1080/01690965.2012.718353

Butler, Y. G. (2019). Teaching vocabulary to young second- or foreign-language learners: What can we learn from the research? Language Teaching for Young Learners, 1(1), 4-33. https://doi.org/10.1075/ltyl.00003

Coventry, K. R., Guijarro-Fuentes, P., & Valdés, B. (2011). Spatial language and second language acquisition. In V. Cook & B. Bassetti (Eds.), Language and bilingual cognition (pp. 263-286). New York: Psychology Press.

Grabe, W. (2009). Reading in a Second Language: Moving from Theory to Practice. Cambridge: Cambridge University Press.

Kroll, J. F., & Stewart, E. (1994). Category interference in translation and picture naming: Evidence for asymmetric connections between bilingual memory representations. Journal of Memory and Language, 33(2), 149-174.

Lotto, L., & de Groot, A. M. (1998). Effects of learning method and word type on acquiring vocabulary in an unfamiliar language. Language Learning, 48(1), 31-69.

Macedonia, M. (2019). Embodied learning: Why at school the mind needs the body. Frontiers in Psychology, 10, 2098.

Malt, B. C., Sloman, S. A., & Gennari, S. P. (2003). Universality and language specificity in object naming. Journal of Memory and Language, 49(1), 20-42. https://doi.org/10.1016/S0749-596X(03)00021-4

Markostamou, I., & Coventry, K. R. (2022). Naming spatial relations across the adult lifespan: At the crossroads of language and perception. Neuropsychology, 36(3), 216-230.

Morett, L. (2014). When hands speak louder than words: The role of gesture in the communication, encoding, and recall of words in a novel second language. The Modern Language Journal, 98(3), 834-853.

Paivio, A., & Csapo, K. (1973). Picture superiority in free recall: Imagery or dual coding? Cognitive Psychology, 5(2), 176-206. https://doi.org/10.1016/0010-0285(73)90032-7

Pulvermüller, F., Cappelle, B., Shtyrov, Y., & Alexopoulou, T. (2010). The word processing deficit in semantic dementia: All categories are equal, but some categories are more equal than others. Journal of Cognitive Neuroscience, 22(9), 2027-2041. https://doi.org/10.1162/jocn.2009.21339

DOES GAME CHARACTER'S LIFE SATISFACTION IN LIFE BOARD GAME REFLECT REAL LIFE?

Kazuhisa Miwa, Hiromu Matsubara and Asaya Shimojo
Graduate School of Informatics, Nagoya University
Nagoya, 4648601 Japan

ABSTRACT

This study explores the potential of "The Game of Life" as a board game for learning of life. Our research question is: to what extent do a board game, such as The Game of Life, that simulates life experiences reflect actual life well-being? Specifically, the study examines whether life satisfaction ratings for a game character made during a board game that simulates human life reflect real-life well-being. The study focuses on two key psychological predictions: the effect of participants' tendency to regret and the effect of autonomous versus imposed choices on life satisfaction. Participants played a life-simulation board game, and the life satisfaction of a game character as their alter ego was estimated based on their in-game experiences. Results indicate that both the tendency to regret and the nature of life choices influence perceived life satisfaction, as predicted by psychological theories. The results are discussed based on the theory of mind and the counterfactual thinking theory.

KEYWORDS

Life Satisfaction, Board Game, Game of Life, Counterfactual Thinking

1. INTRODUCTION

There are several initiatives that use games to help participants deepen their understanding of life and learn life skills. In general, serious games often focus on solving social problems as a learning goal, but in these initiatives, a learning goal is the life we live. In this paper, such learning is referred to as "learning of life." This paper explores the potential of "The Game of Life" as a board game for learning of life. The prototype of the Game of Life was invented in the United States in 1860, arranging real life events on the age-old checkerboard. In 1960, The Game of Life was released to celebrate its 100th anniversary, and has been translated into 21 languages and released in 30 countries around the world (for a description of the development of The Game of Life, see (Bum, 1978)).

In a typical life game, a path symbolizing life is drawn on the game board. By the number of the roulette, players move along the path of life, which determines the course of the path and influences the rest of their lives. Players complete various events in their virtual life and reach the final point in their life. At the end of the game, the player who has the most money wins the game by redeeming items in his or her possession. In this way, a typical life game is more of an entertainment rather than a serious game.

This study answers the following research question about the characteristics of a game for learning of life: To what extent do a board game, such as The Game of Life, that simulates life experiences reflect actual life well-being? In this study, referred by the method employed in media equation studies (Nass & Reeves, 1996), we examine whether factors related to life satisfaction that have been identified in positive and personality psychology are similarly confirmed in life games. Specifically, we examine whether the two predictions regarding the event-effect on well-being are confirmed in the game.

2. TWO PREDICTIONS ON PSYCHOLOGICAL REGRET THEORIES

What events one experiences in life is the most salient factor in determining life satisfaction, along with an individual's demographic variables (e.g., Kettlewell et al., 2020). In general, positive events such as marriage and promotion increase the levels of well-being, and conversely, negative events such as divorce and unemployment decrease the levels of well-being. These effects are confirmed not only for major life events, but also for everyday events (McCullough, Huebner, & Laughlin, 2000). In this study, the increase in well-being due to the experience of positive events relative to the experience of negative events is referred to as Event-Effect-on-Wellbeing.The present study makes two predictions about this Event-Effect-on-Wellbeing based on established psychological theories in the relevant psychological domains.

First Prediction: Regret, along with disappointment, is a negative emotion experienced when the outcome of a decision or action is unfavorable (Zeelenberg, Van Dijk, SR Manstead, & der Pligt, 1998; Zeelenberg
& Pieters, 1999). Numerous wellbeing studies have confirmed a negative correlation between regret tendency and life satisfaction (e.g., Sijtsema, Zeelenberg, & Lindenberg, 2021). The first prediction of this study is that a greater Event-Effect-on-Wellbeing will be observed in the group of participants who are more prone to regret.

Second Prediction: Stronger regret typically occurs when a negative outcome is caused by one's own decision rather than by someone else's choice (Zeelenberg, Van Dijk, Van der Pligt, et al., 1998). The second prediction of this study is that when constructing a situation in which people make their own life choices with a situation in which they are forced to make choices by other people or circumstances, the Event-Effect-on-Wellbeing will be greater in the former situation.

3. EXPERIMENT

3.1 Experimental Environment

The experiment was conducted in an experimental environment running on a web browser. Participants turned the roulette wheel by pressing a button, and moved the character by its number of squares from the square labeled "START" through the 1st, 2nd, 3rd, 4th, and 5th decades of life to the square labeled "GOAL" in Figure 1. The roulette numbers ranged from 1 to 6. After the roulette value was displayed, the character moved over an equal number of squares in the life game. The character then stopped moving, and the content of the event corresponding to the square where the character stopped was displayed on the screen. This procedure led participants to believe that the squares on which the character stopped were randomly selected. In reality, all the roulette values in the game were predetermined, and the same values were displayed to all participants in the same order.

At the end of each decade, "STOP" points were placed. When participants passed through these stop points, they stopped at the square regardless of the roulette number, where they faced the crossroads of their lives in that situation. In each decade, participants experienced, an average of four events, starting from the stop point. (Only the first teenager started at the starting point.)

3.2 Experimental Design

Autonomous Choice Factor: Two factors were manipulated in the experiment. The first factor was the autonomous choice factor, which included a choosable or nonchoosable condition. In the choosable condition, at the stop points, participants could choose between two options at the stop points, based on their preferences. For example, in the teenage year, participants could choose between enrolling in engineering school or economics school. In the non-choosable condition, participants were presented with a choice of life options at the stop points, but were forced to choose one. The choice was an unwanted one for participants. Specifically, before the start of the game, participants completed a pre-questionnaire about their life choice preferences, in which they were shown two life choices and asked to choose their preferred option. Based on the results of the pre-questionnaire, participants were given the unwanted choice.

Life Event Factor: The second factor was the life event factor, which consisted of two conditions: a positive event condition and a negative event condition. In the positive condition, two positive events were set to occur as a result of the choice at the stop point. In the negative condition, two negative events were set to occur. On average, four events occurred at each age stage, including two events that were unrelated to the choice at the beginning of the decade.

3.3 Participants

All participants provided informed consent. Participants were recruited through a crowdsourcing service, and 160 participants (86 males, 73 females, and 1 other) participated in the study (Mage = 39.30, SDage = 8.94). Participants were randomly assigned to one of four groups (choosable/positive life, non-choosable/positive life, choosable/negative life, and non-choosable/negative life). Each group consisted of 42, 36, 41, and 41 participants, respectively. The entire experiment lasted approximately 25 minutes.

3.4 Measurement

The Satisfaction With Life Scale (SWLS) was used to measure life satisfaction (Diener, Emmons, Larsen, & Griffin, 1985). The SWLS consists of five items related to life satisfaction. This study used a Japanese version of the Maximization and Regret Scale (Isobe et al., 2008), which was developed based on the original Maximization and Regret Scale (Schwartz et al., 2002).

3.5 Procedures

At the beginning of the experiment, participants completed a pre-questionnaire about their life choice preferences. Then, they responded to the regret and maximization scale questions.

Before the game, participants were given the instruction, "Please play this game as if it were your life. Please play with a sense of how you would feel if the game character were you. Participants then clicked on the "Start Game" button at the bottom of the page to begin the task. Participants were asked to rate life satisfaction of the game character throughout life in the "GOAL" square.

4. RESULTS

Participants were divided into two groups: the high regret group with a score above the average of all participants' regret scores, and the low regret group with a score below the average. An ANOVA was conducted to examine the effects of the event and regret trait factors and their interaction on the life satisfaction evaluation. Figure 1 shows the result. The difference of life satisfaction scores in the positive and negative conditions represents Event-Effect-on-Wellbeing. There was a significant main effect of the event factor ($F(1,156) = 175.932, p < .001, \eta^2 = .530$). The regret factor also had a significant main effect($F(1,156) = 3.998, p = .047, \eta^2 = .025$). The interaction between the event and regret factors, as a main concern, was also significant ($F(1,156) = 4.665, p = .032, \eta^2 = .029$). Further analyses were conducted to explore a simple effect of the event factor at each of the low and high regret groups. In the higher regret group, there was a significant effect of the event factor ($F(1,156) = 115.745, p < .001, \eta^2 = .426$). In the lower regret group, there was also a significant effect of the regret factor, but the effect size was smaller than that in the high regret group ($F(1,156) = 63.405, p < .001, \eta^2 = .289$). This means that Event-Effect-on-Wellbeing became larger in the group of participants who are more prone to regret. The first prediction was confirmed.

Another ANOVA was conducted to examine the effects of the event and autonomous choice factors and their interaction on the life satisfaction evaluation. Figure 2 shows the result.

There was a significant main effect of the event factor ($F(1,156) = 199.846, p < .001, \eta^2 = .562$). The choice factor also had a significant main effect ($F(1,156) = 33.981, p < .001, \eta^2 = .179$). The interaction between the event and choice factors was significant ($F(1,156) = 4.985, p = .027, \eta^2 = .031$). Further analyses were conducted to explore a simple effect of the event factor at each of the choosable and non-choosable conditions. In the choosable condition, there was a significant effect of the event facto ($F(1,156) = 139.492$, $p < .001, \eta^2 = .472$). In the non-choosable condition, there was also a significant effect of the regret factor ($F(1,156) = 68.159, p < .001, \eta^2 = .304$), but the effect size was smaller than that in the choosable condition.

This means that Event-Effect-on-Wellbeing became larger in the situation in which people make their own life choices. The second prediction was also confirmed.

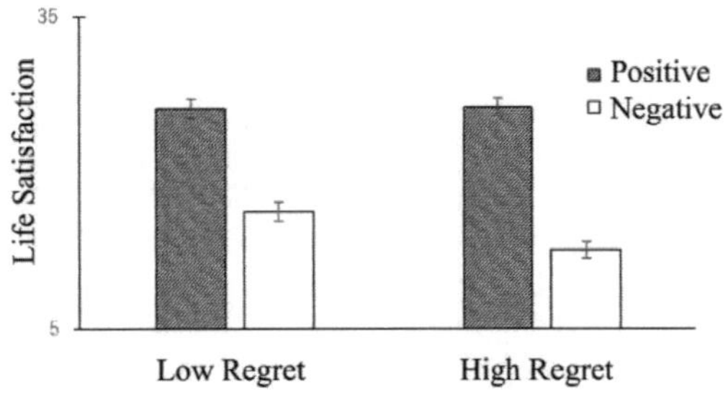

Figure 1. Event-Effect-on-Wellbeing as a function of event and regret trait factors

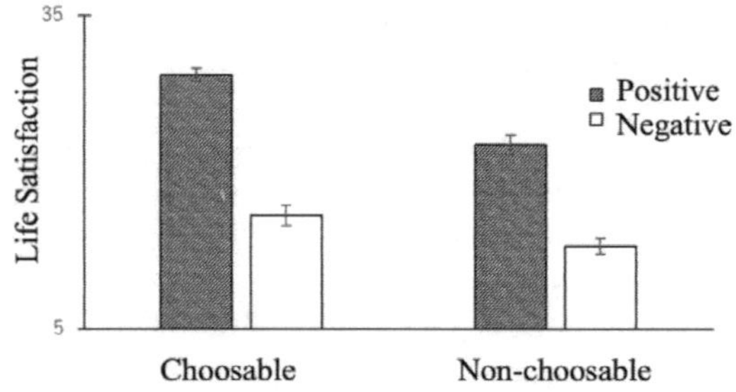

Figure 2. Event-Effect-on-Wellbeing as a function of event and autonomous choice factors

5. CONCLUSIONS

The present study sought to determine whether factors that predict real-life wellbeing, identified in the fields of positive and personality psychology, function similarly in a popular board game, the Game of Life. The study examined factors related to autonomy in life choices and personality factors related to participants' likelihood of regret. The results of the experiment showed that participants who were asked to rate the well-being of the game agent rated the agent's level of well-being similarly to the rating observed in real life. Participants 'personality, in terms of their tendency to regret, adjusted their ratings according to the manner of how they were predicted.

This study is positioned as basic research to explore the possibility of using board games such as the Game of Life as a learning environment for learning of life.

REFERENCES

Bum, T.A. (1978). The game of life: Idealism, reality and fantasy in the nineteenthand twentieth-century versions of a milton bradley game. *Canadian Review of American Studies*, *9*(1), 50–83.

Diener, E., Emmons, R.A., Larsen, R.J., Griffin, S. (1985). The satisfaction with life scale. *Journal of personality assessment*, *49*(1), 71–75.

Isobe, A., Hisatomi, T., Matsui, Y., Ui, M., Takahashi, N., Oba, K., Takemura, K. (2008). Construction of a japanese version of the " regret and maximization scale"in decision making. *The Japanese Journal of Psychology*, *79*(5), 453-458.

Kettlewell, N., Morris, R.W., Ho, N., Cobb-Clark, D.A., Cripps, S., Glozier, N. (2020). The differential impact of major life events on cognitive and affective wellbeing. *SSM-population health*, *10*, 100533.

McCullough, G., Huebner, E.S., Laughlin, J.E. (2000). Life events, self-concept, and adolescents' positive subjective well-being. *Psychology in the Schools*, *37*(3), 281–290.

Nass, C., & Reeves, B. (1996). *The media equation: How people treat computers, television, and new media like real people and places*. CSLI Publications Stanford.

Schwartz, B., Ward, A., Monterosso, J., Lyubomirsky, S., White, K., Lehman, D.R. (2002). Maximizing versus satisficing: happiness is a matter of choice. *Journal of personality and social psychology*, *83*(5), 1178.

Zeelenberg, M., Van Dijk, W.W., SR Manstead, A., der Pligt, J. (1998). The experience of regret and disappointment. *Cognition & Emotion*, *12*(2), 221–230.

Zeelenberg, M., Van Dijk, W.W., Van der Pligt, J., Manstead, A.S., Van Empelen, P., Reinderman, D. (1998). Emotional reactions to the outcomes of decisions: The role of counterfactual thought in the experience of regret and disappointment. *Organizational behavior and human decision processes*, *75*(2), 117–141.

Zeelenberg, M., & Pieters, R. (1999). Comparing service delivery to what might have been: Behavioral responses to regret and disappointment. *Journal of Service Research*, *2*(1), 86–97.

Sijtsema, J.J., Zeelenberg, M., Lindenberg, S.M. (2021). Regret, self-regulatory abilities, and well-being: Their intricate relationships. *Journal of Happiness Studies*, 1–26.

SUCCESSFUL JOB INTERVIEW: GRANULATED MESSAGE FROM INDUSTRY TO IT GRADUATES

Rabab Marouf[4], Iouri Kotorov[1, 2], Hamna Aslam[3], Yuliya Krasylnykova[1] and Manuel Mazzara[4]
[1]*Karelia University of Applied Sciences, Joensuu, Finland*
[2]*Université Paul Sabatier, IRIT, Toulouse, France*
[3]*University of Lincoln, United Kingdom*
[4]*Innopolis University, Innopolis, Republic of Tatarstan*

ABSTRACT

This paper sheds light on the challenge in the Information Technology (IT) and Software Engineering (SE) industries where computer science graduates face a Catch-22 situation, requiring job experience for employment but lacking opportunities to gain it. The literature background and case study examine the demands and dynamics of the IT job market. The case study outcomes are aligned with the insights drawn from the literature. Hence, this paper offers a nuanced exploration of the elements that define a successful applicant profile in the IT sector as well as valuable insights to guide both candidates and employers in navigating job interviews. Focusing on the critical aspect of limited job experience, this study advocates for a strategic alignment of skills transcending formal work history. The gained insights guide both candidates, educational institutions, and employers in navigating the complexities of IT job interviews and contribute to the development of a workforce prepared for future challenges.

KEYWORDS

Information Technology (IT), Software Engineering (SE), Job Experience, Soft Skills, Hiring Practices, Applicant Profile

1. YOU CAN'T GET HERE FROM THERE: THE CATCH-22 IN THE IT JOB MARKET

The growth of IT and software industry has entailed a Catch-22 situation for recent IT graduates setting forth on their professional journeys (Heller & Buckley, 2011). A high demand for qualified IT professionals exists (Bernieri, 2000). Many employers are reluctant to hire graduates with no or limited job experience (Abdul Hamid, 2022). The undeniable demand for practical experience in the hiring process poses a challenge to the entry of talented individuals with academic qualifications and theoretical knowledge into the IT workforce (Aarnikoivu et al., 2019). One main reason for this Catch-22 is that many employers believe that job experience is essential for success in the IT industry, known for its rapid evolution and demand for cutting-edge skills (Abdul Hamid, 2022). While graduates may have theoretical knowledge, they lack the hands-on experience that is necessary to be productive in a real-world setting (Nagy et al., 2023). This requirement for professional experience can be sadly a major obstacle for recent graduates (Tan et al., 2021). The Catch-22 situation arises as recent graduates struggle to gain necessary experience to validate their capabilities and gain traction in the job market (Meruyert et al., 2023; Tsai, 2019). This situation challenges the aspirations of graduates and reflects broader implications for the IT industry, questioning the effectiveness of the current hiring practices and the potential exclusion of highly talented graduates who lack a proven professional track record (Valentino, 2023; Whysall et al., 2019).

1.1 New yet Familiar: Trends in IT Hiring Practices and the Value of Trade-Offs

In recent years, employers have valued professional experience over everything else, considering it a critical factor in hiring decisions, with IT recruiters being among the biggest offenders of this (Aarnikoivu et al., 2019; Meruyert et al., 2023). An experience-based talent acquisition model creates an unnecessary ceiling and using years of experience as an anchor may be detrimental to IT businesses (Kappelman et al., 2016; Schefer-Wenzl & Miladinovic, 2022; Xin et al., 2020). This shift is due to the rapid pace of technological change, the high demand for specialized skills, and the growing recognition that experience can be gained in many various ways (Hughes et al., 2018). Acknowledging that job titles and the number of years of experience are not the actual indicators of a candidate's abilities and potential, forward-thinking IT employers are instead examining the applicant as a person, placing greater importance on a candidate's personal and professional skills and abilities, and taking a more inclusive stance toward candidates with diverse backgrounds (Nagy et al., 2023; Rozario et al., 2019; Swart et al., 2022). Contemporary IT companies have been reevaluating their approach to talent acquisition, moving away from traditional methods of hiring, such as relying on resumes and cover letters or a list of titles, companies, and years in each role to assess a candidate's qualifications (McCann & Selsky, 2012; Nneji & Asikhia, 2021). One notable trend in IT hiring practices is the increasing emphasis on skills and competencies over strict adherence to a predetermined set of job experiences (Kotorov et al., 2023). Internships, apprenticeships, and project-based experiences are gaining prominence as valuable alternatives to traditional work experiences (Madanaguli et al., 2023). Companies are increasingly recognizing the potential of hiring individuals who may not have a lengthy work history but have showcased their abilities through hands-on projects, open-source contributions, or participation in coding bootcamps (Marouf et al., 2023). This shift allows candidates to level the playing field and compete for jobs even without a traditional resume (Nagy et al., 2023). In addition, this shift signifies a departure from rigid prerequisites and a willingness to invest in talent that exhibits potential and a passion for continuous learning (Krasylnykova et al., 2023). Another evolving trend is the growing recognition of the importance of soft skills and cultural fit in addition to technical prowess (Aslam et al., 2023). In response to the increasing demand for diversity and inclusion, companies are redefining their hiring criteria to attract a broader spectrum of talent (Meruyert et al., 2023; Valentino, 2023). By embracing diversity, organizations can benefit from a wealth of perspectives, innovative ideas, and a richer pool of skills (Blaschke et al., 2021a). Employers are becoming more open to recruiting talent from different geographic locations, leveraging technology to build teams that transcend traditional boundaries (Rozario et al., 2019). This trend widens the talent pool and fosters a global perspective within organizations (Blaschke et al., 2021b). Those IT hiring practices reflect a broader recognition of the need for flexibility, inclusivity, and a focus on skills and potential rather than rigid experience requirements (Xin et al., 2020).

1.2 Swim like an Elephant - Landing a Job in IT with the Right Skill Sets

A comprehensive literature review suggests that a robust set of skills is essential for IT graduates aiming to thrive in the ever-evolving landscape of the IT industry (Driskell et al., 2018; Joseph, 2023; Khan et al., 2022; Madanaguli et al., 2023). The IT industry evolves swiftly, and IT professionals need to embrace change and be able to adapt to new technologies, project requirements, or ways of working (Al-Samarraie, 2018). IT graduates must demonstrate an eagerness to acquire new skills and stay abreast of emerging technologies. The IT industry requires a large amount of communication, and IT professionals often need to explain technical concepts to non-technical stakeholders clearly and concisely. Successful IT projects often involve collaboration and working in teams (Shrestha et al., 2023; Swart et al., 2022). Moreover, Effective leadership skills are increasingly in demand and can be one of a candidate's most valuable assets (Hughes et al., 2018). IT professionals need to be self-motivated and able to work independently. As the line between technology and business is increasingly blurring, IT employers increasingly search for candidates with entrepreneurial mindsets and skills for executing strategic partnerships between IT activities and business strategy (Kotorov et al., 2020, 2022).

1.3 In Lieu of Conclusion: Subtracting Obstacles, Adding Success

Overcoming the Catch-22 effect requires a nuanced approach from both aspiring IT professionals and the industry at large. For IT university graduates, success hinges on cultivating a well-rounded skill set that encompasses project management, problem-solving acumen, continuous learning, effective communication, business skills, and adaptability. The ability to collaborate within diverse teams, understand cybersecurity principles, and leverage emerging technologies like cloud computing is increasingly becoming crucial (Kloos et al., 2021). Initiatives such as internships, mentorship programs, and project-based collaborations may also offer graduates opportunities to gain practical experience and bridge the gap between academic knowledge and industry expectations.

2. CASE STUDY: EXPOLORING DYNAMICS TOWARDS OPPORTUNTIES

This case study examines the current needs and trends of the IT job sector as well as interviewer-interviewee dynamics. The data were collected via surveys and interviews among IT industry representatives. The **survey** and **interview qualitative data** have been manually analyzed to identify significant variables of the interviewer-interviewee dynamics.

2.1 Survey

The survey examines the skills that interviewers require in a candidate and the characteristics of a successful job applicant. 11 participants responded to the survey. The survey included questions about what skills are a focus of IT job advertisements and how interviewers meet the candidate (online or offline). Nine participants have been working in the IT sector for more than three years and two participants have around 2 years of experience in the IT industry. In addition to IT skills, participants stated that they focus on the manners of communication, the character of the candidate in communication and negotiation, and critical thinking attributes. Participants highlighted the importance of the professional qualifications, such as the responsible attitude, discipline, openness, honesty, the ability to learn, the ability to recognize mistakes, and passion for the job. The winning factors mentioned by the respondents include confidence, a combination of hard work and skills, and a methodological approach. Thus, the attributes of a successful candidate include traits such as being proactive, calm, confident, supportive, genuine, able to make critical decisions, open, and a good communicator. The participants advised IT undergraduate applicants to be familiar with the employer before the interview, be genuine. and not exaggerate their skills.

2.2 Interviews

Six respondents out of 11 volunteered for the semi-structured interview. The participants are IT industry figures that are involved in recruiting candidates for various IT job roles for computer science graduates. The interviews were conducted both online and offline and ethical considerations have been adhered to. The participants' answers are quoted below. Appendix I has the interview questions. The **themes** generated from the responses to the interview questions are summarized as follows: (1) **Required skills in job advertisements:** Job advertisements for IT applicants focus on various important factors. First, candidates should have IT experience and relevant knowledge in the company's domain. In addition, those job advertisements seek motivated learners. The recruitment process emphasizes the target industry's credibility, state exam grades, and candidate vision. Bachelors are evaluated on math, programming, flexibility, and motivation, while masters are assessed on vision and motivation, with attention to graduates' GPA. Graphic design positions require solid hard skills and the ability to work independently. (2) **Successful applicant profile:** A successful candidate in a job interview in IT should demonstrate technical knowledge and skills such as coding, algorithm problem-solving, database expertise, and design. In addition, soft skills are essential, as different IT companies have various requirements. On the other hand, advanced technical knowledge, motivation towards learning new skills and knowledge and a clear understanding of why the candidate wants to work for the company are significantly crucial. A participant stated, ***"motivation can have the upper hand***

in selecting the candidate among the shortlisted ones" and another participant commented that a successful candidate is someone *who* **"*must be highly motivated... shows that he wants to learn something new. He knows why he wants to work for our company.*"** The overall goal is to showcase one's strengths during the meeting with HR and team leads. The participant adds, ***"I think everybody can find ways where he will show his best sides."*** Another participant suggested that candidates must show resilience and patience, stating, ***"Never give up even if you don't know the answer. Tell the truth, say, I don't know but I think... (and give your ideas)".*** Successful candidates in job interviews entail demonstrating genuine honesty and loyalty in expressing oneself, both verbally and non-verbally, to align with what is written in the cover letter. The candidate's clear and precise answers within a short time frame are important criteria for success, demonstrating determination and clarity about their goals and suitability for the role based on the job description. The participant emphasizes the need for interviewers *to* ***"feel the answer is honest"*** regardless of how accurate the answers of the candidate are; hence, the candidate ***"can answer the questions but you feel there is something that does not work"*** as the participant argues. A participant informed that they give a task called a white board challenge. The task focuses on the candidate's ability to solve a problem related to the job in the real-time. Another important factor for success in job interviews is when candidates admit that they do not know something. The study candidate states that ***"it is fine if he does not know something but if he does not accept it, then this is tricky"***. Therefore, being unwilling to admit that you do not know a certain piece of knowledge, or a skill can be the reason for rejections. The participant adds, ***"We are faster at rejecting than accepting".*** The suggestion in such cases is to say, ***"I do not know, but I guess, or my analysis is...".*** Their approach to problem-solving is also important. A study participant shows the impact of enthusiasm to learn and join the target industry as a winning sign and says, ***"If I see a student with lightning eyes, willing to learn something or do something, then... I am willing to let them join at the trial period".*** Thus, interviews are an opportunity to showcase the skills in the application, with motivation for the target IT industry.

3. CONTRIBUTION AND CONCLUSION

Our interview findings are aligned with the insights drawn from the literature work presented and the survey responses. The insights drawn from the study are outlined below. **Table 1** stipulates the requirements from IT industries to job applicants.

Table 1. Guide for applicants to IT Industries

Prior to job interviews	During job interviews	After job interviews
Do your homework: explore the job you are applying for, visit their website, and familiarize yourself with the technologies they use. **Be** prepared for the interview, keeping in mind that the employer is also looking for each other; it is not just you who need the job; the employer needs your experience and skillset. Hence, such awareness can ensure a high level of confidence. **Familiarize** yourself with the job requirements to draft the cover letter accordingly. **Be** prepared for online meetings: make sure you and your environment show that you are ready. **Ensure** you have submitted an outstanding CV and cover letter that: ***a.*** can have links to any projects or activities you have participated in; ***b.*** highlights your strengths; ***c.*** should be concise, clear, and informative to allow recruiters to identify the major skills they look for among the extensive list of applicants. **Prepare** stories (self-learning experiences) that show your suitability.	**Listen** carefully. **Express** your motivation and enthusiasm to be part of the target industry. **Ask** questions that demonstrate your understanding of the job description and the target IT industry. **Be** clear and honest in your response and maintain a positive attitude. **Admit** when you do not know a specific tool or technical knowledge and give your analysis or relevant knowledge you are familiar with. **Avoid** selecting fuzzy or moving backgrounds that can be distracting remotely. **Make** sure you dress adequately, for online or offline meetings and be confident and relaxed. **Express** willingness to learn new knowledge. **Do** not tell jokes. **Do** not try to impress the interviewers. **Do** not contradict yourself: Make sure your answers are aligned with the information in your application. **Do** not speak negatively about the current or previous employer.	**Keep** applying to other industries. **Do** not give up if you have not been selected. **Reflect** on the interview and anticipate what might be the reason for the rejection. **Improve** the skills that might be the reason for not being selected and communicate with the same industry or other industries after being equipped with the required skillsets. **Ask** for feedback from the recruiters if the result was negative and try again. **Do** not blame yourself for not being selected, as there can be reasons out of control that are only related to the job requirements. Cases of rejections are more than the ones of acceptance.

The proposed message compiles a guideline for a successful job interview for IT applicants. The significance of the study outcome lies in communicating a message to applicants based on an authentic set of criteria for a successful job profile in the IT market. This message from the IT industry serves as a guideline that invites fresh applicants to reflect on the job interview mechanism. Therefore, the applicants can have more awareness of the selecting or rejecting criteria to be able to put foot in the door in the target IT industry. However, as the study findings demonstrate, failures are common in this process and applicants must continue to apply and improve their skills until they win the job they aim for. Moreover, both the IT educational and industrial sectors can take the responsibility in equipping the applicant with the required skills and learning opportunities to contribute to facilitating the IT candidate's employability. This study focuses on the IT job market; nevertheless, some factors focusing on soft skills can be widely applicable to most job sectors. Future work should target a larger sample of study participants as well as wider industries in specific job roles. Additionally, future work should examine the perspective of fresh graduates on IT education and industry. Hence, the investigation of the job interview experience from applicants and employers will contribute to bridging the current gap in employing those fledgling applicants, enabling them to successfully win the job and gifting IT industries with those talents.

REFERENCES

Aarnikoivu, M., Nokkala, T., Siekkinen, T., Kuoppala, K., & Pekkola, E. (2019). Working outside academia? Perceptions of early-career, fixed-term researchers on changing careers. *European Journal of Higher Education*, *9*(2), 172–189. https://doi.org/10.1080/21568235.2018.1548941

Abdul Hamid, R. (2022). The Role of Employees' Technology Readiness, Job Meaningfulness and Proactive Personality in Adaptive Performance. *Sustainability*, *14*(23), Article 23. https://doi.org/10.3390/su142315696

Al-Samarraie, H. (2018). *A systematic review of cloud computing tools for collaborative learning_ Opportunities and challenges to the blended-learning environment*. 15.

Aslam, H., Naumcheva, M., Zhdanov, P., Kotorov, I., Mazzara, M., Akhmetgaraeva, E., Valiev, R., & Krasylnykova, Y. (2023). Perception of the Internationalization Process by the University Employees: The Case Study of Innopolis University. In M. E. Auer, W. Pachatz, & T. Rüütmann (Eds.), *Learning in the Age of Digital and Green Transition* (pp. 873–883). Springer International Publishing. https://doi.org/10.1007/978-3-031-26190-9_89

Bernieri, F. (2000). *The importance of first impressions in a job interview*.

Blaschke, P., Demel, J., & Kotorov, I. (2021a). Innovation performance of Czech and Finnish manufacturing enterprises and their position in the EU. *ACC Journal*, *27*(2), 7–21. https://doi.org/10.15240/tul/004/2021-2-001

Blaschke, P., Demel, J., & Kotorov, I. (2021b). *Innovation Performance of Small, Medium-Sized, and Large Enterprises in Czechia and Finland*. Technical University of Liberec.

Driskell, J. E., Salas, E., & Driskell, T. (2018). Foundations of teamwork and collaboration. *American Psychologist*, *73*(4), 334–348. https://doi.org/10.1037/amp0000241

Heller, J., & Buckley, C. (2011). *Catch-22: 50th Anniversary Edition* (Anniversary edition). Simon & Schuster.

Hughes, D. J., Lee, A., Tian, A. W., Newman, A., & Legood, A. (2018). Leadership, creativity, and innovation: A critical review and practical recommendations. *The Leadership Quarterly*, *29*(5), 549–569. https://doi.org/10.1016/j.leaqua.2018.03.001

Joseph, N. (2023). *Managing a Diverse Workforce: Strategies for Effective Staffing and Inclusion*. https://doi.org/10.13140/RG.2.2.22279.16809

Kappelman, L., Jones, M. C., Johnson, V., McLean, E. R., & Boonme, K. (2016). Skills for success at different stages of an IT professional's career. *Communications of the ACM*, *59*(8), 64–70. https://doi.org/10.1145/2888391

Khan, A., Zaib, S., Khan, F., Khan, J., Khan, J., & Lee, Y. (2022). *Identification and Prioritization of Critical Cyber Security Challenges and Practices for Software Vendor Organizations in Software Development: An AHP-Based Systematic Approach*. https://doi.org/10.21203/rs.3.rs-2250026/v1

Kloos, C. D., Alario-Hoyos, C., Morales, M., Rocael, H. R., Jerez, Ó., Pérez-Sanagustín, M., Kotorov, I., Fernández, S. A. R., Oliva-Córdova, L. M., Solarte, M., Jaramillo, D., Teixeira, A. M., & López, A. H. G. (2021). PROF-XXI: Teaching and Learning Centers to Support the 21st Century Professor. *2021 World Engineering Education Forum/Global Engineering Deans Council (WEEF/GEDC)*, 447–454. https://doi.org/10.1109/WEEF/GEDC53299.2021.9657301

Kotorov, I., Krasylnykova, Y., Demel, J., & Blaschke, P. (2023). The Effect of the Covid-19 Pandemic on Economic Growth and R&D Spending in the EU Countries. *Proceedings of the 16th International Conference*, 68–76. https://doi.org/DOI: 10.15240/tul/009/lef-2023-08

Kotorov, I., Krasylnykova, Y., Zhdanov, P., & Mazzara, M. (2020). Internationalization Strategy of Innopolis University. In J.-M. Bruel, A. Capozucca, M. Mazzara, B. Meyer, A. Naumchev, & A. Sadovykh (Eds.), *Frontiers in Software Engineering Education* (Vol. 12271, pp. 327–340). Springer International Publishing. https://doi.org/10.1007/978-3-030-57663-9_21

Kotorov, I., Pérez-Sanagustín, M., Mansilla, F., Krasylnykova, Y., Hadaou, F. T., & Broisin, J. (2022). Supporting the Monitoring of Institutional Competency in Learning Innovation: The PROF-XXI Tool. *2022 XVII Latin American Conference on Learning Technologies (LACLO)*, 01–08. https://doi.org/10.1109/LACLO56648.2022.10013323

Krasylnykova, Y., Kotorov, I., Demel, J., Mazzara, M., & Bobrov, E. (2023). Innopolis University: An Agile and Resilient Academic Institution Navigating the Rocky Waters of the COVID-19 Pandemic. In G. Jezic, J. Chen-Burger, M. Kusek, R. Sperka, R. J. Howlett, & L. C. Jain (Eds.), *Agents and Multi-agent Systems: Technologies and Applications 2023* (pp. 383–392). Springer Nature. https://doi.org/10.1007/978-981-99-3068-5_36

Madanaguli, A., Dhir, A., Talwar, S., Clauss, T., Kraus, S., & Kaur, P. (2023). Diving into the uncertainties of open innovation: A systematic review of risks to uncover pertinent typologies and unexplored horizons. *Technovation*, *119*, 102582. https://doi.org/10.1016/j.technovation.2022.102582

Marouf, R., Kotorov, I., Aslam, H., Krasylnykova, Y., & Pezer, M. (2023). Thesis Supervision in Computer Science—Challenges and a Gamified Solution. In G. Jezic, J. Chen-Burger, M. Kusek, R. Sperka, R. J. Howlett, & L. C. Jain (Eds.), *Agents and Multi-agent Systems: Technologies and Applications 2023* (pp. 403–412). Springer Nature. https://doi.org/10.1007/978-981-99-3068-5_38

McCann, J., & Selsky, J. W. (2012). *Mastering Turbulence: The Essential Capabilities of Agile and Resilient Individuals, Teams and Organizations* (1st edition). Jossey-Bass.

Meruyert, T., Zhabagin, R., Assylbekov, A., & Nurgalym, J. (2023). *Managing inclusivity and diversity issues*.

Nagy, S., Pelser, A.-M., & Vaiman, V. (2023). *The improvement of Skills & Talents in the workplace*.

Nneji, N., & Asikhia, P. (2021). *Organizational Culture and Organizational Performance: A Review of Literature*. *3*, 361–372. https://doi.org/10.35629/5252-0301361372

Rozario, S. D., Venkatraman, S., & Abbas, A. (2019). Challenges in Recruitment and Selection Process: An Empirical Study. *Challenges*, *10*(2), Article 2. https://doi.org/10.3390/challe10020035

Schefer-Wenzl, S., & Miladinovic, I. (2022). A Structured Process for Supervising Students' Final Theses and Projects in Computer Science. *International Journal of Advanced Corporate Learning (iJAC)*, *15*(1), Article 1. https://doi.org/10.3991/ijac.v15i1.27211

Shrestha, H., Megha, S., Chakraborty, S., Mazzara, M., & Kotorov, I. (2023). Face Mask Recognition Based on Two-Stage Detector. In A. Abraham, S. Pllana, G. Casalino, K. Ma, & A. Bajaj (Eds.), *Intelligent Systems Design and Applications* (pp. 576–585). Springer Nature Switzerland. https://doi.org/10.1007/978-3-031-35507-3_56

Swart, K., Bond-Barnard, T., & Chugh, R. (2022). Challenges and critical success factors of digital communication, collaboration and knowledge sharing in project management virtual teams: A review. *International Journal of Information Systems and Project Management*, *10*(4), Article 4. https://doi.org/10.12821/ijispm100404

Tan, L. M., Laswad, F., & Chua, F. (2021). Bridging the employability skills gap: Going beyond classroom walls. *Pacific Accounting Review*, *34*(2), 225–248. https://doi.org/10.1108/PAR-04-2021-0050

Tsai, C.-Y. (2019). Improving students' understanding of basic programming concepts through visual programming language: The role of self-efficacy. *Computers in Human Behavior*, *95*, 224–232. https://doi.org/10.1016/j.chb.2018.11.038

Valentino, M. A. (2023). *Strengthening the Partnership with Partner Industry towards Data Literate and Collaborative Work Environment*. *7*, 157–159.

Whysall, Z., Owtram, M., & Brittain, S. (2019). The new talent management challenges of Industry 4.0. *Journal of Management Development*, *38*(2), 118–129. https://doi.org/10.1108/JMD-06-2018-0181

Xin, L., Zhou, W., Li, M., & Tang, F. (2020). Career Success Criteria Clarity as a Predictor of Employment Outcomes. *Frontiers in Psychology*, *11*. https://www.frontiersin.org/articles/10.3389/fpsyg.2020.00540

Appendix I

Interview Questions
https://docs.google.com/document/d/1oPtAaiCOORrVx8dlis26ZY3qtEurOcxhcgthwAMXU2U/edit?usp=sharing

Reflection Paper

DEVELOPING A QUALITY ASSURANCE MODEL FOR OER CONVERSION TOOL (CONVOERTER)

Lubna Ali[1], Muhmmad Waseem Khalid[2] and Ulrik Schroeder[1]
[1]*Learning Technologies Research Group, RWTH Aachen University, Aachen, Germany*
[2]*RWTH Aachen University, Aachen, Germany*

ABSTRACT

Applying quality assurance techniques to software applications is important to ensure their quality and develop their functionalities. This paper emphasizes the importance of software quality assurance and the reliability of web-based applications in this digital era, especially in the open education field. It provides a brief overview of the existing literature on software quality assurance and quality metrics. It proposes a testing approach using black-box testing techniques, Goal-Question-Metric for enhancing the quality of a web-based tool (convOERter) developed to convert existing educational materials semi-automatically into OER.

KEYWORDS

Software Quality Assurance, Black-Box Testing, OER, Quality Metrics, Functional Testing, SQA

1. INTRODUCTION

The reliability of software applications is an important element of their overall quality (Pressman, 2014, p. 442). This reflection analyzes brief literature for testing web applications and software quality metrics. It proposes an approach to apply Black-box[1] testing techniques (testing functionality of software application) and GQM[2] (Goal-Question-Metric) model. The main goal of this reflection is to review applied methodologies and develop a quality assurance model for improving web applications' quality and usability. In the following section, an overview of the state of the art will be presented, followed by methodologies and implementation. Finally, conclusions and future research directions will be discussed.

2. STATE OF ART

Various literature discusses the application of software quality metrics to web applications to assure and enhance their quality. Giang et al. (2010) worked on the importance of software quality metrics in web applications for fault prediction. They used metrics to predict errors in web applications using machine learning models. These metrics comprise of Lines of JavaScript (LOJ), Lines of CSS (LOCSS), and Number of Hyperlinks (NOH). In 2010, a study on automated black-box vulnerability testing scanners was made in which the commercial scanners were compared to detect vulnerabilities commonly exist in web applications comprising of SQL Injection(SQLI) and Cross-Site Scripting(XSS) (Bau et al., 2010). These vulnerability scanners were evaluated from various aspects including their potential strengths, weaknesses, effectiveness, and efficiency in detecting vulnerabilities. Lakshmi and Mallika (2017) reviewed various functional and black-box testing methodologies, emphasizing their importance in improving web application reliability and security. They discussed techniques such as model-based mutation testing and user representation models, highlighting their effectiveness in identifying defects and ensuring comprehensive test coverage.

---

[1] BrowserStack. (n.d.). Black-box testing. Available at: https://www.browserstack.com/guide/black-box-testing#:~:text=Black%20box%20testing%20is%20a,to%20its%20internal%20source%20code (Accessed: 17 May 2024).

[2] GeeksforGeeks. (n.d.). Goal Question Metric (GQM) approach in software quality. Available at: https://www.geeksforgeeks.org/goal-question-metric-approach-in-software-quality/ (Accessed: 17 May 2024).

3. METHODOLOGIES AND IMPLEMENTATION

The convOERter is a web-based tool to convert educational material semi-automatically into OER, based on replacing non-OER images with OER images. The reliability of the tool can be improved by applying quality metrics and collecting data related to input files for conversion. Additionally, tracking the frequency of specific types of errors and input files processed can help identify potential errors and allow proactive measures to prevent their occurrence in the future. Implementation of machine learning models on these fault predictors will help to improve the overall performance and user experience application.

Various well-known techniques as explained below can be applied to web-based applications to ensure and enhance their quality. One of these techniques is the GQM (Goal-Question-Metric) model, which primarily focuses on the goals of a software application. It helps to set clear goals, derive relevant questions, and formulate the metrics that can be numerically measured. The data for the metrics will be collected from user feedback and logs produced. These metrics will help in identifying the efficiency and finding the bottlenecks affecting performance. Another technique that can be applied is the Boundary Value Analysis (BVA). BVA is a known black-box testing technique that is focused on how software under test reads the edge cases provided as input during data handling. During this testing, the analysis will focus on how the web application selects files from supported file formats and handles various file sizes. This includes testing edge cases to ensure the application can accept possible user inputs. Cause-effect analysis is a systematic technique to understand the relationships between factors and outcomes in a system. In web applications, it helps identify root causes of issues and develop targeted solutions. For example, if users report inconsistent image recognition, the analysis might reveal factors like insufficient training data or poor input image quality. Addressing these causes can improve the application's efficiency. Use Case Testing which focuses on the end-user's perspective, can also be applied. For the OER conversion tool, we can list all use cases with pre and post-conditions. Since the tool involves user interactions like initiating conversion, deciding on image replacement, and selecting licenses, testing these use cases ensures the application meets user expectations. This helps identify issues during typical interactions, ensuring a seamless user experience.

4. CONCLUSIONS AND FUTURE WORK

The use of software quality assurance models with blackbox techniques and the GQM approach will improve web application quality. This user-centric testing mainly focuses on functional requirements. By continuously refining the testing approach, we can maintain high standards of software quality and security for digital educational resources. Future work will integrate vulnerability testing to identify and address security threats, ensuring better protection and reliability. Additionally, exploring automated testing frameworks can enhance efficiency and consistency in maintaining software quality.

REFERENCES

Bau, J., Bursztein, E., Gupta, D., and Mitchell, J. (2010). State of the Art: Automated Black-Box Web Application Vulnerability Testing. In: *2010 IEEE Symposium on Security and Privacy*. Oakland, CA, USA, pp. 332345.

Giang, L. T., Kang, D., and Bae, D.-H. (2010). Software Fault Prediction Models for Web Applications. In: *2010 IEEE 34th Annual Computer Software and Applications Conference Workshops*. Seoul, Korea (South), pp. 51-56.

Lakshmi, D. R., and Mallika, S. S. (2017). A review on web application testing and its current research directions. *International Journal of Electrical and Computer Engineering*, 7(4), p. 2132.

Lee, M. C. (2014). Software quality factors and software quality metrics to enhance software quality assurance. *British Journal of Applied Science & Technology*, 4(21), pp. 3069-3095.

Pressman, R. S., 2014. *Software Engineering: A Practitioner's Approach*. McGraw-Hill Education, New York, USA.

AUTHOR INDEX

International Association for Development of the Information Society (IADIS)
Rua Sao Sebastiao Da Pedreira
No. 100, 30, 1050-209
Lisbon, Portugal

ISBN 979-8-3313-0936-7

9 798331 309367

CURRAN ASSOCIATES INC.
proceedings.com